# AFRICA

Africa World Press Guide
to Educational Resources
from and about Africa

# AFRICA

Africa World Press Guide
to Educational Resources
from and about Africa

Compiled and edited
by WorldViews

Africa World Press, Inc.

P.O. Box 1892  P.O. Box 48
Trenton, NJ 08607  Asmara, ERITREA

# Africa World Press, Inc.

P.O. Box 1892 Trenton, NJ 08607

P.O. Box 48 Asmara, ERITREA

Resource directories compiled and edited by WorldViews:

*Third World Resource Directory* (1984)
*Asia and Pacific* (1986)
*Latin America and Caribbean* (1986)
*Women in the Third World* (1987)
*Middle East* (1987)
*Africa* (1987)
*Food, Hunger, Agribusiness* (1987)
*Human Rights* (1989)
*Transnational Corporations and Labor* (1989)
*Third World Struggles for Peace with Justice* (1990)
*Third World Resource Directory* (1994)

Copyright © 1997 WorldViews

All rights reserved. No part of this publication may be reproduced, stored in a retrieval system or transmitted in any form or by any means electronic, mechanical, photocopying, recording or otherwise without the prior written permission of the publisher.

Book and cover design: Andrea DuFlon (Berkeley)
Graphics credits: The editors are grateful to all those who granted us permission to use their graphics in this directory. If we have inadvertently omitted any credits please contact WorldViews at 464 19th Street, Oakland, CA 94612-2297, USA.

### Library of Congress Cataloging-in-Publication Data

Africa : Africa world press guide to educational resources from and about Africa / compiled and edited by WorldViews.
    p.    cm.
ISBN 0-86543-643-6 (hbk.). -- ISBN 0-86543-588-X (pbk.)
1. Africa–Bibliography. 2. Africa-Library resources.
I. WorldViews (Organization)
Z3501.A1A37 1997
[DT3]
016.96–dc21                        97-13312
                                     CIP

# CONTENTS

| | |
|---|---|
| Preface | vii |
| Introduction | ix |
| Africa—Overview | 2 |
| Africa's Nations | 4 |
| Africa's Peoples | 8 |
| AIDS in Africa | 12 |
| Belief Systems | 16 |
| Cinema | 20 |
| Conflicts in Africa | 24 |
| Africa's Debt Burden | 28 |
| Democracy | 32 |
| Development | 36 |
| Emergency Relief Aid | 40 |
| Environment | 44 |
| Food and Agriculture | 48 |
| Foreign Intervention | 52 |
| Human Rights | 56 |
| Images of Africa | 60 |
| Labor's Role in Africa | 64 |
| African Literature | 68 |
| Mining in Africa | 72 |
| Music in Africa | 76 |
| Population | 80 |
| Refugees | 84 |
| South Africa | 88 |
| Struggles Unknown | 92 |
| Struggles Won | 96 |
| Visual Arts | 100 |
| The Voice of Women | 104 |
| Women in Africa | 108 |

| | |
|---|---|
| Supplementary Resources | 112 |
|     African Literature | 115 |
|     Films and Videotapes | 118 |
|     Curriculum Resources | 129 |
| Reference List | 139 |
| Directory of Organizations | 180 |
| Names Index | 190 |

# PREFACE

The World Eagle map reproduced on page 1 below is an eye-opener for most people outside the continent of Africa. The map makes the point that there is much indeed that we do not know about Africa. We have little awareness of how large Africa is, how many nations make up the continent, or how rich and varied the societies are that inhabit the continent. Africa receives relatively little coverage in the media and in educational programs, and what coverage there is tends to focus on problem areas such as refugees, famines, and conflicts.

The aim of this directory is to provide educators and others with resource tools that contribute to more informed and enlightened understandings of Africa and its peoples. In this effort we have sought to magnify the voices of those whose perspectives on Africa are not now adequately represented in the mainstream media and in materials used in libraries and schools outside of Africa—especially writers, publishers, filmmakers, educators, and others *from* Africa.

Not content with simply providing access to *more* information about Africa we have selected resource materials that provide critical analyses of the root causes of the "problems" that dominate news coverage about Africa. What are the fundamental reasons for famines and the displacement of people? How are the vestiges of colonialism, the structural adjustment policies of the World Bank, and the presence of anti-personnel landmines related to these "problems"?

An additional aim has been to illustrate—even in problem areas—how much can be learned from the way Africa's peoples are dealing with problems such as AIDS, conflicts, and refugees: community-based initiatives to combat the spread of AIDS/HIV, innovative conflict-resolution measures, and the repatriation of displaced peoples.

Finally, we have deliberately included resource materials that highlight the richness of the African continent in the areas of literature, music, and cinema. We urge educators to tap these resources in order to present a complete and textured picture of Africa's peoples and nations.

The materials in this directory demonstrate the fact that educational resources *are* available to those who wish to learn about Africa. The organizations listed in the Directory of Organizations at the back of the directory are a rich source of resources that will update and complement the materials we have listed and described below. We recommend, in particular, the African Books Collective in Oxford as a key international source for books and pamphlets published *in* Africa.

## On-line Updates

The contents of the chapters in this directory below are available electronically on the Internet at <http://www.igc.org/worldviews/awpguide/afrintro.html>. We intend to post updates and corrections of information in this directory at that Website and we invite readers to visit the site from time to time to keep the material in this directory up-to-date. We also encourage readers to visit the Website of Africa World Press: <http://www.africanworld.com>.

## Acknowledgments

The production of this directory has in every sense of the word been a collective effort. We are grateful to publisher Kassahun Checole and the staff and editors at Africa World Press; to Ed Ferguson and Prexy Nesbitt, who were instrumental in getting this project off the ground; to the staffs of the IDOC documentation center in Rome, the Review of African Political Economy in Sheffield, the African Studies Center in Boston, the African Books Collective in Oxford, the Africa Book Centre in London, and the DataCenter in Oakland; to friend and graphic artist Andrea DuFlon, who designed this directory; and to the many WorldViews interns and volunteers who helped along the way, especially Peggy Mead, Ted von der Ahe, Kyra Ostendorf, Patrika Mani, Ron Nicosia, Anibel Comelo, Robin Cushman, Kristen Rutter, Nancy Gruber, and Michael Heffron Fenton.

Our work on this project was assisted in part by contributions from the Program on Peace and International Cooperation of the John D. and Catherine T. MacArthur Foundation, the African Initiatives program of the Rockefeller Foundation, the South Coast Foundation, the Von der Ahe Family Trust, the Winston Foundation for World Peace, the Mission Context and Relationship division of the General Board of Global Ministries of the United Methodist Church, the Maryknoll Fathers and Brothers, Missionhurst, Comboni Missionaries, OMI Oblates, Missionaries of Africa, and by generous donations from friends and relatives who have supported the work of WorldViews (formerly Third World Resources) throughout the years.

*Thomas P. Fenton and Mary J. Heffron*
*Directors, WorldViews*

# INTRODUCTION

*Africa: Africa World Press Guide to Resources from and about Africa* opens with three chapters that provide general introductory resource materials on Africa, its fifty-three nations (in North and Sub-Saharan Africa), and its diverse peoples. The introductory chapters are followed by twenty-five subject-oriented chapters. These have been arranged in rough alphabetical order according to their topical focus. The topics are deliberately mixed—*belief systems* followed by *cinema* followed by *conflicts*, for example—in order to emphasize the point that, like societies everywhere, African societies are a rich mix of strengths and weaknesses, problems and potential, beauties and tragedies. Each chapter is given four pages (with the exception of the overview chapter).

The resources in the chapters are listed by title, with the author and date in parentheses. Readers should consult the Reference List and the Directory of Organizations at the back of the directory for full bibliographical details for the titles cited and contact information for the publishers and distributors.

Additional resources are cataloged in sections entitled Supplementary Resources (pp. 112-114), African Literature (115-117), Films and Videotapes (118-129), and Curriculum Resources (pp. 129-138). Note that the Reference List (pp. 139-179) contains many more titles than are listed in the body of the directory. The Names Index lists individuals whose works appear in the topical chapters or in the Reference List. No subject index is provided since the chapters themselves are subject-oriented.

We have made every effort to include complete bibliographical data and ordering information for each of the resources, but if information is found to be outdated, insufficient, or inaccurate we invite readers to contact WorldViews at <worldviews@igc.org> or (510) 451-1742.

## Critical educational perspectives

Educating about Africa demands a heightened sensitivity to the abundance of misinformation and stereotypes that cloud perceptions of Africa's nations and peoples. We encourage readers to contact the outreach centers at local colleges or universities for help in evaluating Africa-related print and audiovisual educational resources. The Outreach Center at Boston University's African Studies Center has a particularly good collection of educational materials, along with a valuable checklist for use in evaluating Africa-related educational resources. Contact Barbara Brown, Outreach Director, African Studies Center, Boston University, 270 Bay State Rd., Boston, MA 02215, USA. Tel: (617) 353-7303. Email: <bbbrown@bu.edu>.

Another recommended source for critical perspectives on educational resources is Africa Access, 2204 Quinton Rd., Silver Spring, MD 20910, USA. Tel: (301) 587-5686.

## WorldViews

WorldViews AFRICA is a regional division of WorldViews, a non-profit organization that collects, organizes, publicizes, and promotes the greater use of print and audiovisual materials that offer fresh perspectives on issues of peace and justice in world affairs. WorldViews maintains a clearinghouse of books, pamphlets, periodicals, and organizational information related to these issues and, since 1984, has published a 28-page magazine that alerts readers to new print and audiovisual resources on world affairs: *WorldViews: A Quarterly Review of Resources for Education and Action* (ISSN 1085-7559).

For information, visit the WorldViews Website at <http://www.igc.org/worldviews> or write WorldViews, 464 19th Street, Oakland, CA 94612-2297, USA.

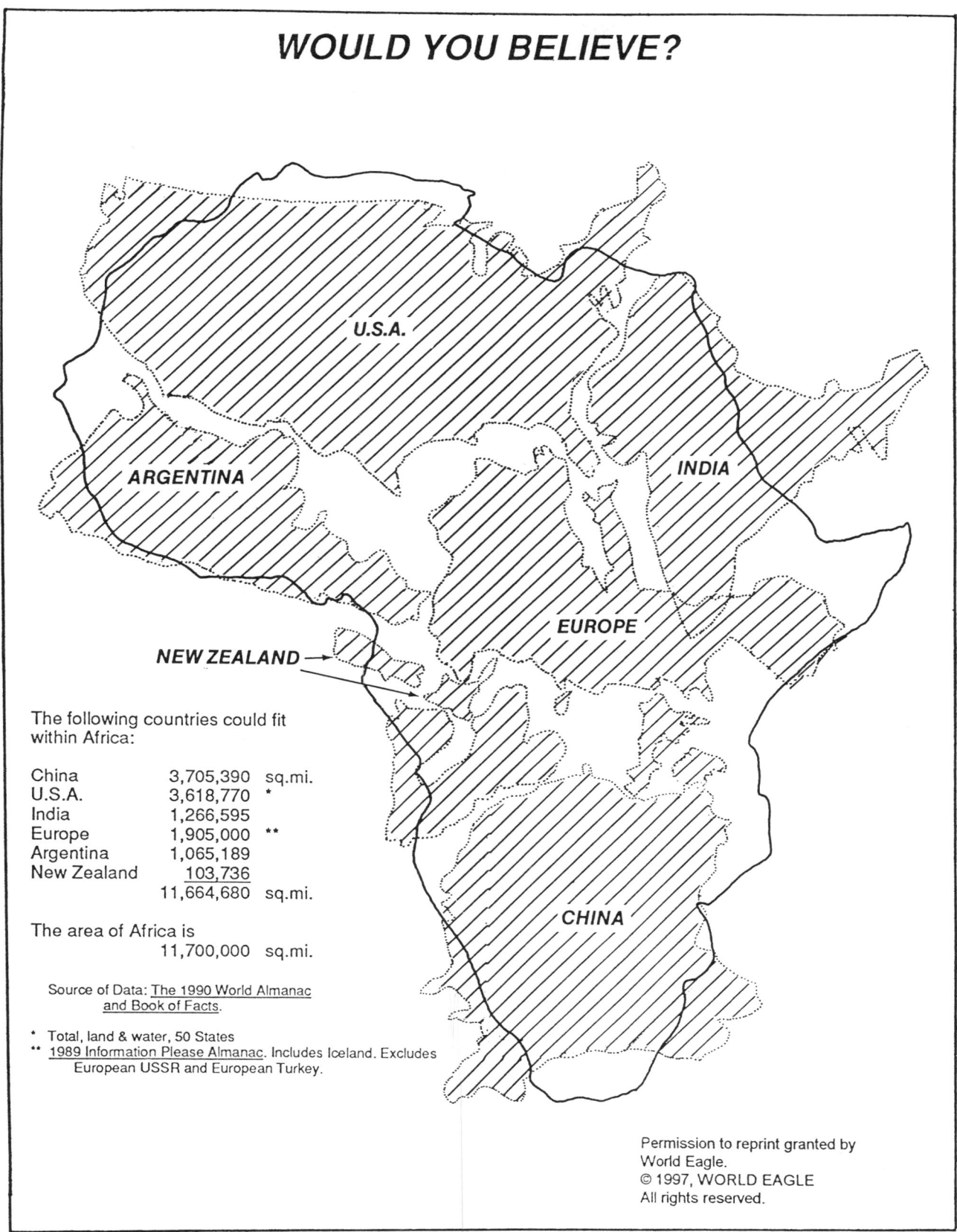

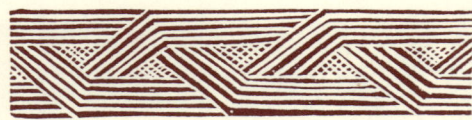

# AFRICA—OVERVIEW
## Approaches to the continent and its history

The resource materials listed in this chapter introduce Africa from a regional perspective. The two chapters that follow focus on the diversity of the peoples and nations of the African continent. See the Supplementary Resources section below for lists of additional materials that are regional in orientation, e.g., atlases, bibliographies, and statistical handbooks.

In a writing career than spanned more than four decades, historian Basil Davidson produced more than twenty books that have helped Western readers understand Africa-behind-the-stereotypes. Any of Davidson's books would be a good starting point for the general reader. His most recent book, *The Search for Africa: History, Culture, Politics* (Davidson 1994), is a collection of short essays that Davidson wrote throughout his illustrious career on controversial topics such as "the invention of racism," the history of Africa, "Africanism," the roots of antiapartheid, pluralism in colonial African societies, African peasants and revolution, and the ambiguities of nationalism.

Other titles by Davidson include *The Black Man's Burden: Africa and the Curse of the Nation-State* (1992), *African Civilization Revisited* (1991), *Modern Africa* (1990), *The Story of Africa* (1984), and *Let Freedom Come: Africa in Modern History* (1978).

A more systematically arranged all-encompassing approach to the history of Africa is found in the eight-volume *General History of Africa* edited by Africa specialists and co-published by UNESCO (Paris), Heinemann Publishers (Oxford), and the University of California Press (Berkeley). "For a long time," Amadou-Mahtar M'Bow (UNESCO Director-General, 1974-87) wrote in his preface to the eighth volume in the series, "all kinds of myths and prejudices concealed the true history of Africa from the world at large. African socities were looked upon as societies that could have no history." In an effort to counter these myths and prejudices and to enlighten the general public, UNESCO undertook the production of this authoritative multi-disciplinary, multi-faceted history of the continent and its peoples.

Titles in the UNESCO *General History of Africa* series are
- *Methodology and African Prehistory* (J. Ki-Zerbo, ed.);
- *Ancient Civilizations of Africa* (G. Mokhtar, ed.);
- *Africa from the Seventh to the Eleventh Century* (M. El Fasi, ed.);
- *Africa from the Twelfth to the Sixteenth Century* (D. T. Niane, ed.);
- *Africa from the Sixteenth to the Eighteenth Century* (B. A. Ogot, ed.);
- *The Nineteenth Century until the 1880s* (J. F. A. Ajayi, ed.);
- *Africa under Foreign Domination, 1880-1935* (A. A. Boahen, ed.); and
- *Africa since 1935* (Ali A. Mazrui, ed.).

Other noteworthy general histories of Africa include The African History in Documents series edited by historian Robert O. Collins (University of California, Santa Barbara). Titles in this series are *Western African History* (Collins 1990), *Eastern African History* (Collins 1990), and *Central and South African History* (Collins 1996).

Collins is also editing another set of historical textbooks in Markus Wiener's Problems in the History of Modern Africa series. The first two volume in the series are entitled *Problems in African History: The Precolonial Centuries* (Collins 1993) and *Historical Problems of Imperial Africa* (Collins 1994). The third volume, *Problems in the History of Modern Africa,* appeared in 1996.

Ali A. Mazrui, the editor of the eighth volume in the UNESCO series, produced a highly acclaimed book and hosted a companion television series in the mid-1980s that have stood the test of time as general introductions to Africa. See *The Africans: A Triple Heritage* (Mazrui 1986) and the 9-part video series with the same title. Another notable video series was produced by Basil Davidson: *Africa* (Davidson 1984; 8 parts). The Mazrui and Davidson videos are available from many university-based African studies centers, and from Church World Service (Elkhart) and other film outlets.

The videotape to view and/or show *before* any other, however, is *What Do We Know about Africa?*, a 25-minute video produced by Barbara Brown and the African Studies Center at Boston University. This eye-opening video challenges viewers to identify and analyze the many stereotypes that exist regarding the African continent and its peoples. Problematic terms such as "tribe," "jungle," "superstitious," and "primitive" are examined in a forthright but non-threatening manner. Even the most enlightened viewers are likely to trip over at least one unexamined bias or misperception brought to light in this video.

*What Do We Know about Africa?* is available for rental or purchase from the African Studies Center, Boston University, 270 Bay State Rd., Boston, MA 02215 USA. Companion study guide included.

Joy to the World Batik detail by Samuel Senkooto of Uganda.
© 1994 Friendship Press. Used with permission.

# AFRICA'S NATIONS
## Africa is *not* a country!

The title of a popular children's book about Africa—*Africa Is Not a Country*—speaks a truth that is lost even on adults who see Africa only as a *continent* and are blind to the individuality of Africa's 53* nations. This skewed perception is evident in educational materials that list Africa—the *continent*—on a par with *countries* in other regions of the world. Thus, "our global studies class sampled foods from Guatemala, Japan, Sweden, Africa, and China."

Approaching the study of Africa through the in-depth analysis of one or two countries is an effective way to counteract the tendency to lump African nations as different as Algeria, Cape Verde, Ghana, Mauritius, South Africa, and Zimbabwe into one undifferentiated mass.

The reference source for African country information that we recommend highly is *The World Guide 1997/98: A View from the South* (1997) and accompanying CD-ROM produced by the Instituto del Tercer Mundo (ITeM) in Montevideo, Uruguay. Produced every two years, this reference book takes pride in presenting the world as seen by "the Third World." ITeM researchers work with a network of correspondents around the world to gather "facts, figures, [and] opinions" on selected international issues and on more than 200 individual countries. The information they provide is meant to combat the "abundant errors, distorted outlooks, [and] racist criteria" that the editors contend are characteristic of many of the almanacs and annual reference books published in Europe and North America.

Numerous reference books contain information arranged in country-by-country order. See, for example:

• *New African Yearbook 1995-96* (Rake 1995-96). The tenth edition of this guide presents information on the political history, economy, and politics of 53 African nations. Statistical data and a country map are included in each

*The World Guide 1997/98*
Instituto del Tercer Mundo (Montevideo)

* The number of nations in Africa varies from source to source. Fifty-three is the number accepted by the United Nations. Western Sahara is not yet recognized as a nation and so is not included in the count.

profile. Each profile is written by one or more Africa specialists. Material in the *New African Yearbook 1995-1996* is clearly presented and will serve the information needs of students and specialists equally well.

- The organization of country profile information in part 2 of *Black Africa: A Comparative Handbook* (Morrison et al. 1989) ensures that comparisons are easy to make between social, political, and economic data for forty-one individual African nations.
- The two volumes in the *Culturgrams: The Nations around Us* series (Skabelund 1995) developed by the David M. Kennedy Center for International Studies, Brigham Young University, place an emphasis on the daily customs and lifestyles of populations in the countries they profile. Four-page "culturgrams" of more than 30 African nations are presented (intermixed with profiles of the nations of Asia and Oceania) in volume 2.
- *Africa South of the Sahara* (Europa Publications) and *The Middle East and North Africa* (Europa Publications). These two long-standing annual publications contain a section of commissioned essays on a variety of topics, an introduction to key organizations related to the region (e.g., Permanent Missions to the United Nations), and alphabetically arranged country surveys that cover the physical and social geography, history, and economy of each nation. Each country survey concludes with a statistical survey, a directory of organizations, and a bibliography of relevant readings.
- The two-volume *Europa World Year Book*, also published annually by Europa Publications, provides a condensed version of the information in the first part of the Africa country surveys (i.e., history, economy, etc.). The information in the second part—the statistical survey, directory of organizations, and bibliography—is essentially the same as in the regional volumes described above.
- Volume 2 in the five-volume *Worldmark Encyclopedia of the Nations* (Gale Research 1995) contains 55 country chapters covering African nations from Algeria to Zimbabwe and, as well, the African dependencies of France and the United Kingdom. Information in the *Worldmark Encyclopedia* is presented in a style that is more accessible to the lay reader than the rather dense prose and detailed data tables of the Europa publications.
- Country profiles of African nations, among others, are also a feature of *The Political Handbook of the World* (Muller), an authoritative reference guide that has been published for more than 65 years. The profiles provide basic facts and data; a guide to top government officials; a concise overview of the country's history, political background, constitutional structure, and foreign relations; informed commentary on "current issues"; and a description of major political parties.
- The Facts on File *Handbooks to the Modern World: Africa* (Moroney 1989) combines country profiles (volume 1) with articles by many of the world's leading Africa specialists on political, economic, and social affairs in Africa

---

**AFRICA'S 53 NATIONS**

Algeria
Angola
Benin
Botswana
Burkina Faso
Burundi
Cameroon
Cape Verde
Central African Republic
Chad
Comoros
Congo
Côte d'Ivoire
Democratic Republic
of the Congo (Zaire)
Djibouti
Egypt
Equatorial Guinea
Eritrea
Ethiopia
Gabon
The Gambia
Ghana
Guinea
Guinea-Bissau
Kenya
Lesotho
Liberia
Libyan Arab Jamahiriya
Madagascar
Malawi
Mali
Mauritania
Mauritius
Morocco
Mozambique
Namibia
Niger
Nigeria
Rwanda
São Tomé and Principe
Senegal
Seychelles
Sierra Leone
Somalia
South Africa
Sudan
Swaziland
United Republic of Tanzania
Togo
Tunisia
Uganda
Zambia
Zimbabwe

(volume 2). The 32 articles in volume 2 cover subjects such as South Africa's wars on its neighbors (Joseph Hanlon), the Organization of African Unity (Colin Legum), Africa's response to International Monetary Fund/World Bank structural adjustment programs (Bade Onimode); banking institutions (Ann Seidman), women (Efua Graham and Wendy Davies), Africa's environmental crisis (Jimoh Omo-Fadaka), labor issues and trade unionism (Nicholas Van Hear and Taffy Adler), and religion and social forces in Africa (Ali Mazrui).

- African nations north of the Sahara are profiled along with the nations of the Middle East in part 2 of *Arab World Notebook: Secondary School Level* (Shabbas and Al-Qazzaz 1989).
- The United Nations is publishing individual volumes of information on nations in Africa and elsewhere in which the United Nations has had significant involvement. Africa-related volumes in the UN's "Blue Book Series" include *The United Nations and Mozambique, 1992-1995; The United Nations and Somalia, 1992-1996;* and *The United Nations and Rwanda, 1993-1996.* See also, *The United Nations and Apartheid, 1948-1994.* Information on the Blue Books series is available from the UN Department of Public Information, United Nations, New York, NY 10017 USA.

Finally, for detailed statistical and other data on African nations consult the various annual guides and reference handbooks compiled and published by the United Nations and its agencies. See, for instance, the *Demographic Handbook for Africa/Guide Demographique de l'Afrique* (United Nations 1992), *African Development Indicators* (United Nations Development Programme and World Bank 1996), and *Human Development Report 1994* (United Nations Development Programme 1994).

**Publishers series**

Various publishing houses have undertaken the regular production of books on individual countries in Africa. See the highly recommended Country Profile series from Oxfam Publications (Oxford), the Historical Dictionary series from Scarecrow Press (Lanham, Md.), the Marxist Regimes series from Pinter Publishers (London and New York), and the Profiles/Nations of Contemporary Africa series from Westview Press (Boulder, Colo.).

Publishers of educational materials provide country-specific elementary school textbooks on various African countries. These are often of varying quality and it is good to check with a source such as *Africa Access* (Silver Spring, Md.) or with the staff at an African studies center at a nearby college or university for help in identifying textbooks that are accurate and fair. Representative elementary school materials with a focus on African *nations* are the Where We Live series from Steck-Vaughn Library (Austin, Texas), the World Focus series from Heinemann (Oxford), and two series from Childrens Press (Chicago): Enchantment of the World and A New True Book.

# COUNTRY-FOCUSED CURRICULUM MATERIALS

See Curriculum Resources section below for ordering information.

**Benin:
Source Pack for Key Stage 2.**
Text written and sources selected by Andrew Forson. Illustrations by Rosemary Forson. Cover design by Julia Forson. Wellingborough: Northamptonshire Black History Group, 1992. ISBN 1-873886-04-7.

**Kenya: The Final Frontier?**
Written by Bernard Dady. Produced by Leeds Development Education Centre, Matrix Multimedia, and the Educational and Multimedia Association. Bradford: Matrix Multimedia, 1996. CD-ROM.

**Eritrea:
Africa's Newest Country.**
Written by Ruth Lewis, with assistance from Claire Booker. London: Christian Aid, 1993. ISBN 0-904379-17-5.

**New Journeys: Teaching about Other Places. Learning from Kenya and Tanzania.**
Written by Sukhvinder Kaur Barhey et al. Edited by Catherine McFarlane and Audrey Osler. Birmingham: Development Education Centre, 1991. ISBN 0-948838-17-5.

**Hanging by a Thread: Trade, Debt and Cotton in Tanzania.** Designed and illustrated by Juliet MacDonald. Leeds: Leeds Development Education Centre, 1992. ISBN 1-871268-35-4.

**Our Country, Our Future:
A Teaching Pack about
South Africa.**
Mbali Ngcobo, Sindisiwe Sabela, and Mduduzi Sishi. Edited by Gillian Symons. London: Research on Education in Southern Africa, Institute of Education, 1994. ISBN 0-85473-401-5.

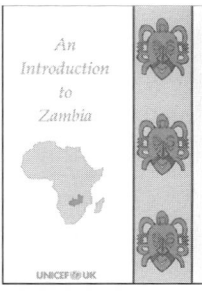

**An Introduction to Zambia.** Written and designed by Heather Jarvis. London: UNICEF-UK, 1992.

**Triumph of Hope: Eritrea's Struggle for Development.
An Activity Pack for
Sixth Forms and
Campaigning Groups.**
Written by Lyn Routledge, Graham Harrison, and Nigel West. Leeds: Leeds Development Education Centre, 1994. ISBN 1-871268-65-6.

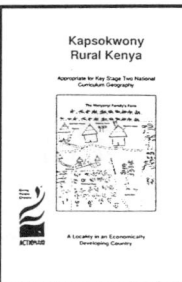

**Kapsokwony, Rural Kenya:
A Locality in an Economically Developing Country.**
Written by Steve Brace. Photographs by Joseph Louw. Illustrations by Harald Smykla. Somerset: ACTION-AID, 1991.

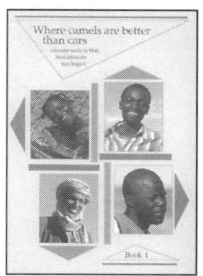

**Where Camels Are Better Than Cars: A Locality Study in Mali, West Africa.**
Written by John and Sarah Snyder with Catherine McFarland. Co-published by Development Education Centre and Save the Children, UK. Birmingham: Development Education Centre, 1992. ISBN 0-948838-25-6.

**AFRICA'S NATIONS 7**

# AFRICA'S PEOPLES
## A rich diversity of ancient and proud societies

There are strengths and weaknesses attached to the study of Africa through a focus on the continent's diverse and numerous *peoples*. The strengths are that the continent is reduced to a more manageable size, the diversity and the rich traditions of Africa's peoples are accentuated, and the similiarities and differences among peoples everywhere in the world can be identified and analyzed. Finally, a study of the particularities of discrete societies throughout the African continent challenges the misperception of Africa as an undifferentiated mass of peoples.

The attendant weaknesses in this approach are that Africa's population of 735 million may be reduced to exotic images and stereotypes of one or another African society or they may remain frozen in the context of the particular historical period or geographic locale being studied. In the introdution to his book, *The Shona and their Neighbours* (Beach 1994), historian David Beach (University of Zimbabwe) clearly delineates the traps that can ensnare the unwary in a study of the peoples of Africa. He takes, as just one example, the rock paintings and stone buildings for which inhabitants of the Zimbabwean plateau are reknowned. "From the standpoint of Shona studies," Beach points out, "[the paintings and buildings] have been both a blessing and a curse. On the one hand, the sheer beauty of the former attracted many of the minority of educated whites into the discipline of archaeology, but it also ensured that they devoted their attention to a period and people fairly remote from the [modern-day] Shona and their recent neighbours." Clearly, as Beach suggests, the particularlities and generalities must be kept in proper balance at all times.

One final caution that is germane to the study of Africa's peoples is that the word "tribe" is an inaccurate and inappropriate way to describe African societies. The term carries negative connotations in the Western mind — primitive peoples, for instance — and is not a designation that Westerners would use to describe distinct ethnic groups in other societies.

The resource materials in this chapter look at the peoples of Africa on three levels. The first level includes general guides to African societies. The second level covers resources that express a focused concern on the state of the world's indigenous peoples, with the peoples of Africa included among them. Finally, we narrow our focus to reference books and other resources that bring individual Africans to life for students and other readers.

## African societies

Several publishers are producing individual studies or series of books that describe the peoples of Africa on a societal level. Among them are Facts on File, Blackwell, Waveland Press, Gale Research, Rosen Publishers, and Africa World Press.

The Peoples of Africa series published in February 1997 by Facts on File aims to help middle and high school students appreciate the diversity of the African continent through the study of the history, language, way of life, social structure, culture and religion, and the political and natural environment of Africa's major ethnic groups. The first five volumes in the series are organized by regions: North Africa, East Africa, West Africa, Central Africa, and Southern Africa. The final volume, entitled *Nations of Africa*, includes profiles of 52 African nations and biographies of 300 African politicians, sports personalities, artists, and ancient kings and queens.

Blackwell's Peoples of Africa series draws on archeological, historical, and anthropological evidence to paint a picture of the culture, society, and history of distinct African peoples from their origins to the present day. "Approaches will vary according to the subject and the nature of the evidence," the publishers explain. "Volumes concerned mainly with culturally discrete peoples will be complemented by accounts which focus primarily on the historical period, on African nations, and contemporary peoples. The overall aim of the series is to offer a comprehensive and up-to-date picture of the African peoples, in books which are at once scholarly and accessible."

Published so far in the Blackwell series is David Beach's study of the Shona peoples and other inhabitants of the Zimbabwean plateau in Southeastern Africa, *The Shona and their Neighbours* (Beach 1994). The following volumes are in preparation: *The Berbers*, by Michael Brett and Elizabeth Fentress; *The Maasai, the Dinka and the East African Pastoralists*, by Peter Robertshaw and Neil Sobania; *The Ethiopians*, by Richard Pankhurst; *The Peoples of the Middle Niger*, by R. J. McIntosh and S. J. McIntosh; and *The Swahili*, by Mark Horton.

Waveland Press, a publisher that specializes in anthropological studies, carries two volumes that are relevant: *A History of the African People* (July 1992) and *Peoples of Africa: Cultures of Africa South of the Sahara* (Gibbs 1965). Robert July's text, which is now in its fourth edition, surveys Africa's diverse peoples from their earliest beginnings through their post-independence

### Some of Africa's Peoples

Afars
Amhara
Asante
Banda
Beja
Bemba
Berbers
Cape Coloured
Chokwe
Dinka
Ewe
Falasha
Fang
Fon
Hausa
Herero
Hutus
Igbo
Karamojong
Kikuyu Maasai
Kongo
Kuba
Lozi
Mbuti
Moors
Ndebele
Ovambo
Shona
Sotho
Swahili
Tswana
Tuareg
Tutsi
Venda
Yoruba
Zulu

struggles to establish politically and economically viable nations. The *Peoples of Africa*, by anthropologist James L. Gibbs Jr., provides profiles of 15 societies of peoples who live in Africa south of the Sahara Desert. Gibbs organizes his presentations around five elements: major forms of subsistence; population sizes and patterns of social and political organization; "cultural areas and ecological zones"; racial stocks; and language families.

*Peoples of the World: Africans South of the Sahara* (Moss and Wilson 1991) profiles 34 contemporary African societies and five "old cultures" (Nok, Ghana, Mali, Songhai, and Bantu). Each of the alphabetically arranged contemporary studies covers the historical background, geographical setting, and present-day culture of the society being examined. A short list of further reading suggestions brings each profile to a close.

The Rosen Publishing Group (New York) is publishing a multi-volume reference set that aims to introduce middle- and high-school students to the culture and history of 56 distinct African societies. Volumes in the Heritage Library of African Peoples series are written by scholars of Africa, under the overall editorial supervision of Professor George Bond, Director of African Studies at Columbia University and professor of anthropology at Teachers College, Columbia University. Each 64-page clothbound volume is illustrated with color photographs and includes links "to important aspects of African and African-American curriculum studies." The Heritage Library of African Peoples is being published in four regional sets: East Africa (available now), and West, Central, and South Africa (forthcoming in late 1997).

Though the aims of this publishing effort are laudable and the credentials of the authors are beyond reproach, it must be noted that the Heritage Library has been criticized by some African studies educators for the disproportionate emphasis it places—through pictures and words—on "exotic" images of relatively small African societies.

Critics ask: What impression would middle-school children in Italy or high-school students in Japan derive of North American societies if their primary sources of information were scholarly studies of the Inuit, Lakota, Cherokee, or other atypical peoples of the Americas?

A similar cautionary note extends to textbooks in the Threatened Cultures series from Wayland Pub-

---

### ENDANGERED PEOPLES

The peoples of Africa are among those studied in resource materials that describe and voice concerns about the state of indigenous and traditional societies around the world. See, for example:

*The Atlas of Endangered Peoples* (Pollock 1995)

*The Indigenous World 1995-96* (International Work Group for Indigenous Affairs—IWGIA 1997)

*Endangered Peoples* (Davidson 1994)

*Enslaved Peoples in the 1990s* (Anti-Slavery International and IWGIA 1997)

*"Never Drink from the Same Cup." Proceedings of the Conference on Indigenous Peoples in Africa. Tune, Denmark 1993* (Veber et al. 1993)

*People of the Tropical Rain Forest* (Denslow and Padoch 1988)

*Populations in Danger* (Jean 1992)

*State of the Peoples: A Global Human Rights Report on Societies in Danger* (Miller 1993)

*Traditional Peoples Today: Continuity and Change in the Modern World* (Burenhult 1994)

Periodicals and other publications from international organizations such as Cultural Survival (Cambridge), International Work Group on Indigenous Affairs (Cophenhagen), and Survival International (London) are recommended sources for up-to-date reports and commentary on the state of peoples in Africa and other parts of the world.

lishers (East Sussex), particularly *Kalahari Bushmen*, produced in 1993 by Dr. Alan Barnard, Senior Lecturer in Social Anthropology at the University of Edinburgh, Scotland.

A highly recommended source for critical appraisals of educational materials such as the aforementioned is *Africa Access Review of K-12 Materials*, published by Africa Access, 2204 Quinton Rd., Silver Spring, MD 20910 USA.

Studies of invididual African societies include *The Swahili: Idiom and Identity of an African People* (Mazrui and Shariff 1994), *The Tuaregs: The Blue People* (Prasse 1995), *The Egyptians* (Donadoni 1997), and *Anioma: A Social History of the Western Igbo People* (Ohadike 1994).

## Personalities

For information on individual African personalities, see *An African Biographical Dictionary* (Brockman 1994). This is the most comprehensive and up-to-date reference directory available on more than 550 African men and women from all walks of life (along with sketches of some "influential" non-Africans). Emphasis is given to the postcolonial contemporary period, with about two-thirds of the alphabetically arranged entries dating from 1950 on. Other reference volumes of this nature include

- *100 Great Africans* (Rake 1994);
- *African States and Rulers: An Encyclopedia of Native, Colonial and Independent States and Rulers Past and Present* (Stewart 1989);
- *Dictionary of African Historical Biography* (Lipschutz and Rasmussen 1986);
- *Peoples of Africa* (Facts on File 1997). Volume 6: *Nations of Africa*;
- *Political Leaders in Black Africa: A Biographical Dictionary of the Major Politicians since Independence* (Wiseman 1991);
- *Who's Who in Africa: Leaders for the 1990s* (Rake 1992);
- *Who's Who in the Arab World 1997-98* (1997).

Noteworthy descriptions and analyses of the lives, times, and thought of various historical and contemporary African individuals include *Amílcar Cabral's Revolutionary Theory and Practice: A Critical Guide* (Chilcote 1991); *The Global African: A Portrait of Ali A. Mazrui* (Kokole 1997); *Haile Sellassie I: The Formative Years, 1892-1936* (Marcus 1995); *Kwame Nkrumah: The Conakry Years. His Life and Letters* (Milne 1990); *The Life and Times of Menelik II: Ethiopia, 1844-1913* (Marcus 1995); *Mwalimu: The Influence of Nyerere* (Legum and Mmari 1995); *The Royal Eagle of the Yoruba* (Olorunnisola and Akinbami 1992); and *Samora Machel: A Biography* (Christie 1989).

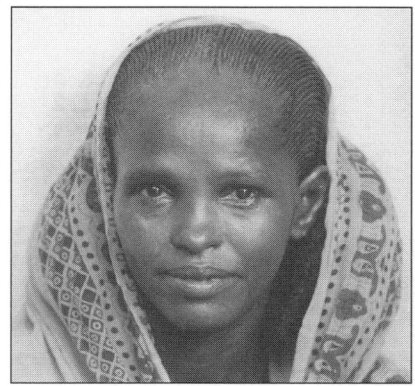

An introduction to African historical and modern-day personalities that is geared to an upper primary-school audience is *African Portraits*, a volume in the Images across the Ages series of textbooks from Raintree Steck-Vaughn publishers (Hoobler and Hoobler 1993).

See also the biographies and autobiographies of African writers, musicians, filmmakers, and others listed elsewhere in this guide.

UN/DPI photos

# AIDS IN AFRICA
## Models of community support

The issue of AIDS in Africa is a troublesome one for educators and for those who struggle to change negative, stereotyped images of Africa. Should AIDS be considered at all in educational programs about Africa? Is it just one more example of the too-easy connection that is made between Africa and apocalyptic crises? Africa educators ask: If you were studying the Americas or giving a course on one or another country in Europe would you include a segment on AIDS? If not, the educators counsel, then it is not fair to isolate Africa in this regard, no matter how grave the crisis.

There is also a concern about the unreliability of AIDS-related statistics. As Doctors David Sanders and Abdulrahman Sambo observe in their article, "AIDS in Africa," in *AIDS, Ethics and Religion: Embracing a World of Suffering* (Overberg 1994), there is little precision in the number of HIV and AIDS cases reported to the World Health Organization (WHO) from the African continent. "Underreporting," they write, "which is common, is due mainly to lack of reliable data and government sensitivity—due to concern for the presumed negative effects on tourism and investment as well as sensationalized (and often racist) reporting of the epidemic" (p. 47).

A final—and very troubling—issue is that of racism. The contention that the Human Immunodeficiency Virus (HIV) had its *origins* in Africa is denounced as racist by some authors and AIDS activists. *AIDS, Africa, and Racism* (Chirimuuta and Chirimuuta 1989) and *Blaming Others: Prejudice, Race and Worldwide AIDS* (Sabatier 1988) are two books that challenge readers to reexamine the accepted wisdom on the origins of the virus.

However troubling the AIDS issue is for Africa educators, researchers, and activists, the fact remains that the AIDS crisis has had a terribly disproportionate impact on the people of Africa. In 1996, the World Health Organization (WHO) estimated that of the 23 million HIV-positive adults worldwide, over 14 million were in sub-Saharan Africa. United Nations figures estimate that another nine million will die as a result of AIDS in the 15

Courtesy Dr. Kapita M. Bila and
Editions Centre de Vulgarisation Agricole

sub-Saharan African countries by 2005. Clearly the spread of AIDS in Africa is a crisis that merits serious study and sensitive concern. No one is helped by ignoring this crisis out of fears—no matter how well-founded—that discussion of the issue will be mishandled by some educators or misunderstood by others.

The resources described below document the nature and extent of the AIDS pandemic in Africa and situate the crisis in the broader context of the spread of AIDS worldwide. The resources also highlight—and this is critical—the innovative and effective ways that Africans are responding to this health challenge.

Three reference books that offer general overviews of the worldwide spread of the AIDS pandemic are *AIDS and the Third World* (Panos 1989), *AIDS in the World: A Global Report* (Mann et al. 1992), and *AIDS in the World Part II* (Mann et al. 1996). None of the books devotes particular attention to the spread of AIDS in Africa, but the data they provide are invaluable for setting the AIDS in Africa crisis in a world context.

**Estimated numbers of persons living with HIV/AIDS (July 1996)**

Total: 21.8 million
Sub-Saharan Africa: 64%
North and South Pacific: 0.2%
Asia: 22%
North America: 3.5%
Caribbean: 1.2%
Latin America: 6%
Europe: 2.1%
North Africa/Middle East: 1%

Courtesy of *Maryknoll Magazine*, May 1997. U.N. statistics

## AIDS in the African context

Three book-length studies examine the AIDS crisis in the African context: *AIDS and STDs in Africa: Bridging the Gap Between Traditional Healing and Modern Medicine* (Green 1994), *AIDS in Africa: Its Present and Future Impact* (Barnett and Blaikie 1992), and *Facing Up to AIDS: The Socio-Economic Impact in Southern Africa* (Cross and Whiteside 1996). *AIDS in Africa and the Caribbean* (Bond et al. 1997) contains ethnographic studies from African and Caribbean nations.

*Facing Up to AIDS* features articles by economists, demographers, and health planners and concentrates its geographical focus on South Africa and Zimbabwe. *AIDS in Africa* deals with the social and economic consequences of AIDS in Africa, with special reference to Uganda. Edward Green's *AIDS and STDs in Africa* critically analyzes various AIDS control programs in Africa and argues that "some sort of collaborative action program involving traditional healers is necessary if we wish to significantly impact the spread of AIDS and other STDs in Africa."

In 1994 the Department for Economic and Social Information and Policy Analysis of the United Nations released a 72-page study of the epidemiology and the demography of HIV and AIDS in Africa: *AIDS and the Demography of Africa*. The UN report features country profiles of fifteen sub-Saharan nations. Each profile contains a one-page narrative overview and a table of demographic indicators (from 1980 to 2005).

Geographer Peter Gould focuses a chapter on Africa ("A Continent in Catastrophe") in his book *The Slow Plague: A Geography of the AIDS Pandemic*

(Gould 1993). Gould argues that we should "throw away the supposed precision of reported statistics [about AIDS], hold onto our commonsense" and analyze how the AIDS pandemic has spread in Africa (and elsewhere) both spatially and temporally."

Anne V. Akeroyd discusses several other books concerned with debates relating to the extent and possible future development of HIV/AIDS in Africa in an article entitled "HIV/AIDS in Eastern and Southern Africa" in the *Review of African Political Economy* (no. 60, pp. 173-184, 1994). Among the books reviewed are *Facing up to AIDS: The Socio-Economic Impact in Southern Africa* (Cross and Whiteside 1993) and *Women and AIDS in Rural Africa: Rural Women's Views of AIDS in Zambia* (Mwale and Burnard 1992).

Case studies of local initiatives to combat AIDS in five African countries are contained in *Community-Based AIDS Prevention and Care in Africa: Building on Local Inititatives* (Leonard and Khan 1994). The countries profiled are Kenya, Tanzania, Uganda, Zambia, and Zimbabwe. Elizabeth Reid's *HIV and AIDS: The Global Inter-Connection* (Reid 1995) contains numerous personal stories about how individuals and communities are living with and working to stop the spread of the virus in Kenya, Lesotho, Nigeria, Tanzania, Uganda, Zaire, Zambia, Zimbabwe, and in other countries of the world.

## AIDS-related issues in Africa

**Children:** Vol. 20, Nos. 2-3/93 of *Children Worldwide* (International Catholic Child Bureau 1993) was devoted to an international survey of children and AIDS. Included in the coverage of Africa were reports entitled "The Fight against AIDS in the Socio-Cultural Context of Africa," "Prenatal Transmission of HIV in Africa," "TASO: Living Positively with AIDS," "AIDS Orphans: Problems and Solutions," and "Anti-AIDS Clubs [in Zambia]."

**Development:** *The Hidden Cost of AIDS: The Challenge of HIV to Development* (Panos 1992) makes several critical points about the relationship between HIV/AIDS and development. The first is that HIV/AIDS is only secondarily a health problem. "The epidemic is driven by social and economic factors which make some individuals more vulnerable to infection." The second point is that poverty fuels the spread of HIV/AIDS. "Communities struggling with inadequate health facilities, high levels of illiteracy, and low incomes are often more at risk." (Quotes found on p. 153.) CAFOD, the overseas development agency of the Roman Catholic Church in England and Wales, produced an "information pack" in 1993 that was designed to help church audiences situate the AIDS crisis within the broader context of development: *AIDS and Development*.

**Women:** *Women and HIV/AIDS: An International Resource Book* (Berer and Ray 1993) describes the impact of HIV/AIDS on the health, sexual relationships, and reproductive rights of women in Africa (see references throughout the book) and contains case studies of women with AIDS in Nigeria, Tanzania,

An inspiring story of one Ugandan woman's encounter with AIDS is told in *We Miss You All. Noerine Kaleeba: AIDS in the Family* (Kaleeba et al. 1991). Kaleeba, a physiotherapist and mother of four, recounts her struggle to come to terms with her husband's AIDS-related suffering and death in mid-1983. Kaleeba speaks forthrightly about her decision to come "out in the open" about her husband's disease, about the "uncomfortable and distressing" experiences she had with hospital staff, and about the difficulties that she and Chris had had in their marriage relationship. Shortly after Chris died (on January 23, 1987), Noerine Kaleeba joined together with 16 friends, 12 of whom had AIDS, to establish the AIDS Support Organisation (TASO) in Kampala, Uganda.

*Graphic credit:* Jane Shepherd

Rwanda, Uganda, South Africa, and Zimbabwe. Examples of creative and effective responses to the HIV/AIDS crisis by women in Africa are found in Brooke Grundfest Schoepf's article, "Action-Research and Empowerment in Africa," in *Women Resisting AIDS* (Schneider and Stoller 1994).

See also *Women and Health in Africa* (Schoepf et al. 1990); *Women and AIDS: Developing a New Health Strategy* (Gupta and Weiss 1993); *Women and AIDS* (Zimbabwe Women's Resource Centre and Network 1993); *Women in the Time of AIDS* (Paterson 1996); *Kampala Women Getting By: Wellbeing in the Time of AIDS* (Wallman 1996); *Women, Poverty and AIDS: Sex, Drug and Structural Violence* (Farmer et al. 1996); and *Women and AIDS: A Bibliography* (Nordquist 1993).

## Keeping up

Various organizations publish magazines and newsletters focused on the AIDS pandemic. See, for example: *AIDS Action*, a quarterly newsletter from AHRTAG/Appropriate Health Resources and Technologies Action Group (London) and *WorldAIDS: A News Magazine Reporting on AIDS and Development*, from Panos (London and Washington, D.C.). Print and audiovisual resources produced on a regular basis in the "Strategies for Hope" series (see below) are recommended for personal and/or group study.

---

### AIDS IN AFRICA—STRATEGIES FOR HOPE

Strategies for Hope produces resource materials that describe the pioneering experiences of African nongovernmental organizations in meeting the challenge of AIDS. Produced with support from various British relief agencies, the resources highlight community-based forms of care, counselling, and support for people with AIDS and their families.

**Booklets:**

• *From Fear to Hope: AIDS Care and Prevention at Chikankata Hospital, Zambia* (Williams 1992)

• *Living Positively with AIDS: The AIDS Support Organization (TASO), Uganda* (Hampton 1991)

• *AIDS Management: An Integrated Approach* (Campbell and Williams 1992)

• *Meeting AIDS with Compassion: AIDS Care and Prevention in Agomanya, Ghana* (Hampton 1991)

• *AIDS Orphans: A Community Perspective from Tanzania* (Mukoyogo and Williams 1993)

• *The Caring Community: Coping with AIDS in Urban Uganda* (Williams and Tamale 1991)

• *All Against AIDS: The Copperbelt Health Education Project, Zambia* (Mouli 1992)

• *Work Against AIDS: Workplace-based AIDS Initiatives in Zimbabwe* (Williams and Ray 1993)

• *Filling the Gaps: Care and Support for People with HIV/AIDS in Côte d'Ivoire* (Williams et al. 1995)

**Videotapes:**

*TASO: Living Positively with AIDS.* A two-part (55 minutes) videotape on the work of The AIDS Support Organization (TASO) in Uganda.

*The Orphan Generation.* A 50-minute video about community-based care and support for children orphaned by AIDS.

*Strategies for Hope* materials are available from TALC, P.O. Box 49, St. Albans, Herts AL1 4AX, England or, in *Kenya,* from Health Education Network, AMREF, P.O. Box 30125, Nairobi, in *Tanzania,* from AIDS Project, AMREF Tanzania, P.O. Box 2773, Dar es Salaam, in *Uganda,* from AMREF Uganda, P.O. Box 51, Entebbe.

# BELIEF SYSTEMS
## Indigenous, Islamic, Christian

*SEDOS Bulletin* 26, nos. 3 and 4 (1994)

Religion, author Tshishiku Tshibangu has observed, "impregnates the entire texture of individual and commercial life in Africa." In his chapter on "Religion and Social Evolution" in *Africa Since 1935* (Mazrui 1993), volume 8 of UNESCO's General History of Africa series, Tshibangu writes: "The African is 'profoundly, incurably a believer, a religious person'. To him, religion is not just a set of beliefs but a way of life, the basis of culture, identity and moral values. Religion is an essential part of the tradition that helps to promote both social stability and creative innovation." Tshibangu's article (chapter 17) identifies and describes the three major strands of religious beliefs in Africa: indigenous (traditional) religions, Christianity, and Islam. An earlier introductory survey, *Religions in Africa* (Stewart et al. 1984), follows the same three-part focus—one that we have adopted for this chapter.

The twenty essays in *Religion in Africa: Experience and Expression* (Blakely et al. 1994) provide a scholarly—yet accessible—overview of the varieties of religious experiences and expressions that are rooted in the African continent. The book is the fruit of a conference entitled "Religion in Africa: The Variety of Religious Experience in Sub-Saharan Africa" held at Brigham Young University in Provo, Utah, 22-25 October 1986. Scholars from four continents who study religious expression throughout all the major regions of Africa and in the African Diaspora in the Americas gave presentations on an array of topics from multi-disciplinary academic perspectives.

Nairobi University professor J. N. K. Mugambi's undergraduate textbook *A Comparative Study of Religions* (Mugambi 1993) presents a wide-ranging survey of religions and belief systems both in and outside Africa (from "the religion of indigenous Australians" to "the rise of Zoroastrianism"). Four essays in section 3—all written by S. G. Kibicho, Associate Professor of Religious Studies, University of Nairobi—cover earlier studies of African religion, the nature and structure of African religion, the conception of God in African religion, and the conceptions of divinities and spirits.

## Indigenous religions

"The importance of traditional African religion," Tshishiku Tshibangu writes (see Mazrui 1993, p. 505), "goes well beyond what the statistical affiliation figure of 20 percent of the total African population may suggest. For many Christians and Muslims," Tshibangu contends, "the basis of moral values still derives more from the old cosmology than from the new beliefs." He cites, as evidence, the continuing respect for ancestors, belief in the continuing involvement of ancestors in the life of their successors, belief in the forces of good and evil that "can be manipulated by direct access to the divinities through prayer and sacrifice, belief in the efficacy of charms and amulets to ward off evil," and, finally, "the vast area of African life which both Islam and Christianity have invaded but have not succeeded in completely displacing," the area of health and healing.

Kenyan theologian John Mbiti's *African Religions and Philosophy* (Mbiti 1990) is acknowledged to be the standard work in the field of systematic studies of traditional African religious and philosophical concepts.

*African Traditional Religion in Biblical Perspective* (Gehman 1993) represents an attempt by a U.S. missionary with more than 30 years' experience in East Africa to search out and understand the positive aspects of African traditional religion in light of the Christian Scriptures.

Recognized books on the history and development of indigenous African religions include *African Religions and Philosophy* (Mbiti 1970); *African Traditional Religion: A Definition* (Idowu 1975); *African Traditional Religions in Contemporary Society* (Olupona 1991); *Introduction to African Religions* (Mbiti 1975); *The Origins and Development of African Theology* (Muzorewa 1985); *Religion, Development and African Identity* (Petersen 1987); and *Religion in Africa* (Parrinder 1969).

## Islam

*The Atlas of the Arab World: Geopolitics and Society* (Boustani and Fargues 1991) is a good starting point for graphic illustrations of the growth of the Islamic faith in nations across the north of Africa. The atlas covers cultural, social, and economic issues in 21 Arab countries—in the Near and Middle East, North Africa, Mauritania, and the Horn of Africa. Chapter 2 focuses on ethnic groups and religions.

Books that introduce Islam in a comprehensive historical and geographical manner include *An Introduction to Islam* (Waines 1995), *Unfolding*

### Distribution of belief systems in Africa

African countries in which one belief system is estimated to have the allegiance of 50 percent or more of the population.
Source: *Worldmark Encyclopedia of the Nations: Africa* (Gale Research)

| | African countries in which one belief system claims 50 percent or more of the population as believers |
|---|---|
| **Traditional Religions** | Benin, Botswana, Burkina Faso, Central African Republic, Cote d'Ivoire, Guinea-Bissau, Madagascar, Mozambique, Sierra Leone, Togo, Zambia |
| **Christianity** | Angola, Burundi, Cameroon, Cape Verde, Equitorial Guinea, Gabon, Kenya, Lesotho, Liberia, Malawi, Namibia, Sao Tome and Principe, Seychelles, South Africa, Swaziland, Uganda, Zimbabwe |
| **Islam** | Algeria, Comoros, Djibouti, Egypt, Gambia, Guinea, Libya, Mali, Mauritania, Morocco, Niger, Senegal, Somalia, Sudan, Tunisis |
| **Mixed*** | Chad, Congo, Democratic Republic of Congo (Zaire), Eritrea, Ethiopia, Ghana, Mauritius, Nigeria, Rwanda, Tanzania |

* no belief system having 50 percent of the population as adherents

Ornate Arabic script centering on the name of God and God's titles of Giver of All Gifts and Most Compassionate One.
Courtesy: Reconciliation International

*Islam* (Stewart 1994), and *Islam in History: Ideas, People, and Events in the Middle East* (Lewis 1993). Professor Gregory Kozlowski's 100-page introduction to Islam is entitled *The Concise History of Islam and the Origin of Its Empires* (Kozlowski 1991). Islam's expansion throughout Africa is covered most completely in *Islam in History* by Professor Bernard Lewis (1993).

The following three volumes concentrate on the influence of Islam in various regions of Africa: *The Heritage of Islam: Women, Religion, and Politics in West Africa* (Callaway and Creevey 1994); *Muslim Identity and Social Change in Sub-Saharan Africa* (Brenner 1993), and *Islamism and Secularism in North Africa* (Ruedy 1996).

Country-specific studies of the nature and political impact of the Islamic movement in Egypt, Sudan, and Tunisia are contained in *Political Islam: Religion and Politics in the Arab World* (Ayubi 1991). The growth of Islamic fundamentalism in Egypt is examined in *Islamic Fundamentalism in Egyptian Politics* (Rubin 1990) and *Islam: The Fear and the Hope* (Boularès 1990).

Recently published reference works on Islam include *Encyclopedia of Islam* (International Union of Academies 1995), *The Oxford Encyclopedia of the Modern Islamic World* (Esposito 1995), and *Islamic Desk Reference* (von Donzel 1994).

## Christianity

Four recently published books cover the growth of Christianity in Africa: *A History of Christianity in Africa: From Antiquity to the Present* (Isichei 1995); *The Church in Africa, 1450-1950* (Hastings 1995); *2000 Years of Christianity in Africa* (Baur 1994); and *Christianity in Africa: The Renewal of a Non-Western Religion* (Bediako 1995).

The Africa Office of the National Council of Churches (USA) and the Washington Office on Africa produced *Christian Witness for Africa: A Guide for Effective Action* in the fall of 1995 in order to encourage informed and effective involvement by U.S. religious institutions in the formulation of U.S. government policies toward Africa. The packet contains background information, liturgical resources, and advocacy strategies designed "to assist church activists and people of conscience interested in refocusing U.S. assistance policy toward Africa. For information, write the Washington Office on Africa, 110 Maryland Ave., NE, Ste. 112, Washington, DC 20002 USA.

Orbis Books (Maryknoll, N.Y.) is the foremost publisher of English-language studies about Christianity and Christian theology in Africa. Among their many titles are *African Cry* (Ela 1986); *The African Synod: Documents, Reflections, Perspectives* (Africa Faith and Justice Network 1996); *African Theology: Inculturation and Liberation* (Martey 1993); *African Theology in Its Social Context* (Bujo 1992); *Faces of Jesus in Africa* (Schreiter 1995); *A Listening Church: Autonomy and Communion in African Churches* (Usukwu 1996); *The Origins and Development of African Theology* (Muzorewa 1985); *Paths of African Theology* (Gibellini 1994); *The Will to Arise: Women, Tradition, and the Church in Africa* (Oduyoye and Kanyoro 1992).

In 1995, Willaim B. Eerdmans (Grand Rapids, Mich.)—another publisher with a strong list of English-language titles on this subject—published what it describes as "the first comprehensive survey of Christian theology in Africa to appear in English," theologian John Parratt's *Reinventing Christianity: African Theology Today* (Parratt 1995).

Books that deal with various facets of the engagement of African Christian churches in the political life of their societies include *The Angels*

*Have Left Us: The Rwanda Tragedy and the Churches* (McCullum 1995); *The Christian Churches and the Democratisation of Africa* (Gifford 1995); *Christianity and Politics in Doe's Liberia* (Gifford 1993); *From Liberation to Reconstruction: African Christian Theology after the Cold War* (Mugambi 1995); *Religion and Politics in East Africa* (Hansen and Twaddle 1995); and *Religion and Politics in Southern Africa* (Hallencreutz and Palmberg 1991).

## Bibliographies and reference works

See the lengthy bibliographies in *Religion in Africa* (Blakely et al. 1994) and in *Africa Since 1935* (Mazrui 1993) for other books and articles on the subject of African belief systems. See also: *Bibliography of New Religious Movements in Primal Societies. Volume 1: Black Africa* (Turner 1977); *A Comprehensive Bibliography of Modern African Religious Movements* (Mitchell and Turner 1967); A. Oded's "A Bibliographic Essay of the History of Islam in Africa" in *A Current Bibliography on African Affairs 8*, no. 1 (1975); *Islam in Sub-Saharan Africa: A Partially Annotated Guide* (Zoghby 1978); and *Bibliography in Contextual Theology in Africa* (Cochrane et al. 1993).

Background on African belief systems can be found in these reference books: *The HarperCollins Dictionary of Religion* (Smith 1995); *Eerdmans' Handbook to the World's Religions: A Comprehensive Guide* (Alexander 1994); *The Illustrated World's Religions: A Guide to Our Wisdom Traditions* (Smith 1994); *Larousse Dictionary of Beliefs and Religions: A Comprehensive Outline of Spiritual Concepts from Prehistory to the Present* (Goring 1994); *The Origins of Religions* (Ries 1994); and *A World Religions Reader* (Markham 1995).

Cluster Publications (Pietermaritzburg Cluster of Theological Institutions)

### SOUTH AFRICA—A CHURCH ENGAGED

*Being the Church in South Africa Today* (Pityana and Villa-Vicencio 1996)

*Civil Disobedience and Beyond: Law, Resistance and Religion in South Africa* (Villa-Vicencio 1990)

*God's Wrathful Children: Political Oppression and Christian Ethics* (Boesak 1995)

*A Long Struggle: The Involvement of the World Council of Churches in South Africa* (Webb 1994)

*Prophetic Christianity and the Liberation Movement in South Africa* (Walshe 1995)

*The Road to Rustenburg: The Church Looking Forward to a New South Africa* (Alberts and Chikane 1991)

*The Spirit of Freedom: South African Leaders on Religion and Politics* (Villa-Vicencio 1996)

*Third Way Theology: Reconciliation, Revolution and Reform in the South African Church During the 1980s* (Balcomb 1993)

*Towards a Democratic Future* (Southern African Catholic Bishops' Conference 1993)

*The Unquestionable Right to be Free: Black Theology from South Africa* (Mosala and Tlhagale 1986)

**Books by and about South African Church Leaders:**

*Beyers Naudé: Pilgrimage of Faith* (Ryan 1990)

*If This Is Treason, I Am Guilty* (Boesak 1987)

*In Transit: Between the Image of God and the Image of Man* (Farisani 1990)

*Priest and Partisan: A South African Journey* (Worsnip 1996)

*The Rainbow People of God: The Making of a Peaceful Revolution* (Tutu 1994)

*Return to South Africa: The Ecstasy and the Agony* (Huddleston 1991)

*The Spirit of Hope: Conversations on Politics, Religion and Values* (Villa-Vicencio 1993)

For additional information on the church in South Africa, see *South Africa as Apartheid Ends: An Annotated Bibliography with Analytical Introductions* (Stultz 1993), pp. 89-93: "Religion and churches."

# CINEMA
## Africa through an African lens

Africa "may not be the most conducive place for film production," author Nwachukwu F. Ukadike notes, "but through hard work and dedication filmmakers have proven that this continent, which was once a filmic cul-de-sac, when given the right opportunity, now produces some of the world's finest films, responsive to the genuine needs and aspirations of its people."

Ukadike's laudatory assessment of the state of African cinema suggests that there is much to be learned about Africa and its peoples by studying films and videos produced by African filmmakers.

Three highly recommended books provide a solid foundation for understanding the development of filmmaking in Africa. They are *Black African Cinema* (Ukadike 1994), which offers an informed and readable survey of the history and development of cinema in sub-Saharan Africa; *Arab and African Film Making* (Malkmus and Armes 1991), which complements Nwachukwu Ukadike's study by including North Africa in its coverage; and *African Experiences of Cinema* (Bakari and Cham 1996), an authoritative collection of documents, testimonies, and essays that address significant aspects of the experiences and challenges of cinema in various parts of the entire African continent over a broad timespan.

Clyde Taylor's opening essay on Africa in *World Cinema since 1945* (Luhr 1987) presents a 21-page history of the development of filmmaking in Africa in the post-colonial period. Taylor's article, "Africa: The Last Cinema," is notable for including North as well as sub-Saharan Africa. Roy Armes also covers North Africa (the Maghreb, or Arab West) and sub-Saharan—or Black— Africa in his groundbreaking survey of film production in the Third World: *Third World Film Making and the West* (Armes 1987).

(Note that most of what has been written about "African" cinema has been produced in French because of the comparative strength of the industry in French-speaking central and west Africa and applies generally to sub-Saharan Africa.)

> "A handsome display of [cinematic] works varying in scope and diverse in creativity has emerged [in Africa] from individual energies out of the concern to decolonize and reassert African identity."
>
> Nwachukwu F. Ukadike,
> *Black African Cinema*
> (Ukadike 1994), p. 308

The history of Black Africa's cinema is given, in brief, in the translated text of a booklet in Cinemedia's French-language series "Cinemas of Black Africa": *To Have a History of African Cinema* (Bachy 1987).

For a concise overview of the subject see Nancy Schmidt's article, "African Filmmakers and Their Films," in *African Studies Review* (Schmidt 1994). Schmidt, who is Librarian for African Studies and Adjunct Professor of Anthropology at Indiana University, has compiled two authoritative and highly recommended bibliographies on African films and filmmakers: *Sub-Saharan African Films and Filmmakers: An Annotated Bibliography* (Schmidt 1988) and *Sub-Saharan African Films and Filmmakers: An Annotated Bibliography, 1987-1992* (Schmidt 1994). Schmidt's two bibliographies contain more than 7,000 entries of English- and French-language books, monographs, academic theses, articles, reviews, pamphlets, and other resource materials on filmmaking in sub-Saharan Africa. The more recent of the two bibliographies includes a reprint of an essay by Schmidt, "Visualizing Africa: The Bibliography of Films by Sub-Saharan African Filmmakers," that describes the nature and scope of printed resources on this topic.

Other noteworthy overviews and bibliographies include *African Cinema: Politics and Culture* (Diawara 1992); *Black and Third Cinema: Film and Television Bibliography* (Vieler-Porter 1991); *Critical Perspectives on Black Independent Cinema* (Cham and Andrade-Watkins 1988); *Bibliography of Film Bibliographies* (Wulff 1987); and "New Discourses of African Cinema," *Iris* (biannual magazine), spring 1995 (no. 18).

## Region/country studies

Nwachukwu Ukadike and Manthia Diawara both devote chapters in their surveys to the study of filmmaking in the Francophone and Anglophone regions of Africa. See *Black African Cinema* (Ukadike 1994), chapters 2 and 3), and *African Cinema: Politics and Culture* (Diawara 1992), chapters 1 and 5. Diawara also covers film production in Portuguese-speaking (Lusophone) Africa, and provides country studies of Zaire and Mozambique.

Africa specialist Nancy J. Schmidt published a review of filmmaking in several African nations in *African Studies Review* 28, no. 1 (1985): 111-114, "African Filmmaking, Country by Country."

The thirty-first edition of the *Variety International Film Guide 1994* (Cowie 1993) contains chapters on filmmaking in four African countries: Burkina Faso, Egypt, South Africa, and Zimbabwe.

*The Cinema in Nigeria* (Balogun 1987) is an introduction to filmmaking in Nigeria by Françoise Balogun, wife of Ola Balogun, "one of Nigeria's most prolific filmmakers and an outspoken advocate of the development of a national film industry in Nigeria" (in the words of Nancy J. Schmidt; see Schmidt's review article, "Recent Perspectives on Sub-Saharan African Filmmaking," in the second quarter 1989 edition of *Africa Today* magazine).

Filmmaking in South Africa is the focus of two studies: *The Cinema of Apartheid: Race and Class in South African Film* (Tomaselli 1988) and *Images of South Africa: The Rise of the Alternative Film* (Botha and van Aswegen 1992). The co-author of *Images of South Africa*—Martin Botha—is a research specialist at the Human Sciences Research Council in Pretoria, South Africa, and is co-editor of *Movies Moguls Mavericks: South African Cinema 1979-1991* (Blignaut and Botha 1992).

For region/country-specific information on filmmaking in North Africa see "Bibliography and Filmography," by Miriam Rosen and Barbara Shahin Batlouni, in *The Arab Image in American Film and Television* (Georgakas and Rosen 1989), and directories published by Arab World and Islamic Resources and School Services (Berkeley, Calif.).

## Biographies and filmographies

Lists of films produced by African filmmakers (continent-wide) are given in the *Directory of African Film-Makers and Films* (Shiri 1992). Entries are arranged alphabetically by the director's surname, with a brief biographical sketch and filmography presented in each entry.

Françoise Pfaff's *Twenty-five Black African Filmmakers* (Pfaff 1988) contains biographical background on African filmmakers, along with lists and descriptions of their films. So, too, does *Chambers Concise Encyclopedia of Film and Television* (Hunter 1991).

---

### Ousmane Sembène: African Filmmaker and Writer

**Ousmane Sembène**
Credit: Pamela Gentile

Born in southern Senegal in 1923, Ousmane Sembène is one of Africa's most popular and prolific filmmakers. His films (two documentary and nine fiction productions) include *L'Empire Sonhrai* (1963), *Borom Sarret* (1963), *Niaye* (1964), *La Noire de...* (1966), *Mandabi* (1968), *Taaw* (1970), *Emitai* (1971), *Xala* (1974), *Ceddo* (1976), *Camp de Thiaroye* (1989), *Guelwaar* (1992). International distributors of Sembène's films are New Yorker Films (New York) and the African Video Centre (London).

Books by Sembène that are available in English translation are *The Black Docker* (1956; trans. Heinemann 1987), *God's Bits of Wood* (1960; trans. Anchor Books/Doubleday 1970), *The Money Order, with White Genesis* (1966; trans. Heinemann 1972), *Xala* (1973; trans. Lawrence Hill 1976), *The Last of the Empire: A Senegalese Novel* (1981; trans. Heinemann 1983), and *Niiwan and Taaw: Two Novellas* (1987; trans Heinemann 1992).

In April 1990 Sembène attended a two-week conference in Amherst, Massachusetts, at the invitation of the Five College African Studies Council. Highlights of the conference, including Sembène's lengthy remarks (in French, with English translation) and critical essays on his work by Mgye Cham, Francoise Pfaff, Frederick Ivor Case, and Claire Andrade-Watkins have been published in *Ousmane Sembène: Dialogues with Critics and Writers* (Gadjigo et al. 1993).

See also: *Evolution of an African Artist: Social Realism in the Works of Ousmane Sembène* (Moore 1973), *The Cinema of Ousmane Sembène: A Pioneer of African Film* (Pfaff 1984), and the listing (under Ousmane) in *A New Reader's Guide to African Literature* (Zell 1983).

The 102-page *Video Catalogue: Africa* (Karlsson 1992) produced by the Educational Resources Information Service, draws on the database of the Media Resource Centre at the University of Natal, (Durban) to present a list of African-made films and videos on a range of subjects including natural science, performing arts, religion, social issues, and visual arts.

Catalogs and guides that contain lists of films from and about Africa include *Africa in Focus: A Video Series on the History and Culture of the Nations of Africa* (Altschul Group 1995); *Africa in the School and Community: Video Resource List* (African Outreach Program, Boston University 1993); *Africa on Film and Videotape: A Guide to Audio-Visual Resources Available in Canada* (RuBlack and Pelletier 1990); *African Films and Videos* (DSR 1997); *African-American and African History and Culture* (Films for the Humanities and Sciences 1994); *Africana Videotape Listings* (Acree 1993); *An Annotated List of Audiovisual Materials* (Council on African Studies, Yale University 1993); *Film and Video Resources about Africa* (University of Illinois Film Center 1985); and *Library of African Cinema* (California Newsreel annual).

The Internet can be used to identify titles and sources of Africa-related audiovisuals. The following sites are noteworthy:
- African Studies Videotapes and Audiocassettes in the Media Resources Center (University of California, Berkeley): http://www.lib.berkeley.edu/MRC/AfricanVid.html
- University of Pennsylvania Audio Visual Center: http://www.sas.upenn.edu/African_Studies/AS.html [and] http://www.sas.upenn.edu/African_Studies/Audio_Visual/menu_Audio_Vis.html
- Guide to Film and Video Resources on the Internet (Lisa R. Wood): http://www-rohan.sdsu.edu/home/olivier/Africa/biblio.html#a9

## Periodicals and reference guides

English-language periodicals that contain news and reviews of African films and videotapes on a regular basis include: *Africa Media Review* (Nairobi), *Black Film Review* (Washington, D.C.), *Cineaste* (New York), *Ecrans d'Afrique/African Screen* (Ouagadougou), *Film Quarterly* (Berkeley), *Focus on Africa* (London), *Media Review* (Lagos), *Guide to Political Videos* (Santa Barbara), *Moving Pictures Bulletin* (London), and *WorldViews: A Quarterly Review of Resources for Education and Action* (Oakland). See *Variety International Film Guide 1994* (Cowie 1993) and *Sub-Saharan African Films and Filmmakers: An Annotated Bibliography, 1987-1992* (Schmidt 1994) for the names of other Africa-related film periodicals.

Reference guides that contain information on African films and filmmakers (as part of their broader coverage) are *Media Review Digest* (Pierian Press annual); *Educational Film and Video Locator* (R. R. Bowker annual); *and The Motion Picture Guide Annual* (Reed Reference Publishing annual); and *The Third World in Film and Video, 1984-1990* (Cyr 1991).

**African Media Program**

The African Studies Center at Michigan State University has reestablished the MSU African Media Program, a major effort to identify high-quality documentary films and television images of Africa. The AMP will create a new, definitive reference database of African films and videotapes by identifying, heavily indexing, and critically reviewing all extant films and videos on Africa released between 1981 and 1996, then continuing the process thereafter. These reviews, with filmographies, will be published in CD-ROM and print formats and disseminated electronically via the Internet.

For more information, contact the African Studies Center, Michigan State University, 100 Center for International Programs, East Lansing, MI 48824-1035 USA. Tel: (517) 353-1700.

# CONFLICTS IN AFRICA
## Causes and prospects for resolutions

Believe the headlines and one would think that the entire continent of Africa is engulfed perpetually in armed conflicts. True, Africa has been judged to be "the most warring region on the planet" (see Project Ploughshares map below), but it is important to put conflicts in African nations into perspective—in regional and global terms—and to exercise extreme caution in drawing conclusions about these conflicts that one would not apply to the incredible devastation of the "world wars" between Western powers in this century or to the social and economic toll that the innocent citizens of many nations have paid as a result of the cold-war arms race between the superpowers.

Another caution in approaching this subject is the need to put to rest the mistaken notion that Africa's conflicts are "tribal" wars. For one thing, the term "tribal" is inaccurate and pejorative, a term that would never be used to describe the warring factions in northern regions (Bosnia or Ireland, for instance). For another reason, the origins and nature of conflicts in African nations are as complex as they are in other parts of the world. They cannot be explained simplistically, as the resources in this chapter make clear.

The resource materials cataloged in this chapter also show that African nations have developed conflict resolution initiatives that are held in high regard worldwide. These breakthroughs deserve to be acknowledged.

### Background on world conflicts

The *Armed Conflicts Report* produced annually by Project Ploughshares Institute of Peace and Conflict Studies (Conrad Grebel College, Waterloo, Ontario) is the best place to begin for a clear and informed presentation of the nature and extent of conflicts on a world scale. The 1997 report (Epps et al.) determined that there were 34 states engaged in "major armed conflicts" in 1996, in varying degrees of intensity. The African continent accounted for 15 armed conflicts in that year.

> "Development is critical to overcoming structural violence which in turn may be crucial to eliminating direct violence... Development is meant to raise the majority above the minimum conditions of existence and eliminate their disadvantages. By so doing it abolishes structural violence and the direct violence that emanates from it."
>
> Okwudiba Nnoli, "Realizing Peace, Development and Regional Security in Africa: A Plan for Action," in *Africa: Perspectives on Peace and Development* (Hansen 1987), p. 216

Handy sources of information on conflicts and related military issues include: *State of the World Conflict Report* for the years 1991 and 1992 (Spencer et al. 1993), produced by the International Negotiation Network of the Carter Center of Emory University (Atlanta, Georgia); *1995 CDI Military Almanac*, compiled by the Washington, D.C.-based Center for Defense Information (CDI 1995); and *World Military and Social Expenditures 1996,* published annually by another Washington, D.C.-based organization, World Priorities (Sivard 1996).

Books that explore the origins and conduct of conflicts on an international scale include *Arms and Warfare: Escalation, De-escalation and Negotiation* (Brzoska and Pearson 1994); *Between Development and Destruction: An Enquiry into the Causes of Conflict in Post-Colonial States* (Van de Goor et al. 1996); *Managing Global Chaos: Sources of and Responses to International Conflict* (Crocker et al. 1996); and *World Security: Challenges for a New Century* (Klare and Thomas 1994).

## Conflicts in Africa

*Arms and Daggers in the Heart of Africa: Studies on Internal Conflicts* (Nyong'o 1993) offers the best overall perspective on internal conflicts in Africa, with particular attention paid to the social forces that cause and perpetuate conflicts. Chapter-length case studies deal with conflicts in Ethiopia, Sudan,

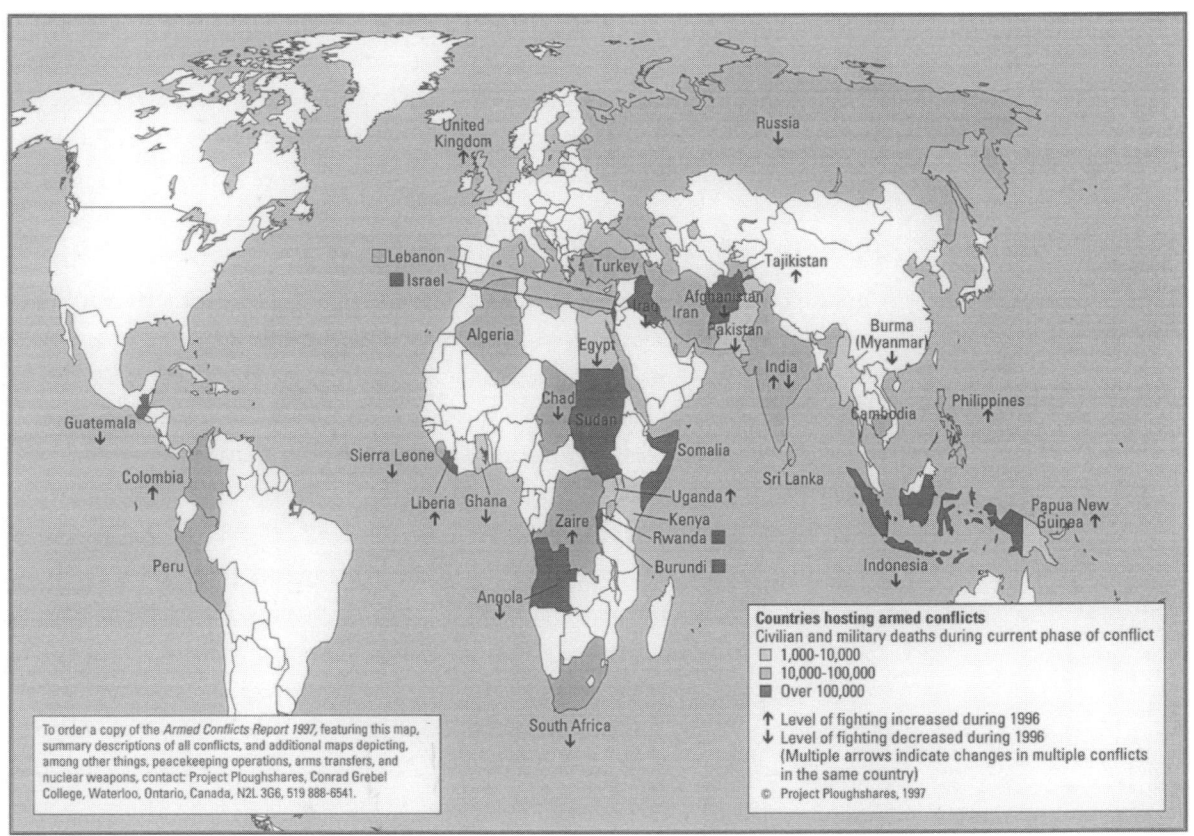

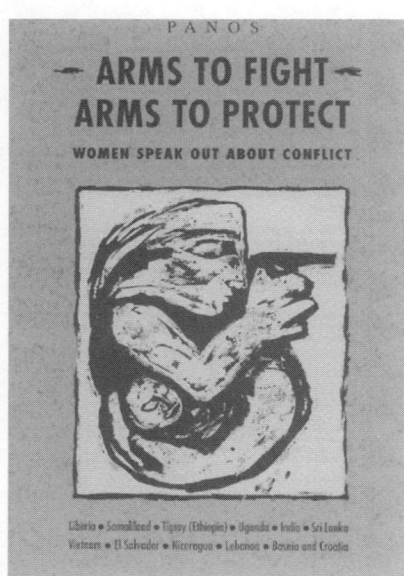

Cover of *Arms to Fight, Arms to Protect: Women Speak Out about Conflict* (Bennett et al. 1995)

Somalia, Uganda, Rwanda, Zimbabwe, Zambia, South Africa, and Liberia.

Other Africa-related studies include *Africa: Perspectives on Peace and Development* (Hansen 1987); *Coups and Army Rule in Africa* (Decalo 1990); *Disarmament and Security in Africa* (United Nations 1993); *No Farewell to Arms? Military Disengagement from Politics in Africa and Latin America* (Welch 1987); *Peace and Security in Africa: A State of the Art Report* (Hansen 1988); *Revolution and Counter-Revolution in Africa: Essays in Contemporary Politics* (Nzongola-Ntalaja 1987); and *The State of War and Peace in Africa in 1992* (Suliman and Verney 1993).

## Issues

**Arms sales:** *Lethal Commerce: The Global Trade in Small Arms and Light Weapons* (Boutwell et al. 1995); *Arms and Warfare: Escalation, De-escalation, and Negotiation* (Brzoska and Pearson 1994); *Armscor: South Africa's Arms Merchant* (McWilliams 1990); *The International Arms Trade* (Laurance 1992)

**Children:** *Child Soldiers: The Role of Children in Armed Conflicts* (Goodwin-Gill and Cohn 1994); *Orphans of the Storm: Peacebuilding for Children of War* (Walker 1993); *Reaching Children in War: Sudan, Uganda, and Mozambique* (Dodge and Raundalen 1991).

**Landmines:** Contact the International Campaign to Ban Landmines, c/o Vietnam Veterans of America Foundation, 1347 Upper Dummerston Rd., Brattleboro, VT 05301, USA, or the Mines Advisory Group, 54a Main St., Cockermouth, Cumbria CA13 9LU, England.

**Women:** *Women and War in South Africa* (Cock 1993); *Not So Innocent: When Women Become Killers* (African Rights 1995); *Arms to Fight, Arms to Protect: Women Speak Out about Conflict* (Bennett et al. 1995). Chapters on Liberia, Somaliland, Tigray, Uganda, among others.

## Region/country studies

*The New Insurgencies: Anticommunist Guerrillas in the Third World* (Radu 1990) contains case studies of Eritrea, Angola, and Mozambique.

**Horn of Africa:** *Arms for the Horn: U.S. Security Policy in Ethiopia and Somalia 1953-1991* (Lefebvre 1991); *Beyond Conflict in the Horn: The Prospects for Peace, Recovery and Development in Ethiopia, Somalia, Eritrea and the Sudan* (Doornbos et al. 1992); *Ethnicity and Conflict in the Horn of Africa* (Fukui and Markakis 1994); *The Horn of Africa* (Gurdon 1994); *Eritrea and Ethiopia: From Conflict to Cooperation* (Tekle); *The Horn of Africa: From War to Peace* (Henze 1991).

**Southern Africa:** *African Nemesis: War and Revolution in Southern Africa, 1945-2010* (Moorcraft 1994); *Recolonization and Resistance in Southern Africa in the 1990s* (Saul 1993); *Conflict in Southern Africa* (Smith 1992); *Front Line Africa: The Right to a Future* (Smith 1990); *A Political History of the Civil War in Angola 1974-1990* (James 1992); *Renamo: Terroris in Mozambique* (Vines 1991); *The Suffering Grass: Superpowers and Regional Conflict in Southern Africa and the*

*Caribbean* (Weiss and Blight 1992); *Southern Africa in a Global Context: Towards a Southern African Security Community* (Nolutshungu 1994).

**Angola:** *Apartheid's Contras: An Inquiry into the Roots of War in Angola and Mozambique* (Minter 1994); *A Political History of the Civil War in Angola, 1974-1990* (James 1992); *UNITA: Myth and Reality* (Conchiglia 1990).

**Burundi:** *Burundi: Breaking the Cycle of Violence* (Reyntjens 1995); *Burundi: Ethnocide as Discourse and Practice* (Lemarchand 1994).

**Kenya:** *Unhappy Valley: Conflict in Kenya and Africa* (Berman and Lonsdale 1992).

**Liberia:** *Enforcing Restraint: Collective Intervention in Internal Conflicts* (Damrosch 1993; chapter 4); *Uprooted Liberians: Casualties of a Brutal War* (Ruiz 1992).

**Mozambique:** *Apartheid's Contras: An Inquiry into the Roots of War in Angola and Mozambique* (Minter 1994); *Invisible Crimes: U.S. Private Intervention in the War in Mozambique* (Austin 1994); *Renamo: Terrorism in Mozambique* (Vines 1991); *Unmasking the Bandits: The True Face of the M.N.R.* (Nilsson 1990).

**Rwanda:** *The Rwanda Crisis: History of a Genocide* (Prunier 1995); *Rwanda: Which Way Now?* (Waller 1996); *Rwanda and Genocide in the Twentieth Century* (Destexhe 1995); *Shattered Lives: Sexual Violence during the Rwandan Genocide and Its Aftermath* (Nowrojee 1996); *The United Nations and Rwanda, 1993-1996* (United Nations 1996). African Rights (London) has published a number of excellent analyses of the conflict in Rwanda, including *Rwanda: Death, Despair and Defiance* (1995).

**Somalia:** *Enforcing Restraint: Collective Intervention in Internal Conflicts* (Damrosch 1993; chapter 5).

## Conflict resolution

The entire April-June 1996 issue of *Africa Today* (Boulder, Colo.) was devoted to studies of "Conflict and Conflict Resolution in Africa" (43, no. 2.) Other publications that feature discussions of conflict resolution in Africa are

- *Beyond Traditional Peacekeeping* (Daniel and Hayes 1995);
- *Conflict Resolution in Africa* (Deng and Zartman 1991);
- *Controlling and Ending Conflict: Issues Before and After the Cold War* (Cimbala and Waldman 1991);
- *Elusive Peace: Negotiating an End to Civil Wars* (Zartman 1995);
- *Ending Mozambique's War: The Role of Mediation and Good Offices* (Hume 1994);
- *Peaceful Settlement of Disputes between States: A Selective Bibliography* (Dag Hammarskjöld Library, United Nations, 1991);
- *Peacemaking in Civil War: International Mediation in Zimbabwe, 1974-1980* (Stedman 1991);
- *Ripe for Resolution: Conflict and Intervention in Africa* (Zartman 1985);
- *Sovereignty as Responsibility: Conflict Management in Africa* (Deng et al. 1996).

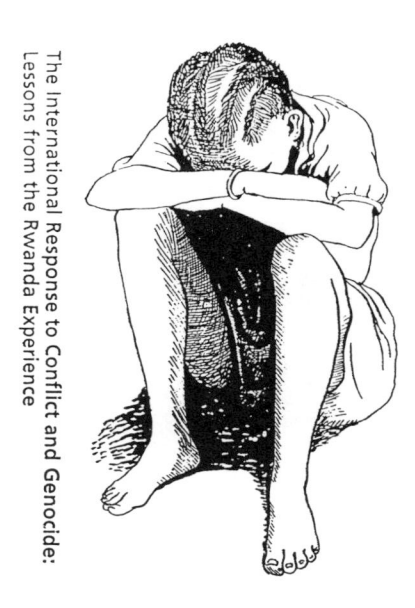

***The International Response to Conflict and Genocide: Lessons from the Rwanda Experience***

In March 1996 a final report was issued by the Joint Evaluation of Emergency Assistance to Rwanda working group.

Titles of volumes in the 5-volume set are:

- *Synthesis Report*
- *Historical Perspective: Some Explanatory Factors*
- *Early Warning and Conflict Management*
- *Humanitarian Aid and Effects*
- *Rebuilding Post-War Rwanda*

*The International Response to Conflict and Genocide: Lessons from the Rwanda Experience* (Eriksson 1996)

# AFRICA'S DEBT BURDEN
## Who suffers? Who benefits?

Explanations for the economic crises that have wracked the nations of Africa in the post-colonial period are many and complex. Some contributing factors are internal, some are external in origin. One area of concern that has received increased attention in recent years is Africa's enormous external debt and programs sponsored by the World Bank and the International Monetary Fund (IMF) to deal with the burden of that debt.

The resources in this chapter provide background on the issue of international debt in the Third World and in Africa. They describe the origins, dimensions, and characteristics of the foreign debt of Third World nations, identify those who benefit from the external debts of these nations, and examine the direct and negative impact of the debt burden on the citizens of Third World countries.

The resources also describe alternative development strategies being devised and promoted by Africans and their supporters in nongovernmental organizations elsewhere in the world. Particular attention is paid to international campaigns to challenge the Structural Adjustment Programs (SAPs) and other policies advocated by the World Bank and IMF.

### Third World debt

Susan George's *A Fate Worse Than Debt: The World Financial Crisis and the Poor* (1990) and Walden Bello's *Dark Victory: The United States, Structural Adjustment and Global Poverty* (1994) are good books to begin with for informed and accessible overviews of the international debt crisis. Two more popularly styled publications on Third World debt are *Freedom from Debt: Peoples' Movements against the Debt* (Culbertson 1991) and *Third World Debt: The Lingering Crisis* (Catholic Institute for International Relations 1991). Concise and readable surveys of debt-related issues may be found in back issues of two popular magazines: "Debt: A Campaign Comic" (*New Internationalist*, no. 243, May 1993) and "Structural Adjustment: Deadly 'Development'" (*The*

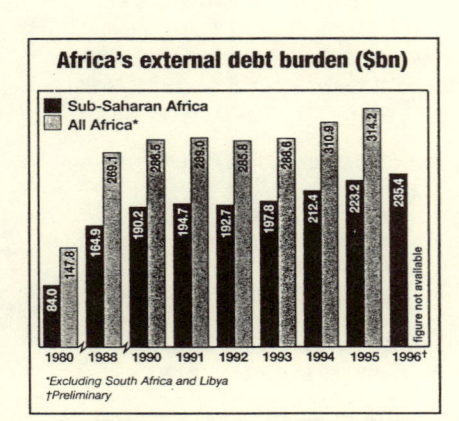

**Africa's external debt burden ($bn)**

| Year | Sub-Saharan Africa | All Africa* |
|---|---|---|
| 1980 | 84.0 | 147.8 |
| 1988 | 164.9 | 269.1 |
| 1990 | 190.2 | 286.5 |
| 1991 | 194.7 | 289.0 |
| 1992 | 192.7 | 285.8 |
| 1993 | 197.8 | 283.6 |
| 1994 | 212.4 | 310.9 |
| 1995 | 223.2 | 314.2 |
| 1996† | 235.4 | figure not available |

*Excluding South Africa and Libya
†Preliminary

*Africa Recovery* 10, no. 4 (January–April 1997), UN Dept. of Recovery, p. 13. Source: World Bank, *Global Development Finance*, 1997.

*Global Advocates Bulletin*, no. 27, October 1994). References to additional resources are found in *International Debt and the Third World* (Nordquist 1989), a 64-page bibliography of about 500 books, articles, and government publications related to Third World debt.

### Debt in Africa

Recommended introductory print resources on the debt crisis in Africa include *Alternative Development Strategies for Africa. Volume 3: Debt and Democracy* (Turok 1991); *African Debt Revisited: Procrastination or Progress?* (Mistry 1991); *The African Response: Adjustment or Transformation* (Turok 1992); and *A Future for Africa: Beyond the Politics of Adjustment* (Onimode 1992). Books published by the Institute for African Alternatives (London), especially those in IFAA's Alternative Development Strategies for Africa series, offer uniformly challenging perspectives from African authors.

The articles in *Africa's Recovery in the 1990s: From Stagnation and Adjustment to Human Development* (Cornia et al. 1992) are noteworthy for the policy alternatives they recommend for a long-term development strategy that features the redistribution of assets and expanded access to basic services.

Numerous published collections of essays cover the full range of debt-related issues in Africa. See, for example, *Adjustments and Democratization in Francophone Africa* (Gervais and Gervais 1993); *The African Debt Crisis* (Parfitt and Riley 1989); *Alternative Development Strategies for Africa. Volume 1: Coalition for Change* (Onimode et al. 1990); *Authoritarianism, Democracy, and Adjustment: The Politics of Economic Reform in Africa* (Gibbon 1992); *Debt, Development and Equity in Africa* (Sonko 1994); *Debt Relief and Sustainable Development in Sub-Saharan Africa* (Abbott 1993); *Development and Democratization in the Third World: Myths, Hopes, and Realities* (Bauzon 1992); *Economic Justice in Africa: Adjustment and Sustainable Development* (Shepherd and Sonko 1994); *From Adjustment to Development in Africa: Conflict, Controversy, Convergence, Consensus?* (Cornia and Helleiner 1994); *Hemmed In: Responses to Africa's Economic Decline* (Callaghy and Ravenhill 1993); *Human Dimensions of Adjustment* (Research Group on African Development Perspectives 1990); *Instruments of Economic Policy in Africa* (African Centre for Monetary Studies 1992); *Negotiating Structural Adjustment in Africa* (Van Der Geest 1994); *Structural Adjustment and Beyond in Sub-Saharan Africa: Research and Policy Issues* (Van Der Hoeven and Van Der Kraaij 1994); and *Social Change and Economic Reform in Africa* (Gibbon 1993).

### Impact

Various books examine the impact of the debt crisis and World Bank/IMF structural adjustment policies on different sectors of Africa's peoples and societies. See, for example,

Graphic image from the 50 Years Is Enough! Campaign
*Credit:* Inter-Church Coalition on Africa (Toronto)

- *The Human Dimension of Africa's Persistent Economic Crisis* (Adedeji et al. 1990) — as its title suggests — is the most topically wide ranging of the books in this category.
- *Beyond Urban Bias in Africa: Urbanization in an Era of Structural Adjustment* (Becker et al. 1994) raises concerns about the impact of structural adjustment programs on Africa's urban future.
- *Structural Adjustment and the African Farmer* (Duncan and Howell 1992) describes the impact of structural adjustment policies upon the incomes and welfare of Africa's peasant farmers, with special emphasis given to this issue in Ghana, Kenya, Madagascar, Malawi, and Niger.

The negative effects of structural adjustment policies on women are analyzed critically in *Mortgaging Women's Lives: Feminist Critiques of Structural Adjustment* (Sparr 1994), *Women Pay the Price: Structural Adjustment in Africa and the Caribbean* (Emeagwali 1995), and *Structural Adjustment and African Women Farmers* (Gladwin 1991). See also *Women and Structural Adjustment*, ZWRCN Bibliographies, no. 8 (Zimbabwe Women's Resource Center and Network 1994).

### Country/regional studies

*The Human Dimension of Africa's Persistent Economic Crisis* (Adedeji et al. 1990) contains seven chapters that examine "country initiatives to sustain the human dimension in spite of the crisis." The countries profiled are: Kenya, Ethiopia, Nigeria, the Sudan, Zambia, Madagascar, and Ghana. For other country- and region-specific studies crisis, see:

**Democratic Republic of the Congo (Zaire):** *The World Bank and Structural Transformation in Developing Countries: The Case of Zaire* (Leslie 1987).

**Egypt:** (1) "Adjustment in Egypt? The Political Economy of Reform." *Review of African Political Economy*, no. 60 (1994), pp. 201-213; (2) *The Mediterranean*

---

### 50 YEARS IS ENOUGH!

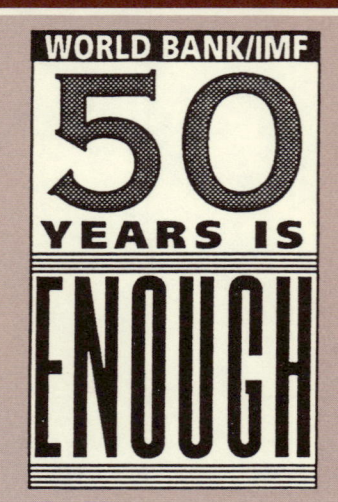

July 1994 marked the 50th anniversary of the founding of the International Monetary Fund (IMF) and the World Bank—the Bretton Woods Institutions (so-called because they were established in Bretton Woods, New Hampshire, in July 1944). Taking the 50th anniversary as their starting point, a diverse group of U.S. nongovernmental organizations launched the "50 Years Is Enough!" campaign in 1994 to marshall efforts to transform the IMF and the World Bank "into democratic, accountable institutions that foster sustainable and people-centered development."

Background resources on the campaign and on the issues the campaign addresses are found in *50 Years Is Enough: The Case Against the World Bank and the International Monetary Fund* (Danaher 1994), *50 Years of Bretton Woods Institutions: Enough!* (Kothari et al. 1994), *The Other Side of the Story: The Real Impact of World Bank and IMF Structural Adjustment Programs* (Hammond and McGowan 1993), and *50 Years Is Enough: A Resource Packet for Action in the Faith Community* (United Church Board of World Ministries 1994).

For more information on the ongoing campaign, contact 50 Years Is Enough Network, 1025 Vermont Ave., NW, Ste. 300, Washington, DC 20005 USA. E-mail: wb50years@igc.org.

*Debt Crescent* (Henry 1996).
**Ghana:** *Adjusting Society: The World Bank, the IMF and Ghana* (Brydon 1996); *Technology and Enterprise Development: Ghana under Structural Adjustment* (Lall et al. 1994).
**Kenya:** *Structural Adjustment and Environmental Linkages: A Case Study of Kenya* (Richardson 1996).
**Malawi:** See volume 2 of *Aid and Power* (Mosley et al. 1991), pp. 201-269.
**Morocco:** *The Mediterranean Debt Crescent* (Henry 1996).
**Mozambique:** *Peace Without Profit: How the IMF Blocks Rebuilding in Mozambique* (Hanlon 1996)
**Nigeria:** *Nigeria: The Politics of Adjustment and Democracy* (Ihonvbere 1994); *The Politics of Structural Adjustment in Nigeria* (Olukoshi 1993).
**Sierra Leone:** Chapter 6 in *The African Debt Crisis* (Parfitt and Riley 1989), pp. 126-147.
**Sub-Saharan Africa:** *Structural Adjustment and Socio-Economic Change in Sub-Saharan Africa* (Gibbon and Olukoshi 1996)
**Sudan:** *Sudan's Debt Crisis* (Brown 1990).
**Tunisia:** *The Mediterranean Debt Crescent* (Henry 1996).
**Uganda:** *Changing Uganda: The Dilemmas of Structural Adjustment and Revolutionary Change* (Hansen and Twaddle 1991).
**West Africa:** *Structural Adjustment in West Africa* (Olukoshi et al. 1994)
**Zimbabwe:** *Structural Adjustment and the Working Poor in Zimbabwe* (Gibbon 1995); *Health and Structural Adjustment in Rural and Urban Zimbabwe* (Bijlmakers et al. 1996).

## World Bank and International Monetary Fund

Michael Barratt Brown's *Africa's Choices: After Thirty Years of the World Bank* (Brown 1996) is the best introduction to this topic. Also recommended is the two-volume set, *Aid and Power: The World Bank and Policy-based Lending* (Mosley et al. 1991), which presents a policy-based overview of the lending practices of the World Bank, with nine country case studies in volume 2.

The case for the success of World Bank and International Monetary Fund (IMF) structural adjustment policies and practices in Africa is made most definitively in *Adjustment in Africa: Reforms, Results, and the Road Ahead* (World Bank 1994).

Critical analyses of World Bank/IMF involvement in Africa's debt crisis include *The Market Tells Them So: The World Bank and Economic Fundamentalism in Africa* (Mihevc 1995), *Africa Beyond Adjustment* (Lipumba 1994), *Resolving Africa's Multilateral Debt Problem: A Response to the IMF and the World Bank* (Mistry 1996), the five volumes in the Rethinking Bretton Woods series, especially *The World Bank: Lending on a Global Scale* (Griesgraber and Gunter 1995), and — more broadly — *Mortgaging the Earth: The World Bank, Environmental Impoverishment, and the Crisis of Development* (Rich 1994).

*SEDOS Bulletin* 26, nos. 3 and 4 (1994)

---

### World Bank/IMF Programs: What's Being Said

Supporters and critics express widely divergent points of view regarding the roles of the World Bank and IMF in the debt crisis in Africa:

**Supporters say:**

"In the African countries that have undertaken and sustained major policy reforms, adjustment is working." (p. 1)

"In African countries that have undertaken some reforms and achieved some increase in growth, the majority of the poor are probably better off and almost certainly no worse off." (p. 7)

*Adjustment in Africa: Reforms, Results, and the Road Ahead.* A World Bank Policy Research Report (World Bank 1994)

**Critics say:**

"Adjustment policies that have been adopted under pressure from the World Bank and the IMF have lacked local ownership. Moreover, they do not explicitly link reform to the development of local human resources and to the institution-building that can make Africans more productive and more capable of designing and implementing poverty-eradicating growth policies." (p. 4)

*Africa Beyond Adjustment* (Lipumba 1994)

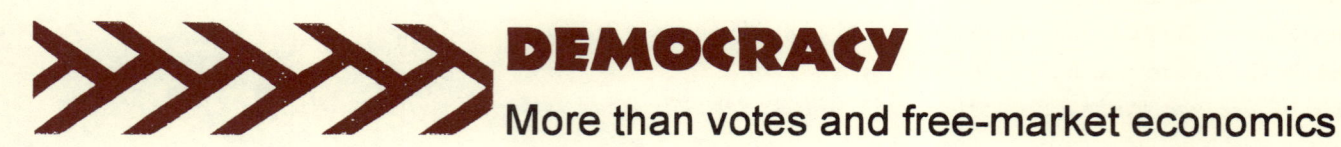

# DEMOCRACY
## More than votes and free-market economics

The story is told of a U.S. citizen chiding the former president of Tanzania, Julius K. Nyerere, about the fact that Tanzania had only one political party. Nyerere is said to have responded: "Well, in the United States, you, too, have only *one* political party, but with your customary extravagance you have created *two* versions of that one party." The study of democracy in Africa challenges Westerners to take a hard look at political institutions and philosophies that are too often taken for granted as the way-things-must-be. At the same time, it broadens and enriches the understanding of the concept of democracy.

Many Africans consider the Western model of political democracy to be extremely narrow and even alien to African cultures. "Democracy is not merely the right to vote and seize power," the Rev. Jose Belo Chipenda, General Secretary, All Africa Conference of Churches (AACC) has said. "It is about a whole complex of rights and duties which citizens must exercise if a government is to be open, accountable, and participatory." Africans like Chipenda find that Western-style democracy "places people into artificial antagonistic boxes, turns friends into enemies, and aims at arousing unnecessary competition." See excerpts from Chipenda's speech to the AACC's 119th General Assembly, in *Development Demands Democracy* (Culbertson 1994), p. 20.

The resource materials in this chapter explore the broader and richer understandings of democracy as they are found in African societies.

### Democracy—African style

Professor Ben O. Nwabueze's book, *Democratisation* (Nwabueze 1993), is the best place to begin for a wide-ranging and textured examination of democratization in African societies. "Democratisation is not only a concept, nor is it synonymous with multi-partyism," Nwabueze writes, "it is also concerned with certain conditions of things, conditions such as a virile civil society, a democratic society, a free society, a just society, equal treatment of all citizens by the state, an ordered, stable society, a society infused with the spirit of liberty, democracy, justice and equality." The stated thesis of Nwabueze's book is that democratization, "in the fullest sense of the term, requires that the society, the economy, politics, the constitution of the state, the electoral system and the practice of government be democratised" (p. ix).

The essays in *Popular Struggles for Democracy in Africa* (Nyong'o 1987) deepen the theoretical and analytical study of democratization with contributions on aspects of the broad theme of "the state, development, and participatory democracy" in Africa by Mahmood Mamdani, Abdelali Doumou, Samir Amin, Harry Goulbourne and other leading African scholars. Case studies are presented of Morocco, Uganda, the People's Republic of Congo, South Africa, Ghana, Liberia, Kenya, and Swaziland. "However repressive regimes have been in Africa," editor Peter Anyang' Nyong'o concludes, "and however successful they might have been in defeating popular attempts at democratic change...the people's impulse to struggle for freedom and social justice can never completely die." (p. 24).

The link between popular struggles and the building of democracy in Africa is developed further in two additional collections of studies. The first is a highly recommended 626-page anthology compiled by Mahmood Mamdani and Ernest Wamba-dia-Wamba, *African Studies in Social Movements and Democracy* (1996). The book's 15 studies emerged from an 8-year-long (1985-1993) "continental dialogue" sponsored by CODESRIA (Council for the Development of Social Science Research in Africa). The second collection, entitled *Democracy, Civil Society and the State* (Sachikonye 1995) analyzes social movements and democratic initiatives in the Southern Africa region.

## AFJN STATEMENT ON DEMOCRATIZATION IN AFRICA

Members of the Africa Faith and Justice Network adopted the following principles regarding democracy in Africa at their annual meeting in Washington, D.C., in October 1993 (excerpts):

- Africans need to define for themselves the meaning of democracy in their own historical and cultural contexts, drawing on their participatory traditions and the experience of democratic societies elsewhere.
- Free-market capitalism and multi-party systems are not synonymous with democracy.
- Grassroots popular movements offer new hope for truly democratic structures in Africa.
- Respect for human, social, and economic rights as well as civil rights is essential if democracy is to take hold in Africa, for democracy cannot survive in a context of stark polarization between rich and poor.
- Economic development and an equitable distribution of resources must go hand-in-hand with the emergence of more democratic structures.
- In brokering negotiations between contending parties, the Church must speak on behalf of the poor and marginated.
- AFJN commits itself to support the move toward democracy in Africa by:
- Listening to and giving voice to African peoples in our common struggle for democracy.
- Supporting networks between Africans and with North Americans in their struggle for justice in Africa.
- Working with others to influence U.S. legislative initiatives supportive of African-defined democratic structures.
- Fostering reflection on and articulation of a theology of democracy within the context of African countries.

*Contact Africa Faith and Justice Network, Box 29378, Washington, DC 20017 USA for a copy of the October 1993 statement.*

## North Africa and the Middle East

Most of the material in the above-mentioned publications concentrates on democratization in sub-Saharan Africa. The scholarly papers presented in *Rules and Rights in the Middle East: Democracy, Law, and Society* (Goldberg et al. 1993) extend the study of democratic structures and processes to include North Africa (the Maghreb). In what is advertised to be "the first sustained look at democracy and democratic movements in the Middle East," contributors analyze the practice of electoral democracy in the Arab East and North Africa and speculate about the prospects for broader democratization in the region.

Two issues of *Middle East Report*, the bimonthly publication of the Middle East Research and Information Project (Washington, D.C.), explore broadened understandings of democracy in North Africa and the Arab East: "Democracy in the Arab World," no. 174 (January/February 1992), and "Islam, the State and Democracy," no. 179 (November/December 1992).

The *Review of African Political Economy* (Sheffield) has carried a number of stimulating articles on democracy in North *and* sub-Saharan Africa in recent years. See, particularly, "Democracy and Development," no. 49 (winter 1990), "Surviving Democracy?," no. 54 (July 1992), and "Democracy, Civil Society and NGOs," no. 55 (November 1992).

## Issues of democracy

The following books examine selected issues related to democracy in Africa:
- *Democracy and Human Rights in Developing Countries* (Arat 1991) explores the theme of social and economic rights as integral elements in democratic societies.
- The academic conference papers reproduced in *Democracy and Pluralism in Africa* (Ronen 1986) offer a variety of perspectives on the problems facing democracy and pluralism in Africa.
- Ethnicity and democracy is the topical concern of two booklets in the Occasional Monograph series published by the Centre for Advanced Social Science (Lagos): *Ethnicity and its Management in Africa: The Democratization Link* (Osaghae 1994) and *Ethnicity and Democracy in Africa: Intervening Variables* (Nnoli 1994).
- The articles in *Democracy and Socialism in Africa* (Cohen and Goulbourne 1991) focus on what the editors identify as "the burning political and social issue facing the [African] continent in the 1990s": the relationship between democracy and socialism.
- Convinced that "no society qualifies as democratic, representative, and progressive until there is free and voluntary participation of all its citizens in all spheres of life" eleven Kenyan women scholars and writers examine the "structural constraints" that have kept women from participating fully and meaningfully in Kenyan society. See their essays in *Democratic Change*

*in Africa: Women's Perspective* (Kabira et al. 1993).
- Several books examine the nature and role of the state as this entity relates to democracy and citizen exercise of political power in Africa. See, among others, *The African State in Transition* (Ergas 1987); *Government and Politics in Africa* (Tordoff 1993); *Political Domination in Africa: Reflections on the Limits of Power* (Chabal 1986); *The Precarious Balance: State and Society in Africa* (Rothchild and Chazan 1988); *The State in Africa: The Politics of the Belly* (Bayart 1993); and *State Building and Democracy in Southern Africa: Botswana, Zimbabwe, and South Africa* (Pierre du Toit 1995).
- The role of the media in the democratic process is examined in a 20-page booklet in the Seminar Paper Series published by SAPES Trust in Harare, Zimbabwe: *Media and Democracy: Theories and Principles with Reference to an African Context* (Ronning 1994).

## Case studies

Studies of democratic processes in individual African nations are found in
- *Democracy: The Challenge of Change* (Chiluba 1995) — Zambia
- *Politics of Democratization: Changing Authoritarian Regimes in sub-Saharan Africa* (Nwokedi 1995) — Benin, Cameroon, Côte d'Ivoire, Congo, Gabon, Kenya, Niger, Nigeria, Mali, Togo, Zaire, and Zambia;
- *Mozambique: A Dream Undone. The Political Economy of Democracy, 1975-84* (Egerö 1990);
- *Governance and Democratisation in Nigeria* (Olowu et al. 1995);
- *Political Parties and Democracy in Tanzania* (Mmuya and Chaligha 1994);
- *Liberalization and Politics: The 1990 Election in Tanzania* (Mukandala and Othman 1994).

### Botswana: An exception that confounds generalizations

"At a time when Africa's dismal economic performance and political corruption and mismanagement have given rise to a new intellectual movement called Afropessimism," Professor Stephen John Stedman writes, "…Botswana stands out as an example of economic development, functioning governance, and multiparty, liberal democracy." Writing in his introduction to *Botswana: The Political Economy of Democratic Development* (Stedman 1993) Professor Stedman explains: "[Botswana] is…a country akin to Switzerland, an exception that confounds generalizations, but whose very exceptionality prompts analysts to see it as a hopeful model for other societies" (p. 1). The ten essays in Stedman's book present the analyses of Africa scholars from Botswana, Germany, and the United States on Botswana's political system and, more generally, on the nature of "good governance in Africa and its relationship to democracy and development" (p. 1).

On Botswana's unique experiment in democratic participation, see also *Democracy in Botswana* (Holm and Molutsi 1989), *Botswana's Search for Autonomy in Southern Africa* (Dale 1995), and *Policy Choice and Development Performance in Botswana* (Harvey and Lewis Jr. 1990).

# DEVELOPMENT
## The search for new forms

Addressing the twenty-first world conference of the Society for International Development (Mexico City, 6-9 April 1994), Thierno H. Kane, Secretary General of Fouta Federation of Village Associations (Senegal) observed that "the picture we have before us today could seem simple, but it is distressing. We see the Africa of granted independence; the Africa of armed liberalization movements; the Africa of enormous mineral resources; the Africa of resource richness; the Africa of drummers; the Africa of the economic recovery sorcerer's apprentices; all these Africas... seem trapped in the same stranglehold that will be getting ever stronger: development" (*Development* 2 [1994], p. 47).

The resource materials in this chapter explain why Africans like Thierno Kane question and challenge the traditional concepts of development. Is development a solution, they ask, or is it, in fact, the *problem*? The resource materials also describe the innovative, alternative development strategies that are being implemented in Africa and elsewhere in the Third World.

### New ways of thinking

Three publications from Zed Books showcase the challenging new viewpoints that are being articulated by contemporary scholars of the international development process: *The Development Dictionary: A Guide to Knowledge as Power* (Sachs 1992), *People First: A Guide to Self-Reliant, Participatory Rural Development* (Burkey 1993), and *Beyond the Impasse: New Directions in Development Theory* (Schuurman 1993). *People First,* which was written by a fieldworker with more than eight years' experience at the village level in Uganda, is the most readable of the three books for a popular audience.

Challenging perspectives by individual African development specialists are found in *One Africa, One Destiny: Towards Democracy, Good Governance and Development* (wa Mutharika 1995) and in a 59-page booklet entitled *The Outlook for Development in the 1990s* (Dadzie 1994).

> "To understand the dynamism of the grassroots we must correct our false and mystified perceptions, move away from our 'development' mentality and stop thinking that external intervention is what is needed."
>
> Thierno H. Kane
> *Development* 2 (1994), p. 48

Bingua wa Mutharika, Secretary-General of the Common Market for Eastern and Southern Africa, draws two lessons from his study of African development. The first is that people must be at the center of all economic and social activity. "Those responsible for political and economic decisions," he contends, "must agree that if development bypasses the common people, then such development is meaningless both morally and spiritually." Wa Mutharika's second lesson is that "Africa cannot be developed using foreign traditions and cultures." Africa needs to learn from its own traditions, wa Mutharika concludes, and it must develop its own development ethics and philosophy.

K.K.S. Dadzie's booklet, *The Outlook for Development in the 1990s*, contains the texts of four lectures Dadzie delivered at the University of Ghana in June 1990 on various aspects of African development. Dadzie is the Secretary-General of the UN Conference on Trade and Development (UNCTAD) in Geneva.

*African Development: Adebayo Adedeji's Alternative Strategies* (Asante 1991) presents the thinking of one of Africa's leading advocates of the need for alternative approaches to African development: Adebayo Adedeji, Under-Secretary-General of the United Nations and Executive Secretary of the UN Economic Commission for Africa (ECA) from 1975 to 1991. Author S. K. B. Asante, himself an ECA senior regional adviser, draws extensively on Adedeji's writings to chart the course of the development debate in Africa since the 1950s.

The viewpoints of various African development theorists and practitioners are well represented in the following collections of papers: *African Perspectives on Development: Controversies, Dilemmas and Openings* (Himmelstrand et al. 1994); *Africa within the World: Beyond Dispossession and Dependence* (Adedeji 1993); *Alternative Development Strategies for Africa. Volume 1: Coalition for Change* (Institute for African Alternatives 1990); *Policy Reform for Sustainable Development in Africa: The Institutional Imperative* (Picard and Garrity 1994); *Social Development in Africa: Strategies, Policies and Programmes after the Lagos Plan* (Mohammed 1991); *Thirty Years of Independence in Africa: The Lost Decades?* (Nyong'o 1992); and *Sustainable Development* (United Nations Non-Governmental Liaison Service 1994). Two clothbound volumes edited by Aguibou Y. Yansané contain papers presented at a Multidisciplinary Colloquium Series held at San Francisco State University in 1990 on "Evaluation of Development Strategies: Prospects for Growth in Africa in the 1990s": *Development Strategies in Africa: Current Economic, Socio-Political, and Institutional Trends and Issues* (Yansané 1996) and *Prospects for Recovery and Sustainable Development in Africa* (Yansané 1996).

Perspectives often at odds with the views expressed in the publications listed above are evident in the conference papers brought together in *The Crisis and Challenge of African Development* (Glickman 1988). Here, academics

"It is not by chance that Africa has remained underdeveloped. Consuming what it does not produce and producing what it does not consume, the continent exhibits an imbalanced, externally oriented economic structure that can, to a large degree, be attributed to the neglect of the development of its human resources and to its colonial legacy."

Hassan Sunmonu, *Africa Within the World* (Adedeji 1993), p. 197.

at U.S. universities, World Bank officials, and the U.S. Ambassador to Nigeria (in 1988), offer their analyses of what has gone wrong with development in Africa and their recommendations for corrective actions.

Two bibliographies of note are *Economic Development in Africa: A Select Bibliography, 1975-1988* (Research and Information System for the Non-Aligned and Other Developing Countries 1989) and *Popular Participation and Development: A Bibliography on Africa and Latin America* (Dow and Barker 1992).

### Issues in African development

Books that focus on particular aspects of development in Africa are:
- *African Capitalists in African Development* (Berman and Leys 1994) — an analysis of the role of capitalist *classes* (as distinct from individual entrepreneurs) in Africa's development.
- *African Politics and Problems in Development* (Sklar and Whitaker 1991) — a call by two U.S. scholars for an Afrocentric approach to the study of African development, one that "does justice to the integrity and complexity of African politics." Sklar and Whitaker devote a good deal of attention to Nigeria.
- *Ambassadors of Colonialism: The International Development Trap* (Information Project for Africa 1993) — a no-holds-barred attack on "the foreign aid and lending program and certain trade activities" as perhaps "the most influential — and the most coercive — tactic in the entire arsenal of political and economic weapons wielded against the developing world by the 'big nations' of the north" (p. 2).

---

**AFRICAN CHARTER FOR POPULAR PARTICIPATION IN DEVELOPMENT**

In February 1990, representatives of African people's organizations, African governments, nongovernmental organizations, and UN agencies met in Arusha, Tanzania, to search for a collective understanding of the role of popular participation in the development and transformation of the Africa region.

The following are excerpts from the document drafted at the Arusha conference:

• "We are united in our conviction that the crisis currently engulfing Africa is not only an economic crisis but also a human, legal, political, and social crisis." (#6)

• "We affirm that nations cannot be built without the popular support and full participation of the people, nor can the economic crisis be resolved and the human and economic conditions improved without the full and effective contribution, creativity, and popular enthusiasm of the vast majority of the people. After all, it is to the people that the very benefits of development should and must accrue." (#7)

• "We, therefore, have no doubt that at the heart of Africa's development objectives must lie the ultimate and overriding goal of human-centred development that ensures the overall well-being of the people through sustained improvement in their living standards and the full and effective participation of the people in charting their development policies, programmes and processes, and contributing to their realization." (#8)

• "We are convinced that to achieve the above objective will require a re-direction of resources to satisfy, in the first place, the critical needs of the people, to achieve economic and social justice, and to emphasize self-reliance on the one hand, and, on the other hand, to empower the people to determine the direction and content of development, and to effectively contribute to the enhancement of production and productivity that are required." (#9)

- *Challenging Rural Poverty: Experiences in Institution-Building and Popular Participation for Rural Development in Eastern Africa* (Kiros 1985) — conference papers that analyze the persistent problem of rural poverty in Eastern Africa and the state of institution-building and grassroots participation in the context of rural development.
- *Gender, Environment, and Development in Kenya: A Grassroots Perspective* (Thomas-Slayter and Rocheleau 1995) — studies on gender, resources, and development in the rural livelihood systems of six Kenyan communities.
- *Moral Philosophy and Development: The Human Condition in Africa* (Kiros 1992) — a novel attempt by a political science professor at Boston University to draw a "moral philosophy of development" from Africa's post-independence development experiences.
- *No Life without Roots: Culture and Development* (Verhelst 1990) — a searing critique of development theories and practices that ignore *culture* as the very basis of sound and integral development.
- *The Significance of the Human Factor in African Economic Development* (Adjibolosoo 1995) — a critical reappraisal of traditional development theory and a call for sub-Saharan African countries to place "a significant emphasis" on "human factor development programs."

The issue of rural development in Kenya and Zimbabwe is examined by African sociologists in *Working with Rural Communities: A Participatory Action Research in Kenya* (Chitere and Mutiso 1991) and *Grassroots Leadership: The Process of Rural Development in Zimbabwe* (Mararike 1995)

Cover of *Voices from Africa* published by the UN Non-Governmental Liaison Service, Palais des Nations, CH-1211 Geneva 10, Switzerland.

## New models in practice

Stories of economic and social accomplishments are found in the following chronicles of sustainable development at the village level in African nations:
- *Against All Odds: Breaking the Poverty Trap* (De Silva 1990) — hope-filled reports on successful, locally based development projects in Kenya, Tanzania, and Zambia (among other Third World nations).
- *Listening to Africa: Developing Africa from the Grassroots* (Pradervand 1990) — an engaging and uplifting chronicle of the village-level "silent revolution" that is changing Africa's development landscape.
- *Let the Dawn Come. Social Development: Looking Behind the Clichés* (Burne and Davies 1995) — the views of ordinary women and men in Uganda, Zimbabwe, and other developing nations, who are striving to improve their lives with the help of nongovernmental organizations.
- *What Works: An Annotated Bibliography of Case Studies of Sustainable Development* (Slocombe et al. 1993) — a catalog of global success stories.

The 4-part television series, *Local Heroes, Global Change* (Church World Service, Elkhart, Ind.), examines "what works in the battle against hunger and poverty in the developing world." Ghana and Zimbabwe are two among the African nations covered in the series.

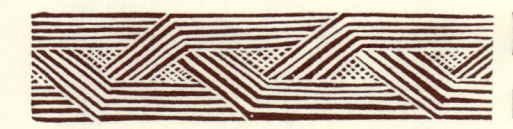

# EMERGENCY RELIEF AID
## Meeting whose needs?

Relief aid. Can't survive without it; can't live with it! Many Africans find themselves trapped in this terrible paradox. International relief assistance has proven to be indispensable in meeting emergency food and health needs in various crises in Africa in the recent past. The famine in the Horn of Africa in 1984-85 and the refugee crisis in Rwanda in the mid-1990s are probably the two examples with the highest public profile.

On the other side, however, emergency aid has come under fire from critics who question its usefulness, its impact, its perpetuation of negative images of Africans as helpless beggars, and its long-term consequences.

The lead article in the September 1994 issue of *IFAD Update*, the bulletin of the International Fund for Agricultural Development of the United Nations, put the question in stark terms: "Faced with disasters yet again in areas like the Horn of Africa, the question is inevitably being asked if it really makes sense to engage in round after round of emergency assistance. In effect, the question is whether, in a certain sense, disaster is normal, and whether emergency response really makes any long-term difference" ("Beyond Emergency Relief," p. 1).

Critics such as aid worker/journalist Michael Maren, author of *The Road to Hell: The Ravaging Effects of Foreign Aid and International Charity* (Maren 1997) and British journalist Graham Hancock, author of *Lords of Poverty* (Hancock 1989), call for a total cut-off of food aid and other foreign assistance, arguing that it is the *donor* countries—and *not* the poor in the Third World— who receive the most benefit from aid as it is presently structured. "Aid is not bad...because it is sometimes misused, corrupt, or crass; rather, it is *inherently* bad, bad to the bone, and utterly beyond reform" (Hancock, p. 183).

The authors of *Foreign Aid Reconsidered* (Riddell 1987) and *Does Aid Work?* (Cassen 1994) acknowledge the numerous weaknesses of the international aid system, but support its continuation with proper safeguards.

> "The massive volumes of emergency aid over the last ten years have certainly reduced suffering and prevented many deaths across Africa. However, it is now finally being recognised that the way that this emergency aid is provided is only worsening the situation."
>
> Ken Wilson, "The Need for More Effective Emergency Aid," in *Emergency Aid and the Refugee* (Irish Mozambique Solidarity, 1993), p. 16

The resource materials in this chapter describe the paradox of African relief aid—with case studies of Ethiopia, Eritrea, and Sudan—and explore some alternative approaches to the delivery of emergency assistance.

## Emergency relief system

David Keen's 86-page booklet, *Refugees: Rationing the Right to Life. The Crisis in Emergency Relief* (Keen 1992) is a good place to begin. Keen describes the macro structure of the international emergency relief system and identifies and examines "shortcomings" in the system as it functions presently. "The quantity and quality of relief for refugees falls short of acceptable standards," Keen states at the start of his final chapter ("An Agenda for Action"). "What we have at present is an unsystematic arrangement where the efficacy of assistance is all too often left to chance, to the vagaries of political agendas and the fluctuating availability of resources. What is needed is a system that will *ensure* refugees' welfare and involve them in determining the nature of aid" (p. 69).

Another popularly accessible introduction to the relief aid dilemma is *Peace, Development, and People of the Horn of Africa*, a report written by John Prendergast and co-published by the Bread for the World Institute on Hunger and Development and the Center of Concern (1992). Prendergast focuses on the distribution of relief aid in war-torn areas in the Horn of Africa region: Sudan, Ethiopia, Eritrea, and Somalia and Somaliland.

In *Beyond Charity: International Cooperation and the Global Refugee Crisis* (Loescher 1994), Professor Gil Loescher (international relations, University of Notre Dame) traces the growth of "the international refugee regime" from 1921, when the League of Nations appointed the first High Commissioner for Refugees, to the post-cold war period of the late 1980s and early 1990s. Loescher's concern is the efficacy of the refugee relief system in its broadest representations (with Africa covered among many other world regions), but his study provides important background for an understanding of the strengths and weaknesses of relief aid in particular situations.

British academic Peter Burnell (lecturer in politics, University of Warwick) narrows the focus of the international relief establishment to British voluntary agencies for overseas aid and development (e.g., Oxfam, Christian Aid, War on Want) in his book *Charity, Politics and the Third World* (1991). Burnell describes the origins and activities of these agencies (at home and abroad) and examines the turbulent international waters in which these charitable institutions swim. "[The cases of] Ethiopia and Sudan, Biafra and Cambodia," Burnell points out, "all demonstrate the willingness of warring parties to make use of hunger and food as instruments of war. In this situation the charities are faced with dilemmas which they cannot possibly resolve to everyone's satisfaction. They risk being damned if they try to intervene and they will be damned if they decide to hold back" (p. 201).

In the early 1990s USA for Africa, a U.S.-based organization that raised and disbursed $49 million in financial assistance for Africa programs during the years from 1985 through 1989, commissioned Africa specialists Michael Scott and Mutombo Mpanya to conduct a thorough-going independent review of USA for Africa operations. The resulting product, *We Are the World: An Evaluation of Pop Aid for Africa* (Scott and Mpanya 1994), will encourage readers at all levels of interest and expertise to re-examine accepted truths about the international emergency relief system.

## Food aid

The relief assistance experiences of eight *recipient* countries (four of them African) and eight *donor* nations are examined in *World Food Aid: Experiences of Recipients and Donors* (Shaw and Clay 1993). Editors John Shaw and Edward Clay focus on food aid—"a controversial form of development assistance," in the words of James Ingram, executive director of the World Food Programme (Rome). Ingram observes that "both donor and recipient governments have displayed an ambivalent attitude to [food aid] that has undermined its usefulness" (see Foreword, p. ix).

Agricultural economist Vernon Ruttan uses the topic of food aid as the binding force for the twelve essays he brings together in *Why Food Aid?* (Ruttan 1993). Contributors trace the development of U.S. government food aid policies and programs, highlighting their humanitarian, political, and (self-serving) commercial features. Africa's experiences with U.S. food aid are described throughout the book.

Author Katarina Tomasevski and editor Robert Gorman approach the issue of relief assistance from two different perspectives in their books *Development Aid and Human Rights* (Tomasevski 1989) and *Refugee Aid and Development: Theory and Practice* (Gorman 1993).

Tomasevski, a consultant researcher with the Danish Center of Human Rights, argues in her book that the observance of human rights law and related standards is a rational basis for working out an overall development assistance policy and implementing individual development projects.

The ten essays in Robert Gorman's collection *Refugee Aid and Development* examine the "twin predicaments" of economic underdevelopment and of refugee movements, making the point that "they are in a very real sense linked and that neither can be fully resolved without taking into account the other" (p. 1). This same theme is developed in a discussion paper published in August 1994 by the Institute of Development Studies at the University of Sussex (Brighton): *Linking Relief and Development* (Ross et al. 1994).

## Case study: Ethiopia and Eritrea

Famine relief in Ethiopia and Eritrea during the period 1983-86 is the subject of numerous critical studies. See *The Ethiopian Famine* (Jansson et al. 1987),

---

**"Consuming Hunger"**

The 3-part video documentary "Consuming Hunger" offers unique insights into issues surrounding famine relief in Africa.

**"Consuming Hunger"**
(Maryknoll World Productions)

*Consuming Hunger*, a 3-part documentary produced by Ilan Ziv and Freke Juijust, analyzes the forces that shape the presentation of hunger issues in the Western media. (Maryknoll World Productions, 1988)

*Fighting the Famine* (Twose 1985), *Peace, Development, and People of the Horn of Africa* (Prendergast 1992), and *Reluctant Aid or Aiding the Reluctant? U.S. Food Aid Policy and Ethiopian Famine Relief* (Varnis 1990).

Background reading on causes of and international responses to famine in the Horn of Africa region may be found in *Environment, Famine, and Politics in Ethiopia: A View from the Village* (Dejene 1990) and *Fau: Portrait of an Ethiopian Famine* (Waller 1990). The latter chronicles the impact of the famine in the mid-1980s on refugees from Ethiopia who settled in a relief camp near the Sudanese town of El Fau, while the former is a detailed field study of environmental degradation in one region of northeastern Ethiopia (Wollo) and an analysis of the relationship between famine and the environment.

## Case study: Sudan

The 1980s, John Prendergast writes, "were a decade of famine, war, and death for Sudan." Drought was the key element in the famine of 1984-86 and conflict was to blame for the famine that wracked southern Sudan from 1988 to 1991. The causes and extent of the two famines in Sudan—and the efforts of outsiders to be of assistance—are analyzed in Prendergast's booklet *Peace, Development, and People of the Horn of Africa* (Prendergast 1992) as well as in books such as *The Benefits of Famine: A Political Economy of Famine and Relief in Southwestern Sudan, 1983-1989* (Keen 1994); *The Challenges of Famine Relief: Emergency Operations in the Sudan* (Deng and Minear 1992); and *Food and Power in Sudan: A Critique of Humanitarianism* (African Rights 1997).

James Morton, a development economist with seven years of field experience in the Darfur region of Sudan, puts Sudan at the center of his hard-hitting critique of development assistance to Africa. See *The Poverty of Nations: The Aid Dilemma at the Heart of Africa* (Morton 1994).

In *Requiem for the Sudan: War, Drought and Disaster Relief on the Nile* (Burr and Collins 1995), authors J. Millard Burr and Robert O. Collins argue that attempts by international and humanitarian governments to aid the victims of Sudan's civil war have been thwarted by bureaucratic infighting, corruption, greed, and ineptitude.

## Other African nations

Joseph Hanlon, author of many books on southern Africa, mounts a withering attack on the policies and programs of the international aid establishment (using Mozambique as a case study) in *Mozambique: Who Calls the Shots?* (1991). Hanlon charges that a "conspiracy of interests" (involving "wealthy aid agencies," the World Bank, well-meaning nongovernmental organizations, and others) has "forced" Mozambique to accept foreign aid and, in the process, is "recolonizing" the former Portuguese colony.

*World Food Aid: Experiences of Recipients and Donors* (Shaw and Clay 1993) contains case studies of Tunisia, Benin, Lesotho, and Tanzania.

---

### Emergency Aid and the Refugee

(Irish Mozambique Solidarity, 1993)

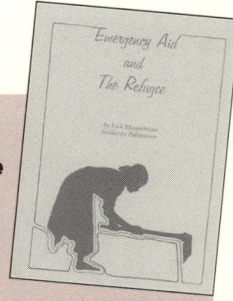

"For most people, the mention of the Third World, Africa, or aid conjures up quite specific and particular images. Starving children, refugees, wars, food aid, volunteers, etc. Images of destruction, helplessness and dependency that very often serve to reinforce racial stereotypes of the Third World, rather than challenge and dispel them."

"The two papers contained in this publication [*Emergency Aid and the Refugee*] spell out many of the difficulties which arise in the provision of emergency aid and highlight the artificial distinction which often exists between what is termed 'development assistance' and 'emergency aid'. In doing so, they are not calling for a cessation of emergency assistance, rather, they advocate a closer, more critical examination of current provision, with a view to improving it."

Irish Mozambique Solidarity
13 Carlisle Street
Dublin 8, Ireland

# ENVIRONMENT
## Africa sets its own priorities

Leave your baggage behind! is the injunction that African analysts like Mohamed Suliman give to environmentalists who come to Africa from developed countries of the North with preconceived notions about environmental protection. Don't transpose your "northern green agenda" onto the continent of Africa, Suliman and others warn, and don't dismiss our efforts to strike a balance between economic development and environmental protection.

"During the 1970s and early 1980s," Mohamed Suliman writes, "many African environmental organisations declared that pollution was their enemy number one, even though there was little evidence to substantiate this claim. Our awareness campaigns looked suspiciously similar to those of Greenpeace and Friends of the Earth, in both content and form. Our northern partners gave us support and encouragement. Our own people scarcely understood what we were talking about." "Besides failing to develop our own environmental priorities," Suliman continues, "the African green movement also failed to consider its specific role as a movement of a developing region. Our people were yearning for a better quality of life and issues of development were paramount to them....[The African green movement] cannot go around preaching to people not to do harm to their environment when their very survival [is] at stake" (Suliman 1993, p. 1).

The London-based Institute for African Alternatives (IFAA), of which Mohamed Suliman is the director, has produced a number of publications that reflect *African* perspectives on environmental issues. The title of one such publication poses the critical question succinctly: *What Does It Mean to Be Green in Africa?* (Suliman 1993). Attempts to draw out the implications of this question—and to search for answers—are found in IFAA publications such as *Alternative Development Strategies for Africa*. Volume 2: *Environment - Women* (Suliman 1991) and *Greenhouse Effect and Its Impact on Africa* (Suliman 1990).

> "The African green movement cannot afford to ignore the mundane issues of development....
> How to save the tree and cut it, that is our question!"
>
> Mohamed Suliman,
> *What Does It Mean to Be Green in Africa?*
> (Suliman 1993), p. 1

The International African Institute (London) shares a similar perspective on environmental issues in Africa. See two recent International African Institute publications in the Africa Issues series edited by Alex de Waal: *The Lie of the Land: Challenging Received Wisdom on the African Environment* (Leach and Mearns 1996) and *Fighting for the Rain Forest: War, Youth and Resources in Sierra Leone* (Richards 1996).

The search for a definition of African environmental priorities is also examined in *Voices from Africa: Local Perspectives on Conservation* (Lewis and Carter 1993) and, on a regular basis, in periodicals issued by ENDA (Environmental Development Action in the Third World), in Dakar, Senegal, and the Environmental Liaison Centre International (ECLI), in Nairobi, Kenya. ENDA's quarterly is entitled *African Environment: Environmental Studies and Regional Planning Bulletin*; *Ecoforum* is the name of the multilingual bimonthly published by the Environmental Liaison Centre.

Contributed essays in *Development and Environment: Sustaining People and Nature* (Ghai 1994) speak to the development issue that Mohamed Suliman raises, as they identify the vital elements of an alternative approach to sustainable development—one that links livelihood, security, environmental protection, and community empowerment. Ghana, Kenya, Zimbabwe, and Madagascar are among the developing nations studied in-depth in *Development and Environment*.

Two books that set the issue of environmental protection in Africa in a larger geographical context are *The Third Revolution: Environment, Population and a Sustainable World* (Harrison 1992) and *Environmental and Economic Dilemmas of Developing Countries: Africa in the Twenty-First Century* (James 1994). *Global Ecology: A New Arena of Political Conflict* (Sachs 1993) and *No Time to Waste: Poverty and the Global Environment* (Davidson et al. 1992) chart a new course in environmental activism, calling for local grassroots involvement in safeguarding and improving the environment (in Africa and elsewhere).

For additional listings on this topic, see *Environmental Issues in the Third World: A Bibliography* (Nordquist 1991).

## Environmental issues in Africa

The role of women in the protection of the environment and the relationship between armed conflicts and environmental destruction are but two of the many issues explored in the resource materials described below.

**Environment and women:** The significant role that women play in managing natural resources in Africa (and in other developing areas) is increasingly becoming a subject of interest. See, for instance, *Close to Home: Women Reconnect Ecology, Health and Development Worldwide* (Shiva 1994); *Women and the Environment* (Rodda 1991); *Ecofeminism* (Mies and Shiva 1993); and *Women and the Environment: A Reader. Crisis and Development in the Third World*

Reproduced with permission of the Association of Christian Lay Centres in Africa (ACLCA), P.O. Box 14126, Nairobi, Kenya. From the cover of *The Taproot of Environmental and Development Crisis in Africa: The Great Challenge* (Otim 1992).

(Sontheimer 1991).

The Zimbabwe Women's Resource Centre and Network (ZWRCN) in Harare has issued a number of resources on this subject: *Fact Sheet on Women and the Environment in Zimbabwe* (Zimbabwe and Regional Network of Environmental Experts 1993); *Women and Environment. ZWRCN Bibliographies, no. 6* (ZWRCN 1993); and *Gender, Environment and Sustainable Development: Zimbabwe's Case. ZWRCN Discussion Paper, no. 8* (Mvududu 1993).

**Environment and conflict:** *Greenwar: Environment and Conflict* (Bennett 1991) explores the role of environmental degradation in "the complex web of causes leading to social and political instability, bloodshed and war" in Africa (p. 1). In chapter 8 of *No Time to Waste* (Davidson et al. 1992) environmental degradation is shown to be the *impetus* for conflicts, as well as the *effect* of armed conflicts. "Environmental degradation can...be a factor generating conflict as pressure on a shrinking natural resource base leads to competition for control of resources," the authors explain. "A vicious circle of environmental degradation and conflict can develop, where inequitable distribution of natural resources leads to environmental degradation, which exacerbates conflict over shrinking resources" (p. 134). Examples of the interrelatedness of poverty, conflict, and environmental degradation are given in the cases of Ethiopia and the Sudan.

**Resource management:** *Wasting the Rain: Rivers, People and Planning in Africa* (Adams 1992) critically examines the ways in which water resources have been developed in Africa (includes dams, wetlands, etc.). *Resource Management in Developing Countries: Africa's Ecological and Economic Problems* (James 1991) explores key resource management issues such as threats to ecological systems, water quality management, and agricultural production, using case studies of Nigeria, Zambia, and other African nations when appropriate.

**Wildlife conservation:** Striking a balance between human needs and wild-

---

## REFERENCE RESOURCES

- *The Conservation Atlas of Tropical Forests: Africa* (Sayer et al. 1992)
- *Dictionary of Environment and Development: People, Places, Ideas and Organizations* (Crump 1993)
- *Dictionary of the Environment* (Allaby 1989)
- *The Environment Encyclopedia and Directory: A World Survey* (Europa Publications 1994)
- *Environmental Profiles: A Global Guide to Projects and People* (Katz et al. 1993)
- *Green Globe Yearbook 1993* (Bergesen and Parmann 1993)
- *International Directory of Non-Governmental Organizations Working for Environmentally, Socially, and Economically Sustainable Development* (WorldWise 1992)
- *The Pocket Green Book* (Rees 1991)
- *The Southern African Environment: Profiles of the SADC Countries* (Moyo et al. 1993)
- *State of the Environment in Southern Africa* (Chenje and Johnson 1994)
- *World Directory of Environmental Organizations: A Handbook of National and International Organizations and Programs—Governmental and Non-Governmental—Concerned with Protecting the Earth's Resources* (Trzyna and Childers 1992)
- *World Resources 1994-95: A Guide to the Global Environment* (Hammond 1994)
- *The World Watch Reader on Global Environmental Issues* (Brown 1991)

For environmental information available on computer networks and bulletin boards see *Ecolinking: Everyone's Guide to Online Environmental Information* (Rittner 1992).

life conservation is an issue taken up in *Wildlands and Human Needs: Reports from the Field* (Stone 1991). This World Wildlife Federation publication describes innovative conservation projects in Cameroon, Zambia, Kenya, Tanzania, and the Central African Republic.

**Eco-tourism:** Environmentally sensitive tourism in Kenya is described in Perez Olindo's article, "The Old Man of Nature Tourism: Kenya," in *Nature Tourism: Managing for the Environment* (Whelan 1991) and in a slim volume by Daniel Nusili Nyeki, Senior Education Officer of the Kenya Wildlife Service, *Wildlife Conservation and Tourism in Kenya* (Nyeki 1993).

**Rainforests:** The range of issues surrounding the preservation and/or appropriate use of Africa's vast rainforests are identified and examined in *The Rainforests of West Africa* (Martin 1991). Swiss biologist Claude Martin underlines the urgency of studying this topic, pointing out that "during the past decade each year has seen an average loss of 7,200 square kilometers of West African forest." Thus it is Africa—and not South America or Southeast Asia—that has suffered the greatest losses to its rainforests in recent times.

In *Paths in the Rainforests: Toward a History of Political Tradition in Equatorial Africa* (Vansina 1990) historian and anthropologist Jan Vansina (University of Wisconsin-Madison) traces the history of the incredibly rich rainforest area of West Africa and describes the many complex societies that came to settle this region. Most of the devastated rainforest land in Africa is in areas that have been opened up by logging interests—an issue that is explored in a pseudonymous article, "Deforestation in Zaire: Logging and Landlessness," in a collection of readings compiled by Marcus Colchester and Larry Lohmann, *The Struggle for Land and the Fate of the Forests* (Colchester and Lohmann 1993).

## African success stories

Success stories of environmental activism in Africa are contained in:
- *Whose Trees? A People's View of Forestry Aid* (Hisham et al. 1991);
- *Women and the Environment* (Rodda 1991);
- *Dying Lake Victoria: A Community-based Prevention Programme* (Akatch 1996).

Two other books are also noteworthy in this regard:
- *More People, Less Erosion: Environmental Recovery in Kenya* (Tiffen et al. 1994); and
- *Portraits in Conservation: Eastern and Southern Africa* (Braun 1995).

Two historical studies show that enlightened environmental protection has a long tradition in the East African region:
- *Custodians of the Land: Ecology and Culture in the History of Tanzania* (Maddox et al. 1996); and
- *Ecology Control and Economic Development in East African History: The Case of Tanganyika, 1850-1950* (Kjekshus 1996).

"Before the end of the century, Nairobi will observe its 100th anniversary. It is our hope that the anniversary will be a celebration of progress towards making the city environment a safer, healthier and more productive place for all its citizens."

Mazingira Institute, Nairobi
quoted in *Nairobi's Environment: A Review of Conditions and Issues* (Lamba 1994)

# FOOD AND AGRICULTURE
## Building another Africa

What captures the media headlines and the popular imagination about the subject of Africa and food is the specter of famine. Famines are real and they are catastrophic. But famines are also as sporadic as volcanic eruptions and major earthquakes in other areas of the world and, when they do occur, they are localized to relatively small areas of the broad African continent.

What goes unnoticed is the fact that when the media rush off to the next cataclysm the people of Egypt, Ghana, Zambia, Mauritius, Sudan, Chad, and other countries in Africa continue—day-in and day-out—to grow the food they need to feed themselves. There *are* problematic questions that need to be examined relative to the topics of food and agriculture in Africa, but these should be set against a backdrop of the sustained effort that Africans invest in providing for their daily needs often against overwhelming odds.

"There is another Africa today," says Father Nzamujo Godfrey Ugwuegmulam, director of the Songhai Project in Benin. "This Africa is not yet known by the mass media. But there are a growing number of communities and nongovernmental organizations and associations that refuse to accept a gloomy picture of the future of Africa....It is our duty to create the human capabilities for solving both the social and economic problems of our African communities. We have no right to decry what is happening in Africa and stop there. The only way to get out of our problems is to build another Africa—our Africa, where we can be recognized as human beings." (*African Farmer*, January 1994, p. 41)

The resource materials in this chapter describe some of the food- and agriculture-related issues that Africans face in building "another Africa." These include control of seeds, distribution of land, export-oriented cash crops, water, sustainable farming techniques, food shortages and war, unavoidable natural phenomena (drought, locusts), the role of foreign agencies in disaster relief, agricultural policies sponsored by the World Bank and

Photo: IFAD/Sierra Leone/ published in "Africa: Sowing the Seeds of Self-Sufficiency," 1986

**"Africa is perfectly capable of producing all the food it needs, as well as an exportable surplus."**

Per Penstrup-Andersen, International Food Policy Research Institute (quoted in *African Farmer*, July 1994, p. 6

International Monetary Fund (IMF), foreign trade and aid, and so forth. The resources also emphasize Africa's accomplishments—the successful projects, the creativity and resiliency of people determined to be self-reliant, the sense of community responsibility for the provision of food and other economic necessities, and the role of women in agricultural production.

## World food system

The best place to begin for an understanding of how the world food system functions is the classic study by Frances Moore Lappé and Joseph Collins, *World Hunger: Twelve Myths* (Lappé and Collins 1986). Their analysis, which has stood the test of time, is reflected in the publications produced by the organization they founded in the San Francisco Bay Area, the Institute for Food and Development Policy/Food First. Publications issued by the World Hunger Educational Service (Washington, D.C.), Bread for the World (Silver Spring, Md.), and World Hunger Year (New York) are also of value.

*Seed and Surplus: An Illustrated Guide to the World Food System* (Delpeuch 1994), co-published by the Catholic Institute for International Relations (London) and Farmers' Link (Norwich), is another introductory guide that presents the workings of the world food system in readable terms and superlative illustrations (more than 50 full-page illustrations in all).

The annual reviews published by the Bread for the World Institute (BFWI) are noteworthy for their analytical essays and their clearly presented charts and tables of statistical data. See *Hunger 1994: Transforming the Politics of Hunger* (BFWI 1993), *Hunger 1995: Causes of Hunger* (BFWI 1994), *Hunger 1996: Countries in Crisis* (BFWI 1995), and *Hunger 1997: What Can Governments Do?* (BFWI 1996).

The 11 essays in *The Color of Hunger: Race and Hunger in National and International Perspective* (Shields 1995) probe for reasons why hunger is concentrated among people of color, both in industrialized and emerging nations. Africa-related essays include Tshenuwani Simon Farisani's "Hunger Amidst Plenty: A South African Perspective" and Mutombo Mpanya's "Stereotypes of Africa in U.S. Hunger Appeals."

## Food and agriculture in Africa

*Myths of African Hunger* (Danaher and Riak 1995) and two related "Food First Backgrounders," *Myths and Root Causes: Hunger, Population, and Development* (Rosset et al. 1994) and *Hunger in the Horn of Africa* (Hammond and Prendergast 1991) sort through the myths and misconceptions that continue to surround this issue in order to identify the "real causes of hunger in Africa."

See also *The Agrarian Question in Southern Africa and "Accumulation from Below": Economics and Politics in the Struggle for Democracy* (Neocosmos 1993); *Agribusiness in Africa: A Study of the Impact of Big Business on Africa's Food and Agricultural Production* (Dinham and Hines 1983); *Agricultural Transformation*

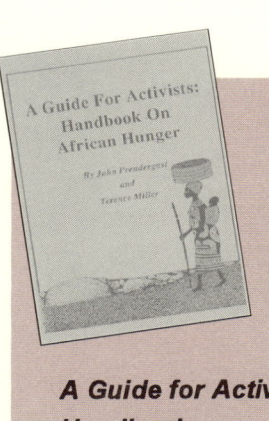

---

### *A Guide for Activists: Handbook on African Hunger*

(Prendergast and Miller 1992)

Designed to meet the information and organizing needs of U.S. activists, this well-organized guide examines the roots of the food crisis in Africa (section 1), analyzes strategies to reduce hunger (section 2), and provides tools that concerned U.S. citizens can use to build a movement against hunger in Africa.

Contact: Maryknoll Justice and Peace Office, P.O. Box 29132, Washington, DC 20017 USA

*World Bank (Washington, D.C.)*

*in Africa* (Seckler 1993); *The Crisis in African Agriculture* (Gakou 1987); *Food in Sub-Saharan Africa* (Hansen and McMillan 1986); *Inducing Food Insecurity: Perspectives on Food Policies in Eastern and Southern Africa* (Salih 1994); and *World Recession and the Food Crisis in Africa* (Lawrence 1986).

The pros and cons of World Bank and IMF involvement in African agriculture are laid out in *Aid to African Agriculture: Lessons from Two Decades of Donors' Experience* (Lele 1992) and *A Blighted Harvest: The World Bank and African Agriculture in the 1980s* (Gibbon et al. 1993).

The following books are particularly useful for delineating the *causes* for African agricultural crises:
- *Africa's Food Crisis: Its Roots, Its Future* (Mpanya and Holdridge n.d.);
- *Famine in East Africa: Food Production and Food Policies* (Seavoy 1989);
- *The Food Question: Profits Versus People?* (Bernstein et al. 1990);
- *Preventing Famine: Policies and Prospects for Africa* (Curtis et al. 1988);
- *Understanding Africa's Food Problems: Social Policy Perspectives* (African Centre for Applied Research and Training in Social Development 1990).

The following studies feature case studies of *initiatives* that are being implemented in Africa to encourage agricultural self-sufficiency:
- *African Agriculture: The Critical Choices* (Amara and Founou-Tchuigoua 1990);
- *From Feast to Famine: Official Cures and Grassroots Remedies to Africa's Food Crisis* (Rau 1991);
- *The Greening of Africa: Breaking Through in the Battle for Land and Food* (Harrison 1990);
- *Living under Contract: Contract Farming and Agrarian Transformation in Sub-Saharan Africa* (Little and Watts 1994);
- *Poverty, Policy, and Food Security in Southern Africa* (Bryant 1988).

## Issues

**Biodiversity and biotechnology:** *Lost Crops of Africa.* Volume 1: *Grains* (Board on Science and Technology for International Development, National Research Council 1996); *New Hope or False Promise? Biotechnology and Third World Agriculture* (Hobbelink 1987).

**Cash crops:** *Food Crops vs. Feed Crops: Global Substitution of Grains in Production* (Barkin et al. 1990).

**Children:** *Intervention in Child Nutrition: Evaluation Studies in Kenya* (Hoorweg and Niemeijer 1989).

**Land ownership and use:** *Land in African Agrarian Systems* (Bassett and Crummey 1993); *Searching for Land Tenure Security in Africa* (Bruce and Migot-Adholla 1993).

**Population:** *Population and Food Security* (Islam et al. 1993-1994).

**Rural development:** *Sustainable Agriculture and Rural Development.* Part 2: *Africa and the North* (FAO 1994).

**Urban agriculture:** *Cities Feeding People: An Examination of Urban Agriculture in East Africa* (Egziabher et al. 1994) contains chapter-length studies of Tanzania, Uganda, Kenya, and Ethiopia.

### Region/country studies

Country studies of Ghana, Nigeria, Kenya, and Zambia are featured in *No Condition is Permanent: The Social Dynamics of Agrarian Change in Sub-Saharan Africa* (Berry 1993). *Food Policy and Agriculture in Southern Africa* (Mkandawire and Matlosa 1993) contains case studies of Zambia, Malawi, Botswana, Tanzania, Mozambique, Zimbabwe, and Swaziland.

**Cameroon:** Chapter 8 in *Institutional Sustainability in Agriculture and Rural Development: A Global Perspective* (Brinkerhoff and Goldsmith 1990): "Policy reform as institutional change."

**Cape Verde:** *History and Hunger in West Africa: Food Production and Entitlement in Guinea-Bissau and Cape Verde* (Bigman 1993).

**Côte d'Ivoire:** *An End to Hunger? The Social Origins of Food Strategies* (Barraclough 1991).

**Egypt:** *Sustainable Agriculture in Egypt* (Faris and Khan 1993).

**Ethiopia:** *Ethiopia: Failure of Land Reform and Agricultural Crisis* (Mengisteab 1990); *Environment, Famine, and Politics in Ethiopia: A View from the Village* (Dejene 1990).

**Guinea Bissau:** *History and Hunger in West Africa: Food Production and Entitlement in Guinea-Bissau and Cape Verde* (Bigman 1993).

**Kenya:** *Intervention in Child Nutrition: Evaluation Studies in Kenya* (Hoorweg and Niemeijer 1989).

**Morocco:** Chapter 9 in *Institutional Sustainability in Agriculture and Rural Development: A Global Perspective* (Brinkerhoff and Goldsmith 1990): "The Three Phases of Sustainability in Morocco's Institut Agronomique et Vétérinaire Hassan II."

**Senegal:** *Gender, Class and Rural Transition: Agribusiness and the Food Crisis in Senegal* (Mackintosh 1989).

**Sudan:** *To Cure All Hunger: Food Policy and Food Security in Sudan* (Maxwell 1991).

**Tanzania:** *Liberalizing Tanzania's Food Trade: Public and Private Faces of Urban Marketing Policy, 1939-1988* (Bryceson 1993); Chapter 5, "Ujamaa: The Failure of a Non-coercive Agricultural Policy in Tanzania," in *Famine in East Africa: Food Production and Food Policies* (Seavoy 1989); *Food Insecurity and the Social Division of Labour in Tanzania, 1919-85* (Bryceson 1990).

**Zimbabwe:** *Seeds for African Peasants: Peasants' Needs and Agricultural Research. The Case of Zimbabwe* (Friis-Hansen 1995); *Zimbabwe's Agricultural Revolution* (Rukuni and Eicher 1994); *Government and Agriculture in Zimbabwe* (Masters 1994).

---

"I grew up in a village of 1,000 people in Tshikapa, Zaire. There were no soldiers, policemen, prisons, or criminals. Everyone had enough food to eat; there were no beggars. Children, elders, and sick people were all taken care of by their families. People grew their own food, built their own homes, and created their own arts and entertainment. Of course, my village was not Korem in Ethiopia [center of the Ethiopian famine in the mid-1980s], or any other village, but this image of peace and self-sufficiency is as valid and real an image of Africa as any other."

— Mutombo Mpanya, "Stereotypes of Africa in U.S. Hunger Appeals," *The Color of Hunger: Race and Hunger in National and International Perspective* (Shields 1995), p. 32

# FOREIGN INTERVENTION
## Case study: Somalia

Foreign "humanitarian" intervention in the crisis in Somalia in the early 1990s brought to light numerous questions about the developing role of various actors in international relief efforts, among them the United Nations, the military forces of countries such as the United States, and the nongovernmental (NGO) community. These questions were much on the minds of many in the fall of 1996 as the United Nations and the governments of Canada, the United States, and other nations contemplated whether or not to intervene in the desperate refugee situation in Zaire and Rwanda.

"Somalia during 1991-93," a November 1994 African Rights discussion paper states, "was the apogee of humanitarianism unbound; an episode when NGOs were groping in the dark to find their role, and testing the limits of their abilities and mandates. Later, the United Nations and the U.S. military found themselves in a similar position, and Somalia became, quite explicitly, a guinea pig for 'humanitarian intervention' in the 'new world order.' Even though the military-humanitarian intervention failed, the precedents in international practice that it set still stand, and there are many who now seek to return to the ideas of a more aggressive international policing role for the United Nations." (*Humanitarianism Unbound? Current Dilemmas Facing Multi-Mandate Relief Operations in Political Emergencies*, p. 17)

The resource materials in this chapter analyze the nature and extent of foreign intervention in emergency situations in Africa and outline the lines of debate regarding the role of the United Nations and other international bodies in such emergencies. Foreign intervention in Somalia from 1991 to 1993 is offered as a case study.

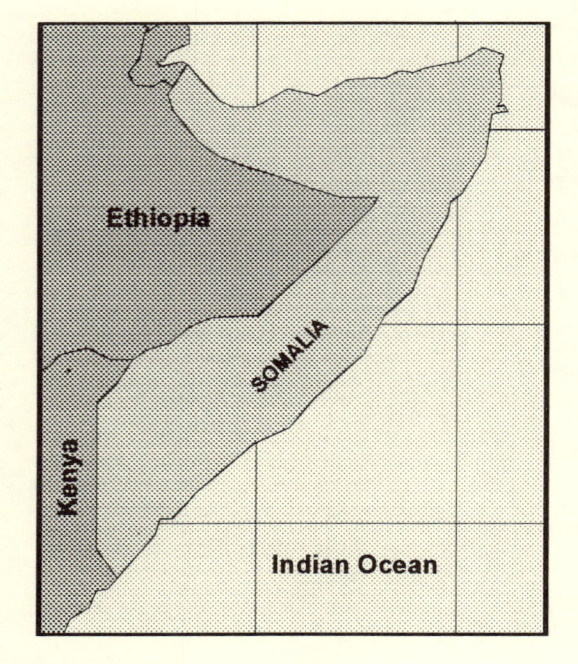

### Humanitarian intervention

Two organizations that are playing pivotal roles in focusing critical attention on issues related to humanitarian intervention are African

Rights (London) and Brown University's Thomas J. Watson Jr. Institute for International Studies (Providence, R.I.).

The Thomas J. Watson Jr. Institute was established in 1986 to provide "a university-wide focus for teaching and research on international relations and foreign cultures and societies." The associate director of the Institute, Thomas Weiss, together with Larry Minear, codirector of Brown University's Humanitarianism and War Project, have been involved in a number of publishing projects that embody the institute's objectives. See, for example: *Humanitarian Emergencies and Military Help in Africa* (Weiss 1990); *Humanitarianism across Borders: Sustaining Civilians in Times of War* (Weiss and Minear 1993); *Humanitarian Action in Times of War: A Handbook for Practitioners* (Minear and Weiss 1993); *Humanitarianism and War: Reducing the Human Cost of Armed Conflict* (Minear and Weiss 1994); *Mercy under Fire: War and the Global Humanitarian Community* (Minear and Weiss 1995); and *The United Nations and Civil Wars* (Weiss 1995).

Other publications that examine issues related to humanitarian intervention—be it military or economic—are *The Politics of Humanitarian Intervention* (Harriss 1995); *Humanitarian Challenges and Intervention: World Politics and the Dilemmas of Help* (Weiss and Collins 1996); *The Ethics and Politics of Humanitarian Intervention* (Hoffmann 1996); *Subduing Sovereignty: Sovereignty and the Right to Intervene* (Heiberg 1994); *Humanitarianism under Seige: A Critical Review of Operation Lifeline Sudan* (Minear 1991); *Making War and Waging Peace: Foreign Intervention in Africa* (Smock 1993); *Without Troops and Tanks: Humanitarian Intervention in Ethiopia and Eritrea* (Duffield and Prendergast 1994); and *New Strategies for a Restless World: Refugees in the 1990s* (Cleveland 1993).

Article-length discussions of interventionism in the post-cold war era are found in *Foreign Affairs* 72, no. 1, 1992/1993, "The New Interventionists," Stephen John Stedman, pp. 1-16); *Current History*, May 1994, "Somaliland: One Thorn Bush at a Time," Rakiya Omaar, pp. 232-236; *New Strategies for a Restless World* (Cleveland 1993), "The Law of Humanitarian Intervention," Nancy C. Arnison, pp. 37-44, and "The Military Role in Emergency Response," Arthur E. Dewey, pp. 45-50; *Middle East Report* 24, nos. 2-3, March-April/May-June 1994, "Can Military Intervention Be 'Humanitarian'?," Alex de Waal and Rakiya Omaar, pp. 3-8, and "Sovereignty and Intervention after the Cold War," Mark Duffield and John Prendergast, pp. 9-23.

For titles of other articles on this topic consult the *Alternative Press Index* (Baltimore, Maryland)—print and CD-ROM versions—and *The Left Index* (Santa Cruz, California).

## United Nations intervention

The UN's own study of its involvement in Somalia in the early 1990s is found in Volume 8 in the United Nations Blue Book series, *The United Nations and*

---

### African Rights

The human rights organization African Rights was established in December 1992 in opposition to Operation Restore Hope in Somalia. The founding directors of African Rights, Rakiya Omaar and Alex de Waal, state that "we believed that the military intervention was not designed to address Somalia's real problems and was in fact destined to make things worse."

"The urgent motivation for setting up African Rights," Omaar and de Waal write, "is that we have become acutely aware of the limitations upon existing human rights, humanitarian, and conflict resolution approaches to Africa's most pressing problems. The United States/United Nations military occupation of much of Somalia has dramatically highlighted the shortcomings of current international approaches to problems of famine and war."

African Rights believes that "any solution to Africa's problems—the emergency humanitarian needs just as much as the long-term demands for political reconstruction and accountability—must be sought primarily among Africans. International organizations should see their principal role as facilitating and supporting attempts by Africans to address their own problems. It is Africa's tragedy that the existing institutions for addressing these problems have not looked to the African people for answers." African Rights "tries to give a voice to Africans concerned with these pressing issues, and to press for more accountability from the international community."

Since its establishment in December 1992, African Rights has issued numerous books, reports, and discussion papers that raise urgent questions about international relief efforts in Africa and elsewhere. These include: *Humanitarianism Unbound? Current Dilemmas Facing Multi-Mandate Relief Operations in Political Emergencies*. Discussion paper, no. 5 (November 1994); *Somalia: Operation Restore Hope. A Preliminary Assessment*. Report (May 1993); *Somalia: Human Rights Abuses by the United Nations Forces*. Report (July 1993); and *Violent Deeds Live On: Landmines in Somalia and Somaliland* (December 1993), a report prepared jointly with the Mines Advisory Group.

AFRICAN RIGHTS, 11 Marshalsea Road, London SE1 1EP, England.

*Somalia, 1992-1996* (United Nations, Department of Public Information 1996).

The years since the beginning of UN involvement in Somalia have seen an outpouring of critical evaluations of the international organization's intervention in complex militarized situations around the world. See, for example,

- *The Next Fifty Years: The United Nations and the United States* (Barry 1996);
- *For a Strong and Democratic United Nations: A South Perspective on UN Reform* (South Centre 1996);
- *Briefing Book on Peacekeeping: The U.S. Role in United Nations Peace Operations* (Holt 1995);
- *The United Nations and Civil Wars* (Weiss 1995);
- *The New UN Peacekeeping: Building Peace in Lands of Conflict after the Cold War* (Ratner 1995);
- *Towards a Theory of United Nations Peacekeeping* (Fetherston 1994);
- *The United Nations in a Turbulent World* (Rosenau 1993).

Jonathan Moore uses Somalia as a case study of UN efforts to rehabilitate war-torn societies in his 106-page booklet, *The UN and Complex Emergencies: Rehabilitation in Third World Transitions* (Moore 1996).

## CASE STUDY: SOMALIA

Studies that focus on the period of foreign humanitarian intervention in Somalia include:
- *The Bones of Our Children Are Not Yet Buried: The Looming Spectre of Famine and Massive Human Rights Abuse in Somalia* (Prendergast 1994);
- *The Cost of Dictatorship: The Somali Experience* (Ghalib 1995);
- *Crisis Management and the Politics of Reconciliation in Somalia: Statements from the Uppsala Forum, 17-19 January 1994* (Salih and Wohlgemuth 1994);
- *The Gun Talks Louder Than the Voice: Somalia's Continuing Cycles of Violence* (Prendergast 1994);
- *Learning from Somalia: The Lessons of Armed Humanitarian Intervention* (Clarke and Herbst 1997);
- *Peacebuilding in Somalia* (Jan 1996)
- *Restoring Hope: The Real Lessons of Somalia for the Future of Intervention* (Oakley and Hirsch 1995);
- *Seeking Peace from Chaos: Humanitarian Intervention in Somalia* (Makinda 1993);
- *Somalia: Human Rights Abuses by the United Nations Forces* (Omaar and de Waal 1993);
- *Somalia: Operation Restore Hope. A Preliminary Assessment* (Omaar and de Waal 1993);
- *Whatever Happened to Somalia? A Tale of Tragic Blunders* (Drysdale 1994).

Books that provide background on Somalia and Somali society include:
- *Blood and Bone: The Call of Kinship in Somali Society* (Lewis 1994);
- *Mending Rips in the Sky: Options for Somali Communities in the 21st Century* (Adam and Ford 1997);
- *Networks of Dissolution: Somalia Undone* (Simons 1995);
- *Road to Zero: Somalia's Self-Destruction* (Omar 1992);
- *Somalia: A Government at War with Its Own People* (Africa Watch 1990);
- *Somalia: A Nation in Turmoil* (Samatar 1991);
- *The Struggle for Land in Southern Somalia: The War Behind the War* (Besteman and Cassanelli 1996);
- *Understanding Somalia: Guide to Culture, History and Social Institutions* (Lewis 1993).

# UNITED NATIONS PEACEKEEPING OPERATIONS PAST AND PRESENT

○ Completed Missions: 25
★ Ongoing Missions: 16
TOTAL MISSIONS: 41

**UNPROFOR**
U.N. Protection Force
March 1992–Jan. 1996

**UNCRO**
U.N. Confidence Restoration Operation in Croatia
April 1995–Jan. 1996

**UNPREDEP**
U.N. Preventative Deployment Force
*April 1995–Present*

**UNTAES**
U.N. Transitional Administration for Eastern Slovonia, Baranja, and Western Sirmium
*Jan. 1996–Present*

**UNTSO**
U.N. Truce Supervision Organization
*June 1948–Present*

**UNOGIL**
U.N. Observation Group in Lebanon
June 1958–Dec. 1958

**UNOMIG**
U.N. Observer Mission in Georgia
*Aug. 1993–Present*

**UNMOT**
U.N. Mission of Observers in Tajikistan
*Dec. 1994–Present*

**UNIPOM**
U.N. India-Pakistan Observation Mission
Sept. 1965–March 1966

**DOMREP**
Mission of the Representative of the Secretary-General in the Dominican Republic
May 1965–Oct. 1966

**UNMOP**
U.N. Mission of Observers in Prevlaka
*Jan. 1996–Present*

**UNFICYP**
U.N. Peacekeeping Force in Cyprus
*March 1964–Present*

**UNIFIL**
U.N. Interim Force in Lebanon
*March 1978–Present*

**UNDOF**
U.N. Disengagement Observer Force
*June 1974–Present*

**UNIIMOG**
U.N. Iran-Iraq Military Observer Group
Aug. 1988–Feb. 1991

**UNIKOM**
U.N. Iraq-Kuwait Observation Mission
*Apr. 1991–Present*

**UNMOGIP**
U.N. Military Observer Group in India & Pakistan
*Jan. 1949–Present*

**UNMIH**
U.N. Mission in Haiti
*Sept. 1993–Present*

**UNMIBH**
U.N. Mission in Bosnia and Herzegovina
*Dec. 1995–Present*

**UNGOMAP**
U.N. Good Offices Mission in Afghanistan and Pakistan
Apr. 1988–March 1990

**UNASOG**
U.N. Aouzou Strip Observer Group
May 1994–June 1994

**ONUCA**
U.N. Observer Group in Central America
Nov. 1989–Jan. 1992

**ONUSAL**
U.N. Observer Mission in El Salvador
July 1991–April 1995

**MINURSO**
U.N. Mission for the Referendum in Western Sahara
*Sept. 1991–Present*

**UNOMUR**
U.N. Observer Mission Uganda-Rwanda
June 1993–Sept. 1994

**UNAMIR**
U.N. Assistance Mission for Rwanda
Oct. 1993–March 1996

**UNYOM**
U.N. Yemen Observation Mission
July 1963–Sept. 1964

**UNSF**
U.N. Security Force in West New Guinea (West Irian)
Oct. 1962–April 1963

**UNEF I**
First U.N. Emergency Force
Nov. 1956–June 1967

**UNAVEM I**
U.N. Angola Verification Mission I
Jan. 1989–June 1991

**ONUC**
U.N. Operation in the Congo
July 1960–June 1964

**UNOSOM I**
U.N. Operation in Somalia I
Apr. 1992–Apr. 1993

**UNAMIC**
U.N. Advance Mission in Cambodia
Oct. 1991–March 1992

**UNOMIL**
U.N. Observer Mission in Liberia
*Sept. 1993–Present*

**UNEF II**
Second U.N. Emergency Force
Oct. 1973–July 1979

**UNAVEM II**
U.N. Angola Verification Mission II
June 1991–Feb. 1995

**UNAVEM III**
U.N. Angola Verification Mission III
*Feb. 1995–present*

**UNTAG**
U.N. Transition Assistance Group
Apr. 1989–March 1990

**ONUMOZ**
U.N. Operation in Mozambique
Dec. 1992–Jan. 1995

**UNOSOM II**
U.N. Operation in Somalia II
May 1993–March 1995

**UNTAC**
U.N. Transitional Authority in Cambodia
March 1992–Sept. 1993

Based on UN information (April 1, 1995). Compiled by the Project on Peacekeeping and the United Nations, Council for a Livable World Education Fund, 110 Maryland Ave., NE, Ste. 201, Washington, DC 20002 USA. Used with permission.

**FOREIGN INTERVENTION**

# HUMAN RIGHTS
## Broader understandings

The traditional human rights emphasis in the West has been on the protection of civil and political rights—to the exclusion of the rights of people everywhere to food, shelter, education, and health. Brendalyn Ambrose, development expert and author of *Democratization and the Protection of Human Rights in Africa: Problems and Prospects* (Ambrose 1995), contends that the Western concept of human rights is too narrow and that an "action plan for human rights and development in Africa must take on a different look. Africa's recovery," Ambrose argues, "calls for the juxtaposition of both political and economic rights because in most countries hunger and diseases kill even more than guns do" (quoted in *CUSO Forum* 12, no. 2, 1994, p. 6).

### African Charter on Human and Peoples' Rights

The resource materials in this chapter describe and analyze the broader conception of human rights that Ambrose calls for and that is enshrined in the 68 articles in the *African Charter on Human and Peoples' Rights*.

The *African Charter* was adopted by the 18th Assembly of the Heads of State and Government of the Organization of African Unity (OAU) in June 1981 and came into force on October 21, 1986, the day that is now marked as Africa Human Rights Day. The text of the *African Charter* is available in *The International Law of Human Rights in Africa: Basic Documents and Annotated Bibliography* (Hamalengwa et al. 1988). An illustrated version of selected articles from the *African Charter* is available from the Legal Research and Resource Development Centre in Lagos, Nigeria.

*The Concept of Human Rights in Africa* (Shivji 1989) is a short but challenging critique of "human rights talk" by a law professor and Head of the Department of Legal Theory in the University of Dar-es-Salaam, Tanzania. African and non-African scholars tackle a broad range of human rights issues in the twelve essays published in *Emerging Human Rights: The African*

---

"While much of the emphasis in the West has been in promoting civil and political rights, the action plan for human rights and development in Africa must take on a different look. Africa's recovery calls for the juxtaposition of both political and economic rights because in most countries, hunger and diseases kill even more than guns do."

Brendalyn Ambrose, author, *Democratization and the Protection of Human Rights in Africa: Problems and Prospects* (1995)

*Political Economy Context* (Shepherd and Anikpo 1990). The articles in *Human Rights and Development in Africa* (Welch and Meltzer 1984) are noteworthy for the attention they give to the human rights situation in the Islamic world and to regional initiatives on human rights in Africa (e.g., the Banjul Charter on Human and People's Rights).

Two other collections of essays—most of them by Western academics—are: *Human Rights and Governance in Africa* (Cohen et al. 1993) and *Human Rights in Africa: Cross-Cultural Perspectives* (An-Na'im and Deng 1990).

In *Human Rights in Commonwealth Africa* (Howard 1986) Rhoda Howard focuses attention on the human rights situation in the nine independent countries of Africa that "at least in their ideals, resemble Western democracies." The human rights debate in North Africa (and in the broader Arab world) is the subject of two studies: *Arab Voices: The Human Rights Debate in the Middle East* (Dwyer 1991)—covering Morocco, Egypt, and Tunisia, and *Islam and Human Rights: Tradition and Politics* (Mayer 1991).

A handy reference collection of human rights documents of African origin and concern is *The International Law of Human Rights in Africa: Basic Documents and Annotated Bibliography* (Hamalengwa et al. 1988). Compiler Munyonzwe Hamalengwa produced a shorter (unannotated) bibliography of professional literature on human rights in Africa in Vol. 8, No. 1 (February 1986) of *Human Rights Quarterly*: "The Human Rights Literature on Africa: A Bibliography" (Cobbah and Hamalengwa 1986).

## Human rights-related issues in Africa

Studies that focus on particular facets of human rights in Africa are:

**Academic freedom:** *Academic Freedom in Africa* (Diouf and Mamdani 1993); *Academic Freedom 2: A Human Rights Report* (Daniel et al. 1993); *The State of Academic Freedom in Africa 1995* (Busia and Dgni-Sgui 1996).

**Children:** *The Rights of the Child in Ghana: Perspectives* (Mensa-Bonsu and Dowuona-Hammond 1994).

**Human rights education:** *Human Rights Education Techniques in Schools: Building Attitudes and Skills* (Nsirimovu 1994).

**Press censorship:** *The Media and Human Rights in Southern Africa* (Inter Press Service, Africa Network 1994); *Truth from Below: The Emergent Press in Africa* (Carver 1991); *Press Freedom in Africa* (Faringer 1991).

**State security:** *Freedom, State Security, and the Rule of Law: Dilemmas of the Apartheid Society* (Mathews 1986); *Individual Freedoms and State Security in the African Context: The Case of Zimbabwe* (Hatchard 1993).

**Women:** *African Women: A General Bibliography, 1976-1985* (Bullwinkle 1989); *The Cross-Cultural Study of Women: A Comprehensive Guide* (Duley and Edwards 1986); *Discrimination against Women: A Global Survey of the Economic, Educational, Social and Political Status of Women* (Rhoodie 1989); *Ours by Right:*

---

### Human Rights Annual Reports

- *Amnesty International Report.* Amnesty International (London)
- *Article 19: World Report.* Article 19 (London)
- *Attacks on the Press: A Worldwide Survey.* Committee to Protect Journalists (New York)
- *Country Reports on Human Rights Practices.* U.S. Department of State (Washington, D.C.)
- *Critique: Review of the U.S. Department of State's Country Reports on Human Rights Practices.* Lawyers Committee for Human Rights (New York and Washington, D.C.)
- *Freedom in the World: The Annual Survey of Political Rights and Civil Liberties.* Freedom House (New York and Washington, D.C.)
- *Freedom of the Press throughout the World.* Reporters Sans Frontières (Paris)
- *Human Rights in Developing Countries: Yearbook.* Nordic Human Rights Publications (Oslo)
- *The Human Rights Watch Global Report on Women's Human Rights.* Human Rights Watch (New York and London)
- *Human Rights Watch World Report.* Human Rights Watch (New York and London)
- *World Survey of Economic Freedom.* Freedom House (New York and Washington, D.C.)

*Women's Rights as Human Rights* (Kerr 1993); *Prisoners of Ritual: An Odyssey into Female Genital Circumcision in Africa* (Lightfoot-Klein 1989); *Uncovering Reality: Excavating Women's Rights in African Family Law* (Armstrong et al. 1992); *Women and Disability* (Boylan 1991); *Women's Rights in International Documents: A Sourcebook with Commentary* (Langley 1991).

### Keeping up

The "Together for Rights, Together Against Poverty" international campaign, which was launched in 1995 by Oxfam (UK and Ireland), offers concerned individuals an opportunity to engage in ongoing human rights initiatives that deal with the full range of social, economic, and political issues in Africa and elsewhere. *Words into Action: Basic Rights and the Campaign against World Poverty* (Simmons 1995) describes the campaign in a well-illustrated fashion.

The Regional Centre for Africa of the Inter Press Service Third World News Agency and the African Centre for Democracy and Human Rights (see below) both publish regular reports on human rights-related issues in Africa.

Other organizations in Africa that monitor human rights developments on a regular basis are listed and described in *National Human Rights Institutions in Africa* (Carver and Hunt 1991), *African Directory: Human Rights Organizations in Sub-Saharan Africa 1996* (Human Rights Internet and Netherlands Institute of Human Rights 1996), and in the *HRI Reporter* published quarterly by Human Rights Internet (Ottawa).

*African Charter on Human and People's Rights.* Booklet published by the Legal Research and Resource Development Centre, Lagos, Nigeria.

---

The **Regional Centre for Africa of the Inter Press Service News Agency** publishes *Human Rights Bulletin,* a monthly bulletin with news reports on human rights situations (broadly defined) throughout Africa.

Inter Press Service (IPS) is the world's leading alternative news agency, with a regional presence in Africa, Asia, Latin America, North America, the Caribbean, and Europe. IPS specializes in "in-depth and contextualized coverage of international processes, events, and issues that affect the Third World with particular emphasis on grassroots actors in development."

**Contact:** IPS Africa Headquarters, 127 Union Ave., P.O. Box 6050, Harare, Zimbabwe. E-mail: ipshre@gn.apc.org.

The **African Centre for Democracy and Human Rights Studies** publishes a quarterly newsletter (in English and French), *African Human Rights Newsletter,* with news reports, commentary and analysis, lists of resources, and a calendar of events related to human rights in Africa. A particularly useful feature of the newsletter is its regular survey of the mission and activities of African nongovernmental organizations working in the field of human rights.

The African Centre also publishes a series of "Occasional Papers" on human rights-related topics.

**Contact:** African Centre for Democracy and Human Rights Studies, Kairaba Ave., K.S.M.D., The Gambia.

# Human Rights Country Reports

Human rights conditions in individual countries in Africa are surveyed on a regular basis by international organizations such as African Rights (AR), Amnesty International (AI), Article 19: International Centre Against Censorship (A19), Committee to Protect Journalists (CPJ), Human Rights Watch (HRW), the Lawyers Committee for Human Rights (LCHR), and Minority Rights Group (MRG). Note, however, that studies such as the following tend to focus only on civil and political human rights.

**Algeria:** *Human Rights Abuses in Algeria: No One Is Spared* (HRW January 1994); *Algeria: Deteriorating Human Rights under a State of Emergency* (AI March 1993).

**Angola:** *Angola: An Appeal for Prompt Action to Protect Human Rights* (AI May 1992).

**Botswana:** *Second Class Citizens: Discrimination against Women under Botswana's Citizenship Act* (HRW September 1994).

**Burundi:** *Burundi: Time for Mass Action to End a Cycle of Mass Murder* (HRW May 1994); *Burundi since the Genocide* (MRG/Kay 1987).

**Cameroon:** *Northern Cameroon: Attacks on Freedom of Expression by Governmental and Traditional Authorities* (A19 July 1995).

**Chad:** *Chad: Never Again? Killings Continue into the 1990s* (AI April 1993); *Chad* (MRG/Whiteman 1988).

**Egypt:** *Egypt: Grave Human Rights Abuses amid Political Violence* (AI May 1993); *The Legal Profession in Egypt* (LCHR January 1993)

**Eritrea:** *Freedom of Expression and Ethnic Discrimination in the Educational System: Past and Future* (HRW January 1993).

**Ethiopia:** *Reckoning under the Law* (HRW December 1994).

**Gambia:** *Democracy Overturned: Violation of Freedom of Expression in The Gambia* (A19 1994)

**Ghana:** *Revolutionary Injustice: Abuses of the Legal System under the PNDC Government* (HRW January 1992).

**Kenya:** *Multipartyism Betrayed in Kenya: Continuing Rural Violence and Restrictions on Freedom of Speech and Assembly* (HRW July 1994); *Kenya: Shooting the Messenger* (A19 October 1993); *The Nightmare Continues: Abuses against Somali Refugees in Kenya* (AR September 1993);

*Kenya: Continuing Human Rights Concerns* (LCHR February 1992).

**Lesotho:** *Lesotho: Torture, Political Killings and Abuses against Trade Unionists* (May 1992).

**Liberia:** *Easy Prey: Child Soldiers in Liberia* (HRW September 1994); *First Steps: Rebuilding the Justice System in Liberia* (LCHR 1991); *Worker Rights Violations in Liberia: GSP Petition before the U.S. Trade Representative* (LCHR May 1989)

**Malawi:** *Malawi: Preserving the One Party State: Human Rights Violations and the Referendum* (May 1993); *Malawi: Ignoring Calls for Change* (LCHR October 1992); *Malawi's Past: The Right to Truth* (A19 November 1993).

**Mauritania:** *Mauritania's Campaign of Terror: State-Sponsored Repression of Black Africans* (HRW April 1994).

**Morocco:** *Human Rights in Morocco* (HRW October 1995); *Cleaning the Face of Morocco: Human Rights Abuses and Recent Developments* (LCHR 1990); *Morocco: Attacks on Freedom of Expression, November 1990-June 1991* (A19 July 1991).

**Mozambique:** *Landmines in Mozambique* (HRW March 1994).

**Nambia:** *Accountability in Namibia: Human Rights and the Transition to Democracy* (HRW August 1992).

**Nigeria:** *Nigeria: Fundamental Human Rights Denied. Report of the Trial of Ken Saro-Wiwa and Others* (A19 June 1995); *The Nigerian Police Force: A Culture of Impunity* (LCHR May 1992); *Nigeria: Attacking Those Who Defend Rights* (LCHR April 1992).

**Rwanda:** *Rwanda: Death, Despair and Defiance* (AR September 1994); *Genocide in Rwanda: April-May 1994* (HRW May 1994); *Rwanda: Who Is Killing? Who Is Dying? What Is to Be Done?* (AR Mary 1994); *Rwanda: Persecution of Tutsi Minority and Repression of Government Critics, 1990-1992* (AI May 1992).

**Sierra Leone:** *Sierra Leone: Political Detainees at the Central Prison, Pademba Road, Freetown* (AI June 1993).

**Somalia:** *Somalia: Update on Disaster-Proposals for Human Rights* (AI April 1993); *Somalia: A Human Rights Disaster* (AI September 1992); *Somalia: A Nation in Turmoil* (MRG/Samatar 1991).

**South Africa:** *Compilation Document* (AI March 1994); *Impunity for Human Rights Abuses in Two Homelands: Reports on KwaZulu and Bophuthatswana* (HRW March 1994); *Prison Conditions in South Africa* (HRW January 1994); *South Africa: Torture, Ill-treatment, and Executions in ANC Camps* (AI December 1992).

**Sudan:** *Civilian Devastation: Abuses by All Parties in the War in Southern Sudan* (HRW June 1994); *Sudan: The Ravages of War: Political Killings and Humanitarian Disaster* (AI September 1993); *Sudan: Patterns of Repression* (AI February 1993); *Sudan: Dismantling Civil Society. Suppression of Freedom of Association* (A19 August 1993); *The Legal Profession in Sudan* (LCHR February 1992); *Sudan: Press Freedom under Siege* (A19 April 1991).

**Tanzania:** *Tanzania: Harassment of Seif Sharif Hamad. Legal Proceedings against Former Zanzibar Chief Minister* (LCHR 1991).

**Tunisia:** *Tunisia: Rhetoric vs. Reality. The Failure of a Human Rights Bureaucracy* (AI January 1994); *Unfulfilled Promises: Human Rights in Tunisia since 1987* (LCHR May 1993); *Mass Trial of Islamists before Military Courts in Tunisia* (LCHR August 1992); *Tunisia: Attacks on the Press and Government Critics* (A19 June 1991).

**Uganda:** *Uganda: The Failure to Safeguard Human Rights* (AI September 1992); *Uganda* (MRG/Hooper and Pirouet 1989).

# IMAGES OF AFRICA
## Stereotypes and distortions

**W**hen one curriculum developer was asked if she intended to produce educational packets on African nations similar to ones she had already published on the Philippines and China, she pointed to a packet on world hunger and responded, "We already have an Africa packet." The educator's response illustrates two not-uncommon problems with the way Africa is perceived. The first is that the African continent—with its 53 countries—is seen to be equivalent to *individual* nations in other parts of the world (i.e., Africa-Philippines or Africa-China). The second problem is that Africa's nations and peoples are often viewed through the lens of dominant media images such as hunger, famine, or refugees.

The resource materials in this chapter examine critically the various ways in which Africa has been portrayed in the media. They also describe efforts to foster "media literacy" in African nations and elsewhere.

### Prevalent misconceptions

The nature, source, and prevalence of misconceptions about the rich and diverse continent of Africa are examined comprehensively in nineteen readable essays in *Africa's Media Image* (Hawk 1992). The essays explore the complexity of the Western journalist's task in understanding and reporting about African realities and then engage in in-depth investigations of media coverage of the Mau Mau peasant uprising in Kenya in 1952, the Algerian war of independence (1954-1962), the Nigerian civil war (1967-1970), superpower rivalries in Africa, and chronic food shortages in parts of Africa in the 1980s. The essays also analyze coverage of Africa in African-American newspapers and in the *New York Times,* popular media notions of the "primitive" and "tribal" in reporting on South Africa, the U.S. media's "promotion" of Angola's Jonas Savimbi as a "freedom fighter" worthy of American support, and the obstacles that block changes in media coverage of Africa-

> "The role of communication and media in the process of development should not be underestimated, nor [should] the function of media as instruments for the citizen's active participation in society. Political and educational systems need to recognize their obligations to promote in their citizens a critical understanding of the phenomena of communication."
>
> UNESCO declaration issued in 1982 at the International Symposium on Media Education (Grunwald, Germany)

related issues. Gretchen Walsh catalogs a range of print and audiovisual resources on this topic in *The Media in Africa and Africa in the Media: An Annotated Bibliography* (Walsh 1996).

### "Freedom fighters," disasters, Mau Mau...

Other studies give individual attention to some of the topics examined in *Africa's Media Image*. *The Cold War Guerrilla: Jonas Savimbi, the U.S. Media, and the Angolan War* (Windrich 1992), for example, casts a critical eye on media coverage of what the *New York Times* called the Reagan administration's "dirty war" in Angola. "What the American public knows about [Jonas] Savimbi and his war to overthrow a government recognized by the entire international community (with the exception of the United States and South Africa),"Elaine Windrich explains, "is what they read in their newspapers, hear on their radios, and see on their televisions. But this 'information' has all too often been derived from official sources, either spokesmen for the Reagan/Bush administrations or agents of the Pretoria regime, both of which have a vested interest in promoting Savimbi's cause" (p. ix).

International media coverage of famines in Africa is scrutinized in *News Out of Africa: Biafra to Band Aid* (Harrison and Palmer 1986), *Disasters, Relief and the Media* (Benthall 1993), and in the three-part video series, *Consuming Hunger: Famine and the Media* (Maryknoll 1988).

*News Out of Africa* offers the informed and personal perspectives of a lecturer and writer on African history (Palmer) and an independent filmmaker (Harrison) on media coverage of three particular famines in Africa: Biafra (1968-70), Ethiopia (1973-74), and Ethiopia, again, in 1984. The short and anecdote-filled book illustrates how commercial interests shape the portrayal of world events and how the selection of stories to be covered and presented is often dictated by random happenings and by strong-willed individuals. *News Out of Africa* also raises disturbing questions about "the present direction of media trends of faster and faster news—of the 'quick and headline-seeking superficial coverage', which seizes on the dramatic and the exceptional, but fails to place it in any meaningful context."

In *Disasters, Relief and the Media*, anthropologist Jonathan Benthall analyzes the diversity of issues facing relief agencies and journalists who report on disasters such as the Nigerian civil war of the late 1960s and the Armenian earthquake of 1988. He considers the different styles and marketing techniques of major relief agencies in the UK, Europe, and the United States, and devotes an entire chapter to a study of "the cultural styles" of humanitarian agencies such as the International Committee of the Red Cross, World Vision, and Médecins san Frontières. Benthall's final chapter focuses on "how disasters and disaster relief are represented across a range of visiual imagery and narrative devices." Special attention is given to the dominant role of television in conveying images of disasters and relief.

### Shaping the Media Image

A 3-part video documentary released in 1988 by Maryknoll World Productions, *Consuming Hunger*, examines the major role that television played in creating awareness of the famine in Ethiopia and in shaping Western images of Africa and its people. (3 segments, 29-minutes each)

> **CHANGING THE DOMINANT IMAGES**
>
> African organizations are taking initiatives on a number of fronts to project positive and more representative images of their realities. Examples of such organizations are: 
>
> The SOUTH → NORTH BOOK PROJECT
>
> The **South-North Book Project** of the Zimbabwe Book Marketing Trust (Harare), which helps African publishers create more and better books for African and non-African readers. 
>
> **The Media Resource Centre and Community Resource Centre Training Project at the University of Natal** (Durban), which has published two excellent media-empowerment tools, *Media Matters in South Africa* (Prinsloo and Criticos 1991) and *Ulwazi: For Power and Courage* (Dreyer and Karlsson 1991).
>
> **The Zimbabwe Women's Resource Centre and Network** (Harare), which seeks to enhance the position of women in Zimbabwe by collecting, compiling, and disseminating written material and information that examine the way gender issues are presented in the media. See *Gender and the Media*, ZWRCN Workshop Report, no. 3 (1992).

*Land, Freedom and Fiction: History and Ideology in Kenya* (Maughan-Brown 1985) looks critically at the "use that is made of fiction as an instrument of propaganda, the way race myths and stereotypes are embodied in fiction." The case study for David Maughan-Brown's study is the "Mau Mau" armed struggle waged by the Gikuyu peasantry against the British colonial forces in Kenya from 1952-56. The term "Mau Mau," Maughan-Brown writes, "perhaps more than any other [term], still signifies for many whites the 'atavism' and 'primitivism' of 'darkest Africa'. This can be attributed in part to the voluminous writings about 'Mau Mau', both fictional and 'non-fictional', produced during the Emergency by Kenyan colonial settlers and their sympathisers." The literary works of Robert Ruark, Elspeth Huxley, Meja Mwangi, Charles Mangua, Ngugi wa Thiong'o, and G. R. Fazakerley, are analyzed.

Patricia Lorcin's scholarly study *Imperial Identities: Stereotyping, Prejudice and Race in Colonial Algeria* (Lorcin 1995) shifts our geographical focus from Kenya in East Africa to Algeria on the north coast of the continent and our historical timeframe from the early 1950s to a 70-year period of French colonial rule in Algeria, 1830-1900. (Algeria won its independence from France in 1962.) Lorcin's investigation shows how French colonial administrators (military and civilian) concocted false images of Algeria's indigenous population and then used these stereotypes to negate the beliefs and values of their colonial subjects and to impose French cultural, social, and political values.

*Africa on Film: Beyond Black and White* (Cameron 1994) surveys the body of more than 400 English-language films that have been made about or in Africa and finds a mixed legacy of racism, sexism, and imperialism, on the one side, and "occasional" accurate portraits of Africa, on the other.

## Flow and control of information

Questioning media images of Africa raises the related issues of imbalances in the worldwide flow of information and concentrated control of the channels of news dissemination by governments and corporate interests.

Two UNESCO-sponsored studies — the first, in 1953, and the second, in 1980 — produced evidence to support the charge that the international flow of information has been dominated by a handful of Western transnational media monopolies whose financial and technological wealth has created a situation whereby Africans and non-Africans learn about African realities through the filtered lens of news agencies based *outside* of Africa. (Two news agencies alone — Reuters and Agence-France Presse — control an estimated 93 percent of the news that flows *into* Africa.)

The two UNESCO studies, *The Flow of News* (UNESCO 1953) and *Many Voices One World* (MacBride 1980), are described and analyzed in *Contra-Flow in Global News* (Boyd-Barrett and Thussu 1992). Boyd-Barrett and Thussu assess the effectiveness of international and regional "news exchange mechanisms" (e.g., the Pan African News Agency and the Union of National Radio and Television Organizations of Africa) that were created as a counter-balance to Western-dominated news gathering and dissemination.

The fourth edition of Pulitzer Prize-winning journalist Ben Bagdikian's *The Media Monopoly* (Bagdikian 1992) transports concerns first raised about monopoly ownership and control in the U.S. media industry to the international level. Bagdikian notes that "the time has come for an international convention to set standards for the modern mass media, one of the most powerful forces in history." He cautions, however, that "with or without an international convention, some governments, openly or not, will always try to retain excessive and inappropriate control."

In their essay in *Africa's Media Image* (Hawk 1992) Thomas Winship and Paul Hemp echo Bagdikian's concern about government control, writing that the Pan African News Agency "has not become a credible source of news to Western readers and editors, in part, because the participating national news agencies often serve as government propaganda mouthpieces." In *Thunder & Silence: The Mass Media in Africa* (Ziegler and Asante 1992) professors Dhyana Ziegler and Molefi Kete Asante situate the problems of media control and censorship by African governments in the broader historical context of colonialism. They quote Africa-specialist Colin Legum, who has observed that "all the colonial governments, without exception, maintained severe forms of censorship, either directly, as in Francophone countries, or indirectly through sedition and other laws."

The legacy of colonial control is described in various publications issued by international human rights organizations such as Article 19 (London) and the Committee to Protect Journalists (New York). See, for example, *Who Rules the Airwaves? Broadcasting in Africa,* a joint publication issued in February 1995 by Article 19 and Index on Censorship.

Louise Bourgault investigates three principal influences on African radio, television, and newspapers in her study *Mass Media in Sub-Saharan Africa* (Bourgault 1995). They are the precolonial legacy of the oral tradition, the presence of an alienated managerial class, and the domination of African nations by systems based on political patronage.

The role of South Africa's white minority government in shaping media images during the apartheid years is the subject of numerous studies, including *Myth, Race and Power: South Africans Imaged on Film and TV* (Tomaselli et al. 1986), *Apartheid Media: Disinformation and Dissent in South Africa* (Phelan 1987), and *Broadcasting in South Africa* (Tomaselli et al. 1989). *History from South Africa: Alternative Visions and Practices* (Brown et al. 1991) represents attempts by South African authors and historians to write their own history of South Africa, using words, photographs, and comic-book illustrations that present images that are in conflict with "official" interpretations of South Africa's history.

### Media Literacy Curricula

Various curricula have been developed to help students identify and examine their images of the developing world, in general, and Africa, in particular.

The Development Education Project at Manchester Polytechnic has published

- *Picturing People: Challenging Stereotypes* (1988)
- *Aspects of Africa: Questioning Our Perceptions* (1988)
- *Investigating Images: Working with Pictures on an International Theme* (1988)
- *Perceptions and Colonialism: Teaching Development Issues* (1986).

See also *Images of Africa* (van der Gaag and Nash 1987) and *This Is Our Africa: Images of Africa by African Photographers* (Joynson and Talbot 1992).

Students can be helped to look critically at the role and function of the media through curricula such as *Whose News? Ownership and Control of the News Media* (Nash and Kirby 1989) and *Frontpage: A Newspaper Simulation Exercise about Ethiopia and Eritrea* (Joynson et al. 1992), as well as through publications produced by organizations such as the Association for Media Education (Wakefield), the Media Resource Centre (Durban), and the Center for Media Literacy (Los Angeles).

# LABOR'S ROLE IN AFRICA
## Policies, laws, and practices

An examination of labor's role in Africa takes us into an area of study wherein the boundary lines are not as sharply drawn as they are in the case of topics like refugees, food and agriculture, and African literature. Issues germane to the subject of labor's role in Africa include the position of labor in the new world economy, the state of industrialization and the manufacturing sector in African economies, broad labor-related issues such as unemployment, work and family, and the role of trade unions in Africa.

### Globalization and worker rights

*Global Village or Global Pillage: Economic Reconstruction from the Bottom Up* (Brecher and Costello 1994) offers a readable and relatively compact introductory survey of the role of work and workers in the new world economy. "All over the world," authors Jeremy Brecher and Tim Costello write, "people are being pitted against each other to see who will offer global corporations the lowest labor, social, and environmental costs. Their jobs are being moved to places with inferior wages, lower business taxes, and more freedom to pollute. Their employers are using the threat of 'foreign competition' to hold down wages, salaries, taxes, and environmental protections and to replace high-quality jobs with temporary, part-time, insecure, and low-quality jobs." A study of labor's role in Africa needs to be set against the background of the global economic and social issues raised and discussed in *Global Village or Global Pillage*.

Other books that analyze labor-related issues on a global level include *Global Dreams: Imperial Corporations and the New World Order* (Barnet and Cavanagh 1995); *Solidarity Across Borders: U.S. Labor in a Global Economy* (Midwest Center for Labor Research 1989); *A Changing International Division of Labor* (Caporaso 1987); *International Labour and the Third World: The Making of a New Working Class* (Boyd et al. 1987); *The New International Labour Studies:*

*An Introduction* (Munck 1988); *Trade Unions and the New Industrialization of the Third World* (Southall 1988). *Global Dreams* is the most popularly accessible book on this list.

*World Labour Report,* produced annually by the International Labour Organization (Geneva 1995), includes Africa in its survey of topics such as employment, working conditions, labor relations, social protection, and the rights of working men and women. The statistical tables at the back of each issue of the report provide country-specific data (noticeably spotty in many cases) for each African nation.

Two other useful reference resources on the subject of international labor are *The Third World Worker in the Multinational Corporation: A Bibliography* (Nordquist 1993) and *World Employment 1995: An ILO Report* (International Labour Office 1995).

## Labor in Africa

The lines of the debate about the role of industry and of the manufacturing sector in Africa's development are clearly articulated in chapter 6 in *Hemmed In: Responses to Africa's Economic Decline* (Callaghy and Ravenhill 1993): "The future of the manufacturing sector in Sub-Saharan Africa," by Roger Riddell. Riddell writes: "The strong contrasts between the emphasis given to the role of manufacturing within Africa by African governments and their advisers, its virtual absence in policy debate emanating from outside Africa, and the, at best, minimal treatment of manufacturing in structural adjustment programs (SAPs), all raise a series of questions for African development in the 1990s." The resolution of these contending points of view on Africa's industrial development will obviously have a direct impact on Africa's working people.

Kwamina Panford's study, *African Labor Relations and Workers' Rights: Assessing the Role of the International Labor Organization* (1994), narrows the focus even further. What is the role of organized labor (unions) in African development? Panford asks. Should workers be encouraged (or forced) to give up their rights to organize, to bargain collectively with employers, and to strike, if it is thought that the exercise of these labor-union rights might impede industrial development? Panford uses the relatively rich labor environment of Ghana as a case study. His particular concern is

Joe Madisia: "Slavery and forced labour" (1992). Used with permission. Joe Madisia, P.O. Box 2587 Walvis Bay, Namibia.

the role and influence of the International Labor Organization (ILO) in the determination of policies, laws, and practices that affect workers' rights in Africa.

Historian Frederick Cooper's 120-page article, "Africa and the World Economy," in *Confronting Historical Paradigms: Peasants, Labor, and the Capitalist World System in Africa and Latin America* (Cooper et al. 1993) looks at labor in Africa in the broader context of the capitalist world system and in the theoretical writings of scholars such as André Gunder Frank, Samir Amin, Walter Rodney, and Immanuel Wallerstein.

Jean-Pierre Lachaud's research study, *The Labour Market in Africa* (Lachaud 1994) summarizes the findings from six African countries on the structuring of the urban labor market and its relationship with poverty and analyzes the relationships between structural adjustment and the labor market. Burkina Faso, Cameroon, Côte d'Ivoire, Guinea, Madagascar, and Mali are the subjects of Lachaud's investigation.

In *The Social History of Labor in the Middle East* (Goldberg 1996) seven social historians study the roots and characteristics of working-class organizing in Turkey, Iran, Syria, Israel, Egypt, and the North Africa region.

## Issues

**Child labor:** *Dance Civet Cat: Child Labour in the Zambezi Valley* (Reynolds 1991); *First Things First in Child Labour: Eliminating Work Detrimental to Children* (Bequele and Myers 1995).

**Migrant labor:** *Forced Labour and Migration: Patterns of Movement within Africa*

### LABOR IN SOUTH AFRICA

*The ANC and Black Workers in South Africa, 1912-1992: An Annotated Bibliography* (Limb 1993)

*Beyond Apartheid: Labour and Liberation in South Africa.* (Fine and Davis 1990)

*Black Women Workers: A Study in Patriarchy, Race and Women Production Workers in South Africa* (Meer 1991)

*Crossing Boundaries: Mine Migrancy in a Democratic South Africa* (Crush and James 1995).

*Hlanganani: A Short History of COSATU.* 1991. 30-minute videotape available from AFSC Film Library (Cambridge).

*The Independent Trade Unions, 1974-1984. Ten Years of the South African Labour Bulletin* (Maree 1987)

*Manufacturing Militance: Workers' Movements in Brazil and South Africa, 1970-1985* (Seidman 1994)

*The Moon Is Dead! Give Us Our Money! The Cultural Origins of an African Work Ethic, Natal, South Africa, 1843-1900* (Atkins 1993)

*Power! Black Workers, Their Unions, and the Struggle for Freedom in South Africa* (MacShane et al. 1984)

*South African Workers Speak* (Tørres 1995)

*Striking Back: A History of COSATU* (Baskin 1991)

*Yours for the Union: Class and Community Struggles in South Africa* (Hirson 1990)

*Threads of Solidarity: Women in South African Industry, 1900-1980* (Berger 1992).

(Zegeye and Ishemo 1989); *Work, Culture, and Identity: Migrant Labourers in Mozambique and South Africa, c. 1860-1910* (Harries 1994); *Labour Export Policy in the Development of Southern Africa* (Paton 1995); *Crossing Boundaries: Mine Migrancy in a Democratic South Africa* (Crush and James 1995).

**Women's labor rights:** *Women and Work in Developing Countries: An Annotated Bibliography* (Ghorayshi 1994); *Black Women Workers: A Study in Patriarchy, Race and Women Production Workers in South Africa* (Meer 1991); *Post Abolished: One Woman's Struggle for Employment Rights in Tanzania* (Mukurasi 1991); *Working Women: International Perspectives on Labour and Gender Ideology* (Redclift and Sinclair 1991); *Women, Employment, and the Family in the International Division of Labour* (Stichter and Parpart 1990); *Threads of Solidarity: Women in South African Industry, 1900-1980* (Berger 1992); *Seeds 2: Supporting Women's Work Around the World* (Leonard 1995).

## Country studies

**Cameroon:** *Labour Resistance in Cameroon: Managerial Strategies and Labour Resistance in the Agro-Industrial Plantations of the Cameroon Development Corporation* (Konings 1993).

**Ethiopia:** *Work and Power in Maale, Ethiopia* (Donham 1994).

**Ghana:** *African Labor Relations and Workers' Rights: Assessing the Role of the International Labor Organization* (Panford 1994); *Trade Union Resource Guide* (Transnationals Information Exchange 1993).

**Mozambique:** *African Workers and Colonial Racism: Mozambican Strategies and Struggles in Lourenço Marques, 1877-1962* (Penvenne 1995).

**Nigeria:** *Labour in the Explanation of an African Crisis. A Critique of Current Orthodoxy: The Case of Nigeria* (Adesina 1994); *The Trades Union Movement in Nigeria* (Otobo 1995).

**Sudan:** *Slaves into Workers: Emancipation and Labor in Colonial Sudan* (Sikainga 1996).

**Tanzania:** *Poverty, Class, and Gender in Rural Africa: A Tanzanian Case Study* (Sender and Smith 1990).

**Tunisia:** *Tunisia: Rural Labour and Structural Transformation* (Radwan et al. 1991); Chapter 3 in *The Labour Market in Africa* (Lachaud 1994).

All of the labor-related issues discussed above are covered regularly in the *Review of African Political Economy*. See, especially, the September 1987 edition of the magazine, entitled *Workers, Unions and Popular Protest* (Baylies and Cohen 1987). ROAPE's diskette-based index—"RIX"—can be used profitably to identify labor-related articles in back issues of the quarterly. Contact the publisher for details. Other labor-oriented periodicals of note are *International Labour Documentation* (Geneva); *Labour, Capital and Society* (Montreal); *South African Labour Bulletin* (Johannesburg); and *World of Work: The Magazine of the ILO* (Geneva).

# AFRICAN LITERATURE
## Voices from "another Africa"

Chinua Achebe
Catherine Obianuju Acholonu
Ama Ata Aidoo
Grace Akello
Amechi Akwanya
Elechi Amadi
Danièle Amrane
Ayi Kwei Armah
Malak'Abd al-Aziz
Mariama Bâ
Biyi Bandele-Thomas
Andrée Chedid
Okey Chigbo
Mia Couto
Tsitsi Danfarembga
Amma Darko
Leila Djabali
Frank Chipasula
Buchi Emecheta
Alda do Espírito Santo
Nuruddin Farah
Nadine Gordimer
Anna Gréki
Abdulrazak Gurnah

In his *Notes on the State of Virginia* (Paris, 1784) Thomas Jefferson observed: "Never yet could I find that a black man had uttered a thought above the level of plain narration; never saw even an elementary trait of painting or sculpture." Responding to this astonishing assertion, Ali A. Mazrui states: "As for Thomas Jefferson's belief that blacks were a people without poetry, black Ethiopians were *writing* poetry before Jefferson's ancestors in the British Isles were taught the Latin alphabet by the Romans" (see Ali Mazrui's article, "The Development of Modern Literature Since 1935," in *Africa Since 1935* [Mazrui 1993], the eighth volume of the *General History of Africa,* pp. 579-80).

Even when Africa's literary accomplishments are acknowledged, problems persist. "Western critical discourse on [Africa's literary output] for centuries has been jaundiced and imperial," Raoul Granqvist observes in his introduction to *Culture in Africa: An Appeal for Pluralism* (Granqvist 1993). "The denigration of [Africa's] productions through misquotation and misrepresentations has been monumental. Western hierarchical notions of literary categories and canonical preferences have tended to obscure the artefacts under consideration" (p. 7).

The resource materials listed and described in this chapter demonstrate the truth of Mazrui's historical reminder and they illustrate the accuracy of Granqvist's critique. They also justify Mazrui's evident pride in the centuries-old literary gifts (verbal and written) of the people of Africa.*

Ali Mazrui's article (reference above, pp. 553-81) is a good place to begin for a concise overview of the state of literature in Africa in the period since 1930—"an era," Mazrui notes, "which has witnessed the most extensive flowering of written literature in Africa." Mazrui identifies and dis-

---
* This chapter is intended to be read in tandem with "The Voice of Women," which highlights the literary and other artistic contributions of African women. Some works by women authors and poets are included in this chapter, "African Literature," but they are covered more fully in "The Voice of Women."

cusses "the most basic forms of creative literature in this period of African history," namely, rhetoric and poetry, drama and theatre, and the novel.

The first ten of the thirteen essays in *A History of Twentieth-Century African Literatures* (Owomoyela 1993) are grouped into three major language divisions (English, French, Portuguese), with an additional chapter entitled "African Language Literatures." Subdivisions within the French- and English-language categories are (a) poetry, (b) fiction, and (c) drama and theater. One chapter is given to a literary history of African women writers, and publisher Hans Zell contributes another chapter entitled "Publishing in Africa: The Crisis and the Challenge."

Robert Cancel's essay on African-language literatures in Oyekan Owomoyela's collection reminds readers "that another Africa exists besides the one that normally preoccupies the world's attention, and that [this other Africa] also produces noteworthy literatures" (p. 3).

Reference guides to African literature include *A New Reader's Guide to African Literature* (Zell et al. 1983); *African Literatures: An Introduction* (Owomoyela 1979); *A New Bibliography of the Lusophone Literatures of Africa/Nova Bibliografía das Literaturas Africanas de Expressão Portuguesa* (Moser and Ferreira 1993); *Black African Literature in English, 1987-1991* (Lindfors 1995); *Cultures Outside the United States in Fiction: A Guide to 2,875 Books for Librarians and Teachers, K-9* (Anderson 1994); and *Africa in Literature for Children and Young Adults: An Annotated Bibliography of English-Language Books* (Khorana 1994).

Two introductory educational guides are *A Handbook for Teaching African Literature* (Gunner 1987) and the older *Teaching of African Literature in Schools* (Gachukia and Akivaga 1978). The recent flourish of published studies (in the United States) on "multicultural literature" yields numerous suggestions for the study/teaching of literary works from and about Africa.

## Poetry and rhetoric

Two anthologies showcase the richness of the poetic tradition in Africa: *The Penguin Book of Modern African Poetry* (Beier and Moore 1984) and *The Heinemann Book of African Women's Poetry* (Chipasula and Chipasula 1995).

Studies and anthologies organized along regional lines include *The Quiet Chameleon: Modern Poetry from Central Africa* (Roscoe and Msiska 1991); *Power and the Praise Poem: Southern African Voices in History* (Vail and White 1991); *New Poets of West Africa* (Sallah 1995); and *When My Brothers Come Home: Poems from Central and Southern Africa* (Chipasula 1985). *An Anthology of Somali Poetry* (Andrzejewski and Andrzejewski 1993) focuses on a country that was once described as "teeming with poets," Somalia.

*A History of Twentieth-Century African Literatures* (Owomoyela 1993) contains two relevant chapters: "English-language poetry" (chapter 4) and "French-language poetry" (chapter 7), with other references to poetry and

---

Hatshepsut
Iyamidé Hazeley
Bessie Head
Saida Hagi-Dirie Herzi
Louis Bernardo Honwana
Rashidah Ismaili
Noni Jabavu
Caroline Ntseliseng Khaketla
Kebbedesh
Ellen Kuzwayo
Alda Lara
Maria Eugénia Lima
Henri Lopes
Rachida Madani
Lina Magala
Naguib Mahfouz
Jamal Mahjoub
Maria Manuela Margarido
Gaele Sobott-Mogwe
Mwana Kupona Msham
Micere Githae Mugo
Citèkù Ndaaya
Njabulo S. Ndebele
Womi Bright Neal
Flora Nwapa
Sekai Nzenza
Ben Okri
Malika O'Lahsen
Amina Saïd
Mongane Serote
Wole Soyinka
Véronique Tadjo
Awa Thiam
Ngugi wa Thiong'o
M. G. Vassanji

rhetoric throughout the book.

Volumes 16 and 18 in the African Literature Today series relate to the poetic and oral forms of African literature: *Oral and Written Poetry in African Literature Today* (Jones et al. 1989) and *Orature in African Literature Today* (Jones et al. 1992).

See also: *Understanding Oral Literature* (Bukenya et al. 1994); *Power and; the Praise Poem: Southern African Voices in History* (Vail and White 1991); *Oral Epics from Africa: Vibrant Voices from a Vast Continent* (Johnson et al. 1997); and *The Tongue Is Fire: South African Storytellers and Apartheid* (Scheub 1996).

## Drama and theatre

*The Cambridge Guide to African and Caribbean Theatre* (Banham et al. 1994 ) is the most up-to-date and authoritative guide to drama and theatre in Africa. Concerned "to redress the bias towards Western theatre evident in many works of reference" the publishers of the *Cambridge Guide* endeavor to offer "a truly international view of theatre — traditional and contemporary." Theatre in 29 African nations is studied, with a short list of further readings given at the end of each country profile.

*The Oxford Illustrated History of Theatre* (Brown 1995) devotes just one part of one chapter to a discussion of theatre in Africa, but Leslie Du S. Read's article — "Beginnings of Theatre in Africa and the Americas" — is particularly noteworthy for the emphasis it gives to the need to put aside Western preconceptions and prejudices when approaching theatre in Africa. "*Theatre as performance*," Read reminds us, "has been emphasized increasingly in the West and *drama as a process of social development* has flourished in the Third World [Africa included]."

A study devoted exclusively to theatre in Africa is *African Popular Theatre: From Pre-colonial Times to the Present Day* (Kerr 1995).

Two engaging studies that help Western readers analyze and judge theatre in Africa on its own terms are *Culture and Development: The Popular Theatre Approach in Africa* (Mlama 1991) and *When People Play People: Development Communication through Theatre* (Mda 1993).

Regionally oriented surveys and studies are *African Drama and the Yoruba World-View* (Ibitokun 1995); *Make Man Talk True: Nigerian Drama in English Since 1970* (Dunton 1992); *Theatre and Cultural Struggle in South Africa* (Kavanagh 1985); *Mother, Sing for Me: People's Theatre in Kenya* (Björkman 1989); *West African Popular Theatre* (Barber et al. 1997); and *Theatre and Drama in Francophone Africa: A Critical Introduction* (Conteh-Morgan 1994).

## Fiction

Individual works and anthologies of African fiction are listed in Appendix 3 below. Readers with Internet access can see an updated version of this list at <www.igc.org/worldviews/awpguide/afrlit.html>.

---

### South Africa

- *Apartheid: Calibrations of Color* (Rosen 1991)
- *Blame Me on History* (Modisane 1986)
- *The Changing Past: Trends in South African Historical Writing* (Smith 1988)
- *Culture in Another South Africa* (Campschreur and Divendal 1989)
- *From South Africa: New Writing, Photographs and Art* (Bunn and Taylor 1987)
- *On Shifting Sands: New Art and Literature from South Africa* (Petersen and Rutherford 1991)
- *The Open Door Omnibus 1993: Selections from New Writers* (Loyson et al. 1993)
- *A People's Voice: Black South African Writing in the Twentieth Century* (Shava 1989)
- *The Song of Jacob Zulu* (Yourgrau 1993)
- *Theatre and Cultural Struggle in South Africa* (Kavanagh 1985)
- *"We Spend Our Years as a Tale That Is Told": Oral Historical Narrative in a South African Chiefdom* (Hofmeyr 1993)
- *Woza Afrika! An Anthology of South African Plays* (Ndlovu 1986)
- *Writing My Reading: Essays on Literary Politics in South Africa* (Horn 1994)

Requesting catalogs from the publishers whose works appear on this list is a good way to keep current. Heinemann's African Writers series is particularly noteworthy. So, too, is the catalog of "New and Recent Titles on African Literature and Languages" published periodically by African Books Collective (Oxford).

## Critical studies

Reference sources of note are the African Literature Today series, published by James Currey (London) and Africa World Press (Lawrenceville); the quarterly *Research in African Literatures*, from Indiana University Press (Bloomington); the New Perspectives on African Literature series from Hans Zell Publishers; and the Studies in African Literature series from Heinemann (Portsmouth) and James Currey (London). The latter series includes *The Marabout and the Muse: New Approaches to Islam in African Literature* (Harrow 1996), *New Writing from Southern Africa: Authors Who Have Become Prominent Since 1980* (Ngara 1996), and *Thresholds of Change in African Literature: The Emergence of a Tradition* (Harrow 1994).

Critical studies in the New Perspectives series (Hans Zell) include *A Mask Dancing: Nigerian Novelists of the Eighties* (Maja-Pearce 1992), *Teachers, Preachers, Non-Believers: A Social History of Zimbabwean Literature* (Veit-Wild 1992), and books listed elsewhere in this chapter.

Studies on individual African authors include *The Art of Ama Ata Aidoo: Polylectics and Reading Against Neocolonialism* (Odamtten 1994); *Critical Perspectives on Ayi Kwei Armah* (Wright 1992); *Rereading Nadine Gordimer* (Wagner 1994); *Studies in the Short Fiction of Mahfouz and Idris* (Mikhail 1992); and *Ancient Songs Set Ablaze: The Theatre of Femi Osofisan* (Richards 1996).

The literature of Francophone Africa is examined in three texts, *Francophone African Fiction: Reading a Literary Tradition* (Ngaté 1988), *African Francophone Writing: A Critical Introduction* (Ibnifassi and Hitchcott 1996), and *Postcolonial Subjects: Francophone Women Writers* (Green et al. 1996).

Other regionally oriented critical studies include *The African Quest for Freedom and Identity: Cameroonian Writing and the National Experience* (Bjornson 1991); *Ghanaian Literatures* (Priebe 1988); *Nigerian Female Writers: A Critical Perspective* (Otokunefor and Nwodo 1989); *Parables and Fables: Exegesis, Textuality, and Politics in Central Africa* (Mudimbe 1991).

See also: *The African Experience in Literature and Ideology* (Irele 1990); *Critical Theory and African Literature Today* (Jones et al. 1994); *The Empire Writes Back: Theory and Practice in Post-Colonial Literatures* (Ashcroft et al. 1989); *The Gong and the Flute: African Literary Development and Celebration* (Ogbaa 1994); *Language and Theme: Essays on African Literature* (Obiechina 1990); *The Question of Language in African Literature Today* (Jones et al. 1991); *Revolutionary Aesthetics and the African Literary Process* (Udenta 1993); and *The Theory of African Literature: Implications for Practical Criticism* (Amuta 1989).

---

### Chinua Achebe

One African writer who has earned a popular following around the world and a privileged position in academic courses on multicultural literature is Nigerian-born novelist, poet, and literary critic Chinua Achebe. Achebe's first novel, *Things Fall Apart*, published in 1958, has been translated into more than 40 languages and has sold more than 3 million copies.

Achebe's other works include *No Longer at Ease*, *Arrow of God*, *A Man of the People*, *Anthills of the Savannah*, *Arrows of God*, *Girls at War and Other Stories*, and *Beware Soul Brother* (a book of his poetry). Heinemann Educational Books (Oxford and Portsmouth, N.H.) and Doubleday/Anchor Books (New York) are sources for Achebe's books.

Cinema Guide distributes a 57-minute videotape about *Chinua Achebe* entitled *Chinua Achebe: The Importance of Stories* (1996). 1697 Broadway, Ste. 506, New York, NY 10019-5904 USA.

A 30-minute film in the "World of Ideas with Bill Moyers" series features Achebe discussing influences on his writings and the impact of colonialism on his culture: *Chinua Achebe* (BMW1-114-CR94. ISBN 1-55951-862-6). PBS Video, 1320 Braddock Pl., Alexandria, VA 22314-1698 USA.

In 1988 American Audio Prose Library (AAPL) produced a 2-cassette tape set that featured a 90-minute interview with Achebe and excerpts read by the author from *Anthills of the Savannah* and *Arrow of God*. P.O. Box 842, Columbia, MO 65205 USA.

One of Achebe's former students, Ezenwa-Ohaeto, has written the first biography of this literary giant: *Chinua Achebe: A Biography* (Ezenwa-Ohaeto 1997).

Photo of Chinua Achebe courtesy of Cinema Guild (New York).

# MINING IN AFRICA
## A wealth of mineral resources

Say gold and diamonds and one African country comes quickly to mind: South Africa. But the African continent's store of mineral resources is much richer and more broadly dispersed than this easy association suggests.

"Sub-Saharan Africa," the authors of *Short Changed: Africa and World Trade* (Brown and Tiffen 1992) note, "exports gold and diamonds, but also large quantities of copper, bauxite, iron ore, uranium, phosphate rock and manganese; smaller quantities of asbestos, beryllium, cadmium, chromite, cobalt, germanium, lead, lithium, nickel, platinum, tantalite, tin, tungsten, vanadium, and zinc" (p. 66).

In an article entitled "African Mining: A Light at the End of the Tunnel" Magnus Ericsson, editor of *Raw Materials Report*, underlines the importance of these mineral resources to the countries of Africa: "Mineral exports contribute between 25 and 90 percent of annual export earnings of 13 countries: Botswana, Ghana, Guinea, Liberia, Senegal, Mauritania, Namibia, Niger, Central African Republic, Sierra Leone, Zaire, Zambia, and Zimbabwe. South Africa is also heavily dependent on exporting its ores and metals" (*Review of African Political Economy* 91, July 1991, p. 98).

The heavy dependence of these African countries on mineral exports means that the lives of many of their citizens are directly affected by the fluctuations in world market prices for tin, copper, and other minerals.

### Third World minerals and mining

For a popular overview of the general state of commodity dependence in Third World countries we recommend two resources. The first is the seven-part series of videos produced by Sue Clayton and Jonathan Curling entitled *Commodities* (First Run/Icarus Films, 1986). The second is the 1994 edition of the

Frances Kelly (Manchester).
From *Past Exposure* (Dropkin and Clark 1992), p. 6

*Third World Atlas* (Thomas 1994), which contains a map on p. 18 that illustrates the extent to which countries in Africa, Asia, the Pacific, Latin America, and the Caribbean are linked to the global economy by virtue of their exports of various commodities, including bauxite, diamonds, and copper.

In *Third World Minerals and Global Pricing: A New Theory* (Nwoke 1987) Dr. Chibuzo Nwoke of the Nigerian Institute of International Affairs narrows the focus from commodities in general to minerals and mining in the Third World context. He explores—in a heavily theoretical and analytical framework—"the issue of the conflictual relationship between foreign mining firms and Third World governments in the sharing of the huge benefits derivable from mining the latter's rich resources." *The New Resource Wars: Native and Environmental Struggles against Multinational Corporations* (Gedicks 1993) is focused primarily on resource exploitation in North America, but chapter 2 offers a readable introduction to many of the political, social, and economic issues related to the mining of natural resources worldwide.

*Raw Materials Report* (Stockholm) is a readable and dependable source of current information on the production and marketing of minerals and other raw materials. Debates about the pros and cons of mineral exploitation in Third World countries are regular features of the attractively designed magazine. The publishers of *Raw Materials Report*, Raw Materials Group, compile an annual reference guide to the major corporate actors in the world mining and refining industry: *Who Owns Who in Mining*.

Two other corporate reference sources are *The Gulliver File. Mines, People and Land: A Global Battleground* (Moody 1992) and chapter 4 of the Institute on Trade Policy's *Wasting the Earth: A Directory of Multinational Corporate Activities* (Draffan 1993).

## Mining in Africa

Mining and mineral extraction issues in Africa are examined in the following books. Some have region or country case studies.

- *African Environments and Resources* (Lewis and Berry 1988). Chapter 11: "Minerals, industry, and the environment."
- *Going for Gold: Men, Mines, and Migration* (Moodie and Ndatshe 1994).
- *King Solomon's Mines Revisted: Western Interests and the Burdened History of Southern Africa* (Minter 1986).

**The Minerals and Metals Market Sub-Saharan Africa's Share**

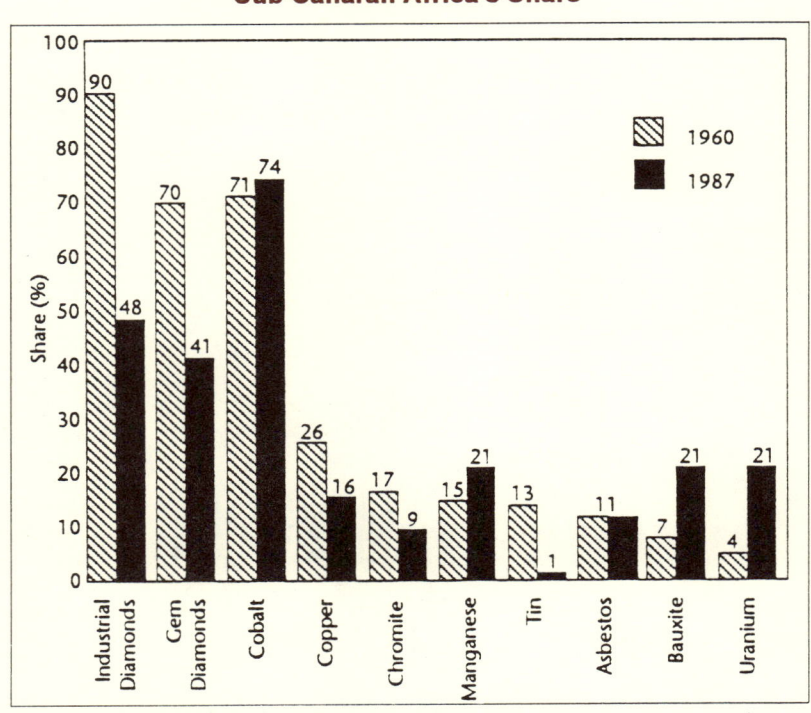

| Mineral | 1960 | 1987 |
|---|---|---|
| Industrial Diamonds | 90 | 48 |
| Gem Diamonds | 70 | 41 |
| Cobalt | 71 | 74 |
| Copper | 26 | 16 |
| Chromite | 17 | 9 |
| Manganese | 15 | 21 |
| Tin | 13 | 1 |
| Asbestos | 11 | 11 |
| Bauxite | 7 | 21 |
| Uranium | 4 | 21 |

*Short Changed: Africa and World Trade* (Brown and Tiffen 1992. Pluto Press, London).
Source: USBM *Mining Annual Review*, World Bureau of Metallurgical Statistics, World Bank from *Mining Development in Sub-Saharan Africa*, Peter M. Fozzard, paper presented at the MEP Conference, Madrid, November 1989. Chart excludes the former Soviet bloc.

- *The Golden Contradiction: A Marxist Theory of Gold. With Particular Reference to South Africa* (Stemmet 1996).
- *Industrialization, Mineral Resources and Energy in Africa* (Khennas 1992).
- *The Last Empire: De Beers, Diamonds, and the World* (Kanfer 1993).
- *Mining in Africa Today: Strategies and Prospects* (Yachir 1988).
- *The Mining Sector in Southern Africa* (Jourdan 1995)
- *Short Changed: Africa and World Trade* (Brown and Tiffen 1992).

## Country studies

A study published by Dakar-based CODESRIA (Council for the Development of Economic and Social Research in Africa), *Industrialization, Mineral Resources and Energy in Africa* (Khennas 1992), contains chapter-length case studies of mining and mineral extraction in Morocco, Tanzania, Nigeria, Algeria, Guinea, Senegal, Niger, Liberia, and Zambia.

**Botswana:** *Policy Choice and Development Performance in Botswana* (Harvey and Lewis 1990). Chapter 6: "Mineral policy and mining development."

**South Africa:** *The History of Black Mineworkers in South Africa* (Allen 1992); *Our Precious Metal: African Labour in South Africa's Gold Industry, 1970-1990* (James 1992); *South Africa Inc.: The Oppenheimer Empire* (Pallister et al. 1987); *Studded with Diamonds and Paved with Gold: Miners, Mining Companies and Human Rights in Southern Africa* (Flynn 1992); *The Political Economy of South Africa* (Fine and Rustomjee 1996), and *Transformation on the South African Gold Mines* (Crush et al. 1992).

---

### CASE STUDY: RÖSSING URANIUM

In 1992 two London-based activist organizations—the Namibia Support Committee and PARTiZANS—published a blockbuster exposé of health, safety, and environmental violations at the world's largest open-pit uranium mine. Located in the desert in western Namibia, the uranium mine is run by Rössing Uranium, a subsidiary of the U.K. mining giant RTZ.

The exposé, entitled *Past Exposure: Revealing Health and Environmental Risks of Rössing Uranium* (Dropkin and Clark 1992), used internal company documents, interviews with workers at the Rössing mine, scientific data, and independent research to level numerous strong charges against the mining multinational and the British government.

Among the charges:

"Throughout the colonial era [Rössing] broke international law, defying UN Security Council resolutions, the International Court of Justice, and a UN decree" (p. 7).

"Dust levels in the Open Pit and Crushers have been known to reach 20-30 times the standard supposedly applied by Rössing (for respirable siliceous dust)." (p. 9)

"Workers in the Final Product Recovery area were exposed to very high levels of radiation in the period up to 1982, and even now their exposures are significant. Their lifetime risk of fatal cancer is probably at least 1 in 25 and possibly as high as 1 in 9" (p. 10)

*Past Exposure* describes the efforts of the Mineworkers Union of Namibia and of an international network of trade union and nongovernmental solidarity organizations to reveal the true state of working and living conditions at the Rössing uranium mine and to take steps to ensure that the newly independent government of Namibia holds Rössing accountable to the "highest standards" the company claims to respect.

The conflicting data and controversial perspectives revealed in *Past Exposure* offer educators and study groups plenty of substance for a case study analysis of one large and influential mining company in Africa.

More up-to-date formulations of the lines of debate regarding Rössing are found in the periodical *Raw Materials Report*, especially volume 9, nos. 3 and 4 (1993).

The Namibia Support Committee no longer exists, but copies of *Past Exposure* (and other information on mining in Africa) are available from PARTiZANS (People Against Rio Tinto Zinc and its Subsidiaries), 218 Liverpool, London N1 1LE, England.

**Tanzania:** *The Mining Industry in Tanzania* (Parker 1992); "Mining and Structural Adjustment: Studies on Zimbabwe and Tanzania." *Research Report,* no. 92 (1993), pp. 9-107; "The Meek Shall Inherit the Earth, but Not the Mining Rights: The Mining Industry and Accumulation in Tanzania," in *Liberalised Development in Tanzania: Studies on Accumulation Processes and Local Institutions* (Gibbon 1995), pp. 37-108.

**Zimbabwe:** "Mining and Structural Adjustment: Studies on Zimbabwe and Tanzania." *Research Report,* no. 92 (1993), pp. 9-78.

### Excerpt from Joseph Diescho's *Born of the Sun: A Namibian Novel* (1988)

Born in northern Namibia to uneducated peasant parents Joseph Diescho went on to study law and political science in South Africa and to become active in movements resisting the apartheid system. Later, while working for a diamond mine company Diescho helped found a workers' union. His novel, *Born of the Sun,* is a story of a dispossessed black majority forced to work in the gold and diamond mines of Namibia and South Africa.

"For four months Muronga has been working in the mine. He has adjusted to the routine and is quite content with his new identity as a mine worker. He has very few opportunities to leave the compound and little free time, so the compound has become almost his entire world.

"At first, he was eager to learn everything he possibly could about his work and his new environment. Because of his youthful physique and good health, Muronga was assigned to work as a lowly shoveler. After the *machineboys* have blasted the rocks off the working face at the new end of the tunnel with dynamite, the choppers break up the larger chunks, and the line of shovelers pass the gravel shovelful by shovelful back to the loaders at the trolley car on its narrow iron rails. To Muronga and all of the other men, the work soon becomes routine, so much so that one day Muronga decides to ask his supervisor if there are any other jobs he can learn.

"'Chiefboss,' Muronga exclaims, careful not to break the rhythm of his shoveling. 'Everything you have taught me here I know how to do. I would like to learn something new—like learning to drive the trolley car.'

"'What? Are you crazy?' the short fat white supervisor shouts. 'You are a shoveler! That's all you were meant to do. You cannot drive that thing, ever. It's dangerous, so only boys who can read and write a little bit can drive it. Not you…it's not for baboons like you. Now get to work! I am busy!' The supervisor shoves Muronga aside with the butt of his flashlight and stalks self-importantly down the tunnel toward the face.

"Taken aback, Muronga swallows hard as the men begin to sing, '*Tsho tsholoza, tshotsholoza,*' the chant they often sing to help them keep a rhythm and feel less tired and more united in the battle with the rocks."

Adebisi Fabunmi, from *Born of the Sun A Namibian Novel* (Diescho 1988), p. 159

**MINING IN AFRICA**    **75**

# MUSIC IN AFRICA
## Breadth and diversity

The music of Africa cannot be squeezed into one mold. There is the traditional music of drums (perhaps the predominant musical reference point in the minds of Westerners); there is the modern or popular music of Mali's Ali Farka Toure, Nigeria's King Sunny Ade and his African Beats, and South Africa's Ladysmith Black Mambazo. In fact, as musicologist John Storm Roberts has observed, "there's no way to write coherently about the music of a continent covering 52 independent nations, between 800 and 1600 languages (depending on your definition), and at least five major cultural groupings."

Roberts, who is founding director of Original Music (Tivoli, N.Y.), is responsible for the World Music chapter of the *All Music Guide: The Best CDs, Albums, and Tapes* (Erlewine and Bultman 1992). The Africa portion of the World Music chapter (pp. 776-795) illustrates the breadth and diversity of African music with a representative sampling of musicians and annotated musical selections displayed under country headings that run from Algeria to Zimbabwe. In his column-long overview of African music and brief introductory essay on world music Roberts highlights the beauties of world and African music ("enriching beyond belief") and issues the necessary cautions against dividing the musical world into *The West* and *The Rest*.

### Guides

*World Music: The Rough Guide* (Broughton et al. 1994) is a useful complement to the *All Music Guide*. The latter is stronger in its annotated lists of individual recordings, while the strength of *World Music* lies in its long and informed narrative overviews of the musical traditions of the Mediterranean and Maghreb (chapter 3), West Africa (chapter 6), Central and East Africa (chapter 7), and Southern Africa (chapter 8). Sidebar material on individual artists and musical instruments and discographies of selected recordings round out each chapter.

> "For the majority of Africans, music remains live and closely tied to their daily lives. The fact that this existence is now under threat from war, famine, invasion and western cultural imperialism in no way diminishes the continuing contribution which Africa makes to the enrichment of our daily lives."
> –Ronnie Graham, *The Da Capo Guide to Contemporary African Music*, p. 15

Scottish historian Ronnie Graham has produced two classic guides to African music: *Stern's Guide to Contemporary African Music* (Graham 1988) (published in the United States as *The Da Capo Guide to Contemporary African Music*, New York: Da Capo Press, 1988) and *The World of African Music: Stern's Guide to Contemporary African Music* (Graham 1992). Graham's guides are organized by country (North African countries are not included), with a map, brief historical introduction, and overview of each country's traditional and modern musical heritage. Graham provides a biographical sketch of key musicians in each country category, along with a short list of recommended musical titles (with date, distributor code, and order number).

The *All Music Guide*, *World Music: The Rough Guide*, and the Graham books are the places to look for informed and trustworthy recommendations of African musical titles on compact discs, records, and cassette tapes. Catalogs from distributors and mail order outlets are another source, though the reliability of recommendations will vary.

## Reference books

Two complementary bibliographical guides to African music were published in 1991 by Greenwood Press and Hans Zell Publishers:
- John Gray's *African Music: A Bibliographical Guide to the Traditional, Popular, Art, and Liturgical Musics of Sub-Saharan Africa* (Gray 1991) is an authoritative reference guide to books and other printed resources *about* African music. Gray, who is the director of the Black Arts Research Center (Nyack, N.Y.), organizes the 5,802 entries in *African Music* into six sections: cultural history and the arts; ethnomusicology; African traditional music (general works; country and regional studies); African popular music (general works; country and regional studies; individual musicians); African art music; and African church music. Three appendixes list other reference works, archives and research centers, and selected commercial recordings (organized under country headings).
- *African Music: A Pan-African Annotated Bibliography* (Lems-Dworkin 1991) is noteworthy for its coverage of music from the entire continent of Africa, including its islands, as well as of African-influenced music of the Western Hemisphere. Editor Carol Lems-Dworkin explains that she is convinced "that African music should not be treated as a thing in itself, but [should be] regarded as the integral part of culture it truly is, playing a major role in African education, history, politics, social life, and frequently associated with religion, dance, art, theater, and oral performance."Another study by the same author is entitled *Videos of African and African-related Performance: An Annotated Bibliography* (Lems-Dworkin 1996).

General reference guides and textbooks with information on African popular music are *Directory of Recorded Sound Resources in the United Kingdom* (Weerasinghe 1989); *Afropop! An Illustrated Guide to Contemporary African*

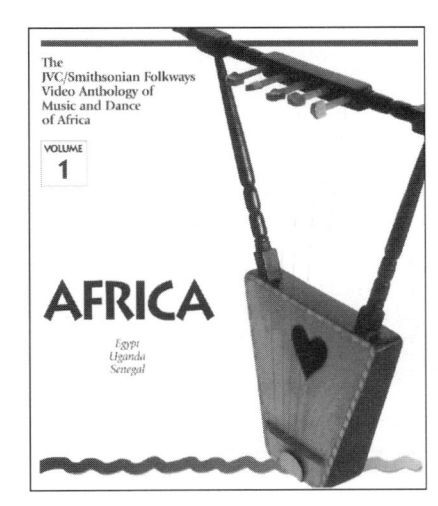

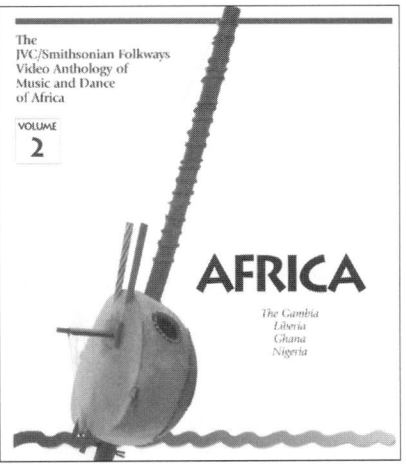

> **Major international distributors of world and African music**
>
> - africassette (Detroit)
> - Allegro Imports (Portland, Ore.)
> - Capitol Records (Hollywood)
> - Celluloid Records (New York, N.Y.)
> - Celluloid/Mélodie (Paris)
> - Gallo (Johannesburg)
> - GlobeStyle (London)
> - Green Linnet Records (Danbury, Conn.)
> - Koch International (Westbury, N.Y.)
> - Ladyslipper (Durham, N.C.)
> - Mango (New York, N.Y.)
> - Natari Music of Africa (W. Sussex)
> - Original Music (Tivoli, N.Y.)
> - Realworld (London)
> - Rogue Records (London)
> - Rounder Records (Cambridge, Mass.)
> - Rykodisc/Hannibal (Salem, Mass.)
> - Shanachie Records (Newton, N.J.)
> - Smithsonian/Folkways (Washington, D.C.)
> - Stern's African Record Centre (London)
> - World Circuit (London)
> - World Music Institute (New York, N.Y.)
>
> See the discography below and the listings of recordings in the books cited above for the names of other distributors. Addresses for U.S. distributors may be found in the back of editions of *Schwann Spectrum*. Addresses for distributors in Europe and the U.K. are given in annual editions of *Kemps International Music Book* (Showcase Publications, annual).

*Music* (Barlow and Eyre 1995); *The Garland Encyclopedia of World Music*. Vol. 1. *Africa* (Stone 1997), and *The Penguin Encyclopedia of Popular Music* (Clarke 1989); *Popular Musics of the Non-Western World: An Introductory Survey* (Manuel 1988); and the quarterly magazine *Schwann Spectrum*.

## Studies of African music

Recommended studies on various aspects of African music include *Contemporary African Music in World Perspectives* (Kofie 1994); *African Stars: Studies in Black South African Performance* (Erlmann 1991); *Breakout: Profiles in African Rhythm* (Stewart 1992); *Jùjú: A Social History and Ethnography of an African Popular Music* (Waterman 1990); *The Music of Africa* (Nketia 1974); *Perspectives on African Music* (Bender 1989); *More than Drumming: Essays on African and Afro-Latin Music* (Jackson 1985); *Studies in African Music* (Jones 1959); and *Where Is the Way: Song and Struggle in South Africa* (Kivnick 1990).

*In the Time of Cannibals: The Word Music of South Africa's Basotho Migrants* (Coplan 1994) and *A Song of Longing: An Ethiopian Journey* (Shelemay 1994) are case studies of music in two distinct African environments, immigrant mine workers from Lesotho and the Falashas of Ethiopia. *Dancing Prophets: Musical Experience in Tumbuka Healing* (Friedson 1996) is focused on the Tumbuka of Malawi, while South Africa and Sierra Leone, respectively, are the locations for two other studies: *Nightsong: Performance, Power, and Practice in South Africa* (Erlmann 1996) and *Seeing with Music: The Lives of Three Blind African Musicians* (Ottenberg 1997).

Studies that set African music in a broader cultural and geographical context include *A Night in Tunisia: Imaginings of Africa in Jazz* (Weinstein 1993); *Music and Black Ethnicity: The Caribbean and South America* (Béhague 1994); *The Rhythms of Black Folk: Race, Religion and Pan-Africanism* (Spencer 1995); and *Muntu: African Culture and the Western World* (Jahn 1989).

## Personalities

For biographical information on African musicians see Eileen Southern's *Biographical Dictionary of Afro-American and African Musicians* (Southern 1982) and Stapleton and May's *African All-Stars: The Pop Music of a Continent* (Stapleton and May 1987).

Africa's musical personalities are featured in *Breakout: Profiles in African Rhythm* (Stewart 1992) and *Musicmakers of West Africa* (Collins 1985).

*Three Kilos of Coffee* (Dibango 1989) is the autobiography of Manu Dibango, composer, producer, performer, film-score writer, and the first African musician ever to record a top 40's hit. *Tears over the Desert* (Kaujeua 1994) is the story—simply told—of Namibia's foremost singer, Jackson Kaujeua. *Makeba: My Story* (Makeba and Hall 1987) chronicles the life and international musical career of one of Africa's best known artists: Miriam Makeba.

# AFRICAN DISCOGRAPHY

## Continental
*Africa Dances.* Original Music
*Africa Never Stands Still.* Ellipsis Arts

## North Africa

### Egypt/Sudan
Various. *Sounds of Sudan.* World Circuit
Ali Hassan Kuban. *From Nubia to Cairo.* Shanachie
Musicians of the Nile. *From Luxor to Isna.* Real World
Oum Kalsoum. (Anything you can find.)

### Algeria
Various. *Songs and Rhythms of Morocco.* Lyrichord
Khaled. *N'ssi N'ssi.* Mango
Djur Djura. *Best of...*Luaka Bop

### Morocco/Mauritania
Various. *Songs and Rhythms of Morocco.* Lyrichord
Master Musicians of Jajouka. *Apocalypse Across the Sky.* Axiom
Khalifa Ould Eide and Dimi Mint Abba. *Moorish Music from Mauritania.* World Circuit

## West Africa

### Senegal/Gambia
Various. *Ancient Heart.* Axiom
Baaba Maal and Mansour Seck. *Djam Leelii.* Mango
Youssou N'Dour. *Immigrés.* Earthworks
Orchestra Baobab. *Bamba.* Stern's
Doudou N'Diaye Rose. *Djabote.* Real World
Dembo Konte and Kausu Kouyate. *Tanante or Simbomba.* Rogue

### Guinea
Bembeye Jazz. *Bembeya Jazz National.* Sonodisc
Fatala. *Gougoma Times.* Real World
Sona Diabaté. *Girls of Guinea.* Shanachie
Jali Musa Jawara. *Yasimika.* Hannibal Rykodisc

### Burkina Faso
Farafina. *Faso Denou* or *Bolomkakote.* Real World and Intuition (respectively)

### Sierra Leone/Côte d'Ivoire
Various. *African Elegant.* Original Music
S. E. Rogie. *Dead Men Don't Smoke Marijuana.* Real World
Le Zagazougou. *Zagazougou Coup.* Piranha

### Ghana
Various. *I've Found My Love: 1960s Guitar Band Highlife.* Original Music
Various. *Various/Giants of Dance Band Highlife.* Original Music
Eric Agyeman. *Highlife Safari.* Stern's
E. T. Mensah. *All For You* or *Day By Day.* Retroafric

### Nigeria
Various. *Azagas and Archibogs.* Original Music
Various. *Yoruba Street Percussion.* Original Music
Various. *Juju Roots.* Rounder
King Sunny Ade. *Juju Music* or *Synchro System.* Mango
Babatunde Olatunji. *Drums of Passion: The Beat.* Rykodisc

### Mali
Various. *Women of Mali.* 1 and 2. Stern's
Salif Keita. *Mansa of Mali: A Retrospective.* Mango
Bajourou. *Big String Theory.* Green Linnet
Ali Farka Toure. *The Source.* Hannibal Rykodisc

## Central Africa

### Cameroon/Gabon/Angola
Various. *African Typic Collection.* Earthworks
Various. *Heart of the Forest.* Hannibal Rykodisc
Les Têtes Brulees. *Hot Heads.* Shanachie
Bonga. *Angola.* Playasound

### Zaire/Congo/Zambia/Burundi/Rwanda
Various. *Sound of Kinshasa.* Original Music
Various. *Roots of Rumba Rock '53-'54.* Crammed Disc
Various. Any one of dozens of "Merveilles du Passe" compilations. Sonodisc
Franco. *20th Anniversaire.* 1 and 2. Sonodisc
Franco and Rochereau. *Omona Wapi.* Shanachie
Tshala Muana. *Soukous Siren.* Shanachie
Papa Wemba. *Papa Wemba.* Stern's
Orchestre Veve. *Best Collections.* Sonodisc
*Mbuti Pygmies of the Ituri Rainforest.* Smithsonian Folkways
Various. *Zambiance!* Globestyle
Tambours du Burundi. *Batimbo.* Playasound
Cecile Kayirebwa. *Rwanda.* Globestyle

## Southern Africa

### South Africa
Various. *Mbube!* Rounder
Various. *Indestructable Beat of Soweto.* 2 through 4. Earthworks
Various. *Siya Hamba.* Original Music
Miriam Makeba. *Sangoma.* Warner Brothers
Obed Ngobeni. *My Wife Bought a Taxi.* Shanachie
Hugh Masekela. *Hope.* Triloka
Dudu Pukwana and Spear. *In the Townships.* Earthworks

### Zimbabwe
Various. *Zimbabwe Frontline.* 1 and 2. Earthworks
Thomas Mapfumo. *Shumba.* Earthworks
Stella Chiweshe. *Ambuya?* Shanachie
Bhundu Boys. *Shabini.* Discafrique

### Mozambique
Ghorwane. *Majuragenta.* Real World
Orchestra Marrabenta. *Independence.* Piranha

### Madagascar
Various. *Madigasikara.* 1 and 2. Globestyle
Various. *World Out of Time.* 1 and 2. Shanachie
Rossy. *One Eye on the Future....* Shanachie
Tarika Sammy. *Fanafody* or *Balance.* Green Linnet

## East Africa

### Taarab Music
Various. *Songs the Swahili Sing.* Original Music
Zuhura Swaleh. *Shani.* Globestyle

### Tanzania
Various. *The Tanzania Sound.* Original Music
Geoffrey Oryema. *Exile.* Real World
Samite. *Pearl of Africa Reborn.* Shanachie

### Kenya
Various. *Before Benga.* 1 and 2. Original Music
Various. *Guitar Paradise of East Africa.* Earthworks
Various. *Kenya Dance Mania.* Earthworks
Ayub Ogada. *En Mana Kuoyo.* Real World

### Somalia/Ethiopia
Various. *Jamiila: Songs from a Somali City.* Original Music
Various. *Music of Ethiopia.* Caprice
Various. *Ethiopian Groove.* Blue Silver

Compiled by B. D. Colwell, producer, Simnadé, Music from Africa, KVMR-FM (Nevada City, California)

# POPULATION
## Questions about policies and programs

Looking over the array of resource materials on the issue of population in Africa it seems, at times, that there is at least one glossy brochure, full-color demographic chart, or population journal for every woman, man, and child in Africa. The topic is well-studied and amply covered in print and audiovisual media. For all the available resources, however, there remain numerous contending points of view on the nature, timing, and relative importance of population-related programs. The quotations below represent just a sample of these divergent points of view.

Professor Aderanti Adepoju, a Nigerian economist and demographer, calls attention to "two broad points of view [that] have dominated the debate on the inter-relationship between population growth and economic development. "One school of thought," Adepoju writes, "holds strongly that fertility rates—the key to slowing the rapid expansion of population—will normally decline only in response to enhanced living conditions, higher incomes, female education and modernization. That is, poverty has to be eradicated before a family-planning culture, in the modern sense, can take root. The other view holds that family planning can be effectively introduced

"Of all the myths about Africa prevailing in the West, none is propagated with more vigor and regularity than the notion that overpopulation is a central cause of African poverty... Indeed, in many African regions the problem is *under*population."
— Djibril Diallo, chief spokesman, UN Office for Emergency Operations in Africa

"Blaming global environmental degradation on population growth helps to lay the groundwork for... top-down, demographically driven population policies and programs which are deeply disrespectful of women, particularly women of color and their children."
— African Centre for Democracy and Human Rights Studies, The Gambia

"There is a very high unmet need for family planning. The economic situation... has brought it home to our people that if they want their children to be educated and well-fed, then they have to begin to do something about children they are going to have."
— Olikoye Ransome-Kuti, Former Minister of Health, Nigeria

irrespective of the level of development; what is needed is an adequate supply of the right methods, backed by intensive awareness and motivational campaigns" (see "Africa's population crisis: Formulating effective policies," *Africa Recovery Briefing Paper* 3, April 1991, p. 4).

The resource materials in this chapter speak to the theoretical and programmatic tug-of-war that Adepoju identifies. They also reflect a broader range of perspectives and issues that policy-makers, development workers, educators, and the general public have about Africa's "population crisis."

## Setting the scene

A few general studies on world population (especially as it relates to the developing nations) set the scene for the focused look at population issues in Africa that follows below.

*Full House: Reassessing the Earth's Population Carrying Capacity* (Brown and Kane 1994) is a balanced and readable summary of the tensions between food production and population growth on a global level. A longer and more thorough analysis of the same topics is *The Future Population of the World: What Can We Assume Today?* (Lutz 1994), an Earthscan publication that includes projections specifically for the Africa region.

Other general studies include *Beyond the Numbers: A Reader on Population, Consumption, and the Environment* (Mazur 1994); *Population: Broadening the Debate* (Bandarage et al. 1994); *Population and Development: Old Debates, New Conclusions* (Cassen et al. 1994); and *Population and Development in Poor Countries* (Simon 1992).

In the revised edition of her 1987 classic study, *Reproductive Rights and Wrongs: The Global Politics of Population Control* (Hartmann 1995), population and development activist Betsy Hartmann makes the case that rapid population growth is a symptom and not a cause of problematic economic and social development, that improvements in the status of women lead to voluntary decreases in family size, and that effective birth control services can only thrive within a comprehensive system of health care delivery that is responsive to people's needs.

Additional feminist criticisms of population programs and policies include *Population Policies Reconsidered: Health, Empowerment, and Rights* (Sen et al. 1994), *Changing the Boundaries: Women-Centered Perspectives on Population and Environment* (Jiggins 1994), *Population and Reproductive Rights: Feminist Perspectives from the South* (Corrêa 1994), and *Private Decisions, Public Debate: Women, Reproduction and Population* (Mirsky and Radlett 1994). The latter contains case studies of

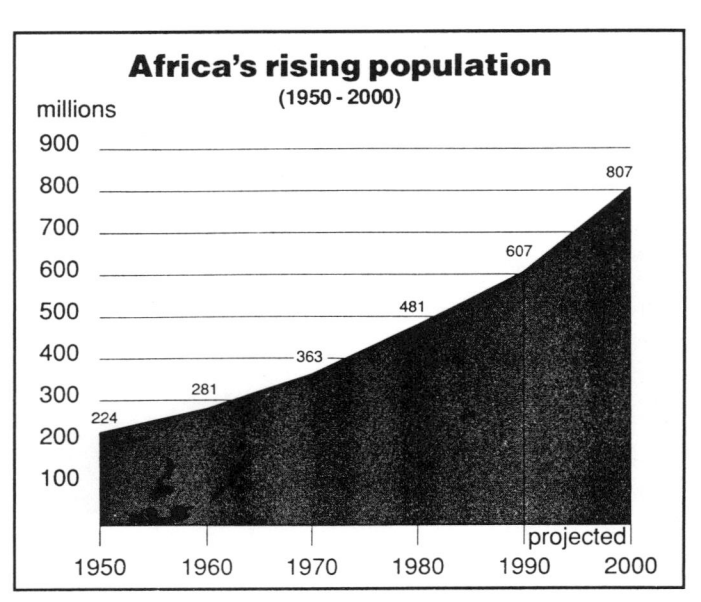

**Africa's rising population**
(1950 - 2000)

millions

| Year | Population |
|------|------------|
| 1950 | 224 |
| 1960 | 281 |
| 1970 | 363 |
| 1980 | 481 |
| 1990 | 607 |
| 2000 | 807 (projected) |

From *Africa Recovery Briefing Paper*, no. 3 (April 1991). Courtesy United Nations Department of Public Information, New York. Source: UN data.

population-related issues in Tanzania, Ghana, Ethiopia, Burkina Faso, and Egypt, among other emerging nations.

Two special issues of *Hunger Notes,* a quarterly newsletter published by World Hunger Education Service (Washington, D.C.), offer a breadth of material on population and development issues in a handy format. The spring 1994 issue, entitled *Population: Broadening the Debate,* contains articles, graphic sidebar materials, and lists of resources that aim to set out the lines of debate regarding population and development. The summer 1994 issue, *Population: The Special Case of Africa* (Adepoju et al. 1994), offers a concise and readable presentation of the issues and debates relative to population issues in Africa.

Other brief, well-designed, and accessible introductions to population-related topics are *Population and Development* (Panos Institute 1994), *We Speak for Ourselves: Population and Development* (Brown et al. 1994), *Why Population Matters* (Population Action International 1996), *World Population Data Sheet* (Population Reference Bureau 1996), and *Is Population the Problem?* (Wheeler 1995).

## Population programs in Africa

Ngozi Onwurah's video documentary, *The Desired Number* (Women Make Movies 1995) uses the Ibu Eze ceremony in Nigeria — Africa's most populous nation — to dramatically illustrate the complexities and difficulties that face family planning advocates as they confront on-the-ground realities in traditional societies in Africa and other regions of the developing world. The Ibu Eze ceremony honors and celebrates Nigerian women who have given birth to nine children. The deeply rooted traditional ceremony brings tangible rewards to the honored woman's family and is perhaps the only recognition a rural woman will receive for her lifetime of labor.

Add to this the influence of the Roman Catholic Church in Nigeria, the economic uncertainties of village life, and nationalist and anti-Western forces who denounce population programs as Western-inspired attempts to limit the growth of Nigerian families, and the logic of the question posed by this video is clear: Why would any woman *not* strive to have as many children as possible?

The need to tackle population management issues in Africa is obvious, but

**Population growth rates**
(annual percentage change)

Source: UN Department of International Economic and Social Affairs.
Reprinted from *Hunger Notes* 20, no. 1 (summer 1994).

the obstacles to the successful implementation of effective programs—as this documentary video makes clear—are numerous and complex.

Books that address population issues in Africa include *African Population and Capitalism: Historical Perspectives* (Cordell and Gregory 1987); *Malthusianism: An African Dilemma. Hunger, Drought, and Starvation in Africa* (Njoku 1986); *Population Growth and Agricultural Change in Africa* (Turner et al. 1993); *Science That Colonizes: A Critique of Fertility Studies in Africa* (Riedmann 1993); and *Gender and Population in the Adjustment of African Economies: Planning for Change* (Palmer 1991).

The Population Reference Bureau (Washington, D.C.) has published a number of booklets on this subject. See, for example, *Africa's Expanding Population: Old Problems, New Policies* (Goliber 1989), *African Population Images* (IMPACT Project 1990), and *Africa Demographic and Health Surveys* (1992).

The Information Project for Africa (Washington, D.C.) has taken a particularly strong interest in developing critical perspectives on population policies and programs in Africa. IPFA's strong point of view—expressed anonymously in the following titles—is evident in publications such as *Ambassadors of Colonialism: The International Development Trap* (1993), *Population Control and National Security: A Review of U.S. National Security Policy on Population Issues, 1970-1988* (1991), and *Unconventional Warfare and the Theory of Competitive Reproduction: U.S. Intervention and Covert Action in the Developing World* (1991). IPFA's research coordinator, Elizabeth Liagin, is the author of the organization's most recent study, *Excessive Force: Power, Politics and Population Control* (Liagin 1996).

### REFERENCE MATERIALS AND PERIODICALS

Reference sources on population-related issues include *The State of World Population 1994* (UNFPA 1994) and *World Resources 1994-95: A Guide to the Global Environment. People and the Environment* (World Resources Institute 1994). Both publications are updated annually.

United Nations publications of note include *Demographic Handbook for Africa 1992* (Economic Commission for Africa, Population Division) and *Family Planning and Population: A Compendium of International Statistics* (Ross et al. 1993). The latter is a joint publication of the UN Population Fund (UNFPA) and the Population Council (New York). *Population and Development: Directory of Non-Governmental Organisations in OECD Countries* (OECD 1994) provides information on more than 700 NGOs active in the fields of population and development. The profiled organizations are based in member nations of the Organization for Economic Cooperation and Development. The OECD membership includes Australia, the United States, Japan, Canada, and most European nations.

Numerous organizations publish journals and magazines on population issues. Chief among these periodicals are:

- *African Population Newsletter.* UN Economic Commission for Africa, Population Division, P.O. Box 3001, Addis Abada, Ethiopia.
- *Canadian Studies in Population.* University of Alberta, Dept. of Sociology, Population Research Laboratory, Edmonton, AB Canada T6G 2H4.
- *Demography.* Population Association of America, 1722 N St., NW, Washington, DC 20036-2983 USA.
- *International Dateline: News of World Population and Development. A Service for Mass Media.* Population Communications International, 777 United Nations Plaza, New York, NY 10017 USA.
- *Population and Development Review.* Population Council, 1 Dag Hammarskjold Plaza, New York, NY 10017 USA.
- *Population Bulletin.* Population Reference Bureau, 1875 Connecticut Ave., NW, Ste. 520, Washington, DC 20009-5728 USA.
- *Population Bulletin of the United Nations.* UN Publications, Sales Section, Rm. DC2 0853, New York, NY 10017 USA.
- *Population Studies: A Journal of Demography.* Population Investigation Committee, London School of Economics, Houghton St., London WC2A 2AE, England.

# REFUGEES
## Multiple causes, terrible consequences

Refugees and Africa, Howard Adelman notes in his introduction to *African Refugees: Development Aid and Repatriation* (Adelman and Sorenson 1994), "seem almost synonymous. Of the over fifteen million refugees in the world," Adelman notes, "Africa has more than five million." Other estimates put the number of refugees and displaced peoples (refugees *within* their national borders) even higher. Whatever the number, Adelman is correct: in the popular mind, as well as in reality, Africa and refugees appear to be inextricably intertwined.

As with all sweeping generalizations about the vast and diverse continent of Africa, however, the too-easy linkage between refugees and Africa needs to be deconstructed. Where are the most intense concentrations of refugees and displaced persons in Africa? What are the causes of these social disruptions? In which instances have refugees been driven from their homes by natural phenomena (e.g., droughts)? In which cases have they been displaced by war? What attendant factors are critical to study in relation to the refugee crisis (e.g., landmines as obstacles to repatriation)? What initiatives are Africans taking to meet the challenge of refugees?

### International refugee problem

The refugee crisis in Africa needs to be situated in an international context. Books that place Africa's refugee crisis in a broader geographical framework include:

- *The Cambridge Survey of World Migration* (Cohen 1995). Substantive essays and up-to-date documentation on world migration from the sixteenth century to the present. Seven essays in chapter six are devoted to migration in Africa, e.g., "Cheap gold: Mine labour in Southern Africa," "People on the move in West Africa: From pre-colonial polities to post-independence states," and "Forced labour and migration in Portugal's African colonies."
- *The World Refugee Problem* (Hakovirta 1991). Finnish scholar Harto Hak-

### Major Asylum Countries

| Country of Asylum | Total number of refugees | Number and country of origin |
|---|---|---|
| Zaire | 774,500 | 370,000 Rwanda<br>76,000 Burundi<br>200,000 Angola<br>110,000 Sudan<br>18,500 Uganda |
| Guinea | 600,000 | 400,000 Liberia<br>200,000 Sierra Leone |
| Tanzania | 256,400 | 5,000 Rwanda<br>31,400 Zaire<br>220,000 Burundi |
| Sudan | 405,400 | 349,000 Eritrea<br>52,000 Ethiopia<br>4,400 Chad |
| Ethiopia | 394,600 | 290,000 Somalia<br>78,000 Sudan<br>18,000 Djibouti<br>8,600 Kenya |
| Côte d'Ivoire | 372,500 | 327,500 Liberia |
| Uganda | 263,000 | 225,000 Sudan<br>28,000 Zaire<br>10,000 Rwanda |
| Kenya | 167,500 | 132,700 Somalia<br>28,700 Sudan<br>5,600 Ethiopia<br>500 Uganda |

*Africa Recovery* 10, no. 4 (1997), p. 23. Source: UNHCR estimates as of February 1997.

ovirta's study of "one of the greatest and saddest global problems of our time."

- *The Global Refugee Crisis* (Loescher and Loescher 1995). A broad survey of the refugee crisis that closes with an outline of the future challenges that refugee movements pose for the international community.
- *Population Movements and the Third World* (Parnwell 1993). The complex interplay between migration and development is the focus of this concise survey of population movements in and from Third World countries.
- *Beyond Borders: Refugees, Migrants and Human Rights in the Post-Cold War Era* (Ferris 1993). A former refugee specialist with the World Council of Churches (Geneva) analyzes movements of people in Africa, Asia, Latin America, and the Middle East and suggests how the international system might respond better to the needs of migrants and refugees.

Two highly recommended educational resources are:

- *Refugees: We Left Because We Had To. An Educational Book for 14-18 Year Olds* (Rutter 1996). A field-tested sourcebook of background readings and curriculum materials on the nature and causes of population displacements in Burundi, Rwanda, Eritrea, Liberia, Sierra Leone, Sudan, Mozambique, and other countries in Africa and Asia.
- *The Refugee Campaign* (CAFOD 1994). A handsome packet of study and worship resources produced for an educational campaign in England and Wales by CAFOD, the Catholic Fund for Overseas Development.

## African context

The conference papers gathered together in *The Migration Experience in Africa* (Baker and Aina 1995) set a helpful historical framework for the study of population movements in Africa by underlining the fact that "the phenomenon of migration is not new in Africa." Africa, as one observer has noted, is—and always has been—a continent "perpetually on the move."

The following books describe and analyze the features of movements of people in Africa today and highlight the numerous and diverse reasons for the displacement of people.

- *African Refugees: Development and Repatriation* (Adelman and Sorenson 1994) identifies and analyzes some of these causes: ideological wars and nationalist conflicts, environmental disasters and ethnic hatreds, and "the brutal ambition for power of a few and the poverty of many."
- In *Protecting the Dispossessed: A Challenge for the International Community* (Deng 1993) Francis M. Deng, formerly Sudan's Minister of State for Foreign Affairs, focuses attention on people in Africa and elsewhere who are internally displaced. "Worldwide," Deng writes, "the number of people displaced within their own countries far exceeds the number of those who have crossed international borders and become refugees. The most recent estimates set the internally displaced population at 25 million and the

> "Landmines are undoubtedly the biggest impediment to refugees going home." This observation by Suzannah Cox, of the British Refugee Council, underlines the importance of broadening the study of refugees to include critical —but little-known— factors like landmines as deadly obstacles to repatriation.
>
> Contact the International Campaign to Ban Landmines, 54A Main St., Cockermouth, Cumbria CA13 9LU England

refugee population at 18 million." (Estimates are that more than 15 million of the 25 million displaced persons worldwide are Africans.) *Protecting the Dispossessed* contains chapter-length country reports on two African nations (Somalia and the Sudan) and an entire chapter—"The Challenge in the African Experience"— that explores ways that the international community can move beyond providing emergency relief to deal with the root causes of displacement.

- The connection between violent conflicts and refugees is examined in *Escape from Violence: Conflict and the Refugee Crisis in the Developing World* (Zolberg et al. 1989). Three of the six regional studies in *Escape from Violence* deal with Africa: (1) Ethnic conflict in the new states of sub-Saharan Africa (Rwanda, Burundi, Sudan, Chad, Uganda); (2) In the long shadow of South Africa (Angola, Mozambique, Zimbabwe, Namibia); and (3) Separatism, revolution, and war in Ethiopia and the Horn (Eritrea, Ethiopia, Somalia).

- *African Exodus: Refugee Crisis, Human Rights and the 1969 OAU Convention* (Carver et al. 1995) reports on the results of a 3-year investigation by the Lawyers Committee for Human Rights (New York) into the state of refugee protection in Africa, with particular reference to the effectiveness of "the most progressive treaty regime in the world," the 1969 Organization of African Unity Convention Governing the Specific Aspects of Refugees in Africa (the "OAU Convention").

- *When Refugees Go Home: African Experiences* (Allen and Morsink 1994) examines the little-noticed fact that millions of African refugees have

## REFERENCE AND PERIODICAL RESOURCES ON

### Displaced Peoples and Refugee Studies: A Resource Guide

Julian Davies, comp. Refugee Studies Programme, University of Oxford. London and New Providence: Hans Zell Publishers, 1990. xii + 219 pp. Cloth. ISBN 0-905450-76-0. Index, list of abbreviations.

Materials are grouped under 10 chapter headings: (1) manuals and reference works; (2) bibliographies; (3) journals and magazines; (4) monographs; (5) dissertations; (6) major libraries and documentation centers; (7) publishers; (8) research and training centers; (9) courses of study; and (10) organizations, networks, and donor agencies.

Listings in chapters 3, 6, 7, 8, and 10 are subdivided by country.

Indexes include names of authors and editors, the titles of written works, and the names of all organizations in the guide.

### World Refugee Survey 1997

U.S. Committee for Refugees. Washington, D.C.: U.S. Committee for Refugees, annual. 160 pp. ISSN 0197-5439. ISBN 0-9365-48-53-3 (1997). Country reports, list of resources, notes, photographs, tables.

The bulk of this annual survey is given to tables and graphs of statistical data (e.g., on the numbers of refugees and asylum seekers in need of protection and/or assistance) and to individual country reports (arranged under regional headings).

The directory of organizations at the back of the oversized handbook contains annotated listings of international organizations, U.S. government offices, and private organizations such as the Center for Migration Studies, the Lawyers Committee for Human Rights, and Refugee Women in Development.

### The State of the World's Refugees 1993: The Challenge of Protection

United Nations High Commissioner for Refugees. New York and London: Penguin Books, 1993. ix + 191 pp. ISBN 0-14-023487-X. List of abbreviations, maps, tables, charts, photographs, end notes, chronology, bibliography.

This report contains an assessment of the plight of the world's 18.2 million refugees (1993) by the Office of the UN High Commissioner for Refugees in Geneva, Switzerland, along with recommended strategies for the future.

Chapter titles include "Information as Protection," "Going Home: Voluntary Repatriation," and "Protection in Times of Armed Conflict."

Annex 1 contains statistical tables and data on refugees; annex 2 provides the texts of and commentary on various international instruments related to refugees.

returned successfully to their homes after periods of internal or external displacement. "It is important for those anxious about the welfare of the world's displaced millions," editors Tim Allen and Hubert Morsink remind their readers, "to seize the opportunity to put returnee as well as refugee needs and aspirations on to the agenda of [international] meetings, and to keep them there by persistent lobbying" (p. 12).

In a follow-up study to *When Refugees Go Home,* editor Tim Allen presents more than 20 papers that question many accepted truths about the situation of displaced peoples in Africa and about international relief and development efforts in Africa. See *In Search of Cool Ground: War, Flight and Homecoming in Northeast Africa* (Allen 1996).

> "In Africa alone, it has been estimated that around 3.5 million refugees were repatriated between 1971 and 1990…[and] during the same years, millions more Africans went home after periods of exile within their own countries."
>
> Tim Allen and David Turton
> *In Search of Cool Ground* (Allen 1996), p. 1

## Keeping up

*Displaced Peoples and Refugee Studies: A Resource Guide* (Davies 1990) is the most thorough and up-to-date guide to library and other documentation sources for further study of involuntary migration on an international scale. Edited by the Refugee Studies Programme, University of Oxford, the clothbound reference book offers expert guidance to directories, handbooks, annuals, teaching aids, journals, monographs, and other printed resources on the worldwide problem of refugees and displaced persons. Names and contact information are also provided for research institutes, donor agencies and foundations, refugee network organizations, and libraries and documentation centers with holdings on the topic of refugees.

---

### REFUGEES AND DISPLACED PEOPLES

**Refugee Survey Quarterly**

Geneva: United Nations High Commissioner for Refugees, Centre for Documentation on Refugees (UNHCR/CDR), quarterly. Journal. By subscription. 150pp. ISSN 0253-1445. Country reports, documentation, literature survey, reviews, editorial, selected bibliography, index, advertisements. Articles appear in English or French.

This successor to the UNHCR's *Refugee Abstracts* publication provides current refugee, legal, and country information that reflects both the evolving nature of refugee protection as reflected in the refugee literature and case-law and the progress made in the development of the UNHCR/CDR's unique databases of refugee-related information.

The Summer/Autumn 1994 issue of *Refugee Survey Quarterly* (Vol. 13, Nos. 2 and 3) was devoted to materials concerning Africa. Country reports in the issue covered Liberia, Somalia, and Rwanda.

**Refugees**

Geneva: United Nations High Commissioner for Refugees, Public Information Section, semi-annual. Magazine. Free. 32pp. ISSN 0252-791X.
Articles, interviews, lists of resources, photographs, tables, charts, maps. Available in the USA from the UNHCR, 1775 K St., NW, Ste. 300, Washington, DC 20006 USA. French-language edition also available.

Each issue of this colorful magazine from the UNHCR is devoted to the study of one aspect of the international situation of refugees and displaced persons. Typical subject areas include refugees and the environment, the costs associated with refugee relief, and the situation of internally displaced peoples.

Other sections in the magazine report on UNHCR activities, bring together a variety of points of view on specific refugee questions, and present the stories of individual refugee workers in the field.

**Refworld CD-ROM**

Geneva: United Nations High Commissioner for Refugees, Centre for Documentation on Refugees (UNHCR/CDR), semi-annual. CD-ROM. Windows/PC version. By subscription.

This Windows-based collection of easy-to-use databases was developed by the CDR to provide access to a variety of sources of public information on refugees around the world. Sources include official speeches of the High Commissioner dating back to February 1992, official publications such as the "State of the World's Refugees," and reports on country situations that are based on fully cited sources such as those from Amnesty International, Human Rights Watch, the Immigration and Naturalization Service of the United States, and WRITENET, a network of regional specialists.

Subscribers receive updates twice a year. A free demonstration version of the CD-ROM is available from the UNHCR/CDR in Geneva.

# SOUTH AFRICA
## A time to build

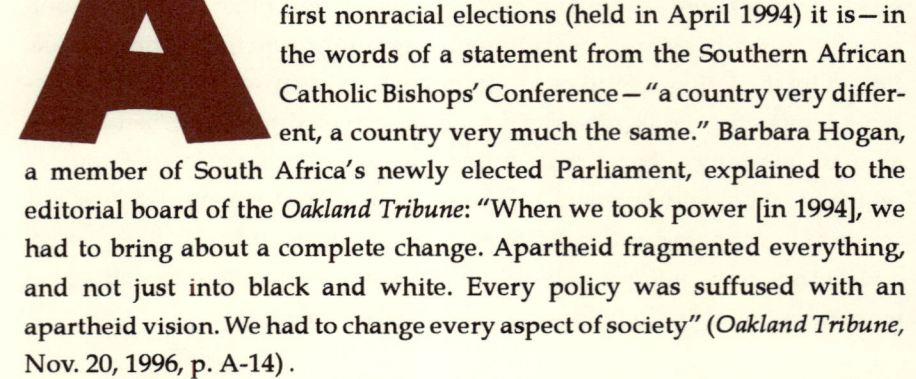

As South Africa emerges from the heady success of its first nonracial elections (held in April 1994) it is—in the words of a statement from the Southern African Catholic Bishops' Conference—"a country very different, a country very much the same." Barbara Hogan, a member of South Africa's newly elected Parliament, explained to the editorial board of the *Oakland Tribune*: "When we took power [in 1994], we had to bring about a complete change. Apartheid fragmented everything, and not just into black and white. Every policy was suffused with an apartheid vision. We had to change every aspect of society" (*Oakland Tribune*, Nov. 20, 1996, p. A-14).

Ahmed Kathrada, another member of the South African Parliament who visited Oakland, California, with Hogan in November 1996, knows better than most how sweet the 1994 victory was over apartheid, for he suffered 26 years as a political prisoner on South Africa's notorious Robben Island. But Kathrada insists that the battle did not end with the defeat of apartheid. In fact, he contends, "The struggle has just started."

The resource materials in this chapter describe the many obstacles that the government of President Nelson Mandela and the people of South Africa face as they struggle to heal the wounds of apartheid and to build a new multiracial nation. The resources also identify the strengths that South Africans bring to these challenges.

### Southern Africa region

Books that situate South Africa in the larger geographical context of the southern Africa region are Professor J. D. Omer-Cooper's highly regarded textbook *History of Southern Africa* (Omer-Cooper 1994), and two collections of essays: the first, by scholar-activist John Saul, *Recolonization and Resistance in Southern Africa in the 1990s* (Saul 1993), and the second, by various international affairs specialists, *The Dynamics of Change in Southern Africa* (Rich 1994).

South African Communication Service, Pretoria 1994

Booklets in the Southern Africa Political Economy series, published by the SAPES Trust (Harare), are useful for the perspectives they offer from social scientists in the region. See, particularly, *Post-Cold War Peace and Security Prospects in Southern Africa* (Rugumamu 1993) and *Southern Africa in the Year 2000: An Overview and Research Agenda* (Mandaza 1993).

## South Africa

We divide the resource materials below into time frames that correspond roughly to twentieth-century South African history before, during, and after the transition period that ended with the historic elections in 1994.

**Apartheid South Africa:** The revised edition of Professor Leonard Thompson's classic *A History of South Africa* (Thompson 1995) is a good place to begin for an overview of the sweep of South Africa's history from the black settlements that pre-dated the arrival of the Europeans to the elections and transition to multi-racial democracy in the 1990s.

Recently published books that shed additional light on the origins and legacy of apartheid include *The Apartheid State in Crisis: Political Transformation in South Africa, 1975-1990* (Price 1991); *Apartheid's Genesis, 1935-1962* (Bonner et al. 1993); *Politics in South Africa: From Vorster to De Klerk* (Maguire 1991); *South Africa: Colonialism, Apartheid and African Dispossession* (Moleah 1993); *South Africa: The Dynamics and Prospects of Transformation, 1900-1994* (Buthelezi 1995); *South Africa: To the Sources of Apartheid* (Debroey 1989); and *The Struggle: A History of the African National Congress* (Holland 1990).

Autobiographies offer unique vantage points for an understanding of apartheid South Africa: *Strikes Have Followed Me All My Life: A South African Autobiography* (Mashinini 1991); *Blame Me on History* (Modisane 1986); *Across Boundaries: The Journey of a South African Woman Leader* (Ramphele 1995); and *Slovo: The Unfinished Autobiography of ANC Leader Joe Slovo* (Slovo 1997).

In his Foreword to *Living Apart: South Africa under Apartheid* (Berry 1996), Archbishop Desmond Tutu compares photo-journalist Ian Berry's stunning collection of black-and-white photographs of South Africa from the late 1950s to the mid-1990s to the emotionally moving museum display Tutu had just visited during a trip to Nuremburg. "These pictures [in Nuremburg]," Archbishop Tutu writes, "were powerful in their impact, more powerful for being so understated. No technicolor. So you can see why Berry's collection fairly took my breath away. It was an extraordinary coincidence, the same medium and cataloguing a further terrible example of our inhumanity to one another. A searing indictment and an important record to counteract amnesia."

**Negotiations and elections:** Books and pamphlets that describe the period of negotiations leading up to the 1994 elections include *The Long Journey: South Africa's Quest for a Negotiated Settlement* (Friedman 1993); *Election '94. South Africa: The Campaigns, Results and Future Prospects* (Reynolds 1994); *The*

### Building Democracy in South Africa

This resource packet was published in early 1994 by the Division of Overseas Ministry of the United Church of Christ (New York) in order to

- provide factual information on the current situation in South Africa
- increase awareness that the process of building democracy in South Africa (and elsewhere) is long-term and complex
- encourage people of faith in the United States to think about how to support the building of democracy in South Africa.

The packet, which was designed to be used for either individual or group study, contains facilitator tips, six issue cards, a map, a handout on the role of the church, a listing of further resources, and action ideas.

*Contact:* DOM-UCBWM Joint Ministry in Africa, 474 Riverside Dr., 7th floor, New York, NY 10115-0109 USA

*Small Miracle: South Africa's Negotiated Settlement* (Friedman and Atkinson 1994); *Launching Democracy: The First Open Election, April 1994* (Johnson and Schlemmer 1996); *The Struggle Continues: South African Women and the Vote* (Kagan and Lippman 1993); *Unfinished Business: South Africa's March to Democracy* (Njanana et al. 1994); *Voting in the Shadow of Apartheid: Questions and Answers on the South African Election* (Landis 1993); and a novel by journalist Mike Nicol, *The Waiting Country: A South African Witness* (1995).

The bibliography, *South Africa. As Apartheid Ends: An Annotated Bibliography with Analytical Introductions* (Stultz 1993), catalogs many additional titles that cover South Africa up to the period of the elections.

**Transition and beyond:** Resource materials that deal with the multitude of specific issues that face South Africans in the future are listed below. Books and pamphlets that feature a broad, multi-issue approach are these:

- *After Apartheid: The Future of South Africa* (Mallaby 1992);
- *Bitter Inheritance: Overcoming the Legacy of Apartheid* (Fleshman 1993);
- *The Catharsis and the Healing: South Africa in the 1990s* (Ergas 1994);
- *Heart of Whiteness:* Afrikaners Face *Black Rule* in the New South Africa (Goodwin and Schiff 1995);
- *The Opening of the Apartheid Mind: Options for the New South Africa* (Adam and Moodley 1993);
- *Peace, Politics and Violence in the New South Africa* (Etherington 1992);
- *Some Are More Equal than Others: Essays on the Transition in South Africa* (Alexander 1993);
- *South Africa: Breaking New Ground* (CIIR Comment 1996);
- *South Africa: The Challenge of Change* (Maphai 1994);
- *South Africa: The Political Economy of Transformation* (Stedman 1994);
- *South Africa: Twelve Perspectives on the Transition* (Kitchen and Kitchen 1994);
- *The South African Tripod: Studies on Economics, Politics, and Conflict* (Odén et al. 1994);
- *Tomorrow Is Another Country: The Inside Story of South Africa's Road to Change* (Sparks 1996).

From 1991 to 1995, Canada's International Development Research Centre (IDRC)—in partnership with the African National Congress, the Congress of South African Trade Unions, and the South African National Civic Organisation—conducted a series of missions in South Africa to assist the government and people of South Africa in their transition to democracy. The reports of these missions have been published by IDRC in a 4-volume set that carries a hearty endorsement by South African President Nelson Mandela. Titles in the *Building a New South Africa* series are given below (under Economy, Environment, Science and Technology, and Urban Policy).

**Free, but still impoverished:** A resident of the Chris Hani squatter settlement, Soweto, South Africa, 1994.
Courtesy of Keith Porter, Stanley Foundation.

## Issues

**Agriculture:** *Modernising Super-Exploitation: Restructuring South African Agriculture* (Marcus 1989)

**Corporate investment:** *Foundations for a New Democracy: Corporate Social Investment in South Africa* (Alperson 1995)

**Democracy:** *Democratization in South Africa: The Elusive Social Contract* (Sisk 1995); *Stabilizing Democracy in South Africa: The Challenges of Post-Apartheid Development* (Southern Africa Grantmakers' Affinity Group, Council on Foundations 1994); *A Democratic South Africa? Constitutional Engineering in a Divided Society* (Horowitz 1991).

**Development:** *Sustainable Development for a Democratic South Africa* (Cole 1994).

**Economy:** *Building a New South Africa.* Volume 1: *Economic Policy* (Van Ameringen 1995); *Managing the Economic Transition in South Africa* (Center for Economic Research on Africa 1994); *South Africa's Economic Crisis* (Gelb 1991).

**Education:** *Pedagogy of Domination: Towards a Democratic Education in South Africa* (Nkomo 1990).

**Environment:** (1) *Building a New South Africa.* Volume 2: *Environment, Reconstruction, and Development* (Whyte 1995); (2) *Restoring the Land: Environment and Change in Post-Apartheid South Africa* (Ramphele 1991).

**Labor:** *Beyond Apartheid: Labour and Liberation in South Africa* (Fine and Davis 1990)

**Media:** *South African Media Policy: Debates of the 1990s* (Louw 1993)

**Police:** *Policing the Conflict in South Africa* (Mathews et al. 1993); *Policing South Africa: The SAP and the Transition from Apartheid* (Cawthra 1993); *South Africa's Police: From Police State to Democratic Policing?* (Cawthra 1992).

**Political institutions:** *South Africa: Designing New Political Institutions* (Faure and Lane 1996).

**Political violence:** *Bargaining for Peace: South Africa and the National Peace Accord* (Gastrow 1995).

**Race and class:** *The Unbreakable Thread: Non-Racialism in South Africa* (Frederikse 1990).

**Rightwing militants:** *Hard Right: The New White Power in South Africa* (van Rooyen 1994).

**Science and Technology:** *Building a New South Africa.* Volume 3: *Science and Technology Policy* (Van Ameringen 1995).

**Urban policy:** *Building a New South Africa.* Volume 4: *Urban Policy* (Van Ameringen 1995).

**Women:** *Women and War in South Africa* (Cock 1993); *Lives of Courage: Women for a New South Africa* (Russell 1989); *Women and Resistance in South Africa* (Walker 1991).

**Youth:** *Heroes or Villains? Youth Politics in the 1980s* (Seekings 1993); *Creating a Future: Youth Policy for South Africa* (Everatt 1994); *Childhood in Crossroads: Cognition and Society in South Africa* (Reynolds 1989).

# STRUGGLES UNKNOWN
## Sudan and Western Sahara

Long-running struggles in two countries in Africa rarely capture headlines in the Western media and thus go unnoticed with their significance unappreciated. The resource materials listed in this chapter describe the origins and nature of the ongoing civil war in Sudan and the struggle for self-determination by the people of the Western Sahara.

### Sudan

Africa's largest country has been wracked by civil wars that have raged in Sudan in modern times, from 1955 to 1972 and from 1983 to the present. The protagonists—broadly defined—have been successive governments in the northern capital of Khartoum (predominantly Islamic fundamentalist in character) and the Sudan People's Liberation Movement (SPLM)—and its military wing, the Sudan People's Liberation Army (SPLA)—in the heavily Christian south of the country.

Oxfam's "Country Profile," *Sudan: A Nation in the Balance* (Peters 1996) is the most up-to-date, balanced, and accessible guide to the country, its people, and its struggles. *Sudan: The Forgotten Tragedy* (Deng et al. 1994), a collection of essays delivered at an October 1993 symposium convened by the U.S. Institute of Peace in Washington, D.C., provides an informed introduction to the history and complexity of the civil war. Authors Ali Abdalla Abbas, Taisier Mohamed Ahmed Ali, Francis M. Deng, Peter Nyot Kok, Bona Malwal, and Kamal El Din Osman Salih all have firsthand knowledge of the struggle, from academic positions in the University of Khartoum to being participants in peace negotiations between the SPLM and the government of Sudan.

Booklets written by John Prendergast, Director of the Horn of Africa Project of the Center of Concern (Washington, D.C.), present the struggle in Sudan in clear and readable terms. See, for example,

*Sudanese Rebels at a Crossroads: Opportunities for Building Peace in a Shattered Land* (1994), *"For Four Years I Have No Rest": Greed and Holy War in the Nuba Mountains of Sudan* (Prendergast and Hopkins 1994), *The Outcry for Peace in the Sudan* (1996), and *Diplomacy, Aid and Governance in Sudan* (1995).

Other readable introductions to the civil war and its consequences are: *Short-Cut to Decay: The Case of the Sudan* (Harir and Tvedt 1994), an analysis of the conflict by academics at universities in Sudan, Norway, Germany, England, and the Netherlands; and *War Wounds: Development Costs of Conflict in Southern Sudan* (Twose and Pogrund 1988), interviews, case studies, photographs, and other materials that portray the conflict as it is seen and felt by Sudanese from different sides of the political spectrum.

Francis M. Deng, a former minister of state for foreign affairs in the Sudan government, and Professor John O. Voll, past president of the Sudan Studies Association, are both prolific and highly respected authors of books on Sudanese affairs. See, for example, Deng's *War of Visions: Conflict of Identities in the Sudan* (1995) and Voll's *Sudan: State and Society in Crisis* (1991).

Other books that provide background on the conflict include *Southern Sudan: Too Many Agreements Dishonoured* (Alier 1992), a perspective on the conflict by a magistrate and government peace negotiator from southern Sudan; *Sudan 1898-1989: The Unstable State* (Woodward 1990), a political analysis of the Sudanese state by a lecturer in the Department of Politics, University of Reading (England); and *Beyond Conflict in the Horn: Prospects for Peace, Recovery and Development in Ethiopia, Somalia and the Sudan* (Doornbos et al. 1992).

Human Rights Watch/Africa has produced two book-length studies of the impact of the civil war: *Civilian Devastation: Abuses by All Parties in the War in Southern Sudan* (Rone 1994) and *Behind the Red Line: Political Repression in Sudan* (Rone 1996).

See also the reports issued regularly in recent years by African Rights (London), Amnesty International (London), Fund for Peace, Human Rights/Horn of Africa Program (New York), Human Rights Watch/Africa (New York), and U.S. Committee for Refugees (Washington, D.C.).

A recommended library reference book on Sudan is *Historical Dictionary of the Sudan* (Fluehr-Lobban et al. 1992).

Finally, lest the large and beautiful country of Sudan and its ancient civilization be reduced unfairly to images of its terrible war we recommend *Sudan: The Passing of Time* (Ribière 1994), a colorful photo-study of the heart-shaped land and the people of Sudan.

**For more information:** The January-March 1996 issue of *World Views* magazine (Oakland, Calif.) contained a guide to Sudan-related organizations and publications, including the *Sudan Democratic Gazette* (London), *Sudan Update* (London), and the Sudan Council of Churches (Khartoum).

## CHRONOLOGY

**1899** Anglo-Egyptian agreement establishes the British-dominated Condominium.

**1922** Britain grants independence to Egypt, but reserves the question of Sudan's future

**1930** "Southern Policy" is introduced secretly to isolate the south culturally and linguistically from the north.

**1947** The Juba conference confirms the abandonment of the "Southern Policy"; south and north are integrated.

**1951** Egypt claims sovereignty over Sudan.

**1956** Sudan becomes independent.

**1958** Military coup led by General Ibrahim Abboud, with support from Western powers.

**1962** Sustained guerrilla war begins in the south.

**1964** The "October Revolution" overthrows Abboud and installs a national government let by Sir al-Khatim al-Khalifa.

**1969** A group of Free Officers in the army, let by Ga'afar al-Numeiri, stage the "May Revolution."

**1972** Southern Sudan becomes a self-governing region.

**1973** Sudan's first Permanent Constitution is proclaimed.

**1975** Following a coup attempt against him, Numeiri centralizes power.

**1976** Exiled Opposition Front defeated as it tries to seize control of country.

**1980** Regional Government is introduced in northern Sudan.

**1983** Civil war erupts again with the Sudan Peoples' Liberation Army led by John Garang. Islamic Shari'a replaces civil penal codes.

**1985** Numeiri is deposed by senior army officers.

**1986-1989** Civilian coalition governments rule Sudan.

**1989** Sudan's third period of democracy ends with military coup on June 30th led by Brigadier General Omar Hassan Ahmad al-Behir. In October, fighting resumes in the south.

**1991** Food shortages and international relief operations.

*See: Chronology of Conflict Resolution Initiatives in Sudan* (Becker and Mitchell 1991), *Historical Dictionary of Sudan* (Fluehr-Lobban et al. 1992), and *Sudan 1898-1989* (Woodward 1990).

## Western Sahara

The people who inhabit the desolate but phosphate-rich desert land between Morocco and Mauritania on the Atlantic Coast of Northwest Africa—the Saharawi (or Sahrawi)—have been fighting for political and economic freedom from Moroccan domination since 1973. The long but little-known struggle in the former Spanish colony of Western Sahara, led by the resistance forces of the Polisario Front, has won for the Saharawi people diplomatic recognition from more than 70 nations for their self-proclaimed Saharan Arab Democratic Republic and a commitment from the United Nations to sponsor a referendum and to monitor the United Nations Peace Plan that was adopted by the UN Security Council in 1991.

Author and political analyst Tony Hodges has studied the Western Saharan issue for many years, traveling extensively in the region. Hodges gave the English-speaking world its first in-depth look at the Polisario struggle against the Western-supported Moroccan regime in *Western Sahara: The Roots of a Desert War* (Hodges 1983).

Hodges later produced the authoritative *Historical Dictionary of Western Sahara* (Pazzanita and Hodges 1994). Now in its second edition, the 564-page reference volume contains a chronology, a 21-page introduction to the Western Sahara (land and people), an alphabetically arranged dictionary of the key actors and movements that have shaped the history of this region, and a comprehensive bibliography of printed materials in English, French, and Spanish.

Minority Rights Group International (London) published its first report on the Saharan struggle by Tony Hodges in November 1984. Updated by the author and republished in 1991, *The Western Saharans* (Hodges 1991) is the most complete and readable summary of the struggle up until 1991. Popularly styled introductions to the Western Sahara conflict that pick up where the MRG reports leave off include *Report of Delegation to Western Sahara* (Woodcraft Folk 1993), *A Briefing Pack on Western Sahara* (Western Sahara Campaign 1995), *Sahrawi Refugees* (Refugee Council n.d.), and *Western Sahara: A Country Fact Sheet* (Western Sahara Awareness Project 1993).

Anthropologist and documentary filmmaker Danielle Smith produced a 30-minute video-documentary in 1994 that gives voice and identity to the refugees who fled to southwest Algeria from the Western Sahara after the invasion and occupation by Morocco in 1975. *Song of Umm Dalaila: The Story of the Sahrawis,* according to Smith, aims "to shatter the wall of silence that has kept the terrors and tragedy of the Sahrawi struggle in darkness." The video captures the spirit of the Sahrawi people's two-decade long struggle for freedom and peace and it celebrates the fantastic accomplishments of the refugees (especially the women) in rebuilding their lives and communities in exile. *Song of Umm Dalaila,* Smith points out, "ap-

**Logo of the Western Sahara Campaign**
Oxford Chambers, Oxford Place, Leeds LS1 3AX, England.

peals to the conscience of the international community to ensure the Sahrawi people exercise their right to self-determination, to regain their homeland. At the same time, the video challenges audiences to reconsider their views of Third World peoples as passive, helpless victims, by presenting an example where the values of hard work and determination persist in spite of great adversity." Filmmaker Danielle Smith is developing a study guide for *Song of Umm Dalaila* for students aged 14 to 18. For information on the video and the guide, write: Danielle Smith, 231 Elgin Ave., Flat 1, London W9 1NH, England. Or contact the Western Sahara Campaign (address below).

English-language studies of the Western Sahara conflict include

- "The Conflict in the Western Sahara," by George Joffé, in *Conflict in Africa* (Furley 1995), pp. 110-133.
- *Fueling the Fire: U.S. Policy and the Western Sahara Conflict* (Kamil 1987), a critical examination of Western support for Morocco's King Hassan.
- *International Dimensions of the Western Sahara Conflict* (Zoubir and Volman 1993), ten essays that include an assessment of the conflict in the post-cold war era and an analysis of the UN-supported plebiscite.
- "The Non-Interventionary Norm Prevails: An Analysis of the Western Sahara," by Karin von Hippel, in *The Journal of Modern African Studies* 33, no. 1 (1995): 67-81.
- *War and Refugees: The Western Sahara Conflict* (Lawless and Monahan 1987), essays that originated from an international symposium organized by the Refugee Studies Programme, Oxford University.

Reports issued by New York-based human rights organizations on the Western Sahara conflict and related topics include *Western Sahara: Keeping It Secret. The United Nations Operation in the Western Sahara* (1995) and *Human Rights in Morocco* (1995), both published by Human Rights Watch/Middle East, and *Cleaning the Face of Morocco: Human Rights Abuses and Recent Developments* (1990), produced by the Lawyers Committee for Human Rights.

Updated reports on the Western Sahara struggle are available from the Western Sahara Campaign, Oxford Chambers, Oxford Place, Leeds LS1 3AX, England. Tel/fax: (0113) 245 4786.

---

### Western Sahara on the Internet

The Internet is the best source for current information on events in Western Sahara.

Begin with the home page of the Swiss solidarity organization, **ARSO** (Association de soutien à un référendum libre et régulier au Sahara Occidental): <http://heiwww.unige.ch/arso/index.htm>.

The ARSO site contains news reports, background information, documents, bibliographies, and links to other Web sites. Much of the English-language information at this site has been translated into Spanish, Portuguese, Italian, and French.

The **Western Sahara Campaign**'s home page is another good source: <http://www.btinternet.com/~donald.macdonald/saharawi.htm>. This site contains news reports from Algerian radio broadcasts, the Agence France Presse news service, and the London office of Polisario. Links to other Web sites are also provided.

Other Web sites:

- **Saharawi Aid Project**
  <http://www.eaglenet.co.uk/sapn/>

- **Amnesty International**
  <http://www.oneworld.org/amnesty/index.html>

- **One World Western Sahara Page**
  <http://www.oneworld.org/guides/sahara/index.html>

- **University of Pennsylvania, African Studies Department**
  <http://www.sas.upenn.edu/African_Studies/Home_Page/../Country_Specific/W_Sahara.html>

# STRUGGLES WON
## Eritrea and Namibia

Two success stories of African liberation struggles to celebrate are those of Eritrea, formerly a province in Ethiopia in the Horn of Africa, and Namibia, known as South West Africa during the decades when the former German colony was occupied by its neighbor, South Africa. In 1994 Scarecrow Press published two volumes in its Historical Dictionaries reference series that integrate some relatively recent information on both Eritrea and Namibia into the detailed and well-organized historical material that is the hallmark of the Scarecrow directories.

The *Historical Dictionary of Ethiopia and Eritrea* (Prouty and Rosenfeld 1994) was completed shortly before Eritrea won its independence from Ethiopia in May 1993. The book contains a fair amount of material on Eritrea, though—as the book's title suggests—the bulk of the historical references in the alphabetically arranged dictionary and in the bibliography are to Eritrea when it was still a region within Ethiopia. The two nations are not treated independently in the dictionary. The final entry in the 4-page chronology in the *Historical Dictionary of Ethiopia and Eritrea* reads "24 May 1993— Eritrea declared itself an independent country after a UN-supervised election."

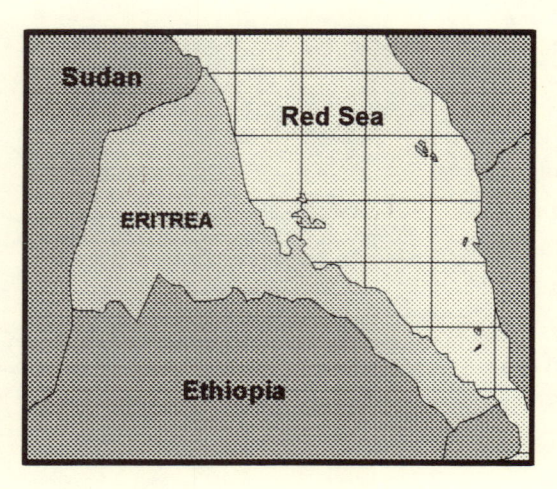

In the case of the Namibia dictionary, by contrast, enough time elapsed between the date of Namibia's independence, March 21, 1990, and the book's publication date to allow for the incorporation of a considerable amount of post-liberation material. Publications on Namibia's long struggle for independence are so voluminous, in fact, that the compilers of the *Historical Dictionary of Namibia* (Grotpeter 1994) had to use a heavy editorial hand to balance this material with other information that painted a broader picture of the nation. "We have been amply informed about [Namibia's] struggle for independence, the debates in the United Nations, and South Africa's role," series editor Jon Woronoff writes. "But many other factors have been largely overlooked. There was an earlier struggle for freedom," Woronoff points out, "one which influenced the more recent phase. Looking further back we must consider how the land was peopled and developed prior to colonization. These aspects are included in [the *Historical Dictionary of Namibia*] and make it broader and deeper than most."

## Eritrea

Pre-liberation books that describe the Eritrean struggle for independence include *The Challenge Road: Women and the Eritrean Revolution* (Wilson 1991), *Eritrea, a Pawn in World Politics* (Yohannes 1991), and *Never Kneel Down: Drought, Development and Liberation in Eritrea* (Firebrace and Holland 1985).

*Eritrea and Ethiopia: From Conflict to Cooperation* (Tekle 1994) is a bridge from pre- to post-liberation Eritrea both in the sense of its time span and its purpose. The book grew out of discussions begun in Atlanta, Georgia, by Eritrean and Ethiopian scholars in 1989—two years before the final victory of the Eritrean Peoples Liberation Army. Convinced that Eritrea's liberation was as imminent as it was certain, the scholars put aside political differences and began to explore ways that Ethiopia and an independent Eritrea could work together cooperatively.

"The major objective of the book," Amare Tekle writes, "is to evaluate the conditions of, and the relationships between, not only Ethiopia and Eritrea but also the rest of the countries in the region with the hope of identifying the real (as opposed to the 'political') root causes of conflict between the peoples of the region and making recommendations which would contribute [among other things] toward the...inauguration of a durable peace based on justice, freedom and equality" (p. ix).

The recent history of Eritrea's liberation struggle is told most accessibly in U.S. journalist Dan Connell's investigation of Eritrea's "unreported" war, *Against All Odds: A Chronicle of the Eritrean Revolution* (Connell 1993), and in a highly recommended video documentary produced in 1993 by Grassroots International (Somerville, Mass.), *Eritrea: Hope in the Horn of Africa*.

*Eritrea: Miracleland* (Ghebrai 1993) is "a very personal account of the visceral pain" suffered by the author, an Eritrean, and by "so many Eritreans" who longed and fought for their national independence from Ethiopia.

Other publications of note include
- *Beyond Conflict in the Horn: The Prospects for Peace, Recovery and Development in Ethiopia, Somalia, Eritrea and the Sudan* (Doornbos et al. 1992);
- *The Challenge Road: Women and the Eritrean Revolution* (Wilson 1991);
- *Emergent Eritrea: Challenges of Economic Development* (Tesfagiorgis 1994);
- *Liberation Politics and External Engagement in Ethiopia and Eritrea* (Prendergast and Duffield 1995);
- *Eritrean Studies Review* (Eritrean Studies Association; ISSN 1086-9174).

**Further information:** Request catalogs from Red Sea Press (Lawrenceville, N.J.) and from the Africa Faith and Justice Network (Washington, D.C.).

## CHRONOLOGY

**1916-30** Empress Zewditu, daughter of Menilek II, is crowned. Ras Teferi Mekonnen is named as her regent and heir.

**1930** After Zewditu's death, Ras Teferi is crowned Emperor Hayle Sellase I (on 2 November).

**1935-36** Italy invades and occupies Ethiopia until 1941; Emperor Hayle Sellase flees to England.

**1941-74** Hayle Sellase I returns to govern as the British army defeats Italy. Despite several attempted coups, he remains on the throne until September 1974, when he is overthrown after a "creeping revolution."

**1974-91** The rule of Mengestu Hayle Maryam and the Derg (Marxist socialists); the People's Democratic Republic is established. Famine and civil war devastate the country.

**1991** Mengestu Hayle Maryam flees to Zimbabwe in May, when the army of the Tigray People's Liberation Front (TPLF) occupies Addis Ababa. In July, the Transitional Government of Ethiopia is established under the leadership of Meles Zenawi, head of TPLF. Some fifteen political-ethnic-regional groups are organized, with the Oromo demanding a separate nation and the relationship of Eritrea to Ethiopia yet to be determined.

**1993** Eritrea declares itself an independent nation on 24 May after a United Nations-supervised election.

Adapted from *Historical Dictionary of Ethiopia and Eritrea* (Prouty and Rosenfeld 1994). Used with permission of Scarecrow Press (Lanham, Md.) See also: *Chronology of Conflict Resolution Initiatives in Eritrea* (Becker and Mitchell 1991).

> "A great future awaits Namibia in the years to come as we continue with my government's policy of national reconciliation, peace, stability, and development."
>
> Speech to the National Assembly, June 10, 1991
> Sam Shafiishuna Nujoma, first president of Namibia

# Namibia

On March 21, 1990, Namibia won its independence from South Africa after decades of war. The "ambience of tranquillity" that has characterized the southwest African nation in the years since the March 1990 elections, Namibian author and educator Joseph Diescho has noted, "distinguishes the country from what it used to be during some 24 years of armed struggle for independence, when the now ruling party, the South West Africa People's Organization (SWAPO), confronted the colonial administration and its politics of racial domination and economic exploitation" ("An Ambience of Tranquillity," in *Namibia Yearbook 1992-93*, p. 13).

The history of Namibia's long struggle for liberation is chronicled in books such as *Namibia: The Violent Heritage* (Soggot 1986); *Changing the History of Africa: Angola and Namibia* (Deutschmann 1989); *The Devils Are among Us: The War for Namibia* (Herbstein and Evenson 1989); *Namibia: The Facts* (International Defence and Aid Fund for Southern Africa 1989); *Namibia: Land of Tears, Land of Promise* (Enquist 1990); and *Namibia in History* (Mbumba and Noisser 1988), a text written for secondary school students.

Helao Shityuwete's autobiography, *Never Follow the Wolf* (Shityuwete 1990), puts Namibia's liberation struggle in personal terms. Shityuwete, one of the first in Namibia to take up arms against the occupying South African armed forces, tells of his involvement in the SWAPO resistance movement, his capture and torture by the South African military, and his imprisonment on South Africa's notorious Robben Island for sixteen years.

*Changing the History of Africa* (Deutschmann 1989) focuses attention on Cuba's political, economic, and military support for the Namibian independence struggle, and *Disengagement from Southwest Africa: Prospects for Peace in Angola and Namibia* (Kahn 1991) examines the role of the Soviet Union and its allies in the conflicts in Angola and Namibia.

In *Namibia: Land of Tears, Land of Promise* (Enquist 1990), theologian Roy Enquist, a former missionary in what is now Namibia, looks at the Namibian independence struggle through the lens of religion. Enquist's concern is how Namibian churches—with their "conservative, apolitical, and pietistic religious traditions"—could have become such ardent supporters of the liberation effort.

The roles of women in Namibia's struggle for independence are described in *Namibia: Women in War* (Cleaver and Wallace 1990) and *"It's Like Holding the Key to Your Own Jail": Women in Namibia* (Allison 1986).

The essays in the highly recommended *Namibia's Liberation Struggle: The Two-Edged Sword* (Leys and Saul 1995) focus attention on the way that Namibia's independence struggle affected "both the liberation movement itself and the political culture bequeathed to the country at independence" (p. vii).

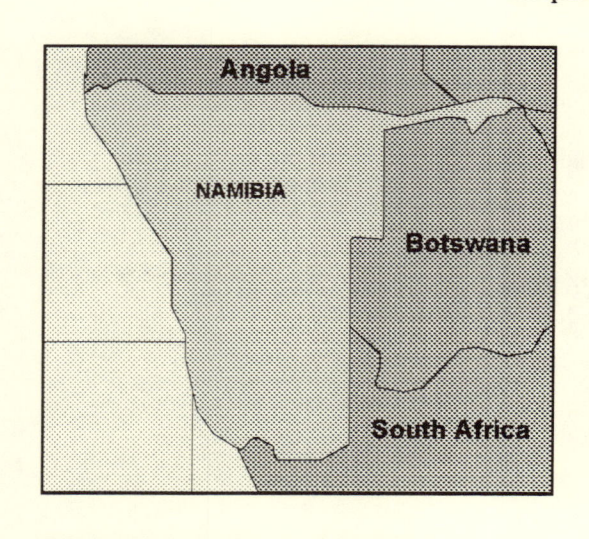

**"The Right to Liberty" (Joe Madisia)**
(Courtesy Joe Madisia, Walvis Bay, Namibia)

## Building a new nation

Two books take up the story of the Namibian people's efforts to build a new nation: *Namibia: The Nation after Independence* (Sparks and Green 1992) and *The Transition to Independence in Namibia* (Cliffe et al. 1994). The Sparks and Green volume surveys the history, politics, economy, society, and culture of Namibia before offering some informed prognostications about what the future might hold for the newly independent nation. *The Transition to Independence in Namibia* concentrates on the period of transition from the "final act of decolonization" (the cease-fire in 1989) to the deliberations of the Constituent Assembly and the March 1990 elections. It was during this transition period, the authors explain, that the majority party, SWAPO, transformed itself "from a largely exile movement of struggle into a political party" and that the country's leadership began to define the institutional structures that would provide the basis of the new state.

*Accountability in Namibia: Human Rights and the Transition to Democracy* (Dicker 1992), a Human Rights Watch report published in August 1992, calls on the governments of South Africa and Namibia "to begin accounting for the abuses [of the past]." By setting forth "the testimony and experiences of the victims of both the South African regime and SWAPO," the report states, "we signify our respect for them and for their suffering" (p. 6).

Anthropologist Wade Pendleton's study of "life in a post-apartheid township in Namibia," *Katutura: A Place Where We Stay* (Pendleton 1996), is a sweeping and engagingly written comparative study of life in Katutura, a township outside of Namibia's capital city, Windhoek, during the occupation by South Africa and after Namibia's independence.

## CHRONOLOGY

**1886-90** Namibia's present international boundaries are established by German treaties with Portugal (1886) and Great Britain (1890).

**1889-90** First German troops arrive; Germany annexes the territory.

**1892-1905** German suppression of uprisings by Herero and Namas; armistice signed on 20 December 1905 ends the German genocide (after the murder of 80 percent of the Herero population).

**1915** South Africa invades and occupies Namibia. Germans surrender at Peace of Korab, 9 July 1915. Namibians try to reclaim land taken by the Germans. South Africa imposes martial law.

**1920** Council of the League of Nations grants South Africa the right to govern Namibia as an integral part of its territory ("South West Africa").

**1946** United Nations refuses to allow South Africa to annex South West Africa (SWA). South Africa refuses to place SWA under UN Trusteeship Council.

**1953** UN General Assembly forms Committee on SWA to supervise mandate without South Africa's cooperation.

**1958** Herman Toivo Ya Toivo and others organize the opposition Ovamboland People's Congress, renamed the Ovamboland People's Organization (OPO) in 1959. OPO becomes the South West Africa People's Organization (SWAPO) in 1960.

**1959** South West Africa Nation Union (SWANU), the oldest Namibian nationalist party, is founded in August.

**1961** UN General Assembly demands South Africa terminate the mandate and sets SWA's independence as objective.

**1966** SWAPO announces plan to begin armed struggle against South African occupation.

**1968** South West Africa officially renamed Namibia by UN General Assembly in April.

**1972** UN General Assembly recognizes SWAPO as "sole legitimate representative" of Namibia's people on 12 December.

**1989** Elections held for a Namibian Constituent Assembly. SWAPO wins.

**1990** Namibia becomes independent on 21 March and joins the United Nations.

Adaped from *Historical Dictionary of Namibia* (Grotpeter 1994). Used with permission of Scarecrow Press (Lanham, Md.).

# VISUAL ARTS
## An integral component of everyday life

Art historian, curator, and educator Jean Kennedy signals the importance of the visual arts in sub-Saharan Africa with her observation that many African societies "take art so much for granted that there is often no one word to describe it." Art in Africa, Kennedy notes, "has always been interwoven—one form with another and all with life itself" (*New Currents, Ancient Rivers: Contemporary African Artists in a Generation of Change* [Kennedy 1992], p. 21). Clearly, then, an understanding of the visual arts in Africa holds the promise of deeper appreciations of the peoples and societies whose everyday lives are so infused with art in all its forms.

Beyond this benefit of studying the visual arts in Africa there is also the fact that an examination of art in African societies is helpful in countering stereotypes about Africa. "[Africa's] new artists wish to abolish stereotypes about Africa," Kennedy writes in her Afterword (p. 185) "Because artists are the bearers of truth [and] the voices by which society is measured they open the doors to cultures about which we know very little. Without them the world is incomplete. They broaden our horizons to include poetic visions which, like the rivers of Africa, run as deep as time."

Jean Kennedy's richly illustrated survey is a good starting point for a journey into the little-explored world of contemporary visual art in sub-Saharan Africa. Kennedy examines the work of more than 150 painters, sculptors, fiber artists, printmakers, and filmmakers primarily from six representative African countries: Nigeria, Senegal, Ethiopia, Sudan, Zimbabwe, and South Africa. (Egypt and North Africa are omitted "not for lack of strong cultural ties to the rest of Africa," Kennedy explains, "but because of space requirements.")

As the title of her survey makes clear, Kennedy is intent on exploring the traditional sources of the diversity of new artistic expression that she finds in the African societies she examines chapter-by-chapter in *New Currents, Ancient Rivers*.

> "Art is, and was always, in the service of man. Our ancestors created their myths and legends and told their stories for a human purpose...; they made their sculptures in wood and terra cotta, stone and bronze to serve the needs of their times. Their artists lived and moved and had their beings in society and created their works for the good of that society."
>
> Chinua Achebe,
> *Morning Yet on Creation Day*
> (New York: Anchor Press/Doubleday, 1975), p. 29

Other general introductions to the visual arts in Africa include the revised edition of Professor Frank Willett's classic one-volume survey, *African Art* (Willett 1993) and Professor Marshall Mount's investigation of painting and sculpture in Africa during the period 1920 to 1965, *African Art: The Years Since 1920* (Mount 1973). Noteworthy books and portfolios published in conjunction with exhibits of African art include *African Art Portfolio: An Illustrated Introduction* (Thompson 1993), *Into the Heart of Africa* (Cannizzo 1989), and *Seven Stories about Modern Art in Africa* (Nicodemus 1995).

Jan Vansina's introductory essay "Arts and society since 1935," in *Africa Since 1935* (Mazrui 1994), provides a succinct overview of artistic developments in Africa in recent times.

## Art of the personal object

Personal objects "fulfill notions of practicality" in human societies and "satisfy the human desire to embellish one's environment," writes Sylvia Williams, director of the National Museum of African Art in Washington, D.C. Personal objects, she continues, "exemplify a widespread human impulse to make and use visually pleasing yet practical objects, objects that bring a sense of order to the diversity and complexity of everyday life" (*The Art of the Personal Object,* Ravenhill 1991, p. 3). Nowhere is the interplay between art and personal objects more prevalent than in African societies.

Utilitarian objects such as baskets, bead jewelry, masks, pots, and textiles "form part of the designed environment that creates a person's feeling of being at home," Philip Ravenhill notes, in his introduction to *The Art of the Personal Object* (1991). "In large part," he explains, "they constitute the most accessible forms of a given society's visual culture. They exemplify the integration of aesthetics and daily life in Africa" (p. 7). The following studies illustrate how particular classes of objects used in everyday life in African societies are charged with artistic meaning:

**Baskets:** *The Dove's Footprints: Basketry Patterns in Matabeleland* (Locke 1995).
**Beads:** *Speaking with Beads: Zulu Arts from Southern Africa* (Morris 1994).
**Masks:** *African Art: An Introduction* (Duerden 1974).
**Pots:** *Smashing Pots: Works of Clay from Africa* (Barley 1994).
**Textiles:** *The Art of African Textiles: Technology, Tradition and Lurex* (Picton 1995); *Cloth that Does Not Die: The Meaning of Cloth in Bùnú Social Life* (Renne 1995); *North African Textiles* (Spring and Hudson 1995).

*Objects: Signs of Africa* (de Heusch 1996) features essays by ethnographers who insist that the form and function of personal objects in African societies must be studied in the complexity of their interrelationships. "It's time we acknowledge," editor Luc de Heusch notes, "that by allowing these [personal] objects to be plucked from their context by a certain type of art history — underpinned by considerable dealer interests — we continue to participate, to a greater or lesser degree, in their intellectual mutilation."

Rigan Gina, Robe of the Elephant

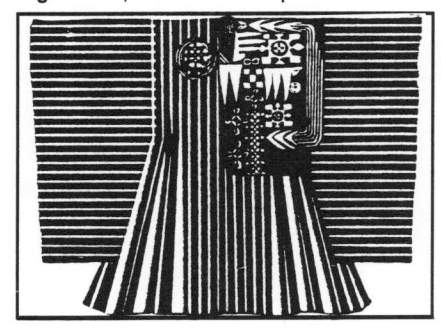

Baule Bracelet

Calabash designs: Djenne

> "African arts have always maintained an historical importance to social and political life projecting a strength of conviction that defines and distinguishes collective aesthetics."
> Michael A. Coronel and Patricia Crane Coronel, *Africa Today* 41:2, p. 4

Published on the occasion of the "Hidden Treasures" exhibition at the Musée royal de l'Afrique centrale in Tervuren, Belgium, de Heusch's volume focuses on the art of personal objects in Western and Central Africa.

## African art and politics

The relationship between politics and a variety of forms of artistic expression in African societies is the subject of the fortieth anniversary edition of the journal *Africa Today*: "Arts and Politics in Africa," *Africa Today* 41, no. 2 (1994). Articles deal with the use of "factory printed textiles" in party politics in Côte d'Ivoire, the politics of performance arts in two areas of Mali, interpretations of the role and function of art in Igbo society (as seen in the works of Chinua Achebe), and the politics of exhibitions of African art.

The powerful role of art in the long struggle against apartheid in South Africa is described and illustrated in the following:

- "Art Against Apartheid: Works for Freedom." *IKON: Creativity and Change* 2, nos. 5 and 6 (1986). This collaborative publishing effort between Art Against Apartheid and the publishers of *IKON* magazine pays tribute to the "extraordinary human strength" of activists in the anti-apartheid struggle through the writings and artistic creations of cultural workers from South Africa and the United States.
- *Resistance Art in South Africa* (Williamson 1989). Artist and activist Sue Williamson illustrates how South African artists (black *and* white) used murals, posters, T-shirt-art, comic strips, graffiti, sculpture, paintings, and linocuts to give expression to a culture of resistance to apartheid during the 1980s.

## Country/region focus

Studies of the visual arts in various countries and regions of Africa are featured in the following:

**Benin and Nigeria:** *The Yoruba Artist: New Theoretical Perspectives on African Arts* (Abiodun et al. 1994).

**Egypt:** *Discovering Ancient Egypt* (David 1994); *Egypt: Ancient Culture, Modern Land* (Malek 1993); *Life of the Ancient Egyptians* (Strouhal 1992); *Monuments of Egypt* (Porter 1990).

**Equatorial Africa:** *East of the Atlantic, West of the Congo: Art from Equatorial Africa* (Siroto 1995).

**Zaire:** *African Reflections: Art from Northeastern Zaire* (Schildkrout and Keim 1990); *Remembering the Present: Painting and Popular History in Zaire* (Fabian 1996).

**Zimbabwe:** *The Hunter's Vision: The Prehistoric Art of Zimbabwe* (Garlake 1995); *Life in Stone: Zimbabwean Sculpture, Birth of a Contemporary Art Form* (Sultan 1994); and *Zimbabwe: Talking Stones*, a videotape distributed by Films for the Humanities and Sciences (Princeton, N.J.).

## Topical issues

**Commerce:** *African Art in Transit* (Steiner 1994) explores the "commodification" and circulation of African art objects in the international art market and analyzes the role of the African middleman who links those who produce and supply works of art in Africa with those who buy and collect so-called "primitive" art in Europe and the United States. On related themes, see Patricia Crane Coronel's essay, "African Art from Earth to Pedestal," in "African Art, Film and Literature," *Africa Today* 36, no. 2 (1989). Coronel explores the ramifications of removing traditional African sculpture from indigenous cultures and isolating it in private collections, storing it in foreign museums, or selling it through auction houses around the world. A related work examines why African artifacts are "disappearing" at a rate perhaps unmatched in any other part of the world: *Plundering Africa's Past* (Schmidt and McIntosh 1996).

**Vodun:** Two recent studies examine the significance of artistic creations in one of the oldest — and most misunderstood — traditions in Africa, the *vodun* (or *voodoo*) cultures of North and West Africa.

- In *African Vodun: Art, Psychology, and Power* (Blier 1995) Harvard University professor Suzanne Preston Blier contributes a lengthy scholarly treatise on "vodun empowerment arts" in two West African nations, Benin and Togo, analyzing the interpenetration of art, society, and psychology in these West African societies.
- *Vital: Three Contemporary African Artists* (Nesbitt 1995) examines the relationship between art and vodun in the works of three contemporary African artists who share a common interest in trance, the rituals, and cultural significance of voodoo, Farid Belkahia, Touhami Ennadre, and Cyprien Tokoudagba.

## Artists

Portraits of individual African artists appear in two books that are at opposite poles in style and intended audience: (1) *Native Artists of Africa* (Moore 1993) is a children's book with five chapters and activity pages on a rug weaver, a painter, a traditional dancer, a basket weaver, and a singer-poet-songwriter-performer from five different areas of the African continent. (2) *Nigerian Artists: A Who's Who and Bibliography* (Kelly 1993) is a weighty library reference volume with biographical profiles and bibliographies of more than 350 twentieth-century professional artists from one African nation, Nigeria.

The life and influence of Nike Davies, one of the few African women artists known internationally in contemporary art circles, are chronicled in *The Woman with the Artistic Brush: A Life History of Yoruba Batki Artist Nike Davies* (Vaz 1995) and a videotape entitled *Batiks by Nike* (Video and Film Distribution, Student Services Bldg., University of South Florida, Tampa, FL 33620, USA).

*The African Dream: Visions of Love and Sorrow: The Art of John Muafangejo* (Levinson 1992) celebrates the life and artistic creations of John Ndevasia Muafangejo (1941-1987). Born in southern Angola in the early 1940s (the date is uncertain), Muafangejo was steeped in the rich cultural traditions of the Kwanyamas, the largest of the eight Owambo groups whose territory now forms part of southern Angola and northern Namibia. Evidence of these cultural traditions, combined with those of the Christian faith that has had a significant influence on Kwanyama society, is found in abundance in the woodcuts and linocuts for which Muagangejo gained international recognition.

# THE VOICE OF WOMEN
## Writers, artists, and musicians

**M**y great hope for African women, South African author Sindiwe Magona writes, "is that one day they will come into their own. That is why I chose to write." As African women struggle to claim their rightful place in African society and in the world, women writers, visual artists, and musicians chart the course of this struggle in a rich variety of artistic works. Through prose, poetry, drama, sculpture, painting, music, and many other forms, African women speak *their* thoughts and share *their* perceptions about their lives and their societies.

"Our problem," Adeola James writes, in her introduction to *In Their Own Voices* (James 1990), "is that we have listened so rarely to women's voices, the noises of men having drowned us out in every sphere of life, including the arts. Yet women too are artists, and are endowed with a special sensitivity and compassion, necessary to creativity" (p. 2).

The resource materials in this chapter introduce the rich variety of artistic works produced by African women. They bring women's voices "to the fore," in Adeola James's words, "not as a token concession, but as a moving and determining force" (ibid.).

## Women's words

The voice of African women is heard through transcriptions of oral testimony, as well as through published literary works.

In *Writing Women's Worlds: Bedouin Stories* (Abu-Lughod 1993) anthropologist Lila Abu-Lughod gives women in a small Bedouin community in Egypt an opportunity to share "conversations, narratives, arguments, songs, [and] reminiscences" about marriage, reproduction, honor, shame, and other elements of their everyday lives. Oral histories from Egypt are also featured in *Khul-Khaal: Five Egyptian Women Tell Their Stories* (Atiya 1982).

*The World and the Word: Tales and Observations from the Xhosa Oral Tradition* (Zenani and Scheub 1992) showcases the rich oral tradition of the

**Nongenile Masithathu Zenani**
**Storyteller of the Xhosa people**

Courtesy: Professor Harold Scheub,
University of Wisconsin Press

Xhosa people of South Africa in the person of master storyteller and healer Nongenile Masithathu Zenani. Professor Harold Scheub (African languages and literature, University of Wisconsin-Madison) worked with Zenani over a period of 15 years to record her rich tales of the origins of Xhosa customs, how they order their world and deal with transgressors, and how they manage all of life's transitions from birth to death. *The World and the Word* combines Zenani's tales together with her own commentary and analyses and Scheub's introductory comments and photographs.

The fall 1994 issue of *Research in African Literatures* (25, no. 3) was devoted entirely to the subject of women as oral artists. "There are clearly many barriers left to be broken," guest editors Molara Ogundipe-Leslie and Carole Boyce Davies observe, "if we are to move to a more developed understanding of the entire field of African literatures" (p. 2). Recognizing the important role that women play in Africa's oral tradition—as the essays in this periodical do—destroys one of the barriers to a full appreciation of Africa's literary heritage.

*In Their Own Voices: African Women Writers Talk* (James 1990) provides a convenient transition between oral histories and written literary works by giving African women writers a forum in which to reflect upon their literary works in their own words. Adeola James, Head of the Department of English at the University of Guyana, interviews 15 women authors and literary critics seeking to uncover "the particular cultural constraints the writers have had to overcome as Africans and women" and to illuminate and clarify other influences on their work (e.g., how does the writer cope with the multifaceted roles of parent, wife, and writer). "In the course of the interviews," Dr. James notes, "we discover that women writers have been no less concerned than men to articulate and denounce the poverty, corruption, and destructive practices that have impeded development in Africa. At the same time, women writers appear to treat more intimately the themes of love and death, transcendence and the struggle to rise above the traditional limitations responsible for women's underdevelopment and oppression" (p. 4).

Literary works by individual African women authors are available through the African Books Collective (Oxford) and from publishers such as James Currey (London), Heinemann (Oxford and Portsmouth, N.H.), and Africa World Press (Lawrenceville, N.J.). See, especially, the African Writers series (Heinemann) and the African Women Writers series (Africa World Press).

Recommended anthologies of literature by African women are
- *Anthology: Over One Hundred Works by Zimbabwe Women Writers* (Kitson 1994);
- *Daughters of Africa: An International Anthology of Words and Writings by Women of African Descent from the Ancient Egyptian to the Present* (Busby 1992);

---

### Independence

When I got home
from the war
I realised
our tradition had not changed
We were still second to men
being told
what to do

We had to wash
and to cook
and to clean the house
we had to bear a child every year

When I risked my life
during the war
I thought
liberation
was meant for men and women

Indeed
we got rid of the white oppressor
but today I see
we women are still not free

But as a person cannot walk
with only one leg
this country cannot develop
without us!
We are Zimbabwe's other leg
we are needed oh yes, we are!

Equality
Dignity
and love
Equality!

Danhiko Women's Group (Zimbabwe)

Courtesy: *IDEX Update*, International Development Exchange (San Francisco)

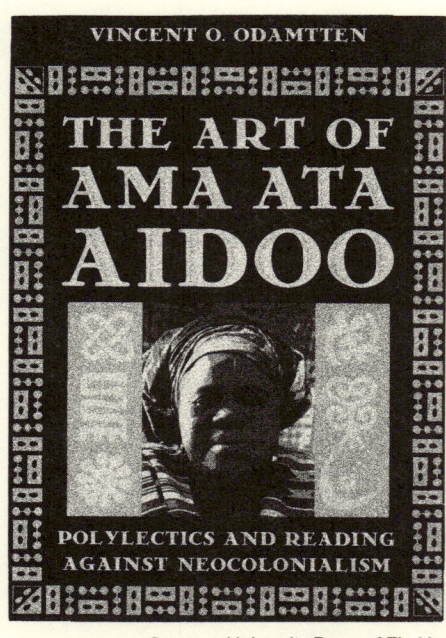

*Courtesy University Press of Florida*

- *The Heinemann Book of African Women's Poetry* (Chipasula and Chipasula 1995).
- *The Heinemann Book of African Women's Writing* (Bruner 1993).
- *Unwinding Threads: Writing by Women in Africa* (Bruner 1983).

In addition there are two collections that bring together writings by Black women writers in Africa and in the Diaspora: *Binding Cultures: Black Women Writers in Africa and the Diaspora* (Wilentz 1992) and *Motherlands: Black Women's Writing from Africa, the Caribbean and South Asia* (Nasta 1991).

See also *Third World Women's Literatures: A Dictionary and Guide to Materials in English* (Fister 1995).

## Literary criticism

In the published edition of her doctoral dissertation, *Gender Voices and Choices: Redefining Women in Contemporary African Fiction* (Chukukere 1995), Gloria Chukukere argues cogently and passionately for due recognition to be given to the enormous contributions that African women have made both in life and literature. Chukukere analyzes the literary works of male and female authors to make her case. Flora Nwapa, Buchi Emecheta, and Bessie Head are among the African women authors she discusses.

Other critical studies of African women authors include

- *Africa Wo/man Palava: The Nigerian Novel by Women* (Ogunyemi 1996).
- *The Art of Ama Ata Aidoo: Polylectics and Reading against Neocolonialism* (Odamtten 1994).
- *Bessie Head: Thunder Behind Her Ears. Her Life and Writing* (Eilersen 1995)

### AFRICA THROUGH THE EYES OF WOMEN

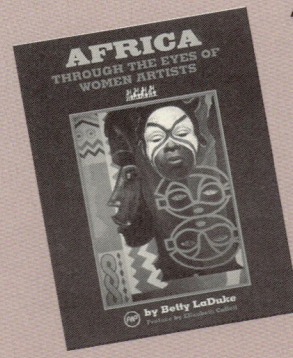

Artist, critic, and educator Betty LaDuke has compiled two illustrated books that showcase the artistic achievements of women throughout the African continent and in the Diaspora.

In *Africa through the Eyes of Women Artists* (LaDuke 1991) LaDuke interviews the artists and presents representative selections from their works. Women from Nigeria, Mali, Senegal, Morocco, Egypt, South Africa, Uganda, and other areas, are represented.

"The art expression of the twelve women artists," LaDuke notes, "contains a variety of images and themes that reveal multifaceted roles within contemporary African society....Their art is composed of intimate and universal themes that touch upon all our lives and expand our vision of humanity" (p. 1).

*Africa: Women's Art, Women's Lives* (LaDuke 1997) grew out of LaDuke's visits to Burkina Faso, Mali, Togo, Cameroon, Zimbabwe, and Eritrea, from 1990 to 1994. LaDuke concludes that whether women in these countries weave, sew, sketch, paint, create fabric applique or stone sculptures, their art work often incorporates the duality of myth and reality as the women artists express their hopes, fears, humor, and frustrations.

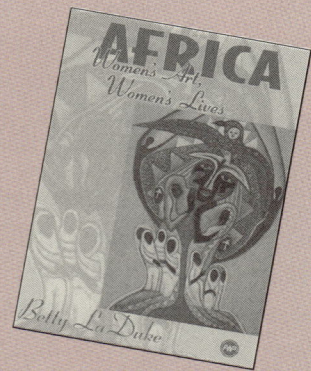

- *Emerging Perspectives on Ama Ata Aidoo* (Azodo and Wilentz 1997).
- *Emerging Perspectives on Buchi Emecheta* (Umeh 1996).
- *Emerging Perspectives on Flora Nwapa* (Umeh 1997).
- *Gender in African Women's Writing: Identity, Sexuality, and Difference* (Mfah-Abbenyi 1997).
- *The Healing Imagination of Olive Schreiner: Beyond South African Colonialism* (Berkman 1989).
- *Men, Women, and God(s): Nawal El Saadawi and Arab Feminist Poetics* (Malti-Douglas 1995).
- *Nigerian Female Writers: A Critical Perspective* (Otokunefor and Nwodo 1989).
- *The Novels of Nadine Gordimer: History from the Inside* (Clingman 1993).
- *A Poetics of Resistance: Women Writing in El Salvador, South Africa, and the United States* (DeShazer 1994).

## Personal stories

The personal stories of African women—told in autobiographies and other literary forms—offer a window on African society as seen through the eyes of women. See, for example, *Aman: The Story of a Somali Girl* (Barnes and Boddy 1994); *Lives of Courage: Women for a New South Africa* (Russell 1989); *Doria Shafik: Egyptian Feminist. A Woman Apart* (Nelson 1996); *The Abandoned Baobab: The Autobiography of a Senegalese Woman* (Bugul 1991); *Woman Between Two Worlds: Portrait of an Ethiopian Rural Leader* (Olmstead 1997); and *Singing Away the Hunger: The Autobiography of an African Woman* (Kendall 1997).

## Music

The Ladyslipper music catalog is a one-stop source for recordings of music by African women vocal and instrumental artists: Ladyslipper, P.O. Box 3124, Durham, NC 27715 USA. The Ladyslipper on-line catalog is available on the Internet at <http://www.ladyslipper.org>. See also the catalogs of distributors listed in the music chapter in this guide.

## Visual arts

In addition to the books by Betty LaDuke (see above), three videotapes introduce the lives and work of African women visual artists. These are:
- *African Art and Women Artists*. 17-minute video from Films for the Humanities and Sciences (New Jersey)
- *The Art of the Weya Women* (Noy 1992)
- *Batiks by Nike*, a companion video to the book *The Woman with the Artistic Brush: A Life History of Yoruba Batik Artist Nike Davies* (Vaz 1995) from University of South Florida (Tampa, Florida).

**"Acada," life-size cement, 1979
by Princess Elizabeth Olowu, Nigeria**

Photograph courtesy of Betty LaDuke (Ashland, Oregon)
from *Africa through the Eyes of Women Artists*, p. 23

# WOMEN IN AFRICA
## Weaving new patterns of life and work

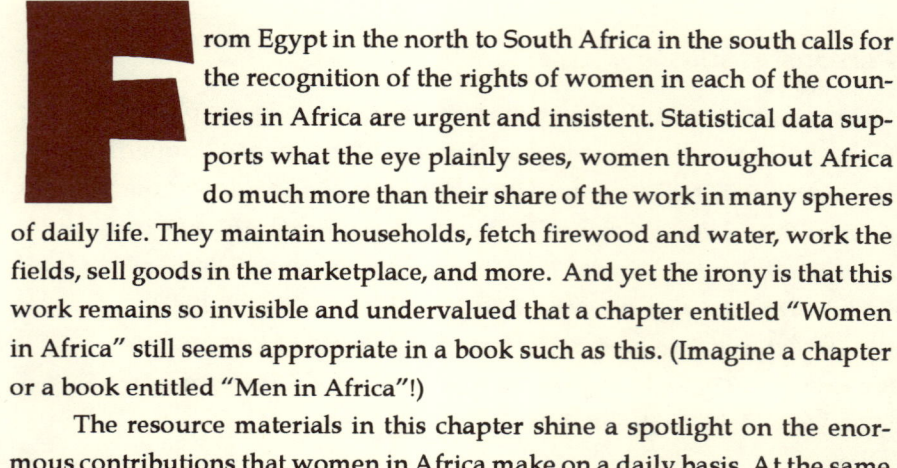

From Egypt in the north to South Africa in the south calls for the recognition of the rights of women in each of the countries in Africa are urgent and insistent. Statistical data supports what the eye plainly sees, women throughout Africa do much more than their share of the work in many spheres of daily life. They maintain households, fetch firewood and water, work the fields, sell goods in the marketplace, and more. And yet the irony is that this work remains so invisible and undervalued that a chapter entitled "Women in Africa" still seems appropriate in a book such as this. (Imagine a chapter or a book entitled "Men in Africa"!)

The resource materials in this chapter shine a spotlight on the enormous contributions that women in Africa make on a daily basis. At the same time they underline the fact that "women's work" continues to be circumscribed by traditional boundaries, even in situations where they have been actively involved in largescale political movements such as in South Africa. Viviene Taylor, National Social Welfare Policy Coordinator of the African National Congress, notes that "Women in South Africa are in the majority and have played a crucial role in the liberation struggle, yet they are underrepresented in all spheres of life except at the lower end....The political and economic empowerment of women, both as representatives of the majority...and as representatives of the most exploited and oppressed class must be given concrete form and content" (*Development* 1994:2, p. 36).

The books and other resource materials in this chapter also call attention to the fact that women in Africa are defining and working out their "liberation" in their own terms. Mercy Amba Oduyoye describes the unique character and trajectory of women's liberation in Africa in these terms: "While the [UN-sponsored] Nairobi meeting was in session [in 1985], African men were still snickering. But something new had touched the women of Africa, and they began to voice their presence. Women were standing up, abandoning the crouched positions from which their life-breath stimulated

Courtesy: SEDOS (Rome).

the wood fires that burned under the earthenware pots of vegetables they had grown and harvested. The pots, too, were their handiwork. Standing up straight, women of Africa stretched their hands to the global sisterhood of life-loving women. In no uncertain terms, African women announced their position on the liberation struggle and their solidarity with other women." Oduyoye goes on to describe what *their* position and *their* solidarity means in the African context. See *Daughters of Anowa: African Women and Patriarchy* (Oduyoye 1995), pp. 1-2 and following.

## Women in the world

Several global resources on women are recommended for the comparative background they provide for the study of women's rights in Africa. See, especially, *The Challenge of Local Feminisms: Women's Movements in Global Perspective* (Basu 1995); *Women, the Environment and Sustainable Development: Towards a Theoretical Synthesis* (Braidotti et al. 1994); *Women and Children First: Environment, Poverty, and Sustainable Development* (Steady 1993); *Women and Politics Worldwide* (Nelson and Chowdhury 1994); *Women at the Center: Development Issues and Practices for the 1990s* (Young et al. 1993); *Women in Developing Economies: Making Visible the Invisible* (Massiah 1993); *Women and Revolution in Africa, Asia, and the New World* (Tétreault 1994); and *The Women and International Development Annual*, Volume 3 (Gallin et al. 1993).

Volumes in the Women and World Development series from Zed Books (London) are uniformly good introductions to aspects of the women's movement worldwide. Titles published include *Women and the Environment*, by Annabel Rodda; *Women and the World Economic Crisis*, by Jeanne Vickers; *Women and Health*, by Patricia Smyke; *Refugee Women*, by Susan F. Martin; *Women and Literacy*, by Marcela Ballara; *Women and Human Rights*, by Katarina Tomasevski; *Women and Work*, by Susan Bullock; and *Women and Empowerment*, by Marilee Karl.

Oxfam (UK and Ireland) publishes a Focus on Gender series of booklets, all edited by Caroline Sweetman. See *Women and Rights* (1995), *Women and Culture* (1995), and *Women, Employment and Exclusion* (1996).

Two periodicals published by and about women in Third World regions are noteworthy: *Women's World* (Isis-WICCE, Kampala) and *Women in Action* (Isis International, Santiago and Quezon City). For names and contact information for additional organizations and periodicals, see *Directory of Third World Women's Publications* (Isis International 1990) and *Womanwise: A Popular Guide and Directory to Women and Development in the "Third World"* (Gray 1993).

## Women in Africa

French historian Catherine Coquery-Vidrovitch's *African Women: A Modern History* (1997) is the most up-to-date and accessible introduction to "the full

*Credit:* UNDP Report 1990.
Used in "Is Population the Problem?"
Community Aid Abroad (Fitzroy, Australia)

### African Women and Development: A History

(Snyder and Tadesse 1995)

This book chronicles the growth of the women's movement in Africa against the background of the establishment and development of one of the most influential women's organizations in Africa, the African Training and Research Centre for Women, now the African Centre for Women, Addis Ababa, Ethiopia).

"If there has been a momentous period in the history of African women," Gertrude Mongella, Secretary-General of the Fourth World Conference on Women, writes in her preface to *African Women and Development*, "it is in the last thirty years covered by this book. For the first time, the spotlight has shone on the ordinary woman of the continent, highlighting the crucial roles she plays in her community and nation. In this book the authentic voices of women are heard, and their aspirations and their struggles for survival are described.

"The African woman has always worked outside her home, in the fields, in marketplaces and in community action. This book tells how a United Nations entity participated in bringing her rich experience to centre-stage, to the national, regional and global forums."

---

history of women in sub-Saharan Africa" from the eve of the colonial period to the present. The book's 20-page bibliography is particularly useful: "Bibliography: African Women in Modern History."

Women's issues in northern Africa are explored in titles such as *Arab Women: Old Boundaries, New Frontiers* (Tucker 1993); *Both Right and Left Handed: Arab Women Talk About Their Lives* (Shaaban 1988); *Modernizing Women: Gender and Social Change in the Middle East* (Moghadam 1993); *Women in Middle Eastern History: Shifting Boundaries in Sex and Gender* (Keddie and Baron 1991); and *Women of the Arab World: The Coming Challenge* (Toubia 1988).

Books that survey the status of women in northern *and* sub-Saharan Africa are relatively few and are somewhat dated. See, for example, *African Women: Their Struggle for Economic Independence* (Obbo 1980), *Women and Class in Africa* (Robertson and Berger 1986), and *Women of Africa: Roots of Oppression* (Cutrufelli 1983). Studies of "women in Africa" have matured beyond the stage of generalities (true as they may once have been) to become more focused investigations of particular issues and regional/national situations such as those listed below.

### Issues

See other chapters throughout this directory for resource materials that link women and issues such as development, environment, and population.

**Agriculture:** *The Shamba Is Like a Child: Women and Agriculture in Tanzania* (Aarnink and Kingma 1991).

**Circumcision:** *Cutting the Rose. Female Genital Mutilation: The Practice and Its Prevention* (Dorkenoo 1994); *The Falling Dawadawa Tree: Female Circumcision in Developing Ghana* (Knudsen 1994); *Female Genital Mutilation: Proposals for Change* (Dorkenoo and Elworthy 1992); *Prisoners of Ritual: An Odyssey into Female Genital Circumcision in Africa* (Lightfoot-Klein 1989).

**Development (economic):** *African Market Women and Economic Power: The Role of Women in African Economic Development* (House-Midamba and Ekechi 1995); *Money-Go-Rounds: The Importance of Rotating Savings and Credit Associations for Women* (Ardener and Burman 1995). Part 1: Africa (pp. 21-124).

**Development (sustainable):** *Women and Sustainable Development in Africa* (James 1995).

**Family law:** *Uncovering Reality: Excavating Women's Rights in African Family Law* (Armstrong et al. 1992).

**Gender violence:** *Gender Violence and Women's Human Rights in Africa* (Center for Women's Global Leadership 1994).

**Health:** *Women and Health in Africa* (Turshen 1991).

**Markets:** *Cultivating Customers: Market Women in Harare, Zimbabwe* (Horn 1994); *Onions Are My Husband: Survival and Accumulation by West African Market Women* (Clark 1994).

## Region/country studies

**East/Central Africa:** *Strategies of Slaves and Women: Life-Stories from East/Central Africa* (Wright 1993).

**Southern Africa:** *Struggling over Scarce Resources: Women and Maintenance in Southern Africa* (Armstrong 1992); *The Legal Situation of Women in Southern Africa* (Stewart and Armstrong 1990).

**Cameroon:** *Men Own the Fields, Women Own the Crops: Gender and Power in the Cameroon Grassfields* (Goheen 1996).

**Egypt:** *The Nubians of West Aswan: Village Women in the Midst of Change* (Jennings 1995); *Women in Society: Egypt* (Samaan 1993).

**Ethiopia/Eritrea:** *A Painful Season and A Stubborn Hope: The Odyssey of an Eritrean Mother* (Tesfagiorgis 1992).

**Ghana:** *The Falling Dawadawa Tree: Female Circumcision in Developing Ghana* (Knudsen 1994).

**Nigeria:** *The Role of Nigerian Women in Politics: Past and Present* (Uchendu 1993); *Women in Nigeria Today* (Bappa et al. 1985).

**South Africa:** *Women and Resistance in South Africa* (Walker 1991); *African Women: Three Generations* (Mathabane 1994); *Women in Society: South Africa* (Rissik 1993).

**Tanzania:** *The Shamba Is Like a Child: Women and Agriculture in Tanzania* (Aarnink and Kingma 1991).

## Reference resources

For additional sources of information on women in Africa see the following bibliographies: *African Women: A General Bibliography, 1976-1985* (Bullwinkle 1989); *African Women in Development: An Annotated Bibliography* (African Training and Research Centre for Women 1990); *Women in Botswana: An Annotated Bibliography* (Erickson 1993); *Women in Development in Southern Africa: Botswana, Lesotho, Malawi and Zambia: An Annotated Bibliography* (CTA Technical Centre for Agricultural and Rural Cooperation 1991); *Women in International Studies: A Bibliographic Guide* (Dickstein 1989); and *Feminism Worldwide: A Bibliography* (Nordquist 1996).

*Bibliographies for African Studies, 1987-1993* (Scheven 1994) contains country-specific bibliographies on women in Botswana, Ghana, Lesotho, Liberia, Mali, Nigeria, Rwanda, South Africa, Tunisia, Uganda, Zambia. The bibliographies and discussion papers published by the Zimbabwe Women's Resource Centre and Network (Harare) cover numerous issues (see sidebar).

Handy reference sources for information on the situation of women worldwide are *Discrimination Against Women: A Global Survey of the Economic, Educational, Social and Political Status of Women* (Rhoodie 1989); *The Human Rights Watch Global Report on Women's Human Rights* (Human Rights Watch 1995); and *Sisterhood Is Global: The International Women's Movement Anthology* (Morgan 1996).

---

**Zimbabwe Women's Resource Centre and Network** (ZWRCN) is a nongovernmental organization that was established in 1990 in order "to enhance the position of women in Zimbabwe" through the collection and dissemination of written material and information. Since mid-1991 ZWRCN has been compiling and publishing bibliographies, discussion papers, and workshop reports on issues related to gender and development.

**ZWRCN bibliographies:**
- *Women and health* (1991)
- *Women's income-generating projects* (1991)
- *Women entrepreneurs* (1991)
- *Women and housing* (1992)
- *Women and AIDS* (1993)
- *Women and environment* (1993)
- *Women and education* (1993)
- *Women and structural adjustment* (1994)
- *Abortion* (1994)
- *Women and land* (1994)
- *Women, science and technology* (1994)
- *Gender and development theories and gender analysis* (1994)
- *Research theories* (1994)

**ZWRCN discussion papers:**
- *Women's income-generating projects* (Chigudu 1991)
- *Gender and the media* (Zinanga 1992)
- *Collection-building and dissemination* (Poulsen 1992)
- *Strategies for empowering women* (Chigudu 1992)
- *From WID to GAD. More than a change in terminology?* (Zwart 1992). (Note: WID = women in development; GAD = gender and development.)
- *Participatory self-evaluation: A tool for empowering women at the community level* (Chigudu 1992)
- *Women, literacy and education* (Silverthorne 1993)
- *Gender, environment and sustainable development: Zimbabwe's case* (Mvududu 1993)
- *The gender dimension of access and land-use rights in Zimbabwe: Evidence to the Land Commission* (January 1994)

**ZWRCN workshop reports:**
- *Women's income-generating projects* (August 1991)
- *Women's income-generating projects: Empowerment* (September 1992)

# SUPPLEMENTARY RESOURCES

## General Studies

*Africa* (Bever 1996)
*Africa* (Martin and O'Meara 1996)
*Africa: Endurance and Change South of the Sahara* (Coquery-Vidrovitch 1988)
*Africa: The Challenge of Transformation* (McCarthy 1995)
*Africa and Africans* (Bohannan and Curtin 1995)
*Africa and the Modern World* (Wallerstein 1986)
*Africa Betrayed* (Ayittey 1992)
*Africa Now: People, Policies, Institutions* (Ellis 1996)
*Africa to 2000 and Beyond: Imperative Political and Economic Agenda* (Ndegwa 1994)
*Africa Within the World: Beyond Dispossession and Dependence* (Adedeji 1993)
*Africa's Way: A Journey from the Past* (Cockcroft 1990)
*African Intellectual Heritage: A Book of Sources* (Asante and Abarry 1996)
*African Philosophy: Myth and Reality* (Hountondji 1996)
*The African Possibility in Global Power Struggle* (Nwankwo 1995)
*African Socialism or Socialist Africa?* (Babu 1981)
*African Youth Speak* (Darmani 1994)
*Agenda for Africa's Economic Renewal* (Ndulu et al. 1996)
*At the Desert's Edge: Oral Histories from the Sahel* (Cross n.d.)
*The Atlas of African Affairs* (Griffiths 1994)
*Between State and Civil Society in Africa* (Osaghae 1994)
*Black Africa: The Economic and Cultural Basis for a Federated State* (Diop 1987)
*Black Man's Burden: Africa and the Curse of the Nation-State* (Davidson 1992)
*Burning Hunger: Three Decades of Personal Struggles Against Poverty: A West African Experience* (Knight 1994)
*Capitalism and Slavery* (Williams 1994)
*The Cultural Unity of Black Africa: The Domains of Patriarchy and of Matriarchy in Classical Antiquity* (Diop 1978)
*Economic Change and Political Liberalization in Sub-Saharan Africa* (Widner 1994)
*Enough Is Enough! For an Alternative Diagnosis of the African Crisis* (Lopes 1994)
*Global Dimensions of the African Diaspora* (Harris 1993)
*I Am Because We Are: Readings in Black Philosophy* (Hord 1995)
*The Idea of Africa* (Mudimbe 1994)
*Not Out of Africa: How Afrocentrism Became an Excuse to Teach Myth as History* (Lefkowitz 1996)
*Organizing African Unity* (Woronoff 1970)
*Political Domination in Africa: Reflections on the Limits of Power* (Chabal 1986)
*The Quest for Regional Cooperation in Southern Africa: Problems and Issues* (Mhone 1993)
*Roots of Time: A Portrait of African Life and Culture* (Jefferson and Skinner 1990)
*The Search for Africa: History, Culture, Politics* (Davidson 1994)
*The Ties That Bind: African-American Consciousness of Africa* (Magubane 1987)
*The Two Faces of Civil Society: NGOs and Politics in Africa* (Ndegwa 1996)
*United States Foreign Policy Toward Africa: Incrementalism, Crisis and Change* (Schraeder 1994)

## Historical Studies

*Africa Since 1800* (Oliver 1994)
*African Decolonization* (Wilson 1994)
*African History for Beginners* (Boyd 1991)
*African History on File* (Diagram Visual Information 1994)
*African People in World History* (Clarke 1993)
*The Africans: A Triple Heritage* (Mazrui 1986)
*Africans: The History of a Continent* (Iliffe 1995)
*Black Folk Here and There: An Essay in History and Anthropology* (Drake 1990)
*A Concise History of Africa* (Garfield 1994)
*The Decolonization of Africa* (Birmingham 1995)
*Dictionary of Portuguese-African Civilization. Vol. 1: From Discovery to Independence* (Nuñez 1994)
*General History of Africa* (Various editors 1981- )
*A History of Africa* (Jaffe 1985)
*History of Africa* (Shillington 1989)
*History of Southern Africa* (Omer-Cooper 1994)
*The Making of Modern Africa. Vol. 1: The Nineteenth Century* (Afigbo 1986)
*Modern Africa: A Social and Political History* (Davidson 1994)

*The New Atlas of African History* (Freeman-Grenville 1991)
*The Scramble for Africa: White Man's Conquest of the Dark Continent from 1876 to 1912* (Pakenham 1991)
*A Short History of Africa* (Oliver and Fage 1988)

## Geographical Studies

*Africa South of the Sahara: A Geographical Interpretation* (Stock 1995)
*The Atlas of the Arab World: Geopolitics and Society* (Boustani and Fargues 1990)
*The New Atlas of African History* (Freeman-Grenville 1991)
*The Peopling of Africa: A Geographic Interpretation* (Newman 1995)

## Organization Guides and Directories

*The African Book World and Press: A Directory* (Zell 1989)
*African Directory: Human Rights Organizations in Sub-Saharan Africa* (Human Rights Internet and Netherlands Institute of Human Rights 1996)
*Directory of African and Afro-American Studies in the United States* (Rana and Disetefano 1987)
*Directory of Development Research and Training Institutes in Africa* (International Development Information Network 1992)
*Handbook of Regional Organizations in Africa* (Söderbaum 1996)
*Historical Dictionary of International Organizations in Sub-Saharan Africa* (DeLancy and Mays 1994)
*Historical Dictionary of Refugee and Disaster Relief Organizations* (Gorman 1994)
*International Directory of African Studies Research* (Baker 1994)
*The SCOLMA Directory of Libraries and Special Collections on Africa in the United Kingdom and Europe* (French 1993)
*The Southern African Development Directory* (Barnard 1994)

## Resource and Research Guides

*The African Studies Companion: A Resource Guide and Directory* (Zell and Lomer 1997)
*African Studies Information Resources Directory* (Gosebrink 1986)
*Handbook of Political Science Research on Sub-Saharan Africa. Trends from the 1960s to the 1990s* (DeLancey 1992)
*Third World Resource Directory, 1994-1995. A Guide to Print, Audiovisual and Organizational Resources on Africa, Asia and Pacific, Latin America and Caribbean, and the Middle East* (Fenton and Heffron 1994)

## Bibliographies

*Bibliographies for African Studies, 1970-1986* (Scheven 1988)
*Bibliographies for African Studies, 1987-1993* (Scheven 1994)
*Publishing and Book Development in Sub-Saharan Africa: An Annotated Bibliography* (Zell and Lomer 1996)
*Zimbabwe Books in Print 1995* (Zimbabwe Book Publishers' Association 1995)

## Statistical Studies and Handbooks

*The African Business Handbook: A Practical Guide to Business Resources for U.S./Africa Trade and Investment* (Sudarkasa 1993)
*African Development Indicators 1996* (World Bank 1996)
*African Economic and Financial Data* (United Nations Development Programme and the World Bank 1989)
*African Industry in Figures, 1993* (United Nations Industrial Development Organization 1993)
*Biennial Report of the Executive Secretary, 1992-1993* (United Nations Economic Commission for Africa 1994)
*Black Africa: A Comparative Handbook* (Morrison 1989)
*Economic Report on Africa 1994* (United Nations Economic Commission for Africa 1994)
*The State of World Rural Poverty: A Profile of Africa* (Haralambous 1993)
*The State of World Rural Poverty: A Profile of the Near East and North Africa* (Abdouli 1994)
*UN Economic Commission for Africa: Annual Report* (United Nations Economic Commission for Africa 1994)

For reference titles about the nations and peoples of Africa see the relevant chapters in the *Africa World Press Guide*.

## Periodicals

The following is a very selective list of periodicals from and about Africa. We include periodicals mentioned in the body of the *Africa World Press Guide* along with a few titles that are not likely to be known to most readers.

*AFJN Issue Papers*. Africa Faith and Justice Network, P.O. Box 29378, Washington, DC 20017, USA.
*Africa Access Review of K-12 Materials*. Africa Access, 2204 Quinton Rd., Silver Spring, MD 20910, USA.
*The Africa Book Centre Book Review*. Africa Book Centre, 38 King St., Covent Garden, London WC2E 8JT, England.
*Africa Recovery Briefing Papers*. UN Department of Information, Communications and Project Management Division, United Nations, Rm. S-931, New York, NY 10017, USA.
*Africa Today*. Africa Today, c/o Graduate School of International Studies, University of Denver, Denver, CO 80208, USA.
*AfricaNews Online*. Africa News Service, P.O. Box 3851, Durham, NC 27702, USA.
*African Human Rights Newsletter*. African Centre for Democracy and Human Rights Studies, Kairaba Ave., K.S.M.D., The Gambia.
*African Publishing Review*. African Publishers' Network (APNET), P.O. Box 3773, Harare, Zimbabwe.
*African Topics: Monitoring Human Rights, Democracy and Development*. Periscope Communications, Skillion Commercial Centre, Ste. 106, Lomond Grove, London SE5 7HN, England.
*APIC Background Paper*. Africa Policy Information Center, 110 Maryland Ave., NE, #509, Washington, DC 20002, USA.
*CAFA Newsletter*. Committee for Academic Freedom in Africa, c/o Sylvia Federici, New College, 130 Hofstra University, Hempstead, NY 11550, USA.
*Echo*. Association of African Women for Research and Development, B.P. 3304, Dakar, Senegal.

*EDICESA News.* Ecumenical Documentation and Information Centre for Eastern and Southern Africa, P.O. Box H94 Hatfield, Harare, Zimbabwe. Also: *EDICESA Briefing: A Bi-monthly Update on Human Rights and Refugees.*

*FocusAfrica.* Inter-Church Coalition on Africa, 129 St. Clair Ave. West, Toronto, ON Canada M4V 1N5.

*Empowerment.* Legal Research and Resource Development Centre, 386, Murtala Muhammed Way, Yaba, P.O. Box 75242, Victoria Island, Lagos, Nigeria.

*GenderReview: Kenya's Women and Development Quarterly.* Women and Media Project of Interlink Rural Information Service, P.O. Box 12871, Nairobi, Kenya.

*Human Rights Watch/Africa.* Human Rights Watch, 485 Fifth Ave., New York, NY 10017-6104, USA.

*Irohin: Bringing Africa to the Classroom.* University of Florida, Center for African Studies, 427 Grinter Hall, Gainesville, FL 32611, USA.

*Journal of Social Development in Africa.* School of Social Work, P/Bag 66022 Kopje, Harare, Zimbabwe.

*PRODDER Newsletter.* Programme for Development Research, P.O. Box 32410, Braamfontein, 2017, South Africa.

*Review of African Political Economy.* ROAPE Publications, P.O. Box 678, Sheffield S1 1BF, England.

*Sauti Ya Siti: Tanzania Women's Magazine.* Tanzania Media Women's Association, P.O. Box 8981, Dar es Salaam, Tanzania.

*Southern Africa Report.* Toronto Committee for the Liberation of Southern Africa, 603 1/2 Parliament St., Toronto, ON Canada M4X 1P9.

*Southscan: A Bulletin of Southern African Affairs.* SouthScan, P.O. Box 724, London N16 5RZ, England.

*Voices from Africa.* United Nations Non-Governmental Liaison Service, Palais des Nations, CH-1211 Geneva 10, Switzerland.

*Washington Notes on Africa.* Washington Office on Africa, 110 Maryland Ave., NE, Ste. 112, Washington, DC 20002, USA.

*WorldViews: A Quarterly Review of Resources for Education and Action.* WorldViews, 464 19th St., Oakland, CA 94612-2297, USA.

## Electronic Sources of Information

The July 1996 issue of *APIC Background Paper* (no. 6), entitled "Africa on the Internet: Starting Points for Policy Information," is a good place to begin a search for Africa-related information in electronic forms. See also:

*Africa South of the Sahara: Selected Internet Resources. An Annotated Guide for Students, Faculty, Librarians, Teachers, Journalists, Business People, and Others,* compiled by Karen Fung. Africa Collection, Hoover Library, Stanford University, Stanford, CA 94305, USA. Web site: http://www-sul.stanFord.edu/depts/ssrg/africa/guide.html.

*Internet Resources on Africa.* African Studies Center, University of Pennsylvania, 642 Williams Hall, Philadelphia, PA 19104-6305, USA. Web site: http://www.sas.upenn.edu/African_Studies/AS.html.

# AFRICAN LITERATURE

The following is a selection of titles of African novels and poetry. Books published in African countries are available internationally from the African Books Collective, The Jam Factory, 27 Park End St., Oxford OX1 1HU England.

Addresses for non-African publishers appear in the Directory of Organizations (below).

*Advance, Retreat.* Richard Rive. New York: St. Martin's Press, 1989. vii + 121 pp. ISBN 0-312-03689-2.

*African Laughter: Four Visits to Zimbabwe.* Doris Lessing. New York: HarperCollins Publishers, 1992. xii + 442 pp. ISBN 0-06-016854-4.

*African Stories.* Doris Lessing. New York: Simon and Schuster, 1981. 666 pp. ISBN 0-671-42809-8.

*And a Threefold Cord.* Alex La Guma. London: Kliptown Books, 1988. 112 pp. ISBN 0-904759-90-3.

*And They Didn't Die.* Lauretta Ngcobo. New York: George Braziller, 1991. 245 pp. ISBN 0-8076-1263-4.

*At The Desert's Edge: Oral Histories From The Sahel.* Nigel Cross and Rhiannon Barker, eds. London: Panos Publications, viii + 248 pp. ISBN 1-870670-26-4.

*Bai Bureh's Countrymen.* Masee Touré. London: Janus Publishing, 1995. ix + 128 pp. ISBN 1-85756-189-9.

*Black + Blues.* Kamau Brathwaite. New York: New Directions Publishing Corporation, 1995. Rev. ed. 69 pp. ISBN 0-8112-1313-7.

*The Blood of Our Silence.* Kelwyn Sole. Johannesburg: Ravan Press, 1988. 123 pp. ISBN 0-86975-338-x.

*Bloodsong: And Other Stories of South Africa.* Ernst Havemann. Boston: Houghton Mifflin, 1987. 134 pp. ISBN 0-395-43296-0.

*The Cardinals: With Meditations and Short Stories.* Bessie Head. Oxford: Heinemann Publishers, 1993. xvi + 141 pp. ISBN 0-435-90967-3.

*The Case of the Socialist Witchdoctor and Other Stories.* Hama Tuma. Oxford: Heinemann Publishers, 1993. x + 227 pp. ISBN 0-435-90590-2.

*Cemetery of Mind.* Dambudzo Marechera. Harare: Baobab Books, 1992. 222 pp. ISBN 0-908311-45-1. Distributed by African Books Collective (Oxford).

*Changes: A Love Story.* Ama Ata Aidoo. New York: Feminist Press, 1993. 196 pp. ISBN 1-55861-065-0.

*Children of Wax: African Folk Tales.* Alexander McCall Smith. New York: Interlink Books, 1991. viii + 119 pp. ISBN 0-940793-73-3.

*Chirundu.* Es'kia Mphahlele. Johannesburg: Ravan Press, 1994, 2nd ed. xvi + 158 pp. ISBN 0-86975-449-1.

*The Colour of Anger.* Naiwu Osahon. Lagos: Heritage Books, 1991. 123 pp. ISBN 978-2358-00-2.

*Conduct Unbecoming.* T. M. Aluko. Ibadan: Heinemann Educational Books, 1993. 165 pp. ISBN 978-129-369-1.

*Corruption.* Tahar Ben Jelloun. Trans. Carol Volk. New York: New Press, 1995. 136 pp. ISBN 1-56584-296-0.

*Cry Amandla.* D. Rowan. Harare: College Press, 1988. 116 pp. ISBN 0-86925-745-5.

*The Curse of the Sacred Cow.* Mary Karooro Okurut. Kampala: Fountain Publishers, 1994. v + 65 pp. ISBN 9970-02-034-X. Distributed by African Books Collective (Oxford).

*The Dancing Tortoise.* Naa Otua Codjoe-Swayne. Accra: Afram Publications, 1994. 293 pp. ISBN 9964-70-136-7. Distributed by African Books Collective (Oxford).

*Dreams of Trespass: Tales of a Harem Girlhood.* Fatima Mernissi. Reading: Addison-Wesley Publishing, 1994. 242 pp. ISBN 0-201-62649-7.

*Dumba Nengue: Run for Your Life. Peasant Tales of Tragedy in Mozambique.* Lina Magaia. Trans. Michael Wolfers. Trenton: Africa World Press, 1988. 113 pp. ISBN 0-86543-074-8.

*Dusk of Dawn.* Freedom Nyamubaya. Harare: College Press, 1995. 60 pp. ISBN 1-77900-214-9.

*Effortless Tears.* Alexander Kanengoni. Oxford: African Books Collective, 1993. 114 pp. ISBN 0-908-31161-3. Distributed by African Books Collective (Oxford).

*The Famished Road.* Ben Okri. New York: Bantam Doubleday Dell, 1992. 500 pp. ISBN 0-385-42476-0.

*The Fire of Africa.* D. Rowan. Harare: College Press, 1995. 91 pp. ISBN 1-77900-105-3.

*Flowers and Shadows.* Ben Okri. Harlow: Longman Group UK, 1989. xv + 208 pp. ISBN 0-582-03536-8.

*Fools and Other Stories.* Njabulo Ndebele. New York: Readers International, 1983. 280 pp. ISBN 0-930523-20-2.

*The Girl from Uganda.* Tengio Urrio. Nairobi: East African Educational Publishers, 1993. 137 pp. ISBN 9966-46-965-6. Distributed by African Books Collective (Oxford).

*Girls at War: And Other Stories.* Chinua Achebe. New York: Anchor Books, 1991. 120 pp. ISBN 0-385-41896-5.

*Goatsmell.* Nevanji Madanhire. Harare: Anvil Press, 1992. 135 pp. ISBN 0-7974-1063-5.

*God's Bits of Wood.* Sembène Ousmane. Trans. Francis Price. Oxford: Heinemann Publishers, 1986. 245 pp. ISBN 0-435-90892-8.

*Guanya Pau: A Story of an African Princess.* Joseph J. Walters. Lincoln: University of Nebraska Press, 1994. xxiii + 111 pp. ISBN 0-8032-9755-6.

*Gwebede's Wars.* William Saidi. Harare: College Press, 1989. 232 pp. ISBN 0-86925-895-8.

*Head Above Water: An Autobiography.* Buchi Emecheta. Oxford: Heinemann Publishers, 1994. x + 229 pp. ISBN 0435-90993-2.

*The Heart of the Ngoni: Heroes of the African Kingdom of Segu.* Harold Courlander and Ousmane Sako. Amherst: University of Massachusetts Press, 1994. xii + 178 pp. ISBN 0-87023-929-5.

*The Herdsman's Daughter.* Bernard Chahilu. Nairobi: East African Educational Publishers, 1995. 228 pp. ISBN 9966-46-680-0. Distributed by African Books Collective (Oxford).

*Homing In.* Marjorie Oludhe Macgoye. Nairobi: East African Educational Publishers, 1994. 205 pp. ISBN 9966-46-547-2. Distributed by African Books Collective (Oxford).

*Hyena and the Moon: Stories to Tell From Kenya.* Heather McNeil. Englewood: Libraries Unlimited, 1994. xvi + 171 pp. ISBN 1-56308-169-5.

*I Remember: A Collection of Short Stories.* Chintamanee Chummun. Port Louis: Editions de l'Ocean Indien, 1993. 146 pp. ISBN 9990-334-013. Distributed by African Books Collective (Oxford).

*I Saw the Sky Catch Fire.* T. Obinkaram Echewa. New York: Penguin Books, 1992. 324 pp. ISBN 0-525-93398-0.

*In the Ditch.* Buchi Emecheta. Oxford: Heinemann Publishers, 1994. 135 pp. ISBN 0435-90994-0.

*Incarnation of Hope.* Agwuncha A. Nwankwo. Enugu: Fourth Dimension Publishers, 1993. x + 166 pp. ISBN 978-156-365-6. Distributed by African Books Collective (Oxford).

*Jesus is Indian: And Other Stories.* Agnes Sam. Oxford: Heinemann Publishers, 1994. 134 pp. ISBN 0435-90921-5.

*Jit.* Michael Raeburn. Harare: Anvil Press, 1991. iv + 111 pp. ISBN 0-7974-1020-1.

*The Joys of Motherhood.* Buchi Emecheta. Oxford: Heinemann Publishers, 1994. 224 pp. ISBN 0-435-90972-x.

*Kalulu's Counting Book.* Tomas and Paul. Harare: Anvil Press, 1993. 22 pp. ISBN 0-7974-1277-8.

*Kandaya: Another Time, Another Place.* Angus Shaw. Harare: Baobab Books, 1993. xi + 209 pp. ISBN 0-908311-60-5. Distributed by African Books Collective (Oxford).

*Kehinde.* Buchi Emecheta. Oxford: Heinemann Publishers, 1994. 144 pp. ISBN 0435-90985-1.

*Lady in Chains.* F. M. Genga-Idowu. Nairobi: Spear Books, 1993. 198 pp. ISBN 9966-46-606-1. Distributed by African Books Collective (Oxford).

*Lamentation at the Shrine: Quo Vadis Africa?.* Eze Chi Chiazo. Enugu: Fourth Dimension Publishers, 1995. 26 pp. ISBN 978-156-397-4. Distributed by African Books Collective (Oxford).

*The Laughing Cry: An African Cock and Bull Story.* Henri Lopes. Trans. Gerald Moore. New York: Readers International, 1987. 259 pp. ISBN 0-930523-33-4.

*Let My People Play!.* Masitha Hoeane. Maseru: Institute of South African Studies, 1994. 158 pp. ISBN 99911-31-11-6. Distributed by African Books Collective (Oxford).

*The Little Karoo.* Pauline Smith. New York: St. Martin's Press, 1990. xvii + 150 pp. ISBN 0-312-04729-0.

*Living, Loving and Lying Awake at Night.* Sindiwe Magona. London: Women's Press, 1992. 168 pp. ISBN 0-7043-4321-5.

*Lodu's Escape and Other Stories from Africa.* Phoebe Mugo, ed. New York: Friendship Press, 1994. iv + 60 pp. ISBN 0-377-00269-0.

*Matters of Dignity.* Ken Mufuka. Harare: Anvil Press, 1993. 142 pp. ISBN 0-7974-1171-2.

*Missing in Action and Presumed Dead.* Rashidah Ismaili. Trenton: Africa World Press, 1992. xi + 100 pp. ISBN 0-86543-297-x.

*Mixed Signals.* Thabo Nkosinathi Masemola. Johannesburg: Skotaville Publishers, 1993. 189 pp. ISBN 0947-4798-64. Distributed by African Books Collective (Oxford).

*Monnew.* Ahmadou Kourouma. Trans. Nidra Poller. San Francisco: Mercury House, 1993. xiv + 254 pp. ISBN 1-56279-027-7.

*My Village Captured Hitler.* Augustus Adebayo. Oxford: African Books Collective, 1993. 135 pp. ISBN 9-78246-158-x. Distributed by African Books Collective (Oxford).

*Nehanda.* Yvonne Vera. Harare: Baobab Books, 1993. 118 pp. ISBN 0-908-311-621. Distributed by African Books Collective (Oxford).

*Never Again.* Flora Nwapa. Trenton: Africa World Press, 1992. 85 pp. ISBN 0-86543-319-4.

*Ngunga's Adventures: A Story of Angola.* Pepetela. Harare: Anvil Press, 1988. 56 pp. ISBN 0-7974-0842-8.

*None to Accompany Me.* Nadine Gordimer. New York: Farrar, Straus and Giroux, 1994. 324 pp. ISBN 0-374-22297-5.

*One is Enough.* Flora Nwapa. Trenton: Africa World Press, 1992. 154 pp. ISBN 0-86543-323-2.

*The Oriki of a Grasshopper and Other Plays.* Femi Osofisan. Washington, D.C.: Howard University Press, 1995. xxxviii +195 pp. ISBN 0-88258-181-3.

*A Pattern of Dust: Selected Poems 1965-1990.* Timothy Wangusa. Kampala: Fountain Publishers, 1994. 87 pp. ISBN 9970-02-028-5. Distributed by African Books Collective (Oxford).

*The Plight of Succession.* Prosper Rwegoshora. Dar es Salaam: Dar es Salaam University Press, 1993. 146 pp. ISBN 9976-6019-56. Distributed by African Books Collective (Oxford).

*Quills of Desire.* Binwell Sinyangwe. Harare: Baobab Books, 1993. 171 pp. ISBN 0-908311-59-1. Distributed by African Books Collective (Oxford).

*A Rainbow on the Paper Sky.* Mandla Langa. London: Kliptown Books, 1989. 192 pp. ISBN 1-871863-01-5.

*Rainbows Are For Lovers.* Wale Okediran. Ibadan: Spectrum Books, 1993. Rev. ed. 211 pp. ISBN 978-246-080-X. Distributed by African Books Collective (Oxford).

*Ramza.* Out El Kouloub. Trans. Nayra Atiya. Syracuse: Syracuse University Press, 1994. ixx + 201 pp. ISBN 0-8156-0280-4.

*Return of No Return and Other Poems.* Kwesi Brew. Accra: Afram Publications, 1995. iv + 47 pp. ISBN 9964-70-152-7. Distributed by African Books Collective (Oxford).

*The Rise and Shine of Comrade Fiasco.* Andrew Whaley. Harare: Anvil Press, 1991. viii + 63 pp. ISBN 0-7974-1018-x.

*Sankofa: Stories, Proverbs and Poems of an African Childhood.* David Abdulai. Denver: Konkori International, 1995. vi + 126 pp. ISBN 0-9647012-0-0.

*Sardines.* Nuruddin Farah. St. Paul: Graywolf Press, 1992. 263 pp. ISBN 1-55597-161-X.

*The Scaffold.* Edward Lurie. Atlantic Highlands: Humanities Press, 1986. 237 pp. ISBN 0-86232-601-x.

*Scrapiron Blues.* Dambudzo Marechera. Harare: Baobab Books, 1994. xv + 250 pp. ISBN 0-908311-70-2. Distributed by African Books Collective (Oxford).

*Season of Hurricane.* Agwuncha A. Nwankwo. Enugu: Fourth Dimension Publishers, 1993. ii + 190 pp. ISBN 978-156-122-X. Distributed by African Books Collective (Oxford).

*The Seed Yams Have Been Eaten.* Phanuel Egejuru. Ibadan: Heinemann Publishers, 1993. iv + 260 pp. ISBN 978 129 183 4. Distributed by African Books Collective (Oxford).

*The Seven Solitudes of Lorsa Lopez.* Sony Labou Tansi. Trans. Clive Wake. Oxford: Heinemann Publishers, 1995. 129 pp. ISBN 0435-905945. Distributed by African Books Collective (Oxford).

*Shadow Over Breaking Waves.* Agwuncha Arthur Nwankwo. Enugu: Fourth Dimension Publishers, 1993. 296 pp. ISBN 978-156-378-8. Distributed by African Books Collective (Oxford).

*Snares Without End.* Olympe Bhely-Quenum. Trans. Dorothy S. Blair. Charlottesville: University Press of Virginia, 1988. xxvi + 204 pp. ISBN 0-8139-1189-3.

*Son of Fate.* John Kiriamiti. Nairobi: East African Publishing, 1994. 276 pp. ISBN 9966-46-439-5. Distributed by African Books Collective (Oxford).

*Song of Farewell.* Jane Okot p'Bitek. Kampala: Fountain Publishers, 1994. 71 pp. ISBN 9970-02-018-8. Distributed by African Books Collective (Oxford).

*The Song of Jacob Zulu.* Tug Yourgrau. New York: Arcade Publishing, 1993. xvi + 106 pp. ISBN 1-55970-237-0.

*Sophiatown: Coming of Age in South Africa.* Don Mattera. Boston: Beacon Press, 1989. xxii + 151 pp. ISBN 0-8070-0206-2.

*Sozaboy: A Novel in Rotten English.* Ken Saro-Wiwa. Harlow, Essex: Longman Group, 1994. 188 pp. ISBN 0-582-23699-1.

*The Stillborn.* Zaynab Alkali. Harlow: Longman Group UK, 1989. xxi + 106 pp. ISBN 0-582-02657-1.

*Study Guide to: Harvest of Thorns.* Beverley Abrahams and Lesley Humphrey. Harare: Academic Books, 1993. iv + 106 pp. ISBN 0-949229-26-1. Distributed by African Books Collective (Oxford).

*Study Guide to: In the Fog of the Season's End.* Pat Made and Beverley Abrahams. Harare: Academic Books, 1993. 42 pp. ISBN 0-949229-25-3. Distributed by African Books Collective (Oxford).

*Sweet & Sour Milk.* Nuruddin Farah. St. Paul: Graywolf Press, 1992. 242 pp. ISBN 1-55597-159-8.

*Tales of an Ashanti Father.* Peggy Appiah. Boston: Beacon Press, 1967. 156 pp. ISBN 0-8070-8313-5.

*This is Lagos and Other Stories.* Flora Nwapa. Trenton: Africa World Press, 1992. 135 pp. ISBN 0-86543-321-6.

*Tides.* Isidore Okpewho. Harlow: Longman Group UK, 1993. 201 pp. ISBN 0-582-10276-6.

*Victory.* George Mujajati. Harare: College Press, 1993. 120 pp. ISBN 1-77900-132-0.

*The Village Bridge.* Andre Proctor. Harare: Anvil Press, 1989. 25 pp. ISBN 0-7974-0897-5.

*Vultures in the Air: Voices from Northern Nigeria.* Zaynab Alkali and Al Imfeld, eds. Ibadan: Spectrum Books, 1995. vii + 150 pp. ISBN 978-246-260-8. Distributed by African Books Collective (Oxford).

*West Africa Folk Tales.* Richard Spears, ed. Trans. Jack Berry. Evanston: Northwestern University Press, 1991. xxvi + 229 pp. ISBN 0-8101-0993-x.

*West African Folktales.* Steven H. Gale. Lincolnwood: NTC Publishing Group, 1995. xx + 203 pp. ISBN 0-8442-5812-1.

*West African Folktales: Instruction Manual.* Steven H. Gale. Lincolnwood: NTC Publishing Group, 1995. 56 pp. ISBN 0-8442-5814-8.

*Without a Name.* Yvonne Vera. Harare: Baobab Books, 1994. 103 pp. ISBN 0-908311-78-8. Distributed by African Books Collective (Oxford).

*Woman of the Aeroplanes.* Kojo Laing. New York: William Morrow and Company, 1988. 196 pp. ISBN 0-688-07941-5.

*Women are Different.* Flora Nwapa. Trenton: Africa World Press, 1992. 138 pp. ISBN 0-86543-326-7.

*Women of Algiers in Their Apartment.* Assia Djebar. Trans. Marjolijn De Jager. Charlottesville: University Press of Virginia, 1992. 211 pp. ISBN 0-8139-1402-7.

*The World of "Mestre" Tamoda.* Uanhenga Xitu. Trans. Annella McDermott. Luanda: Uniao dos Escritores Angolanos, 1988. vi + 158 pp. ISBN 0-930523-43-1.

*Writing Women's Worlds: Bedouin Stories.* Lila Abu-Lughod. Berkeley: University of California Press, 1993. xxiii + 266 pp. ISBN 0-520-07946-9.

*You Can't Get Lost in Cape Town.* Zoe Wicomb. New York: Pantheon Books, 1987. 185 pp. ISBN 0-394-75309-7.

*You Cannot Unsneeze a Sneeze and Other Tales from Liberia.* Esther Warner Dendel. Niwot: University Press of Colorado, 1995. xv + 171 pp. ISBN 0-87081-414-1.

*Yungba Yungba and the Dance Contest.* Femi Osofisan. Ibadan: Heinemann Educational Books, 1993. xviii + 126 pp. ISBN 978-129-249-0. Distributed by African Books Collective (Oxford).

# FILMS AND VIDEOTAPES

The following is a list of recent films and videotapes from and about Africa, along with listings of some classic documentaries. California Newsreel (San Francisco), Full Frame Film and Video Distribution (Toronto), and IDERA Film and Video (Vancouver) regularly produce useful guides to Africa-related films and videos. We have not listed all of the individual audiovisuals cataloged in their guides, so we encourage readers to contact these organizations directly for complete details on their Africa cinema collections.

California Newsreel: *Library of African Cinema, 1993-1994, Library of African Cinema, 1995-96,* and *The Decolonized Eye: Six Films from Africa and the Caribbean.* 149 Ninth St., Ste. 420, San Francisco, CA 94130, USA.

Full Frame Film and Video Distribution: *New African Media* and *The Big Picture: Film and Video for Global Education.* 394 Euclid Ave., Ste. 201, Toronto, ON Canada M6G 2S9.

IDERA Film and Video: *Reel Africa.* 2678 West Broadway, Ste. 200, Vancouver, BC Canada V6K 2G3.

Most of the other major distributors whose films and videos are listed below produce catalogs or catalog supplements that are Africa-focused. See, for example, *African Films & Videos* from DSR (Columbia, Md.) and *African Studies Video Collection* from Cinema Guild (New York). Addresses for these and other distributors of audiovisuals appear in the Directory of Organizations.

The African Media Program (AMP) at Michigan State University is building a definitive reference database of African films and videotapes produced after 1981. This database picks up where the earlier *Africa on Film and Videotape: A Compendium of Reviews* (1982) left off. The updated edition of the AMP reference guide will appear in both compact disk (CD-ROM) and print formats and it will be disseminated in electronic forms through the Internet. African Media Program, Michigan State University, Africa Studies Center, 100 Center for International Programs, East Lansing, MI 48824-1035 USA.

International Broadcasting Trust is a recommended source for high-quality videotapes and complementary print materials on issues such development, environment, and human rights. International Broadcasting Trust (IBT), 2 Ferdinand St., London NW1 8EE, England.

Periodicals that regularly contain listings and/or reviews of Africa-related films and videos include:

*Guide to Political Videos.* Pacifica Communications, P.O. Box 4426, Santa Barbara, CA 93140-4426, USA.

*Images Nord-Sud Bulletin: Guide Trimestriel de Films sur le Développement.* Association des Trois Mondes, 63 bis rue du Cardinal-Lemoine, 75005 Paris, France.

*Moving Pictures Bulletin.* Television Trust for the Environment (TVE), Prince Albert Rd., London NW1 4RZ, England.

*Video Librarian.* Video Librarian, P.O. Box 2725, Bremerton, WA 98310, USA.

*WorldViews: A Quarterly Review of Resources for Education and Action.* WorldViews, 464 19th St., Oakland, CA 94612-2297 USA.

*Zebra News.* Zebra Information Center, Elmegade 5, 1st floor, DK-2200 Copenhagen N, Denmark.

Noteworthy film magazines include *Ecrans d'Afrique/African Screen* (01B.p. 2524 Ouagadougou, 01 Burkina Faso) and *Cineaste* 200 Park Ave. South, New York, NY 10003-1503, USA.

Decriptors in the "topics" field in the listings are keyed to the chapter headings in the *Africa World Press Guide.*

**ABOUT THE UNITED NATIONS: AFRICA RECOVERY.** Produced by United Nations. 1990. 15 minutes. Videocassette. Distributor: Church World Service (Elkhart).
Topic(s): Conflicts / Food and agriculture / Women
Country/region: Zambia / Horn of Africa region

**AFRICA CLOSE-UP.** 1997. 28 minutes. Videocassette. Distributor: Maryknoll World Productions (Maryknoll). Children of the Earth series.
Topic(s): Nations
Country/region: Egypt, Tanzania

**AFRICA I REMEMBER: A MUSICAL SYNTHESIS OF TWO CULTURES.** Produced by A Music on Earth Production. 1996. 30 minutes. Videocassette. Distributor: Filmakers Library (New York).
Topic(s): Music
Country/region: Mali, Senegal, Gambia

**AFRICA ON THE MOVE.** Directed by Galen Films for the Hunger Project. 1992. 55 minutes. Videocassette. Distributor: Bullfrog Films (Oley). ISBN 1-56029-451-5.
Topic(s): Images and media
Country/region: Uganda

*AFRICA, I WILL FLEECE YOU.* Directed by Jean-Marie Teno. 1993. 88 minutes. French with English subtitles. Distributor: Full Frame Film and Video Distribution (Toronto). Distributed also by California Newsreel (San Francisco).
Topic(s): Literature / Human rights
Country/region: Cameroon

*AFRICA: SIERRA LEONE, GHANA, KENYA.* 26 minutes. Videocassette. Distributor: Films for the Humanities and Sciences (Princeton). ARM6631. Our Developing World series.
Topic(s): Africa's peoples / Environment / Nations
Country/region: Sierra Leone, Ghana, Kenya, Liberia

*AFRICA: TANZANIA, MOZAMBIQUE, LESOTHO.* 29 minutes. Videocassette. Distributor: Films for the Humanities and Sciences (Princeton). ARM6632. Our Developing World series.
Topic(s): Conflicts / Human rights / Nations
Country/region: Tanzania, Mozambique, South Africa, Lesotho

*AFRICA: TUNISIA, LIBYA, EGYPT.* 31 minutes. Videocassette. Distributor: Films for the Humanities and Sciences (Princeton). ARM6630. Our Developing World series.
Topic(s): Women / Population / Nations
Country/region: Tunisia, Libya, Egypt

*AFRICAN ART AND WOMEN ARTISTS.* 1993. 17 minutes. Videocassette. Distributor: Films for the Humanities and Sciences (Princeton).
Topic(s): Visual arts / Women
Country/region: Kenya

*AN AFRICAN RECOVERY.* Produced by Sandra Nichols. Co-produced by United Nations. 1988. 26 minutes. Videocassette. Distributor: Church World Service (Elkhart). Also from First Run/Icarus Films (New York).
Topic(s): Environment / Development / Population

*AFRICAN VOICES.* Produced by Mennonite Central Committee. 1986. 40 minutes. Videocassette. Distributor: Mennonite Central Committee (Akron).
Topic(s): Belief systems
Country/region: Burkina Faso, Kenya, Lesotho, Zaire

*THE AFRICANS.* Produced by Peter Bate. Co-produced by BBC Television/WETA-TV. 1986. Videocassette. 9 parts. Distributor: Church World Service (Elkhart). Hosted by Ali A. Mazrui. Available also from Mennonite Central Commitee.
Topic(s): Overview and/or multi-issue

*AFTER RWANDA.* Produced by CKCO-TV. 1995. 30 minutes. Videocassette. Distributor: Mennonite Central Committee (Akron).
Topic(s): Conflicts
Country/region: Burundi, Rwanda, Democratic Republic of the Congo (Zaire)

*AHMED BEN BELLA SPEAKS ON WAR AND SANCTIONS.* 1995. 29 minutes. Videocassette. Distributor: Peoples Video Network (New York).
Topic(s): Democracy
Country/region: Algeria

*AIDS IN AFRICA.* Produced by Roger Pyke Productions/National Film Board of Canada. 1991. 52 minutes. Videocassette. Distributor: Filmakers Library (New York).
Topic(s): AIDS
Country/region: Uganda, Zaire, Côte d'Ivoire, Burundi, Rwanda, South Africa

*AIDS IN AFRICA: LIVING WITH A TIME BOMB.* 33 minutes. Videocassette. Distributor: Films for the Humanities and Sciences (Princeton). QB3165.
Topic(s): AIDS

*AIDS: A RACE AGAINST TIME.* Produced by Plan International. 27 minutes. Videocassette. Distributor: DSR/Development through Self-Reliance (Columbia).
Topic(s): AIDS
Country/region: Nigeria, Zimbabwe

*ALGERIA: WOMEN AT WAR.* Produced by Parminder Vir. 1992. 52 minutes. Videocassette. Subtitled. Distributor: Women Make Movies (New York). No. 97009.
Topic(s): Women / Conflicts
Country/region: Algeria

*ALLAH TANTOU (GOD'S WILL).* Produced by David Achkar. 1991. 62 minutes. Videocassette. In French and Soussou with English subtitles. Distributor: California Newsreel (San Francisco). Distributed also by IDERA Films (Vancouver).
Topic(s): Human rights
Country/region: Guinea

*ANGOLA IS OUR COUNTRY.* Produced by Jenny Morgan. 1988. 45 minutes. Videocassette. Distributor: Women Make Movies (New York). No. 97061.
Topic(s): Women / Nations
Country/region: Angola

*APARTHEID'S LAST STAND.* Produced by David Harrison. 1993. 60 minutes. Videocassette. Distributor: PBS Video (Alexandria). Closed captioned for the hearing impaired.
Topic(s): South Africa / Democracy
Country/region: South Africa

*THE ASHANTI KINGDOM.* 14 minutes. Videocassette. Distributor: Films for the Humanities and Sciences (Princeton). ARM3076.
Topic(s): Africa's peoples
Country/region: Ghana

*BENIN: AN AFRICAN KINGDOM.* 115 minutes. Videocassette. 5 parts. Distributor: Films for the Humanities and Sciences (Princeton). ARM5099-5103.
Topic(s): Nations
Country/region: Benin

*BETWEEN TWO WORLDS.* 1986. 50 minutes. Videocassette. Distributor: Landmark Films (Falls Church). The Arabs: A Living History.
Topic(s): Nations
Country/region: Morocco

*BEYOND THE PLAINS.* Produced by Michael Raeburn. 53 minutes. Videocassette. Distributor: DSR/Development through Self-Reliance (Columbia).
Topic(s): Development
Country/region: Tanzania

*BIRTH OF DEMOCRACY.* Produced by Bassek Ba Khobio. Co-produced by South Productions and Channel 4 Television (UK). 1991. 25 minutes. Videocassette. Distributor: First Run/Icarus Films (New York). The South series.
Topic(s): Democracy
Country/region: Cameroon

*BLACK GIRL.* Directed by Ousmane Sembène. 1965. 60 minutes. Videocassette. In French with English subtitles. Distributor: New Yorker Films (New York).
Topic(s): Cinema

*BLACK SUGAR: SLAVERY FROM AN AFRICAN PERSPECTIVE.* 26 minutes. Videocassette. Distributor: Films for the Humanities and Sciences (Princeton). ARM3256.
Topic(s): Overview and/or multi-issue

*BLOOD AND SAND.* Produced by Sharon Sopher. 57 minutes. Videocassette. Distributor: DSR/Development through Self-Reliance (Columbia).
Topic(s): Western Sahara struggle
Country/region: Western Sahara, Morocco, Mauritania

*BLUE EYES OF YONTA (UDJU AZUL DI YONTA).* Produced by Flora Gomes. 1992. 90 minutes. Color film. In Creole and Portuguese with English subtitles. Distributor: IDERA Film and Video (Vancouver).
Topic(s): Overview and/or multi-issue
Country/region: Guinea-Bissau

*BORN IN AFRICA.* Produced by Frontline/WGBH with Canadian Broadcasting Co. 90 minutes. Videocassette. Available for Africa in English, French, Swahili. Distributor: DSR/Development through Self-Reliance (Columbia).
Topic(s): AIDS
Country/region: Uganda

*BOROM SARRET.* Directed by Ousmane Sembène. 1964. 20 minutes. Videocassette. Distributor: New Yorker Films (New York).
Topic(s): Cinema
Country/region: Senegal

*BREAKING THE SILENCE.* Produced by Deborah d'Entremont and Sylvia Spring. Co-produced by Making WAVES Productions. 56 minutes. Videocassette. Distributor: DSR/Development through Self-Reliance (Columbia).
Topic(s): AIDS
Country/region: Zimbabwe

*BUILDING A NATION.* 1986. 50 minutes. Videocassette. Distributor: Landmark Films (Falls Church). The Arabs: A Living History.
Topic(s): Nations
Country/region: Algeria

*BURDEN ON THE LAND.* Produced by Roger Pyke Productions. 1992. 52 minutes. Videocassette. Distributor: Filmakers Library (New York).
Topic(s): Food and agriculture / Development
Country/region: Mozambique, Malawi, Rwanda, Burundi, Zaire, Côte d'Ivoire, Mali, Ethiopia, Uganda

*ÇA TWISTE A POPENGUINE (ROCKING POPENGUINE).* Directed by Moussa Sene Absa. 1993. 90 minutes. Videocassette. Distributor: California Newsreel (San Francisco). in French with English subtitles.
Topic(s): Overview and/or multi-issue
Country/region: Senegal

*CAMP DE THIAROYE.* Directed by Ousmane Sembène. 1987. 152 minutes. Videocassette. In Wolof and French with English subtitles. Distributor: New Yorker Films (New York).
Topic(s): Cinema
Country/region: Senegal

*CAN TROPICAL RAINFORESTS BE SAVED?* Produced by Robert Richter. 119 minutes. Videocassette. Available in English for Africa only. Distributor: DSR/Development through Self-Reliance (Columbia).
Topic(s): Environment
Country/region: Cameroon

*CARVING A FUTURE IN KENYA.* Produced by Mennonite Central Committee. 1994. 7 minutes. Videocassette. Distributor: Mennonite Central Committee (Akron).
Topic(s): Visual arts
Country/region: Kenya

*CEDDO.* Directed by Ousmane Sembène. 1977. 120 minutes. Videocassette. In Wolof with English subtitles. Distributor: New Yorker Films (New York).
Topic: Cinema

*CHAIN OF TEARS.* Produced by Adrian Pennick. 52 minutes. Videocassette. Available in English for Africa only. Distributor: DSR/Development through Self-Reliance (Columbia).
Topic(s): Conflicts
Country/region: Mozambique, Angola

*CHINUA ACHEBE.* 1994. 30 minutes. Videocassette. Distributor: Films for the Humanities and Sciences (Princeton). ARM4936.
Topic(s): Literature
Country/region: Nigeria

*CHINUA ACHEBE: THE IMPORTANCE OF STORIES.* Directed by Cambiz Khosravi. 57 minutes. 1996. Videocassette. Distributor: Cinema Guild (New York).
Topic(s): Literature
Country/region: Nigeria

*THE CITY VICTORIOUS?* 1986. 50 minutes. Videocassette. Distributor: Landmark Films (Falls Church). The Arabs: A Living History.
Topic(s): Overview and/or multi-issue
Country/region: Egypt

*THE COLOR OF GOLD.* Produced by Don Edkins and Mike Schlomer. 1992. 52 minutes. Videocassette. Distributor: First Run/Icarus Films (New York).
Topic(s): Mining
Country/region: South Africa

*CONSEQUENCES.* Produced by Media for Development Trust. 54 minutes. Color film and videocassette. English, French, and many African languages. Distributor: DSR/Development through Self-Reliance (Columbia).
Topic(s): Population
Country/region: Zimbabwe

*CONSUMING HUNGER.* Produced by Ilan Ziv and Freke Juijust. 90 minutes. Videocassette. 3 parts. Distributor: Maryknoll World Productions (Maryknoll). Available also from Full Frame Film and Video Distribution (Toronto).
Topic(s): Food and agriculture / Images and media
Country/region: Ethiopia

*DAUGHTERS OF THE NILE.* Produced by Hillie Joop van Wijk. 1993. 46 minutes. Videocassette. Distributor: Filmakers Library (New York).
Topic(s): Women / Voice of women / Belief systems
Country/region: Egypt

***THE DEBT CRISIS: AN AFRICAN DILEMMA.*** Produced by Steve Whitehouse. Co-produced by United Nations. 1988. 20 minutes. Videocassette. Distributor: Mennonite Central Committee (Akron). Also from First Run/Icarus Films (New York).
Topic(s): Debt
Country/region: Zambia.

***DEFIANCE IN THE TOWNSHIPS.*** Directed by Keith Bowen. Produced by Meridian Communications. 1994. 25 minutes. Videocassette. Distributor: Churchill Media (Van Nuys). The Last Days of Apartheid series.
Topic(s): South Africa / Conflicts
Country/region: South Africa

***THE DESIRED NUMBER.*** Produced by Ngozi Onwurah. 1995. 28 minutes. Videocassette. Distributor: Women Make Movies (New York). No. 97072.
Topic(s): Population / Women
Country/region: Nigeria

***DEVELOPING STRATEGIES.*** Produced by African Forum for Children. 56 minutes. Videocassette. Distributor: DSR/Development through Self-Reliance (Columbia).
Topic(s): AIDS
Country/region: Uganda, Zimbabwe, Tanzania

***THE DREAM BECOMES A REALITY.*** Produced by Eva Egensteiner. 45 minutes. Videocassette. Distributor: DSR/Development through Self-Reliance (Columbia).
Topic(s): Struggles won
Country/region: Eritrea, Ethiopia

***THE EARTH AT RISK.*** Produced by Schlessinger Video. 1993. 30 minutes. Videocassette. Distributor: Schlessinger Video (Bala Cynwyd). Series of 10 videos.
Topic(s): Environment

***ECOLOGY AND THE ENVIRONMENT: GALAPAGOS, MAURITANIA, MADAGASCAR.*** 30 minutes. Videocassette. Distributor: Films for the Humanities and Sciences (Princeton). ARM6637. Global Issues in Our Developing World series.
Topic(s): Environment / Nations
Country/region: Mauritania, Madagascar

***EGYPT, LAND OF ANCIENT WONDERS.*** 1993. 58 minutes. Videocassette. Distributor: African Video Centre (London).
Country/region: Egypt

***EGYPT: THE FEAR AND THE FAITH.*** Produced by Journeyman Pictures. 1996. 40 minutes. Videocassette. Distributor: Filmakers Library (New York).
Topic(s): Belief systems
Country/region: Egypt

***EMITAI.*** Directed by Ousmane Sembène. 1971. 101 minutes. Videocassette. In Diola and French with English subtitles. Distributor: New Yorker Films (New York).
Topic(s): Cinema
Country/region: Senegal

***THE EMPEROR'S BIRTHDAY: THE RASTAFARIANS CELEBRATE.*** Produced by Volcano Films. 1996. 52 minutes. Videocassette. Distributor: Filmakers Library (New York).
Topic(s): Belief systems
Country/region: Ethiopia

***ENDANGERED SPECIES.*** Produced by Philip Cayford. Co-produced by Central TV. 102 minutes. Videocassette. Available in English for Africa only. Distributor: DSR/Development through Self-Reliance (Columbia).
Topic(s): Environment
Country/region: Rwanda, Zimbabwe

***THE ENIGMA OF THE DEAD SEA SCROLLS.*** Produced by Biblical Productions. 1993. 50 minutes. Videocassette. Distributor: Filmakers Library (New York).
Topic(s): Belief systems

***ERITREA.*** Produced by Susan Kalish. 1990. 30 minutes. Videocassette. Distributor: Cinema Guild (New York).
Topic(s): Struggles won / Conflicts
Country/region: Eritrea, Ethiopia

***ERITREA: HOPE IN THE HORN OF AFRICA.*** Produced by Grassroots International. 1993. 30 minutes. Videocassette. Distributor: First Run/Icarus Films (New York).
Topic(s): Struggles won
Country/region: Eritrea, Ethiopia

***ETHIOPIA: NO EASY WALK.*** Directed by Bernard Odjidja. 1988. 57 minutes. Videocassette. Distributor: Full Frame Film and Video Distribution (Toronto). No Easy Walk series. Also from Cinema Guild (New York).
Topic(s): Nations
Country/region: Ethiopia

***EVERYONE'S CHILD.*** Produced by Media for Development Trust and Plan International. 90 minutes. Videocassette. Distributor: DSR/Development through Self-Reliance (Columbia).
Topic(s): AIDS
Country/region: Zimbabwe

***THE FACES OF AIDS.*** Produced by FHI with support from USAID. 20 minutes. Color film and videocassette. Comes with discussion guidelines. Distributor: DSR/Development through Self-Reliance (Columbia). English, French, Swahili, or Vietnamese.
Topic(s): AIDS
Country/region: Cameroon, Zimbabwe

***FACING THE FUTURE.*** Produced by African Journey. 1990. 15 minutes. Videocassette. Distributor: Church World Service (Elkhart). Journey to Understanding series.
Topic(s): Images and media / Development
Country/region: Zimbabwe

***FATMA'S PRAYER.*** Produced by Sarah Errington. Co-produced by BBC Television. 40 minutes. Videocassette. Available in English for Africa only. Distributor: DSR/Development through Self-Reliance (Columbia).
Topic(s): Refugees
Country/region: Sudan

***FEMMES AUX YEUX OUVERTS (WOMEN WITH OPEN EYES).*** Directed by Anne-Laure Folly. 1994. 52 minutes. Videocassette. Distributor: California Newsreel (San Francisco). in French with English subtitles.
Topic(s): Women / Voice of women
Country/region: Togo, Mali, Burkina Faso, Senegal, Benin

***FIELDS OF TREES.*** Produced by Television Trust for the Environment. 31 minutes. Videocassette. English or French. Distributor: DSR/Development through Self-Reliance (Columbia).
Topic(s): Food and agriculture
Country/region: Zambia, Uganda

**FIRE EYES.** Produced by Soraya Mire. 1995. 60 minutes. Color film and videocassette. Distributor: Filmakers Library (New York).
Topic(s): Women / Belief systems
Country/region: Somalia

**FIRST FREE ELECTION.** Directed by Keith Bowen. Produced by Meridian Communications. 1994. 25 minutes. Distributor: Churchill Media (Van Nuys). The Last Days of Apartheid series.
Topic(s): South Africa / Democracy
Country/region: South Africa

**FOR THOSE WHO SAIL TO HEAVEN.** Produced by Elizabeth Wickett. 1990. 48 minutes. Videocassette. Distributor: First Run/Icarus Films (New York).
Topic(s): Nations
Country/region: Egypt

**THE FORBIDDEN LAND.** Produced by Daniele Lacourse and Yvan Patry. 1989. 55 minutes. Color film and videocassette. Distributor: First Run/Icarus Films (New York).
Topic(s): Conflicts / Struggles won
Country/region: Eritrea, Ethiopia

**FRAGILE RICHES.** Produced by Herremagasinet Films. 34 minutes. Videocassette. Available in English for Africa only. Distributor: DSR/Development through Self-Reliance (Columbia).
Topic(s): Environment
Country/region: Zimbabwe

**FROM SUNUP.** 1987. 28 minutes. Videocassette. Study guide included. Distributor: Maryknoll World Productions (Maryknoll).
Topic(s): Women
Country/region: Tanzania

**GETTING THE STORY.** 1988. 29 minutes. Videocassette. Study guide included. Distributor: Maryknoll World Productions (Maryknoll). Consuming Hunger.
Topic(s): Food and agriculture / Images and media
Country/region: Ethiopia

**THE GODS OF OUR FATHERS.** Produced by Anne Henderson. 1995. 51 minutes. Videocassette. In 2 parts for classroom use. Distributor: Bullfrog Films (Oley). The Human Race series. ISBN 0-7722-0589-2.
Topic(s): Women
Country/region: Egypt

**GOLDWIDOWS.** Produced by Don Edkins et al. 1991. 52 minutes. Videocassette. Distributor: First Run/Icarus Films (New York).
Topic(s): Mining
Country/region: South Africa, Lesotho

**GORÉE: DOOR OF NO RETURN.** 30 minutes. Videocassette. Distributor: Films for the Humanities and Sciences (Princeton). ARM3064.
Topic(s): Overview and/or multi-issue

**GOSPEL OF AIDS: DYING IS NOT A SIN.** Directed by Gil Courtemanche. 1993. 57 minutes. Videocassette. Distributor: IDERA Film and Video (Vancouver). Also from Cinema Guild (New York).
Topic(s): AIDS
Country/region: Rwanda

**GROWING UP.** Produced by Julian Ware and Bruno Sorrentino. 54 minutes. Videocassette. Available in English for Africa only. Distributor: DSR/Development through Self-Reliance (Columbia).
Topic(s): Development
Country/region: Kenya, South Africa

**GUELWAAR.** Produced by Ousmane Sembène. 1993. 115 minutes. Distributor: New Yorker Films (New York). in Wolof and French with English subtitles.
Topic(s): Cinema
Country/region: Senegal

**HADO.** Produced by Gaston Kabore. Co-produced by South Productions and Channel 4 Television (UK). 1991. 13 minutes. Videocassette. Distributor: First Run/Icarus Films (New York). The South.
Topic(s): Women / Music
Country/region: Burkina Faso

**THE HAND THAT FEEDS THE WORLD: WOMEN'S ROLES IN GLOBAL FOOD SECURITY.** Produced by World Food Day Association of Canada. 1993. 19 minutes. Videocassette. Distributor: Mennonite Central Committee (Akron). Available from Manitoba office only.
Topic(s): Food and agriculture / Women

**THE HARD EDGE.** Produced by Philip Roberts. 27 minutes. Videocassette. Available in English for Africa only. Distributor: DSR/Development through Self-Reliance (Columbia).
Topic(s): Environment

**HARVEST THE RAIN.** Produced by World Food Programme. 17 minutes. Videocassette. Available in English for Africa only. Distributor: DSR/Development through Self-Reliance (Columbia).
Topic(s): Environment
Country/region: Kenya

**HEALERS OF GHANA.** 58 minutes. Videocassette. Distributor: Films for the Humanities and Sciences (Princeton). ARM6135.
Topic(s): Belief systems
Country/region: Ghana

**HONONUI TODD: A LIVING LEGEND IN ZIMBABWE.** Produced by Limehurst Films. 1993. 50 minutes. Videocassette. Distributor: Filmakers Library (New York).
Topic(s): Democracy
Country/region: Zimbabwe

**HOPE IN AFRICA.** Produced by Mennonite Central Committee. Photo exhibit. Distributor: Mennonite Central Committee (Akron).
Topic(s): Overview and/or multi-issue

**I HAVE A PROBLEM, MADAM.** Produced by Maarten Schmidt and Thomas Doebele. 1995. 59 minutes. Color film and videocassette. Distributor: First Run/Icarus Films (New York).
Topic(s): Women
Country/region: Uganda

**IMAGES OF HIV/AIDS AROUND THE WORLD.** Produced by Deborah Johnson. 25 minutes. Videocassette. Distributor: DSR/Development through Self-Reliance (Columbia).
Topic(s): AIDS
Country/region: Burkina Faso, Ghana, Côte d'Ivoire, Uganda, Zimbabwe

**IMPERFECT JOURNEY.** Produced by Haile Gerima and Ryszard Kapuscinski. 1994. 88 minutes. Videocassette. Distributor: First Run/Icarus Films (New York).
Topic(s): Nations
Country/region: Ethiopia

**IN A TIME OF VIOLENCE.** Produced by Jeremy Nathan. Directed by Brian Tilley. 1994. 150 minutes. Videocassette. Distributor: California Newsreel (San Francisco). In English, Zulu and Afrikaans with English subtitles.
Topic(s): South Africa / Conflicts
Country/region: South Africa

**IN DANKU THE SOUP IS SWEETER: WOMEN AND DEVELOPMENT IN GHANA.** Produced by Gary Beitel. 1993. 30 minutes. Videocassette. Distributor: Filmakers Library (New York).
Topic(s): Development / Women
Country/region: Ghana

**IN DARKEST HOLLYWOOD: CINEMA AND APARTHEID.** Directed by Daniel Riesenfeld and Peter Davies. 1993. 112 minutes. Distributor: Nightingale/Villon Productions (Hurleyville).
Topic(s): Images and media / South Africa / Visual arts
Country/region: South Africa

**IN THE NAME OF GOD: HELPING CIRCUMCISED WOMEN.** Produced by Cadmos Film. 1997. 29 minutes. Videocassette. Distributor: Filmakers Library (New York).
Topic(s): Women / Belief systems
Country/region: Ethiopia

**ISILILO.** Directed by Molefi Wa Moleli. 1993. 5 minutes. Videocassette. Distributor: Full Frame Film and Video Distribution (Toronto).
Topic(s): South Africa / Human rights
Country/region: South Africa

**ISINGIRO HOSPITAL.** 40 minutes. Videocassette. Distributor: Films for the Humanities and Sciences (Princeton). QB4118.
Topic(s): AIDS
Country/region: Tanzania

**ISLAMIC CONVERSATIONS.** 180 minutes. Videocassette. 6 parts. Distributor: Films for the Humanities and Sciences (Princeton). QB5166.
Topic(s): Belief systems

**IT'S NOT EASY.** 48 minutes. Color film and videocassette. English, French, Luganda, Swahili, siSwati, Zulu. Distributor: DSR/Development through Self-Reliance (Columbia). Discussion guidelines, research report, and photonovela available.
Topic(s): AIDS
Country/region: Uganda

**KEEPING A LIVE VOICE: 15 YEARS OF DEMOCRACY IN ZIMBABWE.** Produced by Edwina Spicer. 1995. 54 minutes. Videocassette. Distributor: First Run/Icarus Films (New York).
Topic(s): Democracy
Country/region: Zimbabwe

**KEITA: THE HERITAGE OF THE GRIOT.** Directed by Dani Kouyate. 1995. 94 minutes. Videocassette. Distributor: California Newsreel (San Francisco).
Topic(s): Belief systems
Country/region: Burkina Faso

**KEN SARO-WIWA: AN AFRICAN MARTYR.** 23 minutes. Videocassette. Distributor: Films for the Humanities and Sciences (Princeton). ARM6475.
Topic(s): Environment / Human rights
Country/region: Nigeria

**KENYA: NO EAST WALK.** Directed by Bernard Odjidja. 1988. 57 minutes. Videocassette. Distributor: Full Frame Film and Video Distribution (Toronto). No Easy Walk series. Also from Cinema Guild (New York).
Topic(s): Images and media / Nations
Country/region: Kenya

**KHULUMANI: SPEAK OUT.** Produced by Lauren Segal. 26 minutes. Videocassette. Distributor: DSR/Development through Self-Reliance (Columbia).
Topic(s): Human rights
Country/region: South Africa

**LAGOS: RICH MAN, POOR MAN.** 20 minutes. Videocassette. Distributor: Films for the Humanities and Sciences (Princeton). QB5095. Geographical Eye Over Africa series.
Topic(s): Development
Country/region: Nigeria

**A LAND OF IMMENSE RICHES: MOZAMBIQUE.** Produced by South African Broadcasting. 1996. 30 minutes. Videocassette. Distributor: Filmakers Library (New York). Living in Africa: African Solutions to African Problems series.
Topic(s): Environment
Country/region: Mozambique

**THE LAST COLONIALS.** Produced by Thierry Michel. 1995. 61 minutes. Color film and videocassette. Distributor: First Run/Icarus Films (New York).
Topic(s): Nations
Country/region: Democratic Republic of the Congo (Zaire)

**THE LAST MILE: MANDELA, AFRICA AND DEMOCRACY.** 1993. 30 minutes. Videocassette. Distributor: Landmark Films (Falls Church).
Topic(s): Democracy / South Africa
Country/region: South Africa, Ghana, Côte d'Ivoire, Senegal

**LISTENING TO THE SILENCE: AFRICAN CROSS RHYTHMS.** 52 minutes. Videocassette. Distributor: Films for the Humanities and Sciences (Princeton). ARM6434.
Topic(s): Music
Country/region: Ghana

**A LITTLE FOR MY HEART AND A LITTLE FOR MY GOD: A MUSLIM WOMEN'S ORCHESTRA.** 1994. 60 minutes. Videocassette. Distributor: Filmakers Library (New York).
Topic(s): Women / Music
Country/region: Algeria

**LIVING WITH DROUGHT.** Produced by BBC Television/Open University. 49 minutes. Videocassette. Available in English for Africa only. Distributor: DSR/Development through Self-Reliance (Columbia).
Topic(s): Environment
Country/region: Niger, Kenya

**THE LOST CITY OF ZIMBABWE.** 1993. 28 minutes. Videocassette. Distributor: Films for the Humanities and Sciences (Princeton).
Topic(s): Africa's peoples

Country/region: Zimbabwe

***LUMUMBA: DEATH OF A PROPHET.*** Produced by Raoul Peck. 1992. 69 minutes. Videocassette. In French with English subtitles. Distributor: California Newsreel (San Francisco). Distributed also by IDERA Films.
Topic(s): Africa's peoples
Country/region: Congo, Zaire

***MAMA AWETHU!*** Produced by Bethany Yarrow. 1993. 53 minutes. Color film and videocassette. Distributor: First Run/Icarus Films (New York).
Topic(s): South Africa / Women
Country/region: South Africa

***MAMA BENZ: AN AFRICAN MARKET WOMAN.*** Produced by SFINX FILM/TV. 1994. 48 minutes. Videocassette. Distributor: Filmakers Library (New York).
Topic(s): Women
Country/region: Togo

***MAN, GOD AND AFRICA.*** Directed by Don Boyd. 1995. 51 minutes. Videocassette. Distributor: Filmakers Library (New York).
Topic(s): Belief systems / South Africa
Country/region: South Africa

***MANDABI.*** Directed by Ousmane Sembène. 1968. 90 minutes. Videocassette. In Wolof with English subtitles. Distributor: New Yorker Films (New York).
Topic(s): Cinema

***MANDELA.*** Produced by Indra de Laneroile and Mike Dutfield. 1994. 60 minutes. Videocassette. Distributor: PBS Videos (Alexandria).
Topic(s): South Africa
Country/region: South Africa

***MANDELA: FROM PRISON TO PRESIDENT.*** 52 minutes. Videocassette. Distributor: Films for the Humanities and Sciences (Princeton). ARM5340.
Topic(s): South Africa
Country/region: South Africa

***MASAI IN THE MODERN WORLD: KENYA.*** Produced by South African Broadcasting. 1996. 30 minutes. Videocassette. Distributor: Filmakers Library (New York). Living in Africa: African Solutions to African Problems.
Topic(s): Africa's peoples
Country/region: Kenya

***MAURITANIA: THE VANISHING OASIS.*** Produced by SRC Television. 1997. 57 minutes. Videocassette. Distributor: Filmakers Library (New York).
Topic(s): Africa's peoples / Environment
Country/region: Mauritania

***THE MEN OF NDOLERA.*** Produced by Belbo Film Productions/NOVIB. 47 minutes. Videocassette. Available in English for Africa only. Distributor: DSR/Development through Self-Reliance (Columbia).
Topic(s): Development
Country/region: Zaire

***THE MESSAGE OF THE BAOBAB TREE.*** Directed by Leopold Togo. 1992. 24 minutes. Videocassette. Distributor: Full Frame Film and Video Distribution (Toronto).
Topic(s): Environment

***MONDAY'S GIRLS.*** Produced by Lloyd Gardner. Directed by Ngozi Onwurah. 1993. 50 minutes. Videocassette. In Waikiriki and English with English subtitles. Distributor: California Newsreel (San Francisco). Also from Women Make Movies (New York).
Topic(s): Women / Belief systems
Country/region: Nigeria

***MOPIOPIO, THE BREATH OF ANGOLA.*** Directed by Zeze Gamboa. 1991. 54 minutes. Videocassette. Distributor: Full Frame Film and Video Distribution (Toronto).
Topic(s): Music
Country/region: Angola

***MORE TIME.*** Produced by Media for Development Trust. 1994. 90 minutes. Color film and videocassette. Distributor: DSR/Development through Self-Reliance (Columbia).
Topic(s): AIDS / Women

***MOROCCO, BODY AND SOUL.*** Produced by Izza Genini. Five 26-minute parts. 1987-1992. Distributor: First Run/Icarus Films (New York).
Topic(s): Music / Nations
Country/region: Morocco

***MOROCCO: THE PAST AND PRESENT OF DJEMMA EL FNA.*** 1996. 18 minutes. Videocassette. Distributor: Filmakers Library (New York).
Topic(s): Nations
Country/region: Morocco

***MR. FOOT.*** Produced by Jean-Marie Teno. Co-produced by South Productions and Channel 4 Television (UK). 1991. 20 minutes. Videocassette. Distributor: First Run/Icarus Films (New York). The South.
Topic(s): Nations
Country/region: Cameroon

***NADINE GORDIMER: ON BEING A LIBERAL WHITE SOUTH AFRICAN.*** 1994. 30 minutes. Videocassette. Distributor: Films for the Humanities and Sciences (Princeton).
Topic(s): Literature / South Africa / Conflicts
Country/region: South Africa

***NAMIBIA: REBIRTH OF A NATION.*** Directed by Kevin Harris. 1990. 45 minutes. Videocassette. Distributor: Cinema Guild (New York).
Topic(s): Conflicts / Struggles won
Country/region: Namibia

***NDEBELE WOMEN: THE RITUALS OF REBELLION.*** Produced by Shelagh Lubbock. 1997. 52 minutes. Videocassette. Distributor: Filmakers Library (New York).
Topic(s): Women / Africa's peoples / Visual arts

***NEED TO KNOW.*** Produced by Jann Turner. 1993. 25 minutes. Videocassette. Distributor: First Run/Icarus Films (New York).
Topic(s): South Africa
Country/region: South Africa

***NELSON MANDELA: THE LONG WALK TO FREEDOM.*** 1990. 28 minutes. Videocassette. Distributor: Landmark Films (Falls Church).
Topic(s): South Africa
Country/region: South Africa

***NERIA.*** Produced by Media for Development Trust. 103 minutes. Color film and videocassette. English, Portuguese, Swahili. Distributor: DSR/Development through Self-Reliance (Columbia). Comes with audio cassette, poster, and press kit. Available also from Full Frame (Toronto).

Topic(s): Women
Country/region: Uganda

***THE NEW SOUTH AFRICA: A PERSONAL JOURNEY.*** Produced by Tug Yourgrau and Joel Olicker. 1996. 58 minutes. Videocassette. Distributor: Filmakers Library (New York).
Topic(s): South Africa
Country/region: South Africa

***NIGERIA: A TALE OF TWO FAMILIES.*** 20 minutes. Videocassette. Distributor: Films for the Humanities and Sciences (Princeton). QB5093. Geographical Eye Over Africa series.
Topic(s): Food and agriculture / Nations
Country/region: Nigeria

***NIGERIA: DAMMED WATER.*** 20 minutes. Videocassette. Distributor: Films for the Humanities and Sciences (Princeton). QB5094. Geographical Eye Over Africa series.
Topic(s): Environment / Nations
Country/region: Nigeria

***THE OCRE PEOPLE: NOMADS OF NAMIBIA.*** Produced by Abraham Vorster. 1995. 32 minutes. Videocassette. Distributor: Filmakers Library (New York).
Topic(s): Africa's peoples
Country/region: Namibia

***ORDINARY PEOPLE.*** Produced by Harriet Gavshon. Directed by Clifford Bestall. Co-produced by Weekly Mail and Guardian Television. Videocassette. Distributor: First Run/Icarus Films (New York). Seven 27-minute parts. 1993-1995.
Topic(s): South Africa
Country/region: South Africa

***OUR WAY OF LOVING.*** Produced by Joanna Head. 1996. 50 minutes. Videocassette. Distributor: Filmakers Library (New York).
Topic(s): Africa's peoples

***PAIN, PASSION AND PROFIT.*** Produced by Gurinder Chadha. 1992. 49 minutes. Videocassette. Distributor: Women Make Movies (New York). No. 97360.
Topic(s): Women

***PAST AND PRESENT: TRADERS, THE CITY AND MEN FROM OVER THE SEA.*** 1994. 15 minutes. Videocassette. Distributor: Films for the Humanities and Sciences (Princeton).
Topic(s): Overview and/or multi-issue
Country/region: Morocco, Benin

***PERSPECTIVES ON VIOLENCE.*** Produced by Bailey and Associates. 90 minutes. Videocassette. Includes a 45-page booklet. Distributor: DSR/Development through Self-Reliance (Columbia).
Topic(s): South Africa
Country/region: South Africa

***PORTRAIT OF AN AFRICAN ARTIST: ELIMO NJAU THE ANTELOPE-MAN.*** 21 minutes. Videocassette. Distributor: Films for the Humanities and Sciences (Princeton). QB3340.
Topic(s): Visual arts

***PRAYING FOR RAIN.*** Produced by Sharon Sopher and Trust Mashoro. 1993. 55 minutes. Videocassette. Distributor: DSR/Development through Self-Reliance (Columbia).
Topic(s): Food and agriculture / Relief aid
Country/region: Zimbabwe

***THE PRESENT: BENIN'S PEOPLE.*** 1994. 15 minutes. Videocassette. Distributor: Films for the Humanities and Sciences (Princeton).
Topic(s): Nations / Belief systems

***THE PRICE OF CHANGE.*** Produced by Marilyn Gaunt. 1982. 26 minutes. Color film and videocassette. Study guide included. Distributor: First Run/Icarus Films (New York). Women in the Middle East series.
Topic(s): Women
Country/region: Egypt

***PRICE OF SURVIVAL: A JOURNEY TO THE WAR ZONE OF SOUTHERN SUDAN.*** 1996. Videocassette. Distributor: Bright Star Productions (London).
Topic(s): Struggles unknown / Conflicts
Country/region: Sudan

***PYGMY IN THE MIDDLE.*** Produced by Ingrid Kvale. 1993. 24 minutes. Videocassette. Distributor: African Video Centre (London).
Topic(s): Africa's peoples

***QUARTIER MOZART.*** Produced by Jean-Pierre Bekolo. 1992. 80 minutes. Color film and videocassette. In French with English subtitles. Distributor: California Newsreel (San Francisco). Distributed also by IDERA Film and Video
Topic(s): Overview and/or multi-issue
Country/region: Cameroon

***QUEST FOR CHANGE.*** Produced by Augustus Richard Norton and Steven R. Talley. 1994. 28 minutes. Videocassette. Distributor: First Run/Icarus Films (New York).
Topic(s): Democracy / Images and media
Country/region: Egypt, Algeria

***RABI.*** Produced by Gaston Kaborè. Co-produced by Cinecom Productions/BBC Television. 1994. 60 minutes. Videocassette. Distributor: Bullfrog Films (Oley). Developing Stories series. ISBN 1-56029-538-4.
Topic(s): Environment
Country/region: Burkina Faso

***REASSEMBLAGE.*** Produced by Trinh T. Minh-ha. 1982. 40 minutes. Color film and videocassette. Distributor: Women Make Movies (New York). No. 97375.
Topic(s): Women
Country/region: Senegal

***RECONCILIATION IN ZIMBABWE.*** Produced by Mark Kaplan. 1990. 34 minutes. Videocassette. Distributor: Cinema Guild (New York).
Topic(s): Conflicts
Country/region: Zimbabwe

***A REPUBLIC GONE MAD: RWANDA 1894-1994.*** Produced by Luc de Heusch and Kathleen de Bethune. 1996. 60 minutes. Videocassette. Distributor: First Run/Icarus Films (New York).
Topic(s): Conflicts
Country/region: Rwanda

***RETURN TO CAMEROON.*** Produced by Edward Guthmann. 1993. 56 minutes. Distributor: Filmakers Library (New York).
Topic(s): Overview and/or multi-issue
Country/region: Cameroon

**THE RIFT VALLEY.** 44 minutes. Videocassette. Distributor: Films for the Humanities and Sciences (Princeton). ARM2271.
Topic(s): Environment

**THE RIGHT TO BE NUBA.** Produced by Peekaboo Pictures Production. 1996. 45 minutes. Videocassette. Distributor: Filmakers Library (New York).
Topic(s): Struggles unknown
Country/region: Sudan

**RIVERS OF SAND.** Produced by Bruno Sorrentino. 1991. 58 minutes. Videocassette. Distributor: First Run/Icarus Films (New York).
Topic(s): Environment
Country/region: Mali

**RWANDAN NIGHTMARE.** Produced by Simon Gallimore. 1994. 41 minutes. Videocassette. Distributor: First Run/Icarus Films (New York).
Topic(s): Conflicts
Country/region: Rwanda

**SAINTS AND SPIRITS.** Produced by Melissa Llewelyn-Davies. 1979. 26 minutes. Color film and videocassette. Study guide included. Distributor: First Run/Icarus Films (New York). Women in the Middle East series.
Topic(s): Belief systems / Women
Country/region: Morocco

**SAMBA TRAORE.** Produced by Idrissa Ouedraogo. 1993. 85 minutes. Distributor: New Yorker Films (New York).
Topic(s): Overview and/or multi-issue
Country/region: Sahel region

**SANKARA.** Produced by Balufa Bakupa-Kanyinda. Co-produced by South Productions and Channel 4 Television (UK). 1991. 20 minutes. Videocassette. Distributor: First Run/Icarus Films (New York). The South series.
Topic(s): Overview and/or multi-issue
Country/region: Burkina Faso

**SELBE: ONE AMONG MANY.** Produced by Safi Faye. 1983. 30 minutes. Color film and videocassette. Distributor: Women Make Movies (New York). No. 97044.
Topic(s): Women
Country/region: Senegal

**SELLING THE FEELING.** 1988. 29 minutes. Videocassette. Distributor: Maryknoll World Productions (Maryknoll). Consuming Hunger series.
Topic(s): Images and media / Food and agriculture
Country/region: Ethiopia

**THE SEVEN AGES OF MUSIC.** 1994. 52 minutes. Videocassette. Distributor: Films for the Humanities and Sciences (Princeton). ARM4007.
Topic(s): Music
Country/region: South Africa

**SEX, LEMURS AND HOLES IN THE SKY.** Produced by Lawrence Moore and Robbie Stamp. Co-produced by Central TV. 52 minutes. Videocassette. Available in English for Africa only. Distributor: DSR/Development through Self-Reliance (Columbia).
Topic(s): Environment
Country/region: Madagascar

**SHAHIRA: NOMADS OF THE SAHARA.** 1993. 52 minutes. Videocassette. Distributor: Filmakers Library (New York).
Topic(s): Africa's peoples / Women
Country/region: Egypt, Sahara

**SHAPING THE IMAGE.** 1988. 29 minutes. Videocassette. Distributor: Maryknoll World Productions (Maryknoll). Consuming Hunger series.
Topic(s): Images and media / Food and agriculture
Country/region: Ethiopia

**SIDE BY SIDE: WOMEN AGAINST AIDS IN ZIMBABWE.** Produced by Harvey McKinnon Productions. 1993. 47 minutes. Videocassette. Distributors: Mennonite Central Committee (Akron) and DSR/Development through Self-Reliance (Columbia).
Topic(s): AIDS / Women
Country/region: Zimbabwe

**SIDET: FORCED EXILE.** Produced by Salem Mekuria. 1991. 60 minutes. Videocassette. Distributor: Full Frame Film and Video Distribution (Toronto). Also from Women Make Movies (New York).
Topic(s): Refugees / Women
Country/region: Ethiopia, Eritrea

**THE SINGING SHEIKH.** Produced by Heiny Srour. Co-produced by South Productions and Channel 4 Television (UK). 1991. 11 minutes. Videocassette. Distributor: First Run/Icarus Films (New York). The South series.
Topic(s): Music / Nations
Country/region: Egypt

**SOMALIA.** Produced by Jane Balfour Films. 1993. 29 minutes. Videocassette. Distributor: New Dimension Media (Eugene).
Topic(s): Foreign intervention
Country/region: Somalia

**SONG OF UMM DALAILA: THE STORY OF THE SAHRAWIS.** Produced by Danielle Smith. 1994. 30 minutes. Videocassette. Distributor: Documentary Educational Resources (Watertown).
Topic(s): Western Sahara struggle
Country/region: Western Sahara, Morocco

**SONGOLOLO: VOICES OF CHANGE.** Directed by Marianne Kaplan. 1990. 54 minutes. Color film and videocassette. Distributor: Cinema Guild (New York).
Topic(s): Music / South Africa
Country/region: South Africa

**SONGS OF THE TALKING DRUM.** Directed by Robbie Leppzer. 57 minutes. Videocassette. Also available in 30-minute version. Distributor: Turning Tide Productions (Wendell). ISBN 1-881626-09-1.
Topic(s): Music
Country/region: South Africa

**SORCERERS OF ZAIRE.** 51 minutes. Videocassette. Distributor: Films for the Humanities and Sciences (Princeton). ARM6136.
Topic(s): Belief systems
Country/region: Democratic Repubic of the Congo (Zaire)

**THE STORY OF EMAN.** Produced by Robbie Hart and Luc Côté. Co-produced by Adobe Foundation. 1994. 26 minutes. Videocassette. Distributor: Bullfrog Films (Oley). Turning series. ISBN 1-56029-598-8.
Topic(s): Women
Country/region: Egypt

***THE STORY OF IDRISSA.*** Produced by Robbie Hart and Luc Côté. Co-produced by Adobe Foundations. 1994. 26 minutes. Videocassette. Distributor: Bullfrog Films (Oley). Turning series. ISBN 1-56029-598-8.
Topic(s): Africa's peoples
Country/region: Niger

***STREET CHILDREN OF AFRICA.*** 1993. 52 minutes. Videocassette. Distributor: Films for the Humanities and Sciences (Princeton).
Topic(s): Human rights

***SUDAN: THE HARSHER FACE OF ISLAM.*** Directed by Mark Stucke. 1996. 40 minutes. Videocassette. Distributor: Filmakers Library (New York).
Topic(s): Belief systems / Struggles unknown
Country/region: Sudan

***THE SULTAN'S BURDEN.*** Directed by Jon Jerstad. Produced by Northern Lights Film Productions. 1995. 50 minutes. Videocassette. Distributor: Filmakers Library (New York).
Topic(s): Democracy
Country/region: Cameroon

***THE SURVIVAL AGE: TANZANIA.*** Produced by South African Broadcasting. 1996. 30 minutes. Videocassette. Distributor: Filmakers Library (New York). Living in Africa: African Solutions to African Problems series.
Topic(s): Development / Environment
Country/region: Tanzania

***TAUW.*** Directed by Ousmane Sembène. 1969. 27 minutes. Videocassette. In Wolof with English subtitles. Distributor: New Yorker Films (New York).
Topic(s): Cinema
Country/region: Senegal

***THESE GIRLS ARE MISSING: THE GENDER GAP IN AFRICA'S SCHOOLS.*** Produced by Shari Robertson and Michael Camerini. 1996. 60 minutes. Videocassette. Distributor: Filmakers Library (New York).
Topic(s): Women
Country/region: Malawi

***THESE HANDS.*** Directed by Flora M'Mbugu-Schelling. 1993. 30 minutes. Color film and videocassette. Distributor: Full Frame Film and Video Distribution (Toronto).
Topic(s): Women
Country/region: Tanzania, Mozambique

***TO BE A WOMAN: AFRICAN WOMEN'S RESPONSE TO THE ECONOMIC CRISIS.*** Produced by Visafric Productions. 1992. 42 minutes. Videocassette. Distributor: Mennonite Central Committee (Akron).
Topic(s): Debt / Women
Country/region: Ghana, Uganda, Zambia

***TODAY'S AFRICA: THE CHURCH AND THE PEOPLE.*** Produced by Christian Aid, BBC/UCTV. 1993. 50 minutes. Videocassette. Distributor: Friendship Press Distribution Office (Cincinnati).
Topic(s): Belief systems / Overview and/or multi-issue

***TOIVO: CHILD OF HOPE.*** Produced by Danièle Lacourse and Yvan Patry. 1990. 28 minutes. Color film and videocassette. Distributor: Full Frame Film and Video Distribution (Toronto).
Topic(s): Struggles won
Country/region: Namibia

***THE TREE OF OUR FOREFATHERS.*** Produced by Evano Multimedia Lda. Directed by Licinio Azevedo. Co-produced by BBC Television/TV Trust for the Environment. 1994. 53 minutes. Videocassette. Distributor: Bullfrog Films (Oley). ISBN 1-56029-593-7.
Topic(s): Conflicts / Refugees
Country/region: Mozambique

***THE TRIBAL MIND.*** Produced by Catherine Mullins and Marrin Cannell. Directed by Garry Greenwald. 1994. 52 minutes. Videocassette. Distributor: Bullfrog Films (Oley). The Human Race series.
Topic(s): South Africa
Country/region: South Africa

***TWO GIRLS GO HUNTING.*** Produced by Joanna Head. 1996. 50 minutes. Videocassette. Distributor: Filmakers Library (New York).
Topic(s): Africa's peoples

***UNDERSTANDING EACH OTHER.*** Produced by African Journey. 1990. 15 minutes. Videocassette. Distributor: Church World Service (Elkhart). Journey to Understanding series.
Topic(s): Images and media / Development
Country/region: Zimbabwe

***A VEILED REVOLUTION.*** Produced by Marilyn Gaunt. 1982. 26 minutes. Color film and videocassette. Study guide included. Distributor: First Run/Icarus Films (New York). Women in the Middle East series.
Topic(s): Women
Country/region: Egypt

***VOICES FROM THE SAND.*** Produced by Stephen Rooke. 1992. 58 minutes. Color film and videocassette. Distributor: Sahara Fund (Washington).
Topic(s): Struggles unknown
Country/region: Western Sahara, Algeria, Morocco

***WAITING FOR THE CARIBOU.*** Produced by Peter Entell. Co-produced by UN Disaster Relief Office. 1991. 30 minutes. Videocassette. Distributor: First Run/Icarus Films (New York).
Topic(s): Relief aid
Country/region: Mozambique

***WARRIOR MARKS.*** Produced by Pratibba Parmar and Alice Walker. 1993. 54 minutes. Color film and videocassette. Distributor: Women Make Movies (New York). No. 97220.
Topic(s): Women / Belief systems
Country/region: Senegal, Gamiba, Burkina Faso

***WATER FOR TONOUMASSÉ.*** Produced by Gary Beitel. 1990. 28 minutes. Videocassette. Distributor: Filmakers Library (New York).
Topic(s): Women
Country/region: Togo

***WE JIVE LIKE THIS.*** Produced by Cinecontact/Kinoki Production. 1993. 52 minutes. Videocassette. Distributor: Filmakers Library (New York).
Topic(s): Music / South Africa
Country/region: South Africa

***WELCOME TO THE HUMAN RACE.*** Produced by Wolpert Productions. 1996. 52 minutes. Videocassette. Distributor: Filmakers Library (New York).
Topic(s): South Africa

Country/region: South Africa

**WHAT DO WE KNOW ABOUT AFRICA?** Produced by Barbara Brown. 25 minutes. Videocassette. Distributor: African Studies Center, Boston University (Boston).
Topic(s): Overview and/or multi-issue

**WINNING THE PEACE.** Produced by Danièlle Lacourse and Yvan Patry. 1992. 30 minutes. Videocassette. Distributor: Full Frame Film and Video Distribution (Toronto).
Topic(s): Struggles won
Country/region: Eritrea, Ethiopia

**WITH THESE HANDS: HOW WOMEN FEED AFRICA.** Produced by Chris Sheppard and Claude Sauvageot. 1987. 33 minutes. Color film and videocassette. Distributor: Full Frame Film and Video Distribution (Toronto) and Filmakers Library (New York).
Topic(s): Food and agriculture / Women
Country/region: Kenya, Zimbabwe, Burkina Faso

**WITNESS TO APARTHEID.** Produced by Sharon Sopher. 58 minutes. Videocassette. Distributor: DSR/Development through Self-Reliance (Columbia).
Topic(s): South Africa
Country/region: South Africa

**WOMEN AT RISK.** Produced by Radio-Television Society of Quebec. 1991. 56 minutes. Videocassette. Distributor: Filmakers Library (New York).
Topic(s): Women / Refugees
Country/region: Zambia, Mozambique

**WOMEN AT WORK.** Produced by Belbo Productions. 51 minutes. Videocassette. Distributor: DSR/Development through Self-Reliance (Columbia).
Topic(s): Environment / Women
Country/region: Kenya

**WOMEN OF NIGER.** Directed by Anne-Laure Folly. 1993. 26 minutes. Videocassette. Distributor: Full Frame Film and Video Distribution (Toronto). Also from Women Make Movies.
Topic(s): Women / Human rights / Democracy
Country/region: Niger

**WOMEN OF THE SAHEL.** Produced by Paolo Quaregna and Mahamane Souleymane. 1995. 52 minutes. Videocassette. Distributor: First Run/Icarus Films (New York).
Topic(s): Women
Country/region: Niger

**THE WOMEN WHO SMILE.** Produced by Joanna Head. 1996. 50 minutes. Videocassette. Distributor: Filmakers Library (New York).
Topic(s): Africa's peoples / Women

**WOMEN: CHANGING OUR ROLE.** Produced by African Journey. 1990. 15 minutes. Videocassette. Distributor: Church World Service (Elkhart). Journey to Understanding series.

Topic(s): Overview and/or multi-issue / Women
Country/region: Zimbabwe

**THE WORLD OF ISLAM.** 180 minutes. Videocassette. 5 parts. Distributor: Films for the Humanities and Sciences (Princeton). QB707.
Topic(s): Belief systems

**XALA.** Directed by Ousmane Sembène. 1974. 123 minutes. Videocassette. In Wolof and French with English subtitles. Distributor: New Yorker Films (New York).
Topic(s): Cinema
Country/region: Senegal

**YOU CAN'T EAT POTENTIAL: BREAKING AFRICA'S CYCLE OF POVERTY.** Directed by Tony Freeth. 1997. 56 minutes. Videocassette. Distributor: Filmakers Library (New York).
Topic(s): Food and agriculture
Country/region: Tanzania, Ghana, Benin

**YOU, AFRICA!** Directed by Ndiouga Moctar Ba. 1993. 43 minutes. Videocassette. Distributor: California Newsreel (San Francisco). In Wolof and French with English subtitles.
Topic(s): Music
Country/region: Senegal

**ZAIRE: THE CYCLE OF THE SERPENT.** Produced by Thierry Michel. 1992. 58 minutes. Videocassette. Distributor: First Run/Icarus Films (New York).
Topic(s): Nations
Country/region: Democratic Republic of the Congo (Zaire)

**ZAMBIA: A COPPER MINER'S FAMILY.** 20 minutes. Videocassette. Distributor: Films for the Humanities and Sciences (Princeton). QB5097. Geographical Eye Over Africa series.
Topic(s): Mining / Nations
Country/region: Zambia

**ZIMBABWE: NO EASY WALK.** Directed by Bernard Odjidja. 1988. 57 minutes. Videocassette. Distributor: Full Frame Film and Video Distribution (Toronto). No Easy Walk series. Also from Cinema Guild (New York).
Topic(s): Conflicts / Nations
Country/region: Zimbabwe

**ZIMBABWE: TALKING STONES.** 58 minutes. Videocassette. Distributor: Films for the Humanities and Sciences (Princeton). QB3341.
Topic(s): Visual arts
Country/region: Zimbabwe

**ZIMBABWE: TOURISM ALONG THE ZAMBEZI RIVER.** 20 minutes. Videocassette. Distributor: Films for the Humanities and Sciences (Princeton). QB5096. Geographical Eye Over Africa series.
Topic(s): Environment / Development / Nations
Country/region: Zimbabwe

# CURRICULUM RESOURCES

WorldViews is grateful to Ron Nicosia for writing the majority of the annotations below, to Anibel Comelo for data entry, and to Peggy Mead, Robin Cushman, and Christine Lampe for editing and proofreading.

WorldViews does not necessarily endorse the content and educational approach of all of the curriculum materials listed below. Educators should consult with African studies centers at nearby colleges or universities for help in evaluating particular materials for classroom use. See also the print and electronic review materials produced by Africa Access, 2204 Quinton Rd., Silver Spring, MD 20910 USA.

*Note:* References in the descriptions to "key stages" indicate grade levels in the national curriculum in the United Kingdom.

***AFRICA DATA SAMPLER: A GEO-REFERENCED DATABASE FOR ALL AFRICAN COUNTRIES.*** Produced by World Resources Institute, World Conservation Monitoring Center, and PADCO, Inc. World Resources Institute, 1709 New York Ave, NW, Washington, DC 20006, USA. Windows format. With 148-page User's Guide. 1995. $179.

This World Resources Institute CD-ROM is a sophisticated research tool that makes use of digital mapping to visualize and analyze environment and development information for 53 countries in Africa. A typical use of the *Africa Data Sampler* would be to call up a country map on screen and then click on one or more of the number of items on a "map legend" to see the lines of a road or railroad transportation network in a country or to display the physical extent and population density of large urban areas or to study the country's system of rivers, lakes, and reservoirs. Users interested in environmental issues might use the *Africa Data Sampler* to examine a country's protected areas, wetlands, or production forests, and then use visual representations of information from related "data sets" to do comparative surveys of environmental features. Similarly, a user with an interest in population could display population density information on a country map and then prepare detailed calculations based on a variety of spatial selections. The spiral-bound User's Guide provides clear instructions on how to navigate around the numerous features of the *Africa Data Sampler.* The CD-ROM uses the ArcView software program to display its data. The User's Guide tells where and how to find and download this free software. For university and other students at advanced levels.

***AFRICA FILE: NOTES, QUOTES AND QUESTIONS ABOUT AFRICA AND DEVELOPMENT.*** Susan Gage. Victoria International Development Education Association (VIDEA). VIDEA, 407-620 View St., Victoria, BC V8W 1J6, Canada. 1989. ISBN 0-921783-08-6.

The ten units of this text cover a wide range of topics, including development, the consequences of colonialism, food and health, aid and debt, the environment, population growth, and human rights. Short readings, provocative quotations, graphics, and statistical tables stimulate interest. Each unit includes several activities for individual and group work. Teacher's notes at the end of each unit provide an overview of the topic and of key concepts. An annotated list of audio-visual resources, bibliography, and index are included. High school and above.

***AFRICA IN CRISIS.*** Peter White. Save the Children, Education Unit, 17 Grove Lane, London SE5 8BRD, England. 1993. £ 4. ISBN 1-870322-59-2.

Includes four posters that question assumptions about Africa; five topic sheets: "Food and Water," "Aid," "Debt and Trade," "Famine," "Population and the Environment"; a crisis scenario, "Famine in Your Town"; and four quiz cards with eight questions each. The materials provide a stimulating starting point for discussion about the causes of famines and the relationship between African countries and other countries that provide aid. High school level.

***AFRICA'S FOOD CRISIS: ITS ROOTS, ITS FUTURE.*** Mutombo Mpanya and David Holdridge. Catholic Relief Services Global Education Office, 209 West Fayette St., Baltimore, MD 21201-3403, USA. Text = 32 pp. Teacher's guide = 28 pp.

The text has five parts—"Ecological Conditions," "Traditional Methods," "Colonial Influences," "Post-Independence Policies," and "The Future"—each followed by questions. Maps, photographs, and a glossary enhance the text's usefulness. The teacher's guide summarizes the main points of each part and includes additional discussion questions and stories relevant to each chapter. An appendix to the teacher's guide includes additional activities and a list of audio-visual resources. High school level.

***AFRICA: FACT, FICTION AND OPINION.*** Andy Scott and Dave Thomas. Nottinghamshire Education Committee, Centre for Multicultural Education, The Melbourne Centre, Melbourne Rd., Leicester LE2 0GU, England.

Uses brief readings and illustrations from European and Arab historical sources to stimulate thinking about African history and some of the misconceptions about it. Exercises ask students to compare the sources and account for differences, considering such factors as the background of the author. Difficult words and phrases are defined. High school level.

***THE AFRICAN ANTHEM: NKOSI SIKELEL' IAFRIKA.*** Enoch Mankayi Sontonga. Trans. African Arts Trust. African Arts Trust, 86 Cambridge Gardens, London W10 6HS, England. 1994. £6.95.

This small packet contains a cassette recording of the African Anthem titled "God Bless Africa." Included in the packet are a brief history of the anthem, words and music, an English translation, and a phonetic guide to the song in two Nguni languages, Xhosa and Zulu.

***AFRICAN HISTORY ON FILE.*** Diagram Visual Information/Diagram Group. Facts on File, 460 Park Ave. South, New York, NY 10016, USA. 1994. Looseleaf bound. ISBN 0-8160-2910-5. Maps, bibliography, chronology, index.

"Much of what is commonly cited as 'African history'," the compilers of this reference book so accurately observe, "details the exploits of peoples other than Africans themselves—usually Arabs or Europeans—and their views of the societies they encountered." The 500+ maps and charts assembled in *African History on File*—particularly those in the book's first seven sections—demonstrate graphically that Africa can boast of having had "many powerful, rich, and sophisticated civilizations which flourished quite independently of Middle Eastern or Western influences." The graphical materials and accompanying narrative introductions in the looseleaf-bound book are divided into ten sections, beginning with the prehistory of the African continent and the early history of the Nile area. In the center sections (3-7), the history of Africa is analyzed by geographical region: North, West, East, Central, and Southern Africa. The concluding sections focus on the history of European exploration and colonialism (section 8), trade and produce exchange within Africa, and between the continent and the rest of the world (section 9), and twentieth-century Africa (section 010).

***AFRICAN STUDIES AND THE UNDERGRADUATE CURRICULUM.*** Lynne Rienner Publishers, 1800 30th St., Boulder, CO 80301, USA. 1994. 335 pp. $25. ISBN 1-55587-445-2.

This multi-disciplinary collection of 23 scholarly essays addresses four topics: interculturalism and African studies, pedagogical and curriculum issues, study programs in Africa, and the evolution of undergraduate programs in African studies.

***AFRICAN STUDIES: CURRICULUM MATERIALS FOR TEACHERS.*** Center for African Studies, University of Illinois, 1208 West California, #101, Urbana, IL 61801, USA. 1987. 2nd ed. 353 pp. $15.

Topically arranged readings written by University of Illinois faculty. Topics include "Government and Politics," "Agricultural and Economic Development," "Health, Science, and the Environment," and "Language and Literature." The readings include references and the text concludes with a chapter of specialized bibliographies and lists of resources. The Table of Contents indicates the level of the materials (elementary school, middle school, senior high school and adult, general interest).

***AFRICAN STUDIES HANDBOOK FOR ELEMENTARY AND SECONDARY SCHOOL TEACHERS.*** Center for International Education, School of Education, University of Massachusetts, Hills House South, Amherst, MA 01003, USA. January 1983. 221 pp. ISBN 0-932288-69-3.

Focusing on African culture, this text provides detailed instructions for lessons on a range of themes: the generation gap, women's roles, Liberian and Kenyan cities, Senegalese clothing, education through folk tales. There are appendixes on clothing, food, and games. The lists of resources are outdated.

***AFRICAN STUDIES ON CD-ROM.*** National Information Services Corporation, 3100 St. Paul St., Baltimore, MD 21218, USA. MS-DOS format. 1996. $995, plus $18 shipping. 2 issues/year.

This compilation of African studies-related databases, produced by NISC South Africa, contains more than 180,000 records from sources in Africa, Europe, and North America. Institutions that supplied their database records include the Africa Institute in Pretoria (1981-1996), the School of African and Oriental Studies at the University of London (1989-1996), the Africana Library at the University of California at Los Angeles (1981-1992), and the International Library of African Music at Rhodes University in Grahamstown, South Africa. (NISC's "ROMWright" software creates a unique composite record when similar records are supplied by two or more of the originating sources.) The CD-ROM offers three search-level options (novice, advanced, and expert) and a variety of display, editing, and printing possibilities. Use of NISC's "rotated index" shows users lists of related terms that might contain information being sought in the search. The rotated index aids in searching for information on South Africa's Bishop Desmond Tutu, for instance, by steering users to the "politics-Tutu" category, in addition to the more obvious "Tutu, Desmond" records in the database. Each record in the database contains title, author, keyterms, source, annotation, and location fields. Materials in the various databases are in numerous languages and formats (e.g., books, articles, reading lists). The results of random searches suggest the riches to be mined from this unique database. A search on "traditional religion" yielded 222 hits; "Mandela" turned up more than 575 references to Nelson Mandela, from 1992 to 1996; and a search on "Egypt" produced almost 1800 database records. Two additional references to "Egypt" in the database were misspelled as "Egptian" and "Egpyt," underlining the fragility of these databases in terms of their foolproof accuracy.

*ASPECTS OF AFRICA: QUESTIONING OUR PERCEPTIONS.* Cathy Nash. Manchester Education Project, Manchester Polytechnic, Manchester M20 8RG, England. 1988. 72 pp. £ 13. Includes slides. ISBN 1-869818-32-6.

Slides and photographs provide the basis for questions and activities intended to help students build visual analysis skills, recognize and challenge stereotypes, and develop an understanding of the society, politics, economy, and geography of several African countries. Students are introduced to such topics as agriculture, education, everyday life, nature, work, and towns and villages. In a final section, students are asked to evaluate media coverage of Africa. Includes slides, maps, statistics, a glossary, and lists of resources. High school level.

*BALANCING THE BOOKS: DEVELOPMENT CHOICES IN NAMIBIA.* Richard Borowski and Cath Sanders. Leeds Development Education Centre, 151-153 Cardigan Road, Leeds LS6 1LJ, England. 1993. 15 pp. £ 2.50. ISBN 1-871268-40-0.

This role-play and decision-making exercise, requiring about an hour and a half, introduces students to the complexity of development issues. The new Republic of Namibia serves as an example of a developing country for which students, acting as the heads of goverment ministries, have to allocate national resources and tackle issues such as unemployment, improvement of health and education, and rural development. The text provides instructions for the teacher, background information, descriptions of ministers' roles, and budget figures, and includes an overview of Namibia's history and economy and a list of resources. Written for 14 to 18 year olds.

*BARICHO: A VILLAGE IN KENYA.* Richard Wright. Warwickshire World Studies Centre, Manor Hall, Sandy Lane, Warks CV32 6RD, England. 84 pp. £ 13.50.

The activity pack provides materials for the study of a community in a developing country. The book first looks at the geography and climate of Kenya as a whole, then focuses on the Kariuki family, who live near Baricho, a village in central Kenya. The book contains maps, rainfall and temperature graphs, and instruction sheets for students to use in group activities that explore aspects of farming and village life. A set of 16 photosheets, each consisting of three to five black-and-white photographs with captions, and a set of 16 color photographs provide the basis for numerous activities. Key Stage 2 in geography.

*BENIN SOURCE PACK FOR KEY STAGE 2.* Andrew Forson. Northamptonshire Black History Group, c/o Wellingborough REC, Wellingborough NN8 1HT, England. 1992. 20 pp. £ 16.95. ISBN 1-873886-04-7.

The focus of this teaching pack is the Kingdom of Benin, today part of the Edo state in southern Nigeria, during the period of its greatest power, from the mid-1400s to the mid-1600s. The pack contains five booklets: "Geography and the Environment," "Rulers and Court Life," "The Empire," "Society and Industry," and "Culture." Each 10- to 12-page booklet contains an introductory section for teachers, background information sheets (with quotations from historical sources), and suggestions for activities. Black-and-white photographs of plaques and artefacts highlight Benin's material culture and artistic tradition. Key Stage 2.

*BENIN: AN AFRICAN KINGDOM.* Cathy Midwinter. World Wide Fund for Nature, Panda House, Weyside Park, Godalming, Surrey GU7 1XR, England. 1994. 100 pp. $19.95. ISBN 1-85850-006-0.

The text provides numerous pair, group, and role-play activities for exploring the history, geography, culture and environment of Benin. The first section, "Learning to Use Evidence," introduces students to using maps, listening to oral histories, and gathering information from photographs. The second section explores four themes: "People and the Environment," "City and Village Life," "Court Life and Government," and "Trade and Markets." The third focuses on the British invasion of Benin in 1897. Teacher's notes provide detailed instructions for all activites. The pack contains a set of 24 large color photographs taken in and around Benin, a color timeline comparing important events in Benin and British history from 1440 to 1700, a poster-sized map of Benin City, a hand-drawn map of the city's main marketplace, and an informational poster on brasscasting, for which Benin City is famous. Key Stage 2 in history and geography.

*BENIN: STUDY OF AN AFRICAN KINGDOM.* Sandra Baker et al., comps. Newman and Westhill Colleges, National Primary Centre, Balden Rd., Harbourne, Birmingham, B32 2EH, England.

Using a cooperative learning model, this text provides numerous pair and group activities for introducing students to the geography, history, and material culture of Benin. The text has five sections—"Geographers," "Storytellers," "European Visitors," "Archaeologists," and "Craft Workers"—each designed to give students practice in evaluating different kinds of information. The sections include general instructions for the teacher and copy masters of activity sheets. Primary level.

*A CASE FOR CHANGE: RIGHTS, REPRESSION, AND RESPONSES IN SOUTH AFRICA.* Caroline Willems et al. Leeds Development Education Centre, 151-153 Cardigan Rd., Leeds LS6 1LJ, England. 1988. 108 pp. ISBN 1-871268-00-1.

Written almost a decade ago, this text was intended to provide an introduction to apartheid, repression, and violence in South Africa. An introductory chapter that explores the relevance of studying South Africa is followed by five thematic chapters: "Human Rights," "Repression and Protest," "Women and Apartheid," "Repression and the Media," and "International Protest." Twenty activities, including discussions of case studies and sophisticated role-plays, are explained in detail. The book includes a glossary, a map of South Africa, evaluation questions, and a list of resources. Developed for students aged 16 and over.

*COMPREHENSIVE MAPWORK FOR SOUTHERN AFRICAN SCHOOLS.* G. K. Erbynn. Heinemann Educational Publishers, Halley Court, Jordan Hill, Oxford OX2 8EJ, England. 1993. 170 pp. ISBN 0-435-95912-3.

This text provides secondary school students with a thorough introduction to geography. Exercises give practice in interpreting a variety of maps, including contour and topographical maps. Full color maps from Botswana, Lesotho, Mauritius, South Africa, Swaziland, Tanzania, Zambia, and Zimbabwe provide the basis for review and examination questions.

**CONFLICT IN SOMALIA AND ETHIOPIA.** Patrick Gilkes. Wayland (Publishers) Ltd., 61 Western Road, Hove, East Sussex BN3 1JD, England. 1994. 48 pp. £8.99. ISBN 0-7502-1179-2.

Part of a series for young readers on socio-political conflicts around the world, this heavily illustrated book briefly examines the origins and consequences of the recent crises in the Horn of Africa. The book discusses the Ethiopian revolution of 1974, the war between Ethiopia and Somalia, the Eritrean struggle for independence, and the civil war in Somalia. It also provides an overview of famines in the Horn of Africa and of international relief aid. Includes a short glossary and list of resources.

**CONTEMPORARY ISSUES FOR WOMEN IN AFRICA SOUTH OF THE SAHARA.** Susan Hill Gross and Mary Hill Rojas. Upper Midwest Women's History Center, 6300 Walker St., St. Louis Park, MN 55416, USA. 1992. Rev. ed. 284 pp. Spiral-bound.

This manual provides a wide range of materials with detailed lesson plans focusing on the issues of family (infancy and sex preference, polygyny, childbearing, motherhood, widowhood), work, and the empowerment of women through organizing. Materials include statistical sheets, case studies, group exercises, and a glossary. Detailed notes are provided for the video "Women and Work in Africa South of the Sahara" to be used with the text. All handouts are reprinted in a separate binder. For secondary to adult-level students.

**DOING IT OURSELVES: A TEACHING PACK FOR SECONDARY SCHOOLS ON THE THEME OF SELF-RELIANCE.** Richard Wright, Julie Bradley, and Myf Hodkin. Warwickshire World Studies Centre, Manor Hall, Sandy Lane, Leamington Spa, Warks CV32 6RD, England. £7.50.

This teaching pack explores the affects of colonial rule and development on formerly self-sufficient communities, focusing on the Maasai of Kenya. Book 1 (36 pp.) introduces the concepts of basic needs, rights, and self-reliance; provides historical background on the Maasai under British rule and after Kenya's independence; examines Kenya's economy and trade; and provides teacher's notes and answers to the activities in Book 2. The topics explored in Book 2 (36 pp.) include secondary school education, village health care, and the role of women in development. A set of 16 black-and-white photo-cards illustrates aspects of traditional Maasai culture.

**ERITREA: AFRICA'S NEWEST COUNTRY.** Ruth Lewis and Claire Booker. Christian Aid, P.O. Box 100, London SE1 7RT, England. 1993. 20 + pp. £10.

This pack introduces students to ordinary family life in Eritrea and to the effects of drought and war. The student textbook profiles two families in two different regions of Eritrea, provides an overview of customs, and includes maps of Eritrea and Africa. The daily lives of the two families are reflected in a set of 28 color photographs. The teacher's guide provides historical and statistical information on Eritrea and detailed instructions for activities that ask students to compare the lives of the two families and to consider some of the problems refugees face. Includes a list of resources. Key Stage 2 in geography.

**ETHIOPIA.** Leslie Semaan. Victoria International Development Association (VIDEA), 407-620 View St., Victoria, BC V8W 1J6, Canada. 1988. 114 pp. Illustrated by Ross Pomeroy. ISBN 0-921783-07-8.

The goal of this text is to give students "the opportunity to go beyond the media coverage that has led to the perception of the whole of Ethiopia as a famine-stricken land." Seventeen short chapters provide an overview of Ethiopian history, geography, culture, and contemporary life. Twenty-five pages of activities corresponding to each of the chapters follow the main text; these consist of discussion questions, problem-solving activities, and research projects. Includes a fact sheet, map, and glossary. Elementary school.

**THE FINAL FRONTIER: LAND, ENVIRONMENT AND PASTORALISM IN KENYA.** Richard Borowski, Peter Kisopia, and Geoff Sayer. Leeds Development Education Centre, 151-153 Cardigan Road, Leeds LS6 1LJ, England. 1993. 48 pp. £9.50. ISBN 1-871268-50-8. See "Kenya: The Final Frontier" CD-ROM below.

The text provides instructions and materials for five activities focusing on the Maasai pastoralists: "Lifestyle," a ranking and photo activity based on 24 color photgraphs; "Frontiers of Freedom," a role-play that explores the effects of colonialism on Maasai settlement and movement patterns; "Economically Speaking," a photo activity followed by a true/false quiz that introduces the issues of development and tourism; Fate Worse than Debt," a role-play showing the link between international debt and environmental damage; and a cost/benefit exercise that addresses land rights issues ("All for One or One for All?"). Includes a list of resources. Key Stages 3 and 4.

**FISH AND SHIPS: A TEACHING PACK ABOUT FISHING AND THE ENVIRONMENT IN BRITAIN AND SIERRA LEONE.** Patrick McDaniel et al. Hull Development Education Centre, c/o David Lister School, Rustenburg Street, Hull HU9 2PR, England. 1991. £6.95.

This educational pack explores the impact of technology on resource exploitation by contrasting the fishing industries of Godrich in Sierra Leone and Hull, an English town. The text contains background on renewable resources, worksheets comparing fishing methods and fish-processing in the two cities, and suggested activities. Includes set of 10 color photos.

**FRONTPAGE: A NEWSPAPER SIMULATION EXERCISE ABOUT ETHIOPIA AND ERITREA.** Angela Johnson et al., eds. and comps. Development Education (DEED), East Dorset Professional Education Centre, Bournemouth BH8 8NR, England. 1992. 20 pp. £2.25. ISBN 0-9515118-2-3.

In this role-play exercise, students play journalists from several newspapers assigned to do an article on Ethiopia and Eritrea since the end of the war in 1991. The authors suggest that the roles of the Ethiopian and Eritrean interviewees be played by people with knowledge of the countries. Detailed descriptions of the roles and historical and statistical information on Ethiopia and Eritrea are provided. In an introductory exercise, students examine newspapers for style, content, and political orientation. After the interviews, students write front-page articles and headlines appropriorate to the style and sympathies of the paper they represent.

***HANGING BY A THREAD: TRADE, DEBT AND COTTON IN TANZANIA.*** Richard Borowski and Nigel West. Leeds Development Education Centre, 151-153 Cardigan Road, Leeds LS6 1LJ, England. 1992. 31 pp. £ 6.50. ISBN 1-871268-35-4.

The text contains instructions and materials for five activities focusing on a cotton-growing area of Tanzania: a photo activity based on a set of 16 black-and-white photographs of rural life; a decision activity concerning food crops and cash crops; a role-play about the production and pricing of jeans; a role-play that explores the effects of World Bank and IMF policies; and a ranking activity concerning ways of addressing the problems of the cotton farmers. Includes a list of resources. For 13 to 19 year-olds.

***THE HORN: PEOPLE, POVERTY AND ENVIRONMENT.*** Produced by SCET. SCIAF: Scottish Catholic International Aid Fund, 5 Oswald St., Glasgow G1 4QR, Scotland. CD-ROM. Windows format. 1995.

This professionally produced high-quality multi-media guide—intended for use in school settings in Scotland, England, and Wales—introduces users to the "people, poverty, and environment" of the Horn of Africa. The educational CD-ROM is divided into eight thematic sections: country profiles (Sudan, Somalia, Eritrea, Ethiopia, and Djibouti); people and the environment (urbanization, environmental degradation, etc.); North-South relations (aid, trade, debt, the role of the United Nations); politics of food (e.g., the causes of famine); women (their role in development, for instance); human rights (emphasis on abuse of political rights, with case studies); health (focuses on "the major health problems of the area"); and education (looks at the provision of education in the Horn, its importance in the development of the region, and the factors that "make providing education difficult"). The disc makes effective use of 200 captioned photographs and offers helpful utilities such as bookmarks and a pop-up notepad. Each multi-layered section offers access to a glossary, statistical tables, and resource listings related to the subject under investigation.

***AN INTRODUCTION TO ZAMBIA.*** Heather Jarvis. UNICEF-UK, Unit 1, Rignals Lane, Galleywood, Chelmsford Essex CM2 8TU, England. £ 11.95. Line illustrations by Elaine Nipper. ISBN 1-871440-08-4.

This resource pack for primary school teachers includes two booklets, 28 high-quality photographs (24 in color), a color map of Africa, and a poster, "Education in Zambia." A 19-page booklet, "An Introduction to Zambia," provides an overview of Zambian history and geography, the educational system, and everyday life for Zambian children, and includes a song and a folk tale. "Palm Grove," a 51-page booklet, offers a detailed look at a town in Zambia, focusing on the lives of two seventh graders at Palm Grove Basic School. The photo set and the maps and illustrations in the booklet serve as the basis for lessons on a broad range of topics, including school, weather and landscape, science and technology, tourism, trade, work, and music and crafts. Resource sheets include instructions for doing basic scientific experiments and for making simple musical instruments and a camera.

***INTRODUCTORY GUIDE TO AFRICA.*** Unitarian Universalist Service Committee, 130 Prospect St., Cambridge, MA 02139-1813, USA. January 1990. 251 pp. $14.95.

This six-session program contains short readings, discussion questions, brainstorming exercises, and role-plays that explore U.S.-Africa cultural, economic, political, and military connections and address the issues of children and youth, the environment, food and hunger, and health. The readings are from *Africa News, Africa Report, New York Times, Washington Post,* and other sources. Includes a chronology of important events in African history, maps and statistics for every African country, profiles of African regional organizations, a list of African studies programs and U.S. organizations working on African issues, and a bibliography.

***KAPSOKWONY RURAL KENYA.*** Steve Brace. ActionAid, Old Church House, Church Steps, Frome, Somerset BA11 1PL, England. 1992. £ 10.99.

This activity pack focuses on the lifestyle of a family in Kapsokwony, a rural region of western Kenya. Booklets on Kenya and Kapsokwony provide geographical information, historical background, and information on health and eduction, and a teacher's guide contains instructions for eight activities that explore farming life. Materials for the activities, including 30 large color photographs, illustrations, and maps, are provided. Key Stage 2 in geography.

***KENYA.*** David Marshall and Geoff Sayer. Heinemann Publishers, Halley Court, Oxford OX2 8EJ, England. 1994. 32 pp. ISBN 0-431-07255-8.

This overview of the people and customs of Kenya is heavily illustrated with color photos and includes a glossary and index. A good introduction for very young readers.

***KENYA: A COUNTRY IN TRANSITION.*** Nancy Jakubowski. Zero Population Growth, 1601 Connecticut Ave., NW, Washington, DC 20009, USA. $10. One teaching guide and 11 copies of a student handout.

The illustrated, 8-page student handout offers an overview of population growth and modernization issues, along with a glossary. The 4-page teacher's guide contains discussion questions and five group activities for reinforcing basic concepts. Intended for high school social science and science classes.

***KENYA: THE FINAL FRONTIER?*** Bernard Dady. Produced by Leeds Development Education Centre, Educational and Multimedia Association, Matrix Multimedia. Matrix Multimedia, 10 Hey St., Bradford BD7 1DQ, England. Windows format. 1996. £ 79.

This "active learning resource" was designed by Matrix Multimedia, in association with Educational & Multimedia Associates, to fit in with geography requirements in the National Curriculum in England and Wales for students aged 11 to 16. The CD-ROM focuses on the lives of Maasai pastoralists in Kenya, raising questions about land use, economic and human development, and environmental degradation as they affect the Maasai. Students explore these issues through five interactive modules: (1) "Lifestyle": an activity based on the examination of photographs to answer questions about the Maasai lifestyle; (2) "Change and development": an activity that explores outside influences on the Maasai people; (3) "Frontiers of freedom": a study of the influence of colonialism on Maasai land use and the grazing patterns of

CURRICULUM RESOURCES

Maasai livestock; (4) "A fate worse than debt": a simulation that demonstrates the link between economic difficulties and environmental degradation; (5) "All for one or one for all": a cost-benefit activity that analyzes the arguments for and against the subdividing of group ranches in Maasai pastoral areas. Student activities on the CD-ROM include government roleplays, investigative assignments, photo hotspot screens, grazing land tests, and drag and drop exercises. Ample supplementary materials are available to the teacher, including worksheets that can be printed from the CD-ROM for classroom use. The "Matrix Geography Series" CD-ROM is based on an award-winning educational packet produced and distributed by the Leeds Development Education Centre.

***KNOWHOW: A SKILLS STUDY PACK.*** Jean Bareham. Sead, 23 Castle St., Edinburgh EH2 3DN, Scotland. 55 pp. £ 4.95.

This pack contains a booklet on women organising in Scotland, a booklet on women organizing in South Africa, and a guide for using the materials. The booklets include background, case studies, and photographs. They provide an overview of the social and political problems facing women in each country and describe attempts to overcome the problems through collective action. A list of useful publications is also included.

***LESSON PLANS ON AFRICAN HISTORY AND GEOGRAPHY: A TEACHING RESOURCE.*** The Center for African Studies University of Florida, 427 Grinter Hall, Gainesville, FL 32611-2037, USA. 1992. 88 pp.

Introductory chapters offer a geographical and cultural overview. Among the historical topics treated are early Christianity in Egypt and Ethiopia, the origin and spread of Islam, the Saharan caravan route, the African diaspora, and the history of Zimbabwe. Each chapter includes an essay of several pages, discussion questions, short answer and/or true-false questions, essay topics, and a bibliography. Intended for secondary school students.

***LET YOUR VOICE BE HEARD! SONGS FROM GHANA AND ZIMBABWE.*** Abraham Kobena Adzinyah, Dumisani Maraire, and Judith Cook Tucker. World Music Press, Multicultural Materials for Educators, P.O. Box 2565, Danbury, CT 06813, USA. 1986. 116 pp. Musical transcriptions by Judith Cook Tucker. ISBN 0-937203-00-9.

Cassette contains 19 game songs, call-and-response songs, and multipart recreational songs from the Akan people of Ghana and the Shona of Zimbabwe. The text provides transcriptions, notes on the cultural context, performance notes, a pronunciation guide, a glossary, and a bibliography.

***LIVING AND LEARNING IN A TANZANIAN VILLAGE: A CHILD'S PERSPECTIVE.*** Rick Dodgson and Cathy Midwinter. Manchester Development Education Project c/o Manchester Polytechnic, 801 Wilmslow Road, Manchester M20 8RG, England. 1992. 25 + pp. £ 11. ISBN 1-869818-47-4.

This activity pack for elementary school students provides a set of 24 large black-and-white photographs that "show positive aspects of life in Tanzania." The aims of this cross-curricular pack are "to counteract generalised and stereotyped images children may hold about Africans and to develop children's visual awareness and understanding of how to 'read' photographs." A handbook for teachers contains 20 activities, detailed descriptions of the photos and questions about them, background information on Tanzania, and a short glossary of basic Swahili words. Included in the pack are a general educational poster on Tanzania, maps of Africa, Tanzania and Kirua (a northern Tanzanian village), and a simplified version of the Peter's Projection world map. Key Stage 2.

***MAPPING AFRICA: A CURRICULUM UNIT FOR GRADES 6-10.*** Stephen Cummins and Tara Washburn. Africa Project, Stanford Program on International and Cross-Cultural Education (SPICE). Africa Project/SPICE Institute for International Studies (IIS), Littlefield Center, Rm. 14, Stanford, CA 94305-5013, USA. 1994. 72 pp.

Lessons and handouts introduce students to the physical and political geography of Africa and to basic environmental and ecological terms. "Map hunts" give students practice using maps and globes. Includes suggestions for group work and answer keys to exercises.

***MATERIAL CULTURE OF KENYA.*** Sultan Somjee. East African Educational Publishers, Brick Court, Mpaka Road/Woodside Grove, Nairobi, Kenya. 1993. 116 pp. $17. ISBN 9966-46-749-1.

This text provides an introduction to the traditional culture of Kenya through an analysis of the forms and functions of dress, tools, ornaments, and furniture. Numerous photographs (some of poor quality) and illustrations accompany the text. Exercises at the end of each chapter test students' understanding and ask students to examine their own material culture.

***MEETING THE THIRD WORLD THROUGH WOMEN'S PERSPECTIVES: CONTEMPORARY WOMEN IN SOUTH ASIA, AFRICA, AND LATIN AMERICA.*** Susan Hill Gross and Mary Hill Rojas. Upper Midwest Women's History Center, 6300 Walker St., St. Louis Park, MN 55416, USA. 1988. 110 pp.

The text focuses on women in the Third World and the issues of family, work, and empowerment. The first part provides teachers with detailed lesson plans using a wide range of materials, including statistical sheets, descriptions of a woman's work day in various countries, brief descriptions of several women's organizations, and a 6-page glossary. There is also a lesson plan for a slide presentation on women as heads of households in the Third World. The second part contains detachable copies of all handouts. Includes a list of resources and a bibliography. For grades 8 through 12. See *Third World Women: Family, Work, and Empowerment* below.

***MOZAMBIQUE: APARTHEID'S SECOND FRONT: A RESOURCE KIT.*** Canadian Council for International Cooperation (COCAMO), 1 Nicholas St., Ottawa, ON K1N 7B7, Canada. 1988. $10.

This resource kit includes nine illustrated background papers (8 to 12 pages each) that focus on the history, society, and economy of Mozambique since the revolution and discuss the background and devastating consequences of the war being waged against the government by the South-African supported MNR in 1988, when these materials were compiled. Nine illustrated brochures, intended for public distribution, cover essentially the same material. A map, a poster, and a user's guide with a resource list are also enclosed.

*MUSIC IN A MULTICULTURAL SOCIETY: EXPLORING AFRICAN MUSIC.* Mark Bradsgaw, comp. Leicestershire Multiculural Centre, Harrrison Road, Leicester, England. 1990. 32 pp. £ 2.95.

This handbook raises awareness of the wealth of African music and provides a guide to compositional techniques. The recommended starter pack of music from Africa features ten records that include traditional and modern music in various styles by both men and women. Brief descriptions of the riff, the drone, vocals, lyrics, chord sequence and instrumentation are included. An appendix provides useful addresses, phone numbers, and contacts in the United Kingdom for those interested in buying records and instruments and for those who would want to tune into radio programs that feature African music.

*NAIROBI: KENYAN CITY LIFE.* Steve Brace. ActionAid, Old Church House, Church Steps, Frome, Somerset BA11 1PL, England. 1992. £ 10.99.

The purpose of this pack is to contrast the lives of the middle class and the poor in Nairobi, Kenya's capital. Booklets provide background on Kenya and Nairobi. A teacher's guide contains instructions for eight classroom activities. Materials for the activities include a set of 30 color photographs, maps, and illustrations. Intended for Key Stage Two of the (UK) Geography National Curriculum.

*NEW JOURNEYS: TEACHING ABOUT OTHER PLACES: LEARNING FROM KENYA AND TANZANIA.* Sukhvinder Kaur Barhey et al. Development Education Centre, Selly Oak Colleges, Bristol Road, Birmingham B29 6LE, England. 1991. 64 pp. £ 14.69. ISBN 0-948838-17-5.

This is a teacher's resource for introducing primary school students to the geography, society, and history of Kenya and Tanzania. Through photo activities, games, group work, and role-plays, students are introduced to the issues of tourism, self-reliance, and land use. Includes 24 color photos and a map. Key Stage 2.

*NILE: PASSAGE TO EGYPT.* Michael McKinnon et al. Produced by Human Code (Austin, Texas). Discovery Channel Multimedia, 7700 Wisconsin Ave., Bethesda, MD 20814-3579, USA. Windows and Macintosh formats. June 1995. $49.95.

This production by Discovery Channel Multimedia takes students on an educational and entertaining trip on Africa's Nile River, from the source of the White Nile at Lake Victoria in Central Africa to the mouth of the river in Alexandria, Egypt. Students board an Egyptian sail boat, a *felucca*, and travel along the mighty river in the company of Samia, a guide who provides instructions on how to navigate the *felucca* and to get the most out of the journey using equipment on board such as a camera, map, and a journal in which they can keep a multimedia record of their trip. The full sweep of Egypt's 5,000 years of history is spread before the travellers. At any point along the way the travellers can elect to take special "tours" that are narrated by such famous travellers as Mark Twain. They can also take a virtual 3-D tour of the Temple of Ramses II, and, while there, they can challenge the famous Pharoah to a game of *Senet*, the ancient Egyptian board game. The compact disc offers numerous possibilities for interactive engagement with the environment and historical features of the Nile as the trip progresses.

Those who prefer to sit back and watch can call up more than 30 minutes of high-quality video and audio from the Discovery Channel documentary from which this CD-ROM product was created, *Nile: River of Gods. Nile: Passage to Egypt* was produced by Human Code (Austin, Texas), an award-winning multimedia development company that has also produced Putnam New Media's *Cartooon History of the Universe.*

*OUR COUNTRY, OUR FUTURE: A TEACHING PACK ABOUT SOUTH AFRICA.* Mbali Ngcobo, Sindisiwe Sabela, and Mduduzi Sishi Symons. Gillian Research on Education in Southern Africa, Institute of Education, University of London, 1994. 88 pp. ISBN 0-85473-401-5. Distributor: Development Education Dispatch Unit, 153, Cardigan Rd., Leeds LS6 1LJ, England.

Written by three South African teachers, these materials explore the history of apartheid and violence in South Africa and analyze strategies for development. Photo activities ask students to look critically at media images. A timeline exercise familiarizes students with the crucial events in the colonization of South Africa, the establishment of apartheid, and the history of resistance to it. A sophisticated "Who Dunnit?" activity examines the responsibility for election violence in South Africa; groups are asked to evaluate evidence and motives and to distinguish fact from opinion. Through group-work and role-playing in a "Who Decides?" activity, students learn about the threat to the environment posed by "development" and look at ways for reconciling conflicting interests. Includes a bibliography. Appropriate for high school and adult students.

*PEOPLE MAKING HISTORY: Book 4.* M. Prew et al., Edited by Nevanji Madanhire, Zimbabwe Publishing House, P.O. Box 350, Harare, Zimbabwe. 1993. 313 pp. £ 15/$27. ISBN 1-779010-48-6. Distributor: African Books Collective, The Jam Factory, 27 Park End St., Oxford OX1 1HU, England.

Written for high school students in Zimbabwe, this history text has four sections: "Colonialism and Resistance," which begins with Western imperialism in the late nineteenth century and includes chapters on underdevelopment in Ghana and Kenya; "Zimbabwe under Colonial Rule"; "Revolution and Transformation," with chapters on the World War II, Zimbabwe's struggle for independence, the Soviet Union , and China; and "World Anti-Imperialist Struggles," which includes chapters on African liberation movements and on the war in Vietnam. Each chapter contains numerous exercises, many of them based on quotations from historical documents. Heavily illustrated with photos and maps.

*PICTURING PEOPLE: CHALLENGING STEREOTYPES.* Cathy Nash and Bob Kirby. Manchester Development Education Project, c/o Manchester Polytechnic, 801 Wilmslow Rd., Manchester M2O 8RG, England. 1988. 48 pp. ISBN 1-869818-37-7.

Focusing on images of young people in the popular media, this text aims at developing students' ability to recognize and question stereotypes. Introductory exercises ask students to examine photos of themselves and their families as a way of showing how values are reflected in images. Worksheets help students analyze how newspapers and magazines represent gender roles and youth violence. Ten black-and-white photographs of school children from Africa, Britain, and the Netherlands are included. Intended for ages 13 to 16.

***A RIVER CHILD: AN ACTIVE LEARNING PACK FOR 8-13 YEAR OLDS.*** Sue Lyle and David Hendley. Faculty of Education, Swansea Institute of Higher Education, Townhill Road, Swansea SA2 0UT, England. 42 + pp. £20. ISBN 0-9522193-0-1.

This cross-curricular pack introduces students to the importance of rivers, focusing on Gashaka, a village in Nigeria. The pack consists of a teacher's handbook, full-size activity cards of animals in Gashaka, a handbook of student activity sheets, a color poster with scenes of daily life in Gashaka, and the story of a ten-year-old boy in the village. The teacher's guide has three sections. The first introduces the students to the major rivers of the world and contains suggestions for a field trip to a local river. The second focuses on village life in Gashaka and contains activities based on the poster and the story. The third examines problems facing the village and encourages students to explore solutions.

***A ROUGH ROAD TO FREEDOM: THE LIFE AND TRAVELS OF THE EIGHTEENTH CENTURY NIGERIAN OLAUDAH EQUIANO.*** Lucy MacKeith. Royal Albert Memorial Museum, Queen Street, Exeter, Devon England. iii + 30 pp. £5.

This thirty-page handbook focuses on the life of Olaudah Equiano, an Ibo taken in slavery to the West Indies. Designed to be used in a participatory theatre program this booklet brings to life the horrors of the transatlantic slave trade through excerpts from Equiano's autobiography and from contemporary sources.

***RURAL BLACKSMITH, RURAL BUSINESSMAN: MAKING AND SELLING METAL GOODS IN MALAWI.*** Intermediate Technology. Development Technology Development Group, 103-105 Southampton Row, London WC1B 4HH, England. 7 + pp. £19.15.

This activity pack examines the work of a blacksmith/businessman in Malawi in order to encourage students to think about the application of technology in a different cultural context. The teacher's notes provide a curriculum guide to technical activities. Also included are technical diagrams, a booklet of background information on Malawi, a booklet that addresses the issue of prejudice and specific assumptions that may need to be countered, a profile of a blacksmith, and two sets of slides (20 and 10 slides each), with descriptive notes. Key Stage 3 in Design and Technology.

***SOMALI STUDY MATERIALS: AN EDUCATION RESOURCE PAK.*** Anita Suleiman and Ali Suleiman. HAAN Associates, P.O. Box 607, London SW16 1EB, England. 1994. £35.95. 9 booklets, posters, and teacher notes.

Three books for students aged 7 to 11 provide an introduction to Somali myths and legends, traditional nomadic culture, and Somali geography. Three books for students aged 11 to 16 focus on Somalia's early history, its people and language, and its food. The packet also includes a Somali-English phrasebook, a reference guide for teachers, a map, and a traditional weather chart. Key stages 2 to 4.

***SONGS AND STORIES FROM UGANDA.*** W. Moses Serwadda. Transcribed and edited by Hewitt Pantaleoni. World Music Press, Multicultural Materials for Educators, P.O. Box 2565, Danbury, CT 06813, USA. 1987. 82 pp. Illus. Leo and Diane Dillon. Tape narrated by Moriah Vecchia, sung by Moses Serwadda and others. ISBN 0-937203-15-7).

The cassette contains 13 songs from the people of Baganda, in southern Uganda. The book provides transcriptions of the songs, traditional stories, and a pronunciation guide to Luganda.

***SOUTH AFRICAN STUDIES.*** Jan Smuts House Library. NISC: National Information Services Corporation, 3100 St. Paul St., Baltimore, MD 21218, USA. MS-DOS format. 1996. $745 annual subscription. Quarterly updates.

This disc in the NISC family of CD-ROMs provides access to 350,000 records from eleven databases of information published in and about South Africa. The databases include the "Index to South African Periodicals" (159,000 records, from 1987 to the present), "South African National Bibliography" (55,000 records compiled by the South African State Library in Pretoria, 1988-present), "National English Literary Museum" (comprehensive since 1990, retrospective to the nineteenth century), and the "Index to South African Theses and Dissertations" (58,000 records compiled by the University of Potchefstroom Library). The CD-ROM comes with information about how to acquire actual copies of the indexed documents from the South African State Library and other document delivery sites in South Africa. The *South African Studies* compact disc is updated quarterly.

***STRUGGLING TO SURVIVE: SCHOOL PACK ON MOZAMBIQUE.*** Mozambique News Agency, 7 Old Bailey, London EC4M 7NB, England. £6.95.

The aim of this pack is to show students how Mozambique, which is one of the poorest countries in the world, suffering from war, natural disasters, underdevelopment and economic crisis, "manages to survive—at a cost." The pack includes teacher's notes, information sheets, role-play sheets, maps, 12 black-and-white photographs with descriptions and questions, a board game of "Snakes and Ladders"—Mozambique style—and a reading list. Intended for students 14 and over, though much of the pack will be accessible to younger students.

***STUDY GUIDE TO CLAIMING THE PROMISE: AFRICAN CHURCHES SPEAK.*** L. Cecile Adams. Friendship Press, P.O. Box 37844, Cincinnati, OH 45222-0844, USA. 1994. 42 pp. $5.95. ISBN 0-377-00268-2.

Intended for a church audience, this text explores issues faced by the churches in Africa. Includes many activities based on the Bible.

***THIRD WORLD SCIENCE.*** For information on ordering, contact Prof. Iolo Wyn Williams, School of Education, University College of North Wales, Lon Pobty, Bangor. Gwynedd, LL 57 IDZ, Wales.

This pack offers "examples of science in action in the Third World." There are six handbooks: "Carrying Loads on Heads" (7 pp.), "Clay Pots" (11 pp.) "Fermentation" (17 pp.), "Housing" (32 pp.), "Iron Smelting" (20 pp.) and "Salt" (38 pp.). Each focuses on a different region of Africa and contains illustrations and technical diagrams. An additional handbook, "Pupils' Projects from Zambia" (69 pp.), also heavily illustrated, provides descriptions of 18 science projects carried out by students at Lubishi Seminary in Zambia. The projects include obtaining oil from castor seeds, iron smelting, and making traditional musical instruments.

***THIRD WORLD WOMEN: FAMILY, WORK, AND EMPOWERMENT.*** Susan Hill Gross and Mary Hill Rojas. Upper Midwest Women's History Center, 6300 Walker St., St. Louis Park, MN 55416, USA. 1989. 131 pp.

A revised and expanded version of *Meeting the Third World Through Women's Perspectives* (see above), this manual includes new material on the issues of gender and the distribution of family resources, gender and work, and women and economic planning. There is also a chapter for educators, "Teaching Contemporary Third World Women's Issues." Same format as the earlier text, with detachable handouts. Intended for adult students

***THIS IS ETHIOPIA: A RESOURCE PACK FOR PRIMARY SCHOOLS.*** CAFOD, Romero Close, Stockwell Road, London SW9 9TY, England. 38 pp. Includes 14 color slides. ISBN 1-871549-38-8.

Through slides and brief readings, students explore life in a contemporary Ethiopian village. There are six sections—"Village Life," "Culture," "Children," "Problems and Progress," "Water," and "Celebration"—each with numerous classroom activities. Notes are provided for the slides.

***THIS IS OUR AFRICA: IMAGES OF AFRICA BY AFRICAN PHOTOGRAPHERS.*** VSO, Development Education Unit, 317 Putney Bridge Road, London SW15 2PN, England. 1992. 13 + pp. £9.50. ISBN 0-9509050-4-6.

This pack includes 27 black-and-white photographs of scenes of everyday life from several African countries—Gambia, Ghana, Malawi, Nigeria, São Tomé e Principe, Sudan, Uganda, and Zimbabwe. The booklet contains annotations by the African photographers, more than 20 activities based on the photos, and a list of resources.

***THIS LAND IS OUR LAND: LAND REFORM IN POST-APARTHEID SOUTH AFRICA.*** Richard Borowski et al. Leeds Development Education Centre, 151-153 Cardigan Road, Leeds LS6 1LJ, England. 1994. 16 pp. £2.75. ISBN 1-871268-55-9.

Through a sophisticated role-play exercise, students consider the effects of apartheid and the problem of land reform. Materials include detailed descriptions of the roles to be played in the exercise (e.g., rural women, commercial farmers, business executives), a list of options, and a map. A time-line exercise introduces students to the history of South Africa. Includes a list of resources. For students 14 to 18.

***TRIUMPH OF HOPE: ERITREA'S STRUGGLE FOR DEVELOPMENT.*** Lyn Routledge, Graham Harrison, and Nigel West. Leeds Development Education Centre, 151-153 Cardigan Rd., Leeds LS6 1LJ, England. 1994. 24 pp. ISBN 1-871268-65-6.

Four activities—a photo activity, a timeline exercise, a role-play, and a ranking activity—introduce students to Eritrean history, the role women played in the liberation struggle, the problems facing returnees, the issues of health care and food security, and some of the options available to the new government for developing the country. Additional historical and statistical information is provided for teachers. Includes eight color photographs. For students 16 and older.

***VOICES FROM ERITREA.*** Minority Rights Group, 379 Brixton Road, London SW9 7DE, England. December 1991. 32 pp. ISBN 0-946690-82-0.

These autobiographical narratives collected from refugee students in London schools provide a compelling introduction to recent Eritrean history. Photographs and illustrations enhance the text, which includes a brief introduction and a list of resources for teachers. (The students' narratives are printed in both English and Tigrinya.) Key Stages 2 to 4.

***VOICES FROM SOMALIA.*** Minority Rights Group, 379 Brixton Road, London SW9 7DE, England. December 1991. 28 pp. ISBN 0-946690-83-9.

Collected from young Somali refugees in London schools, these narratives offer moving perspectives on contemporary Somali society and the recent civil war. The text includes photographs and illustrations, as well as a brief historical introduction and a list of resources for teachers. (The narratives are printed in English and Somali.) Key Stages 2 to 4.

***WATER: PHOTOGRAPHS, CASE STUDIES AND ACTIVITIES ABOUT WATER AND DEVELOPMENT.*** Pete Hedges and Scott Sinclair. Development Education Centre, Selly Oak Colleges, Bristol Road, Selly Oak, Birmingham B29 6LE, England. 1990. 77 pp. £9.90. ISBN 0-948838-086.

This activity pack addresses "the complex relationship of environmental, social and political factors which influence the development of water resources" in Africa Through detailed case studies, the text explores such issues as development and the environment, international aid, traditional versus modern irrigation methods, and sanitation. The heavily illustrated text contains cartoons, charts and graphs, maps, and technical diagrams. Thirty-two color photographs are included; suggestions for activities based on the photos are provided in the text. Also included is a list of water industry resources. A challenging text, intended for adults.

***WHERE CAMELS ARE BETTER THAN CARS: A LOCALITY STUDY IN MALI, WEST AFRICA.*** John Snyder, Sarah Snyder, and Catherine McFarlane. Development Education Centre in partnership with Save the Children. Development Education Centre, Gillett Centre, 998 Bristol Rd., Selly Oak, Birmingham B29 6LE, England. 1992. 72 pp. £15.30. 2 volumes. ISBN 0-948838-25-6.

This pack—two books, 24 color photographs, and a poster of a market—provides an introduction to Mali and West Africa. Book 1 provides profiles of four people who live in or around Douentza and who are from different cultural groups but are economically dependent on each other. Book 1 includes background on Douentza, a time-line of important events in Mali's history, and background on the people and places in the photographs. Book 2 has three sections of reproducible material—"Our Daily Lives," Our Work and Environment," and "Journey and the Market" — each with detailed teaching suggestions. The texts are heavily illustrated with photographs, maps, and diagrams. Key Stage 2.

***WORLDS BEHIND THE MUSIC: AN ACTIVITY PACK ON WORLD MUSIC AND DEVELOPMENT.*** Yusuf Mahmoud et al. Reading International Support Centre and Voluntary Service Overseas, 103 London St., Reading RG1 4QA, England. 1995. 40 pp. Includes tape cassette and 8 color slides. ISBN 1-874709-01-7. Distributor: Development Education Unit, VSO, 317 Putney Bridge Rd., London SW15 2PN, England.

This activity pack — a book, a cassette, and eight slides — is intended for upper secondary school teachers, youth and community workers, and development education workers. It aims to promote understanding of the "wider social, economic, political and cultural context" of the music we listen to. The first side of the cassette contains 11 songs, while the second contains developmental rap. Brainstorming, group, and role-playing activities ask students to consider such topics as the role of music in society and its importance to our identities, development and debt, and stereotypes. Other activities include writing rap lyrics and looking at how images on album covers sell recordings. A list of recommended recordings, a glossary, a bibliography, and suggestions for writing a press release are also included.

# REFERENCE LIST

This reference list contains bibliographical information for all of the books and pamphlets mentioned in the body of the directory. The list also contains citations for printed materials that WorldViews gathered during the course of compiling the *Africa World Press Guide*. Titles of periodicals and audiovisuals appear in the Reference List, though bibliographical information for these resources is not given either because the information is easily available from reference guides to periodical literature or is given elsewhere in this guide (in the Films and Videotapes section, for example).

Materials in this Reference List that were issued by publishers in Africa are very often available from the African Books Collective, the premier international distribution source for books and pamphlets from publishers throughout the African continent. Contact: African Books Collective, The Jam Factory, 27 Park End St., Oxford OX1 1HU, England. Tel: +44-(0) 1865-726686. Fax: +44-(0) 1865-793298. E-mail: abc@dial.pipex.com. Another recommended source in England is the Africa Book Centre, 38 King St., Covent Garden, London WC2E 8JT, England. Write for their catalog.

Many of the books listed in this Reference List have been issued by two or more publishers. We regret that we have only been able to supply the name of one publisher in each listing. We encourage readers to ask about local publisher sources for books in this list.

Titles *not* included in this Reference List: human rights reports from the Human Rights chapter, CD-ROMs from the discography in the African Music chapter, curricula, literature, and audiovisuals from the Supplementary Resources chapter.

WorldViews welcomes corrections, updates, suggestions, and recommended additions to this Reference List. Contact WorldViews, 464 19th Street, Oakland, CA 94612-2297 USA. Tel: 1-510-451-1742. Fax: 1-510-835-3017. E-mail: worldviews@igc.org. Web site: <http://www.igc.org/worldviews/>.

*The Abandoned Baobab: The Autobiography of a Senegalese Woman*. Ken Bugul. Trans. Marjolijin de Jager. Chicago: Lawrence Hill Books/Chicago Review Press, 1991. vii + 159 pp. ISBN 1-55652-114-6.

*Academic Freedom 2: A Human Rights Report*. John Daniel et al., eds. London: Zed Books, 1993. viii + 168 pp. ISBN 1-85649-219-2. Cloth.

*Academic Freedom and Human Rights Abuses in Africa*. New York: Human Rights Watch/Africa, April 1991. 176 pp. ISBN 0-929692-77-2.

*Academic Freedom in Africa*. Mamadou Diouf and Mahmood Mamdani, eds. Dakar: CODESRIA, 1993. 370 pp. ISBN 2-86978-030-3.

*Accountability in Namibia: Human Rights and the Transition to Democracy*. Richard Dicker. New York: Human Rights Watch/Africa, August 1992. 121 pp. ISBN 1-56432-077-4.

*Across Boundaries: The Journey of a South African Woman Leader*. Mamphela Ramphele. New York: Feminist Press, 1997. xii + 272 pp. ISBN 1-55861-165-7. Cloth.

*Adjusting Society: The World Bank, the IMF, and Ghana*. Lynne Brydon. New York: St. Martin's Press, 1996. 256 pp. ISBN 1-860640-000-1.

*Adjustment in Africa: Reform, Results, and the Road Ahead*. A World Bank Policy Research Report. Oxford: Oxford University Press, 1994. xix + 284 pp. ISBN 0-19-520994-X. ISSN 1020-0851.

*Adjustments and Democratization in Francophone Africa*. Rosalind Boyd, ed. Montreal: Centre for Developing-Area Studies, McGill University, 139 pp. ISSN 0706-1706. *Labour, Capital and Society*, 26, no. 9 (April 1993).

*Africa*. Edward Bever. Phoenix: Oryx Press, 1996. x + 302 pp. ISBN 0-89774-954-5. International Government and Politics Series.

*Africa*. Phyllis M. Martin and Patrick O'Meara, eds. Bloomington: Indiana University Press, 1995. 3rd ed. 472 pp.

*Africa Access*. [periodical].

*Africa Access Review of K-12 Materials*. Brenda Randolf, ed. Silver Spring, Md.: Africa Access, 1992. 102 pp.

*Africa and Africans*. Paul Bohannan and Philip Curtin. Prospect Heights, Ill.: Waveland Press, 1995. 301 pp. ISBN 0-88133-840-0.

*Africa and the Modern World*. Immanuel Wallerstein. Trenton: Africa World Press, 1986. 209 pp. ISBN 0-86543-024-1.

*Africa Betrayed*. George B. Ayittey. New York: St. Martin's Press, 1992. xx + 412 pp. ISBN 0-312-08058-1. Cloth.

*Africa Beyond Adjustment*. Nguyuru H. I. Lipumba. Washington, D.C.: Overseas Development Council, 1994. ix + 102 pp. ISBN 1-56517-016-4. Policy Essay, no. 15.

*Africa Demographic and Health Surveys: Chartbook.* Washington, D.C.: Population Reference Bureau, International Programs, 1992. 32 pp.

*Africa Faces Democracy.* Washington, D.C.: Africa Faith and Justice Network, March 1994. iii + 67 pp.

*Africa Films and Videos.* Columbia, Md.: DSR, 1997.

*Africa from Real to Reel: An African Filmography.* Steven Ohrn and Rebecca Riley, eds. Waltham: African Studies Association, 1976. iv + 144 pp.

*Africa in Crisis: The Causes, the Cures of Environmental Bankruptcy.* Lloyd Timerlake. Philadelphia: New Society Publishers, 1986. 232 pp. ISBN 0-86571-082-1.

*Africa in Focus: A Video Series on the History and Culture of the Nations of Africa.* Evanston, Ill.: Altschul Group, 1995.

*Africa in Literature for Children and Young Adults: An Annotated Bibliography of English-Language Books.* Meena Khorana. Westport, Conn.: Greenwood Press, 1994. l + 313 pp. ISBN 0-313-25488-5. Bibliographies and Indexes in World Literature, no. 46.

*Africa in the School and Community: Video Resource List.* African Outreach Program, Boston University. Boston: Africa Studies Center, Boston University, 1993.

*Africa Media Review.* [periodical].

*Africa Now: People, Policies, Institutions.* Stephen Ellis, ed. London: James Currey, 1996. xxii + 293 pp. ISBN 0-85255-231-9.

*Africa on Film and Videotape: A Guide to Audio-Visual Resources Available in Canada.* Carol RuBlack and Céline Pelletier. Vancouver: IDERA Films, 1990. 139 pp. ISBN 2-920862-36-7.

*Africa on Film: Beyond Black and White.* Kenneth M. Cameron. New York: Continuum Publishing Company, 1994. 240 pp. ISBN 0-8264-0658-0.

*Africa Recovery Briefing Paper.* [periodical].

*Africa Since 1800.* Roland Oliver and Anthony Atmore. Cambridge and New York: Cambridge University Press, 1994. 4th ed. xii + 308 pp. ISBN 0-521-41946-8. Cloth.

*Africa Since 1935.* Ali A. Mazrui. Paris: UNESCO, 1993. xxviii + 1,025 pp. ISBN 92-3-102758-1. Distributors: University of California Press (Berkeley) and Heinemann (Oxford).

*Africa South of the Sahara, 1996.* London: Europa Publications, 1996. 25th ed. xix + 1084 pp. ISBN 1-85743-010-7. ISSN 0065-3896. Cloth.

*Africa South of the Sahara: A Geographical Interpretation.* Robert Stock. New York: Guilford Press, 1995. x + 435 pp. ISBN 0-89862-406-1. Cloth.

*The Africa that Never Was: Four Centuries of British Writing about Africa.* Dorothy Hammond and Alta Jablow. Prospect Heights, Ill.: Waveland Press, 1992. 251 pp. ISBN 0-88133-690-4.

*Africa through the Eyes of Women Artists.* Betty LaDuke. Trenton: Africa World Press, 1991. 148 pp. ISBN 0-86543-199-0.

*Africa to 2000 and Beyond: Imperative Political and Economic Agenda.* Philip Ndegwa and Reginald Herbold Green. Nairobi: East African Educational Publishers, 1994. viii + 131 pp. ISBN 9966-46-847-1.

*Africa within the World: Beyond Dispossession and Dependence.* Adebayo Adedeji, ed. London: Zed Books, 1993. xvi + 234 pp. ISBN 1-85649-250-8.

*Africa Wo/man Palava: The Nigerian Novel by Women.* Chikwenye Okonjo Ogunyemi. Chicago: University of Chicago Press, 1996. xiii + 353 pp. ISBN 0-226-62085-9.

*Africa's Agrarian Crisis: The Roots of Famine.* Stephen K. Commins, Michael F. Lofchie, and Rhys Payne, eds. Boulder: Lynne Rienner Publishers, 1986. xiii + 237 pp. ISBN 0-931477-60-3.

*Africa's Choices: After Thirty Years of the World Bank.* Michael Barratt Brown. Boulder: Westview Press, 1997. xiv + 433 pp. ISBN 0-8133-333-4. Cloth.

*Africa's Expanding Population: Old Problems, New Policies.* Thomas J. Goliber. Washington, D.C.: Population Reference Bureau, November 1989. 52 pp. ISSN 0032-468X.

*Africa's Food Crisis: Its Roots, Its Future.* Mutombo Mpanya and David Holdridge. Baltimore: Catholic Relief Services, Global Education Office, 60 pp. Oversized.

*Africa's Media Image.* Beverly G. Hawk, ed. New York: Praeger Publishers, 1992. vii + 268 pp. ISBN 0-275-93796-8.

*Africa's Recovery in the 1990's: From Stagnation and Adjustment to Human Development.* Giovanni Andrea Cornia, Rolph van der Hoeven, and Thandika Mkandawire, eds. New York: St. Martin's Press, 1992. xxi + 375 pp. ISBN 0-312-08631-8.

*Africa's Wars and Prospects for Peace.* Raymond W. Copson. Armonk, N.Y. and London: M. E. Sharpe, 1994. xvi + 211 pp. ISBN 1-56324-301-6.

*Africa's Way: A Journey from the Past.* Laurence Cockcroft. London: I. B. Tauris, 1990. xii + 231 pp. ISBN 1-85043-195-7.

*Africa: Endurance and Change South of the Sahara.* Catherine Coquery-Vidrovitch. Trans. David Maisel. Berkeley: University of California Press, 1988. x + 403 pp. ISBN 0-520-07881-0.

*Africa: Perspectives on Peace and Development.* Emmanuel Hansen, ed. London: Zed Books, 1987. x + 237 pp. ISBN 0-86232-703-2.

*Africa: The Challenge of Transformation.* Stephen McCarthy. London: I. B. Tauris, 1994. xx + 257 pp. ISBN 1-85043-820-X.

*Africa: Women's Art, Women's Lives.* Betty LaDuke. Lawrenceville, N.J.: Africa World Press, 1997. 208 pp. ISBN 0-86543-434-4.

*African Agriculture: The Critical Choices.* Hamid Ait Amara and Bernard Founou-Tchuigoua. Trans. A. M. Berrett. London: Zed Books, 1990. 227 pp. ISBN 0-86232-799-7.

*African All-Stars: The Pop Music of a Continent.* Chris Stapleton and Chris May. London and New York: Quartet, 1987. 373 pp.

*African Art.* Frank Willett. New York: Thames and Hudson, 1993. Rev. ed. 288 pp. ISBN 0-500-20267-2.

*African Art.* Richard B. Woodward. Seattle: University of Washington Press, 1997. 94 pp. ISBN 0-917046-37-4.

*African Art and Women Artists.* [audiovisual].

*African Art in Transit.* Christopher B. Steiner. Cambridge: Cambridge University Press, 1994. xv + 220 pp. ISBN 0-521-43447-5.

*African Art Portfolio: An Illustrated Introduction.* Carol Thompson. New York: New Press, 1993. 25 pp. ISBN 1-56584-112-3.

*African Art, Film and Literature.* George W. Sheperd Jr. and Tilden J. LeMelle, eds. Denver: Africa Today Associates, 1989. 96 pp. ISSN 0001-9887. *Africa Today*, 36, no. 2.

*African Art: An Introduction.* Dennis Duerden. London: Hamlyn, 1974. 96 pp. ISBN 0-600-34853-9.

*African Art: The Years Since 1920.* Marshall W. Mount. New York: Da Capo Press, 1989. xviii + 236 pp. ISBN 0-306-80373-9.

*An African Biographical Dictionary.* Norbert C. Brockman. Santa Barbara: ABC-CLIO, 1994. viii + 440 pp. ISBN 0-87436-748-4.

*African Book World and Press: A Directory.* Hans Zell, ed. London: Hans Zell Publishers, 1989. 4th ed. xxi + 306 pp. ISBN 0-905450-50-7. Cloth.

*The African Business Handbook: A Comprehensive Guide to Business Resources for African Trade and Investment.* Michael E. M. Sudarkasa. Washington, D.C.: 21st Century Africa/International Trade and Development Council, 1996. Vol. 3. 408 pp. ISBN 0-9638197-1-2. ISSN 1072-0812.

*African Capitalists in African Development.* Bruce J. Berman and Colin Leys, eds. Boulder: Lynne Rienner Publishers, 1994. vii + 275 pp. ISBN 1-55587-417-7.

*African Charter for Popular Participation in Development and Transformation.* New York: United Nations Economic Commission for Africa, March 1990. iv + 73 pp.

*African Charter on Human and People's Rights.* Lagos: Legal Research and Resource Development Centre, 1993. 18 pp. ISBN 978-31988-5-8. LRRDC Human Rights Education Series.

*African Cinema: Politics and Culture.* Manthia Diawara. Bloomington: Indiana University Press, 1992. ix + 192 pp. ISBN 0-253-20707-X.

*African Civilization Revisited: From Antiquity to Modern Times.* Basil Davidson. Lawrenceville: Africa World Press, 1991. 459 pp. ISBN 0-86543-124-8.

*African Cry.* Jean-Marc Ela. Maryknoll, N.Y.: Orbis Books, 1986. vi + 154 pp. ISBN 0-88344-259-0.

*The African Debt Crisis.* Trevor W. Parfitt and Stephen P. Riley. New York: Routledge, 1989. vii + 228 pp. ISBN 0-415-00441-1.

*African Debt Revisited: Procrastination or Progress?* Percy S. Mistry. The Hague: Forum on Debt and Development (FONDAD), 1991. 84 pp. ISBN 90-74208-01-0.

*African Decolonization.* H. S. Wilson. London: Edward Arnold/Hodder Headline Group, 1994. ix + 222 pp. ISBN 0-340-55929-2. Contemporary History series.

*African Development Bank.* E. Philip English and Harris M. Mule. Boulder: Lynne Rienner Publishers, 1996. xvi + 213 pp. ISBN 1-55587-493-2.

*African Development Indicators 1996.* Washington, D.C.: World Bank, 1996. xv + 431 pp. ISBN 0-8213-3563-4. ISSN 1020-2927.

*African Development Indicators, 1994-95. World Bank Data on Diskette.* Washington, D.C.: World Bank, 1995. ISBN 0-8213-3203-1. Book and diskette.

*African Development Perspectives Yearbook 1989:* Vol. I: *Human Dimensions of Adjustment.* Research Group on African Development Perspectives Bremen. Berlin: Schelzky and Jeep, 1990. xix + 692 pp. ISBN 3-923024-29-0. U.S. distributor: Westview Press (Boulder, Colo.).

*African Development: Adebayo Adedeji's Alternative Strategies.* S.K.B. Asante. London: Hans Zell Publishers, 1991. xvii + 232 pp. ISBN 0-905450-49-3.

*African Development: Lessons From Asia.* Arlington: Winrock International Institute for Agricultural Development, 1991. 260 pp. ISBN 0-933595-55-7.

*African Directory: Human Rights Organizations in Sub-Saharan Africa.* Human Rights Internet and Netherlands Institute of Human Rights. Ottawa: Human Rights Internet, 1996. v + 276 pp. Spiralbound.

*African Drama and the Yoruba World-View.* Benedict M. Ibitokun. Ibadan: Ibadan University Press, 1995. xi + 183 pp. ISBN 978-121-249-7.

*The African Dream: Visions of Love and Sorrow. The Art of John Muafangejo.* Orde Levinson. New York: Thames and Hudson, 1992. 120 pp. ISBN 0-500-27682-X.

*African Economic and Financial Data.* New York and Washington, D.C.: United Nations Development Programme and the World Bank, 1989. xiii + 204 pp. ISBN 0-8213-1251-0.

*African Environment: Environmental Studies and Regional Planning Bulletin.* Gideon Prinsler Omolu, Gregoire Huni, and Joseph Winter, eds. Dakar: Environmental Development Action in the Third World, 1993. 277 pp. ISSN 0850-8518.

*African Environments and Resources.* L.A. Lewis and L. Berry. Boston: Unwin Hyman, 1988. xii + 404 pp. ISBN 0-04-916011-7.

*African Exodus: Refugee Crisis, Human Rights and the 1969 OAU Convention.* New York: Lawyers Committee for Human Rights, 1995. iv + 266 pp. ISBN 0-934143-73-0.

*The African Experience in Literature and Ideology.* Abiola Irele. Bloomington: Indiana University Press, 1990. xv + 217 pp. ISBN 0-253-20569-7.

*African Experiences of Cinema.* Imruh Bakari and Mbye Cham, eds. Bloomington: Indiana University Press, 1996. x + 276 pp. ISBN 0-85170-511-1.

*African Farmer.* [periodical]. Defunct.

*African Francophone Writing: A Critical Introduction.* Laïla Ibnifassi and Nicki Hitchcott, eds. Herndon, Va.: Berg Publishers, 1996. xi + 215 pp. ISBN 1-85973-014-0. ISSN 1354-3636. Berg French Studies.

*African History for Beginners. Part 1: African Dawn — A Diasporan View.* Herb Boyd. New York: Writers and Readers Publishing, 1991. 128 pp. ISBN 0-86316-144-8.

*African Human Rights Newsletter.* [periodical].

*African Images in Juvenile Literature: Commentaries on Neocolonialist Fiction.* Yulisa Amadu Maddy and Donnarae MacCann. Jefferson, N.C.: McFarland, 1996. vi + 154 pp. ISBN 0-7864-0241-5. Cloth.

*African Images: Racism and the End of Anthropology.* Peter Rigby. Oxford: Berg Publishers, 1996. x + 118 pp. ISBN 1-85973-102-3.

*African Industry in Figures, 1993.* Vienna: United Nations Industrial Development Organization, 1993. vii + 167 pp. ISBN 92-1-106284-5.

*African Intellectual Heritage: A Book of Sources.* Molefi Kete Asante and Abu S. Abarry, eds. Philadelphia: Temple University Press, 1996. xvi + 828 pp. ISBN 1-56639-403-1.

*African Labor Relations and Workers' Rights: Assessing the Role of the International Labor Organization.* Kwamina Panford. Westport, Conn.: Greenwood Press, 1994. xviii + 223 pp. ISBN 0-313-29066-0.

*African Literatures: An Introduction.* Oyekan Owomoyela. Waltham, Mass.: Crossroads Press, 1979.

*African Market Women and Economic Power: The Role of Women in African Economic Development.* Bessie House-Midamba and Felix K. Ekechi, eds. Westport, Conn.: Greenwood Press, 1995. xix + 214 pp. ISBN 0-313-29214-0. ISSN 0069-9624. Contributions in Afro-American and African Studies, no. 174.

*The African Mask.* Janet E. Rupert. New York: Clarion Books, 1994. 129 pp. ISBN 0-395-67295-3.

*African Music: A Bibliographical Guide to the Traditional, Popular, Art, and Liturgical Musics of Sub-Saharan Africa.* John Gray. Westport, Conn.: Greenwood Press, 1991. xii + 499 pp. ISBN 0-313-27769-9. ISSN 0749-2308.

*African Music: A Pan-African Annotated Bibliography.* Carol Lems-Dworkin. London and New York: Hans Zell Publishers, 1991. xvii + 382 pp. ISBN 0-905450-91-4.

*African Music: A People's Art.* Francis Bebey. Trans. Josephine Bennett. Brooklyn: Lawrence Hill Books, 1975. viii + 184 pp. ISBN 1-55652-128-6.

*African Music: Journal of the International Library of African Music.* Grahamstown (South Africa): International Library of African Music. 130 pp. ISSN 0065-4019.

*African Nemesis: War and Revolution in Southern Africa, 1945-2010.* Paul L. Moorcraft. London and Washington, DC: Brassey's UK, 1994. xxix + 519 pp. ISBN 1-85753-140-X.

*African Oral Literature: Backgrounds, Character, and Continuity.* Isidore Okpewho. Bloomington: Indiana University Press, 1992. xiii + 392 pp. ISBN 0-253-20710-X.

*African People in World History.* John Henrik Clarke. Baltimore: Black Classic Press, 1993. 92 pp. ISBN 0-933121-77-6.

*African Perspectives on Development: Contraversies, Dilemmas and Openings.* Ulf Himmelstrand, Kabiru Kinyanjui, and Edward Mburugu, eds. London: James Currey, 1994. xi + 342 pp. ISBN 0-312-12087-7.

*African Philosophy: Myth and Reality.* Paulin J. Hountondji. Trans. Henri Evans. Bloomington and Indianapolis: Indiana University Press, 1996. 2nd ed. xxviii + 221 pp. ISBN 0-253-21096-8.

*African Political Economy: Contemporary Issues in Development.* Kempe Ronald Hope Sr. Armonk, N.Y. and London: M. E. Sharpe, 1997. xiii + 230 pp. ISBN 1-56324-942-1.

*African Politics and Problems in Development.* Richard L. Sklar and C.S. Whitaker. Boulder: Lynne Rienner Publishers, 1991. x + 371 pp. ISBN 1-55587-244-1.

*African Popular Theatre: From Pre-colonial Times to the Present Day.* David Kerr. London: James Currey, 1995. x + 278 pp. ISBN 0-85255-533-4.

*African Population and Capitalism: Historical Perspectives.* Dennis D. Cordell and Joel W. Gregory, eds. Madison: University of Wisconsin Press, 1994. 304 pp. ISBN 0-299-14274-4.

*African Population Images.* IMPACT Project. Washington, D.C.: Population Reference Bureau, 1990. 24 pp.

*African Population Newsletter.* [periodical].

*African Portraits.* Dorothy Hoobler and Thomas Hoobler. Austin: 1993. 96 pp. ISBN 0-8114-6378-8.

*African Portraits: Images Across the Ages.* Dorothy Hoobler and Thomas Hoobler. Austin: Steck-Vaughn, 1993. 96 pp. ISBN 0-8114-6378-8.

*The African Possibility in Global Power Struggle.* Agwuncha Arthur Nwankwo. Enugu (Nigeria): Fourth Dimension Publishing, 1995. ix + 302 pp. ISBN 978-156-395-8.

*African Primary Health Care in Times of Economic Turbulence.* J. Chabot et al., eds. Amsterdam: Royal Tropical Institute/KIT Press, 1995. 151 pp. ISBN 90-6832-087-4.

*The African Quest for Freedom and Identity: Cameroonian Writing and the National Experience.* Richard Bjornson. Bloomington: Indiana University Press, 1991. xvii + 507 pp. ISBN 0-253-31194-2.

*African Reflections: Art from Northeastern Zaire.* Enid Schildkrout and Curtis A. Keim. Seattle: University of Washington Press, 1990. 272 pp. ISBN 295-96962-8.

*African Refugees: Development Aid and Repatriation.* Howard Adelman and John Sorenson, eds. Boulder: Westview Press, 1994. xix + 264 pp. ISBN 0-8133-8460-5.

*African Refugees: Reflections on the African Refugee Problem.* Gaim Kibreab. Trenton: Africa World Press, 1985. 129 pp. ISBN 0-865-007-1.

*African Religions and Philosophy.* John S. Mbiti. Portsmouth, N.H.: Heinemann Educational Books, 1989. 2nd ed. xiv + 288 pp. ISBN 0-435-89591-5.

*The African Response: Adjustment or Transformation.* London: Institute for African Alternatives, 1992. viii + 164 pp. ISBN 1-870425-32-4.

*African Rhythm and African Sensibility: Aesthetics and Social Action in African Musical Idioms.* John Miller Chernoff. Chicago: University of Chicago Press, 1981. xviii + 261 pp. ISBN 0-226-10345-5.

*African Socialism or Socialist Africa?* Abdul Rahman Mohamed Babu. London: Zed Books, 1983. xvi + 174 pp. ISBN 0-905762-39-8.

*African Stars: Studies in Black South African Performance.* Veit Erlmann. Chicago: University of Chicago Press, 1991. xxi + 214 pp. ISBN 0-226-21724-8.

*The African State in Transition.* Zaki Ergas, ed. New York: St. Martin's Press, 1987. xviii + 340 pp. ISBN 0-312-00768-X.

*African States and Rulers: An Encyclopedia of Native, Colonial and Independent States and Rulers Past and Present.* John Stewart. Jefferson: McFarland, 1989. xx + 395 pp. ISBN 0-89950-390-X.

*The African Studies Companion: A Resource Guide and Directory.* Hans Zell, ed. London and New Providence, N.J.: Hans Zell Publishers/K. G. Saur, 1997. 2nd ed. Forthcoming.

*African Studies in Social Movements and Democracy.* Mahmood Mamdani and Ernest Wamba-dia-Wamba. Dakar: CODESRIA, 1995. 626 pp. ISBN 2-86978-051-6.

*African Studies Information Resources Directory.* Jean E. Meeh Gosebrink, ed. and comp. London: Hans Zell Publishers, 1986. xiii + 572 pp. ISBN 0-905450-30-2. Cloth.

*The African Studies Review.* R. Hunt Davis Jr., ed. Los Angeles: African Studies Association, March 1986. 78 pp.

*The African Synod: Documents, Reflections, Perspectives.* Africa Faith and Justice Network. Maryknoll, N.Y.: Orbis Books, 1996. ix + 286 pp. ISBN 1-57075-038-6.

*African Theology in Its Social Context.* Benezet Bujo. Maryknoll, N.Y.: Orbis Books, 1992. 144 pp. ISBN 0-88344-805-X.

*African Theology: Inculturation and Liberation.* Emmanuel Martey. Maryknoll, N.Y.: Orbis Books, 1993. xii + 176 pp. ISBN 0-88344-861-0.

*African Traditional Religion in Biblical Perspective.* Richard J. Gehman. Nairobi: East African Educational Publishers, 1993. 310 pp. ISBN 9966-46-678-9.

*African Traditional Religion: A Definition.* E. Bolaji Idowu. London: SCM Press, 1973.

*African Traditional Religions in Contemporary Society.* Jacob K. Olupona. New York: Paragon House, 1991.

*African Vodun: Art, Psychology, and Power.* Suzanne Preston Blier. Chicago: University of Chicago Press, 1995. xi + 476 pp. ISBN 0-226-05860-3.

*African Women and Development: A History.* Margaret C. Snyder and Mary Tadesse. Johannesburg: Witwatersrand University Press, 1995. xiii + 239 pp. ISBN 1-86814-281-7.

*African Women and Pesticides: More Exposed to Risks, Less Informed about Dangers.* Mariam Sow. San Francisco: Pesticide Action Network, September 1994. 3 pp.

*African Women in Development: An Annotated Bibliography.* Addis Ababa: African Training and Research Centre for Women, Economic Commission for Africa, 1990.

*African Women South of the Sahara.* Margaret Jean Hay and Sharon Stichter, eds. Harlow, Essex: Longman Group, 1995. 2nd ed. xvii + 308 pp. ISBN 0-582-21241-3.

*African Women: A General Bibliography, 1976-1985.* Davis A. Bullwinkle, comp. Westport, Conn.: Greenwood Press, 1989. xx + 334 pp. ISBN 0-313-26607-7. ISSN 0749-2308. African Special Bibliographic Series, no. 9.

*African Women: A Modern History.* Catherine Coquery-Vidrovitch. Trans. Beth Gillian Raps. Boulder: Westview Press, 1997. xviii + 308 pp. ISBN 0-8133-2361-4.

*African Women: South of the Sahara.* Margaret Jean Hay and Sharon Stichter, eds. Harlow: Longman Group, 1995. 2nd ed. xvii + 308 pp. ISBN 0-582-21241-3.

*African Women: Their Struggle for Economic Independence.* Christine Obbo. London: Zed Books, 1980. x + 166 pp. ISBN 0-905762-33-9.

*African Women: Three Generations.* Mark Mathabane. New York: HarperCollins, 1994. xviii + 366 pp. ISBN 0-06-016496-4.

*African Workers and Colonial Racism: Mozambican Strategies and Struggles in Lourenço Marques, 1877-1962.* Jeanne Marie Penvenne. Portsmouth, N.H.: Heinemann, 1995. xvii + 229 pp. ISBN 0-435-08954-4.

*African Youth Speak.* Lawrence Darmani. New York: Friendship Press, 1994. 32 pp. ISBN 0-377-00271-2.

*African-American and African History and Culture.* Princeton, N.J.: Films for the Humanities and Sciences, 1994.

*Africana Videotape Listings.* Eric S. Kofi Acree, ed. Ithaca: John Henrik Clarke Africana Library, Cornell University, 1993. 78+ pp.

*The Africans: A Triple Heritage.* Ali A. Mazrui. Boston and Toronto: Little, Brown and Company, 1986. 336 pp. ISBN 0-316-55200-3.

*Africans: The History of a Continent.* John Iliffe. New York: Cambridge University Press, 1995. xi + 323 pp. ISBN 0-521-48235-6. Cloth.

*Afropop! An Illustrated Guide to Contemporary African Music.* Sean Barlow and Banning Eyre. Brooklyn: World Music Productions, 1995. 80 pp. ISBN 0-7858-09443-9.

*After Apartheid: The Future of South Africa.* Sebastian Mallaby. New York: Times Books/Random House, 1992. xii + 275 pp. ISBN 0-8129-1938-6.

*Against All Odds: A Chronicle of the Eritrean Revolution.* Dan Connell. Trenton: Red Sea Press, 1993. xvi + 309 pp. ISBN 0-932415-89-X.

*Against All Odds: Breaking the Poverty Trap.* Donatus De Silva, ed. Alexandria: Panos Institute and Seven Locks Press, 1989. iv + 186 pp. ISBN 0-932020-70-4.

*Agenda for Africa's Economic Renewal.* Benno Ndulu et al. New Brunswick, N.J. and Oxford: Transaction Publishers, 1996. viii + 246 pp. ISBN 1-56000-280-8. U.S.-Third World Policy Perspectives, no. 21.

*Agents of Change: Studies on the Policy Environment for Small Enterprise in Africa.* Philip English and Georges Henault, eds. Ottawa: IDRC Books, 1995. xix + 353 pp. ISBN 0-88936-726-4.

*Agrarian Question in Southern Africa and "Accumulation From Below": Economics and Politics in the Struggle for Democracy.* Michael Neocosmos. Uppsala: Nordiska Afrikainstitutet, 1993. 79 pp. ISBN 91-7106-342-0. ISSN 0080-6714.

*Agribusiness in Africa: A Study of the Impact of Big Business on Africa's Food and Agricultural Production.* Barbara Dinham and Colin Hines. London: Earth Resources Research, 1983. 224 pp. ISBN 0-946281-00-9.

*Agricultural Transformation in Africa.* David Seckler, ed. Arlington: Winrock International Institute for Agricultural Development, 1993. 208 pp. ISBN 0-933595-77-8.

*Aid and Power: The World Bank and Policy-based Lending.* Vol. 1. Paul Mosley, Jane Harrigan, and John Toye. New York: Routledge, 1991. xvii + 317 pp. ISBN 0-415-01548-0.

*Aid and Power: The World Bank and Policy-based Lending.* Vol. 2. Paul Mosley, Jane Harrigan, and John Toye. New York: Routledge, 1991. xiii + 443 pp. ISBN 1-415-06246-2.

*Aid to African Agriculture: Lessons from Two Decades of Donors' Experience.* Uma Lele, ed. Baltimore: John Hopkins University Press, 1992. xix + 627 pp. ISBN 0-8018-4366-9.

*AIDS and Development.* London: CAFOD, March 1993. Not paged.

*AIDS and STDs in Africa: Bridging the Gap Between Traditional Healing and Modern Medicine.* Edward C. Green. Boulder: Westview Press, 1994. x + 276 pp. ISBN 0-8133-7847-8.

*AIDS and the Demography of Africa.* UN Department for Economic and Social Information and Policy Analysis. New York: United Nations Publications, 1994. x + 72 pp. ISBN 92-1-151268-9.

*AIDS and the Third World.* Panos Institute. Philadelphia: New Society Publishers, 1989. v + 198 pp. ISBN 0-86571-144-5.

*The AIDS Epidemic and Its Demographic Consequences.* UN Department of International Economic and Social Affairs. New York: United Nations Publications, 1991. ix + 140 pp. ISBN 92-1-151224-7.

*AIDS in Africa: Its Present and Future Impact.* Tony Barnett and Piers Blaikie. New York: Guilford Press, 1992. ix + 193 pp. ISBN 0-89862-880-6.

*AIDS in Africa: The Social and Policy Impact.* Norman Miller and Richard C. Rockwell, eds. Lewiston, N.Y.: Edwin Mellen Press, 1988. xxxi + 336 pp. ISBN 0-88946-187-2.

*AIDS in Africa and the Caribbean.* George C. Bond et al., eds. Boulder: Westview Press, 1997. xiii + 234 pp. ISBN 0-8133-2879-9.

*AIDS in the World, II : Global Dimensions, Social Roots, and Responses.* Jonathan M. Mann and Daniel J. M. Tarant, eds. New York: Oxford University Press, 1996. xxxiv + 616 pp. ISBN 0-19-509097-7.

*AIDS in the World: A Global Report.* Jonathan Mann, Daniel J. M. Tarantola, and Thomas W. Netter, eds. Cambridge, Mass.: Harvard University Press, 1992. xiv + 1037 pp. ISBN 0-674-01266-6.

*AIDS Is a Kind of Kahungo That Kills: The Challenge of Using Local Narratives When Exploring AIDS among the Tonga of Southern Zambia.* Hanne Overgaard Mogensen. Stockholm: Scandinavian University Press, 1995. 135 pp. ISBN 82-00-22592-5.

*AIDS Management: An Integrated Approach.* Ian D. Campbell and Glen Williams. London: Actionaid, 1992. Rev. ed. 32 pp. ISBN 1-872502-15-6. Strategies for Hope, no. 3.

*AIDS Orphans: A Community Perspective from Tanzania.* M. Christian Mukoyogo and Glen Williams. London: Actionaid, 1991. 36 pp. ISBN 1-872502-09-1. Strategies for Hope, no. 5.

*AIDS, Africa, and Racism.* Richard C. Chirimuuta and Rosalind J. Chirimuuta. London: Free Association Books, 1989. Rev. ed. 192 pp. ISBN 1-85343-077-3.

*AIDS, Ethics and Religion: Embracing a World of Suffering.* Kenneth R. Overberg, ed. Maryknoll, N.Y.: Orbis Books, 1994. ix + 284 pp. ISBN 0-88344-949-8.

*AIDS: A Christian Response.* Ronald Nicolson. Pietermaritzburg: Cluster Publications, 1995. 84 pp. ISBN 1-875053-04-2.

*AIDS: Action Now. Information, Prevention, and Support in Zimbabwe.* Helen Jackson. Harare: AIDS Counselling Trust, 1992, 2nd ed. xvii + 334 pp. ISBN 0-7974-1146-1.

*AIDS: Children Too.* Geneva: International Catholic Child Bureau, 1993. 74 pp. ISSN 0258-9648. Children Worldwide, 20, nos. 2-3.

*Algeria.* James Ciment. New York: Facts on File, 1996. 176 pp. ISBN 0-8160-3340-4. Conflict and Crisis in the Post-Cold War Series.

*All Against AIDS: The Copperbelt Health Education Project, Zambia.* V. Chandra Mouli. London: Actionaid, 1992. 54 pp. ISBN 1-872502-17-2. Strategies for Hope, no. 7.

*All Music Guide: The Best CDs, Albums and Tapes.* Michael Erlewine et al., eds. San Francisco: Miller Freeman Books, 1994. 2nd eds. 1415 pp. ISBN 0-87930-331-X.

*Alms Bazaar: Altruism under Fire. Non-Profit Organizations and International Development.* Ian Smillie. London: Intermediate Technology Publications, 1995. xvi + 286 pp. ISBN 1-85339-301-0.

*Alternative Development Strategies for Africa.* Haroub Othman et al., eds. London: Institute for African Alternatives, Dec. 1989. 25 pp. ISBN 1-870425-19-7.

*Alternative Development Strategies for Africa.* Vol. 1: *Coalition for Change.* London: Institute for African Alternatives, 1990. x + 179 pp. ISBN 1-870425-20-0.

*Alternative Development Strategies for Africa.* Vol. 2: *Environment - Women.* Mohamed Suliman, ed. London: Institute for African Alternatives, 1991. vii + 178 pp. ISBN 1-870425-29-4.

*Alternative Development Strategies for Africa.* Vol. 3: *Debt and Democracy.* Ben Turok, ed. London: Institute for African Alternatives, 1991. viii + 264 pp. ISBN 1-870425-22-7.

*Alternative Press Index.* [periodical]

*Aman: The Story of a Somali Girl.* Virginia Lee Barnes and Janice Boddy. New York: Pantheon Books, 1994. xvi + 350 pp. ISBN 0-679-43606-5.

*Ambassadors of Colonialism: The International Development Trap.* Washington, D.C.: Information Project for Africa, 1993. 153 pp.

*Amilcar Cabral's Revolutionary Theory and Practice: A Critical Guide.* Ronald H. Chilcote. Boulder and London: Lynne Rienner Publishers, 1991. xii + 291 pp. ISBN 1-55587-058-9.

*Amnesty International Report 1996.* London: Amnesty International Publications, 1996. 360 pp. ISBN 1-887204-06-7.

*The ANC and Black Workers in South Africa, 1912-1992: An Annotated Bibliography.* Peter Limb. London: Hans Zell Publishers, 1993. 380 pp. ISBN 1-873836-95-3.

*Ancient Songs Set Ablaze: The Theatre of Femi Osofisan.* Sandra L. Richards. Washington, D.C.: Howard University Press, 1996. xxvi + 210 pp. ISBN 0-88258-109-0. Cloth.

*The Angels Have Left Us: The Rwanda Tragedy and the Churches.* Hugh McCullum. Geneva: WCC Publications, April 1995. xxiv + 115 pp. ISBN 2-8254-1154-X. Risk Book Series, no. 66.

*Anglo American and the Rise of Modern South Africa.* Duncan Innes. New York: Monthly Review Press, 1984. 358 pp. ISBN 0-85345-629-1.

*Angolan Women Building the Future: From National Liberation to Women's Emancipation.* Organization of Angolan Women. Trans. Marga Holness. London: Zed Books, 1984. 151 pp. ISBN 0-86232-263-4.

*Anioma: A Social History of the Western Igbo People.* Don C. Ohadike. Athens: Ohio University Press, 1994. xx + 249 pp. ISBN 0-8214-10772-5.

*An Anthology of Somali Poetry.* Trans. B.W. and Sheila Andrzejewski. Bloomington: Indiana University Press, 1993. ix + 111 pp. ISBN 0-253-30463-6.

*Anthology: Over One Hundred Works by Zimbabwe Women Writers.* Norma Kitson, ed. Harare: Zimbabwe Women Writers, 1994. xiii + 252 pp. ISBN 0-7974-1318-9.

*The Anticlimax in Kwahani, Zanzibar: Participation and Multipartism in Tanzania.* Max Mmuya and Amon Chaligha. Dar es Salaam: Dar es Salaam University Press, 1993. v + 145 pp. ISBN 9976-60-177-8.

*Apartheid Media: Disinformation and Dissent in South Africa.* John M. Phelan. Westport, Conn.: Lawrence Hill and Company, 1987. xi + 220 pp. ISBN 0-88208-245-0.

*The Apartheid State in Crisis: Political Transformation in South Africa, 1975-1990.* Robert M. Price. New York and Oxford: Oxford University Press, 1991. x + 309 pp. ISBN 0-19-506749-5.

*Apartheid's Contras: An Inquiry into the Roots of War in Angola and Mozambique.* William Minter. Johannesburg: Witwatersrand University Press, 1994. 308 pp. ISBN 1-86814-277-9.

*Apartheid's Genesis, 1935-1962.* Philip Bonner, Peter Delius, and Deborah Posel, eds. Braamfontein: Ravan Press, 1993. x + 455 pp. ISBN 0-86975-440-8.

*Apartheid: A Selective Annotated Bibliography, 1979-1987.* Sherman E. Pyatt. New York and London: Garland Publishing, 1990. xix + 169 pp. ISBN 0-8240-7637-0.

*Apartheid: Calibrations of Color.* Roger Rosen, ed. Icarus. York: Rosen Publishing Group, 1991. 173 pp. ISBN 0-8239-1355-4. ISSN 1054-1381.

*Arab and African Film Making.* Lizbeth Malkmus and Roy Armes. London: Zed Books, 1991. ix + 264 pp. ISBN 0-86232-917-5.

*The Arab Image in American Film and Television.* Dan Georgakas and Miriam Rosen, eds. *Cineaste* 17, no. 1 (1989). 24 pp.

*Arab Voices: The Human Rights Debate in the Middle East.* Kevin Dwyer. Berkeley: University of California Press, 1991. ix + 245 pp. ISBN 0-520-07490-3.

*Arab Women: Old Boundaries, New Frontiers.* Judith E. Tucker, ed. Bloomington: Indiana University Press, 1993. xviii + 264 pp. ISBN 0-253-20776-2.

*Arab World Notebook: Secondary School Level.* Audrey Shabbas and Ayad Al-Qazzaz, eds. Berkeley: Arab World and Islamic Resources (AWAIR), 1989. 460 pp. ISBN 0-9624988-07. Looseleaf binder.

*Armed Conflicts Report.* Ken Epps et al. Waterloo: Project Ploughshares Institute of Peace and Conflict Studies, Conrad Grebel College, 1997.

*Arms and Daggers in the Heart of Africa.* P. Anyang' Nyong'o, ed. Nairobi: Academy Science Publishers, 1993. vii + 364 pp. ISBN 9966-831-13-4.

*Arms and Warfare: Escalation, De-Escalation, and Negotiation.* Michael Brzoska and Frederic S. Pearson. Columbia: University of South Carolina Press, 1994. xv + 316 pp. ISBN 0-87249-982-0.

*Arms For the Horn: U.S. Security Policy in Ethiopia and Somalia 1953-1991.* Jeffrey A. Lefebvre. Pittsburgh: University of Pittsburgh Press, 1991. xvi + 351 pp. ISBN 0-8229-3680-1.

*Arms to Fight, Arms to Protect: Women Speak Out about Conflict.* Olivia Bennett, Jo Bexley, and Kitty Warnock, eds. London: Panos Institute, 1995. iv + 282 pp. ISBN 1-870670-36-1.

*Armscor: South Africa's Arms Merchant.* James P. McWilliams. London: Brassey's, 1990.

*Art Against Apartheid: Works for Freedom.* Susan Sherman and Gale Jackson, eds. New York: IKON Inc., 1986. 184 pp.

*Art and Religion in Africa.* Rosalind I. J. Hackett. London: Cassell, 1996. xiv + 226 pp. ISBN 0-304-33752-8. Cloth.

*The Art of African Textiles: Technology, Tradition and Lurex.* Johnb Picton, ed. London: Barbican Art Gallery, 1995. 142 pp. ISBN 0-85331-682-1. Oversized.

*The Art of Ama Ata Aidoo: Polylectics and Reading against Neocolonialism.* Vincent O. Odamtten. Gainesville: University Press of Florida, 1994. x + 202 pp. ISBN 0-8130-1277-5.

*The Art of the Personal Object.* Philip L. Ravenhill. Washington, D.C.: National Museum of African Art, Smithsonian Institution, 1991. 32 pp. ISBN 0-295-97171-1.

*The Art of the Weya Women.* [audiovisual].

*Asia and Africa: Legacies and Opportunities in Development.* David L. Lindauer and Michael Roemer. San Francisco: Institute for Contemporary Studies, 1994. viii + 422 pp. ISBN 1-55815-320-9.

*Asian Industrialization and Africa: Studies in Policy Alternatives to Structural Adjustment.* Howard Stein, ed. New York: St. Martin's Press, 1995. xvii + 284 pp. ISBN 0-312-12433-3.

*Aspects of Africa: Questioning Our Perceptions.* Manchester: Development Education Project, Manchester Polytechnic, 1988.

*At the Desert's Edge: Oral Histories From the Sahel.* Nigel Cross and Rhiannon Barker, eds. London: Panos Publications, n.d. viii + 248 pp. ISBN 1-870670-26-4.

*The Atlas of African Affairs.* Ieuan Ll. Griffiths. London and New York: Routledge, 1994. 2nd ed. 233 pp. ISBN 0-415-05488-5.

*The Atlas of Endangered Peoples.* Steve Pollock. New York: Facts on File, 1995. 64 pp. ISBN 0-8160-3283-1.

*The Atlas of the Arab World: Geopolitics and Society.* Rafic Boustani and Philippe Fargues. New York: Facts on File, 1990. 144 pp. ISBN 0-8160-2346-8.

*Atlas of World Cultures: A Geographical Guide to Ethnographic Literature.* David H. Price. Newbury Park: Sage Publications, 1989. 156 pp. ISBN 0-8039-3240-5.

*Attacks on the Press in 1993: A Worldwide Survey.* New York: Committee to Protect Journalists, 1994. 263 pp. ISBN 0-944823-12-2.

*Authoritarianism Democracy and Adjustment: The Politics of Economic Reform in Africa.* Peter Gibbon, Yusuf Bangura, and Arve Ofstad, eds. Uppsala: Nordiska Afrikainstitutet, 1992. 236 pp. ISBN 91-7106-323-4.

*Bargaining for Peace: South Africa and the National Peace Accord.* Peter Gastrow. Washington, D.C.: U.S. Institute of Peace, 1995. xi + 160 pp. ISBN 1-878379-39-9.

*Batiks by Nike.* [audiovisual].

*Behind the Red Line: Political Repression in Sudan.* Jemera Rone. New York: Human Rights Watch/Africa, 1996. xiv + 343 pp. ISBN 1-56432-164-9.

*Being the Church in South Africa Today.* Barney N. Pityana and Charles Villa-Vicencio, eds. Johannesburg: South African Council of Churches, 1995. xiv + 173 pp.

*The Benefits of Famine: A Political Economy of Famine and Relief in Southwestern Sudan, 1983-1989.* David Keen. Princeton: Princeton University Press, 1994. xvi + 289 pp. ISBN 0-691-03423-0.

*The Berbers.* Michael Brett and Elizabeth Fentress. Cambridge, Mass.: Blackwell Publishers, forthcoming. ISBN 0631-20767-8.

*Bessie Head: Thunder Behind Her Ears. Her Life and Writing.* Gillian Stead Eilersen. Claremont (South Africa): David Philip Publishers, 1995. 312 pp. ISBN 0-86486-279-2.

*Between a Rock and a Hard Place: Discernment in the Search for Justice. Some Concrete Issues.* Chris Chatteris. Pietermaritzburg: Cluster Publications, 1995. 122 pp. ISBN 0-9583807-7-5.

*Between Development and Destruction: An Enquiry into the Causes of Conflict in Post-Colonial States.* Luc Van de Goor, Kumar Rupesinghe, and Paul Sciarone, eds. New York: St. Martin's Press, 1996. xx + 376 pp. ISBN 0-312-16264-2. Cloth.

*Between State and Civil Society in Africa.* Eghosa Osaghae, ed. Dakar: CODESRIA, 1994. 281 pp. ISBN 2-86978-020-6.

*Beyers Naudé: Pilgrimage of Faith.* Colleen Ryan. Grand Rapids: William B. Eerdmans Publishing, 1990. xvi + 230 pp. ISBN 0-8028-0531-0.

*Beyond Apartheid: Labour and Liberation in South Africa.* Robert Fine and Dennis Davis. London: Pluto Press, 1990. xiii + 338 pp. ISBN 0-7453-0045-6.

*Beyond Borders: Refugees, Migrants and Human Rights in the Post-Cold War Era.* Elizabeth G. Ferris. Geneva: WCC Publications, 1993. xxxvi + 310 pp. ISBN 2-8254-1095-0.

*Beyond Charity: International Cooperation and the Global Refugee Crisis.* Gil Loescher. Oxford: Oxford University Press, 1993. x + 260 pp. ISBN 0-19-508183-8.

*Beyond Conflict in the Horn: The Prospects for Peace, Recovery and Development in Ethiopia, Somalia, and the Sudan.* Martin Doornbos et al., eds. Trenton: Red Sea Press, 1992. viii + 243 pp. ISBN 0-932415-82-2.

*Beyond the Boundaries: Text and Context in African Literature.* Mineke Schipper. Chicago: Ivan R. Dee, 1990. x + 212 pp. ISBN 0-929587-36-7.

*Beyond the Impasse: New Directions in Development Theory.* Frans J. Schuurman, ed. London: Zed Books, 1993. ix + 233 pp. ISBN 1-85649-210-9.

*Beyond the Numbers: A Reader on Population, Consumption, and the Environment.* Laurie Ann Mazur, ed. Washington, D.C.: Island Press, 1994. xvi + 444 pp.

*Beyond Traditional Peacekeeping.* Donald C. F. Daniel and Bradd C. Hayes, eds. New York: St. Martin's Press, 1995. xxii + 320 pp. ISBN 0-312-12512-7.

*Beyond Urban Bias in Africa: Urbanization in an Era of Structural Adjustment.* Charles M. Becker, Andrew M. Hamer, and Andrew R. Morrison. Portsmouth, N.H.: Heinemann, 1994. ix + 294 pp. ISBN 0-435-08091-1.

*Bibliographies for African Studies, 1987-1993.* Yvette Scheven, ed. London: Hans Zell Publishers, 1994. xxi + 176 pp. ISBN 1-873836-51-1.

*Bibliography in Contextual Theology in Africa.* J. R. Cochrane et al., comps. Pietermaritzburg (South Africa): Cluster Publications, 1993. 60 pp. ISBN 0-9583141-1-X.

*Bibliography of Film Bibliographies.* Hans Jurgen Wulff, comp. Munich, New York, London: K. G. Saur, 1987. xxix + 326 pp. ISBN 3-598-10630-0.

*Bibliography of New Religious Movements in Primal Societies. Vol. 1: Black Africa.* H. W. Turner. Boston: G. K. Hall, 1977.

*Biennial Report of the Executive Secretary, 1992-1993.* Addis Ababa: United Nations Economic Commission for Africa, 1994. ix + 68 pp.

*Binding Cultures: Black Women Writers in Africa and the Diaspora.* Gay Wilentz. Bloomington: Indiana University Press, 1992. xxxiii +141 pp. ISBN 0-253-20714-2.

*Biographical Dictionary of Afro-American and African Musicians.* Eileen Southern. Westport, Conn.: Greenwood Press, 1982. xviii + 478 pp. ISBN 0-313-21339-9. Greenwood Encyclopedia of Black Music.

*A Biographical Dictionary of Ancient Egypt.* Rosalie David and Antony E. David. Norman: University of Oklahoma Press, 1992. xxvi + 180 pp. ISBN 0-8061-2822-4.

*Birth of a Nation: Press Clippings and Commentaries on the Eritrean Referendum and the Declaration.* Meg Kidane. Berkeley: Eritrea Quarterly, 1993. 92 pp.

*Bitter Inheritance: Overcoming the Legacy of Apartheid.* Mike Fleshman. New York: Africa Fund, 1993. 6 pp. Southern Africa Perspectives, no. 1.

*Black Africa: A Comparative Handbook.* Donald George Morrison, Robert Cameron Mitchell, and John Naber Paden. New York: Paragon House, 1989. 2nd ed. xxxii + 716 pp. ISBN 0-88702-042-9.

*Black Africa: The Economic and Cultural Basis for a Federated State.* Cheikh Anta Diop. Trans. Harold J. Salemson. Lawrenceville, N.J.: Africa World Press, 1987. Rev. ed. 125 pp. ISBN 0-86543-058-6.

*Black African Cinema.* Nwachukwu Frank Ukadike. Berkeley: University of California Press, 1994. x + 371 pp. ISBN 0-520-07748-2.

*Black African Literature in English, 1987-1991.* Bernth Lindfors. London: Hans Zell Publishers, 1995. xxxv + 682 pp. ISBN 1-873636-16-3. Bibliographical Research in African Literatures, no. 3.

*Black and Third Cinema: Film and Television Bibliography.* Chris Vieler-Porter, comp. London: British Film Institute, 1991.

*Black Film Review.* [periodical].

*Black Folk Here and There: An Essay in History and Anthropology.* Vol. 1. St. Clair Drake. Los Angeles: Center for Afro-American Studies, University of California, Los Angeles, 1990. xxiv + 376 pp. ISBN 0-934934-31-2.

*Black Folk Here and There: An Essay in History and Anthropology.* Vol. 2. St. Clair Drake. Los Angeles: Center for Afro-American Studies, University of California, Los Angeles, 1987. xxviii + 387 pp. ISBN 0-934934-21-5.

*The Black Man's Burden: Africa and the Curse of the Nation-State.* Basil Davidson. New York: Times Books/Random House, 1992. xi + 355 pp. ISBN 0-8129-2210-7.

*Black Women Workers: A Study in Patriarchy, Race and Women Production Workers in South Africa.* Fatima Meer et al. Durban: Madiba Publishers, 1991. 2nd ed. 289 pp. ISBN 0-620-13160-8.

*Blame Me on History.* Bloke Modisane. New York: Simon and Schuster, 1986. xi + 311 pp. ISBN 0-671-70067-7.

*Blaming Others: Prejudice, Race and Worldwide AIDS.* Renée Sabatier. Philadelphia: New Society Publishers, 1988. vii + 168 pp. ISBN 0-86571-146-1.

*A Blighted Harvest: The World Bank and African Agriculture in the 1980s.* Peter Gibbon, Kjell J. Havnevik, and Kenneth Hermele. Trenton: Africa World Press, 1993. viii + 168 pp. ISBN 0-86543-388-7.

*Blood and Bone: The Call of Kinship in Somali Society.* Ioan M. Lewis. Lawrenceville, N.J.: Red Sea Press, 1994. ix + 256 pp. ISBN 0-932415-93-8.

*The Bones of Our Children Are Not Yet Buried: The Looming Spectre of Famine and Massive Human Rights Abuse.* John Prendergast. Washington, D.C.: Center of Concern, January 1994. 44 pp.

*Border Crossings: Emigration and Exile.* Icarus. New York: Rosen Publishing Group, Spring 1992. vi + 170 pp. ISBN 0-8239-1366-X. ISSN 1054-1381. World Issues series.

*Born of the Sun.* Joseph Diescho. New York: Friendship Press, 1988. x + 313 pp. ISBN 0-377-00187-2.

*Both Right and Left Handed: Arab Women Talk about Their Lives.* Bouthaina Shaaban. London: Women's Press, 1988. ISBN 0-7043-4102-6.

*Botswana's Search for Autonomy in Southern Africa.* Richard Dale. Westport, Conn.: Greenwood Press, 1995. xxxvii + 256 pp. ISBN 0-313-29571-9.

*Botswana: The Political Economy of Democratic Development.* Stephen John Stedman. Boulder: Lynne Rienner Publishers, 1993. ix + 214 pp. ISBN 1-55587-305-7.

*Breakout: Profiles in African Rhythm.* Gary Stewart. Chicago: University of Chicago Press, 1992. x + 157 pp. ISBN 0-226-77406-6.

*Briefing Book on Peacekeeping: The U.S. Role in United Nations Peace Operations.* Patricia Holt. Washington, D.C.: Council for a Livable World Education Fund, 1995.

*A Briefing Pack on Western Sahara.* Leeds: Western Sahara Campaign, 1995. 8 individual briefings.

*Broadcasting in South Africa: Studies on the South African Media.* Ruth Tomaselli, Keyan Tomaselli, and Johan Muller, eds. London: James Currey, 1989. 227 pp. ISBN 0-85255-311-0.

*The Broken Hoe: Cultural Reconfiguration in Biase, Southeast Nigeria.* David Uru Iyam. Chicago: University of Chicago Press, 1995. x + 237 pp. ISBN 0-226-38849-2.

*Building a New South Africa.* Vol. 1: *Economic Policy.* Marc Van Ameringen, ed. Ottawa: International Development Research Centre, 1995. xv + 86 pp. ISBN 0-88936-756-6.

*Building a New South Africa.* Vol. 2: *Urban Policy.* Marc Van Ameringen, ed. Ottawa: International Development Research Centre, 1995. xv + 88 pp. ISBN 0-88936-757-4.

*Building a New South Africa.* Vol. 3: *Science and Technology Policy.* Marc Van Ameringen, ed. Ottawa: International Development Research Centre, 1995. xv + 95 pp. ISBN 0-88936-758-2.

*Building a New South Africa.* Vol. 4: *Environment, Reconstruction, and Development.* Anne V. Whyte, ed. Ottawa: International Development Research Centre, 1995. xxxiii + 220 pp. ISBN 0-88936-759-0.

*Building Democracy in South Africa.* New York: Division of Overseas Ministries, United Church of Christ, 1994. 10 pp.

*Building Partnerships for Participatory Development: A Report of a Workshop Held in Hargeisa, Somaliland.* International Co-operation for Development. London: CIIR Publications, 1996. 48 pp.

*Building Whole Communities.* Government of Zimbabwe, Ministry of Community and Co-operative Development. Harare: Community Publishing Process, 1991.

*A Burning Hunger. Three Decades of Personal Struggles Against Poverty: A West African Experience.* Derrick Knight. London: Panos Publications/Christian Aid, 1994. viii + 208 pp. ISBN 1-870670-32-9.

*Burundi: Breaking the Cycle of Violence.* Filip Reyntjens. London: Minority Rights Group, 1995. 30 pp. ISBN 1-897693-85-0. ISSN 0305-6252. MRG International Report, no. 95/1.

*Burundi: Ethnocide as Discourse and Practice.* René Lemarchand. Cambridge: Cambridge University Press, 1994. xxiii + 206 pp. ISBN 0-521-45176-0. Woodrow Wilson Center Series.

*Calamity in Sudan: Civilian Versus Military Rule.* Fatima Babiker Mahmoud, ed. London: Institute for African Alternatives, 1988. ii + 78 pp. ISBN 1-870425-06-5.

*Call Me Woman.* Ellen Kuzwayo. Johannesburg: Ravan Press, 1985. xxi + 266 pp. ISBN 0-86975-279-0.

*The Cambridge Guide to African and Caribbean Theatre.* Martin Banham, Errol Hill, and George Woodyard, eds. Cambridge: Cambridge University Press, 1994. vii + 260 pp. ISBN 0-521-41139-4.

*The Cambridge Survey of World Migration.* Robin Cohen, ed. Cambridge: Cambridge University Press, 1995. xxi + 570 pp. ISBN 0-521-44405-5. Cloth.

*Canadian Studies in Population.* [periodical].

*Capitalism and Slavery.* Eric Williams. Chapel Hill and London: University of North Carolina Press, 1994. xxii + 285 pp. ISBN 0-8078-4488-8.

*The Caring Community: Coping with AIDS in Urban Uganda.* Glen Williams and Nassali Tamale. London: Actionaid, 1991. 36 pp. ISBN 1-872502-10-5. Strategies for Hope, no. 6.

*Cast Away Fear: A Contribution to the African Synod.* A. B. T. Byaruhanga-Akiiki et al. Nairobi: New People, 1994. 47 pp.

*The Catharsis and the Healing: South Africa in the 1990s.* Zeki Ergas. London: Janus Publishing Company, 1994. xii + 339 pp. ISBN 1-85756-079-5.

*Cause Celeb.* Helen Fielding. London: Picador/Pan Macmillan Publishers, 1994. 342 pp. ISBN 0-330+33269-4.

*CDI Military Almanac 1995.* Washington, D.C.: Center for Defense Information, 1995. 40 pp.

*Central and South African History.* Robert O. Collins, ed. Princeton: Markus Wiener Publishers, 1990. 289 pp. ISBN 1-55876-017-2. African History in Documents series.

*Challenge for the 1990s: Statements from African Churches on Democracy, Economic Justice, Partnership.* New York: Joint Ministry in Africa, United Church of Christ and Disciples of Christ, June 1992. 52 pp.

*The Challenge of Local Feminisms: Women's Movements in Global Perspective.* Amrita Basu. Boulder: Westview Press, 1995. xiv + 493 pp. Social Change in Global Perspective.

*The Challenge Road: Women and the Eritrean Revolution.* A. Wilson. London: Earthscan Publications, 1991.

*The Challenges of Famine Relief: Emergency Operations in the Sudan.* Francis M. Deng and Larry Minear. Washington, D.C.: Brookings Institution, 1992. xxii + 165 pp. ISBN 0-8157-1792-X.

*Challenging Rural Poverty: Experiences in Institution-Building and Popular Participation for Rural.* Fassil G. Kiros, ed. Trenton: Africa World Press, 1985. vi + 234 pp. ISBN 0-86543-020-9.

*Chambers Concise Encyclopedia of Film and Televison.* Allan Hunter, ed. Edinburgh: Chambers, 1991. xiii + 401 pp. ISBN 0-550-17253-X.

*A Changing International Division of Labor.* James A. Caporaso. Boulder: Lynne Rienner Publishers, 1987. xiii + 249 pp. ISBN 0-86187-679-2.

*The Changing Past: Trends in South African Historical Writing.* Ken Smith. Athens: Ohio University Press, 1989. 240 pp. ISBN 0-8214-0927-1.

*Changing the Boundaries: Woman-centered Perspectives on Population and the Environment.* Janice Jiggins. Washington, D.C.: Island Press, 1994. xx + 291 pp.

*Changing the History of Africa: Angola and Namibia.* David Deutschmann, ed. Melbourne: Ocean Press, 1989. xxii + 153 pp. ISBN 1-875284-00-1.

*Changing Uganda: The Dilemmas of Structural Adjustment and Revolutionary Change.* H. Hansen and M. Twaddle, eds. London: James Currey, 1991.

*Charity, Politics and the Third World.* Peter J. Burnell. New York: St. Martin's Press, 1991. xiii + 314 pp. ISBN 0-312-06185-4.

*Chelewa, Chelewa: The Dilemma of Teenage Girls.* Zubeida Tumbo-Masabo and Rita Liljestrom, eds. Uppsala: Nordiska Afrikainstitutet, 1994. 218 pp. ISBN 91-7106-354-4.

*Child Soldiers: The Role of Children in Armed Conflicts.* Guy Goodwin-Gill and Ilene Cohn. Oxford: Clarendon Press, 1994. 228 pp. ISBN 0-19-825935-2.

*Childhood in Crossroads: Cognition and Society in South Africa.* Pamela Reynolds. Cape Town: David Philip Publishers, 1989. ISBN 0-86486-117-6.

*Children Worldwide.* [periodical].

*Chinua Achebe.* [audiovisual].

*Chinua Achebe: A Biography.* Ezenwa-Ohaeto. Bloomington: Indiana University Press, forthcoming November 1997. 320 pp. ISBN 0-253-33342-3.

*Chinua Achebe: The Importance of Stories.* [audiovisual].

*Christian Churches and the Democratisation of Africa.* Paul Gifford, ed. Leiden and New York: E. J. Brill, 1995. xi + 301 pp. ISBN 90-04-10234-4. ISSN 0169-9814.

*Christian-Muslim Encounters.* Yvonne Yazbeck Haddad and Wadi Z. Haddad, eds. Gainesville: University Press of Florida, 1995. xi + 508 pp. ISBN 0-8130-1359-3.

*Christianity and Politics in Doe's Liberia.* Paul Gifford. Cambridge and New York: Cambridge University Press, 1993. xvi + 349 pp. ISBN 0-521-42029-6.

*Christianity in Africa: The Renewal of a Non-Western Religion.* Kwame Bediako. Edinburgh: Edinburgh University Press, 1995. xii + 276 pp. ISBN 0-7486-0625-4.

*Chronology of Conflict Resolution Initiatives in Eritrea.* Eddie Becker and Christopher Mitchell. Institute for Conflict Analysis and Resolution. Fairfax, Va.: George Mason University, 1991. 145 pp.

*Chronology of Conflict Resolution Initiatives in Somalia.* Eddie Becker and Christopher Mitchell. Fairfax, Va.: Institute for Conflict Analysis and Resolution, 1991. 90 pp.

*Chronology of Conflict Resolution Initiatives in Sudan.* Eddie Becker and Christopher Mitchell. Fairfax, Va.: George Mason University, 1991. 169 pp.

*The Church in Africa.* Adrian Hastings. Oxford: Oxford University Press, 1995. 706 pp. ISBN 0-19-826921-8.

*Church Versus State in South Africa: The Case of the Christian Institute.* Peter Walshe. Maryknoll, N.Y.: Orbis Books, 1983. xv + 234 pp. ISBN 0-88344-097-0.

*Cineaste.* [periodical].

*The Cinema in Nigeria.* Françoise Balogun. Enugu: Delta of Nigeria, 1987. 144 pp.

*The Cinema of Apartheid: Race and Class in South African Film.* Keyan Tomaselli. Brooklyn: Smyrna Press, 1988. 300 pp. ISBN 0-918266-19-X.

*Cinema of Ousmane Sembène, A Pioneer of African Film.* Françoise Pfaff. Westport, Conn.: Greenwood Press, 1984. xx + 207 pp. ISBN 0-313-24400-6.

*Cities Feeding People: An Examination of Urban Agriculture in East Africa.* Axumite G. Egziabher et al. Ottawa: International Development Research Centre, 1994. xiv + 146 pp. ISBN 0-88936-706-X.

*Civil Disobedience and Beyond: Law, Resistance and Religion in South Africa.* Charles Villa-Vicencio. Grand Rapids: William B. Eerdmans Publishing, 1990. xvi + 165 pp. ISBN 0-8028-0526-4.

*Civilian Devastation: Abuses by All Parties in the War in Southern Sudan.* Jemera Rone. New York: Human Rights Watch, 1994. xiv + 279 pp. ISBN 1-56432-129-0.

*Claiming the Promise: African Churches Speak.* Margaret S. Larom, ed. New York: Friendship Press, 1994. vii + 120 pp. ISBN 0-377-00267-4.

*Classroom Resources on Women in South Africa.* Berkeley: Women in the World, 1986. 10 pp.

*Close Sesame.* Nuruddin Farah. Saint Paul: Graywolf Press, 1992. 239 pp. ISBN 1-55597-162-8.

*Close to Home: Women Reconnect Ecology, Health and Development Worldwide.* Vandana Shiva, ed. Philadelphia: New Society Publishers, 1994. 170 pp. ISBN 0-86571-264-6.

*Cloth That Does Not Die: The Meaning of Cloth in Bunu Social Life.* Elisha P. Renne. Seattle: University of Washington Press, 1996. xxi + 269 pp. ISBN 0-295-97392-1.

*Cocoa and Chaos in Ghana.* Gwendolyn Mikell. Washington, D.C.: Howard University Press, 1992. xxvii + 284 pp. ISBN 0-88258-153-8.

*The Cold War Guerrilla: Jonas Savimbi, the U.S. Media, and the Angolan War.* Elaine Windrich. Westport, Conn.: Greenwood Press, 1992. x + 184 pp. ISBN 0-313-27989-6. Contributions to the Study of Mass Media and Communications, no. 31.

*Collapsed States: The Disintegration and Restoration of Legitimate Authority.* I. William Zartman, ed. Boulder: Lynne Rienner Publishers, 1995. vii + 303 pp. ISBN 1-55587-560-2.

*Collection-Building and Dissemination.* Ann Kathrine Poulsen. Harare: Zimbabwe Women's Resource Center and Network, 1992. Discussion Paper, no. 3.

*Colonial Inscriptions: Race, Sex, and Class in Kenya.* Carolyn Martin Shaw. Minneapolis: University of Minnesota Press, 1995. ix + 250 pp. ISBN 0-8166-2525-5.

*The Color of Hunger: Race and Hunger in National and International Perspective.* David L. L. Shields. Lanham, Md. and London: Rowman and Littlefield, 1995. xii + 172 pp. ISBN 0-8476-8005-3.

*Commodities.* [audiovisual].

*Community-Based AIDS Prevention and Care in Africa: Building on Local Initiatives.* Ann Leonard and Arjmandbanu Khan. New York: Population Council, 1994. iv + 66 pp.

*A Comparative Study of Religions.* J. N. K. Mugambi, ed. Nairobi: Nairobi University Press, 1990. xi + 311 pp. ISBN 9966-846-03-8.

*The Complete Guide to Special Interest Videos.* James R. Spencer. Scottsdale, Arizona: James-Robert Publishing, 1995,. 782 pp. ISBN 0-9627836-2-5.

*A Comprehensive Bibliography of Modern African Religious Movements.* Robert Cameron Mitchell and Harold W. Turner, comp. Evanston: Northwestern University Press, 1966. xiv + 132 pp.

*The Concept of Human Rights in Africa.* Issa G. Shivji. London: CODESRIA, 1989. viii + 126 pp. ISBN 1-870784-02-2.

*A Concise History of Africa*. Robert Garfield. Acton, Mass.: Copley Publishing Group, 1994. 78 pp. ISBN 0-87411-751-8.

*The Concise History of Islam and the Origin of its Empires*. Gregory C. Kozlowski. Acton, Mass.: Copley Publishing Group, 1991. xii + 99 pp. ISBN 0-87411-489-6.

*Conflict in Africa*. Oliver Furley, ed. London and New York: I. B. Tauris Publishers, 1995. 324 pp. ISBN 0-85043-690-8.

*Conflict in Southern Africa*. Chris Smith. East Sussex: Wayland Publishers, 1992. 48 pp. ISBN 0-7502-0357-9.

*Conflict Resolution in Africa*. Francis M. Deng and I. William Zartman, eds. Washington, D.C.: Brookings Institution, 1991. xxii + 418 pp. ISBN 0-8157-1798-9.

*Conflict Resolution in Uganda*. Kumar Rupesinghe, ed. Oslo: International Peace Research Institute, 1989. viii + 308 pp. ISBN 0-85255-334-X. Cloth. *Peace Research Monograph*, no. 16.

*Confronting Historical Paradigms: Peasants, Labor, and the Capitalist World System in Africa and Latin America*. Frederick Cooper et al. Madison: University of Wisconsin Press, 1993. vii + 422 pp. ISBN 0-299-13684-1.

*Consensus and Dissent: Prospects for Human Rights and Democracy in the Horn of Africa*. Leah Leatherbee and Dale Bricker. New York: Fund for Peace, January 1994.

*The Conservation Atlas of Tropical Forests: Africa*. Jeffrey A. Sayer et al., eds. New York: Simon and Schuster, 1992. 288 pp. ISBN 0-13-175332-0.

*Contemporary African Music in World Perspectives: Some Thoughts on Systematic Musicology and Aculturation*. Nicholas N. Kofie. Accra: Ghana Universities Press, 1994. 157 pp. ISBN 9964-3-0212-6.

*Contending Ideologies in South Africa*. James Leatt, Theo Kneifel, and Klaus Nurnberger, ed. Grand Rapids: William B. Eerdmans Publishing, 1986. x + 318 pp. ISBN 0-8028-0182-X.

*Contra-Flow in Global News: International and Regional News Exchange Mechanisms*. Oliver Boyd-Barrett and Daya Kishan Thussu. London: John Libbey, 1992. v + 154 pp. ISBN 0-86196-344-X. ISSN 0956-9057.

*Controlling and Ending Conflict: Issues Before and After the Cold War*. Stephen J. Cimbala and Sideny R. Waldman. Westport: Greenwood Press, 1991.

*Coping with Africa's Refugee Burden: A Time for Solutions*. Robert F. Gorman. Dordrecht and Boston: Martinus Nijhoff Publishers, 1987. xiv + 206 pp. ISBN 90-247-3457-6.

*The Cost of Dictatorship: The Somali Experience*. Jama Mohamed Ghalib. New York: Lilian Barber Press, 1995. xvi + 267 pp. ISBN 0-936508-30-2.

*Country Reports on Human Rights Practices for 1993*. Department of State. Washington, D.C.: U.S. Government Printing Office, 1994. xix + 1409 pp. ISBN 0-16-043627-3.

*Coups and Army Rule in Africa*. Samuel Decalo. New Haven: Yale University Press, 1990. xvii + 366 pp. ISBN 0-300-04045-8.

*Cradles of Civilization: Egypt*. Jaromir Malek, ed. Norman: University of Oklahoma Press, 1993. 192 pp. ISBN 0-8061-2526-8.

*Creating a Future: Youth Policy for South Africa*. David Everatt, ed. Johannesburg: Ravan Press, 1994. x + 218 pp. ISBN 0-86975-452-1.

*The Crisis and Challenge of African Development*. Harvey Glickman, ed. New York: Greenwood Press, 1988. xii + 257 pp. ISBN 0-313-25988-7. ISSN 0069-9624.

*The Crisis in African Agriculture*. Mohamed Lamine Gakou. London: Zed Books, 1987. xii + 100 pp. ISBN 0-86232-733-4.

*Crisis Management and the Politics of Reconciliation in Somalia*. M. A. Mohamed Salih and Lennart Wohlgemuth. Uppsala: Nordiska Afrikainstitutet, 1994. 176 pp. ISBN 91-7106-356-0.

*A Critical History of Shona Poetry*. Emmanuel M. Chiwome. Harare: University of Zimbabwe Publications, 1996. xiii + 151 pp. ISBN 0-908307-44-6.

*Critical Perspectives on Ayi Kwei Armah*. Derek Wright, ed. Washington, D.C.: Three Continents Press, 1992. ix + 354 pp. ISBN 0-89410-641-4.

*Critical Perspectives on Black Independent Cinema*. Mbye B. Cham and Claire Andrade-Watkins, eds. Cambridge, Mass.: MIT Press, 1988. 85 pp. ISBN 0-262-53080-5.

*Critical Theory and African Literature Today*. Eldred Durosimi Jones, Eustace Palmer, and Marjorie Jones, eds. Trenton: Africa World Press, 1994. v + 122 pp. ISBN 0-86543-441-7.

*Critique: Review of the U.S. Department of State's Country Reports on Human Rights Practices, 1995*. New York: Lawyers Committee for Human Rights, July 1996. xvii + 256 pp. ISBN 0-934143-82-X.

*The Cross-Cultural Study of Women: A Comprehensive Guide*. Margot I. Duley and Mary I. Edwards, eds. New York: Feminist Press, University of New York, 1986. xv + 440 pp. ISBN 0-935312-02-1.

*Crossing Boundaries: Mine Migrancy in a Democratic South Africa*. Jonathan Crush and Wilmot James, eds. Cape Town: Institute for Democracy in South Africa, 1995. xvii + 233 pp. ISBN 0-88936-764-7.

*Cultivating Customers: Market Women in Harare, Zimbabwe*. Nancy E. Horn. Boulder: Lynne Rienner Publishers, 1994.

*The Cultural Unity of Black Africa: The Domains of Patriarchy and of Matriarchy in Classical Antiquity*. Chicago: Third World Press, 1978. xv + 235 pp. ISBN 0-88378-049-6.

*Culture and Development: The Popular Theatre Approach in Africa*. Penina Muhando Mlama. Uppsala: Nordiska Afrikainstitutet, 1991. 219 pp. ISBN 91-7106-317-X.

*Culture in Africa: An Appeal for Pluralism*. Raoul Granqvist, ed. Uppsala: Nordiska Afrikainstitutet, 1993. 202 pp. ISBN 91-7106-330-7. ISSN 0281-0018. Seminar Proceedings, no. 29.

*Culture in Another South Africa*. Willem Campschreur and Joost Divendal, eds. New York: Olive Branch Press, 1989. 287 pp. ISBN 0-940793-36-9.

*Cultures Outside the United States in Fiction: A Guide to 2,875 Books for Librarians and Teachers, K-9*. Vicki Anderson. Jefferson: McFarland, 1994. viii + 414 pp. ISBN 0-89950-905-3.

*Culturgrams: The Nations Around Us. Vol. 2: Africa, Asia, and Oceania*. David M. Kennedy Center for International Studies, Brigham Young University. Garrett Park: Garrett Park Press, 1995. x + 300 pp. ISBN 0-912048-87-5 (v.2).

*Current Bibliography of African Affairs*. [periodical].

*Current History*. [periodical].

*Custodians of the Land: Ecology and Culture in the History of Tanzania*. Gregory Maddox, James Giblin, and Isaria N.

Kimambo, eds. London: James Currey, 1996. xiv + 271 pp. ISBN 0-8214-1133-0.

*Cutting the Rose: Female Genital Mutilation. The Practice and its Prevention.* Efua Dorkenoo. London: Minority Rights Group, 1994. xi + 196 pp. ISBN 1-873194-60-9.

*The Da Capo Guide to Contemporary African Music.* Ronnie Graham. New York: Da Capo Press, 1988. xii + 315 pp. ISBN 0-306-80325-9.

*Dance Civet Cat: Child Labour in the Zambezi Valley.* Pamela Reynolds. Athens: Ohio University Press, 1991. xxxi + 176 pp. ISBN 0-8214-0947-6.

*Dancing Prophets: Musical Experience in Tumbuka Healing.* Steven M. Friedson. Chicago: University of Chicago Press, 1996. xix + 239 pp. ISBN 0-226-26502-1.

*Dark Victory: The United States, Structural Adjustment and Global Poverty.* Walden Bello, Shea Cunningham, and Bill Rau. London: Pluto Press, 1994. xii + 148 pp. ISBN 0-7453-0833-3.

*Daughters of Africa: An International Anthology of Words and Writings by Women of African Descent from the Ancient Egyptians to the Present.* Margaret Busby, ed. New York: Ballantine Books, 1992. li + 1093 pp. ISBN 0-345-38268-4.

*Daughters of Anowa: African Women and Patriarchy.* Mercy Amba Oduyoye. Maryknoll, N.,Y.: Orbis Books, 1995. ix + 229 pp. ISBN 0-88344-999-4.

*Debt Relief and Sustainable Development in Sub-Saharan Africa.* George C. Abbott. Brookfield: Edward Elgar, 1993. xvi + 189 pp. ISBN 1-85278-513-6.

*Debt, Development and Equity in Africa.* Karamo N. Sonko. Lanham, Md.: University Press of America, 1994. xv + 217 pp. ISBN 0-8191-9312-7.

*Decolonization and Independence in Kenya, 1940-93.* B. A. Ogot and W. R. Ochieng', eds. London: James Currey, 1995. xviii + 270 pp. ISBN 0-8214-1050-4.

*The Decolonization of Africa.* David Birmingham. Athens: Ohio University Press, 1995. viii + 109 pp. ISBN 0-8214-1153-5.

*Democracy and Development in Africa.* Claude Ake. Washington, D.C.: Brookings Institution, 1996. x + 173 pp. ISBN 0-8157-0220-5. Cloth.

*Democracy and Human Rights in Developing Countries.* Zehra F. Arat. Boulder: Lynne Rienner Publishers, 1991. xi + 219 pp. ISBN 1-55587-170-4.

*Democracy and Pluralism in Africa.* Dov Ronen, ed. Boulder: Lynne Rienner Publishers, 1986. xi + 220 pp. ISBN 0-931477-65-4.

*Democracy and Socialism in Africa.* Robin Cohen and Harry Goulbourne, eds. Boulder: Westview Press, 1991. xv + 272 pp. ISBN 0-8133-8052-9.

*Democracy in Botswana.* John Holm and Patrick Molutsi, eds. Athens: Ohio University Press, 1989. 296 pp. ISBN 0-8214-0943-3.

*Democracy in Developing Countries: Africa.* Larry Diamond, Juan J. Linz, and Seymour Martin Lipset, eds. Boulder: Lynne Rienner Publishers, 1988. xxx + 314 pp. ISBN 1-55587-039-2. Cloth.

*Democracy in the Third World.* Robert Pinkney. Boulder: Lynne Rienner Publishers, 1994. viii + 182 pp. ISBN 1-55587-454-1. Issues in Third World Politics.

*Democracy, Civil Society and the State: Social Movements in Southern Africa.* Lloyd Sachikonye, ed. Harare: SAPES Books, 1995. x + 193 pp. ISBN 1-77905-028-3.

*Democracy: The Challenge of Change.* Frederick J. T. Chiluba. Lusaka: Multimedia Publications, 1995. xii + 169 pp. ISBN 9982-30-053-9.

*Democracy, War and Peace in the Middle East.* David Garnham and Mark Tessler, eds. Bloomington: Indiana University Press, 1995. xxv + 294 pp. ISBN 0-253-20939-0.

*Democratic Change in Africa: Women's Perspective.* Wanjiku M. Kabira, Jacqueline A. Oduol, and Maria Nzomo, eds. Nairobi: Association of African Women for Research and Development, 1993. viii + 147 pp. ISBN 9966-41-054-6.

*Democratic South Africa? Constitutional Engineering in a Divided Society.* Donald L. Horowitz. Berkeley: University of California Press, 1991. xviii + 293 pp. ISBN 0-520-07342-8.

*Democratisation.* B. O. Nwabueze. Ibadan: Spectrum Law Publishing, 1993. x + 304 pp. ISBN 978-246-172-5.

*Democratization and the Protection of Human Rights in Africa: Problems and Prospects.* Brendalyn P. Ambrose. Westport, Conn.: Praeger Publishers, 1995. xii + 216 pp. ISBN 0-275-95143-X.

*Democratization in South Africa: The Elusive Social Contract.* Timothy D. Sisk. Princeton: Princeton University Press, 1995. xiii + 342 pp. ISBN 0-691-03622-5.

*Democratization of Disempowerment in Africa.* Claude Ake. Lagos: Malthouse Press, 1994. 23 pp. ISBN 978-023-008-4. CASS Occasional Monograph, no. 1.

*Demographic Handbook for Africa, 1992.* Economic Commission for Africa, Population Division. New York: United Nations Publications, 1992. 117 pp.

*Demography.* [periodical].

*Desert Frontier: Ecological and Economic Change along the Western Sahel, 1600-1850.* James L. A. Webb Jr. Madison: University of Wisconsin Press, 1995. xxvi + 227 pp. ISBN 0-299-14334-1.

*The Desired Number.* [audiovisual].

*Development.* [periodical].

*Development Aid and Human Rights.* Katarina Tomasevski. New York: St. Martin's Press, 1989. xvi + 208 pp. ISBN 0-312-03139-4.

*Development and Democratization in the Third World: Myths, Hopes, and Realities.* Kenneth E. Bauzon, ed. Washington, D.C.: Taylor and Francis, 1992. xix + 344 pp. ISBN 0-8448-1723-6.

*Development and Environment: Sustaining People and Nature.* Dharam Ghai, ed. Cambridge: Blackwell, 1994. 263 pp. ISBN 0-631-19394-4.

*Development Demands Democracy.* Debbie Culbertson, ed. Toronto: Ten Days for World Development, February 1994. 52 pp.

*The Development Dictionary: A Guide to Knowledge as Power.* Wolfgang Sachs, ed. London: Zed Books, 1992. 306 pp. ISBN 1-85649-044-0.

*Development Strategies in Africa: Current Economic, Socio-Political, and Institutional Trends and Issues.* Aguibou Y. Yansané, ed. Westport, Conn.: Greenwood Press, 1996. xiii + 292 pp. ISBN 0-313-28994-8. ISSN 0069-9624. Contributions in Afro-American and African Studies, no. 170. Cloth.

*The Devils Are Among Us: The War for Namibia.* Denis Herbstein and John Evenson. London: Zed Books, 1989. ix + 202 pp. ISBN 0-86232-897-7.

*The Diary of Hamman Yaji: Chronicle of a West African Muslim Ruler.* James H. Vaughan and Anthony H. M. Kirk-Greene. Bloomington: Indiana University Press, 1995. xv + 162 pp. ISBN 0-253-36206-7.

*Dictionary of African Historical Biography.* Mark R. Lipschutz and R. Kent Rasmussen. Berkeley: University of California Press, 1989. 2nd ed. xiii + 328 pp. ISBN 0-520-06611-1.

*Dictionary of Beliefs and Religions: A Comprehensive Outline of Spiritual Concepts from Prehistory to the Present.* Rosemary Goring, ed. Edinburgh and New York: Larousse, 1994. xii + 605 pp. ISBN 0-7523-5000-5.

*Dictionary of Environment and Development: People, Places, Ideas and Organizations.* Andy Crump. Cambridge: MIT Press, 1993. 272 pp. ISBN 0-262-53117-8.

*Dictionary of Portuguese-African Civilization.* Vol. 1: *From Discovery to Independence.* Benjamin Nuñez. London: Hans Zell Publishers, 1994. xxi + 532 pp. ISBN 1-873836-10-4.

*Dictionary of the Environment.* Michael Allaby. New York: New York University Press, 1989. 3rd ed. 423 pp. ISBN 0-8147-0597-9.

*Diplomacy, Aid and Governance in Sudan.* John Prendergast. Washington, D.C.: Center of Concern, March 1995. 19 pp. Horn of Africa Discussion Paper Series, no. 7.

*Directory of African and Afro-American Studies in the United States.* Hanif M. Rana and John A. Distefano, comps. Los Angeles: African Studies Association, 1987. 7th ed. vi + 275 pp. ISBN 0-918456-61-4. Cloth.

*Directory of African Film-Makers and Films.* Keith Shiri, ed. Westport, Conn.: Greenwood Press, 1992. xiv + 194 pp. ISBN 0-313-28756-2.

*Directory of Development Research and Training Institutes in Africa.* International Development Information Network. Paris: OECD Publications, 1992. 248 pp. ISBN 92-64-03539-7.

*Directory of HIV/AIDS Journals and Newsletters.* Thomas Klinke and Susanne Doll, comp. Frankfurt/Main: Archiv fut Sozialpolitik e.V., June 1994. 169 pp.

*Directory of Recorded Sound Resources in the United Kingdom.* Lali Weerasinghe, ed. and comp. London: British Library National Sound Archive, 1989. xxii + 173 pp.

*Directory of Third World Women's Publications.* Quezon City: Isis International, 1990. 197 pp.

*Disarmament and Security in Africa.* New York: United Nations Publications, 1993. Disarmament Topical Papers, no. 12.

*Disasters, Relief and the Media.* Jonathan Benthall. London: I. B. Tauris Publishers, 1993. xiv + 267 pp. ISBN 1-85043-737-8.

*Discovering Ancient Egypt.* Rosalie David. New York: Facts On File, 1993. 192 pp. ISBN 0-8160-3105-3.

*Discrimination Against Women: A Global Survey of the Economic, Educational, Social and Political Status of Women.* Eschel M. Rhoodie. Jefferson: McFarland, 1989. xii + 618 pp. ISBN 0-89950-448-5. Cloth.

*Disengagement from Southwest Africa: Prospects for Peace in Angola and Namibia.* Owen Ellison Kahn, ed. New Brunswick, N.J.: Transaction Publishers, 1991. xx + 244 pp. ISBN 0-99738-361-0.

*Displaced Peoples and Refugee Studies: A Resource Guide.* Julian Davies, comp. Refugee Studies Programme, University of Oxford. London: Hans Zell Publishers, 1990. xii + 219 pp. ISBN 0-905450-76-0. Hans Zell Resource Guides, no. 2. Cloth.

*Disposable People? The Plight of Refugees.* Judy A. Mayotte. Maryknoll, N.Y.: Orbis Books, 1992. xx + 347 pp. ISBN 0-88344-839-4.

*Does Aid Work? Report to an Intergovernmental Task Force.* Robert Cassen et al. Oxford: Clarendon Press, 1994. xvi + 317 pp. ISBN 0-19-877386-2.

*Doria Shafik, Egyptian Feminist: A Woman Apart.* Cynthia Nelson. Gainesville: University Press of Florida, 1996. xxvi + 432 pp. ISBN 0-8130-1455-7. Cloth.

*The Dove's Footprints: Basketry Patterns in Matabeleland.* Marjorie Locke. Harare: Baobab Books, 1995. 140 pp. ISBN 0-908311-74-5.

*Dust to Dust: A Doctor's View of Famine in Africa.* David Heiden. Philadelphia: Temple University Press, 1992. x + 211 pp. ISBN 0-87722-912-0.

*Dying Lake Victoria: A Community-based Prevention Programme.* Samuel O. Akatch, ed. OSIENALA (Friends of Lake Victoria). Nairobi: Initiatives Publishers, 1996. ix + 96 pp. ISBN 9966-42-046-0.

*The Dynamics of Change in Southern Africa.* Paul B. Rich, ed. New York: St. Martin's Press, 1994. xiv + 279 pp. ISBN 0-312-12120-2.

*East of the Atlantic, West of the Congo: Art from Equatorial Africa.* Leon Siroto. Fine Arts Museums of San Francisco. Seattle: University of Washington Press, 1995. 62 pp. ISBN 0-88401-080-5.

*Eastern African History.* Robert O. Collins. Princeton, N.J.: Markus Wiener Publishers, 1997. 252 pp. ISBN 1-55876-016-4. African History in Documents series.

*Ecofeminism.* Maria Mies and Vandana Shiva. London: Zed Books, 1993. 328 pp. ISBN 1-85649-156-0.

*Ecoforum.* [periodical].

*Ecolinking: Everyone's Guide to Online Environmental Information.* Don Rittner. Berkeley: Peachpit Press, 1992. xi + 352 pp. ISBN 0-938151-35-5.

*Ecology Control and Economic Development in East African History: The Case of Tanganyika, 1850-1950.* Helge Kjekshus. London: Heinemann Educational Books, 1996. xxxi + 222 pp. ISBN 0-8214-1132-2.

*Ecology of an African Rain Forest: Logging in Kibale and the Conflict between Conservation and Exploitation.* Thomas T. Struhsaker. Gainesville: University Press of Florida, 1997. xxii + 434 pp. ISBN 0-8130-1490-5. Cloth.

*Economic Change and Political Liberalization in Sub-Saharan Africa.* Jennifer A. Widner, ed. London and Washington, D.C.: Johns Hopkins University Press, 1994. viii + 307 pp. ISBN 0-8018-4758-3.

*Economic Commission for Africa: Annual Report.* Addis Ababa: United Nations Economic Commission for Africa, 1994. v + 116 pp.

*Economic Development in Africa: A Select Bibliography, 1975-1988.* New Delhi: Research and Information System for the Non-Aligned and Other Developing Countries, 1989. RIS Bibliography Series, no. 9.

*Economic Justice in Africa: Adjustment and Sustainable Development.* George W. Shepherd Jr. and Karamo N.M. Sonko, eds. Westport, Conn.: Greenwood Press, 1994. xii + 214 pp. ISBN 0-313-28965-4. ISSN 0146-3586.

*Ecrans d'Afrique/African Screen.* [periodical].

*Educational Film and Video Locator.* Consortium of University Film Centers. New York: R. R. Bowker, 1990. 4th ed. lxxxv + 3,361 pp. ISBN 0-8352-2624-7. 2 volumes.

*Eerdmans' Handbook to the World's Religions.* Pat Alexander, ed. Grand Rapids: William B. Eerdmans Publishing, 1994. Rev. ed. 464 pp. ISBN 0-8028-0853-0.

*Egypt: Ancient Culture, Modern Land.* Jaromir Malek, ed. Norman: University of Oklahoma Press, 1993. 192 pp. Cradles of Civilization.

*The Egyptians.* Sergio Donadoni, ed. Chicago: University of Chicago Press, 1997. xvi + 361 pp. ISBN 0-226-15556-0.

*Election '94: The Campaigns, Results, and Future Prospects.* Andrew Reynolds, ed. Claremont (South Africa): David Philip Publishers, 1994. xvii + 237 pp. ISBN 0-86486-276-8.

*Elusive Peace: Negotiating an End to Civil Wars.* I. William Zartman, ed. Washington, D.C.: Brookings Institution, 1995. x + 353 pp. ISBN 0-8157-9704-4.

*Embargo: Apartheid's Oil Secrets Revealed.* R. Hengeveld and J. Rodenburg, eds. Shipping Research Bureau. Amsterdam: Amsterdam University Press, 1995. xiii + 399 pp. ISBN 90-5356-135-8.

*Emergency Aid and the Refugee.* Dublin: Irish Mozambique Solidarity, 1993. 36 pp. ISBN 0-9519326-1-6.

*Emergent Eritrea: Challenges of Economic Development.* Gebre Hiwet Tesfagiorgis. Lawrenceville, N.J.: Africa World Press, 1994. ISBN 0-932415-91-1.

*Emerging Human Rights: The African Political Economy Context.* George W. Shepherd Jr. and Mark O. C. Anikpo, eds. Westport, Conn.: Greenwood Press, 1990. viii + 244 pp. ISBN 0-313-26853-3.

*Emerging Perspectives on Ama Ata Aidoo.* Ada Uzoamaka Azodo and Gay Wilentz. Lawrenceville, N.J.: Africa World Press, 1997. 500 pp. ISBN 0-86543-580-4. Cloth.

*Emerging Perspectives on Buchi Emecheta.* Marie Umeh, ed. Lawrenceville, N.J.: Africa World Press, 1996. xlii + 490 pp. ISBN 0-86543-454-9. Cloth.

*Emerging Perspectives on Flora Nwapa.* Marie Umeh, ed. Lawrenceville, N.J.: Africa World Press, 1997. 500 pp. ISBN 0-86543-514-6. Cloth.

*The Empire Writes Back: Theory and Practice in Post-Colonial Literatures.* Bill Ashcroft, Gareth Griffiths, and Helen Tiffin. London: Routledge, 1989. viii + 246 pp. ISBN 0-415-01209-0.

*Encyclopedia of African American Religions.* Larry G. Murphy, J. Gordon Melton, and Gary L Ward. New York and London: Garland Publishing, 1993. lxxvi + 926 pp. ISBN 0-8153-05001.

*Encyclopedia of Islam.* International Union of Academics. Leiden: E. J. Brill, 1995. 14 vols. Cloth.

*An End to Hunger? The Social Origins of Food Strategies.* Solon L. Barraclough. London: Zed Books, 1991. iv + 284 pp. ISBN 0-86232-993-0.

*Endangered Peoples.* Art Davidson. San Francisco: Sierra Club Books, 1994. ix + 198 pp. ISBN 0-87156-423-8.

*Ending Mosambique's War: The Role of Mediation and Good Offices.* Cameron Hume. Washington, D.C.: U.S. Institute of Peace, 1994. xv + 162 pp. ISBN 1-878379-37-2.

*Energy and Sustainable Development.* Hans H. Bass et al., eds. Munster and Hamburg: Lit Verlag, 1994. xxiii + 683 pp. ISBN 3-89473-227-X. African Development Perspectives Yearbook, no. 3.

*Enforcing Restraint: Collective Intervention in Internal Conflicts.* Lori Fisler Damrosch, ed. New York: Council on Foreign Relations Press, 1993. xii + 403 pp. ISBN 0-87609-155-9.

*Enough Is Enough! For an Alternative Diagnosis of the African Crisis.* Carlos Lopes. Uppsala: Nordiska Afrikainstitutet, 1994. 38 pp. ISBN 91-7106-347-1. ISSN 1100-2131. Discussion Paper, no. 5.

*Enslaved Peoples in the 1990s: Indigenous Peoples, Debt Bondage and Human Rights.* Anti-Slavery International, with IWGIA. Copenhagen: International Work Group for Indigenous Affairs (IWGIA), 1997. 224 pp. ISBN 0-900-918-40-3. ISSN 0105-4503. IWGIA Document, no. 83.

*The Environment Encyclopedia and Directory.* London: Europa Publications, 1994. xvii + 381 pp. ISBN 0-946653-94-1. ISSN 1352-6480.

*Environment, Famine, and Politics in Ethiopia: A View From the Village.* Alemneh Dejene. Boulder: Lynne Rienner Publishers, 1990. xiv + 151 pp. ISBN 1-55587-240-9.

*Environmental and Economic Dilemmas of Developing Countries: Africa in the Twenty-First Century.* Valentine Udoh James, ed. Westport, Conn.: Praeger Publishers, 1994. xix + 240 pp. ISBN 0-275-94666-5.

*Environmental Development: Facing All Sides.* Dakar: Environmental Development Action in the Third World (ENDA), 1993. 278 pp. ISSN 0850-8518. African Environment, 8, nos. 3-4.

*Environmental Issues in the Third World: A Bibliography.* Joan Nordquist, ed. Santa Cruz: Reference and Research Services, 1991. 72 pp. ISBN 0-937855-42-1. ISSN 0887-3569. Contemporary Social Issues: A Bibliographic Series, no. 22.

*Environmental Profiles: A Global Guide to Projects and People.* Linda Sobel Katz, Sarah Orrick, and Robert Honig. New York: Garland Publishing, 1993. xxvi + 1083 pp. ISBN 0-8153-0063-8. Oversized. Cloth.

*Eritrea and Ethiopia: From Conflict to Cooperation.* Amare Tekle, ed. Lawrenceville, N.J.: Red Sea Press, 1994. x + 229 pp. ISBN 0-932415-97-0.

*Eritrea, a Pawn in World Politics.* Okbazghi Yohannes. Gainesville: University of Florida Press, 1991. x + 331 pp. ISBN 0-8130-1044-6. Cloth.

*Eritrea: Hope in the Horn of Africa.* [audiovisual].

*Eritrea: Miracleland.* Illen Ghebrai. Washington, D.C.: Illen Ghebrai, 1993. xvii + 354 pp. ISBN 0-9635467-0-8.

*Eritrean Studies Review.* [periodical]

*Escape From Violence: Conflict and the Refugee Crisis in the Developing World.* Aristide R. Zolberg, Astri Suhrke, and Sergio Aguayo. New York: Oxford University Press, 1989. xiii + 380 pp. ISBN 0-19-507916-7.

*The Ethics and Politics of Humanitarian Intervention.* Stanley Hoffmann. Notre Dame: University of Notre Dame Press, 1996. 168 pp. ISBN 0-268-00936-8.

*Ethiopia: Breaking New Ground.* Ben Parker. Oxford: Oxfam (UK and Ireland), 1995. 64 pp. ISBN 0-85598-270-5. Oxfam Country Profile series.

*Ethiopia: Failure of Land Reform and Agricultural Crisis.* Kidane Mengisteab. New York: Greenwood Press, 1990. xviii + 216 pp. ISBN 0-313-27423-1. ISSN 0069-9624.

*The Ethiopian Famine.* Kurt Jansson, Michael Harris, and Angela Penrose. London: Zed Books, 1987. xxviii + 196 pp. ISBN 0-86232-745-8.

*The Ethiopian Revolution, 1974-1987: A Transformation from an Aristocratic to a Totalitarian Autocracy.* Andargachew Tiruneh. Cambridge: Cambridge University Press, 1993. xv + 435 pp. ISBN 0-521-43082-8.

*The Ethiopians.* Richard Pankhurst. Cambridge, Mass: Blackwell Publishers, forthcoming.

*Ethnicity and Conflict in the Horn of Africa.* Katsuyoshi Fukui and John Markakis, eds. Athens: Ohio University Press, 1994. xiv + 242 pp. ISBN 0-8214-1080-6.

*Ethnicity and Democracy in Africa: Intervening Variables.* Okwudiba Nnoli. Lagos: Malthouse Press, 1994. 55 pp. ISBN 978-023-011-4. CASS Occasional Monograph, no. 4.

*Ethnicity and its Management in Africa: The Democratization Link.* Eghosa Osaghae. Lagos: Malthouse Press, 1994. 53 pp. ISBN 978-023-009-2. CASS Occasional Monograph, no. 2.

*Europa World Year Book.* London: Europa Publications, annual.

*Evolution of an African Artist: Social Realism in the Works of Ousmane Sembène.* Moore . Carrie Dailey. Ph.D. dissertation, Indiana University, 1973. xxvii + 289 leaves.

*Excessive Force: Power, Politics, and Population Control.* Elizabeth Liagin. Washington, D.C.: Information Project for Africa, 1996. viii + 348 pp. ISBN 1-886719-15-2.

*Exploring African Music.* Mark Bradshaw. Leicestershire: Centre for Multicultural Education, 1990. 32 pp.

*The Eye of the Elephant: An Epic Adventure in the African Wilderness.* Delia Owens and Mark Owens. Boston: Houghton Mifflin Company, 1992. xiii + 305 pp. ISBN 0-395-42381-3.

*Faces of African Independence: Three Plays.* Guillaume Oyono-Mbia and Seydou Badian. Charlottesville: University Press of Virginia, 1988. xxxvi + 127 pp. ISBN 0-8139-1187-7.

*Faces of Jesus in Africa.* Robert J. Schreiter, ed. Maryknoll, N.Y.: Orbis Books, 1991. xiii + 181 pp. ISBN 0-88344-768-1.

*Facets African American Video Guide.* Patrick Ogle, comp. Chicago: Academy Science Publishers, 1994. iii + 228 pp. ISBN 0-89733-402-7.

*Facing Up to AIDS: The Socio-Economic Impact in Southern Africa.* Sholto Cross and Alan Whiteside, eds. New York: St. Martin's Press, 1996. xii + 331 pp. ISBN 0-312-09106-0.

*Fact Sheet on Women and the Environment in Zimbabwe.* Zimbabwe and Regional Network of Environment Experts. Harare: Zimbabwe Women's Resource Centre and Network, 1993. 9 pp.

*The Falling Dawadawa Tree: Female Circumcision in Developing Ghana.* Christiana Oware Knudsen. Hojbjerg: Intervention Press, 1994. x + 230 pp. ISBN 87-89825-07-1. Available also from Smyrna Press (Brooklyn).

*Family Planning and Population: A Compendium of International Statistics.* John A. Ross, W. Parker Mauldin, and Vincent C. Miller. New York: United Nations Population Fund, 1993. vi + 202 pp. ISBN 0-87834-080-7.

*Famine in East Africa: Food Production and Food Policies.* Ronald E. Seavoy. New York: Greenwood Press, 1989. xii + 283 pp. ISBN 0-313-26755-3. ISSN 0069-9624.

*A Fate Worse Than Debt: The World Financial Crisis and the Poor.* Susan George. New York: Grove Weidenfeld/Evergreen Book, 1990. Rev. ed. xi + 300 pp. ISBN 0-8021-3121-2.

*Fau: Portrait of an Ethiopian Famine.* James Waller. Jefferson: McFarland, 1990. xii + 147 pp. ISBN 0-89950-515-5.

*Female Genital Mutilation: Proposals for Change.* Efua Dorkenoo and Scilla Elworthy. London: Minority Rights Group, April 1992. 43 pp. ISBN 0-946690-90-1. MRG Report, no. 92/3.

*Feminism Worldwide: A Bibliography.* Joan Nordquist, comp. Santa Cruz: Reference and Research Services, 1996. 64 pp. ISBN 0-937855-86-3. ISSN 0887-3569. Contemporary Social Issues: A Bibliographic Series, no. 44.

*50 Years Is Enough: A Resource Packet for Action in the Faith Community.* Cleveland: United Church Board of World Ministries, 1994.

*50 Years Is Enough: The Case Against the World Bank and the International Monetary Fund.* Kevin Danaher, ed. Boston: South End Press, 1994. xiii + 210 pp. ISBN 0-89608-495-7.

*50 Years of Bretton Woods Institutions. Enough!* Smitu Kothari, Vijay Pratap, and Shiv Visvanathan, eds. New York: Apex Press, December 1994. 132 pp. *Lokayan Bulletin.*

*Fighting for the Rain Forest: War, Youth, and Resources in Siera Leone.* Paul Richards. International African Institute. Oxford: James Currey, 1996. xxix + 182 pp. ISBN 0-85255-397-8. African Issues series.

*Fighting the Famine.* Nigel Twose. San Francisco: Food First/Institute for Food and Development Policy, 96 pp. ISBN 0-935028-22-6.

*Filling the Gaps: Care and Support for People with HIV/AIDS in Côte d'Ivoire.* Glen Williams, Auguste Didier Blibolo, and Dominique Kerouedan. London: Actionaid, November 1995. 55 pp. ISBN 1-872502-30-X. Strategies for Hope, no. 10.

*Film Quarterly.* [periodical].

*Films and Video for Black Studies.* University Park: Black Studies Program and Audio-Visual Services at Pennsylvania State University, 1987. viii + 24 pp.

*Films and Video for Black Studies.* Compiled and edited by Rebecca A. Hodges. University Park: Pennsylvania State University, Black Studies Program and Audio-Visual Services. 1987. 2nd ed. 24 pp.

*First Things First in Child Labour: Eliminating Work Detrimental to Children.* A. Bequele and W. E. Myers. United Nations Children's Fund and the International Labour Organization. Geneva: ILO Publications, 1995. xi + 163 pp. ISBN 92-2-109197-X.

*The Flow of News.* Paris: UNESCO, 1953.

*Focus on Africa.* [periodical].

*Food and Power in Sudan: A Critique of Humanitarianism.* London: African Rights, 1997. 380 pp. ISBN 1-899-477-13-6.

*Food Crops vs. Feed Crops: Global Substitution of Grains in Production.* David Barkin, Rosemary L. Batt, and Billie R. DeWalt. Boulder: Lynne Rienner Publishers, 1990. xvi + 169 pp. ISBN 1-55587-185-2.

*Food in Sub-Saharan Africa.* Art Hansen and Della E. McMillan, eds. Boulder: Lynne Rienner Publishers, 1986. xvi + 410 pp. ISBN 0-931477-59-X.

*Food Insecurity and the Social Division of Labour in Tanzania, 1919-85.* Deborah Fahy Bryceson. New York: St. Martin's Press, 1990. xvii + 285 pp. ISBN 0-312-04073-3.

*Food Policy and Agriculture in Southern Africa.* Richard Mkandawire and Khabele Matlosa, eds. Harare: SAPES Books, 1993. x + 250 pp. ISBN 0-7974-1225-5.

*The Food Question: Profits Versus People?* Henry Bernstein et al., eds. New York: Monthly Review Press, 1990. vi + 214 pp. ISBN 0-85345-804-9.

*For a Strong and Democratic United Nations: A South Perspective on UN Reform.* Geneva: South Centre, 1996. xvii + 229 pp. ISBN 92-9162-002-5.

*"For Four Years I Have No Rest": Greed and Holy War in the Nuba Mountains of Sudan.* John Prendergast and Nancy Hopkins. Washington, D.C.: Center of Concern, 1994. 58 pp. Horn of Africa Discussion Paper series, no. 5.

*Forced Labour and Migration: Patterns of Movement Within Africa.* Abebe Zegeye and Shubi Ishemo. London: Hans Zell Publishers, 1989. 405 pp. ISBN 0-905450-36-1.

*Foreign Affairs.* [periodical].

*Foreign Aid Reconsidered.* Roger C. Riddell. Baltimore: Johns Hopkins University Press, 1987. x + 309 pp. ISBN 0-8018-3546-1.

*Forty Lost Years: The Apartheid State and the Politics of the National Party, 1948-1994.* Dan O'Meara. Athens: Swallow Press/Ohio University Press, 1996. xxxix + 579 pp. ISBN 0-8214-1173-X.

*Foundations for a New Democracy: Corporate Social Investment in South Africa.* Myra Alperson. Johannesburg: Ravan Press, 1995. 222 pp. ISBN 0-86975-463-7.

*Foundations of the New South Africa.* John Pampallis. London: Zed Books, 1991. viii + 327 pp. ISBN 1-85649-005-X.

*Francophone African Fiction: Reading a Literary Tradition.* Jonathan Ngaté. Trenton: Africa World Press, 1988. xvii + 186 pp. ISBN 0-86543-088-8.

*Freedom from Debt: Peoples' Movements against the Debt.* Debbie Culbertson, ed. Toronto: Ten Days for World Development, 48 pp.

*Freedom in the World: The Annual Survey of Political Rights and Civil Liberties, 1995-1996.* Roger Kaplan et al., eds. New York: Freedom House, 1996. 544 pp. ISBN 0-932088-86-4.

*Freedom of the Press throughout the World.* Reporters Sans Frontières. Paris: annual.

*Freedom, State Security and the Rule of Law: Dilemmas of the Apartheid Society.* Anthony Mathews. Berkeley: University of California Press, 1986. xxx + 312 pp. ISBN 0-7021-1812-5.

*From Adjustment to Development in Africa: Conflict, Controversy, Convergence, Consensus?* Giovanni Andrea Cornia and Gerald K. Helleiner, eds. New York: St. Martin's Press, 1994. xxiv + 417 pp. ISBN 0-312-12135-0.

*From Fear to Hope: AIDS Care and Prevention at Chikankata Hospital, Zambia.* Glen Williams. London: Actionaid, 1992. Rev. ed. 36 pp. ISBN 1-872502-00-8. Strategies for Hope, no. 1.

*From Feast to Famine: Official Cures and Grassroots Remedies to Africa's Food Crisis.* Bill Rau. London: Zed Press, 1991. vii + 213 pp. ISBN 0-86232-927-2.

*From Liberation to Reconstruction: African Christian Theology after the Cold War.* J. N. K. Mugambi. Nairobi: East African Educational Publishers, 1995. xv + 258 pp. ISBN 9966-46-524-3.

*From Protest to Challenge: A Documentary History of African Politics in South Africa, 1882-1990.* Vol. 5: *Nadir and Resurgence, 1964-1979.* Thomas G. Karis and Gail M. Gerhart. Bloomington: Indiana University Press, 1997. xxix + 805 pp. ISBN 0-253-33231-1. Cloth.

*From Slaving to Neoslavery: The Bight of Biafra and Fernando Po in the Era of Abolition, 1827-1930.* Ibrahim K. Sundiata. Madison: University of Wisconsin Press, 1996. xii + 250 pp. ISBN 0-299-14510-7.

*From South Africa: New Writing, Photographs and Art.* David Bunn and Jane Taylor, eds. Evanston: Northwestern University, 1987. 496 pp. ISSN 0041-3097. TriQuarterly, no. 69 (spring/summer).

*From WID to GAD. More than a Change in Terminology?* Gine Zwart. Harare: Zimbabwe Women's Resource Centre and Network. 1992. ZWRCN Discussion Paper, no. 5.

*Front Line Africa: The Right to a Future.* Susanna Smith. Oxford: Oxfam, 1990. x + 386 pp. ISBN 0-85598-104-0.

*Frontpage: A Newspaper Simulation Exercise about Ethiopia and Eritrea.* Joynson et al. Bournemouth: Development Education (DEED), 1992.

*Fueling the Fire: U.S. Policy and the Western Sahara Conflict.* Leo Kamil. Trenton: Red Sea Press, 1987. 104 pp. ISBN 0-932415-23-7.

*Full House: Reassessing the Earth's Population Carrying Capacity.* Lester R. Brown and Hal Kane. New York and London: W. W. Norton, 1994. 261 pp. ISBN 0-393-31220-8.

*Fundamentalism and Militarism: A Report on the Root Causes of Human Rights Violations in the Sudan.* Abdullahi A. An-Na'im and Peter N. Kok. New York: Fund for Peace, 1991. 39 pp.

*A Future for Africa: Beyond the Politics of Adjustment.* Bade Onimode. London: Earthscan Publications, 1992. ix + 177 pp. ISBN 1-85383-100-x.

*The Future Population of the World. What Can We Assume Today?* Wolfgang Lutz, ed. London: Earthscan, 1994. xx + 484 pp. ISBN 1-85383-239-1.

*Garland Encyclopedia of World Music: Africa.* Ruth M. Stone, ed. New York: Garland Publishing, 1997. 760 pp. ISBN 06035-0.

*The Gèlèdé Spectacle: Art, Gender, and Social Harmony in an African Culture.* Babatunde Lawal. Seattle: University of Washington Press, 1997. xxiv + 327 pp. ISBN 0-295-97527-X. Cloth.

*Gender and Development: Theories and Gender Analysis.* Harare: Zimbabwe Women's Resource Centre and Network, July 1994. 25 pp. ZWRCN Bibliographies, no. 12.

*Gender and Population in the Adjustment of African Economies: Planning for Change.* Ingrid Palmer. Geneva: International Labour Office, 1991. xiv + 186 pp. ISBN 92-2-107739-X.

*Gender and the Media.* Evelyn Zinanga. Harare: Zimbabwe Women's Resource Centre and Network, 1992. 6 pp. ZWRCN Discussion Paper, no. 3.

*Gender in African Women's Writing: Identity, Sexuality, and Difference.* Juliana Makuchi Nfah-Abbenyi. Bloomington: Indiana University Press, November 1997. 224 pp. ISBN 0-253-21149-2.

*Gender Research and Urbanisation, Planning, Housing and Everyday Life.* Harare: Zimbabwe Women's Resource Centre and Network, April 1992. 14 pp. ZWRCN Workshop Report, no. 2.

*Gender Violence and Women's Human Rights in Africa.* New Brunswick, N.J.: Center for Women's Global Leadership, Douglass College, 1994. iv + 42 pp.

*Gender Voices and Choices: Redefining Women in Contemporary African Fiction.* Gloria Chukukere. Enugu (Nigeria): Fourth Dimension Publishing, 1995. 341 pp. ISBN 978-156-380-X.

*Gender, Class and Rural Transition: Agribusiness and the Food Crisis in Senegal.* Maureen Mackintosh. London: Zed Books, 1989. xvii + 218 pp. ISBN 0-86232-841-1.

*Gender, Environment, and Development in Kenya: A Grassroots Perspective.* Barbara Thomas-Slayter and Dianne Rocheleau. Boulder: Lynne Rienner Publishers, 1995. xii + 247 pp. ISBN 1-55587-419-3. Cloth.

*Gender, Environment, and Sustainable Development: Zimbabwe's Case.* Sara C. Mvududu. Harare: Zimbabwe Women's Resource Centre and Network, 1993. ii + 16 pp. ZWRCN Discussion Paper, no. 8.

*Gender, Ethnicity, and Social Change on the Upper Slave Coast: A History of the Anlo-Ewe.* Sandra E. Greene. Portsmouth, N.H.: Heinemann Publishers, 1996. xiii + 209 pp. ISBN 0-85255-622-5. Social History of Africa.

*Ghanaian Literatures.* Richard K. Priebe, ed. Westport, Conn.: Greenwood Press, 1988. x + 300 pp. ISBN 0-313-26438-4. Contributions in Afro-American and African Studies, no. 120.

*The Global Advocates Bulletin.* [periodical].

*The Global African: A Portrait of Ali A. Mazrui.* Omari H. Kokole. Lawrenceville, N.J.: Africa World Press, 1997. 350 pp. ISBN 0-86543-532-4. Cloth.

*Global Dimensions of the African Diaspora.* Joseph E. Harris, ed. Washington, D.C.: Howard University Press, 1993. 2nd ed. vii + 532 pp. ISBN 0-88258-149-X.

*Global Dreams: Imperial Corporations and the New World Order.* Richard J. Barnet and John Cavanagh. New York: Touchstone Books/Simon and Schuster, 1995. 480 pp. ISBN 0-684-80027-6.

*Global Ecology: A New Arena of Political Conflict.* Wolfgang Sachs, ed. London: Zed Books, 1993. xvii + 262 pp. ISBN 1-85649-164-1.

*Global HIV/AIDS: A Strategy for U.S. Leadership.* Center for Strategic and International Studies. Washington, D.C.: CSIS Books, August 1994. ix + 63 pp. ISBN 0-89206-254-1.

*The Global Refugee Crisis.* Gil Loescher and Ann Dull Loescher. Boulder: Westview Press, 1995. 225 pp.

*Global Village or Global Pillage.* Jeremy Brecher and Tim Costello. Boston: South End Press, 1994. vii + 238 pp. ISBN 0-89608-493-0.

*God's Wrathful Children: Political Oppression and Christian Ethics.* Willa Boesak. Grand Rapids: William B. Eerdmans Publishing, 1995. xxi + 264 pp. ISBN 0-8028-0621-X.

*Going for Gold: Men, Mines, and Migration.* T. Dunbar Moodie and Vivienne Ndatshe. Berkeley: University of California Press, 1994. xxi + 337 pp. ISBN 0-520-08130-7.

*The Golden Contradiction: A Marxist Theory of Gold. With Particular Reference to South Africa.* Farouk Stemmet. Aldershot: Avebury, 1996. viii + 276 pp. ISBN 1-85972-353-5. Cloth.

*The Gong and the Flute: African Literary Development and Celebration.* Kalu Ogbaa, ed. Westport, Conn.: Greenwood Press, 1994. xvii + 203 pp. ISBN 0-313-29281-7. Contributions in Afro-American and African Studies, no. 173.

*Governance and Democratisation in Nigeria.* Dele Olowu, Kayode Soremekun, and Adebayo Williams, eds. Ibadan: Spectrum Books, 1995. xv + 171 pp. ISBN 978-246-249-7.

*Government and Agriculture in Zimbabwe.* William A. Masters. Westport, Conn.: Praeger Publishishers, 1994. xvi + 236 pp. ISBN 0-275-94755-6.

*Government and Politics in Africa.* William Tordoff. Bloomington: Indiana University Press, 1993. xvii + 340 pp. ISBN 0-253-28916-5.

*Grassroots Leadership: The Process of Rural Development in Zimbabwe.* Claude G. Mararike. Harare: University of Zimbabwe Publications, 1995. xiv + 114 pp. ISBN 0-908307-39-X.

*Green Globe Yearbook of International Co-operation on Environment and Development.* Helge Ole Bergesen and Georg Parmann, eds. Oxford: Oxford University Press, 1994. 344 pp. ISBN 0-19-823324-8.

*Greenhouse Effect and its Impact on Africa.* Mohamed Suliman, ed. London: Institute for African Alternatives, 1990. 90 pp. ISBN 1-870425-24-3.

*Greening of Africa: Breaking through in the Battle for Land and Food.* Paul Harrison. International Institute for Environment and Development-Earthscan. London: Paladin Grafton Books, 1990. 380 pp. ISBN 0-586-08642-0.

*Greenwar: Environment and Conflict.* Olivia Bennett, ed. Washington, D.C.: Panos Institute, 1991. 156 pp. ISBN 1-870670-23-x.

*The Growth of Media in the Third World: African Failures, Asian Successes.* William A. Hachten. Ames: Iowa State University Press, 1993. xi + 129 pp. ISBN 0-8138-0867-7.

*Guanya Pau: A Story of an African Princess.* Joseph J. Walters. Lincoln: University of Nebraska Press, 1994. xxviii + 112 pp. ISBN 0-8032-9755-6.

*A Guide for Activists: Handbook on African Hunger.* John Prendergast and Terence Miller. Washington, D.C.: Center of Concern, 1992. 28 pp.

*Guide to Political Videos.* [periodical].

*Guide to Specialists 1994-95.* Washington, D.C.: U.S. Institute of Peace, 1994. 25 pp.

*The Gun Talks Louder Than the Voice: Somalia's Continuing Cycles of Violence.* John Prendergrest. Washington, D.C.: Center of Concern, July 1994. 56 pp.

*Haile Sellassie I: The Formative Years, 1892-1936.* Harold G. Marcus. Lawrenceville, N.J.: Red Sea Press, 1995. xvii + 242 pp. ISBN 1-56902-008-6.

*Handbook for Teaching African Literature.* Elizabeth Gunner. Oxford: Heinemann Educational Books, 1987. 2nd ed. xvi + 160 pp. ISBN 0-435-92260-2.

*Handbook of Political Science Research on Sub-Saharan Africa.* Mark W. DeLancey, ed. Westport, Conn.: Greenwood Press, 1992. viii + 427 pp. ISBN 0-313-27509-2. Cloth.

*Handbook of Regional Organizations in Africa.* Fredrik Söderbaum. Uppsala: Nordiska Afrikainstitutet, 1996. 161 pp. ISBN 91-7106-400-1.

*Handbooks to the Modern World: Africa.* Sean Moroney, ed. New York: Facts on File, 1989. Vol. 1: 665 pp. Vol. 2: 532 pp. ISBN 0-8160-1632-2.

*Hard Right: The New White Power in South Africa.* Johann van Rooyen. London and New York: I. B. Tauris, 1994. xxiv + 236 pp. ISBN 1-85043-818-8.

*HarperCollins Dictionary of Religion.* Jonathan Z. Smith, ed. San Francisco: HarperSanFrancisco, 1995. xxviii + 115 pp.

*The Healing Imagination of Olive Schreiner: Beyond South African Colonialism.* Joyce Avrech Berkman. Amherst: University of Massachusetts Press, 1989. xi + 317 pp. ISBN 0-87023-676-8.

*Health and Structural Adjustment in Rural and Urban Zimbabwe.* Leon A. Bijlmakers, Mary T. Basset, and David M. Sanders. Uppsala: Nordiska Afrikainstitutet, 1996. 78 pp. ISBN 91-7106-393-5. ISSN 1104-8425. Research Report, no. 101.

*Heart of Whiteness: Afrikaners Face Black Rule in the New South Africa.* June Goodwin and Ben Schiff. New York: Scribner, 1995. 416 pp. ISBN 0-684-81365-3.

*The Heinemann Book of African Women's Poetry.* Stella Chipasula and Frank Chipasula, eds. Oxford: Heinemann Educational Publishers, 1995. xxiv + 230 pp. ISBN 0-435-90680-1.

*The Heinemann Book of African Women's Writing.* Charlotte Bruner, ed. Portsmouth, N.H.: Heinemann, 1993. xi + 211 pp. ISBN 0-435-90673-9.

*The Heinemann Book of Contemporary African Short Stores.* Chinua Achebe and C. L. Innes, eds. Oxford: Heinemann Educational Publishers, 1992. viii + 200 pp. ISBN 0-435-90566-X.

*Helping or Hurting? Humanitarian Intervention and Crisis Response in the Horn.* John Prendergast. Washington, D.C.: January 1995. 36 pp. Discussion Paper, no. 6.

*Hemmed In: Responses to Africa's Economic Decline.* Thomas M. Callaghy and John Ravenhill, eds. New York: Columbia University Press, 1993. xviii + 573 pp. ISBN 0-231-08229-0.

*The Heritage of Islam: Women, Religion, and Politics in West Africa.* Barbara Callaway and Lucy Creevey. Boulder: Lynne Rienner Publishers, 1994. x + 221 pp. ISBN 1-5587-414-2.

*Heroes or Villains? Youth Politics in the 1980s.* Jeremy Seekings. Johannesburg: Raven Press, 1993. xvi + 108 pp. ISBN 0-86975-445-9.

*The Hidden Cost of AIDS: The Challenge of HIV to Development.* Panos Institute. London and Washington, D.C.: Panos Publications, 1992. viii + 168 pp. ISBN 1-870670-29-9.

*Hidden Enemies: Land Mines in Northern Somalia.* Boston: Physicians for Human Rights, 1992. iii + 51 pp. ISBN 1-879707-12-8.

*Historical Dictionary of Ethiopia and Eritrea.* Chris Prouty and Eugene Rosenfeld. Lanham, Md.: Scarecrow Press, 1994. xxvi + 614 pp. ISBN 0-8108-2663-1. African Historical Dictionaries, no. 56. Cloth.

*Historical Dictionary of International Organizations in Sub-Saharan Africa.* Mark W. DeLancey and Terry M. Mays. Lanham, Md.: Scarecrow Press, 1994. lviii + 515 pp. ISBN 0-8108-2751-4. International Organizations Series, no. 3. Cloth.

*Historical Dictionary of Namibia.* John J. Gropeter. Lanham, Md.: Scarecrow Press, 1994. xxxi + 724 pp. ISBN 0-8108-2728-X. African Historical Dictionaries, no. 57. Cloth.

*Historical Dictionary of Refugee and Disaster Relief Organizations.* Robert F. Gorman. Lanham, Md.: Scarecrow Press, 1994. viii + 273 pp. ISBN 0-8108-2876-6. Cloth.

*Historical Dictionary of the Sudan.* Carolyn Fluehr-Lobban, Richard A. Lobban Jr., and John Obert Voll. Lanham, Md.: Scarecrow Press, 1992. cvii + 409 pp. ISBN 0-8108-2547-3. Cloth.

*Historical Dictionary of Western Sahara.* Anthony G. Pazzanita and Tony Hodges. Lanham, Md.: Scarecrow Press, March 1994. lxxii + 564 pp. ISBN 0-8108-2661-5. Cloth.

*Historical Problems of Imperial Africa.* Robert O. Collins. Princeton, N.J.: Markus Wiener Publishers, 1994. 320 pp. ISBN 1-55876-060-1.

*History and Hunger in West Africa: Food Production and Entitlement in Guinea-Bissau and Cape Verde.* Laura Bigman. New York: Greenwood Press, 1993. xx + 149 pp. ISBN 0-313-26746-4. ISSN 0069-9624.

*History from South Africa: Alternative Visions and Practices.* Joshua Brown et al., eds. The Radical History Review and History Workshop. Philadelphia: Temple University Press, 1991. x + 469 pp. ISBN 0-87722-849-3.

*History of Africa.* Kevin Shillington. New York: St. Martin's Press, Scholarly and Reference Division, 1995. Rev. ed. vi + 447 pp. ISBN 0-312-03178-5.

*A History of Africa.* Hosea Jaffe. London: Zed Books, 1985. x + 172 pp. ISBN 0-86232-274-X. Cloth.

*The History of Black Mineworkers in South Africa.* V L Allen. West Yorkshire: The Moor Press, 1992. xx + 491 pp. ISBN 0-907698-05-0.

*A History of Christianity in Africa: From Antiquity to the Present.* Elizabeth Isichei. Grand Rapids: William B. Eerdmans Publishing, 1995. xi + 420 pp. ISBN 0-8028-0843-3.

*A History of South Africa.* Leonard Thompson. New Haven: Yale University Press, 1995. Rev. ed. xx + 332 pp. ISBN 0-300-06542-6.

*History of Southern Africa.* J. D. Omer-Cooper. London: James Currey, 1994. xiv + 310 pp. ISBN 0-85255-715-9.

*A History of the African People.* Robert W. July. Prospect Heights: Waveland Press, 1992. 4th ed. xiii + 593 pp. ISBN 0-88133-631-9.

*A History of Twentieth-Century African Literatures.* Oyekan Owomoyela, ed. Lincoln: University of Nebraska Press, 1993. x + 411 pp. ISBN 0-8032-8604-X.

*HIV and AIDS: The Global Inter-Connection.* Elizabeth Reid, ed. West Hartford, Conn.: Kumarian Press, 1995. xii + 225 pp. ISBN 1-56549-041-X.

*HIV Prevention and AIDS Care in Africa: A District Level Approach.* Japheth Ng'weshemi et al., eds Amsterdam: Royal Tropical Institute/KIT Press, 1997. 400 pp. ISBN 90-6832-108-0.

*Hlanganani: A Short History of COSATU.* [audiovisual].

*The Horn of Africa.* Charles Gurdon, ed. New York: St. Martin's Press, 1994. xii + 123 pp. ISBN 0-312-12063-X.

*The Horn of Africa: From War to Peace.* Seymour M. Henze. New York: St. Martin's Press, 1991.

*HRI Reporter.* [periodical].

*Human Development Report 1994.* United Nations. New York: United Nations Publications,

*The Human Dimension of Africa's Persistent Economic Crisis.* Adebayo Adedeji, Sadig Rasheed, and Melody Morrison, eds. London: Hans Zell Publishers, 1990. xx + 391 pp. ISBN 0-905450-14-0.

*The Human Factor in Developing Africa.* Senyo B-S. K. Adjibolosoo. Westport, Conn.: Praeger Publishers, June 1995. xii + 222 pp. ISBN 0-275-95059-X.

*Human Rights and Development in Africa.* Claude E. Welch Jr. and Ronald Meltzer, eds. Albany: State University of New York Press, 1984. 352 pp.

*Human Rights and Governance in Africa.* Ronald Cohen, Goran Hyden, and Winston P. Nagan, eds. Gainesville: University Press of Florida, 1993. xvii + 285 pp. ISBN 0-8130-1220-1.

*Human Rights Bulletin.* [periodical].

*Human Rights Education Techniques in Schools: Building Attitudes and Skills.* Anyakwee Nsirimovu. Rivers State (South Africa): Institute of Human Rights and Humanitarian Law, 1994. 42 pp. ISBN 978-2083-04-6.

*Human Rights Education: Strategies for Fostering Participatory Democracy in Ethiopia.* New York: Fund for Peace, November 1992. 54 pp.

*Human Rights in Africa: Cross-Cultural Perspectives.* Abdullahi Ahmed An-Na'im and Francis M. Deng, eds. Washington, D.C.: Brookings Institution, 1990. xv + 399 pp. ISBN 0-8157-1795-4.

*Human Rights in Commonwealth Africa.* Rhoda E. Howard. Totowa: Rowman and Littlefield, 1986. 250 pp. ISBN 0-8476-7433-9. Cloth.

*Human Rights in Developing Countries 1993.* Bård-Anders Andreassen and Theresa Swinehart, eds. Oslo: Nordic Human Rights Publications, 1993. xv + 369 pp. ISBN 82-7743-000-0.

*Human Rights in Morocco.* New York: Human Rights Watch/Middle East, 1995.

*Human Rights Quarterly.* [periodical].

*The Human Rights Watch Global Report on Women's Human Rights.* Human Rights Watch Women's Rights Project. New York: Human Rights Watch, August 1995. xxi + 458 pp. ISBN 0-300-06546-9.

*Human Rights Watch World Report.* New York: Human Rights Watch, annual.

*Humanitarian Action in Times of War: A Handbook for Practitioners.* larry Minear and Thomas G. Weiss. Boulder, Colo.: Lynne Rienner Publishers, 1993.

*Humanitarian Challenges and Intervention: World Politics and the Dilemmas of Help.* Thomas G. Weiss and Cindy Collins. Boulder: Westview Press, 1996. xiv + 239 pp. ISBN 0-8133-2845-4.

*Humanitarian Emergencies and Military Help in Africa.* Thomas G. Weiss, ed. New York: St. Martin's Press, 1990. xxi + 136 pp. ISBN 0-312-04735-5.

*Humanitarianism Across Borders: Sustaining Civilians in Times of War.* Thomas G. Weiss and Larry Minear, eds. Boulder: Lynne Rienner Publishers, 1993. xiv + 209 pp. ISBN 1-55587-428-2.

*Humanitarianism and War: Reducing the Human Cost of Armed Conflict.* Larry Minear and Thomas G. Weiss. Boulder, Colo: Lynne Rienner Publishers, 1994.

*Humanitarianism Unbound? Current Dilemmas Facing Multi-Mandate Relief Operations in Political Emergencies.* Rakiya Omaar and Alex de Waal. London: African Rights, 1994. 40 pp. Discussion Paper, no. 5.

*Humanitarianism under Siege: A Critical Review of Operation Lifeline Sudan.* Larry Minear et al. Lawrenceville, N.J.: Red Sea Press, 1991. xviii + 215 pp. ISBN 0-932415-66-0.

*Hunger 1994: Transforming the Politics of Hunger.* Silver Spring: Bread for the World Institute, 1993. iii + 189 pp. ISBN 0-9628058-9-0.

*Hunger 1995: Causes of Hunger.* Silver Spring: Bread for the World Institute, 1994. 1-884361-50-1.

*Hunger 1996: Countries in Crisis.* Silver Spring: Bread for the World Institute, 1995.

*Hunger 1997: What Can Governments Do?* Silver Spring: Bread for the World Institute, 1996.

*Hunger Notes.* [periodical].

*The Hunter's Vision: The Prehistoric Art of Zimbabwe.* Peter Garlake. Seattle: University of Washington Press, 1995. 176 pp. ISBN 0-295-97480-X.

*I Am Because We Are: Readings in Black Philosophy.* Fred Lee Hord and Jonathan Scott Lee, eds. Amherst: University of Massachusetts Press, 1995. x + 390 pp. ISBN 0-87023-965-1.

*The Idea of Africa.* V. Y. Mudimbe. Bloomington and Indianapolis: Indiana University Press, 1994. xvii + 234 pp. ISBN 0-253-33898-0.

*IDEX Update.* [periodical].

*If This Is Treason, I Am Guilty.* Allan A. Boesak. Grand Rapids: William B. Eerdmans Publishing, 1987. ix + 134 pp. ISBN 0-8028-0251-6.

*IFAD Update.* [periodical].

*IKON: Creativity and Change.* [periodical].

*The Illustrated Life of Mahkanda.* Ranko Pudi. Braamfontein: Skotaville Publishers, 1984. 64 pp. ISBN 0-947009-04-3.

*The Illustrated World's Religions: A Guide to Our Wisdom Traditions.* Huston Smith. San Francisco: HarperSanFrancisco, 1994. 255 pp. ISBN 0-06-067453-9.

*Images of Africa: The U.K. Report.* Nikki van der Gaag and Cathy Nash. London: Oxfam: 1987.

*Images of South Africa: The Rise of the Alternative Film.* Martin Botha and Adri van Aswegen. Pretoria: Human Sciences Research Council, 1992. 188 pp.

*IMF Support for African Adjustment Programs: Questions and Answers.* F. L. Osunsade. Washington, D.C.: International Monetary Fund, External Relations Dept., 1993. 20 pp. ISBN 1-55775-353-9.

*Imperial Identities: Stereotyping, Prejudice and Race in Colonial Algeria.* Patricia M. E. Lorcin. London and New York: I. B. Tauris Publishers, 1995. x + 323 pp. ISBN 0-85043-909-5.

*Imposing Aid: Emergency Assistance to Refugees.* B. E. Harrell-Bond. Oxford, New York, and Nairobi: Oxford University Press, 1986. xxvii + 440 pp. ISBN 0-19-261543-2.

*In Defence of Democracy.* Yash Tandon. Dar es Salaam: Dar es Salaam University Press, 1993. 61 pp. ISBN 9976-60-232-4.

*In Harm's Way: When Should We Risk American Lives in World Conflicts?* Mary Lord and Martha L. McCoy, eds. Pomfret: Study Circles Resource Center, 1994. 39 pp.

*In Search of Cool Ground: War, Flight and Homecoming in Northeast Africa.* Tim Allen, ed. Lawrenceville, N.J.: Africa World Press, 1996. xvi + 336 pp. ISBN 0-86543-525-1.

*In Sight of Surrender: The U.S. Sanctions Campaign against South Africa, 1946-1993.* Les de Villiers. Westport, Conn.: Praeger Publishers, 1995. xvii + 224 pp. ISBN 0-275-94982-6.

*In the Shadow of History: The Passing of Lineage Society.* Andrew P. Davidson. New Brunswick: Transaction Publishers, 1996. xvi + 328 pp. ISBN 1-56000-230-1.

*In the Time of Cannibals: The Word Music of South Africa's Basotho Migrants.* David B. Coplan. Chicago and London: University of Chicago Press, 1994. xxi + 300 pp. ISBN 0-226-11574-7.

*In Their Own Voices: African Women Writers Talk.* Adeola James, ed. Portsmouth, N.H.: Heinemann, 1990. 154 pp. ISBN 0-85255-507-5.

*In Transit: Between the Image of God and the Image of Man.* Tshenuwani Simon Farisani. Grand Rapids: William B. Eerdmans Publishing, 1990. xii + 251 pp. ISBN 0-8028-0438-1.

*The Independent Trade Unions 1974-1984: Ten Years of the South African Labour Bulletin.* Johann Maree. Johannesburg: Raven Press, 1987. xvi + 355 pp. ISBN 0-86975-307-X.

*The Indigenous World, 1995-96.* Copenhagen: International Work Group for Indigenous Affairs, 1996. 288 pp. ISSN 1024-0217.

*Individual Freedoms and State Security in the African Context: The Case of Zimbabwe.* John Hatchard. Athens: Ohio University Press, 1993. ix + 209 pp. ISBN 0-8214-1031-8.

*Inducing Food Insecurity: Perspectives on Food Policies in Eastern and Southern Africa.* M. A. Mohamed Salih, ed. Uppsala: Nordiska Afrikainstitutet, 1994. 236 pp. ISBN 91-7106-359-5. ISSN 0281-0018. Seminar Proceedings, no. 30.

*Inducing the Deluge: Zaire's Internally Displaced People.* Renée G. Roberts. Washington, D.C.: U.S. Committee for Refugees, October 1993. 13 pp.

*Industrialisation, Mineral Resources and Energy in Africa.* Smail Khennas, ed. Dakar: CODESRIA, 1992. vi + 340 pp. ISBN 2-86978-014-1.

*Institutional Sustainability in Agriculture and Rural Development: A Global Perspective.* Derick W. Brinkerhoff and Arthur A. Goldsmith, eds. New York: Praeger Publishers, 1990. x + 262 pp. ISBN 0-275-93373-3.

*Instruments of Economic Policy in Africa.* African Centre for Monetary Studies. London: James Currey, 1992. xiv + 238 pp. ISBN 0-435-08074-1.

*The International Arms Trade.* Edward J. Laurance. Lexington: Lexington Books, 1992.

*International Cooperation in Response to AIDS.* Leon Gordenker et al. London: Pinter/Cassell, 1995. x + 166 pp. ISBN 1-85567-282-0.

*International Debt and the Third World.* Joan Nordquist, comp. Santa Cruz: Reference and Research Services, 64 pp. Contemporary Social Issues: A Bibliographic Series.

*International Dictionary of Films and Filmmakers: Films.* Nicholas Thomas and James Vinson, eds. Chicago: St. James Press, 1990. xii + 1105 pp. ISBN 1-55862-037-0.

*International Dimensions of the Western Sahara Conflict.* Yahia Zoubir and Daniel Volman, eds. Westport, Conn.: Praeger Publishers, 1993. xv + 258 pp. ISBN 0-275-93821-2.

*International Directory of African Studies Research.* International African Institute, ed. Philip Baker, comp. New Providence: Hans Zell Publishers/K. G. Saur, 1994. 3rd ed. xxiii + 319 pp. ISBN 1-873836-36-8. Cloth.

*International Directory of Film and TV Documentation Centres.* Frances Thorpe, ed. Chicago: St. James Press, 1988. vii + 140 pp. ISBN 0-912289-29-5.

*International Directory of Non-Governmental Organizations Working for Environmentally, Socially, and Economically Sustainable Development.* WorldWise and Friends of the Earth. Sacramento: WorldWise, 1992. 328 pp.

*International Labour and the Third World: The Making of a New Working Class.* Rosalind E. Boyd, Robin Cohen, and Peter C. W. Gutkind. Aldershot: Gower Publishing Group, 1987. xii + 283 pp. ISBN 0-566-00971-4.

*International Labour Documentation.* [periodical].

*International Law of Human Rights in Africa: Basic Documents and Annotated Bibliography.* M. Hamalengwa, C. Flinterman, and E. V. O. Dankwa, eds. Norwell: Martinus Nijhoff Publishers, 1988. xii + 427 pp. ISBN 90-247-3587-4.

*The International Response to Conflict and Genocide: Lessons from the Rwanda Experience.* David Millwood, ed. Copenhagen: Joint Evaluation of Emergency Assistance to Rwanda, March 1996. ISBN 87-7265-331-0. 5 volumes.

*Intervention in Child Nutrition: Evaluation Studies in Kenya.* Jan Hoorweg and Rudo Niemeijer. London: Kegan Paul International, 1989. xii + 173 pp. ISBN 07103-0276-2.

*Into the Heart of Africa.* Jeanne Cannizzo. Toronto: Royal Ontario Museum, 1989. 96 pp. ISBN 0-88854-350-6.

*Introduction to African Religions.* John S. Mbiti. New York: Praeger Publishers, 1975.

*An Introduction to Islam.* David Waines. Cambridge and New York: Cambridge University Press, 1995. ix + 332 pp. ISBN 0-5210041880-1.

*Investigating Images: Working with Pictures on an International Theme.* Manchester: Development Education Project, Manchester Polytechnic, 1988.

*Invisible Crimes: U.S. Private Intervention in the War in Mozambique.* Kathi Austin. Washington, D.C.: Africa Policy Information Center, 1994. 50 pp. ISBN 0-9634238-2-7.

*The Invisible Epidemic: The Story of Women and AIDS.* Gena Corea. New York: HarperCollins, 1993. 356 pp. ISBN 0-06-092191-9.

*Iris.* [periodical].

*Is Population the Problem?* Christine Wheeler. Fitzroy: Community Aid Abroad, 1995. 8 pp. ISBN 1-87870-05-09. Issues in Development, no. 6.

*Islam and Human Rights: Tradition and Politics.* Ann Elizabeth Mayer. Boulder: Westview Press, 1995. xix + 223 pp. ISBN 0-8133-2131-X.

*Islam and Science: Religious Orthodoxy and the Battle for Rationality.* Pervez Hoodbhoy. London: Zed Books, 1991. xv + 157 pp. ISBN 1-85649-025-4.

*Islam and the West.* Bernard Lewis. Oxford and New York: Oxford University Press, 1993. ix + 217 pp. ISBN 0-19-507619-2.

*Islam in History: Ideas, People, and Events in the Middle East.* Bernard Lewis. Chicago: Open Court Publishing, 1993. 2nd ed. 487 pp. ISBN 0-8126-9217-9.

*Islam in Revolution: Fundamentalism in the Arab World.* R. Hrair Dekmejian. Syracuse: Syracuse University Press, 1985. xi + 249 pp. ISBN 0-8156-2330-5.

*Islam in Sub-Saharan African: A Partially Annotated Guide.* Samir M. Zoghby. Washington, D.C.: U.S. Government Printing Office, 1978. 318 pp. Available from the Superintendent of Documents, U.S. GPO.

*Islam: The Fear and the Hope.* Habib Boulares. London: Zed Books, 1990. xii + 144 pp. ISBN 0-86232-945-0.

*Islam: The View from the Edge.* Richard W. Bulliet. New York: Columbia University Press, 1994. 236 pp. ISBN 0-231-08218-5.

*Islamic Desk Reference.* E. J. von Donzel. Leiden: E. J. Brill, 1994. ISBN 90-04-09738-4.

*Islamic Fundamentalism in Egyptian Politics.* Barry Rubin. New York: St. Martin's Press, 1990. vii + 178 pp. ISBN 0-312-04571-9.

*The Islamic Impulse.* Barbara Freyer Stowasser, ed. London: Croom Helm, 1987. 329 pp. ISBN 0-932568-12-2.

*Islamism and Secularism in North Africa.* John Ruedy, ed. New York: St. Martin's Press, 1994. xxii + 298 pp. ISBN 0-312-12198-9.

*Islamism and Secularism in North Africa.* John Ruedy, ed. New York: St. Martin's Press, Scholarly and Reference Division, 1996. xxii + 298 pp. ISBN 0-312-16087-9.

*It's Like Holding the Key to Your Own Jail: Women in Namibia.* Caroline Allison. Geneva: World Council of Churches, 1986. x + 71 pp. ISBN 2-8254-0841-7.

*Journal of Modern African Studies.* [periodical].

*Jùjú: A Social History and Ethnography of an African Popular Music.* Christopher Alan Waterman. Chicago: University of Chicago Press, 1990. xii + 277 pp. ISBN 0-226-87465-6. Plus audiotape.

*Kalahari Bushmen.* Alan Barnard. East Sussex: Wayland Publishers, 1993. 48 pp. ISBN 0-7502-0877-5.

*Kampala Women Getting By: Wellbeing in the Time of AIDS.* Sandra Wallman. London: James Currey, 1996. x + 246 pp. ISBN 0-85255-241-6.

*Katutura: A Place Where We Stay. Life in a Post-Apartheid Township in Namibia.* Wade C. Pendleton. Athens, Ohio: Center for International Studies, Ohio University, 1996. xix + 217 pp. ISBN 0-89680-188-8. Monographs in International Studies, Africa Series, no. 65.

*Kemps International Music Book 1994.* London: Showcase Publications, 1994. 476 pp. ISBN 0-95162-125-4.

*Kenyan Foreign Policy Behavior Towards Somalia, 1963-1983.* Korwa G. Adar. Lanham, Md.: University Press of America, 1994. viii + 231 pp. ISBN 0-8191-9041-1.

*Khul-Khaal: Five Egyptian Women Tell Their Stories.* Nayra Atiya. Syracuse: Syracuse University Press, 1982. xxx + 177 pp. ISBN 0-8156-0181-6.

*King Leopold's Dream: Travels in the Shadow of the African Elephant.* Jeremy Gavron. New York: Pantheon Books, 1993. xiii + 288 pp. ISBN 0-679-41998-5.

*King Solomon's Mines Revisted: Western Interests and the Burdened History of Southern Africa.* William Minter. New York: Basic Books, 1986. xiii + 401 pp. ISBN 0-465-03723-2.

*Kwame Nkrumah: The Conakry Years. His Life and Letters.* June Milne, comp. London: Panaf/Zed Books, 1990. x + 422 pp. ISBN 0-901787-54-X.

*Labor and the Growth Crisis in Sub-Saharan Africa.* Washington, D.C.: World Bank, 1995. v + 29 pp. ISBN 0-8213-3343-7.

*Labour Export Policy in the Development of Southern Africa.* Bill Paton. Basingstoke: Macmillan, 1995. xii + 397 pp. ISBN 0-333-61695-2.

*Labour in the Explanation of an African Crisis. A Critique of Current Orthodoxy: The Case of Nigeria.* Jimi Adesina. Dakar: CODESRIA, 1994. ix + 131 pp. ISBN 2-86978-036-2.

*The Labour Market in Africa.* Jean-Pierre Lachaud. Geneva: International Institute for Labour Studies, 1994. xiv + 178 pp. ISBN 92-9014-534-X. Research Series, no. 102.

*Labour Resistance in Cameroon.* Piet Konings. Portsmouth, N.H.: Heinemann, 1993. xii + 203 pp. ISBN 0-435-08087-3.

*Labour, Capital and Society.* [periodical].

*Land in African Agrarian Systems.* Thomas J. Bassett and Donald E. Crummey, eds. Madison: University of Wisconsin Press, 1993. xii + 418 pp. ISBN 0-299-13614-0.

*Land in Zimbabwe: A Gender Question?* Harare: Zimbabwe Women's Resource Centre and Network, January 1994. 12 pp. ZWRCN Workshop Report, no. 6.

*Land, Freedom and Fiction: History and Ideology in Kenya.* David Maughan-Brown. London: Zed Books, 1985. x + 284 pp. ISBN 0-86232-408-4.

*Landmines: A Deadly Legacy.* The Arms Project of Human Rights Watch and Physicians for Human Rights. New York: Human Rights Watch, 1993. xii + 510 pp. ISBN 1-56432-113-4.

*Language and Theme: Essays on African Literature.* Emmanuel N. Obiechina. Washington, D.C.: Howard University Press, 1990. vii + 249 pp. ISBN 0-88258-064-7.

*Larousse Dictionary of Beliefs and Religions.* Rosemary Goring, ed. Edinburgh and New York: Larousse, 1994. xii + 605 pp.

*The Last Empire: De Beers, Diamonds and the World.* Stefan Kanfer. New York: Farrar Straus Giroux, 1993. 409 pp. ISBN 0-374-15207-1.

*Launching Democracy in South Africa: The First Open Election, April 1994.* R. W. Johnson and Lawrence Schlemmer, eds. New Haven: Yale University Press, 1996. xiv + 412 pp. ISBN 0-300-06391-1.

*Learning from Somalia: The Lessons of Armed Humanitarian Intervention.* Walter Clarke and Jeffrey Herbst, eds. Boulder: Westview Press, 1997. xi + 276 pp. ISBN 0-8133-2794-6.

*The Left Index.* [periodical]

*The Legal Situation of Women in Southern Africa.* Julie Stewart and Alice Armstrong. Harare: University of Zimbabwe Publications, 1990. xiv + 241 pp. ISBN 0-908307-15-2.

*Let Freedom Come: Africa in Modern History.* Basil Davidson. Boston: Atlantic Monthly Press, 1978. Published elsewhere as *Africa in Modern History: The Search for a New Society* (London: Allen Lane, 1978).

*Let the Dawn Come. Social Development: Looking Behind the Clichés.* Simon Burne and Wendy Davies, eds. London: Panos Publications, 1995. vi + 152 pp. ISBN 1-870670-33-7.

*Let Your Voice Be Heard! Songs From Ghana and Zimbabwe.* Abraham Kobena Adzinyah, Dumisani Maraire, and Judith Cook Tucker. Danbury: World Music Press, 1993. xix + 116 pp. ISBN 0-937203-22-X. Plus audiotape.

*Lethal Commerce: The Global Trade in Small Arms and Light Weapons.* Jeffrey Boutwell, Michael T. Klare, and Laura W. Reed, eds. Cambridge, Mass.: Committee on International Security Studies, American Academy of Arts and Sciences, 1995. 160 pp. ISBN 0-877240-00-0.

*Liberalised Development in Tanzania.* Peter Gibbon, ed. Uppsala: Nordiska Afrikainstitutet, 1995. 176 pp. ISBN 91-7106-370-6.

*Liberalization and Politics: The 1990 Election in Tanzania.* Rwekaza S. Mukandala and Haroub Othman, eds. Dar Es Salaam: Dar Es Salaam University Press, 1994. viii + 319 pp. ISBN 9976-60-236-7.

*Liberalizing Tanzania's Food Trade: Public and Private Faces of Urban Marketing Policy 1939-1988.* Deborah Fahy Bryceson. Geneva: United Nations Research Institute for Social Development, 1993. xiv + 306 pp. ISBN 0-85255-135-5.

*Liberation Movement and Beyond: Challenges for the ANC.* Yunus Carrim. London: Catholic Institute for International Relations, 1991. 29 pp. ISBN 1-85287-086-9. *CIIR Insight.*

*Liberation Politics and External Engagement in Ethiopia and Eritrea.* John Prendergast and Mark Duffield. Washington, D.C.: Center of Concern, April 1995. 20 pp. Horn of Africa Discussion Paper Series, no. 8.

*Library of African Cinema.* California Newsreel. San Francisco: California Newsreel, annual.

*Libya: Desert Land in Conflict.* Ted Gottfried. Brookfield: Millbrook Press, 1994. 159 pp. ISBN 1-56294-351-0.

*The Lie of the Land: Challenging Received Wisdom on the African Environment.* Melissa Leach and Robin Mearns, eds. International African Institute. Oxford: James Currey, 1996. xvi + 240 pp. ISBN 0-85255-409-5. African Issues series.

*The Life and Times of Menelik II: Ethiopia, 1844-1913.* Harold G. Marcus. Lawrenceville, N.J.: Red Sea Press, 1995. viii + 298 pp. ISBN 1-56902-010-8.

*Life in Stone: Zimbabwean Sculpture: Birth of a Contemporary Art Form.* Olivier Sultan. Harare: Baobab Books, 1994. Rev. ed. 86 pp. ISBN 0-908311-71-0.

*Life of the Ancient Egyptians.* Eugen Strouhal. Norman: University of Oklahoma Press, 1992. 279 pp. ISBN 0-8061-2475-X.

*Linking Relief and Development.* Simon Maxwell and Margaret Buchanan-Smith, eds. Sussex: Institute of Development Studies, October 1994. xiv + 114 pp. ISSN 0265-5012. *IDS Bulletin,* 25, no. 4.

*A Listening Church: Autonomy and Communion in African Churches.* Elochukwu E. Uzukwu. Maryknoll, N.Y.: Orbis Books, 1996. x + 182 pp. ISBN 1-57075-060-2.

*Listening to Africa: Developing Africa from the Grassroots.* Pierre Pradervand. New York: Praeger Publishers, 1990. xxiii + 229 pp. ISBN 0-275-93692-9.

*Lives of Courage: Women for a New South Africa.* Diana E. H. Russell. New York: Basic Books, 1989. xiv + 375 pp. ISBN 0-465-04139-6.

*Living Apart: South Africa under Apartheid.* Ian Berry. San Francisco: Phaidon Press/Chronicle Books, 1996. 288 pp. ISBN 0-714835-23-4. Cloth.

*Living Positively with AIDS: The AIDS Support Organization (TASO), Uganda.* Janie Hampton. London: Actionaid, 1991. Rev. ed. 36 pp. ISBN 1-872502-13-X. Strategies for Hope, no. 2.

*Living Under Contract: Contract Farming and Agrarian Transformation in Sub-Saharan Africa.* Peter D. Little and Michael J. Watts, eds. Madison: University of Wisconsin Press, 1994. xviii + 298 pp. ISBN 0-299-14064-4.

*Local Heroes, Global Change.* [audiovisual].

*The Long Journey: South Africa's Quest for a Negotiated Settlement.* Steven Friedman, ed. Centre for Policy Studies. Johannesburg: Ravan Press, 1993. x + 206 pp. ISBN 0-869754-444-0.

*A Long Road to Uhuru: Human Rights and Political Participation in Kenya.* David Gillies and Makau wa Mutua. Montreal: International Centre for Human Rights and Democratic Development, March 1993. 58 pp.

*A Long Struggle: The Involvement of the World Council of Churches in South Africa.* Pauline Webb, ed. Geneva: WCC Publications, 1994. xiv + 133 pp. ISBN 2-8254-1135-3.

*The Lords of Poverty: Free-Wheeling Lifestyles, Power, Prestige and Corruption of the Multi-million Dollar Aid Business.* Graham Hancock. New York: Atlantic Monthly Press, 1989. xvi + 234 pp. ISBN 0-87113-469-1.

*Lost Crops of Africa.* Vol. 1: *Grains.* National Research Council. Washington, D.C.: National Academy Press, 1996. xix + 384 pp. ISBN 0-309-04990-3.

*The Maasai, the Dinka and the East African Pastoralists.* Peter Robertshaw and Neil Sabania. Cambridge, Mass.: Blackwell Publishers, forthcoming.

*Make Man Talk True: Nigerian Drama in English Since 1970.* Chris Dunton. London: Hans Zell Publishers, 1992. 215 pp. ISBN 0-905450-87-6. New Perspectives on African Literature, no. 5.

*Makeba: My Story.* Miriam Makeba. New York: NAL Books/New American Library, 1987. 249 pp. ISBN 0-453-00561-6.

*The Making of Modern Africa.* Vol. 1: *The Nineteenth Century.* A. E. Afigbo et al. Harlow: Longman Group, 1986. 2nd ed. xii + 372 pp. ISBN 0-582-58508-2.

*Making War and Waging Peace: Foreign Intervention in Africa.* David R. Smock, ed. Washington, D.C.: U.S. Institute of Peace, 1993. vi + 290 pp. ISBN 1-878379-28-3.

*Mali: A Prospect of Peace?* Rhéal Drisdelle. Oxford: Oxfam (UK and Ireland), 1997. 64 pp. ISBN 0-85598-334-5. Oxfam Country Profile.

*Mali: Crossroads of Africa.* Philip Koslow. New York: Chelsea House Publishers, 1995. 64 pp. ISBN 0-7910-3127-6.

*Malthusianism: An African Dilemma: Hunger, Drought, and Starvation in Africa.* John E. Eberegbulam Njoku. Lanham, Md.: Scarecrow Press, 1986. xxix + 181 pp. ISBN 0-8108-1906-6.

*Managing Global Chaos: Sources of and Responses to International Conflict.* Chester A. Crocker, Fen Osler Hampson, and Pamela Aall, eds. Washington, D.C.: United States Institute of Peace Press, 1996. xxiii + 642 pp. ISBN 1-878379-59-3.

*Managing the Economic Transition in South Africa.* Montclair: Center for Economic Research on Africa, 1994. vii + 95 pp. ISBN 0-944572-07-3.

*Manichean Aesthetics: The Politics of Literature in Colonial Africa.* Abdul R. JanMohamed. Amherst: University of Massachusetts Press, 1988. xi + 312 pp. ISBN 0-87023-651-2.

*Manufacturing Militance: Workers' Movements in Brazil and South Africa, 1970-1985.* Gay W. Seidman. Berkeley: University of California Press, 1994. x + 361 pp. ISBN 0-520-08303-2.

*Many Voices, One Church: New People Articles on the African Synod.* Nairobi: New People, 1994. 95 pp.

Many Voices, One World. Sean MacBride. International Commission for the Study of Communication Problems. Paris: UNESCO, 1980.

*The Marabout and the Muse: New Approaches to Islam in African Literature.* Kenneth W. Harrow, ed. Portsmouth, N.H.: Heinemann Publishers, 1996. xxiii + 239 pp. ISBN 0-435-08983-8. Studies in African Literature.

*The Market Tells Them So: The World Bank and Economic Fundamentalism in Africa.* John Mihevc. Penang and Accra: Third World Network, 1995. 313 pp. ISBN 983-9747-15-0.

*Marketing Africa's High-Value Foods: Comparative Experiences of an Emergent Private Sector.* Steven Jaffee and John Morton, eds. Dubuque: Kendall/Hunt Publishing, 1995. vi + 503 pp. ISBN 0-8403-9760-7.

*Marriage in Maradi: Gender and Culture in a Hausa Society in Niger, 1900-1989.* Barbara M. Cooper. Portsmouth, N.H.: Heinemann Publishers, 1997. xlix + 228 pp. ISBN 0-43507413-X. Social History of Africa.

*Marxism and African Literature.* Georg M. Gugelberger, ed. Trenton: Africa World Press, 1985. xiv + 226 pp. ISBN 0-86543-031-4.

*A Mask Dancing: Nigerian Novelists of the Eighties.* Adewale Maja-Pearce. London and New York: Hans Zell Publishers, 1992. 198 pp. ISBN 0-905450-92-2. New Perspectives on African Literature, no. 4.

*Mass Media in Sub-Saharan Africa.* Louis M. Bourgault. Bloomington: Indiana University Press, 1995. xv + 294 pp. ISBN 0-253-20938-2.

*Media and Democracy: Theories and Principles with Reference to an African Context.* Helge Ronning. Harare: SAPES Books, 1994. 20 pp. ISBN 1-77905-015-1. Southern African Political Economy Series, no. 8.

*The Media and Human Rights in Southern Africa.* Harare: Inter Press Service, Global News Agency, April 1994. 60 pp.

*The Media in Africa and Africa in the Media: An Annotated Bibliography.* Gretchen Walsh. London: Hans Zell Publishers, 1996. xxv + 291 pp. ISBN 1-873836-81-3. Cloth.

*Media Matters in South Africa.* Jeanne Prinsloo and Costas Criticos, eds. Durban: Media Resource Centre, Community Resource Centre Training Project, 1991. 301 pp. ISBN 0-86980-802-8.

*The Media Monopoly.* Ben Bagdikian. Boston: Beacon Press, 1992. 4th ed. xxxi + 288 pp. ISBN 0-8070-6159-X.

*Media Review.* [periodical].

*Media Review Digest: The Only Complete Guide to Reviews of Non-Print Media.* C. Edward Wall, ed. Ann Arbor: Pierian Press, annual. xxvi + 916 pp. ISBN 0-87650-337-7.

*Mediating Conflict: Decision-making and Western Intervention in Namibia.* Vivienne Jabri. Manchester: Manchester University Press, 1990. vi + 198 pp. ISBN 0-7190-3219-9.

*The Mediterranean Debt Crescent: Money and Power in Algeria, Egypt, Morocco, Tunisia, and Turkey.* Clement M. Henry. Gainesville: University Press of Florida, 1996. xviii + 336 pp. ISBN 0-8130-1380-1.

*Meeting AIDS with Compassion: AIDS Care and Prevention in Agomanya, Ghana.* Janie Hampton. London: Actionaid, 1991. 32 pp. ISBN 1-872502-07-5. Strategies for Hope, no. 4.

*Meeting the Third World Through Women's Perspectives: Contemporary Women in South Asia, Africa, and Latin America.* Susan Hill Gross and Mary Hill Rojas. Saint Louis Park: Glenhurst Publications, 1988. 113 + 110 pp.

*Memoirs from the Women's Prison.* Nawal El Saadawi. Trans. Marilyn Booth. Berkeley: University of California Press, 1994. 204 pp. ISBN 0-520-08888-3.

*Men Own the Fields, Women Own the Crops: Gender and Power in the Cameroon Grassfields.* Miriam Goheen. Madison: University of Wisconsin Press, 1996. xx + 252 pp. ISBN 0-299-14674-X.

*Men, Women, and God(s): Nawal El Saadawi and Arab Feminist Poetics.* Fedwa Malti-Douglas. Berkeley: University of California Press, 1995. xii + 274 pp. ISBN 0-520-20072-1.

*Men Own the Fields, Women Own the Crops: Gender and Power in the Cameroon Grassfields.* Miriam Goheen. Madison: University of Wisconsin Press, 1996. xx + 252 pp. ISBN 0-299-14674-X.

*Mending Rips in the Sky: Options for Somali Communities in the Twenty-first Century.* Hussein M. Adam and Richard Ford, eds. Lawrenceville: Red Sea Press, 1997. 630 pp. ISBN 1-56902-074-4.

*Mercy Under Fire: War and the Global Humanitarian Community.* Larry Minear and Thomas C. Weiss. Boulder: Westview Press, 1995. xviii + 259 pp. ISBN 0-8133-2567-6.

*The Middle East and North Africa, 1995.* London: Europa Publications, 1995. 41st ed. xix + 1022 pp. ISBN 0-946653-99-2. ISSN 0076-8502.

*The Migration Experience in Africa.* Jonathan Baker and Tade Akin Aina, eds. Uppsala: Nordiska Afrikainstitutet, 1995. 353 pp. ISBN 91-7106-366-8.

*Mining and Structural Adjustment: Studies on Zimbabwe and Tanzania.* C. S. L. Chachage, Magnus Ericsson, and Peter Gibbon. Uppsala: Nordiska Afrikainstitutet, 1993. 112 pp. ISBN 91-7106-340-4. ISSN 0080-6714.

*Mining in Africa Today: Strategies and Prospects.* Faysal Yachir. London: Zed Books, 1988. xv + 91 pp. ISBN 0-86232-739-3.

*The Mining Industry in Tanzania.* M. Parker. Dodoma (Tanzania), 1992.

*The Mining Sector in Southern Africa.* Paul Jourdan, ed. Harare: SAPES Books, 1995. 117 pp. ISBN 1-77905-006-2. Southern African Political Economy series.

*The Mobilization of Muslim Women in Egypt.* Ghada Hashem Talhami. Gainesville: University Press of Florida, 1996. xii + 177 pp. ISBN 0-8130-1429-8. Cloth.

*Modern Africa: A Social and Political History.* Basil Davidson. London: Longman Group, 1994. 3rd ed. xi + 300 pp. ISBN 0-582-21288-X.

*A Modern Economic History of Africa. Vol. 1: The Nineteenth Century.* Tiyambe Zeleza. Dakar: CODESRIA, 1993. vii + 501 pp. ISBN 2-86978-027-3.

*Modernising Super-Exploitation: Restructuring South African Agriculture.* Tessa Marcus. London: Zed Books, 1989. x + 207 pp. ISBN 0-86232-845-4.

*Modernizing Women: Gender and Social Change in the Middle East.* Valentine M. Moghadam. Boulder: Lynne Rienner Publishers, 1993. xvi + 309 pp. ISBN 1-55587-354-5.

*Money-Go-Rounds: The Importance of Rotating Savings and Credit Associations for Women.* Shirley Ardener and Sandra Burman, eds. Oxford: Berg Publishers, 1995. xiii + 326 pp. ISBN 0-85496-832-6.

*Monuments of Egypt.* Eliot Porter. Albuquerque: University of New Mexico Press, 1990. 28 + 103 pp. ISBN 0-8263-1232-2.

*Moon is Dead! Give Us Our Money!: The Cultural Origins of an African Work Ethic, Natal, South Africa.* Keletso E. Atkins. Portsmouth, N.H.: Heinemann, 1993. xvi + 190 pp. ISBN 0-435-08078-4.

*Moral Philosophy and Development: The Human Condition in Africa.* Tedros Kiros. Athens: Ohio University Press, 1992. xxi + 178 pp. ISBN 0-89680-171-3.

*More People, Less Erosion: Environmental Recovery in Kenya.* Mary Tiffen, Michael Mortimore, and Francis Gichuki. Chichester: John Wiley and Sons, 1994. xii + 311 pp. ISBN 0-471-94143-3.

*More Than Drumming: Essays on African and Afro-Latin Music and Musicians.* Irene V. Jackson, ed. Westport, Conn.: Greenwood Press, 1985. 207 pp. ISBN 0-313-23093-5. Contributions in Afro-American and African Studies, no. 80.

*Mortgaging the Earth: The World Bank, Environmental Impoverishment, and the Crisis of Development.* Bruce Rich. Boston: Beacon Press, 1994. xiv + 376 pp. ISBN 0-8070-4704-X.

*Mortgaging Women's Lives: Feminist Critiques of Structural Adjustment.* Pamela Sparr, ed. London: Zed Books, 1994. x + 214 pp. ISBN 1-85649-102-1.

*Mother, Sing for Me: People's Theatre in Kenya.* Ingrid Björkman. London: Zed Books, 1989. ix + 107 pp. ISBN 0-86232-671-0.

*Motherlands: Black Women's Writing from Africa, the Caribbean, and South Asia.* Susheila Nasta, ed. London: Women's Press, 1991. xxx + 366 pp. ISBN 0-7043-4269-3.

*Motion Picture Annual.* New Providence, N.J.: Reed Reference Publishing, annual.

*Movies, Moguls, Mavericks: South African Cinema, 1979-1991.* Johan Blignaut and Martin Botha, eds. Cape Town: Showdata, 1992. Various pagings.

*Moving Pictures Bulletin.* [periodical].

*Mozambique: A Dream Undone. The Political Economy of Democracy, 1975-84.* Bertil Egerö. Uppsala: Nordiska Afrikainstitutet, 1990. 230 pp. ISBN 91-7106-302-1.

*Mozambique: Rising from the Ashes.* Rachel Waterhouse. Oxford: Oxfam (UK and Ireland), 1996. 64 pp. ISBN 0-85598-341-8. Oxfam Country Profile series.

*Mozambique: Who Calls the Shots?* Joseph Hanlon. Bloomington: Indiana University Press, 1991. xiv + 301 pp. ISBN 0-253-32696-6.

*Muntu: African Culture and the Western World.* Janheinz Jahn. New York: Grove Weidenfeld, 1990. xxvii + 267 pp. ISBN 0-8021-3208-1.

*Music and Black Ethnicity: The Caribbean and South America.* Gerard H. Béhague, ed. New Brunswick, N.J.: Transaction Publishers, 1994. iii + 335 pp. ISBN 1-56000-708-7.

*The Music of Africa.* J. H. Kwabena Nketia. New York and London: W. W. Norton, 1974. x + 278 pp. ISBN 0-393-09249-6.

*Music of West Africa: Exploring the Music of the World.* Trevor Wiggins. Oxford: Heinemann Educational Books, 1993. 80 pp. ISBN 0-435-81010-3.

*Musicmakers of West Africa.* John Collins. Washington, D.C.: Three Continents Press, 1985. 177 pp. ISBN 0-89410-075-0.

*Muslim Identity and Social Change in Sub-Saharan Africa.* Louis Brenner, ed. Bloomington: Indiana University Press, 1993. x + 250 pp. ISBN 0-253-31271-X.

*Mwalimu : The Influence of Nyerere.* Colin Legum and Geoffrey Mmari. Lawrenceville, N.J.: Africa World Press, 1995. xii + 205 pp.

*My Fight Against Apartheid.* Michael Dingake. London: Kliptown Books, 1987. 241 pp. ISBN 0-904759-82-2.

*Myth, Literature and the African World.* Wole Soyinka. Cambridge: Cambridge University Press, 1990. xii + 168 pp. ISBN 0-521-39834-7.

*Myth, Race and Power: South Africans Imaged on Film and TV.* Keyan Tomaselli et al. Belleville (South Africa): Anthropos Publishers, 1986. xi + 126 pp. ISBN 0-620-09003-0.

*Myths and Root Causes: Hunger, Population, and Development.* Peter Rosset et al. Oakland: Food First Books, 1994.

*Myths of African Hunger.* Kevin Danaher and Abikok Riak. Oakland: Institute for Food and Development Policy, 1995. 4 pp. Food First Backgrounder, (spring 1995).

*Nairobi's Environment: A Review of Conditions and Issues.* Davinder Lamba. Nairobi: Mazingira Institute: 1994. 69 pp. ISBN 9966-9876-65.

*Namibia and External Resources: The Case of Swedish Development Assistance.* Bertil Odén et al. Uppsala: Nordiska Afrikainstitutet, 1994. 122 pp. ISBN 91-7106-351-X. ISSN 1104-8425. Research Report, no. 96.

*Namibia in History: Junior Secondary History Book.* Nangolo Mbumba and Norbert H. Noisser. London: Zed Books, 1988. 294 pp. ISBN 0-86232-769-5.

*Namibia Yearbook.* Windhoek: Guidebook Press, annual.

*Namibia's Liberation Struggle: The Two-Edged Sword.* Colin Leys and John S. Saul. Athens: Swallow Press/Ohio University Press, 1995. xii + 212 pp. ISBN 0-8214-1103-9.

*Namibia: Land of Tears, Land of Promise.* Roy J. Enquist. Cranbury: Associated University Presses, 1990. 174 pp. ISBN 0-945636-09-1.

*Namibia: The Facts.* London: International Defence and Aid Fund, 1989. 112 pp. ISBN 0-904759-94-6.

*Namibia: The Nation After Independence.* Donald L. Sparks and December Green. Boulder: Westview Press, 1992. xii + 204 pp. ISBN 0-8133-1023-7.

*Namibia: The Violent Heritage.* David Soggot. New York: St. Martin's Press, 1986. xvi + 333 pp. ISBN 0-312-55876-7.

*Namibia: Women in War.* Tessa Cleaver and Marion Wallace. London: Zed Books, 1990. xvi + 137 pp. ISBN 0-86232-901-9.

*National and Class Conflict in the Horn of Africa.* John Markakis. London: Zed Books, 1990. xvii + 314 pp. ISBN 0-86232-961-2.

*National Human Rights Institutions in Africa.* Richard Carver and Paul Hunt. Banjul: African Centre for Democracy/Human Rights Studies and Human Rights Studies, 45 pp. Occasional Paper.

*The Nations of Africa.* New York: Facts on File, 1997. ISBN 0-8160-3488-5. Volume 6 in the Peoples of Africa series.

*Native Artists of Africa.* Reavis Moore. Santa Fe: John Muir Publications, 1993. 48 pp. ISBN 1-56261-147-X.

*Natural Connections: Faith Stories from African and African-American Christians.* Ardell Stauffer, Pearl Sensenig, and Howard Good, eds. Akron, Penn.: Mennonite Central Committee, n.d. 58 pp.

*Nature Tourism: Managing for the Environment.* Tensie Whelan, ed. Washington, D.C.: Island Press, 1991. xii + 223 pp. ISBN 1-55963-036-1.

*Negotiating Structural Adjustment in Africa.* Willem Van Der Geest, ed. London: James Currey, 1994. ix + 230 pp. ISBN 0-85255-142-8.

*Nelson Mandela: The Fight Against Apartheid.* Steven Otfinoski. Brookfield: Millbrook Press, 1992. 128 pp. ISBN 1-56294-067-8.

*Networks of Dissolution: Somalia Undone.* Anna Simons. Boulder: Westview Press, 1995. x + 246 pp. ISBN 0-8133-2581-1.

*"..Never Drink from the Same Cup": Proceedings of the Conference on Indigenous Peoples in Africa, Tune, Denmark 1993.* Hanne Veber et al., eds. Copenhagen: International Work Group for Indigenous Affairs, 1993. 326 pp. ISSN 0105-6387.

*Never Follow the Wolf: The Autobiography of a Namibian Freedom Fighter.* Helao Shityuwete. London: Kliptown Books, 1990. x + 254 pp. ISBN 1-871863-06-6.

*Never Kneel Down: Drought, Development and Liberation in Eritrea.* James Firebrace and Stuart Holland. Trenton: Red Sea Press, 1985. 192 pp. ISBN 0-932415-01-6.

*New African Yearbook, 1995-1996.* Alan Rake, ed. London: IC Publications, 1996. 10th ed. 496 pp. ISBN 0-905268-61-X. ISSN 0140-1378.

*The New Atlas of African History.* G. S. P. Freeman-Grenville. New York: Simon and Schuster, Academic Reference Division, 1991. 144 pp. ISBN 0-13-612151-9. Cloth.

*A New Bibliography of the Lusophone Literatures of Africa.* Gerald Moser and Manuel Ferreira. London: Hans Zell Publishers, 1993. 2nd ed. 432 pp. ISBN 1-873836-85-6. Bibliographical Research in African Literatures, no. 2.

*New Currents, Ancient Rivers: Contemporary African Artists in a Generation of Change.* Jean Kennedy. Washington, D.C.: Smithsonian Institution Press, 1992. 204 pp. ISBN 1-56098-037-0.

*New Discourses on African Cinema.* Frank Ukadike, ed. Bloomington: Indiana University Press, 1995. 176 pp. ISSN 0751-7033. *Iris: A Journal of Theory and Image and Sound,* 18 (spring 1995).

*New Hope or False Promise? Biotechnology and Third World Agriculture.* Henk Hobbelink. London: International Coalition for Development Action, 72 pp.

*The New Insurgencies: Anticommunist Guerrillas in the Third World.* Michael Radu. New Brunswick, N.J.: Transaction Publishers, 1990. 306 pp. ISBN 0-88738-307-6.

*The New International Labour Studies: An Introduction.* Ronaldo Munck. London: Zed Books, 1988. xi + 233 pp. ISBN 0-86232-587-0.

*New Internationalist.* [periodical].

*New Poets of West Africa.* Tijan Sallah, ed. Lagos: Malthouse Press, 1995. 236 pp. ISBN 978-2601-98-5.

*A New Reader's Guide to African Literature.* Hans M. Zell, Carol Bundy, and Virginia Coulon, eds. London: Heinemann Educational Publishers, 1983. 2nd ed. xvi + 553 pp. ISBN 0-8419-0640-8. Studies in African Literature.

*The New Resource Wars: Native and Environmental Struggles Against Multinational Corporations.* Al Gedicks. Boston: South End Press, 1993. xv + 270 pp. ISBN 0-89608-462-0.

*New Strategies for a Restless World.* Harlan Cleveland, ed. Minneapolis: American Refugee Committee, 1993. 60 pp.

*New Tigers and Old Elephants: The Development Game in the 1990s and Beyond.* Scott B. MacDonald, Jane E. Hughes, and David Leith Crum. New Brunswick, N.J.: Transaction Publishers, 1995. xi + 263 pp. ISBN 1-56000-204-2. Cloth.

*The New UN Peacekeeping.* Steven R. Ratner. New York: St. Martin's Press, 1995. xiv + 322 pp. ISBN 0-312-12415-5. Council on Foreign Relations Book. Cloth.

*New Writing from Southern Africa: Authors Who Have Become Prominent Since 1980.* Emmanuel Ngara, ed. London: James Currey, 1996. xiii + 172 pp. ISBN 0-435-08971-4.

*News Out of Africa: Biafra to Band Aid.* Paul Harrison and Robin Palmer. London: Hilary Shipman, 1986. x + 147 pp. ISBN 0-948096-03-9.

*The Next Fifty Years: The United Nations and the United States.* Tom Barry. Albuquerque: Resource Center Press, 1996. xvii + 202 pp. ISBN 0-911213-61-9.

*Ngambika: Studies of Women in African Literature.* Carole Boyce Davies and Anne Adams Graves, eds. Trenton: Africa World Press, 1986. xi + 298 pp. ISBN 0-86543-018-7.

*Nigeria in International Peace-keeping, 1960-1992.* M. A. Vogt and A. E. Ekoko, eds. Lagos: Malthouse Press, 1993. xii + 352 pp. ISBN 978-2601-50-0.

*Nigeria: The Politics of Adjustment and Democracy.* Julius O. Ihonvbere. New Brunswick, N.J.: Transaction Publishers, 1994. x + 231 pp. ISBN 1-56000-093-7.

*Nigerian Artists: A Who's Who and Bibliography.* Bernice M. Kelly, comp. London: Hans Zell Publishers, 1993. vii + 600 pp. ISBN 0-905450-82-5.

*Nigerian Female Writers: A Critical Perspective.* Henrietta C. Otokunefor and Obiageli C. Nwodo, eds. Lagos: Malthouse Press, 1989. xii + 160 pp.

*Nigerian Women and the Challenges of Our Time.* Dora Obi Chizea and Juliet Njoku, eds. Lagos: Malthouse Press, 1991. xi + 100 pp. ISBN 978-2601-69-1.

*Nigerian Women in Development: A Research Bibliography.* Catherine M. Coles and Barbara Entwisle. Los Angeles: Crossroads Press/African Studies Association, November 1985. 170 pp. ISBN 0-918456-58-4.

*A Night in Tunisia: Imaginings of Africa in Jazz.* Norman C. Weinstein. New York: Limelight Editions, 1993. xii + 244 pp. ISBN 0-87910-167-9.

*The Nightmare Continues: Abuses Against Somali Refugees in Kenya.* Rakiya Omaar and Alex de Waal. London: African Rights, September 1993. 54 pp.

*Nightsong: Performance, Power, and Practice in South Africa.* Veit Erlmann. Chicago: University of Chicago Press, 1996. xxv + 446 pp. ISBN 0-226-21721-3.

*No Condition Is Permanent: The Social Dynamics of Agrarian Change in Sub-Saharan Africa.* Sara Berry. Madison: University of Wisconsin Press, 1993. xiv + 258 pp. ISBN 0-299-13934-4.

*No Farewell to Arms? Military Disengagement from Politics in Africa and Latin America.* Claude E. Welch Jr. Boulder: Westview Press, 1987.

*No Life Without Roots: Culture and Development.* Thierry G. Verhelst. Trans. Bob Cumming. London: Zed Books, 1990. 189 pp. ISBN 0-86232-849-7.

*No Place Like Home: Mozambican Refugees Begin Africa's Largest Repatriation.* Jeff Drumtra. Washington, D.C.: U.S. Committee for Refugees, December 1993. 43 pp. ISSN 088-9282.

*No Time to Waste: Poverty and the Global Environment.* Joan Davidson, Dorothy Myers, and Manab Chakraborty. Oxford: Oxfam (UK and Ireland), 1992. v + 217 pp. ISBN 0-85598-183-0.

*None But Ourselves: Masses vs. Media in the Making of Zimbabwe.* Julie Frederikse. Harare: Oral Traditions Association of Zimbabwe, 1990. xii + 371 pp. ISBN 0-7974-0961-0.

*North Africa: Development and Reform in a Changing Global Economy.* Dirk Vandewwalle, ed. New York: St. Martin's Press, 1996. xviii + 286 pp. ISBN 0-312-15853-X.

*North African Textiles.* Christopher Spring and Julie Hudson. Washington, D.C.: Smithsonian Institution Press, 1995. 144 pp. ISBN 1-56098-666-2.

*"Not Either an Experimental Doll": The Separate Worlds of Three South African Women.* Shula Marks, ed. Bloomington: Indiana University Press, 1987. xv + 217 pp. ISBN 0-253-28640-9.

*Not Out of Africa: How Afrocentrism Became an Excuse to Teach Myth as History.* Mary Lefkowitz. New York: New Republic Book/Basic Books, 1996. xvii + 222 pp. ISBN 0-465-09837-1. Cloth.

*Not So Innocent: When Women Become Killers.* Rakiya Omaar and Alex de Waal. London: African Rights, 1995. 284 pp.

*Notes on Achebe's "Things Fall Apart."* Joseph L. Mbele. Northfield, Minn.: St. Olaf College, 1996. 28 pp. Available from author: 1170 Cannon Valley Dr., No. 46, Northfield, MN 55057 USA.

*The Novels of Nadine Gordimer: History from the Inside.* Stephen Clingman. Amherst: University of Massachusetts Press, 1992. xxxvii +276 pp. ISBN 0-87023-802-7.

*The Nubians of West Aswan: Village Women in the Midst of Change.* Anne M. Jennings. Boulder: Lynne Rienner Publishers, November 1995. xii + 179 pp. ISBN 1-55587-592-0.

*Oakland Tribune.* [periodical].

*Objects: Signs of Africa.* Luc de Heusch, ed. Seattle: University of Washington Press, 1996. 213 pp. ISBN 0-295-97571-7.

*Okavango: Africa's Last Eden.* Frans Lanting. San Francisco: Chronicle Books, 1993. 169 pp. ISBN 0-8118-0527-1.

*On Shifting Sands: New Art and Literature from South Africa.* Kirsten Holst Petersen and Anna Rutherford, eds. Portsmouth, N.H.: Heinemann, 1992. vii + 180 pp. ISBN 0-435-08070-9.

*On the Run.* Kapache Victor. Windhoek: New Namibia Books, 1994. 69 pp. ISBN 99916-31-22-4.

*One Africa, One Destiny: Towards Democracy, Good Governance and Development.* Bingu Wa Mutharika. Harare: SAPES Books, 1995. xii + 216 pp. ISBN 1-77905-031-3.

*One Day We Had to Run!.* Sybella Wilkes. London: Evans Brothers, 1994. 61 pp. ISBN 0-237-51489-3.

*100 Great Africans.* Alan Rake. Lanham, Md.: Scarecrow Press, 1994. ix + 431 pp. ISBN 0-8108-2929-0.

*Onions Are My Husband: Survival and Accumulation by West African Market Women.* Gracia Clark. Chicago: University of Chicago Press, 1994. xxiv + 464 pp. ISBN 0-226-10780-9.

*The Open Door Omnibus 1993: Selections from New Writers.* Madeleine Loyson et al. Cape Town: Buchu Books, 1993. 213 pp. ISBN 1-874863-06-7.

*The Opening of the Apartheid Mind: Options for the New South Africa.* Heribert Adam and Kogila Moodley. Berkeley: University of California Press, 1993. xvi + 277 pp. ISBN 0-520-08199-4.

*Operation Timber: Pages From the Savimbi Dossier.* William Minter, ed. Trenton: Africa World Press, 1988. x + 117 pp. ISBN 0-86543-104-3.

*Oral and Written Poetry in African Literature Today.* Eldred Durosimi Jones, Eustace Palmer, and Marjorie Jones, eds. Trenton: Africa World Press, 1989. vi + 162 pp. ISBN 0-86543-126-4.

*Oral Epics from Africa: Vibrant Voices from a Vast Continent.* John William Johnson, Thomas A. Hale, and Stephen Belcher, eds. Bloomington: Indiana University Press, 1997. 320 pp. African Epics series.

*Orature in African Literature Today.* Eldred Durosimi Jones, Eustace Palmer, and Marjorie Jones, eds. Trenton: Africa World Press, 1992. vi + 138 pp. ISBN 0-86543-351-8.

*The Organization of African Unity after Thirty Years.* Yassin El-Ayouty, ed. Westport, Conn.: Praeger Publishers, 1994. xiii + 216 pp. ISBN 0-275-94439-5.

*Organizing African Unity.* Jon Woronoff. Lanham, Md.: Scarecrow Press, 1970. x + 703 pp. ISBN 0-8108-0321-6.

*The Origins and Development of African Theology.* Gwinyai H. Muzorewa. Maryknoll, N.Y.: Orbis Books, 1985. xiv + 146 pp. ISBN 0-88344-351-1.

*The Origins of Religions.* Julien Ries. Grand Rapids: William B. Eerdmans Publishing, 1994. 158 pp. ISBN 0-8028-3767-0.

*The Orphan Generation.* [audiovisual].

*Orphan of the Cold War: The Inside Story of the Collapse of the Angolan Peace Process, 1992-3.* Margaret Joan Anstee. New York: St. Martin's Press, 1996. xxv + 566 pp. ISBN 0-312-16015-0. Cloth.

*Orphans of the Storm: Peacebuilding for Children of War.* John R. Walker. Toronto: Between the Lines, 1993. 193 pp. ISBN 0-921284-79-9.

*The Other Side of the Story: The Real Impact of World Bank and IMF Structural Adjustment Programs.* Ross Hammond and Lisa A. McGowan. Washington, D.C.: Development Group for Alternative Policies, 1993. 44 pp.

*Our Precious Metal: African Labour in South Africa's Gold Industry, 1970-1990.* Wilmot G. James. Bloomington: Indiana University Press, 1992. ix + 188 pp. ISBN 0-253-33092-0.

*Ours by Right: Women's Rights as Human Rights.* Joanna Kerr, ed. London: Zed Books, 1993. xii + 180 pp. ISBN 1-85649-228-1.

*Ousmane Sembène: Dialogues with Critics and Writers.* Samba Gadjigo et al., eds. Amherst: University of Massachusetts Press, 1993. xii + 123 pp. ISBN 0-87023-889-2.

*The Outcry for Peace in the Sudan.* John Prendergast. Washington, D.C.: Centre for the Strategic Initiatives of Women, October 1996. 53 pp.

*The Outlook for Development in the 1990s.* K. K. S. Dadzie. Accra: Ghana Universities Press, 1994. ix + 59 pp. ISBN 9964-3-0186-3.

*The Oxford Encyclopedia of the Modern Islamic World.* John L. Esposito. Oxford and New York: Oxford University Press, 1995. 4 vols. ISBN 0-19-506613-8. Cloth.

*The Oxford Illustrated History of Theatre.* John Russell Brown, ed. Oxford and New York: Oxford University Press, 1995. x + 582 pp. ISBN 0-19-212997-X. Cloth.

*A Painful Season and a Stubborn Hope: The Odyssey of an Eritrean Mother.* Abeba Tesfagiorgis. Lawrenceville, N.J.: Red Sea Press, 1992. 210 pp. ISBN 0-932415-84-9.

*Pan-African Chronology: A Comprehensive Reference to the Black Quest for Freedom in Africa, the Americas, Europe and Asia, 1400-1865.* Everett Jenkins Jr. Jefferson: McFarland, 1996. viii + 440 pp. ISBN 0-7864-0139-7.

*Parables and Fables: Exegesis, Textuality, and Politics in Central Africa.* V.Y. Mudimbe. Madison: University of Wisconsin Press, 1991. xxii + 238 pp. ISBN 0-299-13064-9.

*Participatory Self-Evaluation: A Tool for Empowering Women at Community Level.* Hope Bagyendera Chigudu. Harare: Zimbabwe Women's Resource Centre and Network, November 1992. 8 pp. ZWRCN Discussion Paper, no. 6.

*Past Exposure: Revealing Health and Environmental Risks of Rössing Uranium.* Greg Dropkin and David Clark. London: Namibia Support Committee, 1992. 134 pp. ISBN 0-947905-65-0.

*Paths in the Rainforests: Toward a History of Political Tradition in Equatorial Africa.* Jan Vansina. Madison: University of Wisconsin Press, 1990. xx + 428 pp. ISBN 0-299-12574-2.

*Paths of African Theology.* Rosino Gibellini. Maryknoll, N.Y.: Orbis Books, 1994. vi + 202 pp. ISBN 0-88344-974-9.

*Peace and Security in Africa: A State of the Art Report.* Emmanuel Hansen. London: Zed Books, 1988. Out of print.

*Peace without Profit: How the IMF Blocks Rebuilding in Mozambique.* Joseph Hanlon. Irish Mozambique Solidarity and International African Institute. Oxford: James Currey, 1996. xvi + 175 pp. ISBN 0-85255-800-7. African Issues series.

*Peace, Development, and People of the Horn of Africa.* John Prendergast. Washington, D.C.: Center of Concern, 1992. 56 pp. ISBN 0-9628058-2-3.

*Peace, Politics and Violence in the New South Africa.* Norman Etherington, ed. London: Hans Zell Publishers, 1992. xviii + 352 pp. ISBN 1-873836-75-9.

*Peacebuilding in Somalia.* Ameen Jan. New York: International Peace Academy, July 1996. 26 pp. IPA Policy Briefing Series.

*Peaceful Settlement of Disputes Between States: A Selective Bibliography.* New York: United Nations, 1991. ix + 209 pp. ISBN 92-1-100464-0.

*Peacemaking in Civil War: International Mediation in Zimbabwe, 1974-1980.* Stephen John Stedman. Boulder: Lynne Rienner Publishers, 1991. xiii + 254 pp. ISBN 1-55587-200-X.

*Peasants and Nationalism in Eritrea: A Critique of Ethiopian Studies.* Jordan Gebre-Medhin. Trenton: Red Sea Press, 1989. xv + 220 pp. ISBN 0-932415-38-5.

*Pedagogy of Domination: Towards a Democratic Education in South Africa.* Mokubung Nkomo. Lawrenceville, N.J.: Africa World Press, 1990.

*The Penguin Book of Modern African Poetry.* Ulli Beier and Gerald Moore. Baltimore and Harmondsworth: Penguin Books, 1963.

*The Penguin Encyclopedia of Popular Music.* Donald Clarke, ed. London and New York: Penguin Books, 1991. xii + 1,392 pp. ISBN 0-1405-1147-4. Penguin Reference Books.

*People First: A Guide to Self-Reliant, Participatory Rural Development.* Stan Burkey. London: Zed Books, 1993. xix + 244 pp. ISBN 1-85649-082-3.

*People of the Tropical Rain Forest.* Julie Sloan Denslow and Christine Padoch. Berkeley: University of California Press, 1988. 231 pp. ISBN 0-520-06351-1.

*A People's Voice: Black South African Writing in the Twentieth Century.* Piniel Viriri Shava. London: Zed Books, 1989. 179 pp. ISBN 0-86232-687-7.

*Peoples of Africa: Cultures of Africa South of the Sahara.* James L. Gibbs Jr. Prospect Heights: Waveland Press, 1965. xiv + 594 pp. ISBN 0-88133-318-2.

*Peoples of Central Africa.* New York: Facts on File, 1997. ISBN 0-8160-3486-9. Volume 4 in the Peoples of Africa series.

*Peoples of East Africa.* New York: Facts on File, 1997. ISBN 0-8160-3484-2. Volume 2 in the Peoples of Africa series.

*Peoples of North Africa.* New York: Facts on File, 1997. ISBN 0-8160-3483-4. Volume 1 in the Peoples of Africa series.

*Peoples of Southern Africa.* New York: Facts on File, 1997. ISBN 0-8160-3487-7. Volume 5 in the Peoples of Africa series.

*The Peoples of the Middle Niger.* R. J. McIntosh and S. J. McIntosh. Cambridge, Mass.: Blackwell Publishers, forthcoming.

*Peoples of the World: Africans South of the Sahara.* Joyce Moss and George Wilson. Detroit: Gale Research, 1991. xviii + 443 pp. ISBN 0-8103-7942-2.

*Peoples of West Africa.* New York: Facts on File, 1997. ISBN 0-8160-3485-0. Volume 3 in the Peoples of Africa series.

*The Peopling of Africa: A Geographic Interpretation.* James L. Newman. New Haven: Yale University Press, 1995. xiv + 235 pp. ISBN 0-300-06003-3. Cloth.

*Perceptions and Colonialism: Teaching Development Issues.* Manchester: Development Education Project, Manchester Polytechnic, 1986.

*Perspectives on African Music.* Wolfgang Bender, ed. Bayreuth (Germany): Bayreuth University, 1989. 139 pp.

*Picturing People: Challenging Stereotypes.* Manchester: Development Education Project, Manchester Polytechnic, 1988.

*Piety and Power: Muslims and Christians in West Africa.* Lamin Sanneh. Maryknoll, N.Y.: Orbis Books, 1996. xv + 207 pp. ISBN 1-57075-090-4. Faith Meets Faith Series.

*Plundering Africa's Past.* Peter R. Schmidt and Roderick J. McIntosh, eds. Bloomington: Indiana University Press, 1996. xiii + 280 pp. ISBN 0-253-21054-2.

*The Pocket Green Book.* Andrew Rees. London: Zed Books, 1991. vi + 154 pp. ISBN 0-86232-999-X.

*A Poetics of Resistance: Women Writing in El Salvador, South Africa, and the United States.* Mary K. DeShazer. Ann Arbor: University of Michigan Press, 1994. xii + 350 pp. ISBN 0-472-06563-7.

*The Poetry of Wole Soyinka.* Tanure Ojaide. Lagos: Malthouse Press, 1994. 140 pp. ISBN 978-023-006-8.

*Policing South Africa: The SAP and the Transition from Apartheid.* Gavin Cawthra. London: Zed Books, 1993. xiv + 226 pp. ISBN 1-85649-066-1.

*Policing the Conflict in South Africa.* M. L. Mathews, Philip B. Heymann, and A.S. Mathews, eds. Gainesville: University Press of Florida, 1993. ix + 225 pp. ISBN 0-8130-1224-4.

*Policy Choice and Development Performance in Botswana.* Charles Harvey and Stephen R. Lewis. New York: St. Martin's Press, 1990. xxii + 341 pp. ISBN 0-312-04046-6.

*Policy Reform for Sustainable Development in Africa: The Institutional Imperative.* Louis A. Picard and Michele Garrity, eds. Boulder: Lynne Rienner Publishers, 1994. xiii + 183 pp. ISBN 1-55587-449-5.

*Political Domination in Africa: Reflections on the Limits of Power.* Patrick Chabal, ed. Cambridge: Cambridge University

Press, 1986. ix + 211 pp. ISBN 0-521-31148-9. ISSN 0065-406X. African Studies series, no. 53.

*The Political Economy of Nigeria Under Military Rule: 1984-1993.* Said Adejumobi and Abubakar Momoh, eds. Harare: SAPES Books, 1995. 359 pp. ISBN 1-77905-036-4.

*The Political Economy of South Africa: From Minerals-Energy Complex to Industrialisation.* Ben Fine and Zavareh Rustomjee. Boulder: Westview Press, 1996. ix + 278 pp. ISBN 0-8133-2790-3.

*The Political Handbook of the World, 1994-1995.* Johan Muller. Binghamton: CSA Publications, Binghamton University, 1994. ISBN 0-933199-10-4. ISSN 0193-175X. Cloth.

*A Political History of the Civil War in Angola 1974-1990.* W. Martin James III. New Brunswick, N.J.: Transaction Publishers, 1992. ix + 314 pp. ISBN 0-88738-418-8.

*Political Islam: Religion and Politics in the Arab World.* Nazih Ayubi. New York: Routledge, 1991. xi + 291 pp. ISBN 0-415-05442-7.

*The Political Language of Islam.* Bernard Lewis. Chicago: University of Chicago Press, 1988. viii + 168 pp. ISBN 0-226-47693-6.

*Political Leaders in Black Africa: A Biographical Dictionary of the Major Politicians since Independence.* John A. Wiseman. Aldershot: Edward Elgar, 1991. xxiii + 248 pp. ISBN 1-85278-047-9.

*Political Parties and Democracy in Tanzania.* Max Mmuya and Amon Chaligha. Dar Es Salaam: Dar Es Salaam University Press, 1994. iv + 223 pp. ISBN 9976-60-270-7.

*Politics in South Africa: From Vorster to De Klerk.* Keith Maguire. Edinburgh: W & R Chambers, 1991. 151 pp. ISBN 0-550-20752-X.

*Politics of Democratization: Changing Authoritarian Regimes in Sub-Saharan Africa.* Emeka Nwokedi. Munster: Lit Verlag, 1995. 249 pp. ISBN 3-8258-2419-5.

*Politics of Hope and Terror: South Africa in Transition.* Philadelphia: American Friends Service Committee, November 1992. 27 pp.

*The Politics of Humanitarian Intervention.* John Harriss, ed. London: Pinter/Cassell, 1995. xiii + 190 pp. ISBN 1-85567-334-7.

*The Politics of Structural Adjustment in Nigeria.* Adebayo O. Olujoshi, ed. London: James Currey, 1993. xiv + 144 pp. ISBN 0-85255-130-4.

*Poppie Nongena: One Woman's Struggle against Apartheid.* Elsa Joubert. New York: Henry Holt, 1980. 359 pp. ISBN 0-8050-0230-8.

*Popular Music of the Non-Western World: An Introductory Survey.* Peter Lamarche Manuel. New York: Oxford University Press, 1988. x + 287 pp.

*Popular Participation and Development: A Bibliography on Africa and Latin America.* Hugh Dow and Jonathan Barker. Toronto: Centre for Urban and Community Studies, University of Toronto, 1992. Bibliographic Series, no. 16.

*Popular Struggles for Democracy in Africa.* Peter Anyang' Nyong'o, ed. London: Zed Books, 1987. xiii + 288 pp. ISBN 0-86232-737-7.

*Population and Development.* Washington, D.C.: Panos Institute, 1994. 16 pp. ISSN 1064-9034. From Information to Education series, no. 4.

*Population and Development in Poor Countries: Selected Essays.* Julian L. Simon. Princeton: Princeton University Press, 1992. xx + 463 pp. ISBN 0-691-04256-X.

*Population and Development Review.* [periodical].

*Population and Development: Directory of Non-Governmental Organisations in OECD Countries.* Paris: Organisation for Economic Co-operation and Development, Development Centre, 1994. 360 pp. ISBN 92-64-04171-0.

*Population and Development: Old Debates, New Conclusions.* Robert Cassen et al. New Brunswick, N.J.: Transaction Publishers, 1994. x + 282 pp. ISBN 1-56000-740-0.

*Population and Food Security.* Washington, D.C.: World Hunger Education Service, 32 pp. ISSN 0740-1116. *Hunger Notes*, 19, no. 3 (Winter 1993-1994).

*Population and Reproductive Rights: Feminist Perspectives from the South.* Sonia Correa and Rebecca Reichmann. London: Zed Books, 1994. xiii + 136 pp. ISBN 1-85649-284-2.

*Population Bulletin.* [periodical].

*Population Bulletin of the United Nations.* [periodical].

*Population Control and National Security: A Review of U.S. National Security Policy on Population.* Washington, D.C.: Information Project For Africa, 1991. 55 pp.

*Population Growth and Agricultural Change in Africa.* B. L. Turner II, Goran Hyden, and Robert Kates, eds. Gainesville: University Press of Florida, 1993. xvii + 461 pp. ISBN 0-8130-1219-8.

*Population Movements and the Third World.* Mike Parnwell. New York: Routledge, 1993. xii + 158 pp. ISBN 0-415-06953-X.

*Population Policies Reconsidered: Health, Empowerment, and Rights.* Gita Sen, Adrienne Germain, and Lincoln C. Chen, eds. Cambridge: Harvard University Press, 1994. xiv + 280 pp. ISBN 0-674-69003-6.

*Population Studies: A Journal of Demography.* [periodical].

*Population: Broadening the Debate.* Asoka Bandarage et al. Washington, D.C.: World Hunger Education Service, spring 1994. 36 pp. ISSN 0740-1116. *Hunger Notes* 19, no. 4.

*Population: The Special Case of Africa.* Washington, D.C.: World Hunger Education Service, summer 1994. 28 pp. ISSN 0740-1116. *Hunger Notes* 20, no. 1.

*Populations in Danger.* Francois Jean, ed. Medecins Sans Frontieres. London: John Libbey, 1992. vi + 154 pp. ISBN 0-86196-392-X.

*Portraits in Conservation: Eastern and Southern Africa.* Elisabeth Braun. Golden: North American Press, 1995. xxxi + 268 pp. ISBN 1-55591-914-6.

*Post Abolished: One Woman's Struggle for Employment Rights in Tanzania.* Laeticia Mukurasi. Ithaca: ILR Press, 1991. xv + 127 pp. ISBN 0-87546-703-2.

*Post-Cold War Peace and Security Prospects in Southern Africa.* Severine Rugumamu. Harare: SAPES Books, 1993. 37 pp. ISBN 1-77905-010-0.

*Postcolonial Subjects: Francophone Women Writers.* Mary Jean Green et al., eds. Minneapolis: University of Minnesota Press, 1996. xxii + 359 pp. ISBN 0-8166-2629-4.

*The Poverty of Nations: The Aid Dilemma at the Heart of Africa.* James Morton. London: British Academic Press, 1994. ix + 265 pp. ISBN 1-85043-617-7.

*Poverty, Class, and Gender in Rural Africa: A Tanzanian Case Study*. John Sender and Sheila Smith. London: Routledge, 1990. xiv + 194 pp. ISBN 0-415-05246-7.

*Poverty, Policy, and Food Security in Southern Africa*. Coralie Bryant, ed. Boulder: Lynne Rienner Publishers, 1988. xii + 291 pp. ISBN 1-55587-092-9.

*Power and Need in Africa*. Ben Wisner. Lawrenceville, N.J.: Africa World Press, 1989. 351 pp. ISBN 0-86543-102-7.

*Power and the Praise Poem: Southern African Voices in History*. Leroy Vail and Landeg White. Charlottesville: University Press of Virginia, 1991. xviii + 345 pp. ISBN 0-8139-1340-3.

*Power! Black Workers, Their Unions and the Struggle for Freedom in South Africa*. Denis MacShane, Martin Plaut, and David Ward. Boston: South End Press, 1984. 195 pp. ISBN 0-89608-244-X.

*The Practice of Presence: Shorter Writings of Harry Sawyerr*. John Parratt, ed. Grand Rapids: William B. Eerdmans Publishing, 1994. xvi + 149 pp. ISBN 0-8028-4115-5.

*The Precarious Balance: State and Society in Africa*. Donald Rothchild and Naomi Chazan, eds. Boulder: Westview Press, 1988. x + 357 pp. ISBN 0-86531-738-0.

*Press Freedom in Africa*. Gunilla L. Faringer. New York: Praeger Publishers, 1991. xii + 144 pp. ISBN 0-275-93771-2.

*The Press in South Africa. Studies on the South African Media*. Keyan Tomaselli, Ruth Tomaselli, and Johan Muller, eds. Chicago: Lake View Press, 1987. 258 pp. ISBN 0-941702-24-3.

*Preventing Famine: Policies and Prospects for Africa*. Donald Curtis, Michael Hubbard, and Andrew Shepherd. London and New York: Routledge, 1988. xi + 250 pp. ISBN 0-415-00712-7.

*Priest and Partisan: A South African Journey*. Michael Worsnip. Melbourne and Brooklyn: Ocean Press, 1996. 168 pp. ISBN 1-875284-96-6.

*Prisoners of Ritual: An Odyssey into Female Genital Circumcision in Africa*. Hanny Lightfoot-Klein. Binghamton: Harrington Park Press, 1989. xii + 306 pp. ISBN 0-918393-68-X.

*Prisoners of Ritual: An Odyssey into Female Genital Circumcision in Africa*. Hanny Lightfoot-Klein. Binghamton: Harrington Park Press, 1989. xii + 306 pp. ISBN 0-918393-68-X.

*Private Decisions, Public Debate: Women, Reproduction and Population*. Judith Mirsky and Marty Radlett, eds. London: Panos Publications, 1994. vi + 185 pp. ISBN 1-870670-34-5.

*Privatization in Developing Countries: Its Impact on Economic Development and Democracy*. Jacques V. Dinavo. Westport, Conn.: Praeger Publishers, 1995. xvi + 157 pp. ISBN 0-275-95007-7. Cloth.

*Problems in African History*. Vol. 1: *The Precolonial Centuries*. Robert O. Collins, ed. Princeton, N.J.: Markus Wiener Publishers, 1993. 328 pp. ISBN 1-55876-059-8.

*Problems in African History*. Vol. 2: *Historical Problems of Imperial Africa*. Robert O. Collins, ed. Princeton, N.J.: Markus Wiener Publishers, 1994. 320 pp. ISBN 1-55876-060-1.

*Problems in African History*. Vol. 3: *Problems in the History of Modern Africa*. Robert O. Collins et al., eds. Princeton, N.J.: Markus Wiener Publishers, 1996. 320 pp. ISBN 1-55876-124-1.

*Proceedings of the Conference on the African Commission on Human and Peoples' Rights*. New York: Fund for Peace, June 1991. iii + 55 pp.

*Proceedings of the Global Assembly of Women and the Environment "Partners in Life."* Vol. I. Joan Martin-Brown and Waafas Ofosu-Amaah, eds. Washington, D.C.: Global Assembly Project WorldWIDE Network, 1992. 299 pp.

*Proceedings of the Global Assembly of Women and the Environment "Partners in Life."* Vol. II. Waafas Ofosu-Amaah and Wendy Philleo, eds. Washington, D.C.: Global Assembly Project WorldWIDE Network, 1992. 296 pp.

*Promoting Development: Effective Global Institutions for the Twenty-first Century*. Jo Marie Griesgraber and Bernhard G. Gunter, eds. London: Pluto Press, 1995. xv + 147 pp. ISBN 0-7453-1045-1. Rethinking Bretton Woods, no. 1.

*Prophetic Christianity and the Liberation Movement in South Africa*. Peter Walshe. Pietermaritzburg (South Africa): Cluster Publications, 1995. 180 pp. ISBN 0-9583807-9-1.

*Prospects for Recovery and Sustainable Development in Africa*. Aguibou Y. Yansané, ed. Westport, Conn.: Greenwood Press, 1996. xiii + 363 pp. ISBN 0-313-28995-6. ISSN 0069-9624. Contributions in Afro-American and African Studies, no. 169. Cloth.

*Protecting the Dispossessed: A Challenge for the International Community*. Francis M. Deng. Washington, D.C.: Brookings Institution, 1993. xii + 175 pp. ISBN 0-8157-1826-8.

*Publishing and Book Development in Sub-Saharan Africa: An Annotated Bibliography*. Hans M. Zell and Cecile Lomer. London: Hans Zell Publishers, 1996. x + 409 pp. ISBN 1-873836-46-5.

*Quantifying Genocide in the Southern Sudan 1983-1993*. Millard Burr. Washington, D.C.: U.S. Committee for Refugees, October 1993. 66 pp.

*The Quest for Regional Cooperation in Southern Africa: Problems and Issues*. Guy C. Z. Mhone. Harare: SAPES Books, 1993. 33 pp. ISBN 1-77905-011-9. Ocasional Papers series, no. 4.

*The Question of Language in African Literature Today*. Eldred Durosimi Jones, Eustace Palmer, and Marjorie Jones, eds. Trenton: Africa World Press, 1991. ix + 182 pp. ISBN 0-86543-215-5.

*The Quiet Chameleon: Modern Poetry from Central Africa*. Adrian Roscoe and Hangson Msiska. London and New York: Hans Zell Publishers, 1991. 240 pp. ISBN 0-905450-52-3. New Perspectives on Africa Literature, no. 2.

*Radical Islam: Medieval Theology and Modern Politics*. Emmanuel Sivan. New Haven: Yale University Press, 1990. xi + 238 pp. ISBN 0-300-04915-3.

*The Rainbow People of God: The Making of a Peaceful Revolution*. Desmond Tutu. New York: Doubleday, 1994. xxii + 281 pp. Edited by John Allen.

*The Rainforests of West Africa: Ecology - Threats - Conservation*. Claude Martin. Trans. Linda Tsardakas. Boston: Birkhauser Verlag, 1991. 235 pp. ISBN 0-8176-2380-9.

*Raw Materials Report*. [periodical].

*Reaching Children in War: Sudan, Uganda, and Mozambique*. Cole P. Dodge and Magne Raundalen. Bergen: Sigma Forlag, 1991. xiii + 146 pp. ISBN 82-90373-61-9.

*Reading Chinua Achebe: Language and Ideology in Fiction*. Simon Gikandi. London: James Currey, 1991. 192 pp. ISBN 0-85255-527-X.

*The Realm of the Word: Language, Gender, and Christianity in a Southern African Kingdom*. Paul Stuart Landau.

Portsmouth, N.H.: Heinemann Publishers, 1995. xxix + 249 pp. ISBN 0-435-08965-X.

*Rebuilding Societies after Civil War: Critical Roles for International Assistance.* Krishna Kumar, ed. Boulder: Lynne Rienner Publishers, 1997. xii + 328 pp. ISBN 1-55587-652-8.

*Recolonization and Resistance in Southern Africa in the 1990s.* John S. Saul. Lawrenceville, N.J.: Africa World Press, 1993. xiv + 195 pp. ISBN 0-86543-390-9.

*Red Gold of Africa: Copper in Precolonial History and Culture.* Eugenia W. Herbert. Madison: University of Wisconsin Press, 1984. xxiii + 413 pp. ISBN 0-299-09600-9.

*Referata Verano 1994: Bibliografía Del Medio Ambiente/Environmental Bibliography.* Madrid: SPA Publications, 1994. 255 pp. ISBN 84-605-0778-5. ISSN 1133-8989.

*Refugee Aid and Development: Theory and Practice.* Robert F. Gorman, ed. Westport, Conn.: Greenwood Press, 1993. xv + 229 pp. ISBN 0-313-28580-2. ISSN 8755-5360.

*Refugee and Labour Movements in Sub-Saharan Africa: A Review.* Jonathan Baker. Uppsala: Nordiska Afrikainstitutet, 1995. 28 pp. ISBN 91-7106-362-5. ISSN 1400-3120. Studies on Emergencies and Disaster Relief, no. 2.

*The Refugee Campaign.* London: CAFOD, 1993. ISBN 1-871549-41-8.

*Refugee Survey Quarterly.* [periodical].

*Refugee Women.* Susan Forbes Martin. London: Zed Books, 1992. ISBN 1-85649-001-7.

*Refugees.* [periodical].

*Refugees: Rationing the Right to Life. The Crisis in Emergency Relief.* David Keen. London: Zed Books, 1992. x + 86 pp. ISBN 1-85649-092-0.

*Refugees: We Left Because We Had To. An Educational Book for 14-18 Year Olds.* Jill Rutter. London: Refugee Council, 1996. 2nd ed. 248 pp. ISBN 0-946787-04-2.

*Refworld CD-ROM.* [CD-ROM].

*Reinventing Christianity: African Theology Today.* John Parratt. Grand Rapids: William B. Eerdmans Publishing, 1995. x + 217 pp. ISBN 0-8028-4113-9.

*Relevance of Asian Development Experiences to African Problems.* Seiji Naya and Robert McCleery. San Francisco: Institute for Contemporary Studies, 1994. 75 pp. ISBN 1-55815-313-6. Occasional Papers, no. 39.

*Religion and Experience: Experience and Expression.* Thomas D. Blakely, Walter E. A. van Beek, and Dennis L. Thomson, eds. London: James Currey, 1994. xvi + 512 pp. ISBN 0-85255-207-6.

*Religion and Politics in East Africa.* Holger Bernt Hansen and Michael Twaddle, eds. London: James Currey, 1995. ix + 278 pp. ISBN 0-85255-384-6.

*Religion and Politics in Southern Africa.* Carl Fredrik Hallencreutz and Mai Palmberg, eds. Uppsala: Scandinavian Institute of African Studies, 1991. 219 pp. ISBN 91-7106-312-9. ISSN 0281-0018. Seminar Proceedings, no. 24.

*Religion in Africa.* Geoffrey Parrinder. Baltimore: Penguin African Library, 1969.

*Religion in Africa: Experience and Expression.* Thomas D. Blakely, Walter E. A. van Beek, and Dennis L. Thomson, eds. London: James Currey, 1994. xvi + 512 pp. ISBN 0-85255-207-6.

*Religion, Development, and African Identity.* Kirsten Holst Petersen, ed. Uppsala: Scandinavian Institute of African Studies, 1987. 163 pp. ISBN 91-7106-263-7. ISSN 0281-0018. Seminar Proceedings, no. 17.

*Religions in Africa: A Teaching Manual.* C. C. Stewart, Donalf Crummey, and Louise Crane. Urbana: University of Illinois at Urbana-Champaign, 1984. vi + 77 pp.

*Reluctant Aid or Aiding the Reluctant? U.S. Food Aid Policy and Ethiopian Famine Relief.* Steven L. Varnis. New Brunswick, N.J.: Transaction Publishers, 1990. xi + 229 pp. ISBN 0-88738-348-3.

*Remembering the Present: Painting and Popular History in Zaire.* Johannes Fabian. Berkeley: University of California Press, 1996. xv + 348 pp. ISBN 0-520-20375-5. Cloth.

*Renamo: Terrorism in Mozambique.* Alex Vines. Bloomington: Indiana University Press, 1991. xiv + 176 pp. ISBN 0-253-28880-0.

*Report from the Frontier: The State of the World's Indigenous Peoples.* Julian Burger. London: Zed Books, 1987. viii + 310 pp. ISBN 0-86232-391-6.

*Report of Delegation to Western Sahara, April 1993.* London: Woodcraft Folk, 1993. 38 pp.

*Reporters Sans Frontières 1996 Report: Freedom of the Press Throughout the World.* Reporters Sans Frontières. Luton, Bedfordshire: John Libbey Media, 1996. 381 pp. ISBN 1-86020-508-9.

*Reproductive Rights and Wrongs: The Global Politics of Population Control.* Betsy Hartmann. Boston: South End Press, 1995. xxii + 388 pp. ISBN 0-89608-491-4.

*Requiem for the Sudan: War, Drought, and Disaster Relief on the Nile.* J. Millard Burr and Robert O. Collins. Boulder: Westview Press, 1995. xiv + 385 pp. ISBN 0-8133-2121-2.

*Rereading Nadine Gordimer.* Kathrin Wagner. Bloomington: Indiana University Press, 1994. viii + 294 pp. ISBN 0-253-36303-9.

*Research in African Literatures.* [periodical].

*Research Report.* [periodical].

*Research Theories.* Harare: Zimbabwe Women's Resource Centre and Network, August 1994. 10 pp. ZWRCN Bibliographies, no. 13.

*Resistance Art in South Africa.* Sue Williamson. New York: St. Martin's Press, 1989. 160 pp. ISBN 0-312-04142-X.

*Resolving Africa's Multilateral Debt Problem: A Response to the IMF and the World Bank.* Percy S. Mistry. The Hague: Forum on Debt and Development (FONDAD), 1996. 68 pp. ISBN 90-74208-09-6.

*Resource Management in Developing Countries: Africa's Ecological and Economic Problems.* Valentine U. James. New York: Bergin and Garvey, 1991. xv + 158 pp. ISBN 0-89789-227-5.

*Restoring Hope: The Real Lessons of Somalia for the Future of Intervention.* Robert B. Oakley and John L. Hirsch. Washington, D.C.: U.S. Institute for Peace Press, 1995.

*Restoring the Land: Environment and Change in Post-Apartheid South Africa.* Mamphela Ramphele, ed. London: Panos Publications, 1991. viii + 216 pp. ISBN 1-870670-27-2.

*Return to South Africa: The Ecstasy and the Agony.* Trevor Huddleston. Grand Rapids: William B. Eerdmans Publishing, 1991. 140 pp. ISBN 0-8028-0645-7.

*Revealing Prophets: Prophecy in Eastern African History.* David M. Anderson and Douglas H. Johnson, eds. London: James Currey, 1995. x + 310 pp. ISBN 0-85255-717-5.

*Revolution and Counter-Revolution in Africa: Essays in Contemporary Politics.* Nzongola-Ntalaja. London: Zed Books, 1987. x + 130 pp. ISBN 0-86232-751-2.

*Revolutionary Aesthetics and the African Literary Process.* Udenta O. Udenta. Enugu (Nigeria): Fourth Dimension Publishers, 1993. xxiv + 155 pp. ISBN 978-156-364-8.

*The Rhythms of Black Folk: Race, Religion and Pan-Africanism.* Jon Michael Spencer. Lawrenceville, N.J.: Africa World Press, 1995. xxv + 206 pp. ISBN 0-86543-424-7.

*The Rights of the Child in Ghana: Perspectives.* Henrietta J.A.N. Mensa-Bonsu and Christine Dowuona-Hammond, eds. Accra: Woeli Publishing Services, 1994. xiv + 122 pp. ISBN 9964-978-19-7.

*Ripe for Resolution: Conflict and Intervention in Africa.* William Zartman. New York: Oxford Unversity Press, 1985.

*The Road to Hell: The Ravaging Effects of Foreign Aid and International Charity.* Michael Maren. New York: Free Press, 1997. xiv + 302 pp. ISBN 0-684-82800-6. Cloth.

*The Road to Rustenburg: The Church Looking Forward to a New South Africa.* Dr. Louw Alberts and Rev. Dr. Frank Chikane, eds. Cape Town: Struik Christian Books, 1991. 286 pp. ISBN 1-86823-063-5.

*The Road to Zero: Somalia's Self-Destruction.* Mohamed Osman Omar. London: HAAN Associates, 1992. 213 pp. ISBN 1-874209-75-8.

*The Role of Nigerian Women in Politics: Past and Present.* P.K. Uchendu. Enugu: Fourth Dimension, 1993. xvi + 124 pp. ISBN 978-156-368-0.

*The Roman Church and the African Agenda.* Rome: IDOC International, 1994. ISSN 0250-76431. IDOC Internazionale, 94/1 (January-March).

*Roots and Branches: Films and Videos on the African-American, Afro-Caribbean and African Experience.* Filmakers Library. New York: Filmakers Library, no date.

*Roots of Time: A Portrait of African Life and Culture.* Margo Jefferson and Elliott P. Skinner. Lawrenceville, N.J.: Africa World Press, 1990. 127 pp. ISBN 0-86543-169-8.

*The Royal Eagle of the Yoruba.* Funmilola Olorunnisola and Ademola Akinbami. Ibadan: Bookcraft, 1992. xi + 108 pp. ISBN 978-2030-04-X.

*Rules and Rights in the Middle East: Democracy, Law, and Society.* Ellis Goldberg, Resat Kasaba, and Joel S. Migdal, eds. Seattle: University of Washington Press, 1994. vii + 280 pp. ISBN 0-295-97287-4.

*Rwanda and Genocide in the Twentieth Century.* Alain Destexhe. New York: 1995. x + 92 pp. ISBN 0-8147-1873-6.

*The Rwanda Crisis: History of a Genocide.* Gerard Prunier. New York: Columbia University Press, 1995. xiv + 389 pp. ISBN 0-231-10408-1.

*Rwanda: Death, Despair and Defiance.* Rakiya Omaar and Alex de Waal. London: African Rights, 1994. 2nd ed. 1,234 pp.

*Rwanda: Which Way Now?* David Waller. Oxford: Oxfam (UK and Ireland), 1996. 2nd ed. 72 pp. ISBN 0-85598-354-X. Oxfam Country Profile.

*Sahrawi Refugees.* London: Refugee Council, n.d. 6 pp. Silent Voices, no. 2.

*Samora Machel: A Biography.* Iain Christie. London: Panaf/Zed Books, 1989. xix + 181 pp. ISBN 0-901787-52-3.

*Schwann Spectrum.* [periodical].

*Science That Colonizes: A Critique of Fertility Studies in Africa.* Agnes Riedmann. Philadelphia: Temple University Press, 1993. xv + 174 pp. ISBN 1-56639-042-7.

*Scientific Racism in Modern South Africa.* Saul Dubow. Cambridge: Cambridge University Press, 1995. xii + 320 pp. ISBN 0-521-47907-X.

*The SCOLMA Directory of Libraries and Special Collections on Africa in the United Kingdom and in Europe.* Tom French, comp. and ed. London and New York: Hans Zell Publishers, 1993. viii + 355 pp. ISBN 0-905450-89-2. Cloth.

*The Scramble for Africa: White Man's Conquest of the Dark Continent from 1876 to 1912.* Thomas Pakenham. New York: Avon Books, 1991. xxv + 738 pp. ISBN 0-380-71999-1.

*The Search for Africa: History, Culture, Politics.* Basil Davidson. New York: Times Books/Random House, 1994. x + 373 pp. ISBN 0-8129-2278-6.

*Searching for Land Tenure Security in Africa.* John W. Bruce and Shem E. Migot-Adholla, eds. Dubuque: Kendall/Hunt Publishing, 1993. x + 282 pp. ISBN 0-8403-9508-6.

*Seed and Surplus: An Illustrated Guide to the World Food System.* Bertrand Delpeuch. London: Catholic Institute for International Relations, 1994. ix + 124 pp. ISBN 1-85287-125-3.

*The Seed Is Mine: The Life of Kas Maine, a South African Sharecropper, 1894-1985.* Charles Van Onselen. New York: Hill and Wang, 1996. xvi + 649 pp. ISBN 0-8090-9603-X. Cloth.

*Seeds 2: Supporting Women's Work around the World.* Ann Leonard, ed. New York: Feminist Press, 1995. xi + 241 pp. ISBN 1-55861-106-1.

*Seeds for African Peasants: Peasants' Needs and Agricultural Research. The Case of Zimbabwe.* Esbern Friis-Hansen. Uppsale: Nordiska Afrikainstitutet, 1995. 228 pp. ISBN 91-7106-365-X. ISSN 0348-5676. Centre for Development Research Publications, no. 9.

*Seeing with Music: The Lives of Three Blind African Musicians.* Simon Ottenberg. Seattle: University of Washington Press, 1997. xv + 216 pp. ISBN 0-295-97525-3. Samuel and Althea Stroum Book. Cloth.

*Seeking Peace from Chaos: Humanitarian Intervention in Somalia.* Samuel M. Makinda. Boulder: Lynne Rienner Publishers, 1993. 93 pp. ISBN 1-55587-477-0.

*Selected Policy Instruments: African Alternative Framework to Structural Adjustment Programmes for Socio-Economic Recovery and Transformation.* UN Economic Commission for Africa. New York: United Nations Publications, 1991. 53 pp.

*Selected Reports in Ethnomusicology: Volume V, Studies in African Music.* J.H. Kwabena Nketia and Jacqueline Cogdell DjeDje. Los Angeles: University of California Press, 1984. xx + 387 pp. ISBN 0-88287-017-3.

*Senegal: A State of Change.* Robin Sharp. Oxford: Oxfam (UK and Ireland), 1994. 64 pp. ISBN 0-85598-283-7. Oxfam Country Profile series.

*Serengeti II: Dynamics, Management, and Conservation of an Ecosystem.* A. R. E. Sinclair and Peter Arcese, eds. Chicago and London: University of Chicago Press, 1995. xii + 665 pp. ISBN 0-226-76032-4.

*Setting the Gospel Free.* Nicholas King. Pietmaritzburg: Cluster Publications, 1995. 142 pp. ISBN 1-875053-03-4.

*Seven Stories about Modern Art in Africa.* Everlyn Nicodemus et al. New York: Flammarion, 1995. 320 pp. ISBN 0-85488-109-3.

*The Shamba is Like a Child.* Nettie Aarnink and Koos Kingma. Leiden: Women and Autonomy Centre, Leiden University, 1991. xii + 369 pp. ISBN 90-72631-31-5. ISSN 0923-0513.

*Shattered Lives: Sexual Violence during the Rwandan Genocide and its Aftermath.* Binaifer Nowrojee. Human Rights Watch, Women's Rights Project. New York: Human Rights Watch, 1996. vii + 103 pp. ISBN 1-56432-208-4.

*The Shona and their Neighbours.* David Beach. Oxford and Cambridge, Mass.: Blackwell, 1994. xv + 246 pp. ISBN 0-631-17678-0.

*Short Changed: Africa and World Trade.* Michael Barratt Brown and Pauline Tiffen. London: Pluto Press, 1992. xix + 220 pp. ISBN 0-7453-0699-3.

*A Short History of Africa.* Roland Oliver and J. D. Fage. London: Penguin Books, 1988. 6th ed. x + 303 pp. ISBN 0-14-013601-0.

*Short-Cut to Decay: The Case of the Sudan.* Sharif Harir and Terje Tvedt, eds. Uppsala: Nordiska Afrikainstitutet, 1994. 275 pp. ISBN 91-7106-346-3.

*The Significance of the Human Factor in African Economic Development.* Senyo B-S. K. Adjibolosoo. Westport, Conn.: Praeger Publishers, 1995. xvi + 257 pp. ISBN 0-275-94895-1.

*SIHA I: The Outcry for Peace in the Sudan.* John Prendergast. Washington, D.C.: Centre for the Strategic Initiatives of Women, October 1996. 54 pp.

*Singing Away the Hunger: The Autobiography of an African Woman.* K.l. Limakatso Kendall, ed. Bloomington: Indiana University Press, September 1997. 200 pp. ISBN 0-253-21162-X.

*Sisterhood Is Global: The International Women's Movement Anthology.* Robin Morgan, comp. and ed. New York: Feminist Press, 1996. xxiii + 821 pp. ISBN 1-55861-160-6.

*Slaves into Workers: Emancipation and Labor in Colonial Sudan.* Ahmad Alawad Sikainga. Austin: University of Texas Press, 1996. xviii + 276 pp. ISBN 0-292-77694-2.

*Slovo: The Unfinished Autobiography of ANC Leader Joe Slovo.* Joe Slovo. Melbourne and Brooklyn: Ocean Press, 1997. 293 pp. ISBN 1-875284-95-8.

*Slow Plague: A Geography of the AIDS Pandemic.* Peter Gould. Oxford: Blackwell, 1993. xvi + 228 pp. ISBN 1-55786-418-7.

*The Small Miracle: South Africa's Negotiated Settlement.* Steven Friedman and Doreen Atkinson, eds. Johannesburg: Ravan Press, 1994. xiii + 337 pp. ISBN 0-6975-41-1. *South African Review*, no. 7.

*Smashing Pots: Works of Clay from Africa.* Nigel Barley. Washington, D.C.: Smithsonian Institution Press, 1994. 168 pp. ISBN 1-56098-419-8.

*Sobukwe and Apartheid.* Benjamin Pogrund. New Brunswick, N.J.: Rutgers University Press, 1991. vii + 406 pp. ISBN 0-8135-1693-5.

*Social Change and Economic Reform in Africa.* Peter Gibbon, ed. Uppsala: Nordiska Afrikainstitutet, 1993. 381 pp. ISBN 91-7106-331-5.

*Social Development in Africa: Strategies, Policies and Programmes after the Lagos Plan.* Duri Mohammed, ed. London: Hans Zell Publishers, 1991. vi + 257 pp. ISBN 0-905450-28-0.

*The Social History of Labor in the Middle East.* Ellis Jay Goldberg, ed. Boulder: Westview Press, 1996. xiii + 236 pp. ISBN 0-8133-8498-2.

*Somalia Action Kit.* Baltimore: Catholic Relief Services, Development Education Unit, 1993.

*Somalia: A Nation in Turmoil.* Said S. Samatar. London: Minority Rights Group, August 1991. 34 pp. ISBN 0-946690-80-4.

*Somalia: Human Rights Abuses by the United Nations Forces.* Rakiya Omaar and Alex de Waal. London: African Rights, July 1993. ii + 35 pp.

*Somalia: Operation Restore Hope. A Preliminary Assessment.* Rakiya Omaar and Alex de Waal. London: African Rights, May 1993. v + 59 pp.

*Some Are More Equal Than Others: Essays on the Transition in South Africa.* Neville Alexander. Cape Town: Buchu Books, 1993. 106 pp. ISBN 1-874863-09-1.

*The Song of Jacob Zulu.* Tug Yourgrau. New York: Arcade Publishing, 1993. xvi + 106 pp. ISBN 1-55970-237-0.

*A Song of Longing: An Ethiopian Journey.* Kay Kaufman Shelemay. Champaign: University of Illinois Press, 1994. xxii + 177 pp. ISBN 0-252-06432-1.

*Song of Umm Dalaila: The Story of the Sahrawis.* [audiovisual].

*Songs and Stories from Uganda.* W. Moses Serwadda. Danbury: World Music Press, 1987. ix + 81 pp. ISBN 0-937203-17-3. With audiotape.

*Sophiatown: Coming of Age in South Africa.* Don Mattera. Boston: Beacon Press, 1989. xxii + 151 pp. ISBN 0-8070-0206-2.

*South Africa in the Region: A Post-Apartheid Future.* Robert Davies. London: Catholic Institute for International Relations, 1991. 19 pp. ISBN 1-85287-085-0. CIIR Insight.

*South Africa Inc. The Oppenheimer Empire.* David Pallister, Sarah Stewart, and Ian Lepper. New Haven: Yale University Press, 1988. 382 pp. ISBN 0-300-04251-5.

*South Africa's Economic Crisis.* Stephen Gelb, ed. London: Zed Books, 1991. xiv + 289 pp. ISBN 1-85649-023-8.

*South Africa's Moment of Truth.* Edgar Lockwood. New York: Friendship Press, 1988. vi + 183 pp. ISBN 0-377-00180-5.

*South Africa's Police: From Police State to Democratic Policing?* Gavin Cawthra. London: Catholic Institute for International Relations, 1992. 40 pp. ISBN 1-85287-099-0. *CIIR Insight*.

*South Africa's Radical Tradition: A Documentary History. Vol. 1: 1907-1950.* Allison Drew, ed. Cape Town: Buchu Books, 1996. 404 pp. ISBN 0-7992-1613-5.

*South Africa. As Apartheid Ends: An Annotated Bibliography with Analytical Introductions.* Newell M. Stultz. Ann Arbor: Pierian Press, 1993. xii + 228 pp. ISBN 0-87650-330-X.

*South Africa: An Annotated Bibliography with Analytical Introductions.* Newell M. Stultz. Ann Arbor: Pierian Press, 1989. x + 191 pp. ISBN 0-87650-254-0. Resources on Contemporary Issues.

*South Africa: Breaking New Ground.* CIIR Comment. London: Catholic Institute for International Relations (CIIR), 1996. 47 pp. ISBN 1-85287-151-2. *CIIR Comment*, August 1996.

*South Africa: Colonialism, Apartheid and African Dispossession.* Alfred Tokollo Moleah. Wilmington: Disa Press, 1993. xvi + 505 pp. ISBN 0-913255-03-3.

*South Africa: Contemporary Analysis.* Glenn Moss and Ingrid Obery, eds. and comps. London, Munich, New York: Hans Zell Publishers, 1990. xxvii + 490 pp. ISBN 0-905450-42-6. South African Review, no. 5.

*South Africa: Crossing the Rubicon.* Guy Arnold. London: Macmillan Academic and Professional Ltd., 1992. x + 229 pp. ISBN 0-333-53941-9.

*South Africa: The Challenge of Change.* Vincent Maphai, ed. Harare: SAPES Books, 1994. xxiii + 301 pp. ISBN 1-77905-023-2.

*South Africa: Designing New Political Institutes.* Murray Faure and Jan-Erik Lane, eds. London: Sage Publications, 1996. ix + 278 pp. ISBN 0-7619-5303-5.

*South Africa: The Dynamics and Prospects of Transformation (1900-1994).* Sipho Buthelezi, ed. Harare: SAPES Books, 1995. xii + 134 pp. ISBN 1-77905-033-X.

*South Africa: The Political Economy of Transformation.* Stephen John Stedman, ed. Boulder: Lynne Rienner Publishers, 1994. ix + 213 pp. ISBN 1-55587-421-5.

*South Africa: The Sanctions Mission.* James Mutambirwa. Eminent Church Persons Group. London: Zed Books, 1989. xvi + 135 pp. ISBN 0-86232-911-6.

*South Africa: To the Sources of Apartheid.* Steven Debroey. Lanham, Md.: University Press of America, 1989. xii + 612 pp. ISBN 0-8191-7319-3.

*South Africa: Twelve Perspectives on the Transition.* Helen Kitchen and J. Coleman Kitchen, eds. Westport, Conn.: Praeger Publishers, October 1994. xii + 203 pp. ISBN 0-275-95087-5. Washington Papers, no. 165.

*South African Keywords: The Uses and Abuses of Political Concepts.* Emile Boonzaier and John Sharp, eds. Cape Town: David Philip Publishers, 1988. x + 197 pp. ISBN 0-86486-100-1.

*South African Labour Bulletin.* [periodical].

*South African Media Policy: Debates of the 1990s.* P. Eric Louw, ed. Belleville (South Africa): Anthropos Publishers, 1993. 380 pp. ISBN 0-620-176-555.

*South African Tripod: Studies on Economics, Politics, and Conflict.* Bertil Odén et al. Uppsala: Nordiska Afrikainstitutet, 1994. 281 pp. ISBN 91-7106-341-2.

*South African Workers Speak.* Liv Tørres. Oslo: FAFO, Institute for Applied Social Science, 1995. 151 pp. ISBN 82-7422-140-0. Common Security Forum Studies. FAFO Report, no. 182.

*Southern Africa in a Global Context: Towards a Southern African Security Community.* Sam C. Nolutshungu. Harare: SAPES Books, 1994. 35 pp. ISBN 1-77905-021-6. Occasional Paper Series, no. 6.

*Southern Africa in the Year 2000: An Overview and Research Agenda.* Ibbo Mandaza. Harare: SAPES Books, 1993. 16 pp. ISBN 1-77905-005-4.

*Southern Africa: Exploring a Peace Dividend.* Peter Vale. London: CIIR Publications, 1996. 20 pp. ISBN 1-85287-14-0. CIIR Briefing.

*The Southern African Development Directory.* David Barnard, ed. Braamfontein: Programme for Development Research (PRODDER), Human Sciences Research Council, June 1994. 448 pp. ISBN 0-7969-1623-3.

*The Southern African Environment: Profiles of the SADC Countries.* Sam Moyo, Phil O'Keefe, and Michael Sill. London: Earthscan Publications, 1993. x + 354 pp. ISBN 1-85383-171-9.

*Southern African Futures: Critical Factors for Regional Development in Southern Africa.* Bertil Odén. Uppsala: Nordiska Afrikainstitutet, 1996. 35 pp. ISBN 91-7106-392-7. ISSN 1104-8417. Discussion Paper, no. 7.

*Southern Sudan: Too Many Agreements Dishonoured.* Abel Alier. Reading: Ithaca Press, 1992. xi + 326 pp. ISBN 0-86372-163-X.

*Sovereignty as Responsibility: Conflict Management in Africa.* Francis M. Deng et al. Washington, D.C.: Brookings Institution, 1996. xxiii + 265 pp. ISBN 0-8157-1827-6.

*Speaking with Beads: Zulu Arts from Southern Africa.* Jean Morris. New York: Thames and Hudson, 1994. 94 pp. ISBN 0-500-27757-5.

*The Spirit of Freedom: South African Leaders on Religion and Politics.* Charles Villa-Vicencio. Berkeley: University of California Press, 1996. xxxii + 301 pp. ISBN 0-520-20045-4.

*The Spirit of Hope: Conversations on Politics, Religion and Values.* Charles Villa-Vicencio. Braamfontein: Skotaville Publishers, 1993. xv + 285 pp. ISBN 0-947479-93-7.

*Stabilizing Democracy in South Africa: The Challenges of Post-Apartheid Development.* Washington, D.C.: Southern Africa Grantmakers' Affinity Group, February 1994. 63 pp.

*The State and Its Servants: Administration in Egypt from Ottoman Times to the Present.* Nelly Hanna, ed. Cairo: American University in Cairo Press, 1995. 128 pp. ISBN 977-424-364-1.

*The State and the Crisis in Africa: In Search of a Second Liberation.* Dag Hammarskjold Foundation. Uppsala: Dag Hammarskjold Centre, 1992. 32 pp. ISBN 91-85214-19-1.

*State Building and Democracy in Southern Africa: Botswana, Zimbabwe, and South Africa.* Pierre du Toit. Washington, D.C.: U.S. Institute of Peace, October 1995. xiii + 350 pp. ISBN 1-878379-50-X.

*The State in Africa: The Politics of the Belly.* Jean-Francois Bayart. Trans. Mary Harper. London: Longman Group, 1993. xxiii + 370 pp. ISBN 0-582-06421-X.

*The State of Academic Freedom in Africa, 1995.* Nana Busia and Ren Dgni-Sgui. Dakar: CODESRIA, 1996. 189 pp. ISBN 2-86978-061-3.

*State of the Environment in Southern Africa.* Munyaradzi Chenje and Phyllis Johnson, eds. Harare: Southern African Research and Documentation Centre (SARDC), 1994. xx + 332 pp. ISBN 0-7974-137-4-X.

*A State of the Peoples: A Global Human Rights Report on Societies in Danger.* Marc S. Miller, ed. Boston: Cultural Survival, 1993. x + 262 pp. ISBN 0-8070-0220-8.

*State of the World Conflict Report.* Dayle E. Spencer et al. Atlanta: International Negotiation Network, no date. 100 pp.

*The State of the World's Refugees: The Challenge of Protection.* United Nations High Commissioner for Refugees. New York: Penguin Books, 1993. xii + 191 pp. ISBN 0-14-023487-X.

*The State of War and Peace in Africa, 1992.* Mohamed Suliman and Peter Verney. London: Institute for African Alternatives, January 1993. 40 pp.

*The State of World Population 1994.* Alex Marshall, ed. New York: United Nations Population Fund, 1994. 66 pp. ISBN 0-89714-195-4.

*The State of World Rural Poverty: A Profile of Africa.* Sappho Haralambous, comp. and ed. Rome: International Fund for Agricultural Development, 1993. iii + 86 pp.

*The State of World Rural Poverty: A Profile of the Near East and North Africa.* Abdelhamid Abdouli. Rome: International Fund for Agricultural Development (IFAD), 1994. iv + 59 pp.

*The Status of Human Rights Organizations in Sub-Saharan Africa.* Washington, D.C.: International Human Rights Internship Program, September 1994. ii + 230 pp.

*Stern's Guide to Contemporary African Music.* See *The Da Capo Guide to Contemporary African Music.*.

*Still Killing: Landmines in Southern Africa.* Human Rights Watch Arms Project. New York: Human Rights Watch, 1997. xiv + 204 pp. ISBN 1-56432-206-8.

*The Story of Africa.* Basil Davidson. ??: ??, 1984.

*A Story of South Africa: J. M. Coetzee's Fiction in Context.* Susan VanZanten Gallagher. Cambridge: Harvard University Press, 1991. xii + 258 pp. ISBN 0-674-83972-2.

*Strategies for Empowering Women.* Hope Bagyendera Chigudu. Harare: Zimbabwe Women's Resource Centre and Network, June 1992. 8 pp. ZWRCN Discussion Paper, no. 4.

*Strategies of Slaves and Women: Life-Stories from East/Central Africa.* Marcia Wright. New York: Lilian Barber Press, 1993. x + 238 pp. ISBN 0-936508-28-0.

*Strikes Have Followed Me All My Life: A South African Autobiography.* Emma Mashinini. New York: Routledge, 1991. xxxv + 142 pp. ISBN 0-415-90415-3.

*Striking Back: A History of Cosatu.* Jeremy Baskin. London: Verso, 1991. xv + 488 pp. ISBN 0-86091-557-3.

*Structural Adjustment and African Women Farmers.* C. Gladwin, ed. Gainesville: University of Florida Press, 1991.

*Structural Adjustment and Beyond in Sub-Saharan Africa.* Rolph Van Der Hoeven and Fred Van Der Kraaij, eds. The Hague: Ministry of Foreign Affairs, 1994. xix + 270 pp. ISBN 0-85255-150-9.

*Structural Adjustment and Environmental Linkages: A Case Study of Kenya.* Julie A. Richardson. London: Overseas Development Institute, 1996. viii + 124 pp. ISBN 0-85003-233-4.

*Structural Adjustment and Socio-Economic Change in Sub-Saharan Africa: Some Conceptual, Methodological and Research Issues.* Peter Gibbon and Adebayo O. Olukoshi. Uppsala: Nordiska Afrikainstitutet, 1996. 101 pp. ISBN 91-7106-397-8. ISSN 1104-8425. Research Report, no. 102.

*Structural Adjustment and the African Farmer.* Alex Duncan and John Howell, eds. Portsmouth, N.H.: Heinemann Publishers, 1992. x + 214 pp. ISBN 0-435-08071-7.

*Structural Adjustment and the Working Poor in Zimbabwe.* Peter Gibbon, ed. Uppsala: Nordiska Afrikainstitutet, 1995. 283 pp. ISBN 91-7106-369-2.

*Structural Adjustment in West Africa.* Adebayo O. Olukoshi, R. Omotayo Olaniyan, and Femi Arivisala, eds. Lagos: Pumark Nigeria Educational Publishers, 1994. xiv + 224 pp. ISBN 978-2049-17-4.

*The Struggle Continues: South African Women and the Vote.* Rachael Kagan and Lisa Lippman. New York: Africa Fund, August 1993. 4 pp. Southern Africa Perspectives, no. 2.

*The Struggle for Land and the Fate of the Forests.* Marcus Colchester and Larry Lohmann, eds. London: Zed Books, 1993. 389 pp. ISBN 1-85649-140-4.

*The Struggle for Land in Southern Somalia: The War Behind the War.* Catherine Besteman and Lee V. Cassanelli, eds. Boulder: Westview Press, 1996. xi + 222 pp. ISBN 0-8133-2447-5.

*The Struggle for Resources in Africa.* Sheffield: ROAPE Publications, July 1991. 126 pp. ISSN 0305 6244. Review of African Political Economy, no. 51.

*The Struggle: A History of the African National Congress.* Heidi Holland. New York: George Braziller, 1990. 252 pp. ISBN 0-8076-1238-3.

*Struggling Over Scarce Resources: Women and Maintenance in Southern Africa.* Alice K. Armstrong. Women and Law in Southern Africa Trust. Harare: University of Zimbabwe Publications, 1992. xvi + 157 pp. ISBN 0-908307-27-6.

*Studded With Diamonds and Paved With Gold: Miners, Mining Companies and Human Rights in Southern Africa.* Laurie Flynn. London: Bloomsbury Publishing, 1992. 358 pp. ISBN 0-7475-11551.

*Studies in African Music. Volume 1.* A. M. Jones. London and New York: Oxford University Press, 1959. viii + 295 pp. ISBN 0-19-713512-9. Cloth.

*Studies in African Music. Volume 2.* A. M. Jones. London and New York: Oxford University Press, 1959.

*Studies in the Short Fiction of Mahfouz and Idris.* Mona N. Mikhail. New York: New York University Press, 1992. xii + 168 pp. ISBN 0-8147-5474-0. New York University Studies in Near Eastern Civilization, no. 16.

*Sub-Saharan African Films and Filmmakers, 1987-1992: An Annotated Bibliography.* Nancy J. Schmidt. London: Hans Zell Publishers, 1994. ix + 468 pp. ISBN 1-873836-21-X.

*Sub-Saharan African Films and Filmmakers: An Annotated Bibliography.* Nancy Schmidt. London: Hans Zell, 1988.

*Subduing Sovereignty: Sovereignty and the Right to Intervene.* Marianne Heiberg, ed. London: Pinter Publishers, 1994. viii + 154 pp. ISBN 1-85567-267-7.

*Sudan Democratic Gazette.* [periodical].

*Sudan Update.* [periodical].

*Sudan's Debt Crisis.* R. P. C. Brown. The Hague: Institute of Social Studies, 1990.

*Sudan, 1898-1989: The Unstable State.* Peter Woodward. Boulder: Lynne Rienner Publishers, 1990. xiv + 273 pp. ISBN 1-55587-193-3.

*Sudan: A History of Struggle.* London: Christian Aid, 1989. 4 pp.

*Sudan: A Nation in the Balance.* Chris Peters. Oxford: Oxfam (UK and Ireland), 1996. 64 pp. ISBN 0-85598-316-7. Oxfam Country Profile.

*Sudan: Caught in Time: Great Photographic Archives.* M.W. Daly and L.E. Frobes. Barkshire: Garnet Publishing, 1994. 207 pp. ISBN 1-873938-94-2.

*Sudan: Ending the War, Moving Talks Forward.* Washington, D.C.: U.S. Institute of Peace, 1994. 5 pp.

*Sudan: State and Society in Crisis.* John O. Voll, ed. Bloomington: Indiana University Press, 1991. xi + 170 pp. ISBN 0-253-20683-9.

*Sudan: The Forgotten Tragedy.* Francis M. Deng et al. Washington, D.C.: U.S. Institute of Peace, 1994. ix + 89 pp.

*Sudan: The Passing of Time.* Jean-Pierre Ribiere. Reading: Garnet Publishing, 1994. xiii + 102 pp. ISBN 1-873938-79-9.

*Sudan: The Ravages of War: Political Killings and Humanitarian Disaster.* New York: Amnesty International, U.S.A., September 1993. 33 pp.

*Sudan: The Roots of Famine. A Report for Oxfam.* Nick Cater. Oxford: Oxfam (UK and Ireland), 1986. i + 36 pp.

*Sudanese Rebels at a Crossroads: Opportunities for Building Peace in a Shattered Land.* John Prendergast. Washington, D.C.: Center of Concern, 1994. 51 pp.

*The Suffering Grass: Superpowers and Regional Conflict in Southern Africa and the Caribbean.* Thomas G. Weiss and James G. Blight, eds. Boulder: Lynne Rienner Publishers, 1992. x + 182 pp. ISBN 1-55587-276-X.

*Survey of Economic and Social Conditions in Africa, 1990-1991.* Economic Commission for Africa. New York: United Nations Publications, 1993. xv + 180 pp. ISBN 92-1-125063-3.

*Sustainable Agriculture and Rural Development. Part 2: Africa and the North.* Rome: Food and Agriculture Organization of the United Nations (FAO), 1994. 40 pp. ISSN 1020-0339. DEEP: Development Education Exchange Papers.

*Sustainable Agriculture in Egypt.* Mohamed A. Faris and Mahmood Hasan Khan, eds. Boulder: Lynne Rienner Publishers, 1993. ix + 273 pp. ISBN 1-55587-370-7.

*Sustainable Development.* Geneva: United Nations Non-Governmental Liaison Service, June 1994. ix + 120 pp. Voices from Africa, no. 5.

*Sustainable Development for a Democratic South Africa.* Ken Cole, ed. London: Earthscan Publications, 1994. xiv + 247 pp. ISBN 1-85383-230-8.

*Sustainable Development in Third World Countries: Applied and Theoretical Perspectives.* Valentine Udoh James, ed. Westport, Conn.: Praeger Publishers, 1996. xvi + 245 pp. ISBN 0-275-95307-6. Cloth.

*The Swahili.* Mark Horton. Cambridge, Mass.: Blackwell Publishers, forthcoming.

*The Swahili: Idiom and Identity of an African People.* Alamin M. Mazrui and Ibrahim Noor Shariff. Lawrenceville, N.J.: Africa World Press, 1994. x + 187 pp. ISBN 0-86543-311-9.

*Switching on to the Environment: A Critical Guide to Films on Environment and Development.* London: Television Trust for the Environment, n.d. 143 pp. ISBN 0-905347-66-8.

*The Taproot of Environmental and Development Crisis in Africa: The Great Challenge.* J. J. Otim. Nairobi: Association of Christian Lay Centres in Africa, 1992. ACLCA Publication, no. 2.

*Teachers, Preachers, Non-Believers: A Social History of Zimbabwean Literature.* Flora Veit-Wild. London and New York: Hans Zell Publishers, 1992. xii + 408 pp. ISBN 1-873836-15-5. New Perspectives on African Literature, no. 6.

*Teaching about the New South Africa.* Washington, D.C.: National Council for the Social Studies, February 1995. 10 pp. ISSN 0037-7724. Social Education, 59, no. 2.

*Teaching of African Literature in Schools.* Eddah Gachukia and S. Kichamu Akivaga, eds. Nairobi: Kenya Literature Bureau, 1978.

*Tears over the Deserts.* Jackson Kaujeua. Windhoek: New Namibia Books, 1994. 124 pp. ISBN 99916-31-21-6.

*Technology and Enterprise Development: Ghana Under Structural Adjustment.* Sanjana Lall et al. New York: St. Martin's Press, 1994. xiv + 262 pp. ISBN 0-312-12149-0.

*Technology and Enterprise Development: Ghana under Structural Adjustment.* Sanjaya Lall et al. New York: St. Martin's Press, 1994. xiv + 262 pp. ISBN 0-312-12149-0.

*Theatre and Cultural Struggle in South Africa.* Robert Kavanagh. London: Zed Books, 1985. xv + 237 pp. ISBN 0-86232-283-9.

*Theatre and Drama in Francophone Africa: A Critical Introduction.* John Conteh-Morgan. Cambridge: Cambridge University Press, 1994. xii + 244 pp. ISBN 0-521-43453-X.

*The Theory of African Literature: Implications for Practical Criticism.* Chidi Amuta. London: Zed Books, 1989. ix + 206 pp. ISBN 0-86232-547-1.

*The Third Epidemic: Repercussions of the Fear of AIDS.* Panos Institute and the Norwegian Red Cross. Washington, D.C.: Panos Publications, 1990. iv + 320 pp. ISBN 1-870670-12-4.

*Third Revolution: Environment, Population and a Sustainable World.* Paul Harrison. London: I. B. Tauris Publishers, 1992. xi + 359 pp. ISBN 1-85043-501-4.

*Third Way Theology: Reconciliation, Revolution and Reform in the South African Church during the 1980s.* Anthony Balcomb. Pietermaritzburg (South Africa): Cluster Publications, 1993. 291 pp. ISBN 0-9583141-4-4.

*Third World Atlas.* Alan Thomas et al. Bristol, Penn.: Taylor and Francis, 1994. 80 pp. ISBN 1-56032-323-X.

*Third World Debt: The Lingering Crisis.* London: Catholic Institute for International Relations, 26 pp. ISBN 1-85287-087-7. Comment.

*Third World Film Making and the West.* Roy Armes. Berkeley: University of California Press, 1987. 381 pp. ISBN 0-520-05667-1.

*The Third World in Film and Video, 1984-1990.* Helen W. Cyr. Lanham, Md.: Scarecrow Press, 1991. ix + 246 pp. ISBN 0-8108-2380-2.

*Third World Minerals and Global Pricing: A New Theory.* Chibuzo Nwoke. London: Zed Books, 1987. x + 229 pp. ISBN 0-86232-422-4.

*Third World Resource Directory 1994-1995: A Guide to Print, Audiovisual and Organizational Resources on Africa, Asia and Pacific, Latin America and Caribbean and the Middle East.* Thomas P. Fenton and Mary J. Heffron, comps. and eds. Maryknoll, N.Y.: Orbis Books, 1994. 800 pp. ISBN 0-88344-941-2.

*Third World Resurgence.* [periodical].

*Third World Women. Family, Work, and Empowerment: Contemporary Issues for Women in Three World Areas: South Asia, Sub-Saharan Africa, and Latin America.* Susan Hill Gross and Mary Hill Rojas. Saint Louis Park: Glenhurst Publications, 1989. 135 + 128 pp.

*Third World Women's Literatures: A Dictionary and Guide to Materials in English.* Barbara Fister. Westport, Conn.: Greenwood Press, 1995. 408 pp. ISBN 0-313-28988-3.

*The Third World Worker in the Multinational Corporation: A Bibliography.* Joan Nordquist, comp. Santa Cruz, Calif.: Reference and Research Services, 1993. 68 pp. ISBN 0-937855-58-8. ISSN 0887-3569. Contemporary Social Issues: A Bibliographic Series, no. 30.

*Thirty Years of Independence in Africa: The Lost Decades?* Peter Anyang' Nyong'o, ed. Nairobi: Academy Science Publishers, 1992. viii + 254 pp. ISBN 9966-831-10-X.

*This Is Our Africa: Images of Africa by African Photographers.* Angela Joynson and Jane Talbot. London: Development Education Unit, 1992. 13 pp. ISBN 0-9509050-4-6.

*Threads of Solidarity: Women in South African Industry, 1900-1980.* Iris Berger. Bloomington: Indiana University Press, 1992. xi + 368 pp. ISBN 0-253-20700-2.

*Three Kilos of Coffee: An Autobiography.* Manu Dibango. Trans. Beth G. Raps. Chicago: University of Chicago Press, 1994. xii + 146 pp. ISBN 0-226-14490-9.

*Thresholds of Change in African Literature: The Emergence of Tradition.* Kenneth W. Harrow. Portsmouth, N.H.: Heinemann, 1994. xiv + 384 pp. ISBN 0-435-08082-2.

*Through African Eyes. Volume 1, The Past: The Road to Independence.* Leon E. Clark. New York: CITE Books, 1988. 294 pp. ISBN 0-938960-35-0. Cloth.

*Thunder and Silence: The Mass Media in Africa.* Dhyana Ziegler and Molefi K. Asante. Trenton: Africa World Press, 1992. vi + 205 pp. ISBN 0-86543-251-1.

*The Ties That Bind: African-American Consciousness of Africa.* Bernard Makhosezwe Magubane. Lawrenceville, N.J.: Africa World Press, 1987. xi + 251 pp. ISBN 0-86543-037-3.

*To Cure All Hunger: Food Policy and Food Security in Sudan.* Simon Maxwell, ed. London: Intermediate Technology Publications, 1991. xiv + 248 pp. ISBN 1-85339-087-9.

*To Have a History of African Cinema.* Victor Bachy. Trans. Dalice A. Woodford. Brussels: OCIC, 1987. 69 pp. ISBN 92-9080-019-4.

*Today's Refugees, Tomorrow's Leaders: Report of the Saharawi Women Refugees Conference.* London: One World Action, 1993. 40 pp.

*Tomorrow Is Another Country: The Inside Story of South Africa's Road to Change.* Allister Sparks. New York: Hill and Wang, 1995. viii + 254 pp. ISBN 0-090-9405-3.

*Tomorrow Is Built Today: Experiences of War, Colonialism and the Struggle for Collective Co-Operatives.* Andrew Nyathi and John Hoffman. Harare: Anvil Press, 1990. v + 137 pp. ISBN 0-7974-0934-3.

*The Tongue Is Fire: South African Storytellers and Apartheid.* Harold Scheub. Madison: University of Wisconsin Press, 1996. xxvii + 448 pp. ISBN 0-299-15094-1.

*Towards a Democratic Future.* Johannesburg: Southern African Catholic Bishops' Conference, 1993.

*Towards a Science and Technology Policy for a Democratic South Africa. Mission Report, July 1993.* Ottawa: International Development Research Centre, 1993. x + 131 pp.

*Towards a Theory of United Nations Peacekeeping.* A. B. Fetherston. New York: St. Martin's Press, 1994. xvi + 292 pp. ISBN 0-312-12275-6. Cloth.

*Trade Union Resource Guide.* Amsterdam: Transnationals Information Exchange, February 1993. 90 pp.

*Trade Unions and the New Industrialization of the Third World.* Roger Southall. London: Zed Books, 1988. xiv + 378 pp. ISBN 0-86232-579-X.

*The Trades Union Movement in Nigeria.* Dafe Otobo. Lagos: Malthouse Press, 1995. 87 pp. ISBN 978-023-003-3.

*Traditional Healers and Childhood in Zimbabwe.* Pamela Reynolds. Athens: Ohio University Press, 1996. xxxix + 184 pp. ISBN 0-8214-1121-7.

*Traditional Peoples Today: Continuity and Change in the Modern World.* Goran Burenhult, ed. San Francisco: HarperSanFrancisco, 1994. 239 pp. ISBN 0-06-250268-9. Illustrated History of Humankind.

*Transformation on the South African Gold Mines.* Montreal: 172 pp. ISSN 0706-1706. Labour, Capital and Society, 25, no. 1 (April 1992).

*Transition in Burundi: The Context for a Homecoming.* Catharine Watson. Washington, D.C.: U.S. Committee for Refugees, September 1993. 32 pp. ISSN 0882-9287.

*The Transition to Independence in Namibia.* Lionel Cliffe et al. Boulder: Lynne Rienner Publishers, 1994. x + 293 pp. ISBN 1-55587-420-7.

*Travel, Gender, and Imperialism: Mary Kingsley and West Africa.* Alison Blunt. New York: Guilford Press, 1994. x + 190 pp. ISBN 0-89862-546-7.

*Tropical Rainforest: A World Survey of Our Most Valuable and Endangered Habitat with a Blueprint for Its Survival.* Arnold Newman. New York: Facts on File, 1990. 256 pp. ISBN 0-8160-1944-4. Cloth. Oversized.

*The True Cost of Conflict.* Michael Cranna, ed. London: Earthscan Publications, 1995. xx + 208 pp. ISBN 1-85383-254-5.

*Truth From Below: The Emergent Press in Africa.* Richard Carver. London: Article 19, 1991. viii + 91 pp. ISBN 1-870798-51-1.

*The Tuaregs: The Blue People.* Karl-G. Prasse. Copenhagen: Museum Tusculanum Press, University of Copenhagen, 1995. 85 pp. ISBN 87-7289-313-3.

*Tunisia: Rural Labour and Structural Transformation.* Samir Radwan, Vali Jamal, and Ajit Ghose. London: Routledge, 1991. xii + 122 pp. ISBN 0-415-04274-7.

*Twenty-five Black African Filmmakers: A Critical Study, with Filmography and Bio-bibliography.* Françoise Pfaff. Westport, Conn.: Greenwood Press, 1988. sii + 332 pp. ISBN 0-313-24695-5.

*The Two Faces of Civil Society: NGOs and Politics in Africa.* Stephen N. Ndegwa. West Hartford, Conn.: Kumarian Press, 1996. xii + 140 pp. ISBN 1-56549-055-X.

*2000 Years of Christianity in Africa.* John Baur. Nairobi: Paulines Publications Africa, 1994.

*UN Economic Report on Africa 1994.* UN Economic Commission for Africa. New York: United Nations Publications, April 1994. 60+ pp.

*U.S. Economic Policy Toward Africa.* Jeffrey Herbst. New York: Council on Foreign Relations Press, 1992. vi + 82 pp. ISBN 0-87609-121-4.

*U.S. Foreign Relations with the Middle East and North Africa: A Bibliography.* Sanford R. Siverburg and Bernard Reich, comp. Lanham, Md.: Scarecrow Press, 1994. xvii + 586 pp. ISBN 0-8108-2699-2. Cloth.

*Uganda: A Century of Existence.* P. Godfrey Okoth, Manuel Muranga, and Ernesto Okello Ogwang. Kampala: Fountain Publishers, 1995. xv + 278 pp. ISBN 9970-02-022-6.

*Uganda: Landmarks in Rebuilding a Nation.* P. Langseth et al., eds. Kampala: Fountain Publishers, 1995. xi + 354 pp. ISBN 9970-02-070-6.

*Ulwazi: For Power and Courage.* Libby Dreyer and Jenni Karlsson. Durban: Media Resource Centre, Community Resource Centre Training Project, 1991. 80 pp. ISBN 0-86980-831-1.

*The UN and Complex Emergencies: Rehabilitation in Third World Transitions.* Jonathan Moore. Geneva: UNRISD, War-torn Societies Project, 1996. 104 pp. ISBN 92-9085016-7. UNRISD Report, no. 96/1.

*The Unbreakable Thread: Non-Racialism in South Africa.* Julie Frederikse. London: Zed Books, 1990. x + 294 pp. ISBN 0-86232-971-X.

*Unconventional Warfare and the Theory of Competitive Reproduction: U.S. Intervention and Covert Action in the Developing World.* Washington, D.C.: Information Project for Africa,

1991. 72 pp. I.P.F.A. Foreign Policy Series. Working Paper, no. 2.

*Uncovering Reality: Excavating Women's Rights in African Family Law.* Alice Armstrong et al. Harare: Women and Law in Southern Africa, 1992. 62 pp.

*Understanding Africa's Food Problems: Social Policy Perspectives.* African Centre for Applied Research and Training in Social Development. New York: Hans Zell Publishers, 1990. viii + 259 pp. ISBN 0-905450-39-6. Cloth.

*Understanding Oral Literature.* Austin Bukenya, Wanjiku M. Kabira, and Okoth Okombo, eds. Nairobi: Nairobi University Press, 1995. 102 pp. ISBN 9966-846-31-X.

*Understanding Somalia: Guide to Culture, History, and Social Institutions.* I. M. Lewis. London: HAAN Associates, 1993. 115 pp. ISBN 1-874209-41-3.

*Unfinished Business: South Africa's March to Democracy.* Rhoda Njanana et al. Harare: Southern African Research and Documentation Centre (SARDC), May 1994. 45 pp. ISBN 0-7974-1361-8. Update, no. 8.

*Unfolding Islam.* P. J. Stewart. Reading: Garnet Publishing/Ithaca Press, 1994. xiii + 252 pp. ISBN 0-86372-194-X.

*Unhappy Valley: Conflict in Kenya and Africa.* Vol. 2: *Violence and Ethnicity.* Bruce Berman and John Lonsdale. Athens: Ohio University Press, 1992. xvi + 287 pp. ISBN 0-8214-1025-3.

*UNITA, Myth and Reality.* Augusta Conchiglia. Trans. Marga Holness. London: European Campaign Against South African Aggression on Mozambique and Angola (ECASAAMA), 106 pp. ISBN 0-9516052-1-6.

*United Nations and Apartheid, 1948-1994.* New York: United Nations, Dept. of Public Information, 1994. 566 pp. ISBN 92-1-100546-9. United Nations Blue Book Series, no. 1.

*The United Nations and Civil Wars.* Thomas G. Weiss, ed. Boulder: Lynne Rienner Publishers, 1995. x + 235 pp. ISBN 1-55587-527-0. Emerging Global Issues. Cloth.

*The United Nations and Mozambique, 1992-1995.* New York: United Nations Publications, 1995. 321 pp. ISBN 92-1-100559-0. United Nations Blue Book Series, no. 5.

*United Nations and Rwanda, 1993-1996.* New York: United Nations Publications, 1996. 739 pp. ISBN 92-1-100561-2. United Nations Blue Book Series, no. 10.

*The United Nations and Somalia, 1992-1996.* New York: United Nations Publications, 1996. 516 pp. ISBN 92-1-100566-3. United Nations Blue Books Series, no. 8.

*The United Nations in a Turbulent World.* James N. Rosenau. Boulder, Colo.: Lynne Rienner Publishers, 1992. 87 pp. National Peace Academy series.

*United States Foreign Policy Toward Africa: Incrementalism, Crisis and Change.* Peter J. Schraeder. Cambridge and New York: Cambridge University Press, 1994. xxiii + 347 pp. ISBN 0-521-44439-X.

*Unmasking the Bandits: The True Face of the M.N.R.* Anders Nilsson. London: European Campaign Against South African Aggression on Mozambique and Angola (ECASAAMA), 1990. vi + 91 pp. ISBN 0-9516052-0-8.

*The Unquestionable Right to Be Free: Black Theology from South Africa.* Itumeleng J. Mosala and Buti Tlhagale, eds. Maryknoll, N.Y.: Orbis Books, 1986. xviii + 206 pp. ISBN 0-88344-251-5.

*Uprooted Liberians: Casualties of a Brutal War.* Hiram A. Ruiz. Washington, D.C.: U.S. Committee for Refugees, Feb. 1992. 32 pp. ISSN 0882-9281.

*Variety International Film Guide: 1994.* Peter Cowie, ed. London: Hamlyn/Samuel French Trade, 1993. 448 pp. ISBN 0-600-58005-9.

*Video Catalogue: Africa.* Jenni Karlsson. Educational Resources Information Services. Durban: University of Natal, 1992. viii + 102 pp. ISBN 1-874897-15-8. ISSN 0-86980-805-2.

*Video Catalogue: Environmental Studies.* Educational Resources Information Services. Durban: University of Natal, 1992. viii + 109 pp. ISBN 1-874897-39-5.

*Videos of African and African-related Performance: An Annotated Bibliography.* Carol Lems-Dworkin. Evanston, Ill.: Carol Lems-Dworkin Publishers, 1996. xx + 331 pp. ISBN 0-9637048-1-8.

*Violent Deeds Live On: Landmines in Somalia and Somaliland.* London: African Rights and Mines Advisory Group, 1993. 82 pp.

*Vital: Three Contemporary African Artists. Cyprien Tokoudagba, Touhami Ennadre, Farid Belkahia.* Judith Nesbitt, ed. Seattle: University of Washington Press, 1996. 48 pp. ISBN 1-85437-170-3.

*Voices From Africa: Local Perspectives on Conservation.* Dale Lewis and Nick Carter, eds. Baltimore: World Wildlife Fund, 1993. ix + 216 pp. ISBN 0-89164-124-6.

*Votes and Budgets: Comparative Studies in Accountable Governance in the South.* John Healey and William Tordoff, eds. New York: St. Martin's Press, Scholarly and References Division, 1996. xviii + 270 pp. ISBN 0-312-12709-X.

*Voting in the Shadow of Apartheid: Questions and Answers on the South African Election.* Elizabeth Landis. New York: Africa Fund, September 1993. Africa Fund Perspectives, no. 3.

*The Waiting Country: A South African Witness.* Mike Nicol. London: Victor Gollancz, 1995. 211 pp. ISBN 0-575-05915-X.

*War and Refugees: The Western Sahara Conflict.* Richard Lawless and Laila Monahan, eds. London: Pinter Publishers, 1987. xiv + 201 pp. ISBN 0-86187-900-7.

*War of Visions: Conflict of Identities in the Sudan.* Francis M. Deng. Washington, D.C.: Brookings Institution, 1995. ix + 577 pp. ISBN 0-8157-1793-8.

*War Wounds: Development Costs of Conflict in Southern Sudan.* Nigel Twose and Benjamin Pogrund, eds. London and Washington, D.C.: Panos Institute, 1988. iii + 163 pp. ISBN 1-870670-08-6.

*Waste Not Your Tears.* Violet Kala. Harare: Baobab Books, 1994. 73 pp. ISBN 0-908311-64-8.

*Wasting the Earth: A Directory of Multinational Corporate Activities.* George Draffan, comp. Seattle: Institute on Trade Policy, Task Force on Multinational Corporations, 1993. 200 pp.

*Wasting the Earth: A Directory of Multinational Corporate Activities.* George Draffan. Seattle: 1993.

*Wasting the Rain: Rivers, People and Planning in Africa.* W.M. Adams. Minneapolis: University of Minnesota Press, 1992. 256 pp. ISBN 0-8166-2270-1.

*We Are the World: An Evaluation of Pop Aid for Africa.* Michael Scott and Mutombo Mpanya. Washington, D.C.: InterAction, 1994. xiv + 148 pp. ISBN 0-932140-25-4.

*We Miss You All. Noerine Kaleeba: AIDS in the Family.* Noerine Kaleeba, Sunanda Ray, and Brigid Willmore. Harare:

Women and AIDS Support Network, 1991. 103 pp. ISBN 0-7974-1009-0.

*We Speak for Ourselves: Population and Development.* Nicole A. Brown, Anne Cramer, and Elise Storck. London and Washington, D.C.: Panos Institute, 1994. 32 pp. ISBN 1-879358-04-2.

*We Spend Our Years as a Tale That is Told. Oral Historical Narrative in a South African Chiefdom.* Isabel Hofmeyr. Johannesburg: Witwatersrand University Press, 1993. xvi + 328 pp. ISBN 1-86814-216-7.

*West African Popular Theatre.* Karin Barber, John Collins, and Alain Ricard. Bloomington: Indiana University Press, 1997. xix + 285 pp. ISBN 0-253-21077-1.

*Western African History.* Robert O. Collins. Princeton: Markus Wiener Publishers, 1990.

*Western Sahara: A Country Fact Sheet.* Jamaica Plain, Mass.: Western Sahara Awareness Project, 1993. 2 pp.

*Western Sahara: Keeping It Secret. The United Nations Operation in the Western Sahara.* Fatemeh Ziai. New York: Human Rights Watch/Middle East, 1995. 42 pp. Human Rights Watch/Middle East, 7, no. 7 (October 1995).

*Western Sahara: The Roots of a Desert War.* Tony Hodges. Westport, Conn.: Lawrence Hill and Company, 1983. xii + 388 pp. ISBN 0-88208-152-7.

*The Western Saharans.* Tony Hodges. London: Minority Rights Group, 1991. Revised and updated edition. 24 pp. ISBN 0-946690-21-0.

*What Do We Know about Africa?* [audiovisual].

*What Does It Mean to be Green in Africa?* Mohamed Suliman. London: Institute for African Alternatives, 1993. 21 pp.

*What Will My Mother Say: A Tribal African Girl Comes of Age in America.* Dympna Ugwu-Oju. Chicago: Bonus Books, 1995. 414 pp. ISBN 1-55625-042-0.

*What Works: An Annotated Bibliography of Case Studies of Sustainable Development.* D. Scott Slocombe et al. Sacramento: International Center for the Environment and Public Policy, 1993. 55 pp. ISBN 0-912102-99-3.

*Whatever Happened to Somalia? A Tale of Tragic Blunders.* John Drysdale. London: HAAN Associates, 1994. 216 pp. ISBN 1-874209-51-0.

*When My Brothers Come Home: Poems from Central and Southern Africa.* Frank Mkalawile Chipasula, ed. Middletown: Wesleyan University Press, 1985. xv + 278 pp. ISBN 0-8195-6089-8.

*When People Play People: Development Communication through Theatre.* Zakes Mda. London: Zed Books, 1993. x + 250 pp. ISBN 1-85649-200-1.

*When Refugees Go Home: African Experiences.* Tim Allen and Hubert Morsink, eds. Lawrenceville, N.J.: Africa World Press, 1994. xiii + 305 pp. ISBN 0-86543-433-6.

*Where is the Way: Song and Struggle in South Africa.* Helen Q. Kivnick. New York: Penguin Books, 1990. xvii + 378 pp. ISBN 0-1401-2895-6.

*White on Black: Contemporary Literature about Africa.* John Cullen Gruesser. Urbana: University of Illinois Press, 1992. xv + 181 pp. ISBN 0-252-01916-4. Cloth.

*Who Owns Who in Mining: Ownership and Control in the World Mining and Refining Industry.* Raw Materials Group. London: Roskill Information, annual.

*Who Rules the Airwaves? Broadcasting in Africa.* London: Article 19, 1995. iv + 156 pp. ISBN 0-870798-67-8.

*Who's in Control? IMF/World Bank Campaign.* Oxford: Third World First, 1994. 16 pp.

*Who's Who in Africa: Leaders for the 1990s.* Alan Rake. Lanham, Md.: Scarecrow Press, 1992. vii + 448 pp. ISBN 0-8108-2557-0.

*Who's Who in South African Politics, No. 5.* Shelagh Gastrow, ed. Johannesburg: Ravan Press, 1995. xxxiii + 319 pp. ISBN 0-86975-458-0.

*Who's Who in the Arab World, 1997-98.* Publitec Publications. Detroit: Gale Research, 1996. 13th ed. 988 pp. ISBN 2-903188-13-0. ISSN 0083-9752. Cloth.

*Whose News? Ownership and Control of the News Media.* Cathy Nash and Bob Kirby. Manchester: Development Education Project, 1989. 72 pp. ISBN 1-869818-42-3.

*Whose Trees?* Mohamed Ahmed Hisham, Jan Sharma, and Anthony Ngaiza. London: Panos Publications, 1991. v + 138 pp. ISBN 1-870670-25-6.

*Why Food Aid?* Vernon W. Ruttan, ed. Baltimore: John Hopkins University Press, 1993. vii + 281 pp. ISBN 0-8018-4472-X.

*Why Population Matters.* Washington, D.C.: Population Action International, 1996. 55 pp.

*The Widening Circle of Genocide. Genocide: A Critical Bibliographic Review.* Israel W. Charny, ed. New Brunswick, N.J.: Transaction Publishers, 1994. xxvii + 375 pp. ISBN 1-5600-172-0.

*Wildest Africa.* Paul Tingay. New York: St. Martin's Press, 1995. 240 pp. ISBN 0-312-14479-2. Cloth. Oversized.

*Wildlands and Human Needs: Reports from the Field.* Roger D. Stone. Baltimore: World Wildlife Fund, 1991. vii + 151 pp. ISBN 0-942635-17-5.

*Wildlife Conservation and Tourism in Kenya.* Daniel Musili Nyeki. Nairobi: Jacaranda Designs, 1993. iii + 134 pp. ISBN 9966-884-96-3.

*The Will to Arise: Women, Tradition, and the Church in Africa.* Mercy Amba Oduyoye and Musimbi R. A. Kanyoro, eds. Maryknoll, N.Y.: Orbis Books, 1992. viii + 230 pp. ISBN 0-88344-782-7.

*Without Troops and Tanks: Humanitarian Intervention in Ethiopia and Eritrea.* Mark Duffield and John Prendergast. Lawrenceville, N.J.: Red Sea Press, 1994. xx + 215 pp. ISBN 1-56902-003-5.

*Witness to Apartheid.* [audiovisual].

*Witness to Faith: AIDS and Development in Africa.* Sr. Ursula Sharpe and Noerine Kaleeba. London: CAFOD, n.d. 28 pp. ISBN 1-871549-469.

*Woman Between Two Worlds: Portrait of an Ethiopian Rural Leader.* Judith Olmstead. Urbana and Chicago: University of Illinois Press, 1997. xv + 248 pp. ISBN 0-252-06587-5.

*The Woman with the Artistic Brush: A Life History of Yoruba Batik Artist Nike Davies.* Kim Marie Vaz. Armonk, N.Y.: M. E. Sharpe, 1995. xliv + 137 pp. ISBN 1-56324-507-8.

*The Woman with the Artistic Brush: A Life History of Yoruba Batik Artist Nike Davies.* Kim Marie Vaz. Armonk, N.Y.: M. E. Sharpe, 1995. xliv + 137 pp. ISBN 1-56324-507-8.

*Woman, Why Do You Weep? Circumcision and Its Consequences.* Asma El Dareer. London: Zed Books, 1982. vi + 130 pp. ISBN 0-86232-099-2.

*Womanwise: A Popular Guide and Directory to Women and Development in the "Third World."* Linda Gray, ed. Edinburgh: Scottish Education and Action for Development, 1993. viii + 90 pp. ISBN 0-946953-04-X.

*Women and AIDS.* Harare: Zimbabwe Women's Resource Centre and Network, 1993.

*Women and AIDS in Rural Africa: Rural Women's Views of AIDS in Zambia.* G. Mwale and P. Burnard. Aldershot: Avebury, 1992.

*Women and AIDS: A Bibliography.* Joan Nordquist, comp. Santa Cruz, Calif.: Reference and Research Services, 1993. 76 pp. ISBN 0-937855-56-1. ISSN 0887-3569. Contemporary Social Issues: A Bibliographic Series, no. 29.

*Women and AIDS: Developing a New Health Strategy.* Geeta Rao Gupta and Ellen Weiss. Washington, D.C.: International Center for Research on Women, October 1993. 12 pp. ICRW Policy Series, no. 1.

*Women and Children First: Environment, Poverty, and Sustainable Development.* Filomina Chioma Steady, ed. Rochester, Vt.: Schenkman Books, 1993. xix + 475 pp. ISBN 0-87047-065-5.

*Women and Class in Africa.* Claire Robertson and Iris Berger, eds. New York: Africana Publishing/Holmes and Meier Publishers, 1986. x + 310 pp. ISBN 0-8419-0979-2.

*Women and Culture.* Caroline Sweetman, ed. Oxford: Oxfam (UK and Ireland), 1995. 62 pp. ISBN 0-85598-310-8. Gender and Development, 3, no. 1 (February 1995).

*Women and Disability.* Esther Boylan, ed. London: Zed Books, 1991. xi + 111 pp. ISBN 0-86232-987-6.

*Women and Drought.* Harare: Zimbabwe Women's Resource Centre and Network, December 1992. 7 pp. ZWRCN Workshop Report, no. 4.

*Women and Education.* Harare: Zimbabwe Women's Resource Centre and Network, July 1993. 26 pp. ZWRCN Bibliographies, no. 7.

*Women and Empowerment.* Marilee Karl. London: Zed Books, 1995. ISBN 1-85649-192-7.

*Women and Environment.* Harare: Zimbabwe Women's Resource Centre and Network, 1993. 30 pp. ZWRCN Bibliographies, no. 6.

*Women and ESAP.* Harare: Zimbabwe Women's Resource Centre and Network, August 1993. 10 pp. ZWRCN Workshop Report, no. 5.

*Women and Health.* Patricia Smyke. London: Zed Books, 1991. ISBN 0-86232-983-3.

*Women and Health in Africa.* Meredeth Turshen, ed. Lawrenceville, N.J.: Africa World Press, 1991. vi + 250 pp. ISBN 0-86543-181-7.

*Women and HIV/AIDS: An International Resource Book.* Marge Berer, ed. London: Pandora/Harper Collins, 1993. 383 pp. ISBN 0-04-440-876-5.

*Women and Human Rights.* Katarina Tomasevski. London: Zed Books, 1993.

*Women and International Development Annual, Volume 3.* Rita S. Gallin, Anne Ferguson, and Janice Harper, eds. Boulder: Westview Press, 1993. viii + 215 pp. ISBN 0-8133-8512-1. ISSN 1045-893X.

*Women and Land.* Harare: Zimbabwe Women's Resource Centre and Network, May 1994. 16 pp. ZWRCN Bibliographies, no. 10.

*Women and Literacy.* Marcela Ballara. London: Zed Books, 1992. ISBN 0-86232-981-7.

*Women and Politics Worldwide.* Barbara J. Nelson and Najma Chowdhury, eds. New Haven: Yale University Press, 1994. xi + 818 pp.

*Women and Resistance in South Africa.* Cherryl Walker. New York: Monthly Review Press, 1991. xxxiii + 309 pp. ISBN 0-85345-830-8.

*Women and Revolution in Africa, Asia, and the New World.* Mary Ann Tétreault, ed. Columbia: University of South Carolina Press, 1994. x + 456 pp. ISBN 1-57003-016-2.

*Women and Rights.* Caroline Sweetman, ed. Oxford: Oxfam (UK and Ireland), 1995. 64 pp. ISBN 0-85598-317-5. Gender and Development, 3, no. 2 (June 1995).

*Women and Structural Adjustment.* Harare: Zimbabwe Women's Resource Centre and Network, January 1994. 40 pp. ZWRCN Bibliographies, no. 8.

*Women and Sustainable Development in Africa.* Valentine Udoh James, ed. Westport, Conn.: Praeger Publishers, 1995. xvi + 203 pp. ISBN 0-275-95308-4.

*Women and the Environment.* Annabel Rodda, ed. London: Zed Books, 1991. vii + 180 pp. ISBN 0-86232-985-X.

*Women and the Environment: A Reader. Crisis and Development in the Third World.* Sally Sontheimer, ed. New York: Monthly Review Press, 1991. 205 pp. ISBN 0-85345-835-9.

*Women and the Family.* Helen O'Connell. London: Zed Books, 1994. ISBN 1-85649-106-4.

*Women and the World Economic Crisis.* Jeanne Vickers. London: Zed Books, 1991. ISBN 1-85649-230-3.

*Women and War in South Africa.* Jacklyn Cock. Cleveland: Pilgrim Press, 1993. x + 254 pp. ISBN 0-8298-0966-X.

*Women and Work.* Susan Bullock. London: Zed Books, 1994. ISBN 1-85649-118-8.

*Women and Work in Developing Countries: An Annotated Bibliography.* Parvin Ghorayshi, comp. Westport, Conn.: Greenwood Press, 1994. xix + 223 pp. ISBN 0-313-28834-8. ISSN 0742-6941. Bibliographies and Indexes in Women's Studies, no. 20.

*Women are Different.* Flora Nwapa. Trenton: Africa World Press, 1992. 138 pp. ISBN 0-86543-326-7.

*Women Artists: Multi-Cultural Visions.* Betty LaDuke. Trenton: Red Sea Press, 1992. xxii + 170 pp. ISBN 0-932415-78-4.

*Women as Oral Artists.* Molara Ogundipe-Leslie and Carole Boyce Davies, eds. Bloomington: Indiana University Press, 1994. 200 pp. ISSN 0034-5210. Research in African Literatures, 25, no. 3 (Fall).

*Women at the Center: Development Issues and Practices for the 1990s.* Gay Young, Vidyamali Samarasinghe, and Ken Kusterer, eds. West Hartford, Conn.: Kumarian Press, 1993. x + 221 pp. ISBN 1-56549-029-0.

*Women Entrepreneurs Bibliography.* Harare: Zimbabwe Women's Resource Centre and Network, December 1991. 14 pp. ZWRCN Bibliographies, no. 3.

*Women in Action.* [periodical].

*Women in Africa of the Sub-Sahara. Volume I: From Ancient Times to the 20th Century.* Marjorie Wall Bingham and Susan Hill Gross. Women in the World Area Studies. Hudson: Gary E. McCuen, 1982. 143 pp. ISBN 0-86596-031-3.

*Women in Africa of the Sub-Sahara. Volume II: The 20th Century.* Marjorie Wall Bingham and Susan Hill Gross. Women in the World Area Studies. Hudson: Gary E. McCuen, 1982. 117 pp. ISBN 0-86596-007-0.

*Women in African Literature Today.* Eldred Durosimi Jones, ed. Trenton: Africa World Press, 1987. 162 pp. ISBN 0-86543-057-8.

*Women in Botswana: An Annotated Bibliography.* Christine Erickson. Women and Law in Southern Africa Trust. Gaborone: University of Botswana, 1993. vi + 71 pp. ISBN 99912-0-081-9.

*Women in Developing Economies: Making Visible the Invisible.* Joycelin Massiah, ed. Providence & Oxford: Berg Publishers, 1993. 300 pp. ISBN 0-85496-345-6.

*Women in Development in Southern Africa: Botswana, Lesotho, Malawi and Zambia: An Annotated Bibiography.* Wageningen, The Netherlands: CTA Technical Centre for Agricultural and Rural Cooperation, 1991. 4 vols.

*Women in International Studies: A Bibliographic Guide.* Ruth Dickstein. Tucson: Southwest Institute for Research on Women, 1989. 60 pp.

*Women in Middle Eastern History: Shifting Boundaries in Sex and Gender.* Nikki R. Keddie and Beth Baron, eds. New Haven: Yale University Press, 1991. xii + 343 pp. ISBN 0-300-05005-4.

*Women in Nigeria Today.* Editorial Committee Women in Nigeria. London: Zed Books, 1985. 257 pp. ISBN 0-86232-448-3.

*Women in Society: Egypt.* Angele Botros Samaan. New York: Marshall Cavendish, 1993. 128 pp. ISBN 1-85435-505-8.

*Women in Society: South Africa.* Dee Rissik. New York: Marshall Cavendish, 1993. 128 pp. ISBN 1-85435-504-X.

*Women in the Third World: A Historical Bibliography.* Pamela R. Byrne and Suzanne R. Ontiveros, eds. Santa Barbara: ABC-CLIO, 1986. xii + 152 pp. ISBN 0-87436-459-0. Cloth.

*Women in the Time of AIDS.* Gillian Paterson. Maryknoll: Orbis Books, 1996. xvi + 112 pp. ISBN 1-57075-106-4.

*Women of Africa: Roots of Oppression.* Maria Rosa Cutrufelli. Trans. Nicolas Romano. London: Zed Books, 1983. 186 pp. ISBN 0-86232-084-4.

*Women of the Arab World.* Nahid Toubia, ed. London: Zed Books, 1988. xii + 168 pp. ISBN 0-86232-785-7.

*Women Pay the Price: Structural Adjustment in Africa and the Caribbean.* Gloria T. Emeagwali, ed. Lawrenceville, N.J.: Africa World Press, 1995. 165 pp. ISBN 0-86543-429-8.

*Women Resisting AIDS: Feminist Strategies of Empowerment.* Beth E. Schneider and Nancy E. Stoller, eds. Philadelphia: Temple University Press, 1995. xii + 339 pp.

*Women's Income Generating Projects.* Harare: Zimbabwe Women's Resource Centre and Network, August 1991. 6 pp. ZWRCN Workshop Report, no. 1.

*Women's Income Generating Projects.* Hope Bagyendera Chigudu. Harare: Zimbabwe Women's Resource Centre and Network, August 1991. 8 pp. ZWRCN Discussion Paper, no. 1.

*Women's Income Generating Projects: Empowerment.* Harare: Zimbabwe Women's Resource Centre and Network, September 1992. 49 pp. ZWRCN Workshop Report, no. 1 (Follow up).

*Women's Rights in International Documents: A Sourcebook with Commentary.* Winston E. Langley. Jefferson: McFarland, 1991. xxi + 192 pp. ISBN 0-89950-548-1. Cloth.

*Women's Voices on Africa: A Century of Travel Writings.* Patricia W. Romero, ed. Princeton: Markus Wiener Publishing, 1992. 280 pp. ISBN 1-55876-048-2.

*Women's World.* [periodical].

*Women, Employment and Exclusion.* Caroline Sweetman, ed. Oxford: Oxfam (UK and Ireland), 1996. 72 pp. ISBN 0-85598-364-7. Focus on Gender, 4, no. 3 (October 1996).

*Women, Employment, and the Family in the International Division of Labour.* Sharon Stichter and Jane L. Parpart, eds. Philadelphia: Temple University Press, 1990. 253 pp. ISBN 0-87722-739-X. Women in the Political Economy.

*Women, Literacy and Education.* Jessica Silverthorne. Harare: Zimbabwe Women's Resource Centre and Network, July 1993. 12 pp. ZWRCN Discussion Paper, no. 7.

*Women, Poverty, and AIDS: Sex, Drugs, and Structural Violence.* Paul Farmer, Margaret Connors, and Janie Simmons, eds. Monroe: Common Courage Press, 1996. xxi + 473 pp. ISBN 1-56751-074-4.

*Women, Science and Technology.* Harare: Zimbabwe Women's Resource Centre and Network, August 1994. 14 pp. ZWRCN Bibliographies, no. 11.

*Women, the Environment and Sustainable Development: Towards a Theoretical Synthesis.* Rosi Braidotti et al. London: Zed Books, 1994. xiii + 220 pp. ISBN 1-85649-184-6.

*Women: Challenges to the Year 2000.* New York: United Nations Department of Pubic Education, 1991. 96 pp. ISBN 92-1-100458-6.

*Words into Action: Basic Rights and the Campaign against World Poverty.* Pat Simmons. Oxford: Oxfam (UK and Ireland), 1995. 112 pp. ISBN 0-85598-331-0.

*Work Against AIDS: Workplace-based AIDS Initiatives in Zimbabwe.* Glen Williams and Sunanda Ray. London: Actionaid, 1993. 68 pp. ISBN 1-872502-25-3. Strategies for Hope, no. 8.

*Work and Power in Maale, Ethiopia.* Donald L. Donham. New York: Columbia University Press, 1994. 2nd ed. x + 176 pp. ISBN 0-231-10047-7.

*Work, Culture, and Identity: Migrant Laborers in Mozambique and South Africa, c. 1860-1910.* Patrick Harries. Portsmouth, N.H.: Heinemann, 1994. xxiii + 305 pp. ISBN 0-435-08094-6.

*Workers, Unions and Popular Protest.* Carolyn Baylies and Robin Cohen, eds. Sheffield: ROAPE Publications, 1987. 128 pp. ISSN 0305-6244. Review of African Political Economy, no. 39.

*Working with Rural Communities: A Participatory Action Research in Kenya.* Orieko Chitere and Roberta Mutiso, eds. Nairobi: Nairobi University Press, 1991. 206 pp. ISBN 9966-8-46-17-4.

*Working Women: International Perspectives on Labour and Gender Ideology.* Nanneke Redclift and M. Thea Sinclair. London: Routledge, 1991. x + 242 pp. ISBN 0-415-01843-9.

*The World and the Word: Tales and Observations from the Xhosa Oral Tradition.* Nongenile Masithathu Zenani. Madison: University of Wisconsin Press, 1992. xii + 499 pp. ISBN 0-299-13310-9.

*World Bank and Structural Transformation in Developing Countries: The Case of Zaire.* Winsome J. Leslie. Boulder: Lynne Rienner Publishers, 1987. xi + 208 pp. ISBN 1-55587-036-8.

*The World Bank: Lending on a Global Scale.* Jo Marie Griesgraber and Bernhard G. Gunter. Washington, D.C.: Center of Concern, 1996. xix + 240 pp. Rethinking Bretton Woods.

*World Cinema Since 1945.* William Luhr, ed. New York: Unger, 1987. x + 708 pp. ISBN 0-8044-3078-0.

*World Directory of Environmental Organizations: A Handbook of National and International Organizations and Programs — Governmental and Non-Governmental — Concerned with Protecting the Earth's Resources.* Thaddeus C. Trzyna and Roberta Childers, eds. Sacramento: California Institute of Public Affairs, 1992. 4th ed. 231 pp. ISBN 0-912102-97-7. ISSN 0092-0908.

*World Directory of Moving Image and Sound Archives.* Wolfgang Klaue, ed. Munchen: K. G. Saur, 1993. 192 pp. ISBN 3-598-22594-6.

*World Employment 1995: An ILO Report.* Geneva: International Labour Office, 1995. x + 200 pp. ISBN 92-2-109448-0. ISSN 1020-3079.

*World Food Aid.* John Shaw and Edward Clay, eds. Portsmouth, N.H.: Heinemann, 1993. xii + 244 pp. ISBN 0-435-08097-0.

*The World Guide 1997/98: A View from the South.* Instituto del Tercer Mundo. Oxford: New Internationalist Publications, 1997. 10th biennial ed. 628 pp. ISBN 1-869847-43-1.

*World Hunger: Twelve Myths.* Frances Moore Lappé and Joseph Collins. London: Earthscan Publications, 1988. Rev. ed. x + 182 pp. U.S. distributor: Food First (Oakland, Calif.).

*World Labour Report.* Geneva: International Labour Office, 1995. xi + 122 pp. ISBN 92-2-109447-2.

*World Military and Social Expenditures 1996.* Ruth Leger Sivard et al. Washington, D.C.: World Priorities, 1996. 56 pp. ISBN 0-918281-09-1. ISSN 0363-4795.

*World Music in Music Libraries.* Carl Rahkonen, ed. Canton, Mass.: Music Library Association, 1994. xi + 77 pp. ISBN 0-914954-49-0. ISSN 0094-5099. MLA Technical Reports, no. 24.

*World Music: The Rough Guide.* Simon Broughton et al., eds. London: Rough Guides, 1994. 698 pp. ISBN 1-85828-017-6.

*The World of African Music: Stern's Guide to Contemporary African Music.* Ronnie Graham. London: Pluto Press, 1992. viii + 235 pp. ISBN 0-7453-0657-8.

*World of Work: The Magazine of the ILO.* [periodical].

*World Population Data Sheet 1996: Demographic Data and Estimates for the Countries and Regions of the World.* Washington, D.C.: Population Reference Bureau, June 1996. ISSN 0085-8315. Poster.

*World Recession and the Food Crisis in Africa.* Peter Lawrence, ed. Boulder: Westview Press, 1986. vi + 314 pp. ISBN 0-8133-0511-X.

*The World Refugee Problem.* Harto Hakovirta. Tampere: Hillside, 1991. 109 pp. ISBN 951-95484-1-6.

*World Refugee Survey 1995.* Washington, D.C.: U.S. Committee for Refugees, 1994. 196 pp. ISBN 0-9365-48-05-11. ISSN 0197-5439.

*World Refugee Survey 1997: An Annual Assessment of Conditions Affecting Refugees, Asylum Seekers and Internally Displaced People.* Virginia Hamilton, ed. Washington, D.C.: U.S. Committee for Refugees, 1997. 250 pp. ISBN 0-9365-48-53-3. ISSN 0197-5439.

*A World Religions Reader.* Ian Markham. Cambridge, Mass: Blackwell Publishers, 1995. 365 pp. ISBN 0-631-18239-X. Cloth.

*World Resources 1994-95: A Guide to the Global Environment.* Allen L. Hammond, ed. World Resources Institute. Oxford: Oxford University Press, 1994. xii + 400 pp. ISBN 0-19-521045-X. ISSN 0887-0403.

*World Security: Challenges for a New Century.* Michael T. Klare and Daniel C. Thomas. New York: St. Martin's Press, 1994. viii + 408 pp. ISBN 0-312-10265-8.

*World Survey of Economic Freedom, 1995-1996: A Freedom House Study.* Richard E. Messick, ed. New Brunswick, N.J.: Transaction Publishers, 1996. 219 pp. ISBN 1-56000-929-2.

*The World Watch Reader on Global Environmental Issues.* Lester R. Brown, ed. New York: W. W. Norton, 1991. 336 pp. ISBN 0-393-03007-5. Cloth.

*The World's Women: Trends and Statistics, 1970-1990.* New York: United Nations Publications, 1991. xiv + 120 pp. ISBN 92-1-161313-2.

*The World's Women: Trends and Statistics, 1970-1990.* UN Department of International and Economic and Social Affairs. New York: United Nations Publications, 1991. xiv + 120 pp. ISBN 92-1-161313-2. Social Statistics and Indicators, no. 8.

*Worldmark Encyclopedia of the Nations.* Vol. 2: *Africa.* Detroit: Gale Research, 1995. 480 pp. ISBN 0-8103-9880-X. Cloth.

*WorldViews: A Quarterly Review of Resources for Education and Action.* [periodical].

*Woza Afrika! An Anthology of South African Plays.* Duma Ndlovu, ed. New York: George Braziller, 1986. xxx + 272 pp. ISBN 0-8076-1169-7.

*Writing and Being.* Nadine Gordimer. Cambridge: Harvard University Press, 1995. 145 pp. ISBN 0-674-96232-X. Cloth.

*Writing My Reading: Essays on Literary Politics in South Africa.* Peter Horn. Amsterdam: Editions Rodopi, 1994. xi + 172 pp. ISBN 90-5183-723-2. ISSN 0924-1426. Cross/Cultures, no. 15.

*Writing Women's Worlds: Bedouin Stories.* Lila Abu-Lughod. Berkeley: University of California Press, 1993. xxiii + 266 pp. ISBN 0-520-08304-0.

*The Yoruba Artist: New Theoretical Perspectives on African Arts.* Rowland Abiodun, Henry J. Drewal, and John Pemberton III, eds. Washington, D.C.: Smithsonian Institution Press, 1994. ix + 276 pp. ISBN 1-56098-340-X.

*Yours for the Union: Class and Community Struggles in South Africa.* Baruch Hirson. London: Books, 1989. xiv + 230 pp. ISBN 0-86232-370-3.

*Zimbabwe Books in Print, 1995.* Harare: Zimbabwe Book Publishers' Association, 1995. ix + 192 pp. ISBN 0-7974-1456-8.

*Zimbabwe's Agricultural Revolution.* Mandivamba Rukuni and Carl K. Eicher, eds. Harare: University of Zimbabwe Publications, 1994. 418 pp.

*Zimbabwe: The Struggle for Health. A Community Approach for Farmworkers.* Chris McIvor. London: Catholic Institute for International Relations, 1995. ix + 67 pp. ISBN 1-85287-122-9.

# DIRECTORY OF ORGANIZATIONS

ABC-CLIO, 130 Cremona Dr., P.O. Box 1911, Santa Barbara, CA 93116-1911, USA.
Academy Chicago Publishers, 363 W. Erie St., Chicago, IL 60610, USA.
Academy Science Publishers, P.O. Box 14798, Nairobi, Kenya.
ActionAid, Hamlyn House, MacDonald Rd., Archway, London N19 5PG, England.
ActionAid, Old Church House, Church Steps, Frome, Somerset BA11 1PL, England.
Addison-Wesley Longman, One Jacob Way, Reading, MA 01867-3999, USA.
Afram Publications, 9 Ring Rd. East, P.O. Box M18, Accra, Ghana.
Africa Faith and Justice Network, P.O. Box 29378, Washington, DC 20017, USA.
Africa Fund, 198 Broadway, New York, NY 10038, USA.
Africa Policy Information Center, 110 Maryland Ave., NE, Suite 112, Washington, DC 20002, USA.
Africa Project/SPICE Institute for International Studies (IIS), Littlefield Center, Rm. 14, Stanford University, 300 Lasuen St., Stanford, CA 94305-5013, USA.
Africa Today Associates, University of Denver, Graduate School of International Studies, Denver, CO 80208, USA.
Africa World Press, 11 Princess Rd., Ste. D, Lawrenceville, NJ 08648, USA.
African Arts Trust, 86 Cambridge Gardens, London W10 6HS, England.
African Books Collective, The Jam Factory, 27 Park End St., Oxford OX1 1HU, England.
African Language Teachers Association, University of Wisconsin, 866 Van Hise Hall, 1220 Linden Dr., Madison, WI 53706-1447, USA.
African Literature Association, University of Wisconsin, 866 Van Hise Hall, 1220 Linden Dr., Madison, WI 53706-1557, USA.
African Rights, 11 Marshalsea Rd., London SE1 1EP, England.
African Studies Association, Emory University, Credit Union Bldg., Atlanta, GA 30322, USA.
African Studies Center, Boston University, 270 Bay State Rd., Boston, MA 02215, USA.
African Video Centre, 7 Balls Pond Rd., Dalston, London N1 4AX, England.
Africana Publishing, c/o Holmes and Meier, 160 Broadway East, Bldg. 900, New York, NY 10038-4201, USA.
AHRTAG. See Appropriate Health Resources and Technologies Action Group.
AIDS Counselling Trust, P.O. Box 7225, Harare, Zimbabwe.
Altschul Group, 1560 Sherman, Ste. 100, Evanston, IL 60201, USA.
American Academy of Arts and Sciences, Committee on International Security Studies, 136 Irving St., Cambridge, MA 02138, USA.
American Friends Service Committee, Literature Resources, 1501 Cherry St., Philadelphia, PA 19102-1479, USA.
American Refugee Committee, 2344 Nicollet Ave., Ste. 350, Minneapolis, MN 55404, USA.
American University in Cairo Press, 113 Sharia Ksr El Aini, P.O. Box 2511, Cairo, Egypt.
Amnesty International Publications, 1 Easton St., London WC1X 8DJ, England.
Amnesty International USA, 322 Eighth Ave., New York, NY 10001, USA.
Amnesty International, International Secretariat, 1, Easton St., London WC1X 8DJ, England.
Amsterdam University Press, Prinsengracht 747-751, Amsterdam, 1017-JX, The Netherlands.
Anchor Books/Doubleday, 1540 Broadway, New York, NY 10036, USA.
Anthropos Publishers, P.O. Box 636, Belleville 7535, South Africa.
Anti-Slavery International, The Stableyard, Broomgrove Rd., London SW9 9TL, England.
Anvil Press, P.O. Box 4209, Harare, Zimbabwe.
Apex Press, 777 UN Plaza, New York, NY 10017, USA.
Apex Press/New Horizons Press, P.O. Box 337, Croton-on-Hudson, NY 10520, USA.
Appropriate Health Resources and Technologies Action Group (AHRTAG), AIDS Programme, Farringdon Point, 29-35 Farringdon Rd., London EC1M 3JB, England.
Arcade Publishing, 141 Fifth Ave., New York, NY 10010, USA.

Archiv für Sozialpolitik e.V., Postfach 100125, 60001 Frankfurt/M., Germany.
Edward Arnold, Mill Rd., Dunton Green, Sevenoaks, Kent, TN 132YA, England.
Edward Arnold/Hodder Headline Group, 338 Euston Rd., London, NW1 3BH, England.
Article 19, 33 Islington High St., London N1 9LH, England.
Associated University Presses, 440 Forsgate Dr., Cranbury, NJ 08512, USA.
Associated University Presses, 25 Sicilian Ave., London WC1A 2QH, England.
Association of African Studies Programs, Duke University, 2814 Perkins Library, Durham, NC 27706, USA.
Association of African Women for Research and Development, B.P. 3304, Dakar, Senegal.
Association of Christian Lay Centres in Africa, AACC Bldg., Waiyaki Way, Westlands, P.O. Box 14205, Nairobi, Kenya.
Atlantic Monthly Press. See Grove/Atlantic. (New York, N.Y.).
Audio-Visual Services at Pennsylvania State University, Special Services Bldg., University Park, PA 16802, USA.
Avebury, Gower House, Croft Rd., Aldershot, Hampshire GU11 3HR, England
Avon Books/Hearst Corp., 1350 Avenue of the Americas, New York, NY 10019, USA.
Ballantine Books, 201 E. 50 St., New York, NY 10022, USA.
Bantam Doubleday Dell, 1540 Broadway, New York, NY 10036, USA.
Baobab Books, P.O. Box 1559, Harare, Zimbabwe.
Lilian Barber Press, P.O. Box 232, New York, NY 10163, USA.
Barbican Art Gallery, Barbican Centre, London EC2Y 8D5, England.
Basic Books, 10 E. 53rd St., New York, NY 10022, USA.
Bayreuth University (Bayreuth, Germany).
Beacon Press, 25 Beacon St., Boston, MA 02108-2892, USA.
Berg Publishers (UK), 150 Cowley Rd., Oxford OX4 1JJ, England.
Berg Publishers (USA), c/o New York University Press, 70 Washington Square South, New York, NY 10012, USA.
Bergin and Garvey Publishers, c/o Greenwood Publishing Group, 88 Post Rd. West, Box 5007, Westport, CT 06881-5007, USA.
Between the Lines, 720 Bathurst St., Ste. 404, Toronto, ON M5S 2R4, Canada.
Birkhauser Verlag, 675 Massachusetts Ave., Cambridge, MA 02139, USA.
Black Classic Press, P.O. Box 13414, Baltimore, MD 21203, USA.
Black Studies Program, Pennsylvania State University, University Park, PA 16802, USA.
Blackwell Publishers (UK), 108 Cowley Rd., Oxford OX4 1JF, England.
Blackwell Publishers (USA), 238 Main St., Cambridge, MA 02142, USA.
Bloomsbury Publishing, 2 Soho Square, London W1V 5DE, England.
Bonus Books, 160 E. Illinois St., Chicago, IL 60611, USA.
Bookcraft, 29 Moremi Rd., New Bodija, P.O. Box 16279, Ibadan, Nigeria.
Boston University, African Studies Center, 270 Bay State Rd., Boston, MA 02215, USA.
R. R. Bowker, P.O. Box 31, New Providence, NJ 07974, USA.
Brassey's UK, 33 John St., London WC1N 2AT, England.
Brassey's/Maxwell Macmillan, 22883 Quicksilver Dr., Ste. 100, Dulles, VA 20166, USA.
George Braziller, 60 Madison Ave., New York, NY 10010, USA.
Bread for the World Institute, 1100 Wayne Ave., Ste. 1000, Silver Spring, MD 20910, USA.
Bright Star Productions, One St. Luke's Mews, London W11 1DF, England.
E. J. Brill, 24 Hudson St., Kinderhook, NY 12106, USA.
British Academic Press (London). See I. B. Tauris.
Brookings Institution Books, 1775 Massachusetts Ave., NW, Washington, DC 20036, USA.
Buchu Books, P.O. Box 2580, 8000 Cape Town, South Africa.
Bullfrog Films, P.O. Box 149, Oley, PA 19606, USA.
CAFOD, 2 Romero Close, Stockwell Rd., London SW9 9TY, England.
California Newsreel, 149 Ninth St., Ste. 420, San Francisco, CA 94103, USA.
Cambridge University Press (U.K.), The Edinburgh Bldg., Shaftesbury Rd., Cambridge CB2 2RU, England.
Cambridge University Press, 40 W. 20 St., New York, NY 10011-4211, USA.
Canadian Council for International Cooperation (CO-CAMO), 1 Nicholas St., Ottawa, ON K1N 7B7, Canada.
Cassell, Wellington House, 125 Strand, London, WC2R 0BB, England
Catholic Institute for International Relations. See CIIR Publications.
Catholic Relief Services, Global Education Office, 209 West Fayette St., Baltimore, MD 21201-3403, USA.
Center for African Studies, University of Florida, 427 Grinter Hall, Gainesville, FL 32611-2037, USA.
Center for African Studies, University of Illinois, 1208 W. California, #101, Urbana, IL 61801, USA.
Center for Afro-American Studies, University of California—Los Angeles, African Area Studies, Los Angeles, CA 90024, USA.
Center for Economic Research on Africa, Montclair State College, School of Business, Dept. of Economics, Upper Montclair, NJ 07043, USA.
Center for International Education School of Education, University of Massachusetts, Hills House South, Amherst, MA 01003, USA.
Center for International Studies, Ohio University, Athens, OH 45701, USA.
Center for Media Literacy, 4727 Wilshire Blvd., Ste. 403, Los Angeles, CA 90010.
Center for Women's Global Leadership, Douglass College, 27 Clifton Ave., New Brunswick, NJ 08903, USA.
Center of Concern, 3700 13th St., NE, Washington, DC 20017, USA.
Centre for Developing-Area Studies, McGill University, 3715 Pell St., Montreal, Quebec H3A 1X1, Canada.
Centre for the Strategic Initiatives of Women, 1701 K St., NW, 11th floor, Washington, DC 20006, USA.

Chambers, 43-45 Annandale St., Edinburgh, EH7 4A2, Scotland).
Chelsea House/Main Line Book Company, 300 Park Ave. South, 6th floor, New York, NY 10010, USA.
Christian Aid, P.O. Box 100, London SE1 7RT, England.
Chronicle Books, 85 Second St., 6th floor, San Francisco, CA 94105, USA.
Church World Service, P.O. Box 968, 28606 Phillips St., Elkhart, IN 46515, USA.
Churchill Media, 6901 Woodley Ave., Van Nuys, CA 91406, USA.
CIIR Publications, Unit 3, Canonbury Yard, 190a New North Rd., London N1 7BJ, England.
Cineaste, 200 Park Ave. South, New York, NY 10003-1503, USA.
Cinema Guild, 1697 Broadway, Ste. 506, New York, NY 10019, USA.
Clarendon/Oxford University Press, Walton St., Oxford OX2 6DP, England.
Clarion Books, c/o Houghton Mifflin, 215 Park Ave. South, New York, NY 10003, USA.
John Henrik Clarke Africana Library, Cornell University, Ithaca, NY 14850, USA.
Cluster Publications, P.O. Box 2400, Pietermaritzburg 3200, South Africa.
CODESRIA, P.O. Box 3304, rue Leon Damas, Fann-Residence, Dakar, Senegal.
College Press, 15 Douglas Rd., P.O. Box 3041, Workington, Harare, Zimbabwe.
Columbia University Press, 136 South Broadway, Irvington, NY 10533, USA.
Columbia University, Institute of African Studies, 1103 International Affairs Bldg., New York, NY 10027, USA.
Committee on International Security Studies, American Academy of Arts and Sciences, 136 Irving St., Cambridge, MA 02138-1996, USA.
Committee to Protect Journalists, 330 Seventh Ave., 12th floor, New York, NY 10001-5010, USA.
Common Courage Press, P.O. Box 702, Monroe, ME 04951, USA
Community Aid Abroad, 156 George St., Fitzroy, VIC 3065, Australia.
Community Publishing Process, Private Bag 7735, Causeway, Harare, Zimbabwe.
Continuum Publishing Group, 370 Lexington Ave., New York, NY 10017-6503, USA.
Copley Publishing Group, 138 Great Rd., Acton, MA 01720, USA.
Cornell University, Africana Studies and Research Center, 310 Triphammer Rd., Ithaca, NY 14853, USA.
Council on Foreign Relations Press, 58 E. 68 St., New York, NY 10021, USA.
Crossroads Press, University of California, Los Angeles, 255 Kinsey Hall, Los Angeles, CA 90024, USA.
CSA Publications, Binghamton University, P.O. Box 6000, Binghamton, NY 13902-6000, USA.
CSISBOOKS, Center for Strategic and International Studies, 1800 K St., NW, Washington, DC 20006, USA.
Cultural Survival, 96 Mt. Auburn St., Cambridge, MA 02138, USA.

James Curry Publishers, 73 Botley Rd., Oxford OX2 0BS, England.
Da Capo Press, 233 Spring St., New York, NY 10013, USA.
Dag Hammarskjöld Centre, Övre Slottsgatan 2, 753 10 Uppsala, Sweden.
Dar es Salaam University, P.O. Box 35182, Dar es Salaam, Tanzania.
Ivan R. Dee, 1332 N. Halstead St., Chicago, IL 60622, USA.
Delta of Nigeria, 5B Aria Rd., P.O. Box 1172, Enugu, Nigeria.
Development Education DEED, East Dorset Professional Education Centre, Lowther Road, Bournemouth BH8 8NR, England.
Development Education Centre, Gillett Centre, 998 Bristol Rd., Selly Oak, Birmingham B29 6LE, England.
Development Education Dispatch Unit, 153, Cardigan Rd., Leeds LS6 1LJ, England.
Development Group for Alternative Policies, 1400 I St., NW, Ste. 520, Washington, DC 20005, USA.
Development Technology Development Group, Ltd., 103-105 Southampton Row, London WC1B 4HH, England.
Disa Press, 2307 Kennwynn Rd., Wilmington, DE 19810, USA.
Documentary Educational Resources, 101 Morse St., Watertown, MA 02172, USA.
Doubleday, c/o Bantam Doubleday Dell, 1540 Broadway, New York, NY 10036.
DSR/Development through Self-Reliance, 9111 Guilford Rd., Columbia, MD 21046, USA.
Earth Resources Research, 258 Pentonville Rd., London N1 9JX, USA.
Earthscan Publications, 120 Pentonville Rd., London N1 9JN, England.
East African Educational Publishers, Brick Court, Mpaka Road/Woodside Grove, Westlands, P.O. Box 45314, Nairobi, Kenya.
Edinburgh University Press, 22 George Sq., Edinburgh EH8 9LF, Scotland.
Edwin Mellen Press, P.O. Box 450, Lewiston, NY 14092-0450, USA.
Edward Elgar, Old Post Rd., Brookfield, VT 05036, USA.
William B. Eerdmans Publishing, 255 Jefferson Ave., SE, Grand Rapids, MI 49503, USA.
Emory University, Institute of African Studies, 101 Social Sciences Bldg., 1555 Pierce Dr., Atlanta, GA 30322, USA.
Environmental Development Action in the Third World (ENDA), P.O. Box 3370, Dakar, Senegal.
Europa Publications, 18 Bedford Square, London WC1B 3JN, England.
European Campaign Against South African Aggression on Mozambique and Angola (ECASAAMA), P.O. Box 839, London NW1 7EF, England.
Evans Brothers, 2A Portman Mansions, Chiltern Street, London W1M 1LE, England.
Facts on File, 11 Penn Plaza, New York, NY 10001-2006, USA.
Faculty of Education, Swansea Institute of Higher Education, Townhill Road, Swansea SA2 0UT, England.
FAFO, Institute for Applied Social Science, P.O. Box 2947, Tøyen, N-0608, Oslo, Norway.
Farrar, Straus and Giroux, 19 Union Square West, New York, NY 10003, USA.

Feminist Press, City University of New York, 311 E. 94th St., New York, NY 10128-5684, USA.
Filmakers Library, 124 E. 40th St., New York, NY 10016, USA.
Films for the Humanities and Sciences, P.O. Box 2053, Princeton, NJ 08543-2053, USA.
Fireside Books/Simon and Schuster, 1230 Avenue of the Americas, New York, NY 10020, USA.
First Run/Icarus Films, 153 Waverly Pl., 6th floor, New York, NY 10014, USA.
Flammarion, c/o Whitechapel Art Gallery, 80-82 Whitechapel High St., London E1 7QX, England.
Food and Agriculture Organization of the United Nations (FAO), Viale delle Terme di Caracalla, Rome 00100, Italy.
Food First Books, 398 60th St., Oakland, CA 94618, USA.
Forum on Debt and Development, Noordeinde 107a, 2514 GE The Hague, The Netherlands.
Fountain Publishers, 4 Arigidi St., Bodija, Ibadan, Nigeria.
Fourth Dimension Publishers, House 16, Fifth Ave., City Layout, PMB 01164, Enugu, Nigeria.
Free Association Books, 39-41 North Rd., London, N7 9DP, England.
Freedom House, 120 Wall St., 26th floor, New York, NY 10005, USA.
Friendship Press, 475 Riverside Dr., Rm. 772, New York, NY 10115, USA.
Full Frame Film and Video Distribution, 394 Euclid Ave., Ste. 201, Toronto, ON M6G 2S9, Canada.
Fund for Peace, 345 E. 46th St., Ste. 712, New York, NY 10017, USA.
Fund for Peace, Horn of Africa Program, 823 United Nations Plaza, Ste. 717, New York, NY 10017, USA.
Gale Research, P.O. Box 33477, Detroit, MI 48232-9853, USA.
Garland Publishing, 717 Fifth Ave., Ste. 2500, New York, NY 10022-8101, USA.
Garnet Publishing, 8 Southern Ct., South St., Reading RG1 4QS, England.
Garrett Park Press, P.O. Box 190, Garrett Park, MD 20896, USA.
GEM Publications, 411 Mallalieu Dr., Hudson, WI 54016, USA.
George Mason University, Institute for Conflict Analysis and Resolution, Fairfax, VA 22030, USA.
Ghana Universities Press, P.O. Box 4219, Accra, Ghana.
Illen Ghebrai, P.O. Box 53247, Washington, DC 20009-9998, USA.
Glenhurst Publications, Central Community Center, 6300 Walker St., St. Louis Park, MN 55416, USA.
Global Assembly Project, WorldWIDE Network, 1331 H St., NW, Rm. 903, Washington, DC 20005, USA.
Global Pesticide Campaigner, c/o Pesticide Action Network, 116 New Montgomery, Ste. 810, San Francisco, CA 94150, USA.
Gower Publishing Co., Old Post Rd., Brookfield, VT 05036, USA.
Graywolf Press, 2402 University Ave., Ste. 203, St. Paul, MN 55114, USA.
Greenwood Press/Greenwood Publishing Group, 88 Post Rd. West, Box 5007, Westport, CT 06881-5007, USA.
Grove/Atlantic, 841 Broadway, New York, NY 10003-4793, USA.
Grove Weidenfeld, c/o Grove Atlantic, 841 Broadway, New York, NY 10003-4793, USA.
Guidebook Press, P.O. Box 30064, Windhoek, Namibia.
Guilford Press, 72 Spring St., New York, NY 10012, USA.
HAAN Academic Publishing, Eurolink Centre, Ste. 61A, 49 Effra Rd., London SW2 1BZ, England.
HAAN Associates, P.O. Box 607, London SW16 1EB, England.
Hamlyn Samuel French Trade, 34-35 Newman St., London W1P 3PD, England.
HarperCollins Publishers, 10 E. 53 St., New York, NY 10022, USA.
HarperSanFrancisco, 1160 Battery St., San Francisco, CA 94111, USA.
Harvard University Press, 79 Garden St., Cambridge, MA 02138, USA.
Heinemann Educational, Heinemann Publishers (Oxford), Halley Court, Jordan Hill, Oxford OX2 8EJ, England.
Heinemann/Reed Publishing, 361 Hanover St., Portsmouth, NH 03801-3912, USA.
Croom Helm, 51 Washington St., Dover, NH 03820, USA.
Henry Holt and Co., 115 W. 18th St., New York, NY 10011, USA.
Heritage Books, 2-8 Calcutta Crescent, Gate 4, P.O. Box 610, Apapa, Lagos, Nigeria.
Lawrence Hill Books, 611 Broadway, Ste. 530, New York, NY 10012, USA.
Lawrence Hill Books/Chicago Review Press, 814 N. Franklin St., Chicago, IL 60610, USA.
Hill and Wang, c/o Farrar, Strauss & Giroux, 19 Union Sq. W., New York, NY 10003, USA.
Houghton Mifflin, 222 Berkeley St., Boston, MA 02116-3764, USA.
Howard University Press, 1240 Randolph St., NE, Washington, DC 20017, USA.
Howard University, African Studies Program, P.O. Box 231, Washington, DC 20059, USA.
Hull Development Education Centre, c/o David Lister School, Rustenburg Street, Hull HU9 2PR, England.
Human Rights Watch, Publications Dept., 485 Fifth Ave., New York, NY 10017-6104, USA.
Human Rights Watch/Africa, 485 Fifth Ave., New York, NY 10017-6104.
Human Rights Watch/Middle East, 485 Fifth Ave., New York, NY 10017-6104.
Human Sciences Research Council, P/Bag X41, 134 Pretorius St., Pretoria 0001, South Africa.
Humanities Press, 165 First Ave., Atlantic Highlands, NJ 07716-1289, USA.
Ibadan University Press, Publishing House, University of Ibadan, Ibadan, Oyo State, Nigeria.
IC Publications/International Communications, 7 Coldbath Sq., London EC1R 4LQ, England.
IDERA Film and Video, 2678 West Broadway, Ste. 200, Vancouver, BC V6K 2G3, Canada.
IDOC International, Via Santa Maria dell'Anima 30, Rome 0186, Italy.
IDRC Books, 250 Albert St., P.O. Box 8500, Ottawa K1G 3H9, Canada.

Ikon, P.O. Box 1355, Stuyvesant Sta., New York, NY 10009, USA.

ILO Publications, International Labour Office, 4, route des Moreillons, CH-1211 Geneva 22, Switzerland.

ILR Press, Cornell University Press, P.O. Box 6525, Ithaca, NY 14851-6525, USA.

Indiana University Press, 601 N. Morton St., Bloomington, IN 47404-3797, USA.

Indiana University, African Studies Program, 221 Woodburn Hall, Bloomington, IN 47405, USA.

Information Project for Africa, P.O. Box 43345, Washington, DC 20010, USA.

Initiatives Publishers, P.O. Box 69313, Nairobi, Kenya.

Institute for African Alternatives, 23 Bevenden St., London N1 6BH, England.

Institute for Conflict Analysis and Resolution, George Mason University, Fairfax, VA 22030, USA.

Institute for Contemporary Studies/ICS Press, 720 Market St., 4th floor, San Francisco, CA 94102, USA.

Institute for Democracy in South Africa, Albion Spring, 183 Main Rd., Rondebosch, Cape Town 7700, South Africa.

Institute for Food and Development Policy, 398 60th St., Oakland, CA 94618, USA.

Institute of Development Studies, University of Sussex, Sussex BN1 9RE, England.

Institute of Human Rights and Humanitarian Law, 19 Sangana St., Humanity Ste., P.O. Box 2292, Port Harcourt, Rivers State, Nigeria.

Institute on Trade Policy, Task Force on Multinational Corporations, P.O. Box 389, Seattle, WA 98111-0389, USA.

Inter Press Service, Via Panisperna, 207, Rome, Italy.

Inter Press Service, Africa Headquarters, P.O. Box 6050, Harare, Zimbabwe.

InterAction, 1717 Massachusetts Ave., NW, Ste. 801, Washington, DC 20036, USA.

Interlink Books, 43 Crosby, Northhampton, MA 01006, USA.

Intermediate Technology Publications, 103/105 Southampton Row, London WC1B 4HH, England.

Intermediate Technology, The Education Office, Myson House, Railway Terrace, Rugby CV21 3HT, England.

International Broadcasting Trust, 2 Ferdinand St., London NW1 8EE, England.

International Catholic Child Bureau, 63, rue de Lausanne, CH-1202 Geneva, Switzerland.

International Center for Research on Women, 1717 Massachusetts Ave., NW, Ste. 302, Washington, DC 20036, USA.

International Center for the Environment and Public Policy, P.O. Box 189040, Sacramento, CA 95818, USA.

International Centre for Human Rights and Democratic Development, 63, rue de Bresoles, Montreal, QU H2Y 1V7, Canada.

International Defence and Aid Fund, University of the Western Cape, Historical and Cultural Centre, Cape Town, South Africa.

International Development Research Centre, IDRC Publications, P.O. Box 8500, Ottawa, ON K1G 3H9, Canada.

International Fund for Agricultural Development, North American Liaison Office, 1889 F St., NW, Washington, DC 20006, USA.

International Human Rights Internship Program, 1400 K St., NW, Ste. 650, Washington, DC 20005, USA.

International Institute for Labour Studies, P.O Box 6, CH-1211 Geneva 22, Switzerland.

International Labour Office, Washington Branch, 1828 L St., NW, Ste. 801, Washington, DC 20036, USA.

International Labour Organization, 4, route des Moreillons, CH-1211 Geneva, Switzerland.

International Library of African Music, c/o ISER, Rhodes University, P.O. Box 94, Grahamstown 6140, South Africa.

International Monetary Fund, 700-19th St., NW, Rm. C100, Washington, DC 20431, USA.

International Negotiation Network, Carter Center of Emory University, One Copenhill, Atlanta, GA 30307, USA.

International Peace Academy, 777 United Nations Plaza, New York, NY 10017, USA.

International Work Group for Indigenous Affairs (IWGIA), Fiolstraede 10, DK-1171 Copenhagen K, Denmark.

Intervention Press/Forlaget Intervention Press, Castenschioldsvej 7, DK-8270 Hojbjerg, Denmark.

Iowa State University Press, 2121 S. State Ave., Ames, IA 50010-8300, USA.

Irish Mozambique Society, 13 Carlisle St., Dublin 8, Ireland.

Island Press/Center for Resource Economics, 1718 Connecticut Ave., NW, Rm. 300, Washington, DC 20009-1148, USA.

Ithaca Press/Garnet Publishing, 8 Southern Ct., South St., Reading, Berkshire RG1 4QS, England.

Jacaranda Designs, P.O. Box 7936, Boulder, CO 80306, USA.

James-Robert Publishing, 15838 N. 62 St., Scottsdale, AZ 85254-1988, USA.

Janus Publishing Company, Duke House, 37 Duke St., London W1M 5DF, England.

Johns Hopkins University Press, 2715 N. Charles St., Baltimore, MD 21218-4319, USA.

Joint Evaluation of Emergency Assistance to Rwanda (Copenhagen). No address given in publication.

Joint Ministry in Africa, United Church of Christ and Disciples of Christ, 475 Riverside Dr., New York, NY 10115, USA.

Kegan Paul International, P.O. Box 256, London WC1B 3SW, England.

Kendall/Hunt Publishers, 4050 Westmark Dr., P.O. Box 1840, Dubuque, IA 52004-1840, USA.

Kliptown Books, 64 Essex Rd., London N1 8LR, England.

Konkori International (Denver). No address available.

Kumarian Press, 14 Oakwood Ave., West Hartford, CT 06119-2127, USA.

Labour, Capital and Society. See Centre for Developing-Area Studies, McGill University.

Lake View Press, P.O. Box 578279, Chicago, IL 60657, USA.

Landmark Films, 3450 Slade Run Dr., Falls Church, VA 22042, USA.

Larousse, 95 Madison Ave., New York, NY 10016, USA.

Lawyers Committee for Human Rights, 333 Seventh Ave., 13th floor, New York, NY 10001, USA.

Leeds Development Education Centre, 151-153 Cardigan Road, Leeds LS6 1LJ, England.

Legal Research and Resource Development Centre, 386 Murtala Muhammed Way, Yaba, P.O. Box 75242, Victoria Island, Lagos, Nigeria.

Leicestershire Multicultural Centre. See Centre for Multicultural Education (Leicester).

Carol Lems-Dworkin Publishers, P.O. Box 1646, Evanston, IL 60204-1646, USA

John Libbey, 13 Smiths Yard, Summerley St., London SW18 4HR, England.

John Libbey Media, Faculty of Humanities, University of Luton, 75 Castle St., Luton, Bedfordshire, LU1 3AJ, England.

Libraries Unlimited, P.O. Box 6633, Englewood, CO 80155-6633, USA.

Limelight Editions/Proscenium Publications, 118 E. 30 St., New York, NY 10016, USA.

Lit Verlag, Dieckstr. 73, Munster 48145, Germany.

Little Brown and Company, 34 Beacon St., Boston, MA 02106, USA.

Longman (USA). See Addison-Wesley Longman.

Longman Group UK, Longman House, Burnt Mill, Harlow, Essex CM20 2JE, England.

Lynne Rienner Publishers, 1800 30 St., Ste. 314, Boulder, CO 80301-1032, USA.

Macmillan Press, Houndmills, Basingstoke, Hampshire RG21 2XS, England.

Macmillan Publishers, 4 Little Essex St., London WC2R 3LF, England.

Macmillan Publishing (USA), c/o Simon and Schuster, 201 W. 103 St., Indianapolis, IN 46290, USA.

Macmillan Reference, 1633 Broadway, 5th floor, New York, NY 10019, USA.

Madiba Publishers, Dept. of Sociology, University of Natal, King George V Ave., Durban 4000, South Africa.

Malthouse Press, P.O. Box 8917, Lagos, Nigeria.

Manchester Development Education Project, c/o Manchester Polytechnic, 801 Wilmslow Road, Manchester M20 8RG, England.

Manchester University Press, Oxford Rd., Manchester M13 9NR, England.

Marshall Cavendish, 99 White Plains Rd., P.O. Box 2001, Tarrytown, NY 10591-9001, USA.

Martinus Nijhoff Publishers, c/o Kluwer Academic Publishers, 101 Philip Dr., Norwell, MA 02061, USA.

Martinus Nijhoff/Wolters Kluwer Academic Publishers, Spuiboulevard 50, P.O. Box 989, 3000 AZ Dordrecht, Netherlands.

Maryknoll World Productions, P.O. Box 308, Maryknoll, NY 10545, USA.

Gary E. McCuen. See GEM Publications.

McFarland and Co., P.O. Box 611, Jefferson, NC 28640, USA.

Media Resource Centre, University of Natal, Dept. of Education, King George V Ave., Durban 4001, South Africa.

Mennonite Central Committee, 21 South 12th St., P.O. Box 500, Akron, PA 17501-0500, USA.

Mercury House, 201 Filbert St., Ste. 400, San Francisco, CA 94133, USA.

Michigan State University, African Studies Center, 100 Center for International Programs, East Lansing, MI 48824, USA.

Millbrook Press, 2 Old New Milford Rd., Brookfield, CT 06804, USA.

Miller Freeman, 600 Harrison St., San Francisco, CA 94107, USA.

Mines Advisory Group, 54a Main St., Cockermouth, Cumbria CA13 9LU, England.

Ministry of Foreign Affairs, Government of The Netherlands, The Hague, The Netherlands.

Minority Rights Group, 379 Brixton Road, London SW9 7DE, England.

MIT Press, 55 Hayward St., Cambridge, MA 02142-1399, USA.

Monthly Review Press, 122 W. 27 St., New York, NY 10001, USA.

Moor Press, Hainsworth House, Damens Lane, Keighley, West Yorkshire BD22 7AR, England.

Mozambique News Agency, 7 Old Bailey, London EC4M 7NB, England.

John Muir Publications, c/o W.W. Norton, 500 Fifth Ave., New York, NY 10110, USA.

Museum Tusculanum Press, University of Copenhagen, Njalsgade 92, DK-2300 Copenhagen, Denmark.

Music Library Association, P.O. Box 487, Canton, MA 02021, USA.

Nairobi University Press, P.O. Box 30197, Nairobi, Kenya.

NAL Books/New American Library, 1633 Broadway, New York, NY 10019, USA.

Namibia Support Committee, 37-39 Great Guilford St., London SE1 0ES, England.

National Academy Press, c/o National Academy of Sciences, 2101 Constitution Ave., NW, Lockbox 285, Washington, DC 20418, USA.

National Council for the Social Studies, 3501 Newark St., NW, Washington, DC 20016, USA.

National Museum of African Art, Smithsonian Institution, Washington, DC 20560, USA.

National Primary Centre, Balden Rd., Harbourne, Birmingham B32 2EH, England.

New American Library, 1633 Broadway, New York, NY 10019, USA.

New Dimension Media, 85803 Lorane Highway, Eugene, OR 97405, USA.

New Directions Publishing Corporation, 80 Eighth Ave., New York, NY 10011, USA.

New Namibia Books, P.O. Box 21601, Windhoek, Namibia.

New People Media Centre, P.O. Box 21681, Nairobi 21681, Kenya.

New Press, 450 W. 41 St., 6th floor, New York, NY 10036, USA.

New Republic Books/Basic Books, c/o Harper Collins, 10 E. 53rd St., New York, NY 10022, USA.

New Society Publishers, P.O. Box 189, Gabrieola Island, BC V0R 1X0, Canada.

New Society Publishers USA, P.O. Box 3245, New Haven, CT 06515, USA.

New York University Press, 70 Washington Sq. South, New York, NY 10012, USA.

New Yorker Films, 16 W. 61st St., New York, NY 10023, USA.

Newman and Westhill Colleges. See National Primary Centre (Birmingham).

Nigerian Institute of International Affairs, 13-15 Kofo Abayomi Rd., Victoria Island, G.P.O. Box 1727, Lagos, Nigeria.

Nightingale/Villon Production, Brophey Rd., Hurleyville, NY 12747, USA.

Nordiska Afrikainstitutet/Nordic Africa Institute, P.O. Box 1703, S-751 47 Uppsala, Sweden.

North American Press, 350 Indiana St., Ste. S-350, Golden, CO 80401, USA.

Northamptonshire Black History Group, c/o Wellingborough REC, Victoria Centre, Palk Road, Wellingborough NN8 1HT, England.

Northwestern University Press, 625 Colfax St., Evanston, IL 60201, USA.

W.W. Norton, 500 Fifth Ave., New York, NY 10110, USA.

Nottinghamshire Education Committee, Centre for Multicultural Education, The Melbourne Centre, Melbourne Rd., Leicester LE2 0GU, England.

NTC Publishing Group, 4255 W. Touhy Ave., Lincolnwood, IL 60646, USA.

Ocean Press, GPO Box 3279, Melbourne, VIC 3001, Australia.

Ocean Press, P.O. Box 020692, Brooklyn, NY 11202, USA.

OCIC Publications, Rue de l'Orme, 8, 1040 Brussels, Belgium.

Ohio University Press, Scott Quadrangle, Athens, OH 45701, USA.

Olive Branch Press/Interlink Publishing Group, 43 Crosby, Northhampton, MA 01006, USA.

One World Action Publications, 13-14 W. Smithfield, Weddel House, 5th floor, London EC1A 9HY, England.

Open Court Publishing, 315 Fifth St., Peru, IL 61354, USA.

Oral Traditions Association of Zimbabwe, P.O Box 7729, Causeway, Harare, Zimbabwe.

Orbis Books, Walsh Bldg., Maryknoll, NY 10545, USA.

Organisation for Economic Co-operation and Development, Development Centre, 2, rue Andre-Pascal, 75775 Paris Cedex 16, France.

Oryx Press, 4041 North Central, Ste. 700, Phoenix, AZ 85012-3397, USA.

Overseas Development Council, 1875 Connecticut Ave., NW, Ste. 1012, Washington, DC 20009, USA.

Overseas Development Institute, Portland House, Stag Pl., London SW1E 5DP, England.

Oxfam (UK and Ireland), 274 Banbury Rd., Oxford OX2 7DZ, England.

Oxfam Publications, 274 Banbury Rd., Oxford OX2 7DZ, England.

Oxford University Press (Australia), GPO Box 2784Y, Melbourne, Vic 3001, Australia.

Oxford University Press (U.K.), Walton St., Oxford OX2 6DP, England.

Oxford University Press (USA), 200 Madison Ave., New York, NY 10016, USA.

Pacifica Communications, P.O. Box 4426, Santa Barbara, CA 93140-4426, USA.

Paladin Grafton Books (London).

Panaf/Zed Books, 7 Cynthia St., London N1 9JF, England.

Pandora Books, c/o Routledge, Chapman and Hall, 29 W. 35 St., New York, NY 10001, USA.

Pandora/Harper Collins, 77-85 Fulham Pl., Hammersmith, London W6 8JB, England.

Panos Institute (UK), 9 White Lion St., London N1 9PD, England.

Panos Institute (USA), 1025 Thomas Jefferson St., NW, Ste. 105, Washington, DC 20007, USA.

Panos Publications, 9 White Lion St., London N1 9PD, England.

Pantheon Books/Random House, 201 E. 50 St., New York, NY 10022, USA.

Paragon House Publishers, 90 Fifth Ave., New York, NY 10011, USA.

PBS Video, 1320 Braddock Pl., Alexandria, VA 22314-1698, USA.

Penguin USA, 375 Hudson St., New York, NY 10014-3657, USA.

Peoples Video Network Store, 39 W. 14th St., New York, NY 10011, USA.

Pesticide Action Network, 116 New Montgomery, Ste. 810, San Francisco, CA 94105, USA.

Phaidon Press, Regent's Wharf, All Saints St., London N1 9PA, England.

David Philip Publishers, 3 Scott Rd., P.O. Box 23408, Claremont 7735, South Africa.

Physicians for Human Rights, 100 Boylston St., Ste. 702, Boston, MA 02116, USA.

Picador USA/St. Martin's Press, c/o Macmillan Publishers, 175 Fifth Ave., New York, NY 10010, USA.

Pierian Press, P.O. Box 1808, Ann Arbor, MI 48106, USA.

Pilgrim Press/United Church of Christ, 475 Riverside Dr., New York, NY 10115, USA.

Pinter Publishers, 25 Floral St., London WC2E 9DS, England.

Pinter Publishers/St. Martin's, 175 Fifth Ave., New York, NY 10010, USA.

Pinter/Cassell, 25 Floral St., Covent Garden, London, WC2E 9DS, England.

Pluto Press, 345 Archway Rd., London N6 5AA, England.

Pluto Press Australia, P.O. Box 199, Leichhardt, NSW 2040, Australia.

Population Council, One Dag Hammarskjold Plaza, New York, NY 10017, USA.

Population Reference Bureau, P.O. Box 96152, Washington, DC 20090-6152, USA.

Poseidon Press/Simon and Schuster, c/o Paramount Communications, 1230 Avenue of the Americas, New York, NY 10020, USA.

Praeger Publishers/Greenwood Publishing Group, 88 Post Rd. West, Box 5007, Westport, CT 06881-5007, USA.

Princeton University Press, 1445 Lower Ferry Rd., Ewing, NJ 08618, USA.

Programme for Development Research (PRODDER), Human Sciences Research Council, P.O. Box 32410, Braamfontein 2107, South Africa.

Pumark Nigeria Educational Publishers, 15, Ogunsefumni St., Anifowose, P.O. Box 4152, Lagos, Nigeria

Quartet Books, 27 Goodge St., London W1P 1FD, England

Raintree Steck-Vaughan, c/o National Education Corp., P.O. Box 26015, Austin, TX 78755, USA.

Ravan Press, P.O. Box 31334, Braamfontein 2017, South Africa.

Readers International, P.O. Box 959, Columbia, LA 71418-0959, USA.

Reading International Support Centre and Voluntary Service Overseas, 103 London St., Reading RG1 4QA, England.

Red Sea Press, P.O. Box 1892, Trenton, NJ 08607, USA; 11 Princess Rd., Ste. D. Lawrenceville, NJ 08648-2319, USA..
Reference and Research Services, 511 Lincoln St., Santa Cruz, CA 95060, USA.
Refugee Council, Bondway House, 3-9 Bondway, London, SW8, England.
Reporters Sans Frontières, 5, rue Geoffroy-Marie, 75009 Paris, France.
Research Group on African Development Perspectives, Institute for World Economics and International, Management, University of Bremen, P.O. Box 330440, 28334 Bremen, Germany.
Resource Center Press, P.O. Box 4506, Albuquerque, NM 87196, USA.
Review of African Political Economy, P.O. Box 678, Sheffield S1 1BF, England.
ROAPE Publications, P.O. Box 678, Sheffield S1 1BF, England.
Editions Rodopi, Keizersgracht 302-304, 1016 EX Amsterdam, The Netherlands.
Rosen Publishing Group, 29 E. 21 St., New York, NY 10010, USA.
Rough Guides, One Mercer St., London WC2H 9QL, England. Distributor: Penguin Books.
Routledge, 29 W. 35 St., New York, NY 10001-2291, USA.
Routledge (UK), 11 New Fetter Lane, London EC4P 4EE, England.
Routledge Journals, Cheriton House, North Way, Andover SP10 5BE, England.
Rowman and Littlefield Publishers, 4720 Boston Way, Lanham, MD 20706, USA.
Royal Albert Memorial Museum, Queen Street, Exeter, Devon England.
Royal Ontario Museum (Toronto).
Royal Tropical Institute, Mauritskade 63, NL 1092 AD Amsterdam, Netherlands.
Rutgers University Press, Livingston Campus, Bldg. 4161, P.O. Box 5062, New Brunswick, NJ 08903, USA.
Sage Publications, 2455 Teller Rd., Thousand Oaks, CA 91320, USA.
Sahara Fund, 4438 Tindall St., NW, Washington, DC 20016, USA.
St. James Press, 233 E. Ontario, Ste. 600, Chicago, CA 60611, USA.
St. Martin's Press, 175 Fifth Ave., New York, NY 10010, USA.
St. Martin's Press, Scholarly & Reference Division, 275 Park Ave. South, New York, NY 10010, USA.
St. Olaf College, 1170 Cannon Valley Dr., No. 46, Northfield, MN 55057, USA.
Sapes Books, c/o Sapes Trust, P.O. Box MP111, Mount Pleasant, Harare, Zimbabwe.
K.G. Saur/Reed Reference Publishing Company, 121 Chanlon Rd., New Providence, NJ 07974-9903, USA.
Save the Children, Education Unit, 17 Grove Lane, London SE5 8BRD, England.
Scandinavian Institute of African Studies, Dragarbrunnsgatan 24, Box 1703, Uppsala S-751 47, Sweden.
Scarecrow Press/Grolier Educational Corp., 4720 Boston Way, Ste. A, Lanham, MD 20706-4310, USA.
Schelzky and Jeep. See Research Group on African Development Perspectives.

Schenkman Books, 118 Main St., Rochester, VT 05767, USA.
Schlessinger Video (Bala Cynwyd, Wales).
Scottish Education and Action for Development (SEAD), 23 Castle St., Edinburgh EH2 3DN, Scotland.
Charles Scribner's Sons/Macmillan, 1633 Broadway, 5th floor, New York, NY 10019-6785, USA.
Sead, 23 Castle St., Edinburgh EH2 3DN, Scotland.
M. E. Sharpe, 80 Business Park Dr., Armonk, NY 10504, USA.
Hilary Shipman, 19 Framfield Rd., Highbury, London N5 1UU, England.
Sierra Club Books, 100 Bush St., 13th floor, San Francisco, CA 94104, USA.
Sigma Forlag. See Scandinavian Institute of African Studies.
Simon and Schuster/Paramount Communications, 1230 Avenue of the Americas, New York, NY 10020, USA.
Skotaville Publishers, 35 Malle St., 2nd floor, Northside, P.O. Box 32483, Braamfontein 2107, South Africa.
Smithsonian Institution Press, 470 L'Enfant Plaza, Ste. 470, Washington, DC 20560, USA.
Smyrna Press, P.O. Box 1803–GPO, Brooklyn, NY 11202, USA.
Snoeck-Ducaju and Zoon. See University of Washington Press.
South Centre, Chemin du Champ-d'Anier 17, 1211 Geneva 19, Switzerland.
South End Press, 116 St. Botolph St., Boston, MA 02115, USA.
Southern Africa Grantmakers' Affinity Group, c/o Henry J, Kaiser Family Foundation, 1450 G St., NW, Ste. 250, Washington, DC 20005, USA.
Southern African Research and Documentation Centre (Harare). Distributed by African Books Collective (Oxford).
SPA Publications, Guzmán el Bueno, 21, 28015 Madrid, Spain.
Spear Books. See East African Educational Publishers.
Spectrum Books, Sunshine House, 2nd Commercial Rd., Gluyole Estate, PMB 5612, Ibadan, Nigeria.
Spectrum Law Publishing (see above).
Spectrum Publications Pty Ltd, 61 Somerset St, P.O. Box 75, Richmond, Victoria 3121, Australia.
Stanford University, Center for African Studies, 114 Littlefield Hall, 300 Lausen St., Stanford, CA 94305-5013, USA.
Steck-Vaughn, P.O. Box 26015, Austin, TX 78755, USA.
Struik Christian Books, P.O. Box 3755, Cape Town, 8000, South Africa.
Study Circles Resource Center, P.O. Box 203, Pomfret, CT 06258, USA.
Summit Books/Simon and Schuster, c/o Paramount Communications, 1230 Avenue of the Americas, New York, NY 10020, USA.
Swallow Press/Ohio University Press, Ohio University, Scott Quadrangle, Athens, OH 45701, USA.
Swedish NGO Foundation for Human Rights, Drottninggatan 101, S-113 60 Stockholm, Sweden.
Syracuse University Press, 1600 Jamesville Ave., Syracuse, NY 13244-5160, USA.
I.B. Tauris/St. Martin's Press, 175 Fifth Ave., New York, NY 10010, USA.
Taylor and Francis, 1900 Frost Rd., Suite 101, Bristol, PA 19007-1598, USA.

Television Trust for the Environment, Prince Albert Rd., London NW1 4RZ, England.
Temple University Press, Broad and Oxford Streets, Philadelphia, PA 19122, USA.
Ten Days for Global Justice, 77 Charles St. West, Ste. 401, Toronto, ON M5S 1K5, Canada.
Ten Days for World Development. See Ten Days for Global Justice.
Thames and Hudson/W.W. Norton, 500 Fifth Ave., New York, NY 10110, USA.
Third World First, 217 Cowley Rd., Oxford OX4 1XG, England.
Third World Network, 228 Macalister Rd., 10400 Penang, Malaysia.
Third World Network, P.O. Box 8604, Accra-North, Ghana.
Third World Press, 7524 S. Cottage Grove, Chicago, IL 60019, USA.
Three Continents Press, P.O. Box 38009, Colorado Springs, CO 80937-8009, USA.
Times Books/Random House, 201 E. 50 St., New York, NY 10022, USA.
Touchstone Books/Simon and Schuster, c/o Paramount Communications, 1230 Avenue of the Americas, New York, NY 10020, USA.
Transaction Publishers, Rutgers—The State University, New Brunswick, NJ 08903, USA.
Turning Tide Productions, P.O. Box 864, Wendell, MA 01379, USA.
21st Century Africa, 818 18th St., NW, Ste. 810, Washington, DC 20006, USA.
U.S. Committee for Refugees, 1717 Massachusetts Ave., NW, Ste. 701, Washington, DC 20036, USA.
U.S. Government Printing Office, Mail Stop SM, Washington, DC 20401, USA.
U.S. Institute of Peace, 1550 M St., NW, Ste. 700, Washington, DC 20005-1708, USA.
UN Development Program, 1889 F St., NW, Washington, DC 20006, USA.
UN Non-Governmental Liaison Service, DC2, Rm. 1103, New York, NY 10017, USA.
UN Publications, United Nations, Rm. DC2-853, New York, NY 10017, USA.
UN Research Institute for Social Development (UNRISD), Palais des Nations, 1211 Geneva 10, Switzerland.
UNESCO, 1 rue Miollis, 75015 Paris, France.
Ungar Publishing Company, 370 Lexington Ave., New York, NY 10017, USA.
União dos Escritores Angolanos, CP 2767-C, Luanda, Angola.
UNICEF-UK, 55 Lincoln's Inn Fields, London WC2A 3NB, England.
Unitarian Universalist Service Committee, 130 Prospect St., Cambridge, MA 02139-1813, USA.
United Nations Publications, Palais des Nations, Geneva CH-1211, Switzerland.
United States Institute of Peace Press, 1550 M St., NW, Ste. 700, Washington, DC 20005, USA.
University of Botswana, PB 0022, Gaborone, Botswana.
University of California—Berkeley, African Studies Center, 356 Stevens Hall, Berkeley, CA 94720, USA.
University of California—Los Angeles, African Studies Center, 10244 Bunche Hall, 405 Hilgard Ave., Los Angeles, CA 90024, USA.
University of California Press, 2120 Berkeley Way, Berkeley, CA 94720, USA.
University of California, Institute of International Studies, 215 Moses Hall, Berkeley, CA 94720, USA.
University of Chicago Press, 5801 Ellis Ave., Chicago, IL 60637, USA.
University of Florida, Center for African Studies, 427 Grinter Hall, Gainesville, FL 32611-2048, USA.
University of Illinois Press, 1325 South Oak St., Champaign, IL 61820, USA.
University of Illinois, Center for African Studies, 210 International Studies Bldg., 910 S. Fifth St., Champaign, IL 61820, USA.
University of Massachusetts Press, P.O. Box 429, Amherst, MA 01004, USA.
University of Michigan Press, 839 Greene St., P.O. Box 1104, Ann Arbor, MI 48106-1104, USA.
University of Michigan, Center for Near Eastern and North Africa Studies, 144 Lane Hall, Ann Arbor, MI 48109, USA.
University of Minnesota Press, 2037 University Ave., SE, Minneapolis, MN 55414-3092, USA.
University of Natal Library, P.O. Box 375, Pietermaritzburg, Natal 3200, South Africa.
University of Nebraska Press, 901 N. 17th St., Lincoln, NE 68588, USA.
University of New Mexico Press, 1720 Lomas Blvd., NE, Albuquerque, NM 87131-1591, USA.
University of North Carolina Press, P.O. Box 2288, Chapel Hill, NC 27515-2288, USA.
University of Notre Dame Press, P.O. Box L, Notre Dame, IN 46556, USA.
University of Oklahoma Press, 1005 Asp Ave., Norman, OK 73069-0445, USA.
University of Pennsylvania, African Studies Program, University Museum, Rm. 418, 33rd and Spruce Streets, Philadelphia, PA 19104-6398, USA.
University of Pittsburgh Press, 127 N. Bellefield Ave., Pittsburgh, PA 15260, USA.
University of South Carolina Press, 937 Assembly St., Carolina Plaza, 8th floor, Columbia, SC 29208, USA.
University of Texas Press, P.O. Box 7819, Austin, TX 78712-7819, USA.
University of Washington Press, University of Washington, P.O. Box 50096, Seattle, WA 98145-5096, USA.
University of Washington Press, P.O. Box 50096, Seattle, WA 98145-5096, USA.
University of Wisconsin - Milwaukee, 3243 N. Downer Ave., Milwaukee, WI 53211, USA.
University of Wisconsin Press, 114 North Murray St., Madison, WI 53715-1199, USA.
University of Wisconsin, African Studies Program, 1454 Van Hise, 1220 Linden Dr., Madison, WI 53706-1557, USA.
University of Zimbabwe Publications, Publications Office, P.O. Box MP45, Mount Pleasant, Harare, Zimbabwe.
University Press of America, 4720 Boston Way, Lanham, MD 20706, USA.

University Press of Colorado, P.O. Box 849, Niwot, CO 80544, USA.

University Press of Florida, 15 N.W. 15th St., Gainesville, FL 32603, USA.

University Press of Virginia, P.O. Box 3608, University Sta., Charlottesville, VA 22903, USA.

UNRISD, War-torn Societies Project, Palais des Nations, 1211 Geneva 10, Switzerland.

Unwin Hyman, 955 Massachusetts Ave., Cambridge, MA 02139, USA.

Upper Midwest Women's History Center, c/o Hamline University, 1536 Hewitt Ave., St. Paul, MN 55104-1284, USA.

Verso, 180 Varick St., New York, NY 10014-4606, USA.

Verso, 6 Meard St., London W1V 3HR, England.

Victor Gollancz, Villiers House, 41-47 Strand, London WC2N 5JE, England.

Victoria International Development Association (VIDEA), 407-620 View St., Victoria, BC V8W 1J6, Canada.

VSO, Development Education Unit, 317 Putney Bridge Road, London SW15 2PN, England.

Warwickshire World Studies Centre, Manor Hall, Sandy Lane, Leamington Spa, Warks CV32 6RD, England.

Waveland Press, P.O. Box 400, Prospect Heights, IL 60070, USA.

Wayland Publishers, 61 Western Rd., Hove, East Sussex BN3 1JD, England.

WCC Publications, 150 route de Ferney, P.O. Box 2100, 1211 Geneva 2, Switzerland.

Wesleyan University Press, 110 Mount Vernon St., Middletown, CT 06457, USA.

Western Sahara Awareness Project. Closed U.S. office in Jamaica Plain, Massachusetts.

Western Sahara Campaign, Oxford Chambers, Oxford Pl., Leeds, LS1 3AX, England.

Westview Press, 5500 Central Ave., Boulder, CO 80301-2877, USA.

Markus Wiener Publishers, 114 Jefferson Rd., Princeton, NJ 08540, USA.

John Wiley and Sons, 605 Third Ave., New York, NY 10158-0012, USA.

William Morrow and Company, 1350 Avenue of the Americas, New York, NY 10019, USA.

Professor Iolo Wyn Williams, School of Education, University College, of North Wales, Lon Pobty, Bangor, Gwynedd LL57 1DZ, Wales.

Winrock International Institute for Agricultural Development, 1611 Kent St., No. 600, Arlington, VA 22209, USA; Rt. 3, Box 376, Morrilton, AR 72110-9537, USA.

Witwatersrand University Press, 1 Jan Smuts Ave., Johannesbury 2001, South Africa.

Woeli Publishing Services, P.O. Box K601, Accra, New Town Ghana.

Women and AIDS Support Network, 83 Montgomery Rd., Highlands, Harare, Zimbabwe.

Women and Autonomy Centre, Leiden University, P.O. Box 9555, 2300 RB Leiden, The Netherlands.

Women and Law in Southern Africa, P.O. Box UA171, Union Ave., Harare, Zimbabwe.

Women in the World, 1030 Spruce St., Berkeley, CA 94707, USA.

Women Make Movies, 462 Broadway, Ste. 500, New York, NY 10013, USA.

Women's Press, 34 Great Sutton St., London EC1V 0DX, England.

Woodcraft Folk, 13 Ritherdon Rd., London SW17 8QE, England.

World Bank Publications, 1818 H St., NW, Washington, DC 20433, USA.

World Bank, European Office, 66 Avenue d'Iena, Paris 75116, France.

World Council of Churches Publications, P.O. Box 2100, 1211 Geneva 2, Switzerland.

World Food Day Association of Canada, 400 176 Gloucester St., Ottawa, ON K2P 0A6, Canada.

World Health Organization, Global Programme on AIDS, 1211 Geneva 27, Switzerland.

World Hunger Education Service, P.O. Box 29056, Washington, DC 20017, USA.

World Music Press, Multicultural Materials for Educators, P.O. Box 2565, Danbury, CT 06813, USA.

World Music Productions, 688 Union St., Brooklyn, NY 11215, USA.

World Priorities, P.O. Box 25140, Washington, DC 20007, USA.

World Wide Fund for Nature, Panda House, Weyside Park, Godalming, Surrey GU7 1XR, England.

World Wildlife Fund International, World Conservation Centre, Ave. du Mont-Blanc, CH-1196 Gland, Switzerland.

World Wildlife Fund Publications, P.O. Box 4866, Hampden PO, Baltimore, MD 21211, USA.

World Wildlife Fund UK, P.O. Box 963, Slough SL2 3RS, England.

Worldmark Press/John Wiley and Sons, 605 Third Ave., New York, NY 10158, USA.

WorldViews, 464 19th St., Oakland, CA 94612-2297, USA.

Writers and Readers Publishing, P.O. Box 461, Village Sta., New York, NY 10111, USA.

Yale University Press, 92A Yale Station, New Haven, CT 06520, USA.

Yale University, African Studies Center, 85 Trumbull St., P.O. 13A, New Haven, CT 06520, USA.

Zed Books, 7 Cynthia St., London N1 9JF, England.

Hans Zell Publishers, c/o Bowker-Saur/Reed Reference Publishing, 60 Grosvenor St., London W1X 9DA, England.

Hans Zell Publishers/Bowker-Saur, 121 Chanlon Rd., New Providence, NJ 07974, USA.

Zero Population Growth, 1601 Connecticut Ave., N.W., Washington, DC 20009, USA.

Zimbabwe Book Publishers' Association, 12 Selous Ave., Harare, Zimbabwe.

Zimbabwe Publishing House, P.O. Box 350, Harare, Zimbabwe.

Zimbabwe Women Writers, 78 Kaguri St., Harare, Zimbabwe.

Zimbabwe Women's Resource Centre and Network, Stemar House, Rm. 203, Corner Speke Ave., and Kaguvi St., Harare, Zimbabwe.

# NAMES INDEX

Aall, Pamela, 160
Aarnink, Nettie, 110, 111
Abarry, Abu S., 141
Abbas, Ali Abdalla, 92
Abbott, George C., 29, 149
Abdouli, Abdelhamid, 172
Abiodun, Rowland, 102, 180
Abu-Lughod, Lila, 104, 180
Achebe, Chinua, 71, 100, 102, 155
Acree, Eric S. Kofi, 23, 143
Adam, Heribert, 90, 164
Adam, Hussein M., 54, 161
Adams, W. M., 46, 176
Adar, Korwa G., 159
Adedeji, Adebayo, 30, 37, 140, 156
Adejumobi, Said, 165
Adelman, Howard, 84, 85, 142
Adepoju, Aderanti, 80, 82
Adesina, Jimi, 159
Adjibolosoo, Senyo B-S. K., 39, 156, 170
Adler, Taffy, 6
Adzinyah, Abraham Kobena, 159
Afigbo, A. E., 160
Aguayo, Sergio, 152
Aina, Tade Akin, 85, 161
Ajayi, J. F. A., 3
Akatch, Samuel O., 47, 151
Ake, Claude, 150
Akeroyd, Anne V., 14
Akinbami, Ademola, 11, 170
Akivaga, S. Kichamu, 69, 174
Al-Qazzaz, Ayad, 6, 144
Alberts, Dr. Louw, 19, 169
Alexander, Neville, 90, 171
Alexander, Pat, 19, 151
Ali, Taisier Mohamed Ahmed, 92
Alier, Abel, 93, 172
Allaby, Michael, 46, 150

Allen, Tim, 86, 87, 157, 177
Allen, V. L., 74, 156
Allison, Caroline, 98, 158
Alperson, Myra, 91, 153
Amara, Hamid Ait, 50, 140
Ambrose, Brendalyn P., 56, 150
Amin, Samir, 33, 66
Amuta, Chidi, 71, 174
An-Na'im, Abdullahi A., 57, 154, 156
Anderson, David M., 69, 169
Anderson, Vicki, 149
Andrade-Watkins, Claire, 21, 149
Andreassen, Bård-Anders, 156
Andrzejewski, B. W., 69
Andrzejewski, Sheila, 69
Anikpo, Mark O. C., 57, 151
Annison, Nancy C.,
Anstee, Margaret Joan, 164
Arat, Zehra F., 34, 150
Arcese, Peter, 170
Ardener, Shirley, 110, 161
Arivisala, Femi, 173
Armes, Roy, 20, 144, 174
Armstrong, Alice, 58, 110, 111, 159, 173, 175
Arnold, Guy, 171
Asante, Molefi Kete, 63, 141, 174
Asante, S. K. B., 37, 141
Ashcroft, Bill, 71, 152
Atiya, Nayra, 104, 159
Atkins, Keletso E., 66, 161
Atkinson, Doreen, 90, 171
Atmore, Anthony, 140
Austin, Kathi, 27, 158
Ayittey, George B., 139
Ayubi, Nazih, 18, 165
Azodo, Ama Usoamaka, 107, 152

Babu, Abdul Rahman Mohamed, 142
Bachy, Victor, 21, 174
Badian, Seydou, 153
Bagdikian, Ben, 63, 161
Bakari, Imruh, 20, 141
Baker, Jonathan, 85, 161, 167
Baker, Philip, 158
Balcomb, Anthony, 19, 174
Ballara, Marcela, 109, 178
Balogun, Françoise, 21, 148
Bandarage, Asoka, 81
Bangura, Yusuf, 145
Banham, Martin, 70, 147
Barber, Karin, 70, 176
Barhey, Sukhvinder Kaur, 7
Barker, Jonathan, 38, 166
Barker, Rhiannon, 145
Barkin, David, 50, 153
Barley, Nigel, 101, 171
Barlow, Sean, 78, 143
Barnard, Alan, 11, 158
Barnard, David, 172
Barnes, Virginia Lee, 107, 144
Barnet, Richard J., 64, 155
Barnett, Tony, 13, 143
Baron, Beth, 110, 178
Barraclough, Solon L., 51, 152
Barry, Tom, 54, 163
Baskin, Jeremy, 66, 172
Bass, Hans H., 152
Basset, Mary T., 155
Bassett, Thomas J., 50, 159
Basu, Amrita, 109, 147
Batlouni, Barbara Shahin, 22
Batt, Rosemary L., 153
Baur, John, 18
Bauzon, Kenneth E., 29, 150
Bayart, Jean-Francois, 35, 172
Baylies, Carolyn, 67, 179
Beach, David, 8, 9, 170
Becker, Charles M., 30, 145
Becker, Eddie, 93, 97, 148
Bediako, Kwame, 18, 147

Béhague, Gerard H., 78, 162
Beier, Ulli, 69, 165
Belcher, Stephen, 164
Bello, Walden, 28, 149
Bender, Wolfgang, 78, 165
Bennett, Olivia, 26, 46, 145, 155
Benthall, Jonathan, 61, 151
Bequele, A., 66, 153
Berer, Marge, 14, 178
Berger, Iris, 66, 67, 110, 174, 177
Bergesen, Helge Ole, 46, 155
Berkman, Joyce Avrech, 107, 155
Berman, Bruce J., 27, 38, 140, 175
Bernstein, Henry, 50, 153
Berry, Ian, 89, 160
Berry, L., 73, 141
Berry, Sara, 51, 163
Besteman, Catherine, 54, 173
Bever, Edward, 139
Bexley, Jo, 145
Bigman, Laura, 51, 156
Bijlmakers, Leon A., 31, 155
Bingham, Marjorie Wall, 177
Birmingham, David, 150
Björkman, Ingrid, 70, 161
Bjornson, Richard, 71, 142
Blaikie, Piers, 13, 143
Blakely, Thomas D., 16, 19, 169
Blibolo, Auguste Didier, 153
Blier, Suzanne Preston, 103, 142
Blight, James G., 27, 173
Blignaut, Johan, 22, 161
Blunt, Alison, 175
Boahen, A. A., 3
Boddy, Janice, 107, 144
Boesak, Allan A., 19, 157
Boesak, Willa, 19, 155
Bohannan, Paul, 139

190  AFRICA WORLD PRESS GUIDE

Bond, George C., 10, 13, 143
Bonner, Philip, 89, 144
Booker, Claire, 7
Boonzaier, Emile, 171
Botha, Martin, 22, 157, 161
Boulares, Habib, 18, 158
Bourgault, Louis M., 63, 160
Boustani, Rafic, 17, 145
Boutwell, Jeffrey, 26, 159
Boyd, Herb, 141
Boyd, Rosalind E., 64, 139, 158
Boyd-Barrett, Oliver, 62, 148
Boylan, Esther, 58, 109, 178
Brace, Steve, 7
Bradshaw, Mark, 78, 153
Braidotti, Rosi, 109, 179
Braun, Elisabeth, 47, 166
Brecher, Jeremy, 64, 155
Brenner, Louis, 18, 162
Brett, Michael, 9, 145
Bricker, Dale, 148
Brinkerhoff, Derick W., 51, 158
Brockman, Norbert C., 11, 140
Broughton, Simon, 76, 180
Brown, Barbara, 3
Brown, John Russell, 70, 164
Brown, Joshua, 63, 156
Brown, Lester R., 46, 81, 154, 180
Brown, Michael Barratt, 31, 72, 73, 74, 140, 170
Brown, Nicole A., 82, 176
Brown, R. P. C., 31, 173
Bruce, John W., 50, 170
Bruner, Charlotte, 106, 155
Bryant, Coralie, 50, 166
Bryceson, Deborah Fahy, 51, 153, 159
Brydon, Lynne, 31
Brzoska, Michael, 25, 26, 144
Buchanan-Smith, Margaret, 160
Bugul, Ken, 107, 139
Bujo, Benezet, 18, 142
Bukenya, Austin, 70, 175
Bulliet, Richard W., 158
Bullock, Susan, 109, 178
Bullwinkle, Davis A., 57, 111, 142
Bundy, Carol, 163
Bunn, David, 70, 154
Burenhult, Goran, 10, 175
Burger, Julian, 169
Burkey, Stan, 36, 165
Burman, Sandra, 110, 161
Burnard, P., 14, 177

Burne, Simon, 39, 159
Burnell, Peter J., 41, 147
Burr, J. Millard, 43, 167, 169
Busby, Margaret, 105, 149
Busia, Nana, 57, 172
Buthelezi, Sipho, 89, 171
Byaruhanga-Akiiki, A. B. T., 147
Byrne, Pamela R., 111, 179
Callaghy, Thomas M., 29, 65, 156
Callaway, Barbara, 18, 156
Cameron, Kenneth M., 62, 139
Campbell, Ian D., 15, 143
Campschreur, Willem, 70, 149
Cancel, Robert, 69
Cannizzo, Jeanne, 101, 158
Caporaso, James A., 64, 147
Carrim, Yunus, 159
Carter, Nick, 45, 176
Carver, Richard, 57, 58, 86, 162, 175
Cassanelli, Lee V., 54, 173
Cassen, Robert, 40, 81, 151, 166
Cater, Nick, 173
Cavanagh, John, 64, 155
Cawthra, Gavin, 91, 165, 171
Chabal, Patrick, 35, 165
Chabot, J., 142
Chachage, C. S. L., 161
Chakraborty, Manab, 163
Chaligha, Amon, 35, 144, 166
Cham, Mbye B., 20, 141, 149
Charny, Israel W., 177
Chatteris, Chris, 145
Chazan, Naomi, 35, 166
Chen, Lincoln C., 166
Chenje, Munyaradzi, 46, 172
Chernoff, John Miller, 142
Chigudu, Hope Bagyendera, 111, 164, 172, 179
Chikane, Rev. Dr. Frank, 19, 169
Chilcote, Ronald H., 11, 144
Childers, Roberta, 46, 179
Chiluba, Frederick J. T., 35, 150
Chipasula, Frank Mkalawile, 69, 106, 155, 177
Chipasula, Stella, 69, 106, 155
Chipenda, Jose Belo, 32
Chirimuuta, Richard C., 12, 143
Chirimuuta, Rosalind J., 12, 143
Chitere, Orieko, 39, 179

Chiwome, Emmanuel M., 149
Chizea, Dora Obi, 163
Chowdhury, Najma, 109, 178
Christie, Iain, 11, 170
Chukukere, Gloria, 106, 154
Cimbala, Stephen J., 27, 149
Ciment, James, 144
Clark, David, 74, 164
Clark, Gracia, 110, 164
Clark, Leon E., 174
Clarke, Donald, 78, 165
Clarke, John Henrik, 142
Clarke, Walter, 54, 159
Clay, Edward, 42, 43, 179
Clayton, Sue, 72
Cleaver, Tessa, 98, 162
Cleveland, Harlan, 53, 163
Cliffe, Lionel, 99, 175
Clingman, Stephen, 107, 163
Cochrane, J. R., 19, 146
Cock, Jacklyn, 26, 91, 178
Cockcroft, Laurence, 140
Cohen, Robin, 34, 67, 84, 147, 150, 158, 179
Cohen, Ronald, 57, 156
Cohn, Ilene, 26, 147
Colchester, Marcus, 47, 173
Cole, Ken, 91, 173
Coles, Catherine M., 163
Colewell, B. D., 79
Collins, Cindy, 53, 157
Collins, John, 78, 162, 176
Collins, Joseph, 49, 179
Collins, Robert O., 43, 147, 151, 156, 167, 169, 176, 179
Commins, Stephen K., 140
Conchiglia, Augusta, 27, 175
Connell, Dan, 97, 143
Connors, Margaret, 179
Conteh-Morgan, John, 70, 174
Cooper, Barbara M., 160
Cooper, Frederick, 65, 148
Coplan, David B., 78, 157
Copson, Raymond W., 140
Coquery-Vidrovitch, Catherine, 109, 140, 142
Cordell, Dennis D., 83, 142
Corea, Gena, 158
Cornia, Giovanni Andrea, 29, 140, 154
Coronel, Michael A., 102
Coronel, Patricia Crane, 102, 103
Correa, Sonia, 81, 166
Costello, Tim, 64, 155
Coulon, Virginia, 163
Cowie, Peter, 21, 23, 176

Cramer, Anne, 176
Crane, Louise, 169
Cranna, Michael, 175
Creevey, Lucy, 18, 156
Criticos, Costas, 161
Crocker, Chester A., 25, 160
Cross, Nigel, 145
Cross, Sholto, 13, 14, 153
Crum, David Leith, 163
Crummey, Donald E., 50, 159, 169
Crump, Andy, 46, 150
Crush, Jonathan, 66, 67, 74, 149
Culbertson, Debbie, 28, 32, 150, 154
Cunningham, Shea, 149
Curling, Jonathan, 72
Curtin, Philip, 139
Curtis, Donald, 50, 166
Cutrufelli, Maria Rosa, 110, 179
Cyr, Helen W., 23, 174
Dady, Bernard, 7
Dadzie, K. K. S., 34, 36, 164
Dale, Richard, 35, 146
Daly, M, W., 173
Damrosch, Lori Fisler, 27, 152
Danaher, Kevin, 30, 49, 153, 162
Daniel, Donald C. F., 27, 145
Daniel, John, 57, 139
Dankwa, E, V, O., 158
Darmani, Lawrence, 143
David, Antony E., 146
David, Rosalie, 102, 146, 151
Davidson, Andrew P., 157
Davidson, Art, 10, 152
Davidson, Basil, 2, 3, 141, 146, 159, 161, 170, 172
Davidson, Joan, 45, 46, 163
Davies, Carole Boyce, 105, 163, 178
Davies, Julian, 86, 87, 151
Davies, Robert, 171
Davies, Wendy, 6, 39, 159
Davis, R. Hunt, Jr., 142
Davis, Dennis, 91, 145
de Heusch, Luc, 101, 164
De Silva, Donatus, 39
de Villiers, Les, 157
de Waal, Alex, 45, 53, 54, 163, 170, 171
Debroey, Steven, 89, 171
Decalo, Samuel, 26, 149
Dejene, Alemneh, 43, 51, 152
Dekmejian, R. Hrair, 158
DeLancey, Mark W., 155, 156
Delius, Peter, 144

**NAMES INDEX** **191**

Delpeuch, Bertrand, 49, 170
Deng, Francis M., 27, 43, 57, 85, 92, 93, 147, 156, 167, 172, 173, 176
Denslow, Julie Sloan, 10, 165
DeShazer, Mary K., 107, 165
Destexhe, Alain, 27, 170
Deutschmann, David, 98, 147
DeWalt, Billie R., 153
Dewey, Arthur E., 53
Dgni-Sgui, Ren, 57, 172
Diamond, Larry, 150
Diawara, Manthia, 21, 140
Dibango, Manu, 78, 174
Dicker, Richard, 99, 139
Dickstein, Ruth, 111, 178
Diescho, Joseph, 75, 98, 146
Dinavo, Jacques V., 167
Dingake, Michael, 162
Dinham, Barbara, 49, 143
Diop, Cheikh Anta, 146
Diouf, Mamadou, 57, 139
Distefano, John A., 150
Divendal, Joost, 70, 149
DjeDje, Jacqueline Cogdell, 170
Dodge, Cole P., 26, 167
Doll, Susanne, 151
Dolphyne, 107
Donadoni, Sergio, 11, 151
Donham, Donald L., 67, 179
Doornbos, Martin, 26, 93, 97, 145
Dorkenoo, Efua, 110, 149, 153
Doumou, Abdelali, 33
Dow, Hugh, 38, 166
Dowuona-Hammond, Christine, 57, 169
Draffan, George, 73, 176
Drake, St. Clair, 146
Drew, Allison, 171
Drewal, Henry J., 180
Dreyer, Libby, 175
Drisdelle, Rhéal, 160
Dropkin, Greg, 74, 164
Drumtra, Jeff, 163
Drysdale, John, 54, 177
du Toit, Pierre, 35, 172
Dubow, Saul, 170
Duerden, Dennis, 101, 140
Duffield, Mark, 53, 97, 159, 177
Duley, Margot I., 57, 149
Duncan, Alex, 30, 173
Dunton, Chris, 70, 160
Dwyer, Kevin, 57, 144
Edwards, Mary I., 57, 149
Egerö, Bertil, 35, 162

Egziabher, Axumite G., 51, 148
Eicher, Carl K., 51, 180
Eilersen, Gillian Stead, 106, 145
Ekechi, Felix K., 110, 141
Ekoko, A. E., 163
El Dareer, Asma, 176
El Fasi, M., 3
El Saadawi, Nawal, 161
El-Ayouty, Yassin, 164
Ela, Jean-Marc, 18, 141
Ellis, Stephen, 139
Elworthy, Scilla, 110, 153
Emeagwali, Gloria T., 30, 179
Emecheta, Buchi, 106
English, E. Philip, 141, 143
Enquist, Roy J., 98, 162
Entwisle, Barbara, 163
Epps, Ken, 24
Ergas, Zaki, 35, 90, 142, 147
Erickson, Christine, 111, 178
Ericsson, Magnus, 72, 161
Erlewine, Michael, 76, 144
Erlmann, Veit, 78, 142, 163
Esposito, John L., 18, 164
Etherington, Norman, 90, 165
Evenson, John, 98, 150
Everatt, David, 91, 149
Eyre, Banning, 78, 143
Ezenwa-Ohaeto, 71, 147
Fabian, Johannes, 102, 169
Fabunmi, Adebisi, 75
Fage, J. D., 170
Farah, Nuruddin, 148
Fargues, Philippe, 17, 145
Faringer, Gunilla L., 57, 166
Faris, Mohamed A., 51, 173
Farisani, Tshenuwani Simon, 19, 49, 157
Farmer, Paul, 15, 179
Faure, Murray, 91, 171
Fentress, Elizabeth, 9, 145
Ferguson, Anne, 178
Ferreira, Manuel, 69, 162
Ferris, Elizabeth G., 85, 145
Fetherston, A. B., 54, 175
Fielding, Helen, 147
Fine, Ben, 74, 165
Fine, Robert, 66, 91, 145
Firebrace, James, 97, 162
Fister, Barbara, 106, 174
Fleshman, Mike, 90, 146
Flinterman, C., 158
Fluehr-Lobban, Carolyn, 93, 156
Flynn, Laurie, 74, 173
Ford, Richard, 54, 161
Forson, Andrew, 7

Forson, Julia, 7
Forson, Rosemary, 7
Founou-Tchuigoua, Bernard, 50, 140
Frank, Andre Gunder, 66
Frederikse, Julie, 91, 163, 175
Freeman-Grenville, G. S. P., 162
French, Tom, 170
Friedman, Steven, 89, 90, 160, 171
Friedson, Steven M., 78, 149
Friis-Hansen, Esbern, 51, 170
Frobes, L., E., 173
Fukui, Katsuyoshi, 26, 152
Furley, Oliver, 95, 148
Gachukia, Eddah, 69, 174
Gadjigo, Samba, 22, 164
Gakou, Mohamed Lamine, 50, 149
Gallagher, Susan VanZanten, 172
Gallin, Rita S., 109, 178
Garfield, Robert, 148
Garlake, Peter, 102, 157
Garnham, David, 150
Garrity, Michele, 37, 165
Gastrow, Peter, 91, 145
Gastrow, Shelagh, 177
Gavron, Jeremy, 159
Gebre-Medhin, Jordan, 165
Gedicks, Al, 73, 163
Gehman, Richard J., 17, 142
Gelb, Stephen, 91, 171
Georgakas, Dan, 22, 144
George, Susan, 28, 153
Gerhart, Gail M., 154
Germain, Adrienne, 166
Ghai, Dharam, 45, 150
Ghalib, Jama Mohamed, 54, 149
Ghebrai, Illen, 97, 152
Ghorayshi, Parvin, 67, 178
Ghose, Ajit, 175
Gibbon, Peter, 29, 31, 50, 75, 145, 146, 159, 161, 171, 173
Gibbs Jr., James L., 9, 10, 165
Gibellini, Rosino, 18, 164
Giblin, James, 149
Gichuki, Francis, 161
Gifford, Paul, 19, 147
Gikandi, Simon, 167
Gillies, David, 160
Gladwin, C., 30, 172
Glickman, Harvey, 37, 149
Goheen, Miriam, 111, 161
Goldberg, Ellis, 33, 66, 170, 171
Goldsmith, Arthur A., 51, 158

Goliber, Thomas J., 83, 140
Good, Howard, 162
Goodwin, June, 90, 155
Goodwin-Gill, Guy, 26, 147
Gordenker, Leon, 158
Gordimer, Nadine, 180
Goring, Rosemary, 19, 150, 159
Gorman, Robert F., 42, 149, 156, 167
Gosebrink, Jean E. Meeh, 142
Gottfried, Ted, 159
Goulbourne, Harry, 33, 34, 150
Gould, Peter, 13, 14, 171
Graham, Efua, 6
Graham, Ronnie, 76, 77, 149, 180
Granqvist, Raoul, 68, 149
Graves, Anne Adams, 163
Gray, John, 77, 141
Gray, Linda, 109, 177
Green, December, 99, 162
Green, Edward C., 13, 143
Green, Mary Jean, 71, 166
Green, Reginald Herbold, 140
Greene, Sandra E., 154
Gregory, Joel W., 83, 142
Griesgraber, Jo Marie, 31, 167, 179
Griffiths, Gareth, 152
Griffiths, Ieuan Ll., 145
Gropeter, John J., 96, 99, 156
Gross, Susan Hill, 161, 174, 177
Gruesser, John Cullen, 177
Gugelberger, Georg M., 160
Gunner, Elizabeth, 69, 155
Gunter, Bernhard G., 31, 167, 179
Gupta, Geeta Rao, 15, 177
Gurdon, Charles, 26, 156
Gutkind, Peter C. W., 158
Hachten, William A., 155
Hackett, Rosalind I. J., 145
Haddad, Wadi Z., 147
Haddad, Yvonne Yazbeck, 147
Hakovirta, Harto, 84, 180
Hale, Thomas A., 164
Hallencreutz, Carl Fredrik, 19, 169
Hamalengwa, Munyonzwe, 56, 57, 158
Hamer, Andrew M., 145
Hamilton, Virginia, 180
Hammond, Allen L., 46, 180
Hammond, Dorothy, 140

Hammond, Ross, 30, 164
Hampson, Fen Osler, 160
Hampton, Janie, 15, 160, 161
Hancock, Graham, 40, 160
Hanlon, Joseph, 6, 31, 43, 162, 164
Hanna, Nelly, 172
Hansen, Art, 50, 153
Hansen, Emmanuel, 24, 26, 140, 164
Hansen, H., 31, 147
Hansen, Holger Bernt, 19, 169
Haralambous, Sappho, 172
Harir, Sharif, 93, 170
Harper, Janice, 178
Harrell-Bond, B. E., 157
Harries, Patrick, 67, 179
Harrigan, Jane, 143
Harris, Joseph E., 155
Harris, Michael, 152
Harrison, Graham, 7
Harrison, Paul, 45, 50, 61, 155, 163, 174
Harriss, John, 53, 166
Harrow, Kenneth W., 71, 160, 174
Hartmann, Betsy, 81, 169
Harvey, Charles, 35, 74, 165
Hastings, Adrian, 18, 148
Hatchard, John, 57, 157
Havnevik, Kjell J., 146
Hawk, Beverly G., 60, 63, 140
Hay, Margaret Jean, 142, 143
Hayes, Bradd C., 27, 145
Head, Bessie, 106
Healey, John, 176
Heiberg, Marianne, 53, 173
Heiden, David, 151
Helleiner, Gerald K., 29, 154
Hemp, Paul, 63
Henault, Georges, 143
Hengeveld, R., 151
Henry, Clement M., 31, 161
Henze, Seymour M., 26, 156
Herbert, Eugenia W., 167
Herbst, Jeffrey, 54, 159, 175
Herbstein, Denis, 98, 150
Hermele, Kenneth, 146
Heymann, Philip B., 165
Hill, Errol, 147
Himmelstrand, Ulf, 37, 142
Hines, Colin, 49, 143
Hirsch, John L., 54, 168
Hirson, Baruch, 66, 180
Hisham, Mohamed Ahmed, 47, 177
Hitchcott, Nicki, 71, 141
Hobbelink, Henk, 50, 163

Hodges, Tony, 94, 156, 176, 177
Hoffman, John, 174
Hoffmann, Stanley, 53, 152
Hofmeyr, Isabel, 70, 176
Hogan, Barbara, 88
Holdridge, David, 50, 140
Holland, Heidi, 89, 173
Holland, Stuart, 97, 162
Holm, John, 35, 150
Holt, Patricia, 54, 146
Honig, Robert, 152
Hoobler, Dorothy, 11, 142
Hoobler, Thomas, 11, 142
Hoodbhoy, Pervez, 158
Hoorweg, Jan, 50, 51, 158
Hope, Kempe Ronald, Sr., 142
Hopkins, Nancy, 93, 153
Hord, Fred Lee, 157
Horn, Nancy E., 110, 149
Horn, Peter, 70, 180
Horowitz, Donald L., 91, 150
Horton, Mark, 9, 173
Hountondji, Paulin J., 142
House-Midamba, Bessie, 110, 141
Howard, Rhoda E., 57, 156
Howell, John, 30, 173
Hubbard, Michael, 166
Huddleston, Trevor, 19, 169
Hudson, Julie, 101, 163
Hughes, Jane E., 163
Hume, Cameron, 27, 152
Huni, Gregoire, 141
Hunt, Paul, 58, 162
Hunter, Allan, 22, 147
Hyden, Goran, 156, 166
Ibitokun, Benedict M., 70, 141
Ibnifassi, Laïla, 71, 141
Idowu, E. Bolaji, 17, 142
Ihonvbere, Julius O., 31, 163
Iliffe, John, 143
Ingram, James, 42
Innes, C. L., 155
Innes, Duncan, 144
Irele, Abiola, 71, 141
Ishemo, Shubi, 67, 153
Isichei, Elizabeth, 18, 156
Iyam, David Uru, 146
Jablow, Alta, 140
Jabri, Vivienne, 161
Jackson, Gale, 145
Jackson, Helen, 144
Jackson, Irene V., 78, 161
Jaffe, Hosea, 156
Jaffee, Steven, 160
Jahn, Janheinz, 78, 162

Jamal, Vali, 175
James, Adeola, 104, 105, 157
James, Valentine U., 45, 46, 110, 152, 169, 173, 178
James, W. Martin, III, 26, 27, 165
James, Wilmot G., 66, 67, 74, 159, 164
Jan, Ameen, 54, 165
JanMohamed, Abdul R., 160
Jansson, Kurt, 42, 152
Jarvis, Heather, 7
Jean, Francois, 10, 166
Jefferson, Margo, 169
Jenkins Jr., Everett, 164
Jennings, Anne M., 111, 164
Jiggins, Janice, 81, 147
Joffé, George, 95
Johnson, John William, 70, 164
Johnson, Phyllis, 46, 172
Johnson, R. W., 90, 159
Jones, A. M., 78, 173
Jones, Eldred Durosimi, 70, 71, 149, 164, 167, 178
Jones, Marjorie, 149, 164, 167
Joubert, Elsa, 166
Jourdan, Paul, 74, 161
Joynson, Angela, 63, 154, 174
Juijust, Freke, 42
July, Robert W., 9, 156
Kabira, Wanjiku M., 35, 150, 175
Kagan, Rachael, 90, 173
Kahn, Owen Ellison, 98, 151
Kala, Violet, 176
Kaleeba, Noerine, 14, 175, 177
Kamil, Leo, 95, 154
Kane, Hal, 81, 154
Kane, Thierno H., 36
Kanfer, Stefan, 74, 159
Kanyoro, Musimbi R. A., 18, 177
Kaplan, Roger, 154
Karis, Thomas G., 154
Karl, Marilee, 109, 178
Karlsson, Jenni, 23, 175, 176
Kasaba, Resat, 170
Kates, Robert, 166
Kathrada, Ahmed, 88
Katz, Linda Sobel, 46, 152
Kaujeua, Jackson, 78, 174
Kavanagh, Robert, 70, 174
Keddie, Nikki R., 110, 178
Keen, David, 41, 43, 145, 167
Keim, Curtis A., 102, 142
Kelly, Bernice M., 103, 163

Kendall, Kl. Limakatso, 107, 170
Kennedy, Jean, 100, 162
Kerouedan, Dominique, 153
Kerr, David, 70, 142
Kerr, Joanna, 58, 164
Khan, Arjmandbanu, 14, 148
Khan, Mahmood Hasan, 51, 173
Khennas, Smail, 74, 158
Khorana, Meena, 69, 139
Ki-Zerbo, J., 3
Kibicho, S. G., 16
Kibreab, Gaim, 142
Kidane, Meg, 146
Kimambo, Isaria N., 149
King, Nicholas, 170
Kingma, Koos, 110, 111, 170
Kinyanjui, Kabiru, 142
Kirby, Bob, 63, 176
Kirk-Greene, Anthony H. M., 150
Kiros, Fassil G., 39, 147
Kiros, Tedros, 39, 161
Kitchen, Helen, 90, 171
Kitchen, J. Coleman, 90, 171
Kitson, Norma, 105, 144
Kivnick, Helen Q., 78, 177
Kjekshus, Helge, 47, 151
Klare, Michael T., 25, 159, 180
Klaue, Wolfgang, 179
Klinke, Thomas, 151
Kneifel, Theo, 148
Knight, Derrick, 147
Knudsen, Christiana Oware, 110, 111, 153
Kofie, Nicholas N., 78, 148
Kok, Peter N., 92, 154
Kokole, Omari H., 11, 154
Konings, Piet, 67, 159
Koslow, Philip, 160
Kothari, Smitu, 30, 153
Kozlowski, Gregory C., 18, 148
Kumar, Krishna, 167
Kusterer, Ken, 178
Kuzwayo, Ellen, 147
Lachaud, Jean-Pierre, 66, 67, 159
LaDuke, Betty, 106, 107, 140, 178
Lall, Sanjaya, 31, 174
Lamba, Davinder, 47, 162
Landau, Paul Stuart, 167
Landis, Elizabeth, 90, 176
Lane, Jan-Erik, 91, 171
Langley, Winston E., 58, 179
Langseth, P., 175
Lanting, Frans, 164

Lappé, Frances Moore, 49, 179
Larom, Margaret S., 148
Laurance, Edward J., 26, 158
Lawal, Babatunde, 154
Lawless, Richard, 95, 176
Lawrence, Peter, 50, 180
Leach, Melissa, 45, 159
Leatherbee, Leah, 148
Leatt, James, 148
Lee, Jonathan Scott, 157
Lefebvre, Jeffrey A., 26, 145
Lefkowitz, Mary, 163
Legum, Colin, 6, 11, 63, 162
Lele, Uma, 50, 143
Lemarchand, René, 27, 147
LeMelle, Tilden J., 140
Lems-Dworkin, Carol, 77, 141, 176
Leonard, Ann, 14, 67, 148, 170
Lepper, Ian, 171
Leslie, Winsome J., 30, 178
Levinson, Orde, 103, 141
Lewis, Bernard, 18, 158, 165
Lewis, Dale, 45, 176
Lewis, Ioan M., 54, 146, 175
Lewis, L. A., 73, 141
Lewis, Ruth, 7
Lewis, Stephen R., 35, 74, 165
Leys, Colin, 38, 98, 140, 162
Liagin, Elizabeth, 83, 152
Lightfoot-Klein, Hanny, 58, 110, 167
Liljestrom, Rita, 147
Limb, Peter, 66, 144
Lindauer, David L., 145
Lindfors, Bernth, 69, 146
Linz, Juan J., 150
Lippman, Lisa, 90, 173
Lipschutz, Mark R., 11, 150
Lipset, Seymour Martin, 150
Lipumba, Nguyuru H. I., 31, 139
Little, Peter D., 50, 160
Lobban, Richard A., Jr., 156
Locke, Marjorie, 101, 151
Lockwood, Edgar, 171
Loescher, Ann Dull, 85, 155
Loescher, Gil, 41, 85, 145, 155
Lofchie, Michael F., 140
Lohmann, Larry, 47, 173
Lomer, Cecile, 167
Lonsdale, John, 27, 175
Lopes, Carlos, 152
Lorcin, Patricia M. E., 62, 157
Lord, Mary, 157
Louw, Joseph, 7
Louw, P. Eric, 91, 171

Loyson, Madeleine, 70, 164
Luhr, William, 20, 179
Lutz, Wolfgang, 81, 154
MacBride, Sean, 62, 160
MacCann, Donnarae, 141
MacDonald, Juliet, 7
MacDonald, Scott B., 163
Mackintosh, Maureen, 51, 154
MacShane, Denis, 66, 166
Maddox, Gregory, 47, 149
Maddy, Yulisa Amadu, 141
Magona, Sindiwe, 104
Magubane, Bernard Makhosezwe, 174
Maguire, Keith, 89, 166
Mahmoud, Fatima Babiker, 147
Maja-Pearce, Adewale, 71, 160
Makeba, Miriam, 78, 160
Makinda, Samuel M., 54, 170
Malek, Jaromir, 102, 149, 151
Malkmus, Lizbeth, 20, 144
Mallaby, Sebastian, 90, 143
Malti-Douglas, Fedwa, 107, 161
Malwal, Bona, 92
Mamdani, Mahmood, 33, 57, 139, 142
Mandaza, Ibbo, 89, 172
Mandela, Nelson, 88
Mann, Jonathan M., 13, 143
Manuel, Peter Lamarche, 78
Maphai, Vincent, 90, 171
Maraire, Dumisani, 159
Mararike, Claude G., 39, 155
Marcus, Harold G., 11, 155, 159
Marcus, Tessa, 91, 161
Maree, Johann, 66, 157
Maren, Michael, 40, 169
Markakis, John, 26, 152, 162
Markham, Ian, 19, 180
Marks, Shula, 163
Marshall, Alex, 172
Martey, Emmanuel, 18, 142
Martin, Claude, 47, 167
Martin, Phyllis M., 139
Martin, Susan Forbes, 109, 167
Martin-Brown, Joan, 167
Mashinini, Emma, 89, 172
Massiah, Joycelin, 109, 178
Masters, William A., 51, 155
Mathabane, Mark, 111, 143
Mathews, A. S., 165
Mathews, Anthony, 57, 154
Mathews, M. L., 91, 165

Matlosa, Khabele, 51, 153
Mattera, Don, 171
Maughan-Brown, David, 62, 159
Mauldin, W. Parker, 153
Maxwell, Simon, 51, 160, 174
May, Chris, 140
May, Terry M., 78, 156
Mayer, Ann Elizabeth, 57, 158
Mayotte, Judy A., 151
Mazrui, Alamin M., 174
Mazrui, Ali A., 3, 6, 11, 16, 17, 19, 68, 101, 140
Mazur, Laurie Ann, 81, 145
Mbele, Joseph L., 163
Mbiti, John S., 17, 142, 158
Mbumba, Nangolo, 98, 162
Mburugu, Edward, 142
McCarthy, Stephen, 140
McCleery, Robert, 167
McCoy, Martha L., 157
McCullum, Hugh, 19, 144
McFarlane, Catherine, 7
McGowan, Lisa A., 30, 164
McIntosh, R. J., 9, 165
McIntosh, Roderick J., 103, 165
McIvor, Chris, 179
McMillan, Della E., 50, 153
McWilliams, James P., 26, 145
Mda, Zakes, 70, 177
Mearns, Robin, 45, 159
Meer, Fatima, 66, 67, 146
Melton, J. Gordon, 152
Meltzer, Ronald, 57, 156
Mengisteab, Kidane, 51, 152
Mensa-Bonsu, Henrietta J. A. N., 57, 169
Messick, Richard E., 180
Mfah-Abbenyi, Juliana Makuchi, 107
Mhone, Guy C. Z., 167
Mies, Maria, 45, 151
Migdal, Joel S., 170
Migot-Adholla, Shem E., 50, 170
Mihevc, John, 31, 160
Mikell, Gwendolyn, 148
Mikhail, Mona N., 71, 173
Miller, Marc S., 10, 172
Miller, Norman, 143
Miller, Terence, 49, 155
Miller, Vincent C., 153
Millwood, David, 158
Milne, June, 11, 159
Minear, Larry, 43, 53, 147, 157, 161

Minter, William, 27, 73, 144, 159, 164
Mirsky, Judith, 81, 167
Mistry, Percy S., 29, 31, 141, 169
Mitchell, Christopher, 93, 97, 148
Mitchell, Robert Cameron, 19, 146, 148
Mkandawire, Richard, 51, 153
Mkandawire, Thandika, 140
Mlama, Penina Muhando, 70, 149
Mmari, Geoffrey, 11, 162
Mmuya, Max, 35, 144, 166
Modisane, Bloke, 70, 89, 146
Mogensen, Hanne Overgaard, 143
Moghadam, Valentine M., 110, 161
Mohammed, Duri, 37, 171
Mokhtar, G., 3
Moleah, Alfred Tokollo, 89, 171
Molutsi, Patrick, 35, 150
Momoh, Abubakar, 165
Monahan, Laila, 95, 176
Moodie, T. Dunbar, 73, 155
Moodley, Kogila, 90, 164
Moorcraft, Paul L., 26, 141
Moore, Carrie Dailey, 22, 152
Moore, Gerald, 69, 165
Moore, Jonathan, 54, 175
Moore, Reavis, 103, 162
Morgan, Robin, 111, 170
Moroney, Sean, 5, 155
Morris, Jean, 101, 172
Morrison, Andrew R., 145
Morrison, Donald George, 5, 146
Morrison, Melody, 156
Morsink, Hubert, 86, 87, 177
Mortimore, Michael, 161
Morton, James, 43, 166
Morton, John, 160
Mosala, Itumeleng J., 19, 176
Moser, Gerald, 69, 162
Mosley, Paul, 31, 143
Moss, Glenn, 171
Moss, Joyce, 10, 165
Mouli, V. Chandra, 15, 144
Mount, Marshall W., 101, 140
Moyo, Sam, 46, 172
Mpanya, Mutombo, 42, 49, 50, 51, 140, 175
Msiska, Hangson, 69, 167
Muafangejo, John Ndevasia, 103

Mudimbe, V. Y., 71, 157, 164
Mugambi, J. N. K., 16, 19, 148, 154
Mukandala, Rwekaza S., 35, 159
Mukoyogo, M. Christian, 15, 143
Mukurasi, Laeticia, 67, 166
Mule, Harris M., 141
Muller, Johan, 5, 146, 166
Munck, Ronaldo, 65, 163
Muranga, Manuel, 175
Murphy, Larry G., 152
Mutambirwa, James, 171
Mutiso, Roberta, 39, 179
Mutua, Makau wa, 160
Muzorewa, Gwinyai H., 17, 18, 164
Mvududu, Sara C., 46, 111, 154
Mwale, G., 14, 177
Myers, Dorothy, 163
Myers, W. E., 66, 153
Nagan, Winston P., 156
Nash, Cathy, 63, 157, 176
Nasta, Susheila, 106, 161
Naya, Seiji, 167
Ndatshe, Vivienne, 73, 155
Ndegwa, Philip, 140
Ndegwa, Stephen N., 175
Ndlovu, Duma, 70, 180
Ndulu, Benno, 143
Nelson, Barbara J., 109, 178
Nelson, Cynthia, 107, 151
Neocosmos, Michael, 49, 143
Nesbitt, Judith, 103
Netter, Thomas W., 143
Newman, Arnold, 175
Newman, James L., 165
Nfah-Abbenyi, Juliana Makuchi, 154
Ng'weshemi, Japheth, 156
Ngaiza, Anthony, 177
Ngara, Emmanuel, 71, 163
Ngaté, Jonathan, 154
Ngaté, Jonathan, 71, 154
Ngcobo, Mbali, 7
Niane, D. T., 3
Nicodemus, Everlyn, 101, 170
Nicol, Mike, 90, 176
Nicolson, Ronald, 143
Niemeijer, Rudo, 50, 51, 158
Nilsson, Anders, 27, 176
Njanana, Rhoda, 90, 175
Njoku, John E. Eberegbulam, 83, 160
Njoku, Juliet, 163

Nketia, J. H. Kwabena, 78, 162, 170
Nkomo, Mokubung, 91, 165
Nnoli, Okwudiba, 24, 34, 152, 162
Noisser, Norbert H., 98, 162
Nolutshungu, Sam C., 27, 172
Nordquist, Joan, 15, 45, 65, 111, 153, 158, 174, 177
Nowrojee, Binaifer, 27, 170
Nsirimovu, Anyakwee, 57, 156
Nuñez, Benjamin, 150
Nujoma, San Shafishuna, 98
Nurnberger, Klaus, 148
Nwabueze, B. O., 32, 150
Nwankwo, Agwuncha Arthur, 142
Nwapa, Flora, 106, 178
Nwodo, Obiageli C., 71, 107
Nwoke, Chibuzo, 73, 174
Nwokedi, Emeka, 35, 166
Nyathi, Andrew, 174
Nyeki, Daniel Musili, 47, 177
Nyong'o, Peter Anyang', 25, 33, 37, 144, 166, 174
Nzomo, Maria, 26, 150
Nzongola-Ntalaja, 26, 169
O'Connell, Helen, 109, 178
O'Keefe, Phil, 172
O'Meara, Dan, 153
O'Meara, Patrick, 139
Oakley, Robert B., 54, 168
Obbo, Christine, 110, 143
Obery, Ingrid, 171
Obiechina, Emmanuel N., 71, 159
Ochieng', W. R., 149
Odén, Bertil, 90, 162, 172
Odamtten, Vincent O., 76, 106, 145
Oded, A., 19
Oduol, Jacqueline A., 150
Oduyoye, Mercy Amba, 18, 108, 109, 149, 177
Ofosu-Amaah, Waafas, 167
Ofstad, Arve, 145
Ogbaa, Kalu, 71, 155
Ogle, Patrick, 153
Ogot, B. A., 3, 149
Ogundipe-Leslie, Molara, 105, 178
Ogunyemi, Chikwenye Okonjo, 106, 140
Ogwang, Ernesto Okello, 175
Ohadike, Don C., 11, 144
Ojaide, Tanure, 165
Okombo, Okoth, 175
Okoth, P. Godfrey, 175

Okpewho, Isidore, 141
Olaniyan, R. Omotayo, 173
Olindo, Perez, 47
Oliver, Roland, 140, 170
Olmstead, Judith, 107, 177
Olorunnisola, Funmilola, 11, 170
Olowu, Dele, 35, 155
Olukoshi, Adebayo O., 31, 166, 173
Olupona, Jacob K., 17, 142
Omaar, Rakiya, 53, 54, 157, 163, 170, 171
Omar, Mohamed Osman, 54, 169
Omer-Cooper, J. D., 88, 156
Omo-Fadaka, Jimoh, 6
Omolu, Gideon Prinsler, 141
Onimode, Bade, 6, 29, 154
Ontiveros, Suzanne R., 111, 179
Onwurah, Ngozi, 82
Orrick, Sarah, 152
Osaghae, Eghosa, 34, 145, 152
Oster, Audrey, 7
Osunsade, F. L., 157
Otfinoski, Steven, 162
Othman, Haroub, 35, 144, 159
Otim, J. J., 45, 174
Otobo, Dafe, 67, 175
Otokunefor, Henrietta C., 71, 107
Ottenberg, Simon, 78, 170
Overberg, Kenneth R., 143
Owens, Delia, 152
Owens, Mark, 152
Owomoyela, Oyekan, 69, 141, 156
Oyono-Mbia, Guillaume, 153
Paden, John Naber, 146
Padoch, Christine, 10, 165
Pakenham, Thomas, 170
Pallister, David, 74, 171
Palmberg, Mai, 19, 169
Palmer, Eustace, 149, 164, 167
Palmer, Ingrid, 83, 154
Palmer, Robin, 61, 163
Palmer, Robin, 61, 163
Pampallis, John, 153
Panford, Kwamina, 65, 67, 141
Pankhurst, Richard, 9, 152
Parfitt, Trevor W., 29, 31, 141
Parker, Ben, 152
Parker, M., 75, 161
Parmann, Georg, 46, 155
Parnwell, Mike, 85, 166
Parpart, Jane L., 67, 179

Parratt, John, 18, 166, 167
Parrinder, Geoffrey, 17, 169
Paterson, Gillian, 15, 179
Paton, Bill, 67, 159
Payne, Rhys, 140
Pazzanita, Anthony G., 94, 156
Pearson, Frederic S., 25, 26, 144
Pelletier, Céline, 23
Pendleton, Wade C., 99, 159
Penrose, Angela, 152
Penstrup-Andersen, Per, 48
Penvenne, Jeanne Marie, 67, 143
Peters, Chris, 92, 173
Petersen, Kirsten Holst, 17, 70, 164, 169
Pfaff, Françoise, 22, 148, 175
Phelan, John M., 63, 144
Philleo, Wendy, 167
Picard, Louis A., 37, 165
Pinkney, Robert, 150
Pityana, Barney N., 19, 145
Plaut, Martin, 166
Pogrund, Benjamin, 93, 171, 176
Pollock, Steve, 10, 145
Porter, Eliot, 102, 161
Posel, Deborah, 144
Poulsen, Ann Kathrine, 111, 148
Pradervand, Pierre, 39, 160
Prasse, Karl-G., 11, 175
Pratap, Vijay, 153
Prendergast, John, 41, 43, 49, 53, 54, 92, 93, 97, 146, 150, 153, 155, 156, 159, 164, 165, 170, 173, 177
Price, David H., 145
Price, Robert M., 89, 144
Priebe, Richard K., 71, 154
Prinsloo, Jeanne, 161
Prouty, Chris, 96, 97, 156
Prunier, Gerard, 27, 170
Pudi, Ranko, 157
Pyatt, Sherman E., 144
Radlett, Marty, 81, 167
Radney, Walter, 66
Radu, Michael, 26, 163
Radwan, Samir, 67, 175
Rahkonen, Carl, 180
Rake, Alan, 4, 11, 162, 164, 177
Ramphele, Mamphela, 89, 91, 139, 169
Rana, Hanif M., 150
Randolf, Brenda, 139

Rasheed, Sadig, 156
Rasmussen, R. Kent, 11, 150
Ratner, Steven R., 54, 163
Rau, Bill, 50, 149, 154
Raundalen, Magne, 26, 167
Ravenhill, John, 29, 65, 156
Ravenhill, Philip L., 101, 145
Ray, Sunanda, 14, 15, 175, 179
Read, Leslie DuS., 70
Redclift, Nanneke, 67, 179
Reed, Laura W., 159
Rees, Andrew, 46, 165
Reich, Bernard, 175
Reichmann, Rebecca, 166
Reid, Elizabeth, 14, 156
Renne, Elisha P., 101, 148
Reynolds, Andrew, 89, 151
Reynolds, Pamela, 66, 91, 147, 149, 175
Reyntjens, Filip, 27, 147
Rhoodie, Eschel M., 57, 111, 151
Riak, Abikok, 49, 162
Ribiere, Jean-Pierre, 93, 173
Ricard, Alain, 176
Rich, Bruce, 31, 161
Rich, Paul B., 88, 151
Richards, Paul, 45, 153
Richards, Sandra L., 71, 144
Richardson, Julie A., 31, 173
Riddell, Roger C., 40, 65, 153
Riedmann, Agnes, 83, 170
Ries, Julien, 19, 164
Rigby, Peter, 141
Riley, Stephen P., 29, 31, 141
Rissik, Dee, 111, 179
Rittner, Don, 46, 151
Roberts, John Storm, 76
Roberts, Renée G., 158
Robertshaw, Peter, 9, 160
Robertson, Claire, 110, 177
Rocheleau, Dianne, 39, 154
Rockwell, Richard C., 143
Rodda, Annabel, 45, 47, 109, 178
Rodenburg, J., 151
Rodney, Walter, 66
Roemer, Michael, 145
Rojas, Mary Hill, 161, 174
Romero, Patricia W., 179
Rone, Jemera, 93, 145, 148
Ronen, Dov, 34, 150
Ronning, Helge, 35, 160
Roscoe, Adrian, 69, 167
Rosen, Miriam, 22, 144
Rosen, Roger, 70, 144
Rosenau, James N., 54, 176
Rosenfeld, Eugene, 96, 97, 156

Ross, John A., 42, 153
Rosset, Peter, 49, 162
Rothchild, Donald, 35, 166
Routledge, Lyn, 7
Rubin, Barry, 18, 158
RuBlack, Carol, 23
Ruedy, John, 18, 158
Rugumamu, Severine, 89, 166
Ruiz, Hiram A., 27, 176
Rukuni, Mandivamba, 51, 179
Rupesinghe, Kumar, 145, 148
Russell, Diana E., H., 91, 107, 160
Rustomjee, Zavareh, 74, 165
Rutherford, Anna, 70, 164
Ruttan, Vernon W., 42, 177
Rutter, Jill, 85, 167
Ryan, Colleen, 19, 145
Sabania, Neil, 160
Sabatier, Renée, 12, 146
Sabela, Sindisiwe, 7
Sachikonye, Lloyd, 33, 150
Sachs, Wolfgang, 36, 45, 150, 155
Salih, Kamal El Din Osman, 92
Salih, M. A. Mohamed, 50, 54, 149, 157
Sallah, Tijan, 69, 163
Samaan, Angele Botros, 111, 179
Samarasinghe, Vidyamali, 178
Samatar, Said S., 54, 59, 171
Sambo, Abdulrahman, 12
Sanders, David M., 12, 155
Sanneh, Lamin, 165
Saul, John S., 26, 88, 98, 162, 167
Sayer, Jeffrey A., 46, 148
Scheub, Harold, 70, 104, 105, 174
Scheven, Yvette, 111, 145
Schiff, Ben, 90, 155
Schildkrout, Enid, 102, 142
Schipper, Mineke, 145
Schlemmer, Lawrence, 90, 159
Schmidt, Nancy J., 21, 23, 173
Schmidt, Peter R., 103, 165
Schneider, Beth E., 15, 179
Schoepf, Brooke Grundfest, 15
Schraeder, Peter J., 176
Schreiter, Robert J., 18, 153
Schuurman, Frans, 36, 145
Sciarone, Paul, 145

Scott, Michael, 42, 175
Seavoy, Ronald E., 50, 51, 153
Seckler, David, 50, 143
Seekings, Jeremy, 91, 156
Seidman, Ann, 6
Seidman, Gay W., 66, 160
Sembène, Ousmane, 22
Sen, Gita, 81, 166
Sender, John, 67, 166
Sensenig, Pearl, 162
Serwadda, W. Moses, 171
Shaaban, Bouthaina, 110, 146
Shabbas, Audrey, 6, 144
Shariff, Ibrahim Noor, 11, 174
Sharma, Jan, 177
Sharp, John, 171
Sharp, Robin, 170
Sharpe, Sr. Ursula, 177
Shava, Piniel Viriri, 70, 165
Shaw, Carolyn Martin, 148
Shaw, John, 42, 43, 179
Shelemay, Kay Kaufman, 78, 171
Shepherd, George W., Jr., 29, 57, 140, 151
Shepherd, Andrew, 166
Sherman, Susan, 145
Shields, David L. L., 49, 51, 148
Shillington, Kevin, 156
Shiri, Keith, 22, 150
Shityuwete, Helao, 98, 162
Shiva, Vandana, 45, 148, 151
Shivji, Issa G., 56, 148
Sikainga, Ahmad Alawad, 67, 171
Sill, Michael, 172
Silverthorne, Jessica, 111, 179
Simmons, Janie, 179
Simmons, Pat, 58, 179
Simon, Julian L., 81, 166
Simons, Anna, 54, 162
Sinclair, A. R. E., 170
Sinclair, M. Thea, 67, 179
Siroto, Leon, 102, 151
Sishi, Mduduzi, 7
Sisk, Timothy D., 91, 150
Sivan, Emmanuel, 167
Sivard, Ruth Leger, 180
Siverburg, Sanford R., 175
Skinner, Elliott P., 169
Sklar, Richard L., 38, 142
Slocombe, D. Scott, 39, 177
Slovo, Joe, 89, 171
Smillie, Ian, 144
Smith, Chris, 26, 148
Smith, Danielle, 94, 95
Smith, Huston, 19, 157
Smith, Jonathan Z., 19, 155

Smith, Ken, 70, 147
Smith, Sheila, 67, 166
Smith, Susanna, 26, 154
Smock, David R., 53, 160
Smyke, Patricia, 109, 178
Smykla, Harald, 7
Snyder, John, 7
Snyder, Margaret C., 110, 142
Snyder, Sarah, 7
Sobania, Neil, 9
Söderbaum, Fredrik, 155
Soggot, David, 98, 162
Sonko, Karamo N. M., 29, 149, 151
Sontheimer, Sally, 46, 178
Soremekun, Kayode, 155
Sorenson, John, 84, 85, 142
Southall, Roger, 65, 175
Southern, Eileen, 78, 146
Sow, Mariam, 142
Soyinka, Wole, 162
Sparks, Allister, 90, 174
Sparks, Donald L., 99, 162
Sparr, Pamela, 30, 161
Spencer, Dale E., 25
Spencer, James R., 148
Spencer, Jon Michael, 78, 169
Spring, Christopher, 101, 163
Stapleton, Chris, 78, 140
Stauffer, Ardell, 162
Steady, Filomina Chioma, 109, 177
Stedman, Stephen John, 27, 35, 53, 90, 146, 165, 171
Stein, Howard, 145
Steiner, Christopher B., 102, 140
Stemmet, Farouk, 74, 155
Stewart, C. C., 16, 169
Stewart, Gary, 78, 146
Stewart, John, 11, 142
Stewart, Julie, 111, 159
Stewart, P. J., 18, 175
Stewart, Sarah, 171
Stichter, Sharon, 67, 142, 143, 179
Stock, Robert, 140
Stoller, Nancy E., 15, 179
Stone, Roger D., 47, 177
Stone, Ruth M., 78, 154
Storck, Elise, 176
Stowasser, Barbara Freyer, 158
Strouhal, Eugen, 102, 160
Struhsaker, Thomas T., 151
Stultz, Newell M., 19, 90, 171
Sudarkasa, Michael E. M., 140
Suhrke, Astri, 152

Suliman, Mohamed, 26, 44, 45, 144, 155, 172, 177
Sultan, Olivier, 102, 160
Sundiata, Ibrahim K., 154
Sunmonu, Hassan, 37
Sweetman, Caroline, 109, 178, 179
Swinehart, Theresa, 156
Symons, Gillian, 7
Tadesse, Mary, 110, 142
Talbot, Jane, 63, 174
Talhami, Ghada Hashem, 161
Tamale, Nassali, 15, 147
Tandon, Yash, 157
Tarantola, Daniel J. M., 143
Taylor, Clyde, 20
Taylor, Jane, 70, 154
Tekle, Amare, 26, 97, 152
Tesfagiorgis, Abeba, 111, 164
Tesfagiorgis, Gebre Hiwet, 97, 151
Tessler, Mark, 150
Tétreault, Mary Ann, 109, 178
Thomas, Alan, 73, 174
Thomas, Daniel C., 25, 180
Thomas, Nicholas, 158
Thomas-Slayter, Barbara, 39, 154
Thompson, Carol, 101, 140
Thompson, Leonard, 89, 156
Thomson, Dennis L., 169
Thorpe, Frances, 158
Thussu, Daya Kishan, 62, 148
Tiffen, Mary, 47, 161
Tiffen, Pauline, 72, 73, 74, 170
Tiffin, Helen, 152
Timerlake, Lloyd, 139
Tingay, Paul, 177
Tiruneh, Andargachew, 152
Tlhagale, Buti, 19, 176
Tomaselli, Keyan, 22, 63, 146, 148, 162, 166
Tomaselli, Ruth, 63, 146, 166
Tomasevski, Katarina, 42, 109, 150, 178
Tordoff, William, 35, 155, 176
Tørres, Liv, 66, 172
Toubia, Nahid, 110, 179
Toye, John, 143
Trzyna, Thaddeus C., 46, 179
Tshibangu, Tshishiku, 16, 17
Tucker, Judith Cook, 110, 159
Tucker, Judith E., 110, 144

Tumbo-Masabo, Zubeida, 147
Turner, B. L., II, 83, 166
Turner, H. W., 19, 146
Turner, Harold W., 19, 148
Turok, Ben, 29, 144
Turshen, Meredeth, 110, 178
Turton, David, 87
Tutu, Desmond, 19, 167
Tvedt, Terje, 93, 170
Twaddle, M., 31, 147
Twaddle, Michael, 19, 169
Twose, Nigel, 43, 93, 153, 176
Uchendu, P, K., 111, 169
Udenta, Udenta O., 71, 169
Ugwu-Oju, Dympna, 177
Ugwuemulam, Nzamujo Godfrey, 48
Ukadike, Nwachukwu Frank, 20, 21, 146, 163
Umeh, Marie, 107, 152
Uzukwu, Elochukwu E., 18, 160
Vail, Leroy, 69, 70, 166
Vale, Peter, 172
Van Ameringen, Marc, 91, 146
van Aswegen, Adri, 22, 157
van Beek, Walter E. A., 169
Van de Goor, Luc, 25, 145
van der Gaag, Nikki, 63, 157
Van Der Geest, Willem, 29, 162
Van Der Hoeven, Rolph, 29, 140, 172
Van Der Kraaij, Fred, 29, 172
Van Hear, Nicholas, 6
Van Onselen, Charles, 170
van Rooyen, Johann, 91, 155
Vandewwalle, Dirk, 163
Vansina, Jan, 47, 101, 164
Varnis, Steven L., 43, 169
Vaughan, James H., 150
Vaz, Kim Marie, 103, 107, 176
Veber, Hanne, 10, 162
Veit-Wild, Flora, 71, 174
Verhelst, Thierry G., 39, 163
Verney, Peter, 26, 172
Vickers, Jeanne, 109, 178
Victor, Kapache, 164
Vieler-Porter, Chris, 21, 146
Villa-Vicencio, Charles, 19, 145, 148, 172
Vines, Alex, 26, 27, 169

Vinson, James, 158
Visvanathan, Shiv, 153
Vogt, M. A., 163
Voll, John O., 93, 173
Voll, John Obert, 156
Volman, Daniel, 95, 158
von Donzel, E. J., 18, 158
von Hippel, Karin, 95
Wa Mutharika, Bingu, 36, 37, 164
Wagner, Kathrin, 71, 169
Waines, David, 17, 158
Waldman, Sideny R., 27, 149
Walker, Cherryl, 91, 111, 178
Walker, John R., 26, 164
Wall, C. Edward, 161
Wallace, Marion, 98, 162
Waller, David, 27, 170
Waller, James, 43, 153
Wallerstein, Immanuel, 66, 139
Wallman, Sandra, 15, 159
Walsh, Gretchen, 61, 161
Walshe, Peter, 19, 148, 167
Walters, Joseph J., 155
Wamba-dia-Wamba, Ernest, 33, 142
Ward, David, 166
Ward, Gary L, 152
Ward, Gary L., 152
Warnock, Kitty, 145
Waterhouse, Rachel, 162
Waterman, Christopher Alan, 78, 158
Watson, Catharine, 175
Watts, Michael J., 50, 160
Webb, James L. A., Jr., 150
Webb, Pauline, 19, 160
Weerasinghe, Lali, 77, 151
Weinstein, Norman C., 78, 163
Weiss, Ellen, 15, 177
Weiss, Thomas G., 27, 53, 54, 157, 161, 173, 176
Welch, Claude E., Jr., 26, 57, 156, 163
West, Nigel, 7
Wheeler, Christine, 82, 158
Whelan, Tensie, 47, 162
Whitaker, C, S., 38, 142
White, Landeg, 69, 70, 166
Whiteside, Alan, 13, 14, 153
Whyte, Anne V., 91, 146
Widner, Jennifer A., 151

Wiggins, Trevor, 162
Wilentz, Gay, 106, 107, 146, 152
Wilkes, Sybella, 164
Willett, Frank, 101, 140
Williams, Adebayo, 155
Williams, Eric, 147
Williams, Glen, 15, 143, 147, 153, 154, 179
Williams, Sylvia, 101
Williamson, Sue, 102, 169
Willmore, Brigid, 175
Wilson, A., 97, 147
Wilson, George, 10, 165
Wilson, H. S., 141
Wilson, Ken, 40
Windrich, Elaine, 61, 148
Winship, Thomas, 63
Winter, Joseph, 141
Wiseman, John A., 11, 165
Wohlgemuth, Lennart, 54, 149
Wood, Lisa R., 23
Woodward, Peter, 93, 173
Woodward, Richard B., 140
Woodyard, George, 147
Woronoff, Jon, 96, 164
Worsnip, Michael, 19, 167
Wright, Derek, 71, 149
Wright, Marcia, 111, 172
Wulff, Hans Jurgen, 21, 146
Yachir, Faysal, 74, 161
Yansané, Aguibou Y., 37, 150, 167
Yohannes, Okbazghi, 97, 152
Young, Gay, 109, 178
Yourgrau, Tug, 70, 171
Zartman, I. William, 27, 148, 151, 169
Zegeye, Abebe, 67, 153
Zeleza, Tiyambe, 161
Zell, Hans M., 69, 140, 142, 163, 167
Zenani, Nongenile Masithathu, 104, 105, 178
Ziai, Fatemeh, 176
Ziegler, Dhyana, 63, 174
Zinanga, Evelyn, 111, 154
Ziv, Ilan, 42
Zoghby, Samir M., 19, 158
Zolberg, Aristide R., 86, 152
Zoubir, Yahia, 95, 158
Zwart, Gine, 111

# Update the resources in the *Africa World Press Guide* by subscribing to the *WorldViews* quarterly.

The *WorldViews* quarterly magazine features critical reviews and guides to organizations and their print and audiovisual resources about issues covered in *Africa: Africa World Press Guide to Educational Resources from and about Africa*. Each 28-page issue describes a broad range of educational resources including organizations, books, periodicals, pamphlets, films and videos, audiotapes, compact discs, and educational CD-ROMs. Regional coverage focuses on the emerging nations of Africa, Asia and the Pacific, Latin America and the Caribbean, and the Middle East.

> "...the best periodical source for networking, organizations, and publications on the Third World."
> —*Progressive Periodicals Directory* (2nd edition)

> "How can one gain information about the Third World, particularly...new periodicals, books, pamphlets, and even audiovisual materials. The answer is [*WorldViews*]."
> —Bill Katz, *Library Journal,* May 15, 1986

---

**ORDER FORM**: *WorldViews: A Quarterly Review of Resources for Education and Action* [ISSN 1085-7559]

**Subscription rates** (check or money order in U.S. dollars drawn on a U.S. bank)
    **U.S. and Canada:** U.S.$50/year (organizations), U.S.$25/year (individuals)
    **Outside U S. and Canada:** U.S.$65/year (organizations), U.S.$45/year (individuals)

Enclosed please find a check/money order for US$_____ for a one-year subscription to the *WorldViews* quarterly at the (circle one) organizational/individual rate for calendar year 19____.

NAME _____

ADDRESS _____
_____
_____
_____

WorldViews, 464 19th Street, Oakland, CA 94612-2297 USA
Web site: http://www.igc.org/worldviews/    E-mail: worldviews@igc.org